The Power of **Critical Thinking**

The Power of
Critical Thinking

THIRD EDITION

Effective Reasoning About
Ordinary and Extraordinary Claims

LEWIS VAUGHN

NEW YORK | OXFORD
OXFORD UNIVERSITY PRESS | 2010

Oxford University Press, Inc., publishes works that further Oxford University's
objective of excellence in research, scholarship, and education.

Oxford New York
Auckland   Cape Town   Dar es Salaam   Hong Kong   Karachi
Kuala Lumpur   Madrid   Melbourne   Mexico City   Nairobi
New Delhi   Shanghai   Taipei   Toronto

With offices in
Argentina   Austria   Brazil   Chile   Czech Republic   France   Greece
Guatemala   Hungary   Italy   Japan   Poland   Portugal   Singapore
South Korea   Switzerland   Thailand   Turkey   Ukraine   Vietnam

Published by Oxford University Press, Inc.
198 Madison Avenue, New York, New York 10016
http://www.oup.com

Oxford is a registered trademark of Oxford University Press

Library of Congress Cataloging-in-Publication Data

Vaughn, Lewis.
    The power of critical thinking : effective reasoning about ordinary and extraordinary
claims / Lewis Vaughn.—3rd ed.
      p. cm.
    Includes bibliographical references and index.
    ISBN 978-0-19-537792-7 (alk. paper)
1. Critical thinking. I. Title.
    BC177.V38 2010
    160—dc22

                                                                                2009018616

Printing number: 9 8 7 6 5 4 3 2 1

Printed in the United States of America
on acid-free paper

To Kathy, for more than I can say

BRIEF CONTENTS

CONTENTS

Part Three ARGUMENTS

6 Deductive Reasoning: Propositional Logic 217

7 Deductive Reasoning: Categorical Logic 251

THIS THIRD EDITION OF *THE POWER OF CRITICAL THINKING* STAYS TRUE to its core values and—consistent with the insights and needs of many teachers of critical thinking—builds onto and remodels the original sturdy structure. The book's guiding purpose is unchanged: to provide comprehensive coverage of basic critical thinking skills, to include important features and topics often ignored by other texts, and to present all this in a plainspoken, lively style that encourages students to think, reason, and learn.

Each year the spheres of human endeavor that can benefit from a strong dose of critical thinking have multiplied or expanded. Students confront a media-driven, information-loaded, spin-doctored, nonsense-rich world. To meet this challenge, they require a solid grounding in a wide range of critical thinking skills applicable to many kinds of claims, evidence, and arguments. This need arises everywhere but is particularly acute in science, morality, politics, advertising, the news media, the Internet, and personal life. This text tries to provide these basic necessities in the clearest, most straightforward way possible.

Rest assured, the heart of the text—heavy coverage of argument and inference—still strongly beats. The book has a comprehensive introduction to claims and arguments (Chapter 3); good coverage of propositional and categorical logic (Chapters 6 and 7); and full treatment of the fundamentals of inductive reasoning, including Mill's methods, enumerative and analogical induction, causal arguments, and opinion polls (Chapter 8).

Uncommon Features

Distinguishing features of this book that are missing in many other texts are still here. They include:

- **Comprehensive Coverage of Inference to the Best Explanation.** This textbook devotes three chapters to inference to the best explanation because

(1) it is probably the type of inference that students use most, (2) it can be especially fertile ground for diverse cases and examples that students are likely to find intriguing, and (3) it implies a framework for thinking about claims and theories as well as a method for assessing their worth. Step-by-step instructions and plentiful examples show students how to use this kind of inference to assess theories and claims in science, pseudoscience, ethics, medicine, the media, and popular culture.

- **Extensive Treatment of Scientific Reasoning.** The text offers a chapter each on inductive reasoning and causal arguments (Chapter 8), scientific theories and inference (Chapter 9), and scientific method and theory evaluation (Chapter 10). Extended examples show how scientific reasoning applies to an array of questions in many scientific fields, everyday life, and even the realm of extraordinary phenomena.

- **Emphasis on Evaluation of Evidence, Authority, and Credibility.** Throughout this text (and especially in Chapter 4) considerable ink is expended to show students how to assess the evidence and claims proffered by scientists and other experts, the news media, advertising, and personal experience. In each case, the relevant principles or procedures are explained and illustrated. In this edition, photographs accompanied by thought-provoking captions also prompt students to evaluate evidence—the visual evidence contained in images.

- **Progressive, Stand-Alone Writing Modules.** Rather than relegating material on writing to a separate chapter (the usual practice), this text introduces the rudiments of argumentative essay writing in five end-of-chapter writing lessons, or modules. Each one is designed to help the student think about, plan, and write good argumentative essays—and to do so with a minimum of instructor input. The modules are progressive, starting in Chapter 1 with a few fundamentals of the writing process and then later (in Chapters 2, 3, and 4) covering basic guidelines and concepts that can help students think critically and write intelligently about arguments and issues. Topics include essay structure, thesis, outlining, writing and revising drafts, definition, ambiguity, and more. The module in Chapter 5 contains an annotated student paper illustrating many of the points made in the earlier modules. Though most of the modules are linked in some fashion to material in their corresponding chapters, they are meant to serve as a stand-alone (though cumulative) tutorial to be used as the instructor sees fit, and at any point in the course. The point of the modules is to help instructors get students writing quickly and progressing rapidly to more challenging writing assignments—without stopping the course to teach a chapter on writing.

- **Large and Diverse Collections of Exercises.** The exercises number in the hundreds, drawn from a wide range of sources and configured in a variety of forms, with selected answers in the back of the book. For the most part, within each chapter they are presented progressively, from simple to complex, elementary to more advanced, and familiar to unusual. The exercise types vary widely. Some of the more ambitious ones include:

- **Field Problems**—exercises that ask students to apply their new skills to claims, arguments, and essays found outside the classroom on the Internet and in newspapers, magazines, books, and other sources
- **Integrative Exercises**—exercise sets that overlap with material in previous chapters, reinforcing not only the current lessons but earlier ones as well
- **Writing Exercises**—writing assignments that ask students to write argumentative essays on selected topics or on arguments presented in the short essays found in the back of the book (Essays for Evaluation)
- **Self-Assessment Quizzes**—end-of-chapter tests that allow students to gauge their understanding of the material

- **A Chapter on Obstacles to Critical Thinking.** In Chapter 2 students now will find a review of many of the factors that may impede critical thinking—bias, habit, tradition, emotion, skewed perceptions, rationalizations, and certain philosophical outlooks. Along with explanations of how these factors affect thinking are suggestions on how to avoid or minimize them.

- **A Few Less Noticeable but Useful Features:**

  - Guidelines for evaluating news reports (Chapter 4)
  - A discussion of how critical reasoning can be used in the formation of worldviews (Chapter 11)
  - A chapter on moral reasoning covering moral arguments and the evaluation of moral theories (Chapter 11)
  - Guidelines for evaluating occult, paranormal, or supernatural claims (Chapter 10)
  - Advice on how to evaluate Internet sources (Chapter 4)
  - Critiques of subjective relativism, social relativism, and skepticism (Chapter 11)
  - In each chapter: chapter objectives, summaries, and a list of key terms
  - An end-of-book glossary

New Material and Features

This book has been blessed with reviewers who know precisely what they want—a very fine thing since authors often don't know what they want. These veteran teachers of critical thinking said the book would be more useful if we added the following (and they were right):

- **More Essays for Analysis.** The last edition featured fifteen essays for evaluation and discussion, located in Appendix A. Now there are six more—three pairs arranged in a pro/con format, each pair debating a single issue. New topics include torture and student free speech. All the essays are now linked to related writing exercises.

- **An Expanded Chapter on Moral Reasoning.** Thanks to the many teachers who wanted more substance in Chapter 11, it now includes more detailed analysis of moral principles, premises, judgments, and theories—and of how all these relate to one another. It also adds to the material on utilitarianism a discussion of Kant's theory and illustrates how the moral criteria of adequacy can be applied to both of them.
- **A Revamped System of Text Boxes.** Previously almost all the text boxes were informative but not very pedagogical. That's changed. Now there are three types of boxes:

  - **"Newsmakers"**—These focus on current events and issues in the media and illustrate a principle of critical thinking, ending with questions meant to encourage critical thought and discussion. Many of them—such as those on Barack Obama, "Joe the Plumber," and Tom Cruise—are new to this edition.
  - **"From the Web"**—These boxes also aim to teach a lesson about critical thinking but draw their material from websites and blogs.
  - **"Further Thought"**—The book still contains many of these informative boxes, designed to cover interesting supplementary material not covered in the main text.

- **New Photos to Encourage Critical Thinking About Visuals.** Nearly all of the stand-alone photos are now instructive, not just informative, prompting students to critically evaluate images and draw plausible inferences about them. The photos are provocative, their captions making a point and asking questions that drive students from passive seeing to active reflection.
- **Other Helpful Changes:**
  - New material on legal reasoning
  - An expanded discussion of the benefits of critical thinking
  - More guidance on doing research and judging sources
  - Additional coverage of rhetoric
  - More margin quotations

Ancillary Materials

- Computerized Test Bank and Instructor's Manual (including PowerPoint Lecture Outlines) available on CD.
- Printed Instructor's Manual with Test Bank.
- Companion Website (www.oup.com/us/criticalthinking) that has both Student Resources and Instructor Resources sections. The Student Resources include study notes, self-quizzes, additional exercises, and other materials.

The Instructor Resources include the Instructor's Manual, Computerized Test Bank, and the PowerPoint lecture outlines.

- Cartridges for major course management systems are also available containing the Instructor Resources.

Acknowledgments

The author now has more people than ever to thank for the text's good qualities—but, alas, still no one to blame but himself for any errors. First on the list are the capable and dedicated people at Oxford University Press: my extraordinary editors Robert Miller and Linda Harris, as well as Sarah Calabi and Aleksandra Florek. I have benefited from the insights and suggestions of some of the brightest and most helpful reviewers I have ever encountered (and I have encountered many). They include: Jami Anderson, University of Michigan—Flint; David E. Campbell, Humboldt State University; Evgenia Cherkasova, Suffolk University; Carlos Colombetti, Skyline College; Sharon Crasnow, Riverside Community College—Norco; Norman B. Cubbage, University of Louisville; B. Deckard, California State University, Long Beach; S. L. Dwyer, Georgia State University; Daniel Engster, University of Texas at San Antonio; Doug Fraleigh, California State University, Fresno; John Gibson, University of Louisville; Rex Gilliland, Southern Connecticut State University; Ann Glauser, University of Georgia; Cynthia Gobatie, Riverside City College; Jeffrey C. Goodman, James Madison University; Geoffrey Gorham, St. Olaf College; Richard A. S. Hall, Fayetteville State University; Ken Heiges, Allan Hancock College; Paul Herrick, Shoreline Community College; David Hunter, Buffalo State College, SUNY; Donald K. Kazee, Northern Kentucky University; Joanne Kingman-Sanchez, Pima Community College; Michael C. LaBossiere, Flordia A&M University; Ann Lewald, Tennessee Technological University; Stephen Ma, California State University, Los Angeles; James Martin, California State University, San Marcos; Keith O'Neill, Dutchess Community College; Maria Paleologou, California State University, Bakersfield; Jamie Phillips, Clarion University of Pennsylvania; Gregory Rich, Fayetteville State University; Victor Rios Jr., College of the Desert; Frank X. Ryan, Kent State University; Nicholas K. Simmons, University of Kansas; Aeon J. Skoble, Bridgewater State College; Marin Smillov, Santa Fe College; Taggart Smith, Purdue University; Ted Stryk, Roane State Community College; Ana Torres-Bower, Cerritos College; Gaye Walton-Price, Contra Costa College; Jared Welsh, Georgia State University; Karen Williams, San Jose State University; Marie G. Zaccaria, Georgia Perimeter College, Dunwoody Campus; Kevin Zanelotti, Radford University; and Ted Zenzinger, Regis College.

BASICS Part One

The Power of
Critical Thinking

 CHAPTER OBJECTIVES

- Understand the definition of *critical thinking* and the importance of the definition terms "systematic," "evaluation," "formulation," and "rational standards."
- Understand how critical thinking relates to logic, the truth or falsity of statements, knowledge, and personal empowerment.

WHY IT MATTERS

- Appreciate why critical thinking is better than the passive acceptance of beliefs.
- Appreciate the relevance of the claim "The unexamined life is not worth living" to critical thinking.
- Understand why the following claims are dubious: "Critical thinking makes people too critical or cynical," "Critical thinking makes people cold and unemotional," and "Critical thinking is the enemy of creativity."
- Appreciate the pervasive use of critical thinking in all human endeavors.
- Understand how critical thinking empowers people.

HOW IT WORKS

- Distinguish between statements and nonstatements.
- Understand the basic concepts of reasons, argument, inference, premises, and conclusion.
- Know how to use indicator words to help pinpoint premises and conclusions.
- Be able to distinguish between passages that do and do not contain an argument.
- Be able to identify arguments in various contexts and distinguish between arguments and superfluous material, arguments and explanations, and premises and conclusions.

> "The recipe for perpetual ignorance is: be satisfied with your opinions and content with your knowledge."
>
> —ELBERT HUBBARD

We want quality beliefs: p.) those that are true & justified

Concern with how we think

CT is not concerned with the causes of a belief but with the reasons that support it.

—Techniques
— Attitudes
— Principles

CRITICAL THINKING

—systematic
—evaluation
—formulation
—rational standards

CT involves logic but it is broader than logic...

Logic: study of good reasoning, or inference and the rules that govern it...

YOU CAME INTO THIS WORLD WITHOUT OPINIONS OR JUDGMENTS OR values or viewpoints—and now your head is brimming with them. If you tried to write them all down, you would be busy for the rest of your life (and would probably win an award for being the world's biggest bore). They help you make your way through the world. They guide you to both failure and success, ignorance and understanding, good and bad, paralysis and empowerment. Some of your beliefs truly inform you, and some blind you. Some are true; some are not. But the question is, *which ones are which?* This kind of question—a question about the *quality* of your beliefs—is the fundamental concern of **critical thinking.**

Determining the quality or value of your beliefs is a function of thinking, and the kind of thinking that does this job best is critical thinking—a skill that higher education seeks to foster. This means that critical thinking is not about *what* you think, but *how* you think.

Notice also that the question about the quality of beliefs is not about what factors *caused* you to have the beliefs that you do. A sociologist might tell you how society has influenced some of your moral choices. A psychologist might describe how your emotions cause you to cling to certain opinions. Your best friend might allege that you have unconsciously absorbed most of your beliefs directly from your parents. But none of these speculations have much to do with the central task of critical thinking.

Critical thinking focuses not on what *causes* a belief, but on *whether it is worth believing.* A belief is worth believing, or accepting, if we have *good reasons* to accept it. The better the reasons for acceptance, the more likely the belief is to be true. Critical thinking offers us a set of standards embodied in techniques, attitudes, and principles that we can use to assess beliefs and determine if they are supported by good reasons. After all, we want our beliefs to be true, to be good guides for dealing with the world—and critical thinking is the best tool we have for achieving this goal.

Here's one way to wrap up these points in a concise definition:

CRITICAL THINKING: The systematic evaluation or formulation of beliefs, or statements, by rational standards.

Critical thinking is *systematic* because it involves distinct procedures and methods. It entails *evaluation* and *formulation* because it's used to both assess existing beliefs (yours or someone else's) and devise new ones. And it operates according to *rational standards* in that beliefs are judged by how well they are supported by reasons.

Critical thinking, of course, involves **logic.** Logic is the study of good reasoning, or inference, and the rules that govern it. Critical thinking is broader than logic because it involves not only logic but also the truth or falsity of statements, the evaluation of arguments and evidence, the use of analysis and investigation, and the application of many other skills that help us decide what to believe or do.

Ultimately, what critical thinking leads you to is knowledge, understanding, and—if you put these to work—empowerment. In addition, as you're guided by your instructor through this text, you will come to appreciate some other benefits that cannot be fully explored now: Critical thinking enables problem-solving, active learning, and intelligent self-improvement.

In Chapters 2 and 3 (the rest of Part 1) you'll get a more thorough grounding in critical thinking and logical argument plus plenty of opportunities to practice your new skills. Consider this chapter an introduction to those important lessons.

Why It Matters

In large measure, our lives are defined by our actions and choices, and our actions and choices are guided by our thinking—so our thinking had better be good. Almost every day we are hit by a blizzard of assertions, opinions, arguments, and pronouncements from all directions. They all implore us to believe, to agree, to accept, to follow, to submit. If we care whether our choices are right and our beliefs true, if we want to rise above blind acceptance and arbitrary choices, we must use the tools provided by critical thinking.

If a picture is worth a thousand words, it also leaves much unsaid. A photograph by itself, like this one, is a slice of time, without context: events preceding it or following it are unrecorded, surrounding scenes drop from view, and facts that could aid analysis are missing. Good critical thinkers know this and interpret such images with caution. A chain email claimed that this 2007 photo was proof that Barack Obama "refused to not only put his hand on his heart during the pledge of allegiance, but refused to say the pledge." Actually the photo, taken at a steak fry in Iowa, was snapped while the onlookers were listening to the national anthem. Does this picture prove that Obama "refused" to recite the pledge and to put hand to heart? Does it prove that he is unpatriotic? What, if anything, does it demonstrate?

We, of course, always have the option of taking the easy way out. We can simply glom onto whatever beliefs or statements come blowing by in the wind, adopting viewpoints because they are favored by others or because they make us feel good. But then we forfeit control over our lives and let the wind take us wherever it will, as if we had no more say in the outcome than a leaf in a storm.

A consequence then of going with the wind is a loss of personal freedom. If you passively accept beliefs that have been handed to you by your parents, your culture, or your teachers, then those beliefs are *not really yours*. You just happened to be in a certain place and time when they were handed out. If they are not really yours, and you let them guide your choices and actions, then they— not you—are in charge of your life. Your beliefs are yours only if you critically examine them for yourself to see if they are supported by good reasons.

To examine your beliefs in this way is to examine your life, for your beliefs in large measure define your life. To forgo such scrutiny is to abandon your

> "Are you not ashamed of caring so much for the making of money and for fame and prestige, when you neither think nor care about wisdom and truth and the improvement of your soul?"
> —SOCRATES

Socrates: "the unexamined life
is not worth living..."

① Skills for learning & exploring

② Defense against error, manipulation and prejudice...

③ Tools for self-discovery

Worldview

chance of making your life deliberately and authentically meaningful. The great philosopher Socrates says it best: "The unexamined life is not worth living."

Thus in the most profound sense, critical thinking is not only enlightening, but empowering. This empowerment can take several forms:

Skills for learning and exploring. Some species of critical thinking is essential in every intellectual endeavor, every profession, and every college course. Economics, literature, philosophy, ethics, science, medicine, law—these and many other fields require you to understand and use argument, evaluation, analysis, logic, and evidence. Critical thinking is the common language of many worlds, and practicing it will help you make your way in them.

Defense against error, manipulation, and prejudice. For lack of good critical thinking, many intelligent people have been taken in by clever marketers, dubious "experts," self-serving politicians, charming demagogues, skillful propagandists, misinformed bloggers, wooly conspiracy theorists, misguided gurus, reckless alarmists, knee-jerk partisans, and smooth-talking xenophobes. For want of a little logic and careful reflection, you can easily choose the wrong career, wrong friends, wrong spouse, wrong investments, wrong religion, and wrong leaders. Without some skill in moral reasoning (critical thinking applied to ethics), you risk making bad decisions about right and wrong, about good and bad. Critical thinking is no guarantee against any of these errors, but it does provide your best possible defense.

Tools for self-discovery. A central goal of higher education is to enable students to think critically and carefully for themselves, to confront issues and problems and then devise their own warranted, defensible answers. This means you must be able not only to critically examine the arguments and assertions of others but also to apply these critical powers to your own ideas. To discover what to believe—that is, to find out which claims are worthy of belief—you must weigh them in the balance of critical reasoning. A central question of a mature intellect is, "What should I believe?" This is the fundamental query at the heart of all your conscious life choices. Only you can answer it, and ultimately only critical thinking can guide you to justified answers.

Critical thinking applies not just to some of your individual beliefs, but to all of them together. It applies to your worldview, the vast web of fundamental ideas that help you make sense of the world, what some people call a philosophy of life. We all have a worldview, and most of us want the beliefs that constitute it to be true and coherent (to fit together without internal contradictions). As you will see in Chapter 11, devising a coherent worldview is the work of a lifetime—and can only be done with the help of critical thinking.

Our choice whether to apply critical thinking skills is not an all-or-nothing decision. Each of us uses critical thinking to some degree in our lives. We often evaluate reasons for (and against) believing that someone has committed a crime, that an earnest celebrity is deluded, that one candidate in an election is better than another, that gun control laws should be strengthened or weakened, that we should buy a car, that the legendary Bigfoot does not exist, that a friend is trustworthy, that one university is superior to another, that the bill being considered in Congress would be bad for the environment, that Elvis is living the good life in a witness-protection program. But the more urgent consideration is not just whether we sometimes use critical thinking, but how well we use it.

Many people, however, will have none of this—and perhaps you are one of them. They believe that critical thinking—or what they take to be critical thinking—makes one excessively critical or cynical, emotionally cold, and creatively constrained.

For example, there are some who view anything that smacks of logic and rationality as a negative enterprise designed to attack someone else's thinking and score points by putting people in their place. A few of these take the word *critical* here to mean "faultfinding" or "carping."

Now, no doubt some people try to use critical thinking primarily for offensive purposes, but this approach goes against critical thinking principles. The *critical* in critical thinking is used in the sense of "exercising or involving careful judgment or judicious evaluation." Critical thinking is about determining what we are justified in believing, and that involves an openness to other points of view, a tolerance for opposing perspectives, a focus on the issue at hand, and fair assessments of arguments and evidence. To paraphrase a bumper-sticker slogan: Good critical thinking does not make cynics—people make cynics.

Some people fear that if they apply critical thinking to their lives, they will become cold and unemotional—just like a computer abuzz with logic and rote functions. But this is a confused notion. Critical thinking and feelings actually complement one another. Certainly part of thinking critically is ensuring that we don't let our emotions distort our judgments. But critical thinking can also help us clarify our feelings and deal with them more effectively. Our emotions often need the guidance of reason. Likewise, our reasoning needs our emotions. It is our feelings that motivate us to action, and without motivation our reasoning would never get off the ground.

Then there's this dubious assumption: Critical thinking is the enemy of creativity. To some people, critical thinking is a sterile and rigid mode of thought that constrains the imagination, hobbles artistic vision, and prevents "thinking

[Handwritten margin notes:]

OBJECTIONS AND
RESPONSES TO CT

①

O: CT is cynical
and fault finding

R: People can use CT in a way
that defeats the purpose of CT

②

O: CT can erode our emotions

R: CT can help clarify them

Emotion needs reasoning;
reasoning needs emotions

③

O: CT undermines creativity
R: CT enhances creativity

C.S. Peirce on musement

"Never, ever, think outside the box."

CT enables us to think outside the box of stereotypes, superstition & wishful thinking

outside the box." But critical thinking and creative thinking are not opposed to one another. Good critical thinkers can let their imaginations run free just like anyone else. They can create and enjoy poetry, music, art, literature, and plain old fun in the same way and to the same degree as the rest of the world. Critical thinking can complement creative thinking because it is needed to assess and enhance the creation. Scientists, for example, often dream up some very fanciful theories (which are an important part of doing science). These theories pop into their heads in the same sort of ways that the ideas for a great work of art appear in the mind of its creator. But then scientists use all of their critical thinking skills to evaluate what they have produced (as artists sometimes do)—and this critical examination enables them to select the most promising theories and to weed out those that are unworkable. Critical thinking perfects the creation.

In a very important sense, critical thinking is thinking outside the box. When we passively absorb the ideas we encounter, when we refuse to consider any alternative explanations or theories, when we conform our ideas to the wishes of the group, when we let our thinking be controlled by bias and stereotypes and superstition and wishful thinking—we are deep, deep in the box. But we rise above all that when we have the courage to think critically. When we are willing to let our beliefs be tried in the court of critical reason, we open ourselves to new possibilities, the dormant seeds of creativity.

REVIEW NOTES

☑ Why Critical Thinking Matters

- Our thinking guides our actions, so it should be of high quality.
- If you have never critically examined your beliefs, they are not truly yours.
- To examine your beliefs is to examine your life. Socrates: "The unexamined life is not worth living."
- Critical thinking involves determining what we're justified in believing, being open to new perspectives, and fairly assessing the views of others and ourselves.
- Critical thinking provides skills for learning and exploring; defense against error, manipulation, and prejudice; and tools for self-discovery.
- Critical thinking complements both our emotions and our creativity.
- Critical thinking is thinking outside the box.

Critical thinking covers a lot of territory. It's used across the board in all disciplines, all areas of public life, all the sciences, all sectors of business, and all vocations. It has played a major role in all the great endeavors of human-kind—scientific discoveries, technological innovations, philosophical insights, social and political movements, literary creation and criticism, judicial and legal reasoning, democratic nation building, and more. The *lack* of critical thinking has also left its mark. The great tragedies of history—the wars, massacres, holocausts, tyrannies, bigotries, epidemics, and witch hunts—grew out of famines of the mind where clear, careful thinking was much too scarce.

How It Works

As you can see, critical thinking has extremely broad application. Principles and procedures used to evaluate beliefs in one discipline or issue can be used to assess beliefs in many other arenas. Good critical thinking is the same everywhere. Here are the common threads that make it universal.

CLAIMS AND REASONS

Critical thinking is a rational, systematic process that we apply to beliefs of all kinds. As we use the term here, *belief* is just another word for statement, or claim. A **statement** is an assertion that something is or is not the case. The following are statements:

handwritten note: ① STATEMENT: Assertion that something is/is not the case

- A triangle has three sides.
- I am cold.
- You are a liar.
- You are not a liar.
- I see blue spots before my eyes.
- $7 + 5 = 12$
- You should never hit your mother with a shovel.
- The best explanation for his behavior is that he was in a trance.
- Rap music is better than punk rock.
- There are black holes in space.

So statements, or claims, are the kinds of things that are either true or false. They assert that some state of affairs is or is not actual. You may know that a specific statement is true, or you may not. There may be no way to find out at the time if the statement is true or false.

"What some people fail to grasp, Larry, is the difference between 'thinking outside of the box' and just being a weirdo."

© 2002 by Randy Glasbergen

There may be no one who believes the statement. But it would be a statement nonetheless.

Some sentences, though, do *not* express statements:

- Does a triangle have three sides?
- Is God all-powerful?
- Turn that music off.
- Stop telling lies.
- Hey, dude.
- Great balls of fire!

The first two sentences are questions. The second two are commands or requests. The fifth sentence is a greeting. The sixth one is an exclamation. None asserts that something is or is not the case.

When you're engaged in critical thinking, you're mostly either evaluating statements or formulating them. In both cases your primary task is to figure out how strongly to believe them. The strength of your belief should depend on the quality of the reasons in favor of the statements. Statements backed by good reasons are worthy of strong acceptance. Statements that fall short of this standard deserve weaker acceptance.

Sometimes you may not be able to assign any substantial weight at all to the reasons for or against a statement. There simply may not be enough evidence to rationally decide. Generally when that happens, good critical thinkers don't arbitrarily choose to accept or reject a statement. They suspend judgment until there is enough evidence to make an intelligent decision.

REASONS AND ARGUMENTS

Reasons provide support for a statement. That is, they provide us with grounds for believing that a statement is true. Reasons are themselves expressed as statements. So a statement expressing a reason or reasons is used to show that another statement is true or likely to be true. This combination of statements—a statement (or statements) supposedly providing reasons for accepting another statement—is known as an **argument.** Arguments are the main focus of critical thinking. They are the most important tool we have for evaluating the truth of statements (our own and those of others) and for formulating statements that are worthy of acceptance. Arguments are therefore essential for the advancement of knowledge in all fields.

Often people use the word *argument* to indicate a quarrel or heated exchange. In critical thinking, however, *argument* refers to the assertion of reasons in support of a statement.

The statements (reasons) given in support of another statement are called the **premises.** The statement that the premises are intended to support is called the **conclusion.** We can define an argument, then, like this:

ARGUMENT: A group of statements in which some of them (the premises) are intended to support another of them (the conclusion).

The following are some simple arguments:

1. Because banning assault rifles violates a constitutional right, the U.S. government should not ban assault rifles.
2. The *Wall Street Journal* says that people should invest heavily in stocks. Therefore, investing in stocks is a smart move.
3. When Judy drives her car, she's always late. Since she's driving her car now, she will be late.
4. Listen, any movie with clowns in it cannot be a good movie. Last night's movie had at least a dozen clowns in it. Consequently it was awful.
5. The war on terrorism must include a massive military strike on nation X because without this intervention, terrorists cannot be defeated. They will always be able to find safe haven and support in the X regime. Even if terrorists are scattered around the world, support from nation X will increase their chances of surviving and launching new attacks.
6. No one should buy a beer brewed in Canada. Old Guzzler beer is brewed in Canada, so no one should buy it.

Here are the same arguments where the parts are easily identified:

1. [Premise] Because banning assault rifles violates a constitutional right, [Conclusion] the U.S. government should not ban assault rifles.
2. [Premise] The *Wall Street Journal* says that people should invest heavily in stocks. [Conclusion] Therefore, investing in stocks is a smart move.
3. [Premise] When Judy drives her car, she's always late. [Premise] Since she's driving her car now, [Conclusion] she will be late.
4. [Premise] Any movie with clowns in it cannot be a good movie. [Premise] Last night's movie had at least a dozen clowns in it. [Conclusion] Consequently it was awful.
5. [Premise] Without a military intervention in nation X, terrorists cannot be defeated. [Premise] They will always be able to find safe haven and support in the X regime. [Premise] Even if terrorists are scattered around the world, support from nation X will increase their chances of surviving and launching new attacks. [Conclusion] The war on terrorism must include a massive military strike on nation X.
6. [Premise] No one should buy a beer brewed in Canada. [Premise] Old Guzzler beer is brewed in Canada. [Conclusion] So no one should buy it.

What all of these arguments have in common is that reasons (the premises) are offered to support or prove a claim (the conclusion). This logical link between premises and conclusion is what distinguishes arguments from all other kinds of discourse. This process of reasoning from a premise or premises to a conclusion based on those premises is called **inference**. Being able to identify arguments, to

"What danger can ever come from ingenious reasoning and inquiry? The worst speculative skeptic ever I knew was a much better man than the best superstitious devotee and bigot."
—DAVID HUME

pick them out of a block of nonargumentative prose if need be, is an important skill on which many other critical thinking skills are based.

Now consider this passage:

The cost of the new XJ fighter plane is $650 million. The cost of three AR21 fighter bombers is $1.2 billion. The administration intends to fund such projects.

Is there an argument here? No. This passage consists of several claims, but no reasons are presented to support any particular claim (conclusion), including the last sentence. This passage can be turned into an argument, though, with some minor editing:

The GAO says that any weapon that costs more than $50 million apiece will actually impair our military readiness. The cost of the new XJ fighter plane is $650 million dollars. The cost of three AR21 fighter bombers is $1.2 billion. We should never impair our readiness. Therefore, the administration should cancel both these projects.

Now we have an argument because reasons are given for accepting a conclusion.

Here's another passage:

Allisha went to the bank to get a more recent bank statement of her checking account. The teller told her that the balance was $1725. Allisha was stunned that it was so low. She called her brother to see if he had been playing one of his twisted pranks. He wasn't. Finally, she concluded that she had been a victim of bank fraud.

Where is the conclusion? Where are the reasons? There are none. This is a little narrative hung on some descriptive claims. But it's not an argument. It could be turned into an argument if, say, some of the claims were restated as reasons for the conclusion that bank fraud had been committed.

Being able to distinguish between passages that do and do not contain arguments is a very basic skill—and an extremely important one. Many people think that if they have clearly stated their beliefs on a subject, they have presented an argument. But a mere declaration of beliefs is not an argument. Often such assertions of opinion are just a jumble of unsupported claims. Search high and low and you will not find an argument anywhere. A writer or speaker of these claims gives the readers or listeners no grounds for believing the claims. In writing courses, the absence of supporting premises is sometimes called "a lack of development."

Here are three more examples of verbiage sans argument:

Attributing alcohol abuse by children too young to buy a drink to lack of parental discipline, intense pressure to succeed, and affluence incorrectly draws attention to proximate causes while ignoring the ultimate cause: a culture that tolerates overt and covert marketing of alcohol, tobacco and sex to these eas-

FROM THE WEB

Critical Thinking and Fake Blogs

Fake blogs offering parodies of celebrities or other famous people can be fun: Remember the parody blog called Fake Steve Jobs? But another kind of fake blog—the phony business blog—is less amusing. As one report says,

[S]ome firms have been trying to con the consumer by pushing their own propaganda on websites while pretending to be the voice of the people.

Companies caught out posting these bogus blogs—or "flogs"—include Sony, L'Oreal and Wal-Mart. . . .[1]

Have you been a victim of flogging? Probably. Will you get flogged again? Perhaps. The good news is that critical thinking skills provide excellent anti-flog protection. How? Try answering that question for yourself after studying this chapter.

"He who knows only his own side of the case, knows little of that. His reasons may be good, and no one may have been able to refute them. But if he is equally unable to refute the reasons on the opposite side; if he does not so much as know what they are, he has no ground for preferring either opinion."
—JOHN STUART MILL

ily manipulated, voracious consumers. [Letter to the editor, *New York Times*]

[A recent column in this newspaper] deals with the living quarters of Bishop William Murphy of the Diocese of Rockville Centre. I am so disgusted with the higher-ups in the church that at times I am embarrassed to say I am Catholic. To know that my parents' hard-earned money went to lawyers and payoffs made me sick. Now I see it has also paid for a high-end kitchen. I am enraged. I will never make a donation again. [Letter to the editor, *Newsday*]

I don't understand what is happening to this country. The citizens of this country are trying to destroy the beliefs of our forefathers with their liberal views. This country was founded on Christian beliefs. This has been and I believe still is the greatest country in the world. But the issue that we cannot have prayer in public places and on public property because there has to be separation of church and state is a farce. [Letter to the editor, *Douglas County Sentinel*]

The passage on alcohol abuse in children is not an argument but an unsupported assertion about the causes of the problem. The passage from the disappointed Catholic is an expression of outrage (which may or may not be justified), but no conclusion is put forth, and no reasons supporting a conclusion are offered. Note the contentious tone in the third passage. This passage smells like an argument. But, alas, there is no argument. Each sentence is a claim presented without support.

Sometimes people also confuse **explanations** with arguments. An argument gives us reasons for believing *that something is the case*—that a claim is true or probably true. An explanation, though, tells us *why or how something is the case*. Arguments have something to prove; explanations do not. Ponder this pair of statements:

1. Adam obviously stole the money, for three people saw him do it.
2. Adam stole the money because he needed it to buy food.

Statement 1 is an argument. Statement 2 is an explanation. Statement 1 tries to show that something is the case—that Adam stole the money. And the reason offered in support of this statement is that three people saw him do it. Statement 2 does not try to prove that something is the case (that Adam stole the money). Instead, it attempts to explain why something is the case (why Adam stole the money). Statement 2 takes for granted that Adam stole the money and then tries to explain why he did it. (Note: Explanations can be used as integral *parts* of arguments. As such they are powerful intellectual and scientific tools that help us understand the world, which is why this text has several chapters [Part 4] devoted to explanations used in this way.)

It's not always easy to recognize an argument, to locate both premises and conclusion, but there are a few tricks that can make the job more manageable. For one, there are **indicator words** that frequently accompany arguments and signal that a premise or conclusion is present. For example, in argument 1, cited earlier in this chapter, the indicator word *because* tips us off to the presence of the premise "Because banning assault rifles violates a Constitutional right." In argument 2, *therefore* points to the conclusion "Therefore, investing in stocks is a smart move."

Here are some common premise indicators:

because	due to the fact that	inasmuch as
in view of the fact	being that	as indicated by
given that	since	for
seeing that	assuming that	the reason being
as	for the reason that	

[Handwritten margin notes:]

ARGUMENTS VS. EXPLANATIONS
Explanation: tells us why or how something is the case...

INDICATOR WORDS

① Premise Indicators

And here are some common conclusion indicators:

therefore	it follows that	it must be that
thus	we can conclude that	as a result
which implies that	so	which means that
consequently	hence	ergo

Conclusion Indicators ②

Using indicator words to spot premises and conclusions, however, is not foolproof. They're just good clues. You will find that some of the words just listed are used when no argument is present. For example,

- I am here *because* you asked me to come.
- I haven't seen you *since* Woodstock.
- He was *so* sleepy he fell off his chair.

Note also that arguments can be put forth without the use of *any* indicator words:

CAVEAT: Arguments can be put forth w/o indicator words

> We must take steps to protect ourselves from criminals. We can't rely on the government—law enforcement is already stretched thin. The police can't be everywhere at once, and they usually get involved only after a crime has been committed.

As you may have noticed from these examples, the basic structure of arguments can have several simple variations. For one thing, arguments can have any

STRUCTURE
- number of premises
- location of conclusion
- disguised premises and/or conclusion
- missing premises and/or conclusion

" NEWSMAKERS "

Political Straw

Political discourse bristles with bad arguments, logical fallacies, rhetorical manipulations, and flat-out lies—the very things that critical thinking can help us defend against. Consider these examples of one of the politician's favorite ploys—the fallacy of the *straw man*, the distorting, weakening, or oversimplifying of someone's position so it can be more easily attacked or refuted (discussed in detail in Chapter 5).

BARACK OBAMA

> "[John McCain] says that he is willing to send our troops into another hundred-year war in Iraq."

> "When John McCain said we could just 'muddle through' in Afghanistan, I argued for more resources."

JOHN McCAIN

"Senator Obama claimed that the threat Iran poses to our security is 'tiny' compared to the threat once posed by the former Soviet Union. Obviously, Iran isn't a superpower and doesn't possess the military power the Soviet Union had. But that does not mean that the threat posed by Iran is insignificant."

"The question is what kind of change? Will we go back to the policies of the '60s and '70s that have failed? Or will we go forward? Will we enact the largest single tax increase since the Second World War as my opponent [Obama] proposes, or will we keep taxes low—low for families and employers?"

GEORGE W. BUSH

"There is a certain attitude in the world, by some, that says that it's a waste of time to try to promote free societies in parts of the world. . . . And I fully understand that that might rankle some, and be viewed by some as folly. I just strongly disagree."

"Some people believe the answer to this problem is to wall off our economy from the world. I strongly disagree."

Can you tell how each position is being distorted? How common is the strawman fallacy? Do you think it is effective as a tool of persuasion? Would you fall for this tactic?   ∎

number of premises. Arguments 1 and 2 have one premise. Arguments 3, 4, and 6, two premises; argument 5, three premises. In extended arguments that often appear in essays, editorials, reports, and other works, there can be many more premises. Also, the conclusion of an argument may not always appear after the premises. As in argument 5, the conclusion may be presented first.

Occasionally the conclusion of an argument can be disguised as a question—even though we would usually expect a question not to be a claim at all. (For purposes of examining such arguments, we may need to paraphrase the conclusion; in some arguments, we may also need to paraphrase premises.) Most of the time readers have no difficulty discerning what the implicit conclusion is. See for yourself:

> Do you think for one minute that liberal Democrats in Congress will support a bill that makes gun control legislation impossible? They have never voted that way. They have already declared that they will not allow such a bill. And their leadership has given them their marching orders: Don't support this bill.

Rhetorical Question

Probably the best advice for anyone trying to uncover or dissect arguments is this: *Find the conclusion first.* Once you know what claim someone is trying to prove, isolating the premises becomes much easier. Ask yourself, "What claim is this writer or speaker trying to persuade me to believe?" If the writer or speaker is not trying to convince you of anything, there is no argument to examine.

RULE ONE: Find the conclusion first...

What claim is the writer trying to persuade me to believe..?

ARGUMENTS IN THE ROUGH (BASIC ANALYSIS)

As you've probably guessed by now, in the real world, arguments almost never appear neatly labeled as they are here. As suggested earlier, they usually come imbedded in a thicket of other sentences that serve many other functions besides articulating an argument. They may be long and hard to follow. And sometimes a passage that sounds like an argument is not. Your main challenge is to identify the conclusion and premises without getting lost in all the "background noise."

Real world arguments are rarely presented in a neat way

Ponder this passage:

[1] A. L. Jones used flawed reasoning in his letter yesterday praising this newspaper's decision to publish announcements of same-sex unions. [2] Mr. Jones asserts that same-sex unions are a fact of life and therefore should be acknowledged by the news media as a legitimate variation on social partnerships. [3] But the news media are not in the business of endorsing or validating lifestyles. [4] They're supposed to report on lifestyles, not bless them. [5] In addition, by validating same-sex unions or any other lifestyle, the media

> "Ignorance is an evil weed, which dictators may cultivate among their dupes, but which no democracy can afford among its citizens."
>
> —WILLIAM HENRY BEVERIDGE

Premise 1 – [3]
Premise 2 – [5]
Conclusion – [6]

REVIEW NOTES

☑ Claims, Reasons, and Arguments

- **Statement (claim):** An assertion that something is or is not the case
- **Premise:** A statement given in support of another statement
- **Conclusion:** A statement that premises are used to support
- **Argument:** A group of statements in which some of them (the premises) are intended to support another of them (the conclusion)
- **Explanation:** A statement or statements asserting why or how something is the case
- **Indicator words:** Words that frequently accompany arguments and signal that a premise or conclusion is present

abandon their objectivity and become political partisans—which would destroy whatever respect people have for news outlets. [6] All of this shows that the news media—including this newspaper—should never (explicitly or implicitly) endorse lifestyles by announcing those lifestyles to the world.

There's an argument here, but it's surrounded by extraneous material. The conclusion is sentence 6—"All of this shows that the news media—including this newspaper—should never (explicitly or implicitly) endorse lifestyles by announcing those lifestyles to the world." Since we know what the conclusion is, we can identify the premises and separate them from other information. Sentences 1 and 2 are not premises; they're background information about the nature of the dispute. Sentence 3 presents the first premise, and sentence 4 is essentially a restatement of that premise. Sentence 5 is the second premise.

Stripped clean of nonargumentative material, the argument looks like this:

Irony

FURTHER THOUGHT

💡 Go Ahead, Make My Day

Occasionally you will come across an argument that makes its case by way of irony. Both the premises and conclusion may be clearly implied but nowhere stated directly. Here's an excerpt from a full-page ad in the *New York Times* featuring a big picture of Osama bin Laden, the man thought to be responsible for the terrorist attacks of September 11. Osama is addressing America:

> I want you to invade Iraq. Go ahead. Send me a new generation of recruits. Your bombs will fuel their hatred of America and their desire for revenge. Americans won't be safe anywhere. Please attack Iraq. Distract yourself from fighting Al Qaeda. Divide the international community. Go ahead. Destabilize the region. Maybe Pakistan will fall—we want its nuclear weapons. Give Saddam a reason to strike first. He might draw Israel into a fight. Perfect! So please—invade Iraq. Make my day.

Here, an advocacy group is arguing for the opposite of what "Osama" is saying: Don't invade Iraq. This message is the implied conclusion. The basic idea is that invading Iraq is exactly what terrorists want—so don't do it.

[Premise] But the news media are not in the business of endorsing or validating lifestyles. [Premise] In addition, by validating same-sex unions or any other lifestyle, the media abandon their objectivity and become political partisans—which would destroy whatever respect people have for news outlets. [Conclusion] All of this shows that the news media—including this newspaper—should never (explicitly or implicitly) endorse lifestyles by announcing those lifestyles to the world.

Argument

Now see if you can spot the conclusion and premises in this one:

[1] You have already said that you love me and that you can't imagine spending the rest of your life without me. [2] Once, you even tried to propose to me.

FURTHER THOUGHT

💡 Dumb and Dumber

Many times when we don't know something, that's bad. But when we don't know that we don't know something, that's worse. At least, that's the view of researchers who studied the effects of this kind of double-edged ignorance (*Journal of Personality and Social Psychology*, Dec. 1999). In several studies, the researchers assessed the ability of study participants in areas that demanded

Harry and Lloyd (Jim Carrey and Jeff Daniels) from the movie *Dumb & Dumber* (1994).

"knowledge, wisdom, or savvy"—logical reasoning, English grammar, and humor.

The results: People whose abilities were very weak tended to greatly overestimate them. Those who got the lowest test scores thought that they achieved much higher scores. The data suggested that the overestimations arose because the subjects couldn't distinguish accuracy from error. They didn't know what they didn't know. Ironically, when the researchers helped the participants improve their abilities and increase their knowledge, the participants could recognize their limitations.

Hmm. Increase your knowledge and recognize your limitations—isn't that what critical thinking helps you do?

[3] And now you claim that you need time to think about whether we should be married. [4] Well, everything that you've told me regarding our relationship has been a lie. [5] In some of your letters to a friend you admitted that you were misleading me. [6] You've been telling everyone that we are just friends, not lovers. [7] And worst of all, you've been secretly dating someone else. [8] Why are you doing this? [9] It's all been a farce, and I'm outta here.

And you thought that romantic love had nothing to do with critical thinking! In this passionate paragraph, an argument is alive and well. The conclusion is in sentence 4: "Well, everything that you've told me . . . has been a lie." Sentence 9, the concluding remark, is essentially a repetition of the conclusion. Sentences 1, 2, and 3 are background information on the current conflict. Sentences 5, 6, and 7 are the premises, the reasons that support the conclusion. And sentence 8 is an exasperated query that's not part of the argument.

You will discover that in most extended argumentative passages, premises and conclusions make up only a small portion of the total wordage. A good part of the text is background information and restatements of the premises or conclusion. Most of the rest consists of explanations, digressions, examples or illustrations, and descriptive passages.

Of all these nonargumentative elements, explanations are probably most easily confused with arguments. As we've seen, arguments try to prove or demonstrate that a statement is true. They try to show *that* something is the case. Explanations, however, do not try to prove that a statement is true. They try to show *why* or *how* something is the way it is. Consider these two statements:

* People have a respect for life because they adhere to certain ethical standards.
* People should have a respect for life because their own ethical standards endorse it.

The first statement is an explanation. It's not trying to prove anything, and no statement is in dispute. It's trying to clarify why or how people have respect for life. The second statement, though, is an argument. It's trying to prove, or provide support for, the idea that people should have a respect for life.

We discuss the basics of explanations in Chapter 9, and we deal with the other nonargumentative elements in Chapters 4 and 5. In the meantime, you should be able to locate the conclusion and premises of an argument—even when there is a lot of nonargumentative material nearby.

Finally, as you can see, learning the principles of critical thinking or logic requires at least some prior knowledge and ability. But, you may wonder (especially if this is your first course in critical or logical reasoning), Where does this prior knowledge and ability come from—and do you have these prerequisites? Fortunately, the answer is yes. Since you are, as Aristotle says, a rational animal, you already have the necessary equipment, namely, a logical sense that helps you reason in everyday life and enables you to begin honing your critical reasoning.

🔑 KEY WORDS

argument	inference
conclusion	logic
critical thinking	premise
explanation	statement
indicator words	

Summary

- Critical thinking is the systematic evaluation or formulation of beliefs, or statements, by rational standards. It is *systematic* because it involves distinct procedures and methods. It entails *evaluation* and *formulation* because it's used to both assess existing beliefs (yours or someone else's) and devise new ones. And it operates according to *rational standards* in that beliefs are judged according to the reasons and reasoning that support them.

- Critical thinking matters because our lives are defined by our actions and choices, and our actions and choices are guided by our thinking. It helps guide us toward beliefs that are worthy of acceptance, that can help us be successful in life, however we define success.

- Critical thinking empowers learning and exploring; defense against error, manipulation, and prejudice; and self-discovery.

- A consequence of not thinking critically is a loss of personal freedom. If you passively accept beliefs that have been handed to you by your family and your culture, then those beliefs are not really yours. If they are not really yours, and you let them guide your choices and actions, then they—not you—are in charge of your life. Your beliefs are yours only if you critically examine them for yourself to see if they are supported by good reasons.

- Some people believe that critical thinking will make them cynical, emotionally cold, and creatively constrained. But there is no good reason to believe that this is the case. Critical thinking does not necessarily lead to cynicism. It can complement our feelings by helping us sort them out. And it doesn't limit creativity—it helps perfect it.

- Critical thinking is a rational, systematic process that we apply to beliefs of all kinds. As we use the term here, *belief* is just another word for statement, or claim. A *statement* is an assertion that something is or is not the case. When you're engaged in critical thinking, you are mostly either evaluating a statement or trying to formulate one. In both cases your primary task is to figure out how strongly to believe the statement (based on how likely it is to be true). The strength of your belief will depend on the strength of the reasons in favor of the statement.

- In critical thinking an argument is not a feud but a set of statements—statements supposedly providing reasons for accepting another statement. The statements given in support of another statement are called the *premises*. The statement that the premises are used to support is called the *conclusion*. An argument, then, is a group of statements in which some of them (the premises) are intended to support another of them (the conclusion).
- Being able to identify arguments is an important skill on which many other critical thinking skills are based. The task is made easier by indicator words that frequently accompany arguments and signal that a premise or conclusion is present. Premise indicators include *for, since,* and *because.* Conclusion indicators include *so, therefore,* and *thus.*

EXERCISES

Exercises marked with * have answers in "Answers to Exercises" (Appendix B). Quizzes, integrative exercises, and writing assignments are not supplied with answers.

Exercise 1.1

REVIEW QUESTIONS

* 1. What is critical thinking?
  2. Is critical thinking primarily concerned with *what* you think or *how* you think?
  3. Why is critical thinking systematic?
* 4. According to the text, what does it mean to say that critical thinking is done according to rational standards?
  5. According to the text, how does a lack of critical thinking cause a loss of personal freedom?
* 6. What does the term *critical* refer to in critical thinking?
  7. In what way can feelings and critical thinking complement each other?
* 8. What is a statement?
  9. Give an example of a statement. Then give an example of a sentence that is not a statement.
  10. According to the text, by what standard should we always proportion our acceptance of a statement?
* 11. What is an argument?
  12. Give an example of an argument with two premises.
  13. What is a premise?

*14. What is a conclusion?

15. Why can't a mere assertion or statement of beliefs constitute an argument?

16. True or false: All disagreements contain an argument.

*17. Does the following passage contain an argument? *Sample passage:* I couldn't disagree more with Olivia. She says that video games provoke young men to violence and other insensitive acts. But that's just not true.

18. Does the following passage contain an argument? *Sample passage:* Alonzo asserts that the government should be able to arrest and imprison anyone if they are suspected of terrorist acts. But that's ridiculous. Doing that would be a violation of basic civil liberties guaranteed in the Bill of Rights.

*19. What are indicator words?

20. List three conclusion indicator words.

21. List three premise indicator words.

22. Give an example of a short argument that uses one or more indicator words.

*23. What is probably the best strategy for trying to find an argument in a complex passage?

24. True or false: You can almost always find an argument in narrative writing.

Exercise 1.2

For each of the following sentences, indicate whether it is or is not a statement.

*1. Now that you're mayor of the city, do you still believe that the city government is a waste of time? ✕

2. Do not allow your emotions to distort your thinking. ✕

3. If someone wants to burn the American flag, they should be able to do it without interference from the police. Ⓢ

*4. Do you think that I'm guilty? ✕

5. Should our religious beliefs be guided by reason, emotion, or faith? ✕

6. Stop driving on the left side of the road! ✕

*7. The Vietnam War was a terrible mistake. Ⓢ

8. The Vietnam War was not a terrible mistake. Ⓢ

9. I shall do my best to do my duty to God and my country. Ⓢ

*10. Are you doing your best for God and country? ✕

Exercise 1.3

For each of the following passages indicate whether it constitutes an argument. For each argument specify what the conclusion is.

*1. Rene hates Julia, and she always upsets him, so <u>he should avoid her.</u> Ⓐ

✗ 2. Rene hates Julia, and his feelings against her cause him tremendous pain.

✗ 3. I pledge allegiance to the flag of the United States of America and to the republic for which it stands, one nation under God, indivisible, with liberty and justice for all.

✗* 4. Why do you think you have the right to park your car anywhere you please?

✗ 5. Drop your gun! You're under arrest.

✗ 6. If you smoke that cigarette in here, I will leave the room.

✗* 7. The *Titanic* sank, and no one came to save it.

Ⓐ 8. Jesus loves me, for the Bible tells me so.

Ⓐ 9. Spiderman is a better superhero than Superman because kryptonite can't hurt him, and he doesn't have a Lois Lane around to mess things up.

Ⓐ 10. "Whether our argument concerns public affairs or some other subject we must know some, if not all, of the facts about the subject on which we are to speak and argue. Otherwise, we can have no materials out of which to construct arguments." [Aristotle, *Rhetoric*]

Ⓐ* 11. If guns are outlawed, then only outlaws will have guns. Don't outlaw guns.

Ⓐ 12. If someone says something that offends me, I should have the right to stop that kind of speech. After all, words can assault people just as weapons can.

Ⓐ 13. "Citizens who so value their 'independence' that they will not enroll in a political party are really forfeiting independence, because they abandon a share in decision-making at the primary level: the choice of the candidate." [Bruce L. Felknor, *Dirty Politics*]

Ⓐ 14. If someone says something that offends me, I cannot and should not try to stop them from speaking. After all, in America, speech—even offensive speech—is protected.

Ⓐ* 15. "Piercing car alarms have disturbed my walks, café meals or my sleep at least once during every day I have lived in the city; roughly 3,650 car alarms. Once, only once, was the wail a response to theft. . . . Silent car alarms connect immediately to a security company, while the noisy ones are a problem, not a solution. They should be banned, finally." [Letter to the editor, *New York Times*]

Ⓐ 16. "If history is a gauge, the U.S. government cannot be trusted when it comes to sending our children to war. It seems that many years after Congress sends our children to war, we find out that the basic premise for the war was an intentional lie." [Letter to the editor, *L.A. Daily News*]

Exercise 1.4

For each of the following passages indicate whether it constitutes an argument. For each argument specify both the conclusion and the premises.

Ⓐ * 1. Faster-than-light travel is not possible. It would violate a law of nature.

(A) 2. You have neglected your duty on several occasions, and you have been absent from work too many times. Therefore, <u>you are not fit to serve</u> in <u>your current capacity.</u>

X 3. Racial profiling is not an issue for white people, but it is an issue for African Americans.

(A) * 4. The <u>flu epidemic on the East Coast is real.</u> Government health officials say so. And I personally have read at least a dozen news stories that characterize the situation as a "flu epidemic."

X 5. Communism is bunk. Only naïve, impressionable pinheads believe that stuff.

(A) 6. "Current-day Christians use violence to spread their right-to-life message. These Christians, often referred to as the religious right, are well known for violent demonstrations against Planned Parenthood and other abortion clinics. Doctors and other personnel are threatened with death, clinics have been bombed, there have even been cases of doctors being murdered." [Letter to the editor, *Arizona Daily Wildcat*]

X * 7. "I am writing about the cost of concert tickets. I am outraged at how much ticket prices are increasing every year. A few years ago, one could attend a popular concert for a decent price. Now some musicians are asking as much as $200 to $300." [Letter to the editor, *Buffalo News*]

X 8. "Homeland security is a cruel charade for unborn children. Some 4,000 per day are killed in their mother's womb by abortion. This American holocaust was legalized by the Supreme Court in an exercise of raw judicial power." [Letter to the editor, *Buffalo News*]

(A) 9. <u>Witches are real.</u> They are mentioned in the Bible. There are many people today who claim to be witches. And historical records reveal that there were witches in Salem.

X * 10. Stretched upon the dark silk night, bracelets of city lights glisten brightly.

(A) 11. Vaughn's car is old. It is beat up. It is unsafe to drive. Therefore, <u>Vaughn's car is ready for the junkyard.</u>

Exercise 1.5

For each of the following conclusions, write at least two premises that can support it. Your proposed premises can be entirely imaginary. To concoct the premises, think of what kind of statement (if true) would convince you to believe the conclusion.

EXAMPLE

Conclusion: Pet psychics can diagnose a dog's heartburn 100 percent of the time.
Premise 1: In the past fifty years, in hundreds of scientific tests, pet psychics were able to correctly diagnose heartburn in dogs 100 percent of the time.
Premise 2: Scientists have confirmed the existence of energy waves that can carry information about the health of animals.

1. What this country needs is more family values.
2. All animals—rodents, dogs, apes, whatever—have moral rights, just as people do.
* 3. Every woman has the right to abort her fetus if she so chooses.
4. When I looked into your eyes, time stood still.
5. All medical patients have the right to end their own lives.
* 6. When it comes to animals, Vaughn doesn't know what he's talking about.
7. Suspicion has arisen regarding the financial dealings of Governor Spendthrift.
8. The Internet is the most dangerous tool that terrorists have in their arsenal.
* 9. The Internet is the best tool that law enforcement officials have against terrorists.
10. Pornography is good for society because it educates people about sexuality.
11. Pornography is bad for society because it misleads people about sexuality.
* 12. *The Sopranos* is the greatest series in the history of TV.
13. It is the duty of every student to prevent this arbitrary tuition increase.
14. Ling cannot hold her liquor.

Exercise 1.6

For each of the following sets of premises, write a conclusion that would be supported by the premises (your conclusion should depend on both premises). Neither the conclusion nor the premises need to be statements that are true. To formulate an appropriate conclusion, try to think of a statement (conclusion) that could reasonably be supported by the premises.

EXAMPLE

Premise 1: The price of your shares in the stock market will continue to decline for at least a year.
Premise 2: Anyone with shares whose price will continue to decline for at least a year should sell now.
Conclusion: You should sell now.

1. Premise 1: You are afraid of heights.
   Premise 2: Anyone who is afraid of heights will fall if he or she climbs a tree.
* 2. Premise 1: School vouchers are being used in four states.
   Premise 2: School vouchers have decreased the quality of education in every state where they've been used.
3. Premise 1: School vouchers are being used in four states.
   Premise 2: School vouchers have improved the quality of education in every state where they've been used.
* 4. Premise 1: All married people are happier than unmarried people.
   Premise 2: You are married.

(handwritten notes in margin):
You will fall if you climb a tree

SV have decreased the quality of Education in towns.

SV have improved the quality of Education in towns

As a M P you are happier than people who are not M

5. Premise 1: If stem-cell research is banned, Edgar will be very happy.
   Premise 2: Stem-cell research is banned.

Edgar will be very happy

6. Premise 1: If there is no God, then there is no morality.
   Premise 2: There is no God.

There is no morality

7. Premise 1: There is a God.
   Premise 2: If there is a God, then life has meaning.

Life has meaning

* 8. Premise 1: There is a great deal of pornography of all kinds on the Internet.
   Premise 2: The government has essentially established a hands-off policy toward pornography on the Internet.
   Premise 3: Kids everywhere have access to pornography of all kinds on the Internet.

The govt. does not do anything re: pornography on the Internet even though kids have access to all kinds of porn

9. Premise 1: People in favor of capital punishment have a complete disregard for human life.
   Premise 2: Anyone who has a complete disregard for human life cannot be trusted.
   Premise 3: Nancy favors capital punishment.

Nancy cannot be trusted

Exercise 1.7

For each of the following passages, determine if there is an argument present. If so, identify the premises and the conclusion.

* 1. "[T]he Religious Right is *not* 'pro-family'. . . . Concerned parents realize that children are curious about how their bodies work and need accurate, age-appropriate information about the human reproductive system. Yet, thanks to Religious Right pressure, many public schools have replaced sex education with fear-based 'abstinence only' programs that insult young people's intelligence and give them virtually no useful information." [Rob Boston, *Free Inquiry Magazine*]

2. "[Francis Bacon] is the father of experimental philosophy. . . . In a word, there was not a man who had any idea of experimental philosophy before Chancellor Bacon; and of an infinity of experiments which have been made since his time, there is hardly a single one which has not been pointed out in his book. He had even made a good number of them himself." [Voltaire, *On Bacon and Newton*]

* 3. "Is there archaeological evidence for the [Biblical] Flood? If a universal Flood occurred between five and six thousand years ago, killing all humans except the eight on board the Ark, it would be abundantly clear in the archaeological record. Human history would be marked by an absolute break. We would see the devastation wrought by the catastrophe in terms of the destroyed physical remains of pre-Flood human settlements. . . . Unfortunately for the Flood enthusiasts, the destruction of all but eight of the world's people left no mark on the archaeology of human cultural evolution." [Kenneth L. Feder, *Frauds, Myths, and Mysteries*]

There is archaeological evidence for the [Biblical] Flood.

4. "Subjectivism claims that what makes an action [morally] right is that a person approves of it or believes that it's right. Although subjectivism may seem admirably egalitarian in that it takes everyone's moral judgments to be as good as everyone else's, it has some rather bizarre consequences. For one thing, it implies that each of us is morally infallible. As long as we approve of or believe in what we are doing, we can do no wrong. But this cannot be right. Suppose that Hitler believed that it was right to exterminate the Jews. Then it was right for Hitler to exterminate the Jews. . . . But what . . . Hitler did was wrong, even if [he] believed otherwise." [Theodore Schick, Jr., *Free Inquiry Magazine*]

Field Problems

1. Obtain the "Letters to the Editor" section of any newspaper (including student newspapers and online newspapers). Select a letter that contains at least one argument. Locate the conclusion and each premise.

   Next go through the letters again to find one that contains no argument at all. Rewrite the letter so that it contains at least one argument. Try to preserve as much of the original letter as possible. Stay on the same topic.

2. Go to www.townhall.com or www.usatoday.com and select an opinion essay on any issue. Identify its premises and conclusion, and decide whether you think the argument is a good one, providing reasons for your judgment.

Self-Assessment Quiz

Answers appear in "Answers to Self-Assessment Quizzes" (Appendix C).

1. What is an argument?
2. Name at least three premise indicators and three conclusion indicators.
3. Select the sentence that is *not* a statement:

   a. When I met you, you didn't know anything about logic.
   b. Read the story and write a complete review of it.
   c. Four score and seven years ago our fathers brought forth on this continent a new nation.
   d. The best pizza in town can be had at Luigi's.

4. From the following list, select the conclusion that is supported by the premises in the following argument:

   When conservative Pat Buchanan last spoke on this campus, he was shouted down by several people in the audience who do not approve of his politics. He tried to continue but finally had to give up and walk away. That was unfortunate, but he's not the only one. This kind of treatment has also happened to other unpopular guest speakers. How easily the students at this university forget that free speech is guaranteed by the Bill of Rights. University regulations also support free speech for all students, faculty, and visitors and strictly forbid the harassment of speakers. And this country was founded on the idea that citizens have the right to freely express their views—even when those views are unpopular.

a. Pat Buchanan is a fascist.

b. We should never have guest speakers on campus.

c. Campus speakers should be allowed to speak freely without being shouted down.

d. Some guest speakers deserve to have the right of free speech and some don't.

5. Indicate whether the following passage contains an argument. If it does, specify the conclusion.

> We live in an incredibly over-reactionary society where the mindless forces of victim demagoguery have unfortunately joined with the child-worship industry. It is obviously tragic that a few twisted kids perpetuated such carnage there in Columbine. [Letter to the editor, Salon.com]

6. Indicate whether the following passage contains an argument. If it does, specify the conclusion.

> "War doesn't solve problems; it creates them," said an Oct. 8 letter about Iraq. World War II solved problems called Nazi Germany and militaristic Japan and created alliances with the nations we crushed. . . . The Persian Gulf war solved the problem of the Iraqi invasion of Kuwait. The Civil War solved the problem of slavery. These wars created a better world. War, or the threat of it is the only way to defeat evil enemies who are a threat to us. There is no reasoning with them. There can be no peace with them . . . so it's either us or them. What creates true peace is victory. [Letter to the editor, *New York Times*]

7. Indicate whether the following passage contains an argument. If so, specify the conclusion.

> Paul Krugman will always reach the same answer, namely that President Bush is wrong about everything. This time, he asserts that the federal government is "slashing domestic spending." Really? The president's budget request for 2003 would raise domestic spending 6 percent. Even setting aside spending that is related to homeland security, the president's request was for more than 2 percent growth, or nearly $7 billion in new dollars. In total, over the last five years, domestic spending will have skyrocketed by more than 40 percent. [Letter to the editor, *New York Times*]

For questions 8–12, indicate which sentences or sentence fragments are likely to be conclusions and which are likely to be premises.

8. Therefore, the Everglades will be destroyed within three years.
9. Assuming that you will never reach Boston.
10. This implies that you are not driving as safely as you should.
11. Given all the hoopla surrounding the football team.
12. It follows that sexual harassment should be a crime.

For questions 13–15, write at least two premises for each of the numbered conclusions. You can make up the premises, but you must ensure that they support the conclusion.

13. DNA evidence should be disallowed in cases of capital murder.
14. Computers will never be able to converse with a human being well enough to be indistinguishable from humans.
15. The great prophet Nostradamus (1503–1566) predicted the September 11 terrorist attacks.

Read the following argument. Then in questions 16–20, supply the information requested. Each question asks you to identify by number all the sentences in the argument that fulfill a particular role—conclusion, premise, background information, example or illustration, or reiteration of a premise or the conclusion. Just write down the appropriate sentence numbers.

[1] Is global warming a real threat? [2] Or is it hype propagated by tree-hugging, daft environmentalists? [3] The president apparently thinks that the idea of global climate change is bunk. [4] But recently his own administration gave the lie to his bunk theory. [5] His own administration issued a report on global warming called the *U.S. Climate Action Report 2002.* [6] It gave no support to the idea that global warming doesn't happen and we should all go back to sleep. [7] Instead, it asserted that global warming was definitely real and that it could have catastrophic consequences if ignored. [8] For example, global climate change could cause heat waves, extreme weather, and water shortages right here in the United States. [9] The report is also backed by many other reports, including a very influential one from the United Nations. [10] Yes, George, global warming is real. [11] It is as real as typhoons and ice storms.

16. Conclusion.
17. Premise or premises.
18. Background information.
19. Example or illustration.
20. Repetition of conclusion or premise.

Critical Thinking and Writing
MODULE 1

This is the first of five end-of-chapter lessons, or modules, designed to help you think about, plan, and write good argumentative essays. The modules are progressive, starting here with a few fundamentals of the writing process and then later covering basic guidelines and concepts that can help you think critically and write intelligently about arguments and issues. Though the modules are linked in some fashion to material in their corresponding chapters, they are meant to serve as a stand-alone (though cumulative) tutorial to be used as your instructor sees fit.

ARGUMENTS AND ARGUMENTATIVE ESSAYS

As we note in this chapter, an argument is a group of statements in which some of them (the premises) are intended to support another of them (the conclusion). This configuration of statements-supporting-another-statement is not only the basic structure of an argument—it's the general design of an argumentative essay. An argumentative essay tries to support a particular conclusion or position on an issue by offering reasons to support that conclusion. Arguments (in the critical thinking sense) are not passionate exchanges of unsupported views, pointless contests of the is-too-is-not variety. And neither are argumentative essays. A mere sequence of statements expressing your views is not an argument, just as several pages of such statements do not constitute an argumentative essay.

So in an argumentative essay, your main task is to provide rational support for a claim. If you are successful, you will have shown that there are good reasons to accept your view of things. Readers who think critically may well be persuaded by your arguments. If you write well, you may be able to make your essay even more persuasive through rhetorical or stylistic devices that add emphasis, depth, and vividness to your prose. No one wants to read a boring essay. What you should not do, however, is rely entirely on non-argumentative elements to persuade your audience. Strong emotional appeals, for example, can indeed persuade some people, but they prove nothing. In truly effective argumentative essays, the primary persuasive device is critical reasoning.

BASIC ESSAY STRUCTURE

Good argumentative essays generally contain the following elements, though not necessarily in the order shown here:

- Introduction (or opening)
- Statement of thesis (the claim to be supported)

- Argument supporting the thesis
- Assessment of objections
- Conclusion

In the *introduction*, you want to do at least two things: (1) grab the reader's attention and (2) provide background information for the thesis. Effective attention-grabbers include startling statistics, compelling quotations, interesting anecdotes, opinions of experts, shocking or unexpected claims, and vivid imagery. Whatever attention-grabbers you use, *they must relate to the topic of the essay*. No use telling a good story if it has nothing to do with your thesis. Providing background for your thesis often means explaining why your topic is important, telling how you became concerned, or showing that there is a problem to be solved or a question to be answered. Very often the introduction is laid out in the first paragraph of the essay, sometimes consisting of no more than a sentence or two. In general, the briefer the introduction, the better.

The *thesis statement* also usually appears in the first paragraph. It's the statement that you hope to support or prove in your essay, the conclusion of the argument that you intend to present. You want to state the thesis in a single sentence and do so as early as possible in the essay. Your thesis statement is like a compass to your readers, guiding them through your essay from premise to premise, showing them a clear path. It also helps *you* stay on course, reminding you to keep every part of the essay related to your single unifying idea. Your thesis statement should be restricted to a claim that can be defended in the space allowed (often only 750 to 1000 words). Not restricted enough: "Tuition is too high." Better: "Tuition increases at Podunk College are unacceptable." Better still: "The recent tuition increase at Podunk College is unnecessary for financial reasons." (More on how to devise a properly restricted thesis statement in a moment.)

The main body of the essay is the fully developed *argument supporting the thesis*. This means that the basic essay structure consists of the thesis statement followed by each premise or reason that supports the thesis. Each premise in turn is clearly stated, sufficiently explained and illustrated, and supported by examples, statistics, expert opinion, and other evidence. Sometimes you can develop the essay very simply by devoting a single paragraph to each premise. At other times, each premise may demand several paragraphs. In any case, you should develop just one point per paragraph, with every paragraph clearly relating to the thesis statement.

A sketch of the argument for the Podunk College essay, then, might look like this:

Premise: If the college has a budget surplus, then a tuition increase is unnecessary.

Premise: The college has had a budget surplus for the last five years.

Premise: If the college president says that the school is financially in good shape and therefore doesn't need a tuition increase, then it's probably true that the school doesn't need a tuition increase.

Premise: In an unguarded moment, the president admitted that the school is financially in good shape and therefore doesn't need a tuition increase.

Thesis statement: Therefore, the recent tuition increase at Podunk College is probably unnecessary for financial reasons.

Good argumentative essays include an *assessment of objections*—an honest effort to take into account any objections that readers are likely to raise about the thesis statement or its premises. When you deal with such objections in your essay, you lend credibility to it because you're making an attempt to be fair and thorough. In addition, when you carefully examine objections, you can often see ways to make your argument or thesis statement stronger. It isn't necessary to consider every possible objection, just the strongest or the most common ones. Sometimes it's best to deal with objections when you discuss premises that relate to them. At other times it may be better to handle objections near the end of the essay after defending the premises.

Finally, your essay—unless it's very short—must have a *conclusion*. The conclusion usually appears in the last paragraph of the essay. Typically it reiterates the thesis statement (though usually not in exactly the same words). If the argument is complex or the essay is long, the conclusion may contain a summary of the argument. Good conclusions may reassert the importance of the thesis statement, challenge readers to do something about a problem, tell a story that emphasizes the relevance of the main argument, or bring out a disturbing or unexpected implication of a claim defended in the body of the essay.

GUIDELINES FOR WRITING THE ESSAY

1. *Determine your thesis statement.* Do *not* write on the first thesis idea that pops into your head. Select a topic you're interested in and narrow its scope until you have a properly restricted thesis statement. Research the topic to find out what issues are being debated. When you think you have an idea for a thesis statement, stop. Dig deeper into the idea by examining the arguments associated with that claim. Choose a thesis statement that you think you can defend. If you come to a dead end, start the process over.

2. *Create an outline.* Establish the basic framework of your outline by writing out your thesis statement and all the premises that support it. Then fill in the framework by jotting down what points you will need to make in defense of each premise. Decide on what objections to your argument you will consider and how you will respond to them.

3. *Write a first draft.* As you write, don't be afraid to revise your outline or even your thesis statement. Writing will force you to think carefully about the strengths and weaknesses of your argument. If need be, write a second draft and a third. Good writers aren't afraid of revisions; they depend on them.

4. *Stay on track.* Make sure that each sentence of your essay relates somehow to your thesis statement and argument.

5. *Zero in on your audience.* Determine for what audience your essay is intended, and *write to them.* Is it readers of the local paper? fellow students? people who are likely to disagree with you?

6. *Support your premises.* Back up the premises of your argument with examples, expert opinion, statistics, analogies, and other kinds of evidence.

7. *Let your final draft sit.* If possible, when you've finished writing your paper, set it aside and read it the next day. You may be surprised how many mistakes this fresh look can reveal. If you can't set the essay aside, ask a friend to read it and give you some constructive criticism.

Writing Assignments

1. Read Essay 1 ("Death Penalty Discriminates Against Black Crime Victims") in Appendix A and outline the argument presented. Specify the thesis statement and each supporting premise.

2. Write a two-page essay in which you defend a claim that *contradicts* the thesis statement in Essay 1. Pretend that all the evidence cited in Essay 1 actually supports *your* thesis statement. You may alter the description of the evidence accordingly.

3. Study the argument presented in Essay 2 ("Marine Parks") in Appendix A. Identify the conclusion and the premises and objections considered. Then write a two-page rebuttal to the essay. That is, defend the claim that marine mammals should continue to be kept in marine parks.

4. Select an issue from the following list and write a three-page paper defending a claim pertaining to the issue.

   • Should there be a constitutional amendment banning the desecration of the American flag?
   • Should a representation of the Ten Commandments be allowed to be displayed in a federal courtroom?
   • Should the legal drinking age be lowered?
   • Should the private ownership of fully automatic machine guns be outlawed?

Obstacles to Critical Thinking

- Appreciate that there are ways to (1) detect errors in our thinking, (2) restrain the attitudes and feelings that can distort our reasoning, and (3) achieve a level of objectivity that makes critical thinking possible.
- Understand that the most common impediments to critical thinking can be sorted into two categories: (1) those hindrances that arise because of *how* we think and (2) those that occur because of *what* we think.

PSYCHOLOGICAL OBSTACLES

- Learn how to detect and overcome self-interested thinking by (1) watching out for instances when your deliberations get personal, (2) being alert to ways that critical thinking can be undermined, and (3) ensuring that no relevant evidence or ideas have been left out.
- Appreciate how group thinking can distort critical thinking.
- Understand the meaning and be able to cite examples of *peer pressure*, *appeal to popularity*, *appeal to common practice*, and *stereotyping*.

PHILOSOPHICAL OBSTACLES

- Know what a worldview is and how certain pivotal ideas in a worldview can undermine critical thinking.
- Be able to critique the doctrine of subjective relativism.
- Be able to critique the doctrine of social relativism.
- Know the definition of philosophical skepticism and how the view relates to critical thinking.

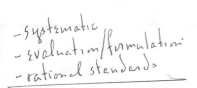

Environment is hostile to CT

- systematic
- evaluation/formulation
- rational standards

Fallibility

Training in CT
① Detect errors in our thinking
② Retrain attitudes & feelings that can distort our reasoning
③ Cultivate an objective view.

Requirements
① Awareness
② Practice
③ Motivation

Sources of Error
① Psychological Obstacles: How we think...
② Philosophical Obstacles: What we think...

CRITICAL THINKING DOES NOT HAPPEN IN A VACUUM BUT IN AN "environment" that's often hostile to it. It takes place in the real world in the minds of real people who almost always have thoughts and feelings and experiences that, given half a chance, would sabotage critical reasoning at every turn. The sparkling palace of our mind is grand—except for the demons chained in the basement.

Recall our definition of critical thinking: *The systematic evaluation or formulation of beliefs, or statements, by rational standards.* This means, of course, that several factors must be present for the process of critical thinking to be fully realized. If the process fails to be systematic, or falls short of being a true evaluation or formulation, or ignores rational standards, critical thinking can't happen. Because we are fallible, there are a thousand ways that this failure of reason could come about. And there is no cure for our fallibility.

We should expect then that thinking critically will often be difficult and even unpleasant (as painful truths sometimes are), and indeed it is. But there are ways to (1) detect errors in our thinking (even subtle ones), (2) restrain the attitudes and feelings that can distort our reasoning, and (3) achieve a level of objectivity that makes critical thinking possible.

Doing all this—and doing it consistently—requires *awareness*, *practice*, and *motivation*. If we are to think critically, we must be *aware* of not only what good critical thinking involves but also what sloppy thinking entails. Then we must *practice* avoiding the pitfalls and using the skills and techniques that critical thinking requires. And we must be *motivated* to do all of this, for it is unlikely that we will use critical thinking very much if we can't appreciate its value and therefore have little motivation to make the extra effort.

We can sort the most common impediments to critical thinking into two main categories: (1) those hindrances that arise because of *how* we think and (2) those that occur because of *what* we think. There is some overlap in these categories; how people think is often a result of what they think and vice versa. But in general, category 1 obstacles are those that come into play because of psychological factors (our fears, attitudes, motivations, and desires), and category 2 impediments are those that arise because of certain philosophical ideas we have (our beliefs about beliefs). For example, a category 1 hindrance is the tendency to conform our opinions to those of our peers. This conformism often grows out of some psychological need that is part of our personality. A common category 2 problem is the belief that objectivity in thinking is impossible or that we really don't know anything or that we don't know what we think we know.

In this chapter we review the most common category 1 and 2 barriers to critical thinking and practice uncovering and neutralizing them. The motivation to learn these lessons well is up to you.

FURTHER THOUGHT

💡 Francis Bacon on Critical Thinking

Francis Bacon (1561–1626), the godfather of modern science, articulated basic principles and methods of science and advocated their use in the careful pursuit of reliable knowledge. He also warned about common mistakes in thinking that can doom the scientific enterprise and lead to biased perceptions and serious error. Bacon asserted that preventing these mistakes is possible through scientific, down-to-earth thinking —approximately what we would call *critical thinking*, a necessary and powerful tool in the search for truth. He termed the mistakes "the idols of the mind" because he thought that people not only commit the errors but revere them as one would revere a false god.

Bacon focused on four kinds of idols that he considered especially prevalent and destructive. The first type is "The Idols of the Tribe"—the problems in thinking that arise from human nature generally. This is the fallacy of presuming that our biased perceptions are automatically a true reflection of the objective world, that knowledge is to be found inside us without any reference to the real world.

The second group consists of "The Idols of the Cave"—the biases that are unique to each individual. These develop from each person's personality, education, and experiences. Bacon claimed that we each live in our own cave, "which refracts and discolors the light of nature."

Then there are "The Idols of the Marketplace"—the impediments to clear thinking that develop from our imprecise and careless use of language. As Bacon said "the ill and unfit choice of words wonderfully obstructs the understanding."[1]

Finally are "The Idols of the Theater"—the ideologies or systems of thought that are "but so many stage-plays, representing worlds of their own creation after an unreal and scenic fashion."[2] These barriers to good critical thinking have little or nothing to do with the real world but are nevertheless thought to be accurate and profound.

Idols of the Mind
① Idols of the Tribe:

② Idols of the Cave

③ Idols of the Marketplace

④ Idols of the Theater

Psychological Obstacles

No one is immune to category 1 obstacles. We are all heir to psychological tendencies and habits that affect our behavior and channel our thinking. They tend to persist or recur, haunting our minds until we have the awareness and the will to break free of them.

THE ALMIGHTY SELF

As humans we spend a great deal of time protecting, maintaining, and comforting our own mental life, our own *selves*—a perfectly natural urge that does no harm until we push our self-serving efforts too far. How far is too far? From the standpoint of critical thinking, we have taken things too far when we accept claims for no good reason—when our thinking is no longer systematic and rational. In the service of our almighty selves, we distort our judgment and raise our risk of error, which is ironically a risk to ourselves.

Self-interested thinking takes several forms. We may decide to accept a claim *solely on the grounds that it advances, or coincides with, our interests.* You may think, "I believe the city should lower the sales tax for convenience stores because I own a convenience store," or, "I am against all forms of gun control because I am a hunter," or, "This university should not raise tuition because I am a student, and I don't want to pay more tuition." There is nothing inherently wrong with accepting a claim that furthers your own interests. The problem arises when you accept a claim *solely because* it furthers your interests. Self-interest alone simply cannot establish the truth of a claim. To base your beliefs on self-interest alone is to abandon critical thinking.

Here's a classic example of self-interested thinking depicted in the film *Twelve Angry Men*:

> Twelve jurors sit in a room deliberating over whether to find the defendant guilty of murder. The accused is a teenage boy who has grown up in the rough and impoverished streets of the inner city. At first, all but one juror (the jury foreman) vote guilty. The foreman convinces the other jurors to examine the evidence once again. Their deliberations go on for hours, and as they do, the prosecution's case slowly falls apart. Damning evidence that had seemed so strong earlier was now shown to be full of holes. They take another vote, but this time eleven jurors, including the foreman, vote not guilty, while one man (juror number 3) insists that the other jurors are deluded and that the boy is undoubtedly guilty. The jurors ask him to explain his reasons. He angrily insists again that the boy is guilty, but he can't provide any evidence or reasons that suggest the boy's guilt. He just rants at the other jurors. Finally the other jurors think they understand what's behind the seemingly irrational stance of juror number 3: He wants to convict the boy for personal reasons—

[Handwritten margin notes:]

See Schopenhauer: Counsels & Maxims "Our Relations to Others" see section 26

① Self-Interested Thinking (SIT)

Self-interest cannot establish the truth of a claim...

Twelve Angry Men

perhaps because of a troubled relationship with his own son or because of some other bias that has nothing to do with the guilt or innocence of the defendant.

In this example, the other members of the jury eventually realize that the judgments of juror number 3 are self-serving, linked to his own emotional needs. What gave him away? An obvious clue is his emotional protestations. But an even more telling clue is his rejection of all relevant evidence. The reasons for acquitting are perfectly clear to the other jurors, but he won't (or can't) consider them. In everyday life, these two clues often signal the presence of powerful self-interest at work.

The influence of self on your thinking can take another form. You may be tempted to accept claims *for no other reason than that they help you save face*. We all like to think of ourselves as excelling in various ways. We may believe that we are above average in intelligence, integrity, talent, compassion, physical beauty, sexual prowess, athletic ability, and much more. But we not only like to think such things about ourselves, we want others to think the same about us. The rub comes, however, when we accept or defend claims just to cover up the cracks in our image. You make a mistake, and so you blame it on someone or something else. You behave badly, and you try to justify your behavior. You make a judgment or observation that turns out to be wrong, and you're too embarrassed or proud to admit it. (In Chapter 4 we'll learn that sometimes self-interested thinking can even alter our perceptions.)

The consequences of self-centered thinking can be, well, self-destructive. In the realm of critical thinking, this devotion to yourself can prevent careful evaluation of claims, limit critical inquiry, blind you to the facts, provoke self-deception, engender rationalizations, lead you to suppress or ignore evidence, and beget wishful thinking. And these mistakes can decrease your chances of success (however you define success) and hamper your personal growth, maturity, and self-awareness. Such egocentricism can also leave you wide open to propaganda and manipulation by people who appeal to your personal desires and prejudices. How easy would it be for people to control your choices and thoughts if they told you exactly what you wanted to hear? (There are in-depth discussions of these lapses in critical thinking in Chapters 4 and 5.)

Often what we think we see in vague stimuli turns out to be something that our minds have made up. We see bunnies, bearded men, and Elvis in formless clouds and smoke. We hear words and animal noises in garbled audio (like records played backward). This phenomenon is known as *pareidolia*. A good example is this stunning photo taken by NASA's Hubble Space Telescope showing the Cone Nebula, a massive pillar of gas and dust, the breeding ground for stars. Some Christians say they perceive something else in the picture: the head of Jesus Christ crowned with a ring of stars. The "Jesus Nebula" they call it. What image do you think would be picked out by Hindus or Muslims? What do you see?

Pareidolia

Saving Face

Self-centered thinking can be self-destructive...

"To be conscious that you are ignorant is a great step to knowledge."
—BENJAMIN DISRAELI

FURTHER THOUGHT

When We Construct the Facts Ourselves

Psychologists have long known that a great deal of what we experience is *fabricated by ourselves*. That is, our own desires and expectations help form an impressive proportion of our perceptions, memories, and beliefs. Here are two examples documented by scientific research:

- There are probably hundreds of stories about ghosts and aliens showing up in people's bedrooms. Whatever is going on here, it certainly doesn't need to be supernatural. Researchers have shown that when people are in that drowsy state just before sleep, they often have weird hallucinations known as *hypnogogic imagery*. These images come on suddenly, are not under the sleeper's control, and can seem as realistic as physical objects in the room. Images range from faces in the dark to ghostly shapes and colored geometric shapes.
- Research has shown that our memories aren't exact copies of past events. The recall of eyewitnesses, for instance, is notoriously iffy. In the act of recall, they try to reconstruct a memory—but the reconstruction is frequently inexact, resulting in distortions and missing details. Stress can exaggerate these problems. Our memories can be drastically changed if we later come across new information—even if the information is brief and wrong. Most amazing of all, our expectations about the way things should be can insert or delete elements of a memory. If we expect to see a gun in the hand of a bank robber, we may remember exactly that even though no gun was involved.

Part of the job of critical thinking, of course, is to counteract all these tendencies—or help you recognize them when they happen.

Other people (especially those who know you fairly well) may be amused or puzzled by your stubborn adherence to claims that obviously conflict with the evidence. Or they may think it odd that you cling to ideas or behaviors that you loudly condemn in others.

When examining a claim or making a choice, how can you overcome the excessive influence of your own needs? Sometimes you can do it only with great effort, and sometimes the task is much easier, especially if you remember these three guidelines:

- Watch out when things get very personal.
- Be alert to ways that critical thinking can be undermined.
- Ensure that nothing has been left out.

DILBERT: © Scott Adams/Dist. By United Feature Syndicate, Inc.

Watch Out When Things Get Very Personal

You are most likely to let your self-interest get in the way of clear thinking when you have a big personal stake in the conclusions you reach. You may be deeply committed to a particular view or belief, or you may want desperately for a particular claim to be false or unjustified, or you may be devoted not to particular claims but to *any* claims that contradict those of someone you dislike. Such zeal can wreck any attempt at careful, fair evaluation of a claim.

The twentieth-century philosopher Bertrand Russell asserts that the passionate holding of an opinion is a sure sign of a lack of reasons to support the opinion:

> When there are rational grounds for an opinion, people are content to set them forth and wait for them to operate. In such cases, people do not hold their opinions with passion; they hold them calmly, and set forth their reasons quietly. The opinions that are held with passion are always those for which no good ground exists; indeed the passion is the measure of the holder's lack of rational conviction.[3]

The dead giveaway that you are skewing your thinking is a surge of strong emotions (like the one that gripped juror number 3). If your evaluation or defense of a position evokes anger, passion, or fear, your thinking could be prejudiced or clouded. It is possible, of course, to be emotionally engaged in an issue and still think critically and carefully. But most of the time, getting worked up over a claim or conclusion is reason enough to suspect that your thinking is not as clear as it should be.

The rule of thumb is: If you sense a rush of emotions when you deal with a particular issue, stop. Think about what's happening and why. Then continue at a slower pace and with greater attention to the basics of critical reasoning,

Bertrand Russell: Passion sometimes masks a failure of rationality...

Rule of Thumb: If there is a rush of emotion—stop & think.

W.K. Clifford: It is morally
wrong to believe on in-
sufficient evidence...
(Note William James' objection)

Is It Wrong to Believe Without Good Reasons?

Some philosophers have asserted that it is morally wrong to believe a proposition without justification or evidence. One of these is the famous biologist Thomas Henry Huxley. Another is mathematician W. K. Clifford (1845–1879). This is how Clifford states his view:

> It is wrong always, everywhere, and for anyone, to believe anything upon insufficient evidence. If a man, holding a belief which he was taught in childhood or persuaded of afterwards, keeps down and pushes away any doubts which arise about it in his mind . . . and regards as impious those questions which cannot easily be asked without disturbing it—the life of that man is one long sin against mankind.[4]

Clifford thinks that belief without evidence is immoral because our actions are guided by our beliefs, and if our beliefs are unfounded, our actions (including morally relevant actions) are likely to be imprudent.

double-checking to ensure that you are not ignoring or suppressing evidence or getting sloppy in your evaluations.

Be Alert to Ways That Critical Thinking Can Be Undermined

If you understand the techniques and principles of critical thinking, and you have practiced applying them in a variety of situations, you are more likely than not to detect your own one-sided self-centered thinking when it occurs. An alarm should go off in your head: "Warning—faulty reasoning."

When your alarm sounds, double-check your thinking, look for lapses in arguments and claims, and weed them out.

Ensure That Nothing Has Been Left Out

A common flaw in reasoning is the failure to consider evidence or arguments that *do not support* preferred claims or positions. For example, you may secretly want a particular claim to be true, so you knowingly or unknowingly look for evidence in its favor but ignore evidence against it. The chances of making this mistake increase markedly when you are reasoning for the sake of self.

This kind of preferential treatment for some statements and not others is part of a common phenomenon called *selective attention* (see Chapters 4 and 5). In

Selective attention
& confirmation bias...

REVIEW NOTES

☑ Avoiding Self-Interested Thinking

- Watch out when things get personal and you become emotionally vested in an issue.
- Beware of the urge to distort your thinking to save face.
- Be alert to ways that critical thinking can be undermined.
- Ensure that nothing has been left out of consideration.
- Avoid selective attention.
- Make a conscious effort to look for opposing evidence.

FURTHER THOUGHT

💡 Are You a Conformist? Take This Test and Find Out

To some extent we all conform our ideas and behavior to group influences, but some people go overboard. Take the following test to find out if you're one of them. Check off each statement that applies to you, then add up the numbers of each checked statement to get your score. The lower your score, the more conformist you are.

+100   You usually change your beliefs for good reasons.
+1   You change your beliefs for good reasons only when money is involved.
−10   You usually change your beliefs for no reason whatsoever.
−15   You automatically change your beliefs when your friends ridicule them.
−30   You automatically change your beliefs when total strangers ridicule them.
−40   You change your beliefs whenever you see a TV ad.
−42   You change your beliefs to be accepted into a group.
−50   You change your clothes to be accepted into a group.
−50   You would change your car to be accepted into a group.
−100   You would change your beliefs *and* your physical features to be accepted into a group.

If your score is below zero, *do not* drop your course in critical thinking. If it's *way, way* below zero, you need more than a course in critical thinking. Is this a bogus test? Yes, totally. If you figured that out by the second statement, give yourself 1000 points.

"The fact that an opinion has been widely held is no evidence whatever that it is not absurd; indeed in view of the silliness of the majority of mankind, a widespread belief is more likely to be foolish than sensible."

—BERTRAND RUSSELL

Make a conscious effort to look for opposing evidence

Power of the Borg

Group Think: Cults are an extreme example, yet group think occurs on a daily basis...
See Arthur Deikman...

selective attention, we notice certain things and ignore others—usually without even being aware that we're doing it. We may ignore facts that contradict our beliefs and search out facts that support them. Scientific research has repeatedly confirmed this behavior. In a typical study, researchers showed subjects both *evidence for* and *evidence against* the reality of extrasensory perception (ESP). Subjects who already doubted the existence of ESP accurately recalled both kinds of evidence. But subjects who already believed in ESP remembered both kinds of evidence as *proving* ESP. They somehow recalled even the disconfirming evidence as supporting their belief in ESP!

The remedy for this problem is to *make a conscious effort to look for opposing evidence.* Don't consider your evaluation of a statement or argument finished until you've carefully considered *all the relevant reasons.* Ask yourself, "What is the evidence or reasons against this statement?"

This approach is at the heart of science. A basic principle of scientific work is not to accept a favored theory until competing (alternative) theories are thoroughly examined. (More on this in Chapter 10.)

THE POWER OF THE GROUP

In the television series *Star Trek: The Next Generation,* the crew of the starship *Enterprise* encounters an unusual threat: the Borg. The Borg is a collective of individual minds that have been stripped of individuality and merged into a single group-mind with evil intentions. Much of the Borg storyline (which spans several episodes) is about the dignity and importance of individualism as opposed to the conformism of the Borg hive. The thought of losing one's self in the monolithic Borg is presented as a profound tragedy—a theme that strikes a cord with humans. Individualism, independence, and freedom of thought are what we want, what we must have.

Or so we say. Despite our apparent longings, we humans spend a great deal of our time trying to conform to, or be part of, groups. We want to belong, we want the safety and comfort of numbers, we want the approval of our beloved tribe. All of which is perfectly normal. We are, after all, social creatures. Conformist tendencies are a fact of life. But trouble appears when our conformism hampers—or obliterates—critical thinking.

We all belong to multiple groups—family, employees, gender, church, club, professional society, political party, advocacy group, you name it—and we can be susceptible to pressure from all of them. Much of the time, there is intense pressure to fit into groups and to adopt ideas, attitudes, and goals endorsed by them. Sometimes the influence of the group is subtle but strong and can occur in the most casual, "unofficial" gatherings. The claims and positions adopted by the group can be implicit, never spoken, but well understood. The political chat group online, the group of Christians or Muslims or Jews who happen to meet on the bus, the collection of peers who support the same political cause—all these can exert a noticeable influence on our beliefs.

Group pressure to accept a statement or act in a certain way has several overlapping subtypes (some of which we'll cover in more detail in later chapters). When the pressure to conform comes from your peers, it's called—surprise—**peer pressure.** When the pressure comes from the mere popularity of a belief, it's known as—believe it or not—an **appeal to popularity** (also known as an appeal to the masses). When the pressure comes from what groups of people do or how they behave, it's called an **appeal to common practice.** In all cases, the lapse in critical thinking comes from the use of group pressure *alone* to try to support a claim (see Chapter 5).

www.CartoonStock.com

Group pressure can happen quickly. For example, if you're listening to a speech by a member of your own political party, you may immediately find yourself positively disposed toward the speaker—not because you agree with him but because he's a member of your group.

Group pressure can also take a while. Consider:

Lillian has just become a new member of the Democratic Club on campus, an association of Democrats and political liberals. She has been trying to join the club ever since her freshman year. She likes being in a group that shares most of her beliefs, and she feels that just being a member of the club—whose members include many of the brightest students on campus—boosts her up a notch or two socially. She soon finds out that she agrees with club members on every political and social issue—except one. Everyone else in the group is adamantly opposed to capital punishment. Lillian favors it because she researched all the arguments for and against it and concluded that the pro side was stronger. But she doesn't want to jeopardize her membership because of her stand on this one issue. So she never mentions it. Whenever she hears arguments against the death penalty, she believes them to be faulty. But after a few months, she learns to ignore the arguments. In fact, she tries not to think about the subject at all. Over time, her views on the subject change, until finally she finds herself being whole-heartedly against the death penalty.

Here, the need to belong slowly usurps critical reasoning in a specific subject area (capital punishment). On other topics, Lillian may be an astute critical thinker.

"Believe nothing, no matter where you read it, or who said it, no matter if I said it, unless it agrees with your own reason and your own common sense."
—THE BUDDHA

The Types of Group Think
① Peer pressure
② Appeal to popularity
③ Appeal to common practice

FURTHER THOUGHT

Prejudice, Bias, and Racism

Group pressure often leads to prejudice, bias, and racism. (To a lesser extent, so does self-interest.) But what do these terms mean?

Prejudice in its broadest sense is a judgment or opinion—whether positive or negative—based on insufficient reasons. But usually the term is used in a more narrow way to mean a negative, or adverse, belief (most often about people)

Critical thinking against racism. In 1957 during efforts to integrate schools in Little Rock, Arkansas, a black student is jeered as she attempts to attend classes at an all-white high school.

without sufficient reasons. At the heart of prejudice, then, is a failure of critical thinking. And the use of critical thinking is an important part of eradicating prejudiced views.

Bias is another word for prejudice, both in the general and the narrow sense. Sometimes the word is also used to mean an inclination of temperament or outlook—as in "My bias is in favor of tougher laws."

Racism is a lack of respect for the value and rights of people of different races or geographical origins. Usually this attitude is based on prejudice—specifically an unjustified belief that one group of people is somehow superior to another.

Ethnocentricism:
"We are better" Group Think

"A great many people think they are thinking when they are really rearranging their prejudices."
—WILLIAM JAMES

There's another kind of group influence that we have all fallen prey to: the pressure that comes from presuming that our own group is the best, the right one, the chosen one, and all other groups are, well, not as good. You can see this kind of ethnocentrism in religions, political parties, generations, social classes, and many other groups. The assumption that your group is better than others is at the heart of prejudice.

This we-are-better pressure is probably the most powerful of all. We all have certain beliefs not because we have thought critically about them but because

REVIEW NOTES

☑ Avoiding Group Pressure on Your Thinking

- Group pressure can come in the form of peer pressure, appeals to popularity, and appeals to common practice.
- Group-centered thinking can degenerate into narrow-mindedness, resistance to change, and stereotyping.
- The best way to defend yourself against group thinking is to always proportion your acceptance of a claim according to the strength of reasons.

"NEWSMAKERS"

Left-Wing/Right-Wing Bias

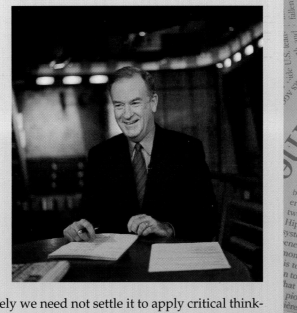

Is there a left-wing bias in the news media? A right-wing bias? Some swear the *New York Times* and PBS slant the news to the left; others say *Fox News* tilts it to the right. The charge that the news is politically slanted—left or right—regularly starts arguments (the nasty, pointless kind) and usually lacks supporting evidence. Whether the allegation is true is not an issue we can settle here, and fortunately we need not settle it to apply critical thinking to the news media.

As detailed in Chapter 4, many factors can render news reports unreliable, incomplete, or misleading—even when no political bias is at work. Critical thinking requires that we not assume without good reason that a report gives us an entirely accurate picture. The best way to ensure that we get the whole story is to read a variety of newspapers, newsmagazines, opinion journals, and websites. ▼

The worst approach is to rely only on news sources that reinforce our existing political views. People have a natural tendency to seek out only evidence that supports their treasured beliefs and to resist evidence that contradicts them. They want to watch, hear, and read only what is psychologically comforting—and to avoid what disturbs their worldview. But this strategy undermines serious inquiry and reflection, stunts our understanding, and blights independent thinking.

Do you ever read magazines, newspapers, or websites that run counter to your political beliefs? Do you associate only with people who share your political views? Do you ever seriously consider plausible objections to your positions? Do you think the availability of other points of view online helps open up the debate beyond older media biases? Or does it just reinforce what readers of each blog already think they know?

our parents raised us to believe them or because the conceptual push and pull of our social group has instilled them in us. That is, we may believe what we believe—and assume that our beliefs are better than anyone else's—because we were born into a family or society that maintains such views. We may be a Catholic or a Democrat or a racist primarily because we were born into a Catholic or Democratic or racist family or society. Like the influence of the self, this endemic pressure can lead to wishful thinking, rationalization, and self-deception. Group thinking can also easily generate narrow-mindedness, resistance to change, and **stereotyping** (drawing conclusions about people without sufficient reasons). (Again, more on these problems in Chapters 4 and 5.)

But as comfortable as our inherited beliefs are, when we accept them without good reason, we risk error, failure, and delusion. And as we discussed in Chapter 1, if we have certain beliefs solely because they were given to us, they are not really our beliefs. The sign of a maturing intellect is having the will and the courage to gradually prune beliefs that are groundless.

For critical thinkers, the best way to deal with the power of the group is to proportion your belief to the strength of reasons.

After thinking critically about claims favored by groups, you may find that the claims are actually on solid ground, and you really do have good reason to accept them. Or you may find that there is no good reason for believing them, and so you don't accept them. Either way, critical thinking will give you a clearer view of the group and yourself.

Critical thinking then is independent thinking. And in the West and many other parts of the world, those who achieve independent thinking—the Aristotles, the Einsteins, the Shakespeares, the Michaelangelos—are revered.

Philosophical Obstacles

A **worldview** is a philosophy of life, a set of fundamental ideas that helps us make sense of a wide range of important issues in life. The ideas are fundamental because they help guide us in the evaluation or acceptance of many other less basic ideas. They are answers to the "big questions" of life, such as, What do I know? Is knowledge possible? What is real and what is not? How do I know which actions are morally right?

The interesting thing about worldviews is that we all have one, for we all have adopted (or inherited) certain fundamental ideas about the world. You may have unknowingly absorbed the ideas from your family or society, and you may not have thought much about them, but you have a worldview nonetheless. Even the rejection of all worldviews is a worldview.

In Chapter 11 we discuss how critical thinking can help you construct a worldview that is founded on good reasons. For now, we need to investigate how some elements of a worldview—certain fundamental but problematic ideas—may undermine critical thinking. These notions can give rise to category 2 obstacles to critical reason, for they may affect our thinking through the content of our beliefs.

SUBJECTIVE RELATIVISM

Like science, critical thinking may be underpinned by a number of propositions that few people would think to question. Science, for example, is based on the proposition that the world is publicly understandable—that it has a certain structure (independent of what anyone thinks), that we can know the structure, and that this knowledge can be acquired by anyone. Critical thinking is based on similar ideas. Among the most basic is the notion that the truth of a claim does not depend on what a person thinks. That is, your believing that something is true *does not make it true.*

The idea that truth depends on what someone believes is called **subjective relativism,** and if you accept this notion or use it to try to support a claim, you're said to commit the **subjectivist fallacy.** This view says that truth depends not on the way things are but solely on what someone believes. Truth, in other words, is relative to persons. Truth is a matter of what a person believes—not a matter of how the world is. This means that a proposition can be true for one person, but not for another. If you believe that dogs can fly, then it is true (for you) that dogs can fly. If someone else believes that dogs cannot fly, then it is true (for him) that dogs cannot fly.

You've probably encountered subjective relativism more often than you realize. You may have heard someone (maybe even yourself!) say, "This is *my* truth, and that's *your* truth," or, "This statement is true *for me.*"

Many critics of subjective relativism maintain that it can undermine critical thinking in a fundamental way. In large part, critical thinking is about determining whether statements are true or false. But if we can make a statement true just by believing it to be true, then critical thinking would seem to be unnecessary. The subjectivist fallacy, they say, may be an excuse to forgo the tough job of critical inquiry.

Most philosophers see the situation this way: We use critical thinking to find out whether a statement is true or false—*objectively* true or false. Objective truth is about the world, about the way the world is regardless of what we may believe about it. To put it differently, there is a way the world is, and our beliefs do not make it. The world is the way it is, regardless of how we feel about it.

These same philosophers would probably be quick to point out that some objective truths *are* about our subjective states or processes. It might be true, for example, that you're feeling pain right now. But if so, the claim that you are feeling pain right now is an objective truth about your subjective state.

Also, they would readily admit that there are some things about ourselves that obviously *are* relative because they are one way for us and another way for someone else. You may like ice cream, but someone else may not. Your liking ice cream is then relative to you. But the truth about these states of affairs is not relative.

Subjective relativism (as well as other forms of relativism) is controversial, and we needn't spend much time on it here. But you should know at least that many philosophers have (through the use of critical thinking!) uncovered some

---

Subjective Relativism,
Subjective relativism :
the subjectivist fallacy :
mistaken view that truth
is relative to the individual

"Man is a credulous animal, and must believe *something*; in the absence of good grounds for belief, he will be satisfied with bad ones."

—BERTRAND RUSSELL

Subjectivist thinking as way
to avoid critical thinking

Realism: there is a way the
world is: we use CT to
discover the way the world is

Some objective truths are
about our subjective
states or processes...

My liking ice cream is
relative to me, but the truth
about this fact about me is
an objective truth re: the world

Critique of Subjectivism

① It entails personal in-
fallibility, which is absurd

② It is self-defeating...

odd implications that seem to render the view implausible. First, they point out that if we could make a statement true just by believing it to be true, we would be infallible. We could not possibly be in error about anything that we sincerely believed. We could never be mistaken about where we parked the car or what we said about jelly beans or what some general said about carpet bombing. Personal infallibility is, of course, absurd, and this possibility seems to weigh heavily against subjective relativism.

Social relativism implies that societies are infallible—even about such horrors as the Nazis' imprisonment and murder of millions of people in World War II.

Many critics think that subjective relativism's biggest problem is that it's self-defeating. It defeats itself because its truth implies its falsity. The relativist says, "All truth is relative." If this statement is objectively true, then it refutes itself because if it is objectively true that "All truth is relative," then the statement itself is an example of an objective truth. So if "All truth is relative" is objectively true, it is objectively false.

SOCIAL RELATIVISM

To escape the difficulties of subjective relativism, some people posit **social relativism,** the view that truth is relative to societies. The claim is that truth depends not on an individual's beliefs, but on society's beliefs. So a claim can be true for the Chinese but false for Americans, true for college students but false for public officials, true for Baptists but false for atheists. To many, this kind of relativism, like the subjective kind, also seems to render critical thinking superfluous.

Social relativism is attractive to many because it seems to imply an admirable egalitarianism—the notion that the beliefs of different societies are all equal. But a lot of philosophers maintain that it has most of the same defects that subjective relativism has. For example, according to social relativism, individuals aren't infallible, but societies are. The beliefs of whole societies cannot be mistaken. But this notion of societal infallibility is no more plausible than the idea of individual infallibility. Is it plausible that no society has ever been wrong about anything—never been wrong about the causes of disease, the best form of government, the number of planets in our solar system, the burning of witches, the Nazi policy of killing six million Jews?

"What we need is not the will to believe, but the will to find out."
—BERTRAND RUSSELL

Social Relativism:
Mistaken view that truth is relative to a society or culture

Social relativism seems to support tolerance but this view is mistaken...

Critique of Social Relativism
① It entails infallibility, which is absurd...
② It is self-defeating

Critics like to point out that just as subjective relativism is self-defeating, so is social relativism. The claim that "All truth is relative to societies" is self-defeating because if it is objectively true, then it is an example of an objective truth—and that means that the claim is objectively false.

If you accept relativism, you may be tempted to care very little about critical thinking, and that would be your loss. Fortunately, there is no good reason why you should neglect critical thinking in the name of relativism.[6]

SKEPTICISM

If knowledge were impossible, critical thinking—as a way of coming to know the truth or falsity of claims—would seem to be out of a job. Most of us, though, believe that we *can* acquire knowledge. We think that we know a great many things—that we are alive, that our shoes are a certain color, that there is a tree on the lawn, that the Earth is not flat, that rabbits cannot fly, that 2 + 2 = 4. But not everyone would agree. There are some who believe that we know much less than we think we do or nothing at all. This view is known as **philosophical skepticism,** and thinkers who raise doubts about how much we know are known as **philosophical skeptics.**

This is no place to dive into a debate on skepticism, but we can take a quick look at the most important type of philosophical skepticism and see what, if anything, it has to do with critical thinking. This form of skepticism says that knowledge requires certainty—if we are to know anything, we must be certain of it. This means that our knowledge isn't knowledge unless it is beyond any *possibility* of doubt. If knowledge requires certainty, however, there is very little that we know because there are always considerations that can undermine our certainty.

But it seems that our knowledge *does not* require certainty. All of us can cite many situations in which we do seem to have knowledge—even though we do not have absolutely conclusive reasons. We usually would claim to know, for example, that it is raining, that our dog has spots, that we were born, that the moon is not made of green cheese—even though we are not absolutely certain of any of these. These situations suggest that we do know many things. We know them not because they are beyond all *possible* doubt, but because they are beyond all *reasonable* doubt. Doubt is always possible, but it is not always reasonable. Rejecting a reasonable claim to knowledge just because of the bare possibility that you may be wrong is neither reasonable nor necessary.

Critical thinking does have a job to do in our efforts to acquire knowledge. Its task, however, is not to help us find claims that we cannot possibly doubt but to help us evaluate claims that vary in degrees of reasonable doubt—that is, from weak reasons (or no reasons) to very strong reasons.

Philosophical Skepticism Assumes that knowledge requires certainty. If this is so, there is very little we can know

Response to Skepticism Knowledge does not require certainty: belief must pass the reasonable doubt test; not the possible doubt test

KEY WORDS

appeal to common practice	social relativism
appeal to popularity (or to the masses)	stereotyping
peer pressure	subjective relativism
philosophical skepticism	subjectivist fallacy
philosophical skeptics	worldview

Summary

- Critical thinking takes place in a mental environment consisting of our experiences, thoughts, and feelings. Some elements in this inner environment can sabotage our efforts to think critically or at least make critical thinking more difficult. Fortunately, we can exert some control over these elements. With practice, we can detect errors in our thinking, restrain attitudes and feelings that can disrupt our reasoning, and achieve enough objectivity to make critical thinking possible.

- The most common of these hindrances to critical thinking fall into two main categories: (1) those obstacles that crop up because of *how* we think and (2) those that occur because of *what* we think. The first category is comprised of psychological factors such as our fears, attitudes, motivations, and desires. The second category is made up of certain philosophical beliefs.

- None of us is immune to the psychological obstacles. Among them are the products of egocentric thinking. We may accept a claim solely because it advances our interests or just because it helps us save face. To overcome these pressures, we must (1) be aware of strong emotions that can warp our thinking, (2) be alert to ways that critical thinking can be undermined, and (3) ensure that we take into account *all* relevant factors when we evaluate a claim.

- The first category of hindrances also includes those that arise because of group pressure. These obstacles include conformist pressures from groups that we belong to and ethnocentric urges to think that our group is superior to others. The best defense against group pressure is to proportion our beliefs according to the strength of reasons.

- We may also have certain core beliefs that can undermine critical thinking (the second category of hindrances). Subjective relativism is the view that truth depends solely on what someone believes—a notion that may make critical thinking look superfluous. But subjective relativism leads to some strange consequences. For example, if the doctrine were true, each of us would be infallible. Also, subjective relativism has a logical problem—it's self-defeating. Its truth implies its falsity. There are no good reasons to accept this form of relativism.

- Social relativism is the view that truth is relative to societies—a claim that would also seem to make critical thinking unnecessary. But this notion is undermined by the same kinds of problems that plague subjective relativism.

- Philosophical skepticism is the doctrine that we know much less than we think we do. One form of philosophical skepticism says that we cannot know anything unless the belief is beyond all possible doubt. But this is not a plausible criterion for knowledge. To be knowledge, claims need not be beyond all possible doubt but beyond all *reasonable* doubt.

EXERCISES

Exercises marked with * have answers in "Answers to Exercises" (Appendix B). Quizzes, integrative exercises, and writing assignments are not supplied with answers.

Exercise 2.1

REVIEW QUESTIONS

*1. According to the text's definition of critical thinking, what factors must be present for critical thinking to be realized?

2. What are the two main categories of common obstacles to critical thinking?

3. What did W. K. Clifford say about the morality of believing claims?

4. What is stereotyping?

*5. From the standpoint of critical thinking, what event signals that we have allowed our bias in favor of our selves go too far?

6. According to the text, what effect can our urge to save face have on our thinking?

*7. When are you most likely to let your self-interest get in the way of clear thinking?

8. According to the text, what should you do if you sense a rush of emotion when you think about a particular issue?

9. What is selective attention?

10. According to the text, how might selective attention affect your thinking when you are examining evidence for or against a claim?

* 11. How might the influence of a group that you belong to affect your attempts to think critically?

12. According to the text, what is the most powerful group pressure of all?

13. What is the appeal to popularity?

* 14. What is a worldview?

15. What is subjective relativism?

16. According to the text, how could subjective relativism make critical thinking unnecessary?

* 17. Is critical thinking concerned with the *objective* or the *subjective* truth of claims?

18. What is social relativism?

19. What is philosophical skepticism?

20. Does our knowledge require certainty?

* 21. What kind of doubt is involved in the acquisition of knowledge?

Exercise 2.2

For each of the following passages, indicate whether it contains examples of self-interested thinking, face-saving, or group pressure. Some of these are really tough. (SIT)   (FS)   (GP)

* 1. Mary: Animals have the same rights as humans.
   Jenna: What makes you think that?
   SIT Mary: I love animals, and there are so many that are treated horribly all over the world. It's heartbreaking.

2. Jonathan: My essay is better than Julio's.
   Betty: Why do you think that yours is better than all the others? Do you
   SIT agree that the content and writing of all the essays are similar?
   Jonathan: Well, yes.
   Betty: Do you agree that all the other benchmarks of quality are nearly identical?
   Jonathan: Yes, but mine is still better.

3. Dear friends, as your state senator I will continue my tireless work on
   SIT your behalf. I will continue to use my considerable talents to make this district even better. I will continue to let my integrity be the guide for all my actions.

GP * 4. We cannot allow those people to move into this neighborhood. They're not like us.

GP 5. I oppose women becoming members of this club. If I endorsed their claims, every friend I've got in the club would turn his back on me.

GP   6. His statements about the West Bank are all false, of course. He's an
            Israeli.

GP/SIT * 7. Christianity is superior to all other religions. I was raised Christian, and
            all my relatives are Christians. This is the only religion I've known, and
            the only one I need.

SIT   8. I'm due for tenure next year, so I am in favor of continuing the tradition
            of tenure at this university.

GP   9. The United States is the greatest nation on the face of the earth. I don't
            know anything about other countries, and I don't want to know.

SIT   * 10. If Joan is appointed to the committee, I am guaranteed to have a job for
            the rest of my life. I wholeheartedly favor Joan's appointment.

GP   11. Free speech should not extend to pornographers. Right now they are
            allowed to espouse their smut on the Internet and many other places.
            That's just not how I was raised.

Exercise 2.3

Read each of the following claims. Then select from the list any statements that,
if true, would constitute good reasons for accepting the claim. Be careful: In
some questions, none of the choices is correct.

* 1. John: The newspaper account of the charges of pedophilia lodged against
     Father J. Miller, a Catholic priest in our town, should never have been
     printed.

    a. The charges are false.
    b. John is a Catholic.
    c. Important evidence that would exonerate Father Miller was not men-
       tioned in the newspaper account.
    d. The town is predominately Catholic.

  2. Alice: The speed limit on I-95 should be 70 mph.

    a. Raising the speed limit to 70 mph would result in faster and safer traffic.
    b. The state commission on highways did a study showing that I-95
       should have a limit of 70 mph.
    c. Alice travels I-95 every day and needs to drive 70 mph to get to work
       on time.
    d. Alice drives I-95 every day.

* 3. Janette: Women are less violent and less emotional than men.

    a. A study from Harvard shows that women are less violent and less
       emotional than men.
    b. Janette is a woman.
    c. Janette is a member of a group of women who are fighting for the rights
       of women.
    d. Janette and all her friends are women.

4. Brie: People should buy stock in IBM, an action that will push the price per share higher.

   a. Brie owns a large proportion of IBM stock.
   b. Brie is chair of the board at IBM.
   c. The stock market is weak.
   d. Brie has a large family to support.

   No Good Reasons

5. Colonel Stockton: The United States should attack the terrorists in Iran, even at the risk of a full-scale war with Arab states.

   a. The terrorists have humiliated Colonel Stockton's forces.
   b. The terrorists have humiliated the United States.
   c. Colonel Stockton is loyal to his troops, all of whom want to attack the terrorists in Iran.
   d. Attacking the terrorists in Iran would cause no casualties and would result in world peace.

* 6. Morgan: Capital punishment is always wrong.

   a. All of Morgan's friends agree that capital punishment is wrong.
   b. If Morgan favored capital punishment, her friends would abandon her.
   c. Morgan is president of the Anti-Capital Punishment League.
   d. Morgan has already made her views known and cannot change her mind without seeming to be inconsistent.

   No Good Reasons

7. Angelo: Marijuana should be legalized.

   a. All of Angelo's friends smoke marijuana.
   b. Legalizing marijuana would reduce the consumption of marijuana and save lives, money, and resources.
   c. Angelo has already said on television that marijuana should be legalized.
   d. Angelo likes to smoke marijuana.

Exercise 2.4

Read each of the following passages. Indicate whether it contains examples of the kind of group pressure that encourages people to conform (peer pressure or appeal to popularity) or the type that urges people to think that one's own group is better than others. For each example of group pressure, specify the possible negative consequences. A couple of these are very difficult to classify.

* 1. Ortega is deeply religious, attending church regularly and trying to abide by church law and the Scriptures. He has never considered any other path. He believes that laws should be passed that forbid people to shop on Sunday and that designate Easter as a national holiday.

   Better than Others

GP/Peer

2. John goes to a prestigious college where many students use illegal drugs. Nearly everyone in John's frat house uses them. So far, he hasn't tried any, but his frat brothers frequently ask if he wants some. And he has noticed that he is rarely invited to any frat parties.

GP/ Better Than Others

* 3. A northeast college has invited a famous writer to be a guest speaker in the campuswide distinguished speaker series. She is an accomplished poet and essayist. She is also a Marxist and favors more socialism in the United States. During her speech she is shouted down by a small group of conservative students and faculty.

Peer Pressure or Popularity

4. Yang Lei is a conservative columnist for one of the best conservative journals in the country. But she yearns for greener pastures—namely, a regular column for a weekly news magazine. She gets her dream job, though the magazine does have liberal leanings. The first few columns she writes for the magazine are a shock to her friends. Politically they are middle-of-the-road or even suspiciously liberal.

We Are Better

5. Alex is a fourth-grade teacher at a suburban elementary school in Tennessee. He is liked by students and teachers alike, and he has superior teaching skills. He is also a homosexual. When a group of fundamentalist Christians learn that Alex is gay, they pressure the school board to fire him.

Popularity

6. Sylvia writes a column for the university newspaper. In her last installment, she argues that in a time of national crisis, the U.S. justice department should have the power to arrest and detain literally anyone suspected of terrorism. Her arguments are well supported and presented with a tone of tolerance for those who disagree with her. And most students do disagree—vehemently. Hundreds of letters to the editor arrive at the newspaper, each one denouncing Sylvia and calling her a fascist and a few names that could not be published. In Sylvia's next column, she apologizes for her statements, says that she made serious errors, and declares that her statements should be viewed as hypothetical.

Popularity

* 7. Advertisement: When you make the best car in the world, everyone wants it. Audi XK2. A car in demand.

Exercise 2.5

Read each of the following scenarios. Indicate whether it contains examples of self-interested thinking or face-saving and, for each instance, specify the possible negative consequences.

FS

* 1. Barbara thinks that she is a superior student with excellent writing and math skills. She frequently says so to her friends and sometimes ridicules other people's grades and test scores. She predicts that her SAT scores will be in the 1400s. When she finally takes the test, she's calm, alert, and eager to get a fantastic score. Afterwards she says that she feels great.

Her scores come back in the 800s. She explains that the test doesn't count because it's obviously scored wrong and, besides, she's not a good test taker.

* 2. City assemblyman Jackson is in a position to cast the deciding vote on two proposals for the development of a new city park. Proposal 1 offers a parcel of land near the assemblyman's house, which affords him a beautiful view. Its drawbacks are that it costs twice as much as proposal 2 and cannot be easily accessed by most of the public. Proposal 2 suggests a parcel of land near the center of town. It is convenient to the public, has a more beautiful setting, and will raise property values in the area. Assemblyman Jackson says that the obvious best choice is proposal 1.

SIT

3. Antonio is a college student who responds predictably to his scores on tests. If the score is high, he remarks that he hardly studied at all and that his score ranks among the highest in the class. If the scores are low, he says that the instructor grades unfairly, that the test was flawed, and that he intends to protest his grade to the grade-review committee.

FS

4. Sheila is a bright medical scientist. For years she has been working on a series of clinical studies that could establish her favorite medical hypothesis—that high doses of vitamin E can cure skin cancer. Each study in the series has added more evidence suggesting that the hypothesis is probably true. The last study in the series is crucial. It is a much larger study than the others, and it will confirm or invalidate the usefulness of vitamin E for skin cancer. When the study is completed, she examines the data. Instead of confirming her hypothesis, the study suggests not only that her pet idea is unfounded but also that the doses of vitamin E used are toxic, causing terrible side effects in patients. She concludes, though, that the study results do not disconfirm her hypothesis but are merely inconclusive.

FS

5. David and Max are in a heated debate about the theory of biological evolution. David rejects the theory in favor of creationism, which says that life on earth was created or facilitated by a supreme intelligence. Max rejects creationism in favor of evolution. David marshals an abundance of facts that seem to prove his case. In addition, he alleges that evolution is false because there are huge gaps in the fossil record suggesting that there has never been a smooth, tidy progression of species from earlier forms to later forms. Max has no answer for this fossil-record gap argument and looks exasperated. David is about to declare victory when Max suddenly begins to quote the research findings of reputable biologists showing that there really are no gaps. After the debate some of Max's friends quietly congratulate him for being clever enough to quote research findings that are fictitious.

FS

Field Problems

1. Recall a situation in your past in which your beliefs were skewed by self-interest, face-saving, or group pressure. Think about (1) how one or more of these three factors affected your beliefs, (2) what consequences (negative or positive) resulted from the event, and (3) what beliefs you might have acquired if you had used critical thinking. Take notes to help you remember the facts and be prepared to present your story in class.

2. Recall a situation in which the beliefs of someone you know were skewed by self-interest, face-saving, or group pressure to conform. Identify the three factors mentioned in the preceding question.

 Self-Assessment Quiz

Answers appear in "Answers to Self-Assessment Quizzes" (Appendix C).

1. According to the definition of critical thinking given in the text, what factors must be present for critical thinking to be realized?

2. From the standpoint of critical thinking, what event signals that we have allowed our bias in favor of our selves to go too far?

3. According to the text, how might selective attention affect your thinking when you are examining evidence for or against a claim?

4. According to the text, what is probably the most powerful group pressure of all?

5. According to the text, what is a worldview?

6. What kind of doubt is involved in the acquisition of knowledge?

7. According to the text, why is it important to look for opposing evidence when evaluating claims?

Read each of the following scenarios. Indicate whether it contains examples of self-interested thinking, face-saving, or both.

8. Edgar predicts that Horace Windblower will win the 2008 presidential election. In fact, he bets money on it and brags that he always predicts the winners. Windblower loses by the widest margin in U.S. history. At first, Edgar refuses to pay the bet but finally relents. He claims that the election was rigged from the very beginning.

9. Lois strongly believes in UFO abductions—people being kidnapped by space aliens. She says that she has absolute proof: a small piece of metal that she says is "not of this earth" and a cut on her shin that she says came from alien probes. However, several metallurgists in the area say that the piece of metal is ordinary aluminum. And her daughter reminds her that she got the cut on her shin when she ran into a desk drawer.

Lois doesn't say anything else about her "evidence," and she asserts that the real proof is in the skies in the form of alien spacecraft.

10. One day Julie and Jill hear their instructor read a list of arguments for and against abortion. Half the arguments are pro, and half con. Julie is in on the pro side, Jill on the con side. Later when they discuss the abortion arguments, they recall the facts differently. Julie remembers that most of the arguments were for abortion rights. Jill remembers only the arguments against abortion and can't recall any pro arguments.

Specify whether the following passages are examples of face-saving, self-serving, or group-pressure thinking, or a combination of these.

11. The world would be better off if everything were run by Republicans.

12. Everyone believes in affirmative action. That fact alone ought to convince you to do the same.

13. Look, every student I know cheats on exams once in a while. So why not you? Why do you have to be such a Boy Scout?

14. People should do whatever makes them happy.

15. Congressman Hornblower: Anyone who doesn't believe in God shouldn't have a say in how this nation is run. I don't think that atheists should even be citizens.

16. Yes, I smoked marijuana in college, but I didn't inhale.

17. In the United States about 90 percent of the population has some kind of religious belief or denominational affiliation. In light of this, how can you say you're an unbeliever? If you're an unbeliever, you're un-American.

Read each of the following passages and indicate whether it is an example of the subjectivist fallacy or social relativism.

18. This may not be your truth, but it's my truth.

19. It's true for me that killing innocent civilians is morally wrong. It may not be true for you.

20. Chinese diplomat: My country cannot be judged by some universal standard. It must be judged by its own unique criteria and norms.

 Integrative Exercises

These exercises pertain to material in Chapters 1 and 2.

1. What is an argument?

2. What is a statement, or claim? (Give an example of a statement and an example of a sentence that is not a statement.)

3. In what ways can a group that you belong to affect your evaluation of a claim?

4. According to the text, what critical thinking principle should you invoke when you're trying to think clearly under group pressure?

For each of the following passages, indicate whether it contains an argument. For each argument, specify what the conclusion is and whether the passage contains an appeal to popularity or peer pressure.

5. You can never escape your past because your memory will always remind you of it.

6. Cloning any biological entity (including humans) is not worth the risk involved. Scientists have already reported some unexpected, dangerous side effects in the cloning of plants, and the clone of the famous Dolly the sheep has exhibited some cellular abnormalities.

7. Cloning is perfectly safe. It's only religious nuts and conservative politicians who are making a big fuss about it.

8. It will be a great day when the Pentagon has to have a bake sale to raise money for bombs and guns and education gets billions of dollars.

9. Capitalism is an immoral, oppressive system. That's just the way I was raised.

10. If you burn the American flag, you are guilty of treason. The flag is our country, and harming our flag is harming our country. Harming our country is treason.

11. Most Canadians believe that the prime minister is doing a great job. You can't argue with the people. Therefore, he is doing a great job.

12. All your friends think your views on abortion are ridiculous. That should be proof enough that you're wrong.

Read each of the following claims. Then select from the list any statements that, if true, would constitute good reasons for accepting the claim. Some statements may have no good reasons listed.

13. Corporation executives who cook the books should be imprisoned.

   a. Everyone in the business world believes that cooking the books should be punished by imprisonment.
   b. Polls show that most Americans are in favor of imprisoning executives who cook the books.
   c. In Russia it is common practice to imprison executives who cook the books.
   d. Imprisoning executives who cook the books is the only way to save American business from disaster and the only morally correct course of action.

14. Psychic predictions in tabloid newspapers are almost always accurate.

   a. This claim is true for me, even if it isn't true for you.

    b. It is impossible to know anything, so there is no way that anyone can legitimately claim that tabloid psychics are almost always right.

    c. Massive amounts of research into psychic phenomena prove that tabloid psychics are usually correct in their predictions.

    d. Believing that psychics cannot predict anything accurately is close-minded and petty. I refuse to be that way.

15. There is an afterlife. After you die, your essence lives on.

    a. I have to believe in an afterlife. The alternative is too terrible to contemplate.

    b. Over 80 percent of Americans believe in an afterlife.

    c. This society believes that there is an afterlife.

    d. On the radio I told two million people that there is an afterlife. So I have to believe in it. Otherwise, I'll look like a fool.

For each of the following passages, determine whether an argument is present and whether peer pressure or an appeal to popularity is being used. Some passages may not contain arguments, and some may not contain examples of group pressure.

16. "Barbara Ehrenreich wrote tongue-in-cheek in her June column, 'First, challenge anyone to find in the Bible . . . a single phrase or sentence forbidding the fondling or sodomizing of altar boys.' . . . In fact, the Bible does have at least a single phrase or sentence forbidding just such a thing. In 1 Corinthians 6:9 (New International Version), Paul has a list of those who will not inherit the Kingdom. Although far from settled, one of the words in the list suggests that men in a mentoring relationship with young boys are 'wicked' if they engage in sexual acts with the boys." [Letter to the editor, *The Progressive,* July 2002]

17. "[A] political scientist at the Massachusetts Institute of Technology says, 'I expect robust Internet voting by 2010.' He may be right, but would this be a good thing? Remote voting by way of the Internet would privatize one of our few remaining civic rituals. Balloting technology is not politically neutral. The history of elections administration in this country shows that different ways of voting allocate political values differently." [Letter to the editor, *New York Times*]

18. You must reject the proposition that violence in this country proves we need stronger gun-control laws. First, there is no documented connection between violence and the availability of guns. Second, if you accept the proposition, you will be the laughingstock of all of your fellow conservatives.

19. To teens, getting fake IDs to sneak into clubs and taverns may seem like a good idea, but it's not. I think every teenager who tries it should be arrested.

20. Every thinking person in this country would disagree with you.

Critical Thinking and Writing
MODULE 2

FROM ISSUE TO THESIS

For many students, the biggest challenge in writing an argumentative essay is deciding on an appropriate thesis—the claim, or conclusion, that the essay is designed to support or prove. Very often, when an essay runs off the track and crashes, the derailment can be traced to a thesis that was bad from the beginning.

Picking a thesis out of the air and beginning to write is usually a mistake. Any thesis statement that you craft without knowing anything about the subject is likely to be ill-formed or indefensible. It's better to begin by selecting an issue—a question that's controversial or in dispute—then researching it to determine what arguments or viewpoints are involved. To research it, you can survey the views of people or organizations involved in the controversy. Read articles and books, talk to people, go online. This process should not only inform you about various viewpoints but also tell you what arguments are used to support them. It should also help you narrow the issue to one that you can easily address in the space you have.

Suppose you begin with this issue: whether the United States has serious industrial pollution problems. After investigating this issue, you would probably see that it is much too broad to be addressed in a short paper. You should then restrict the issue to something more manageable—for example: whether recent legislation to allow coal-burning power plants to emit more sulfur dioxide will harm people's health. With the scope of the issue narrowed, you can explore arguments on both sides. You cannot examine every single argument, but you should assess the strongest ones, including those that you devise yourself. You can then use what you've already learned about arguments to select one that you think provides good support for its conclusion. The premises and conclusion of this argument can then serve as the bare-bones outline of your essay. Your argument might look like this:

[Premise 1] Excessive amounts of sulfur dioxide in the air have been linked to increases in the incidence of asthma and other respiratory illnesses.
[Premise 2] Many areas of the country already have excessive amounts of sulfur dioxide in the air.
[Premise 3] Most sulfur dioxide in the air comes from coal-burning power plants.
[Conclusion] Therefore, allowing coal-burning power plants to emit more sulfur dioxide will most likely increase the incidence of respiratory illnesses.

For the sake of example, the premises of this argument are made up. But your essay's argument must be for real, with each premise that could be called into question supported by an additional argument. After all, your readers are not likely to accept your argument's conclusion if they doubt your premises.

In some cases, your paper may contain more than one argument supporting a single conclusion, or it may offer a critique of someone else's argument. In either case, investigating an issue and the arguments involved will follow the pattern just suggested. In a critique of an argument (or arguments), you offer reasons why the argument fails and thus support the thesis that the conclusion is false.

This process of devising a thesis statement and crafting an argument to back it up is not linear. You will probably have to experiment with several arguments before you find one that's suitable. Even after you decide on an argument, you may later discover that its premises are dubious or that they cannot be adequately supported. Then you will have to backtrack to investigate a better argument. Backtracking in this preliminary stage is relatively easy. If you postpone this rethinking process until you are almost finished with your first draft, it will be harder—and more painful.

ARGUMENT AND EMOTION

As we saw earlier, the point of an argument is to provide rational support for a claim, to supply good reasons for accepting a conclusion. And argument, of course, is the main focus of a good argumentative essay. Nonetheless, experienced writers often enhance the persuasive power of their argumentative essays through the use of various emotional appeals. Inexperienced writers, though, sometimes get the argumentative and emotional elements confused or out of balance. To avoid such problems, try to stick to these rules of thumb:

- Be fair to the opposing view. Summarize or restate the opposing arguments accurately. Avoid sarcasm, ridicule, or loaded (emotive) words in describing other viewpoints. Don't say, for example, "this so-called argument," "that ridiculous view," or "this idiotic proposal."
- Be fair to your opponent. Avoid personal attacks, insults, stereotyping, and innuendo. Keep the main focus on the quality of your opponent's arguments, not his or her character.
- Avoid appeals to your own self-interest or the wishes of your preferred group.
- If you have strong feelings about an issue, try to channel those feelings into creating the best arguments possible—not into emotional displays on paper.

Writing Assignments

1. Read Essay 3 ("The Wrong Ruling on Vouchers") in Appendix A and write a summary of the essay in 75-100 words. Mention the thesis statement and each supporting premise.

2. Study the argument presented in Essay 6 ("Misleading the Patient for Fun and Profit") in Appendix A. Identify the conclusion and the premises and objections considered. Then write a two-page rebuttal to the essay. That is, defend the claim that it is morally right to promote unproven treatments.

3. Select an issue from the following list and write a three-page paper defending a statement pertaining to the issue. Follow the procedure discussed in the text for identifying a thesis and an appropriate argument to defend it.

   - Are the media biased?
   - Should a single corporation be allowed to own as many media outlets (newspapers, radio and TV stations, publishers, etc.) as it wants?
   - Should the U.S. government be allowed to arrest and indefinitely imprison without trial any American citizen who is suspected of terrorism?
   - Should racial profiling be used to do security screening of airline passengers?

4. Study Essay 12 ("Marriage Still Evolving, as Ever") in Appendix A. Identify the conclusion and premises of the essay's argument, and write a rebuttal to it.

Making Sense of Arguments

 CHAPTER OBJECTIVES

ARGUMENT BASICS

- Distinguish between deductive and inductive arguments.
- Understand the terms *valid*, *invalid*, and *sound*.
- Understand the terms *strong*, *weak*, and *cogent*.

JUDGING ARGUMENTS

- Be able to follow the four-step procedure for determining whether an argument is deductive or inductive, good or bad.
- Be familiar with indicator words that suggest that an argument is deductive or inductive.

FINDING MISSING PARTS

- Know how to use the three-step procedure for uncovering implicit premises.

ARGUMENT PATTERNS

- Memorize and be able to recognize the argument patterns known as *modus ponens*, *modus tollens*, *hypothetical syllogism*, *denying the antecedent*, *affirming the consequent*, and *disjunctive syllogism*.
- Be able to use the counterexample method for determining if a deductive argument is valid or invalid.

DIAGRAMMING ARGUMENTS

- Understand the definition of *dependent* and *independent premises*.
- Be able to follow the five-step procedure to diagram arguments, both simple and complex ones, including those embedded in extraneous material.

ASSESSING LONG ARGUMENTS

- Understand the challenges involved in assessing long arguments.
- Be able to follow the four-step procedure for diagramming long arguments.

IN THIS CHAPTER WE RESUME OUR DISCUSSION OF ARGUMENTS begun in Chapter 1, delve deeper into the dynamics and structure of different argument types, and get a lot more practice in identifying and critiquing simple (and not so simple) arguments in their "natural habitat."

Remember, in Chapter 1 we defined an argument as a group of statements in which some of them (the premises) are intended to support another of them (the conclusion). An essential skill is the ability to identify arguments in real-life contexts and to distinguish them from nonarguments. To recognize an argument you must be able to identify the premises and the conclusion. Indicator words such as *because* and *since* often signal the presence of premises, and words such as *therefore* and *thus* can point to a conclusion.

Argument Basics

The point of *devising* an argument is to try to show that a statement, or claim, is worthy of acceptance. The point of *evaluating* an argument is to see whether this task has been successful—whether the argument shows that the statement (the conclusion) really is worthy of acceptance. When the argument shows that the statement is worthy of acceptance, we say that the argument is *good*. When the argument fails to show that the statement is worthy of acceptance, we say that the argument is *bad*. There are different ways, however, that an argument can be good or bad. There are different ways because there are different types of arguments.

Arguments come in two forms—**deductive** and **inductive.** A deductive argument is intended to provide logically *conclusive* support for its conclusion. An inductive argument is intended to provide *probable*—not conclusive—support for its conclusion.

A deductive argument that succeeds in providing such decisive logical support is said to be **valid;** a deductive argument that fails to provide such support is said to be **invalid.** A deductively valid argument is such that if its premises are true, its conclusion *must* be true. That is, if the premises are true, there is *no way* that the conclusion can be false. In logic, *valid* is not a synonym for true. A deductively valid argument simply has the kind of logical structure that *guarantees* the truth of the conclusion *if* the premises are true. "Logical structure" refers not to the content of an argument but to its construction, the way the premises and conclusion fit together. Because of the guarantee of truth in the conclusion, deductively valid arguments are said to be **truth-preserving.**

(margin handwritten notes)

① Identify Argument

② Analyze Argument

③ Evaluate Argument

Evaluation requires ability to recognize the different types of arguments...

① Deductive Argument: provides logically conclusive support for its conclusion...

② Inductive Argument provides probable support for its conclusion...

Ⓐ
DEDUCTIVE ARGUMENT
Valid vs. Invalid

FURTHER THOUGHT

 Persuading or Reasoning?

A fundamental distinction in critical thinking is this: Persuading someone to agree with you is not the same thing as presenting them with a good argument. You can influence people's opinions by using words to appeal to their ego, gullibility, bigotry, greed, anger, prejudice, and more. You just have to use emotional language, psychological ploys, semantic or syntactic tricks, and outright lies. But having done so, you would not have demonstrated that *any* belief is true or warranted. You would not have shown that a claim is *worthy of acceptance*. This latter task is a matter of logic and argument. The machinations of raw persuasion are not.

Great persuaders aren't necessarily great critical thinkers.

Certainly the presentation of a good argument (in the critical thinking sense) can sometimes be psychologically compelling. And there are times when persuasion through psychological or emotional appeals is appropriate, even necessary. You just have to keep these two functions straight in your mind.

Persuading is not the same as reasoning!!

Here's a simple deductively valid argument:

All dogs have fleas.
Bowser is a dog.
So Bowser has fleas.

And here's a golden oldie.

All men are mortal.
Socrates is a man.
Therefore, Socrates is mortal.

And one in regular paragraph form:

[Premise] If abortion is the taking of a human life, then it's murder.
[Premise] It is the taking of a human life. [Conclusion] So it necessarily follows that abortion is murder.

Examples of DVAs

Order of the premises
does not matter...

Invalid Arguments

Ⓑ
INDUCTIVE ARGUMENT
Strong vs. Weak

In each of these arguments, if the premises are true, the conclusion must be absolutely, positively true. It is impossible for the premises to be true and the conclusions false. The conclusion *logically follows* from the premises. And the order of the premises makes no difference.

A deductively *invalid* version of these arguments might look like this:

All dogs are mammals.
All cows are mammals.
Therefore, all dogs are cows.

If Socrates has horns, he is mortal.
Socrates is mortal.
Therefore, Socrates has horns.

In each of these, the conclusion does *not* logically follow from the premises. Each is an attempt at a deductively valid argument, but the attempt fails. And, again, this would be the case regardless of the order of the premises.

An inductive argument that succeeds in providing probable—but not conclusive—logical support for its conclusion is said to be **strong.** An inductive argument that fails to provide such support is said to be **weak.** An inductively

"In the midst of chaos, Larry is the clear voice of reason. Get him the hell out of here."

strong argument is such that if its premises are true, its conclusion is *probably* or *likely* to be true. The structure of an inductively strong argument cannot guarantee that the conclusion is true if the premises are true—but the conclusion can be rendered probable and worthy of acceptance. (Here again, the structure and content of an argument are distinct elements.) Because the truth of the conclusion cannot be guaranteed by the truth of the premises, inductive arguments are not truth-preserving.

Let's turn our first two deductively valid arguments into inductively strong arguments:

> Most dogs have fleas.
> Therefore, Bowser, my dog, probably has fleas.

> Ninety-eight percent of
>   humans are mortal.
> Socrates is human.
> Therefore, Socrates is likely to be mortal.

Notice that in the first argument, it's entirely possible for the premise to be true and the conclusion false. After all, if only *most* dogs have fleas, there is no guarantee that Bowser has fleas. Yet the premise, if true, makes the conclusion probably true. Likewise, in the second argument it is possible that even if 98 percent of humans are mortal and Socrates is human, the conclusion that Socrates is mortal could be false. But the premises, if true, make it likely that the conclusion is true.

Logical validity or logical strength is an essential characteristic of good arguments. But there is more to good arguments than having the proper structure. Good arguments also have *true premises*. A good argument is one that has the proper structure—*and* true premises. Take a look at this argument:

Statistical Syllogisms

TRUE PREMISES
Validity and Strength are necessary but not sufficient for a good argument: Premises must also be true...

An emotionally powerful photograph can shock us into vivid awareness of suffering, then empathy for the victim, then an informed moral response. But the emotional reaction to some photos—like this notorious one of a hooded, wired, and posed Iraqi prisoner at Abu Ghraib prison near Baghdad—can be so incendiary as to short-circuit reasoning. Rage and horror block critical thinking. Rage and horror unchecked by reason can lead to lynchings. When such photographs confront us, we should not be afraid to *feel*—nor should we forget to *think*, to guide our feelings with critical reasoning. If you have seen this photo before, what was your immediate emotional response to it? How did your feelings affect your judgments about the morality of the actions depicted, or the treatment of Iraqi prisoners in general, or of the overall conduct of the war in Iraq?

All pigs can fly.
Vaughn is a pig.
Therefore, Vaughn can fly.

The premises of this argument are false—but the conclusion follows logically from those premises. It's a deductively valid argument with all the parts in the right place—even though the premises are false. But it is not a good argument. A good argument must have true premises, and this argument doesn't. A deductively valid argument that has true premises is said to be **sound.** A sound argument is a good argument, which gives you good reasons for accepting its conclusion.

Note, however, that deductively valid arguments can have true or false premises and true or false conclusions. Specifically, deductively valid arguments can have false premises and a false conclusion, false premises and a true conclusion, and true premises and a true conclusion. A valid argument, though, cannot have true premises and a false conclusion—that's impossible. See for yourself:

False Premises, False Conclusion
All dogs have flippers.
All cats are dogs.
Therefore, all cats have flippers.

False Premises, True Conclusion
Bowser is a cat.
All cats are mammals.
Therefore, Bowser is a mammal.

True Premises, True Conclusion
Bowser is a dog.
All dogs are mammals.
Therefore, Bowser is a mammal.

A good inductive argument must also have true premises. For example:

Scientific studies show that 99 percent of dogs have three eyes.
So it's likely that the next dog I see will have three eyes.

This is an inductively strong argument, but it's not a good argument because its premise is false. When inductively strong arguments have true premises, they are said to be **cogent.** Good inductive arguments are cogent. Bad inductive arguments are not cogent.

You may have noticed another important difference between deductive and inductive arguments. The kind of support that a deductive argument can give a conclusion is *absolute.* Either the conclusion is shown to be true, or it is not. There is no sliding scale of truth or falsity. The support that an inductive argument can provide a conclusion, however, can vary from weak to extremely strong.

☑ Deductive and Inductive Arguments

- A deductive argument is intended to provide conclusive support for its conclusion.
- A deductive argument that succeeds in providing conclusive support for its conclusion is said to be valid. A valid argument is such that if its premises are true, its conclusion must be true.
- A deductively valid argument with true premises is said to be sound.
- An inductive argument is intended to provide probable support for its conclusion.
- An inductive argument that succeeds in providing probable support for its conclusion is said to be strong. A strong argument is such that if its premises are true, its conclusion is probably true.
- An inductively strong argument with true premises is said to be cogent.

Both deductive and inductive arguments can be manipulated in various ways to yield new insights. For example, let's say that you have formulated a valid deductive argument, and you know that the conclusion is false. From these facts you can infer that at least one of the premises is false. Using this tack, you can demonstrate that a premise is false because in a valid argument it leads to an absurd conclusion. Or let's say that you've fashioned a valid argument, and you know that your premises are true. Then you can infer that the conclusion must be true—even if it's contrary to your expectations. Or maybe you put forth a strong inductive argument, and you know that the premises are questionable. Then you know that the conclusion also can't be trusted.

Creative Critical Thinking

If you don't already have a sense of the wide-ranging usefulness of deductive and inductive arguments, the coming pages will make the point clear. You will find abundant evidence that the utility of both types of arguments is *universal*. They apply everywhere, work everywhere, and instruct everywhere—in everyday and professional life (Chapters 4-8), in scientific and extraordinary realms (Chapters 9-10), and in moral and philosophical explorations (Chapter 11).

Exercise 3.1

1. What is a deductive argument?
2. What is an inductive argument?
3. Are inductive arguments truth-preserving? Why or why not?
* 4. The terms *valid* and *invalid* apply to what types of arguments?

5. What kind of guarantee does a deductive argument provide when it is valid?

6. Can an inductive argument guarantee the truth of the conclusion if the premises are true? Why or why not?

7. What is the difference between an inductively strong argument and an inductively weak one?

* 8. What is the term for valid arguments that have true premises?

9. What is the term for strong arguments that have true premises?

10. Can a valid argument have false premises and a false conclusion? false premises and a true conclusion?

11. What logical conclusion can you draw about an argument that is valid but has a false conclusion?

* 12. Is it possible for a valid argument to have true premises and a false conclusion?

13. In what way are conclusions of deductive arguments absolute?

Judging Arguments

When it comes to deductive and inductive arguments, the most important skills you can acquire are being able to identify them and determining whether they are good or bad. Much of the rest of this text is devoted to helping you become proficient in these skills. This chapter will serve as your first lesson and give you a chance to practice what you learn.

So the obvious questions here are: When you come face to face with an argument to evaluate, (1) how can you tell whether it's deductive or inductive, and (2) how can you determine whether it gives you good reasons for accepting the conclusion (whether it's sound or cogent)? The following is a suggested four-

DILBERT: © Scott Adams/Dist. By United Feature Syndicate, Inc.

step procedure for answering these questions, one that will be elaborated on here and in later chapters.

Step 1. Find the argument's conclusion and then its premises. Use the techniques you learned in Chapter 1. You'll have plenty of chances to hone this skill in upcoming chapters.

Step 2. Ask: Is it the case that if the premises are true the conclusion *must* be true? If the answer is yes, treat the argument as *deductive,* for it is very likely meant to offer conclusive support for its conclusion. The argument, then, is deductively valid, and you should check to see if it's sound. If the answer is no, proceed to the next step.

Step 3. Ask: Is it the case that if the premises are true, its conclusion is *probably* true? If the answer is yes, treat the argument as *inductive,* for it is very likely meant to offer probable support for its conclusion. The argument, then, is inductively strong, and you should check to see if it's cogent. If the answer is no, proceed to the next step.

Step 4. Ask: Is the argument intended to offer conclusive or probable support for its conclusion but *fails* to do so? If you reach this step, you will have already eliminated two possibilities: a valid argument and a strong one. The remaining options are an invalid argument or a weak one. So here you must discover what type of (failed) argument is intended. These two guidelines can help you do that:

> **GUIDELINE 1:** Generally if an argument looks deductive or inductive because of its form, assume that it is intended to be so.

Bad arguments may sometimes look like good arguments because the arrangement of their premises and conclusion—their form—is similar to that found in reliable arguments. (You saw some of these reliable argument forms in the argument examples presented earlier in this chapter.) Such argument forms are an indication of what kind of argument is intended, and that fact gives you some guidance on determining argument type.

> **GUIDELINE 2:** Generally if an argument looks deductive or inductive because of indicator words (and its form yields no clues), assume that it is intended to be so.

Arguments are often accompanied by words or phrases that identify them as deductive or inductive. Terms that signal a deductive argument include "It necessarily follows that," "it logically follows that," "absolutely," "necessarily," and "certainly." Words signaling an inductive argument include "likely," "probably," "chances are," "odds are," and "it is plausible that." Such indicator words, though, are not foolproof clues to argument type because they are sometimes used in misleading ways. For example, someone might end an inductively strong argument with a conclusion prefaced with "it necessarily follows that,"

Four Step Procedure

Look for indicator words

"He who strikes the first blow admits he's lost the argument."
—CHINESE PROVERB

suggesting that the argument is deductively valid. But argument-type indicators may still be useful, especially when the argument form yields no clues (when guideline 1 doesn't apply).

Inconsistent to a Fault

In case you didn't know already, because of strong bias, public figures often make pronouncements that are logically inconsistent (as well as moronic, offensive, and mystifying). Worse, the rest of the world may swallow the contradictory statements without noticing anything amiss. For example:

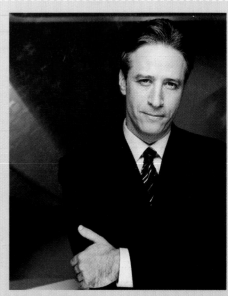

- If a TV pundit finds that his favorite politician has been having an extramarital affair, he declares the episode a "personal matter" that should not be publicly discussed. But if a politician he loathes is guilty of the same indiscretion, he declares it an outrage and can't stop talking about it on the air.
- In support of a vice presidential candidate whose only executive experience is a term as mayor of a small town, a radio talk show host insists that such experience is perfect preparation for being vice president. But she asserts that another vice presidential candidate whom she opposes and who has almost identical credentials is unsuitable for the office—because he doesn't have enough executive experience.
- Commentators criticize a woman televangelist for making sexist remarks about a another woman—but they use the same sexist language to deride the televangelist.

Such contradictions abound in the public square and go largely unnoticed by the media. A few astute commentators, though, are happy to point out such addled thinking. Jon Stewart, host of the popular *Daily Show*, regularly mocks pundits and politicians who try to have it both ways, often juxtaposing film clips of them soberly affirming one thing and then piously proclaiming the opposite.

No matter who is guilty of it, this brand of inconsistency shows that bias is hard at work, undercutting clear thinking. And when we inconsistently apply a rule or standard of judgment, the rule or standard itself is called into question. If we take an extramarital affair or blatant sexism seriously only when it suits our rhetorical aims, do we really believe these issues are important?

How can we detect this problem in ourselves? We can manage it only through careful reflection on the logic of what we say. One trick is what can be called the "turned tables" test. If you criticize someone or something you dislike for violating some standard, ask yourself: Would I judge someone or something I like in the same way for the same reasons? Logic demands that you treat equals equally.

Try this: Think of the strongest criticism you could make about the behavior of the political leader you respect the least. Now suppose your favorite political leader is guilty of the same behavior. Would you be willing to criticize him or her just as strongly? ■

In step 4, once you discover which kind of argument is intended, you will know that it is either invalid or weak (because in steps 2 and 3 we eliminated the possibility of a valid or strong argument). The only remaining task is to determine whether the premises are true.[1]

Are the premises true?

Let's try out the four-step procedure on a few arguments. Consider this one:

> [Premise] Unless we do something about the massive AIDS epidemic in Africa, the whole continent will be decimated within six months. [Premise] Unfortunately we won't do anything about the AIDS epidemic in Africa. [Conclusion] It necessarily follows that the whole of Africa will be decimated within six months.

EXAMPLE I

Step 1 is already done for us; the premises and conclusion are clearly labeled. In step 2, we must ask, "Is it the case that if the premises are true, the conclusion must be true?" The answer is yes: If it's true that the AIDS epidemic in Africa will decimate the population in six months unless "we do something," and it's true that "we won't do anything," then the conclusion that Africa will be decimated in six months *must* be true. So this argument is deductively valid. To determine if it's sound, we would need to check to see if the premises are true. In this case, the first premise is false because, under current conditions, it would take longer than six months for the epidemic to decimate the whole continent.

Analysis & Evaluation
① The argument is DV.
② The argument is unsound.
Verdict: bad argument

The other premise ("we won't do anything") is at least dubious since we can't predict the future. So what we have here is a deductively valid argument that's unsound—a bad argument.

Now let's analyze this one:

[Premise] This week, under pressure from the American Civil Liberties Union, the school board rescinded its policy of allowing school-sponsored public prayers at football games. [Premise] All the school board members agreed with the policy change. [Premise] And a memo from the board was circulated to all students, teachers, and coaches declaring that there will be no more public prayers at football games. [Conclusion] Let's face it, the days of public prayers at our school football games are over.

From step 2 we can see that even if this argument's three premises are all true, the conclusion can still be false. After all, even if everything described in the premises happens, there still could be a public prayer at a football game (perhaps because of some mistake or an act of protest on the part of school-prayer advocates). So the argument can't be deductively valid. But if we go through step 3, we can see that if all the premises are true, the conclusion is likely to be true, making the argument inductively strong. If the premises *are* true, the argument would be cogent.

See what you think of this one:

[Premise] If you act like Bart Simpson, you will be respected by all your classmates. [Premise] But you don't act like Bart Simpson. [Conclusion] It follows that you will not be respected by all of your classmates.

This argument flunks the tests in steps 2 and 3: It is not deductively valid, and it is not inductively strong. But it does resemble a deductive argument in two ways. First, it displays a pattern of reasoning that can, at first glance, seem deductive. Actually, it uses an argument pattern that is always deductively *in-*

EXAMPLE II

Analysis and Evaluation
① The argument is an ISA.
② If the premises were true, we would say it is cogent.

EXAMPLE III

The argument is invalid (DA)

FURTHER THOUGHT

When Reasoning Wrecks . . . Leave the Scene of the Accident

Sometimes arguments go off into a ditch and you don't know why. Here's an example of a wrecked argument from the great American satirical writer Ambrose Bierce (1842–1914?). What's wrong here?

Sixty men can do a piece of work sixty times as quickly as one man.
One man can dig a posthole in sixty seconds.
Therefore, sixty men can dig a posthole in one second.

valid (called denying the antecedent, an argument form we will look at shortly). This alone should be evidence enough that the argument is indeed deductive but invalid. But it also contains an argument indicator phrase ("it follows that") that suggests an attempt at a deductive form.

You'll get a lot more exposure to argument forms and indicator words in the rest of this chapter (and the rest of this text). Ultimately, practice in distinguishing different types of arguments and their relative worth is the only way to gain proficiency (and confidence!) in making these judgments.

So far we've spent most of our time assessing the logical structure of arguments—that is, whether they are valid/invalid or strong/weak. We haven't focused as much attention on evaluating the truth of premises because that's a big issue best considered separately—which is what we do in Part 2 of this book.

Exercise 3.2

For each of the following arguments, follow the four-step procedure to determine whether it is deductive or inductive, valid or invalid, and strong or weak. Indicate the results of applying each step.

EXAMPLE 1

Colonel Mustard did not commit the murder. Someone who had committed the murder would have dirt on his shoes and blood on his hands. Colonel Mustard has neither.

Step 1: Conclusion: Colonel Mustard did not commit the murder. Premises: Someone who had committed the murder would have dirt on his shoes and blood on his hands. Colonel Mustard has neither.
Step 2: Deductively valid.
Step 3: Does not apply.
Step 4: Does not apply.

EXAMPLE 2

Most people who smoke pot are irresponsible and forgetful. Looks like you smoke pot all the time. Ergo, you're irresponsible and forgetful. Can you remember that?

Step 1: Conclusion: Ergo, you're irresponsible and forgetful. Premises: Most people who smoke pot are irresponsible and forgetful. Looks like you smoke pot all the time.
Step 2: Not deductively valid.
Step 3: Inductively strong.
Step 4: Does not apply.

DV 1. Either Jack is lying or he is not. If his ears turn red, he's lying. If they don't turn red, he's telling the truth. His ears are red. <u>Jack is lying</u>.

IS *2. Ethel graduated from Yale. If she graduated from Yale, she probably has a superior intellect. <u>She has a superior intellect</u>.

DV 3. If you go to that party you're completely nuts. You're going to the party. It <u>necessarily follows that <u>you're nuts</u></u>.

IW 4. "<u>Good sense is of all things in the world the most equally distributed</u>, for everybody thinks himself so abundantly provided with it, that even those most difficult to please in all other matters do not commonly desire more of it than they already possess."[René Descartes, *A Discourse on Method*]

DI 5. All philosophers are absent-minded. All philosophers are teachers. It necessarily follows that <u>all absent-minded people are teachers</u>.

DV *6. Every musician has had special training, and everyone with special training has a college degree. Thus, <u>every musician has a college degree</u>.

? 7. People with high IQs also have psychic abilities. <u>People with high SAT scores</u>—which are comparable to high IQ scores—<u>also probably have psychic abilities</u>.

DV 8. If Elvis Presley's name is spelled wrong on his tombstone, there must be some kind of conspiracy surrounding the death of the King. His name is spelled wrong. Therefore, <u>there's a conspiracy</u>.

NDV/NIS *9. Some actors sing, and some play a musical instrument. So <u>some actors who sing also play a musical instrument</u>.

DV 10. Anyone who is not a bigot will agree that Chris is a good fellow. Some people in this neighborhood think that he's anything but a good fellow. <u>Some people in this neighborhood are bigots</u>.

NDV/NIS 11. "In the actual living of life there is no logic, for life is superior to logic." [Daisetz Teitaro Suzuki, *Essays in Zen Buddhism*]

IS 12. A vase was found broken on the floor; some money had been taken out of the safe; and there were strange scratches on the wall. It therefore follows that <u>someone obviously burglarized the place</u>.

IS 13. All the evidence in this trial suggests that Lizzy Borden is guilty of murder. Let's face it: <u>She's probably guilty</u>.

DV 14. If everything was all right, there would be no blood on the floor. Of course, there is plenty of blood on the floor. Therefore, <u>everything is not all right</u>.

DV *15. If minds are identical to brains—that is, if one's mind is nothing but a brain—androids could never have minds because they wouldn't have brains. Clearly, a mind is nothing but a brain, so <u>it's impossible for androids to have minds</u>.

IW 16. "From infancy, almost, the average girl is told that marriage is her ultimate goal; therefore <u>her training and education must be directed towards that end</u>." [Emma Goldman, "Marriage and Love"]

DV 17. If you have scratches on your body that you can't account for, and you feel that you have been visited by space aliens, then you really have been visited by space aliens. You have such scratches, and you have experienced such feelings. Doubtless you have been visited by space aliens.

DV 18. If bombs are falling on London, war has started. The bombs are falling now. War has begun.

Exercise 3.3

For each of the following arguments, indicate whether it is valid or invalid, strong or weak.

W 1. Joe says that the food in the restaurant is first-rate. So it's first-rate.

V 2. Social welfare is by definition a handout to people who have not worked for it. But giving people money that they have not earned through labor is not helping anyone. It follows then that social welfare does not help anyone.

V * 3. If CNN reports that war has started in Iraq, then war has started in Iraq. CNN has reported exactly that. War must have started.

V 4. If $r = 12$, then $s = 8$; $r = 12$; therefore, $s = 8$.

S 5. Any sitcom that tries to imitate *Seinfeld* is probably a piece of trash. All of this season's sitcoms try to ape *Seinfeld*. They've gotta be trash.

? 6. "Poetry is finer and more philosophical than history; for poetry expresses the universal and history only the particular." [Aristotle, *Poetics*]

V 7. Either you're lying or you're not telling the whole story. You're obviously not lying, so you're just relating part of the story.

V * 8. Either your thinking is logical or it is emotional. It's obviously not logical. It's emotional.

S 9. It is unwise to touch that electrical wire. It might be hot.

W 10. A recent Gallup poll says that 80 percent of Americans believe in the existence of heaven, but only 40 percent say they believe in hell. People are just too willing to engage in wishful thinking.

V 11. Stem-cell research encourages abortions because abortions are a prime source for stem cells. Anything that encourages abortions should be banned. We ought to ban all stem-cell research.

V 12. "We say that a person behaves in a given way because he possesses a philosophy, but we infer the philosophy from the behavior and therefore cannot use it in any satisfactory way as an explanation, at least until it is in turn explained." [B. F. Skinner, *Beyond Freedom and Dignity*]

S 13. You flunked the last three tests. You didn't show up for the last eight classes. And you haven't written any of the essays. Looks like you don't know the material.

? * 14. Bachelors are unmarried. George is a bachelor. He has never taken a wife.

W   15. Bachelors are unmarried, and George acts like he's not married. He's a bachelor for sure.

V   16. If there is a tax cut this year, the deficit will rise. There has already been a tax cut. The deficit is sure to rise.

V   17. If the universe had a beginning, then it was caused to begin. We know that the universe did have a beginning in the form of the Big Bang. So it was caused to come into existence. If it was caused to come into existence, that cause must have been God. God caused the universe to come into existence.

V *18. If the United States is willing to wage war in the Middle East, it can only be because it wants the oil supplies in the region. Obviously the United States is willing to go to war there. The United States wants that oil.

W   19. "Someone must have been telling lies about Joseph K., for without having done anything wrong he was arrested one fine morning." [Franz Kafka, *The Trial*]

V   20. Anyone willing to take the lives of innocent people for a cause is a terrorist. Many Christians, Jews, and Muslims have taken innocent lives in the name of their religious cause. Many Christians, Jews, and Muslims have been terrorists.

S   21. If he comes back, it's probably because he wants money. There he is. He wants money.

I   22. If you're eighteen, you're eligible to vote. But you're only seventeen. You're not eligible to vote.

I *23. I like geometry. My geometry teacher likes me. Therefore I will pass my geometry course with flying colors.

Finding Missing Parts

Sometimes arguments not only are faulty but also have a few pieces missing. Premises (and sometimes even conclusions)—material needed to make the argument work—are often left unstated. These implicit premises, or assumptions, are essential to the argument. Of course, certain assumptions are frequently left unsaid for good reason: They are obvious and understood by all parties to the argument, and boredom would set in fast if you actually tried to mention them all. If you wish to prove that "Socrates is mortal," you normally wouldn't need to explain what *mortal* means and that the name Socrates does not refer to a type of garden tool. But many arguments do have unstated premises that are not only necessary to the chain of reasoning but also must be made explicit to fully evaluate the arguments.

For instance:

The easy availability of assault rifles in the United States has increased the risk of death and injury for society as a whole. Therefore, assault rifles should be banned.

Sometimes premises are missing because they are commonsense...

Sometimes they are not commonsense and we need to supply them...

Missing premise

FURTHER THOUGHT

Legal Reasoning

Though arguments and critical thinking are used (and abused) everywhere, their presence is especially obvious in law. Arguments are essential parts of legal reasoning at several levels—in the making of laws, in criminal and civil

proceedings, in judicial rulings, in the weighing of evidence, and in the application of legal precedent.

- **Legislation.** The making of new laws usually involves considerable debate about the wisdom of the legislation, and reasoned argument is the presumed medium of the deliberations. For example:

  Suppose . . . that there is currently no law requiring children to wear bicycle helmets. Assume moreover that the American Medical Association (AMA), acting on the belief that we ought to prevent unnecessary injuries and/or deaths of children, convinces the legislature to hold hearings to consider the merits of adopting such a law. What would be the major content of such hearings? Obviously, *arguments* regarding the pros and cons of bicycle helmet legislation. The AMA might testify, for example, that we can save children from serious injury and even death by implementing such a law; some parents may share the concerns of the AMA, while other parents might argue that this constitutes an illegitimate intrusion by the government into what are private family matters; legal authorities might point out the difficulty they would face in enforcing such a law . . . and some might argue that the policy would place an unfair burden on the poor who cannot afford high-priced helmets.[2]

- **Legal proceedings.** In civil matters, litigation takes the form of opposing parties arguing the merits of their side. The point of the arguments is to show that a litigant did (or did not) legally transgress in some way. In criminal cases, prosecutors argue that the defendant did in fact commit a crime, marshalling evidence and testimony to support that conclusion.

▼

Defending attorneys argue against the conclusion, trying to cast doubt on the supporting reasons or showing why the conclusion must be false. The arguments are mainly inductive, often including the inductive pattern known as inference to the best explanation (see Chapter 9). Using this latter kind of argument, the prosecutor contends that the best explanation of the evidence is that the defendant committed the crime; the defense may then maintain that there is a better explanation (that the defendant was framed, was mistaken for someone else, etc.).

- **Judicial rulings.** The thinking involved in judicial decisions is complex, entailing judgments about the meaning and application of statutes, assessments of the relevance and implications of cases, and reasoning of both the deductive and inductive kind. The overarching pattern is that of argument: the conclusion is the final judicial judgment, and the premises (the reasons behind the judgment) generally refer to statutes, previous cases, or other sources of judicial authority. A common argument pattern is *analogical induction*, or argument by analogy (see Chapter 8). A judge first decides that the present case is relevantly similar (analogous) to a previously decided case; then she reasons that since the earlier case was treated in a particular fashion, the present case should be treated in a similar way. In Anglo-American law, decisions in previous cases (legal precedents) carry considerable judicial weight, and arguments by analogy reflect this fact. ∎

Notice that there is a kind of disconnect between the premise and the conclusion. The conclusion follows from the premise *only* if we assume an additional premise, perhaps something like this: "Anything that increases the risk of death and injury for society as a whole should be banned." With this additional premise, the argument becomes:

> The easy availability of assault rifles in the United States has increased the risk of death and injury for society as a whole. (Anything that increases the risk of death and injury for society as a whole should be banned.) Therefore, assault rifles should be banned.

Now we have an argument that we can evaluate...

Now that all the premises are spelled out, you can evaluate the *full* argument just as you would any other. Not only that, but you can see that the unstated premise is questionable, which is the case with many implicit premises. Not everyone would agree that anything raising the risk of death or injury should be banned, for if that were the case we would have to outlaw automobiles, airplanes, most prescription drugs, most occupations, and who knows how many kitchen appliances! Many unstated premises are like this one: They're controversial and therefore should not be left unexamined.

People sometimes omit premises because they are questionable...

Here's another one:

Anyone who craves political power cannot be trusted to serve the public interest. Senator Blowhard can't be trusted to serve the public interest.

As stated, this argument seems like a rush to judgment because the first premise concerns *anyone* who craves power, and suddenly Senator Blowhard is denounced as untrustworthy. Something's missing. What we need is another premise connecting the first premise to the conclusion: "Senator Blowhard craves political power." Now let's plug the implicit premise into the argument:

Anyone who craves political power cannot be trusted to serve the public interest. Senator Blowhard craves political power. He can't be trusted to serve the public interest.

I've never met anyone like you. You're just wrong about everything.

www.CartoonStock.com

So exactly when should we try to ferret out an unstated premise? The obvious answer is that we should do so when there appears to be something essential missing—an implied, logical link between premises and conclusion that is not a commonsense, generally accepted assumption. Such implicit premises should never be taken for granted because, among other things, they are often deliberately hidden or downplayed to make the argument seem stronger.

Be aware, though, that many times the problem with an argument is not unstated premises, but invalid or weak structure. Consider this:

Invalid or weak arguments cannot be fixed by adding a missing premise.

If Tariq works harder, he will pass his calculus course. But he will not work harder, so he will not pass calculus.

This argument is invalid; the conclusion does not follow from the premises. Like most invalid arguments, it can't be salvaged without altering it beyond what is clearly implied. It's just a bad argument. The same goes for weak arguments. They usually can't be fixed up without adding or changing premises gratuitously. Remember, the point of articulating unstated premises is to make explicit what is already implicit. Your job as a critical thinking is *not* to make bad arguments good; that task falls to the one who puts forth the argument in the first place.

"The difficult part in an argument is not to defend one's opinion, but rather to know it."
—ANDRÉ MAUROIS

To make sure that your investigation of implicit premises is thorough and reasonable, work through the following three-step process.[3]

THREE STEP PROCESS

Step 1. Search for a credible premise that would make the argument *valid,* one that would furnish the needed link between premise (or premises) and conclusion. Choose the supplied premise that

a. is most plausible

and

b. fits best with the author's intent.

The first stipulation (a) means that you should look for premises that are either true or, at least, not obviously false. The second stipulation (b) means that premises should fit—that is, at least not conflict—with what seems to be the author's point or purpose (which, of course, is often difficult to discern). If the premise you supply is plausible and fitting (with author's intent), use it to fill out the argument. If your supplied premise is either not plausible or not fitting, go to step 2.

Step 2. Search for a credible premise that would make the argument as *strong* as possible. Choose the supplied premise that fulfills stipulations a and b. If the premise you supply is plausible and fitting, use it to fill out the argument. If your supplied premise is either not plausible or not fitting, consider the argument beyond repair and reject it.

Step 3. Evaluate the reconstituted argument. If you're able to identify a credible implicit premise that makes the argument either valid or strong, assess this revised version of the argument, paying particular attention to the plausibility of the other premise or premises.

Now let's apply this procedure to a few arguments:

> If the Fed lowers interest rates one more time, there will be a deep recession. I'm telling you there's going to be a deep recession.

The first step is to see if there's a credible premise that would make the argument valid. We can see right away that one premise will do the trick: "The Fed has lowered interest rates again." Adding it to the argument will supply the needed link between the existing premise and the conclusion. We also can see that our new premise is plausible (the Fed has lowered interest rates again) and seems to fit with the point of the argument (to prove that there will be a recession). Our resulting argument, though, is probably not a good one because the premise about the effect of the Fed's lowering interest rates is dubious.

Now examine this one:

> Security officer Jones lied on her employment application about whether she had a criminal record. Security officer Jones will do a lousy job of screening passengers for weapons.

The sentence "Security officer Jones will do a lousy job of screening passengers for weapons" is the conclusion here. To try to make this argument valid, we would need a premise like "Any security officer at La Guardia airport who has lied on his or her employment application about having a criminal record will do a lousy job of screening passengers for weapons." This premise fits the point of the argument, but it isn't plausible. Surely it cannot be the case that *any* security officer who has lied will do a lousy job of screening. A more plausible premise is "Most security officers at La Guardia airport who have lied on their employment applications about having a criminal record will do a lousy job of

[handwritten margin notes: Example I; We can make the argument valid...; Example II; We can make the argument strong...]

screening passengers for weapons." This premise will do, and this is now a good argument—assuming that the other premise is true.

What about this one:

> The use of marijuana should be legal because it's an act that brings pleasure to people's lives.

EXAMPLE III

To make this argument valid, we would need to add this premise (or one like it): "Any act that brings pleasure to people's lives should be legal." But this premise is hard to accept since many heinous acts—such as murder and theft—may bring pleasure to some people, yet few of us would think those acts should be legal. To try to make the argument strong, we might add this premise instead: "Some acts should be legal simply because they bring pleasure to people's lives." This premise is actually controversial in some quarters, but it at least is not obviously false. It also fits with the point of the argument. If we decide that the premise is neither plausible nor fitting, we would declare the argument beyond repair.

Exercise 3.4

I. For each of the following arguments, identify the implicit premises that will make the argument valid.

EXAMPLE

The engine is sputtering. It must be out of gas.
Implicit premise: Whenever the engine sputters, it's out of gas.

* **1.** Any senator who is caught misusing campaign funds should resign his seat. Senator Greed should resign.
  S. Greed was caught misusing c. funds.

  2. Jenna is a highly motivated runner, so she is sure to finish the race.
  Any highly motivated runner will finish.

  3. In the first week at the box office, the movie grossed over $30 million. So it's sure to win at least one Oscar.
  Any movie that grosses over 30 mil in the first week @ BO will win...

  4. The FBI doesn't have a very serious focus on stopping terrorism. Another major terrorist attack will happen in this country.
  If the FBI... then another major terrorist attack

* **5.** The author of the book on interventionist wars is either biased or incompetent as a journalist. So she's biased.
  She's not incompetent

  6. The conflict in Indonesia is a genuine war. So it can't possibly be morally justified.
  No genuine war can be morally just.

  7. The Taliban regime fell because it persecuted women.
  If the Taliban regime falls, it will...

  8. The United States government should limit its activities to the Western Hemisphere because it doesn't have the resources to cover the whole world.
  Any WG that doesn't have resources...

* **9.** If the engine starts right away, it's because of the tune-up I gave it. Must be because of the tune-up I gave it.
  The engine started right away.

10. Taslima did not criticize U.S. military action in the Gulf War or in the war in Afghanistan. She must be a hawk.

II. To each of the following arguments, change or add a premise that will make the argument strong.

1. Coach Johnson once fell asleep during a game. He's probably not a very good coach.

2. Aziz regularly eats at McDonald's, so Aziz is likely to gain a few pounds.

* 3. Six out of ten of my teenage friends love rap music. So 60 percent of all teens love rap music.

4. Seventy-one percent of the faculty and staff at Goddard Community College are Democrats. So most of the students are probably Democrats.

5. Miriam was in the library when the books were stolen from the librarian's desk. She was also seen hanging around the desk. So she's probably the one who stole them.

* 6. If Assad's fingerprints are on the vase, then he's probably the one who broke it. He's probably the one who broke it.

7. If the president needs more money to balance the federal budget, he will get it from Social Security. Well, he's almost certainly going to get it from Social Security.

8. Ninety percent of students at Boston College graduate with a B.A. degree. Li Fong will probably graduate from Boston College with a B.A. degree.

* 9. The murder rates in most large American cities on the East Coast are very high. The murder rates in most large cities in the West and Midwest are very high. So the murder rate in New Orleans must be very high.

10. John has a typical American diet. His fat intake is probably excessively high.

Argument Patterns

Earlier we discussed the importance of being familiar with argument patterns, or forms, the structures on which the content is laid. The point was that knowing some common argument forms makes it easier to determine whether an argument is deductive or inductive. But being familiar with argument forms is also helpful in many other aspects of argument evaluation. Let's take a closer look at some of these forms.

Since argument forms are structures distinct from argument content, we can easily signify different forms by using letters to represent statements in the arguments. Each letter represents a different statement in much the same way

FROM THE WEB

(((□))) Arguments on the Net

The Internet is fertile ground for all manner of arguments—good, bad, benign,
and benighted. Here's one that has gone
around the world a few times in cyberspace:

> Hillary Clinton supports gun-control
> legislation.
> All fascist regimes of the twentieth
> century have passed gun-control legis-
> lation.
> Therefore, Hillary Clinton is a fascist.

What's wrong with this argument? If
you don't know, the following section
on argument patterns will help you. An

Secretary of State Hillary Rodham
Clinton.

important clue that something is fishy here is that any argument of this
form can be used to try to "frame" anybody. Consider:

> Vaughn likes salads and can be trained to do tricks.
> Hamsters like salads and can be trained to do tricks.
> Therefore, Vaughn is a hamster.

that letters are used to represent values in a mathematical equation. Consider
this argument:

> *If the job is worth doing, then it's worth doing well.*
> *The job is worth doing.*
> *Therefore, it's worth doing well.*

We can represent this argument like this:

> *If p, then q.*
> p.
> *Therefore, q.*

Notice that the first line in the argument is a compound statement—it's composed of at least two constituent statements, which are represented in this case
by *p* and *q*. So we have three statements in this argument that are arranged into
an argument form, one that is both very common and always valid. We can plug
any statements we want into this form, and we will still get a valid argument.
The premises may be true or false, but the form will be valid.

① *Modus Ponens*

Conditional Arguments

Some of the more common argument patterns that you encounter are like this pattern—they're deductive, and they contain one or more **conditional**, or if-then, premises. The first statement in a conditional premise (the *if* part) is known as the **antecedent.** The second statement (the *then* part) is known as the **consequent.**

The pattern shown here is called **affirming the antecedent** or, to use the Latin term, *modus ponens.* Any argument in the *modus ponens* form is valid—if the premises are true, the conclusion absolutely must be true. This means that if "If *p*, then *q*" and "*p*" are both true, the conclusion has to be true also. These facts, then, provide a way to quickly size up an argument. If it's in the form of *modus ponens*, it's valid, regardless of the content of the statements.

Another common argument form is called **denying the consequent,** or *modus tollens:*

② Modus tollens

> If Austin is happy, then Barb is happy.
> Barb is not happy.
> Therefore, Austin is not happy.

The form of *modus tollens* is:

> If *p*, then *q*.
> Not *q*.
> Therefore, not *p*.

REVIEW NOTES

☑ Valid Argument Forms

AFFIRMING THE ANTECEDENT

(Modus Ponens) — EXAMPLE

> If *p*, then *q*.
> *p*.
> Therefore, *q*.

> If Spot barks, a burglar is in the house.
> Spot is barking.
> Therefore, a burglar is in the house.

DENYING THE CONSEQUENT

(Modus Tollens) — EXAMPLE

> If *p*, then *q*.
> Not *q*.
> Therefore, not *p*.

> If it's raining, the park is closed.
> The park is not closed.
> Therefore, it's not raining.

Hypothetical Syllogism — EXAMPLE

> If *p*, then *q*.
> If *q*, then *r*.
> Therefore, if *p*, then *r*.

> If Ajax steals the money, he will go to jail.
> If Ajax goes to jail, his family will suffer.
> Therefore, if Ajax steals the money, his family will suffer.

Like *modus ponens*, *modus tollens* is always valid. If the premises are true, the conclusion must be true. So any argument that's in the *modus tollens* pattern is valid.

A third common argument form is called **hypothetical syllogism.** "Hypothetical" is just another term for conditional. A **syllogism** is a deductive argument made up of three statements—two premises and a conclusion. (*Modus ponens* and *modus tollens* are also syllogisms.) In a hypothetical syllogism, all three statements are conditional, and the argument is always valid:

If the ball drops, the lever turns to the right.
If the lever turns to the right, the engine will stop.
Therefore, if the ball drops, the engine will stop.

Here's the symbolized version:

If p, then q.
If q, then r.
Therefore, if p, then r.

People often use hypothetical syllogisms to reason about causal chains of events. They try to show that one event will lead inexorably to a sequence of events, finally concluding in a single event that seems far removed from the first. This linkage has prompted some to label hypothetical syllogisms "chain arguments."

There are two common argument forms that are *not* valid, though they strongly resemble valid forms. One is called **denying the antecedent.** For example:

If Einstein invented the steam engine, then he's a great scientist.
Einstein did not invent the steam engine.
Therefore, he is not a great scientist.

Denying the antecedent is represented like this:

If p, then q.
Not p.
Therefore, not q.

You can see the problem with this form in the preceding argument. Even if the antecedent is false (if Einstein did not invent the steam engine), that doesn't show that he's not a great scientist because he could be a great scientist on account of some other great achievement. Thus, denying the antecedent is clearly an invalid pattern: It's possible for the premises to be true and the conclusion false.

Here's another example of this form:

If science can prove that God is dead, then God is dead.
Science cannot prove that God is dead.
Therefore, God is not dead.

③ Hypothetical Syllogism

Chain arguments

Two FORMAL FALLACIES

① Denying The Antecedent

AFFIRMING THE CONSEQUENT

If *p*, then *q*.
q.
Therefore, *p*.

EXAMPLE

If the cat is on the mat, she is asleep.
She is asleep.
Therefore, she is on the mat.

DENYING THE ANTECEDENT

If *p*, then *q*.
Not *p*.
Therefore, not *q*.

EXAMPLE

If the cat is on the mat, she is asleep.
She is not on the mat.
Therefore, she is not asleep.

---

② *Affirming the Consequent*

"Mistakes are made on two counts: an argument is either based on error or incorrectly developed."

—THOMAS AQUINAS

A Final Valid Form

④ *Disjunctive Syllogism*

Even if science cannot prove that God is dead, that in itself does not show that God is not dead. Perhaps God is dead even though science cannot prove it. In other words, it's possible for both premises to be true while the conclusion is false.

There's another common invalid form you should know about: **affirming the consequent.** Here's an instance of this form:

> If Buffalo is the capital of New York, then Buffalo is in New York.
> Buffalo is in New York.
> Therefore, Buffalo is the capital of New York.

We represent this form like this:

> If p, then q.
> q.
> Therefore, p.

Obviously, in this form it's possible for the premises to be true while the conclusion is false, as this example shows. This pattern, therefore, is invalid.

Finally, we come to a common argument form called **disjunctive syllogism.** It's valid and extremely simple:

> Either Ralph walked the dog, or he stayed home.
> He didn't walk the dog.
> Therefore, he stayed home.

The symbolized form:

> Either p or q.
> Not p.
> Therefore, q.

Keep in mind that in a disjunctive syllogism, either disjunct can be denied, not just the first one.

These six deductive argument forms (four valid ones and two invalid ones) can help you streamline the process of argument evaluation. If you want to find out quickly if a deductive argument is valid, you can use these patterns to do that. (Remember, a good deductive argument has both a valid form and true premises.) You need only to see if the argument fits one of the forms. If it fits a valid form, it's valid. If it fits an invalid form, it's invalid. If it doesn't fit any of the forms, then you need to find another way to evaluate the argument. The easiest way to regularly apply this form-comparison technique is to memorize all six forms so you can identify them whenever they arise.

Summary

Sometimes you can see right away that an argument has a valid or invalid form. At other times, you may need a little help figuring this out, or you may want to use a more explicit test of validity. In either case, the *counterexample method* can help. With this technique you check for validity by simply devising a parallel argument that has the same form as the argument you're evaluating (the test argument) but has obviously *true premises and a false conclusion*. Recall that any argument having true premises and a false conclusion cannot be valid. So if you can invent such an argument that also has the same pattern as the test argument, you've proved that the test argument is invalid.

Counterexample Method

Let's say that you are confronted with this argument:

If *crime is increasing, then our nation has abandoned God.*
Our nation has abandoned God
Therefore, crime is increasing.

And to check this test argument, you come up with this parallel argument:

If *George is a dog, then he is warm-blooded.*
George is warm-blooded.
Therefore, he is a dog.

This argument has the same pattern as the previous one—but the premises are true, and the conclusion is false. So the test argument is invalid. You may have already guessed that it is an instance of affirming the consequent. The counterexample method, though, works not just for the deductive forms we've discussed but for all deductive forms. (We will discuss other deductive forms in upcoming chapters.)

See Famous Deductive Arguments (p. 225)

REVIEW NOTES

☑ Disjunctive Syllogism

SYMBOLIZED VERSION	EXAMPLE
Either *p* or *q*.	Either we light the fire or we will freeze.
Not *p*.	We will not light the fire.
Therefore, *q*.	Therefore, we will freeze.

Exercise 3.5

For each of the following arguments, determine whether it is valid or invalid and indicate the argument pattern.

V|MT   *1. If the Pilgrims built that wall, there would be archeological evidence of that.
But there is no such evidence.
So the Pilgrims did not build that wall.

V|MP   2. If the butler didn't kill the master, then the maid did.
The butler didn't kill him.
So the maid killed him.

V|DS   3. Either John drove home or he stayed late.
He didn't drive home.
Therefore, he stayed late.

I|AC   4. If the South Africans have nuclear weapons, the South African jungle will be radioactive.
The South African jungle is radioactive.
Therefore, the South Africans have nuclear weapons.

I|DA   5. If the South Africans have nuclear weapons, the South African jungle will be radioactive.
The South Africans do not have nuclear weapons.
Therefore, the South African jungle is not radioactive.

V|MT   *6. If CNN News omits important news stories, then it is irresponsible.
It is not irresponsible.
So CNN News does not omit important news stories.

I|AC   7. If ESP (extrasensory perception) were real, psychic predictions would be completely reliable.
Psychic predictions are completely reliable.
Therefore, ESP is real.

I|DA   8. If ESP (extrasensory perception) were real, psychic predictions would be completely reliable.
ESP is not real.
Therefore, psychic predictions are not completely reliable.

V|MP   *9. If ESP (extrasensory perception) were real, psychic predictions would be completely reliable.
ESP is real.
Therefore, psychic predictions are completely reliable.

V|MT   10. If laws could stop crime, there would be no crime.
But there is crime.
Therefore, laws cannot stop crime.

I|AC   11. If I perceive what appears to be a red door, then there really is a red door there.
There really is a red door there.
Therefore, I perceive what appears to be a red door.

V|HS

12. If it rains, Alex will get wet.
    If Alex gets wet, he will be upset.
    Therefore, if it rains, Alex will be upset.

Exercise 3.6

For each of the following premises, fill out the rest of the argument to make it valid in two different ways—*modus ponens* and *modus tollens*.

1. If the theory of evolution was untrue, biology would make no sense.
* 2. If Lino is telling the truth, he will admit to all charges.
3. If some wars are just, then pacifism is false.
4. If the new vaccine prevents the spread of the virus, the researchers who developed the vaccine should get the Nobel Prize.
* 5. If religious conflict in Nigeria continues, thousands more will die.
6. If *p*, then *q*.
7. If the glaciers are melting, global warming has increased.
8. If there is such a thing as moral progress—that is, social changes in which we judge states of affairs to be "better" now than before—then the Enlightenment ideal of moral perfection is possible.
* 9. If solar power can supply six megawatts of power in San Francisco (which is certainly not the sunniest place in the world), then solar power can transform the energy systems in places like Texas and Arizona.
10. If my honorable colleague would stop listening to only his own voice for less than sixty seconds, he would doubtless be astonished that there are other minds in the world with other ideas.

Exercise 3.7

Use the counterexample method to create a parallel argument for each of the invalid arguments in Exercise 3.5. Write out each parallel argument and represent its form using letters as discussed earlier. Answers are provided for 4, 5, 7, 8, and 11.

EXAMPLE

Test Argument:
    If the president cuts taxes again, there will be a long-term recession.
    There will be a long-term recession.
    Therefore, the president will cut taxes.

Parallel Argument:
    If Donald Trump could fly, he would be famous.
    He is famous.
    Therefore, he can fly.

    If *a*, then *b*.
    b.
    Therefore, *a*.

Diagramming Arguments

Most of the arguments we've looked at so far have been relatively simple. When arguments are more complex (in real life they usually are!), you may find it increasingly difficult to sort out premises from conclusions and argument parts from nonargumentative background noise. If you can visualize an argument's structure, though, the job gets much easier. That's where argument diagramming comes in.

Let's begin by diagramming the following argument:

> *There is no question in my mind. I therefore maintain that Colonel Mustard is the murderer. Because if he did it, he would probably have blood stains on the sleeve of his shirt. The blood stains are tiny, but they are there. Any observant person could see them. Also the murder weapon was within the colonel's reach for quite a while before the crime was committed. And since of all the people in the house at the time he alone does not have an airtight alibi, he must be the killer.*

The first thing we do is underline (or circle) any premise or conclusion indicator words (e.g., "therefore," "since," and "because"):

> *There is no question in my mind. I <u>therefore</u> maintain that Colonel Mustard is the murderer. <u>Because</u> if he did it, he would probably have blood stains on the sleeve of his shirt. The blood stains are tiny, but they are there. Any observant person could see them. Also the murder weapon was within the colonel's reach for quite a while before the crime was committed. And <u>since</u> of all the people in the house at the time he alone does not have an airtight alibi, he must be the killer.*

Next we number all the statements (and *only* the statements) in the passage in sequential order. (For the purposes of diagramming, an if-then statement is considered one statement, and multiple statements in a single compound sentence are to be counted as separate statements. Such statements are usually joined by "and," "or," and "but.") Then we look for the conclusion and draw a <u>wavy line</u> under it. Only after we've zeroed in on the conclusion should we try to locate the premises, which we can indicate by <u>underlining</u> them:

> *(1) There is no question in my mind. (2) I therefore maintain that Colonel Mustard is the murderer. (3) Because if he did it, he would probably have blood stains on the sleeve of his shirt. (4) The blood stains are tiny, but they are there. (5) Any observant person could see them. (6) Also the murder weapon was within the colonel's reach for quite a while before the crime was committed. (7) And since of all the people in the house at the time he alone does not have an airtight alibi, he must be the killer.*

And then we cross out all extraneous statements—those that are neither premises nor conclusions, those that are redundant, and those that are nothing more than background information or other logically irrelevant material.

> (1) ~~There is no question in my mind.~~ (2) *I therefore maintain that Colonel Mustard is the murderer.* (3) *Because if he did it, he would probably have blood stains on the sleeve of his shirt.* (4) *The blood stains are tiny, but they are there.* (5) ~~Any observant person could see them.~~ (6) *Also the murder weapon was within the colonel's reach for quite a while before the crime was committed.* (7) *And since of all the people in the house at the time he alone does not have an airtight alibi,* ~~he must be the killer~~.

Allen is far less argumentative since Angie's introduction to falconry.

By permission of the Jerry Van Amerongen and Creators Syndicate, Inc.

Finally, we draw the diagram. Place the numbers of the premises above the number for the conclusion. Then draw arrows from the premises to the conclusion they support. Each arrow represents a logical relationship between premise and conclusion, a relationship that we normally indicate with the word "therefore" or "is a reason or premise for."

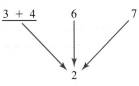

In this diagram you can see that premises 3 and 4 are handled differently from premises 6 and 7. The reason is that some premises are **independent** and some are **dependent.**

An independent premise offers support to a conclusion *without the help of any other premises.* If other premises are omitted or undermined in an argument, the support supplied by an independent premise does not change. We represent this fact in the diagram by drawing separate arrows from premises 6 and 7 to the conclusion. Premise 6 gives independent support to the conclusion, and premise 7 gives independent support to the conclusion. If we delete one of these premises, the support that the other one gives does not change.

Premises 3 and 4 are dependent premises. They do depend on each other to jointly provide support to a conclusion. If either premise 3 or 4 is removed, the support that the remaining premise supplies is undermined or completely canceled out. By itself, premise 3 ("Because if he did it, he would probably have blood stains on the sleeve of his shirt") offers no support whatsoever to the conclusion ("Colonel Mustard is the murderer"). And by itself, premise 4 ("The blood stains are tiny, but they are there") doesn't lend any support to the conclusion. But together, premises 3 and 4 offer a good reason to accept the conclusion. We represent dependent premises by joining them with a plus sign ("+") and underlining them, as in our diagram. Since dependent premises together act as a single premise, or reason, we draw a single arrow from the combined premises ("3 + 4") to the conclusion. With the diagram complete, we can see clearly that two independent premises and one set of dependent premises provide support for the conclusion (statement 2).

Now, consider this argument:

> *(1) The famous trial lawyer Clarence Darrow (1857–1938) made a name for himself by using the "determinism defense" to get his clients acquitted of serious crimes. (2) The crux of this approach is the idea that humans are not really responsible for anything they do because they cannot choose freely—they are "determined," predestined, if you will, by nature (or God) to be the way they are. (3) So in a sense, Darrow says, humans are like wind-up toys with no control over any action or decision. (4) They have no free will. (5) Remember that Darrow was a renowned agnostic who was skeptical of all religious claims. (6) But Darrow is wrong about human free will for two reasons. (7) First, in our moral life, our own commonsense experience suggests that sometimes people are free to make moral decisions. (8) We should not abandon what our commonsense experience tells us without good reason—and (9) Darrow has given us no good reason. (10) Second, Darrow's determinism is not confirmed by science, as he claims—but actually conflicts with science. (11) Modern science says that there are many things (at the subatomic level of matter) that are not determined at all: (12) They just happen.*

Indicator words are scarce in this argument, unless you count the words "first" and "second" as signifying premises. After we number the statements consecutively, draw a wavy line under the conclusion, underline the premises, and cross out extraneous statements, the argument looks like this:

> *(1) ~~The famous trial lawyer Clarence Darrow (1857–1938) made a name for himself by using the "determinism defense" to get his clients acquitted of serious crimes.~~ (2) ~~The crux of this approach is the idea that humans are not really responsible for anything they do because they cannot choose freely—they are "determined," predestined, if you will, by nature (or God) to be the way they are.~~ (3) ~~So in a sense, Darrow says, humans are like wind-up toys with no control over any action or decision. (4) They have no free will. (5) Remember that Darrow was a renowned agnostic who was skeptical of all religious claims.~~ (6) But Darrow is wrong about human free will for two reasons. (7) First, in our moral life, our own commonsense experience suggests that sometimes*

people are free to make moral decisions. (8) We should not abandon what our commonsense experience tells us without good reason—and (9) Darrow has given us no good reason. (10) Second, Darrow's determinism is not confirmed by science, as he claims—but actually conflicts with science. (11) Modern science says that there are many things (at the subatomic level of matter) that are not determined at all: (12) ~~They just happen.~~

To simplify things, we can eliminate several statements right away. Statements 1 through 4 are just background information on Darrow's views. Statement 5 is irrelevant to the argument; his agnosticism has no logical connection to the premises or conclusion. Statement 12 is a rewording of statement 11.

After this elimination process, only the following premises and conclusion (statement 6) remain:

(6) But Darrow is wrong about human free will for two reasons.
(7) First, in our moral life, our commonsense experience suggests that sometimes people are free to make moral decisions.
(8) We should not abandon what our commonsense experience tells us without good reason
(9) Darrow has given us no good reason.
(10) Darrow's determinism is not confirmed by science, as he claims—but actually conflicts with science.
(11) Modern science says that there are many things (mostly at the subatomic level of matter) that are not determined at all:

The question is, how are these premises related to the conclusion? Well, premises 7, 8, and 9 are dependent premises supporting the conclusion. Taken separately, these premises are weak, but together they constitute a plausible reason for accepting statement 6. Premise 10 directly supports the conclusion,

REVIEW NOTES

☑ Diagramming Arguments: Step by Step

1. Underline all premise or conclusion indicator words, such as "since," "therefore," and "because." Then number the statements.
2. Find the conclusion and draw a wavy line under it.
3. Locate the premises and underline them.
4. Cross out all extraneous material—redundancies, irrelevant sentences, questions, exclamations.
5. Draw the diagram, connecting premises and conclusions with arrows showing logical connections. Include both dependent and independent premises.

and it in turn is supported by premise 11. These logical relationships can be diagrammed like this:

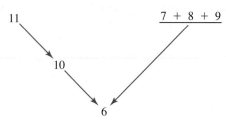

Now read this one:

As the Islamic clerics cling to power in Iran, students there are agitating for greater freedom and less suppression of views that the clerics dislike. Even though ultimate power in Iran rests with the mullahs, it is not at all certain where the nation is headed. Here's a radical suggestion: The Islamic republic in Iran will fall within the next five years. Why do I say this? Because the majority of Iranians are in favor of democratic reforms, and no regime can stand for very long when citizens are demanding access to the political process. Also, Iran today is a mirror image of the Soviet Union before it broke apart—there's widespread dissatisfaction and dissent at a time when the regime seems to be trying to hold the people's loyalty. Every nation that has taken such a path has imploded within five years. Finally, the old Iranian trick of gaining support for the government by fomenting hatred of America will not work anymore because Iran is now trying to be friends with the United States.

When we number the statements and underline the indicators, we get this:

(1) As the Islamic clerics cling to power in Iran, students there are agitating for greater freedom and less suppression of views that the clerics dislike. (2) Even though ultimate power in Iran rests with the mullahs, it is not at all certain where the nation is headed. Here's a radical suggestion: (3) The Islamic republic in Iran will fall within the next five years. Why do I say this? (4) <u>Because</u> the majority of Iranians are in favor of democratic reforms, (5) and no regime can stand for very long when citizens are demanding access to the political process. (6) Also, Iran today is a mirror image of the Soviet Union before it broke apart—there's widespread dissatisfaction and dissent at a time when the regime seems to be trying to hold the people's loyalty. (7) Every nation that has taken such a path has imploded within five years. (8) Finally, the old Iranian trick of gaining support for the government by fomenting hatred of America will not work anymore (9) <u>because</u> Iran is now trying to be friends with the United States.

And here's the passage with the premises and conclusion underlined and the extraneous material crossed out:

(1) ~~As the Islamic clerics cling to power in Iran, students there are agitating for greater freedom and less suppression of views that the clerics dislike. (2) Even~~

~~though ultimate power in Iran rests with the mullahs, it is not at all certain where the nation is headed. Here's a radical suggestion:~~ *(3) The Islamic republic in Iran will fall within the next five years.* Why do I say this? *(4) Because the majority of Iranians are in favor of democratic reforms, (5) and no regime can stand for very long when citizens are demanding access to the political process. (6) Also, Iran today is a mirror image of the Soviet Union before it broke apart—there's widespread dissatisfaction and dissent at a time when the regime seems to be trying to hold the people's loyalty. (7) Every nation that has taken such a path has imploded within five years. (8) Finally, the old Iranian trick of gaining support for the government by fomenting hatred of America will not work anymore (9) because Iran is now trying to be friends with the United States.*

The conclusion is statement 3, and the premises are statements 4 through 9. The first two statements are extraneous. Statements 4 and 5 are dependent premises, and so are statements 6 and 7. Statements 8 and 9 constitute an argument that gives support to the passage's conclusion. Statement 8 is the conclusion; statement 9, the premise. Notice also that the sentence "Why do I say this?" is not diagrammed at all because it's not a statement. The diagram of this argument is as follows:

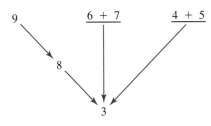

By the time you work through the diagramming exercises in this chapter, you will probably be fairly proficient in diagramming arguments of all kinds. Just as important, you will have a better appreciation of how arguments are built, how they're dissected, and how you can judge their value in a penetrating, systematic way.

Exercise 3.8

For each of the following diagrams, devise an argument whose premises and conclusion can be accurately depicted in the diagram. Write out the argument, number each statement, and insert the numbers into the diagram at the appropriate places.

*1. ( )   ( )   ( )

( )

Exercise 3.9

Diagram the following arguments using the procedure discussed in the text.

1. ①I shouldn't take physics this semester. ②My course load is already too heavy. ③There's no room for the course in my schedule. And ④I don't like physics.

2. ①The president is soft on the environment. ②He has weakened clean-air regulations and ③lifted restrictions on logging in the West.

3. ①Congressman Porkbarrel is either dishonest or incompetent. ②He's not incompetent, though, because ③he's expert at getting self-serving legislation through Congress. ④I guess he's just dishonest.

4. ①If an individual in a coma is no longer a person, then giving him a drug to kill him is not murder. ②Such an individual is in fact not a person. ③Therefore, giving him the drug is not murder.

5. ①"The City Council deserves the gratitude of all New Yorkers for introducing a bill to ban the use of cell phones in places of public performance. . . . ②These rules may be hard to enforce, but so are bans on littering, auto horn honking and other quality-of-life offenses. ③By changing the law, the city will send a clear message that cell phone abuse is not just an etiquette issue but robs audience members of their right to enjoy the performance they paid for." [Letter to the editor, *New York Times*, November 28, 2002]

＊ 6. ①If Marla buys the house in the suburbs, she will be happier and healthier. ②She is buying the house in the suburbs. So ③she will be happier and healthier.

7. ①If you gain too much weight, your blood pressure will increase. ②If your blood pressure increases, your risk of stroke or heart attack rises. ③Therefore, gaining too much weight can increase your risk of stroke and heart attack.

8. ①"Grow accustomed to the belief that death is nothing to us, since ②every good and evil lie in sensation. ③However, death is the deprivation of sensation. ④Therefore . . . death is nothing to us." [Epicurus]

9. ①"A cause-and-effect relationship is drawn [by those opposed to pornography] between men viewing pornography and men attacking women, especially in the form of rape. ②But studies and experts disagree as to whether any relationship exists between pornography and violence, between images and behavior. ③Even the pro-censorship Meese Commission Report admitted that the data connecting pornography to violence was unreliable." [*Free Inquiry*, Fall 1997] ④ So the C-E relation is doubtful.

＊ 10. ①The existence of planets outside our solar system is a myth. ②There is no reliable empirical evidence at all showing that planets exist outside our solar system.

11. If Li Yang gets a high score on her test, she will have a perfect grade point average. If she gets a low score, she will drop out of school. She

will get a high score on the test, so she will have a perfect grade point average.

12. Most atheists are liberals, and George is an atheist. Therefore, George is probably a liberal. Therefore, George is probably in favor of increased welfare benefits because most liberals are in favor of increased welfare benefits.

13. Bill is a student at Yale. No student at Yale has won the Nobel Prize. Therefore, Bill has not won the Nobel Prize.

14. "An international agreement proscribes the use of gas and so germ warfare must be developed." [Germaine Greer, *The Female Eunuch*]

15. The only valid reasons for dishonorably discharging someone from the Army are health problems and violations of Army regulations. So if Amal says that he was dishonorably discharged for simply being gay, he is lying or is mistaken. He is not lying. So he is mistaken.

16. "It is clear that archaeologists have not yet come to terms with dowsing [the alleged ability to detect underground water or treasure by paranormal means]. Where it has been the subject of tests, the tests have been so poorly designed and executed that any conclusion whatsoever could have been drawn from them. The fact that such tests are usually carried out only by researchers with a prior positive view of dowsing means that the conclusions will likely also be positive. The normal processes of peer review and scholarly discussion have also failed to uncover the lack of properly controlled test conditions in such studies as those of Bailey et al. and Locock, causing a generation of students and general readers in the United Kingdom, at least, to remain under the impression that the reality of archaeological dowsing had been all but confirmed by science." [*Skeptical Inquirer*, March/April 1999]

* 17. There are at least two main views regarding the morality of war. Pacifism is the view that no war is ever justified because it involves the taking of human life. Just-war theory is the view that *some* wars are justified for various reasons—mostly because they help prevent great evils (such as massacres, "ethnic cleansing," or world domination by a madman like Hitler) or because they are a means of self-defense. I think that our own moral sense tells us that sometimes (in the case of World War II, for example) violence is occasionally morally justified. It would be hard for anyone to deny that a war to prevent something like the Holocaust is morally right.

18. Some say that those without strong religious beliefs—nonbelievers in one form or another—cannot be moral. But millions upon millions of people have been nonbelievers or nontheists and yet have produced some of the most noble and most morally principled civilizations in history. Consider the Buddhists of Asia and the Confucianists of China. Consider also the great secular philosophers from the ancient Greeks to the likes of Bertrand Russell and John Searle of the twentieth century.

19. Either Maggie, Jose, or Ling broke the window. Jose couldn't have done it because he was studying in his room and was observed the whole time. Maggie couldn't have done it because she was out of town at the time and has witnesses to prove it. So the thief had to be Ling.

* 20. The picnic will probably be spoiled because there is a 90 percent probability of rain.

21. The Golden Gate Bridge will probably be attacked by terrorists within the next two years. The latest intelligence reports from the Justice Department confirm this prediction. Plus terrorists have already stated publicly that they intend to destroy various symbolic structures or monuments in the United States, including Mount Rushmore and the Golden Gate.

22. We shouldn't pay Edward an allowance because he never does any work around the house, and he will probably just waste the money because he has no conception of the value of anything.

Assessing Long Arguments

The general principles of diagramming can help you when you have to evaluate arguments that are much longer and more complicated than most of those in this chapter. Some arguments are embedded in extended passages, persuasive essays, long reports, even whole books. In such cases, the kind of *detailed* argument diagramming we use to analyze short passages won't help you much. In very lengthy works, our five-step diagramming procedure would be tedious and time-consuming—if not maddening. But the *general approach* used in the procedure is relevant to longer arguments.

When you have to evaluate a very long passage, you're almost always faced with three obstacles:

1. Only a small portion of the prose may contain statements that serve as the premises and conclusion. (The rest is background information, reiterations of ideas, descriptions, examples, illustrations, asides, irrelevancies, and more.)

2. The premises or conclusion may be implicit.

3. Many longer works purporting to be filled with arguments contain very few arguments or none at all. (It's common for many books—even best sellers—to pretend to make a case for something but to be devoid of genuine arguments.)

Fortunately, you can usually overcome these impediments if you're willing to put in some extra effort. The following is a four-step procedure that can help.

Step 1. Study the text until you thoroughly understand it. You can't locate the conclusion or premises until you know what you're looking for—and that requires having a clear idea of what the author is driving at. Don't attempt to find the conclusion or premises until you "get it." This understanding entails having an overview of a great deal of text, a bird's-eye view of the whole work.

Step 2. Find the conclusion. When you evaluate extended arguments your first task, as in shorter writings, is to find the conclusion. There may be several main conclusions or one primary conclusion with several subconclusions (as depicted in some of the previous argument diagrams). Or the conclusion may be nowhere explicitly stated but embodied in metaphorical language or implied by large tracts of prose. In any case, your job is to come up with a single conclusion statement for each conclusion—even if you have to paraphrase large sections of text to do it.

Step 3. Identify the premises. Like the hunt for a conclusion, unearthing the premises may involve condensing large sections of text into manageable form—namely, single premise statements. To do this you need to disregard extraneous

---

FURTHER THOUGHT

💡 No Arguments, Just Fluff

Once you get really good at spotting arguments in a variety of passages, you may be shocked to see that a massive amount of persuasive writing contains no arguments at all. Apparently many people—including some very good writers—think that if they clearly express their opinions, then they have given an argument. You could look at this state of affairs as evidence that people are irrational—or you could view it as a time-saver: No need to waste your time on a bunch of unsupported opinions.

Unsupported opinions are everywhere, but they seem to permeate political writing, letters to the editor, and anything that's labeled "spiritual." Sometimes opinions are so weakly supported that they're almost indistinguishable from completely unsupported ones. Here's a taste:

My family and friends have season tickets for the Buffalo Bandits. The disrespect that is shown to America by this team is appalling, particularly in this time of war. As both the Canadian and American national anthems are sung before each game, members of the team are hopping around, tugging at their uniforms, talking and carrying on amongst themselves. The players can't even wait for the national anthem to finish before they run off to their respective field positions. Whether one is for or against the war is irrelevant. Have some respect for America and what it stands for. [Letter to the editor, *Buffalo News* website]

No argument here, just indignation.

> So after a decade of progress, we have our smog problem back (as if it ever left). Another problem overlooked? Couldn't be because of all the giant behemoths (SUVs) on the road, could it? Nah. Or letting all the trucks from south of the border into our country without safety and smog inspections could it? Nah. It couldn't be because the government needs to have control of all it surveys? Nah. It must be something simpler, you think? Nah. [Letter to the editor, *Daily News* (Los Angeles) website]

No argument here either.

> How little is said of the soul-life and its complete identification with the human being! To most men the soul is something apart from themselves that is only to be talked of and trusted in on special occasions: There is no real companionship, no intimate affiliation, between men's minds and souls in their everyday existence. Now there is in every man a divine power, and when that divinity, which is real self, is acknowledged and understood by the mind, it takes a very active part in man's life—indeed, it could fill at the very least one-half of his thought-life. [Theosophy website]

Nope.   ■

material and keep your eye on the "big picture." Just as in shorter arguments, premises in longer pieces may be implicit. At this stage you shouldn't try to incorporate the details of evidence into the premises, though you must take them into account to fully understand the argument.

Step 4. Diagram the argument. After you identify the premises and conclusion, diagram them just as you would a much shorter argument.

Let's see how this procedure works on the following selection:

The Case for Discrimination

Edgardo Cureg was about to catch a Continental Airlines flight home on New Year's Eve when he ran into a former professor of his. Cureg lent the professor his cell phone and, once on board, went to the professor's seat to retrieve it. Another passenger saw the two "brown-skinned men" (Cureg is of Filipino descent, the professor Sri Lankan) conferring and became alarmed that they, and another man, were "behaving suspiciously." The three men were taken off the plane and forced to get later flights. The incident is now the subject of a lawsuit by the ACLU.

Several features of Cureg's story are worth noting. First, he was treated unfairly, in that he was embarrassed and inconvenienced because he was wrongly suspected of being a terrorist. Second, he was not treated unfairly, because he was not wrongly suspected. A fellow passenger, taking account of his apparent ethnicity, his sex and age, and his behavior, could reasonably come to the conclusion that he was suspicious. Third, passengers' anxieties, and their inclination to take security matters into their own hands, increase when they have good reason to worry that the authorities are not taking all reasonable steps to look into suspicious characters themselves. . . .

Racial profiling of passengers at check-in is not a panacea. John Walker Lindh could have a ticket; a weapon could be planted on an unwitting 73-year-old nun. But profiling is a way of allocating sufficiently the resources devoted to security. A security system has to, yes, discriminate—among levels of threat. [*National Review,* July 1, 2002]

In this example, the author has given us a break by alluding to the conclusion in the title: Discrimination by racial profiling is a justified security measure. Notice that this conclusion is not explicitly stated in the text but is implied by various remarks, including "A security system has to, yes, discriminate." Given this conclusion, we can see that the entire first paragraph is background information—specifically, an example of racial profiling. The first premise is implicit. We glean it from the comments in the second paragraph: Racial profiling is a reasonable response in light of our legitimate concerns about security. The second premise is explicit: Profiling is a way of allocating sufficiently the resources devoted to security.

Laid out in neat order, this argument looks like this:

(1) Racial profiling is a reasonable response in light of our legitimate concerns about security.
(2) Profiling is a way of allocating sufficiently the resources devoted to security.
(3) Therefore, discrimination by racial profiling is a justified security measure.

The diagram of this argument looks like this:

A fact that can further complicate the argument structure of a long passage is that complex arguments can sometimes be made up of simpler arguments (subarguments). For example, the conclusion of a simple argument can serve as a premise in another simple argument, with the resulting chain of arguments constituting a larger complex argument. Such a chain can be long. The complex argument can also be a mix of both deductive and inductive arguments. Fortunately, all you need to successfully analyze these complex arguments is mastery of the elementary skills discussed earlier.

The best way to learn how to assess long passages is to practice, which you can do in the following exercises. Be forewarned, however, that this skill depends heavily on your ability to understand the passage in question. If you do grasp the author's purpose, then you can more easily paraphrase the premises and conclusion and uncover implicit statements. You will also be better at telling extraneous stuff from the real meat of the argument. In the "Critical Thinking and Writing" section for this chapter, we continue this discussion of evaluating long arguments.

Exercise 3.10

For each of the following passages, (1) list the conclusion and premises and (2) diagram the argument.

* 1. "There are those who maintain . . . that even if God is not required as the author of the moral law, he is nevertheless required as the enforcer of it, for without the threat of divine punishment, people will not act morally. But this position is [not plausible]. In the first place, as an empirical hypothesis about the psychology of human beings, it is questionable. There is no unambiguous evidence that theists are more moral than nontheists. Not only have psychological studies failed to find a significant correlation between frequency of religious worship and moral conduct, but convicted criminals are much more likely to be theists than atheists. Second, the threat of divine punishment cannot impose a moral obligation, for might does not make right. Threats extort; they do not create a moral duty." [*Free Inquiry*, Summer 1997]

2. "I love *Reason* [magazine], but [regarding a previous article by Nick Gillespie] I'm wondering if all the illegal drugs that Nick Gillespie used to take are finally getting to him. He has a right to speak out against President Bush, but when he refers to him as "the millionaire president who waited out the Vietnam War in the Texas Air National Guard," it reminds me of the garbage rhetoric that I might see if I were reading Ted Rall, or Susan Sontag, or one of the other hate-mongering, America-bashing, leftist whiners. That kind of ad hominem attack is not only disrespectful to a man who is doing a damned good job as commander-in-chief (with approval ratings of more than 80 percent); it detracts from the whole point of the article." [Letter to the editor, *Reason*, July 2002]

3. "The fifth way [of proving that God exists] is taken from the governance of the world. We see that things which lack knowledge, such as natural

bodies, act for an end, and this is evident from their acting always, or nearly always, in the same way, so as to obtain the best result. Hence it is plain that they achieve their end, not fortuitously, but designedly. Now whatever lacks knowledge cannot move towards an end, unless it be directed by some being endowed with knowledge and intelligence; as the arrow is directed by the archer. Therefore some intelligent being exists by whom all natural things are directed to their end; and this being we call God." [Thomas Aquinas, *Summa Theologica*]

4. "The first thing that must occur to anyone studying moral subjectivism [the view that the rightness or wrongness of an action depends on the beliefs of an individual or group] seriously is that the view allows the possibility that an action can be both right and not right, or wrong and not wrong, etc. This possibility exists because, as we have seen, the subjectivist claims that the moral character of an action is determined by individual subjective states; and these states can vary from person to person, even when directed toward the same action on the same occasion. Hence one and the same action can evidently be determined to have—simultaneously—radically different moral characters. . . . [If] subjectivism . . . does generate such contradictory conclusions, the position is certainly untenable." [Phillip Montague, *Reason and Responsibility*]

5. A Florida judge dismissed a lawsuit that accused the Vatican of hiding instances of sexual abuse by priests. The suit was thrown out because Florida's statute of limitations had run out on the case. I submit that the dismissal was proper and ethical considering the community stature and function of priests and the benefits that accrue to society in the aftermath of the decision. Let's consider community stature first. The community stature of priests must always be taken into account in these abuse cases. A priest is not just anybody; he performs a special role in society—namely, to provide spiritual guidance and to remind people that there is both a moral order and a divine order in the world. The priest's role is special because it helps to underpin and secure society itself. Anything that could undermine this role must be neutralized as soon a possible. Among those things that can weaken the priestly role are publicity, public debate, and legal actions. Abuse cases are better handled in private by those who are keenly aware of the importance of a positive public image of priests. And what of the benefits of curtailing the legal proceedings? The benefits to society of dismissing the legal case outweigh all the alleged disadvantages of continuing with public hearings. The primary benefit is the continued nurturing of the community's faith, without which the community would cease to function effectively.

KEY WORDS

affirming the antecedent

affirming the consequent

antecedent

cogent argument

conditional statement

consequent

deductive argument

denying the antecedent

denying the consequent

dependent premise

disjunctive syllogism

hypothetical syllogism

independent premise

inductive argument

invalid argument

modus ponens

modus tollens

sound argument

strong argument

syllogism

truth-preserving

valid argument

weak argument

Summary

- Arguments come in two forms: deductive and inductive. A deductive argument is intended to provide logically conclusive support for a conclusion; an inductive one, probable support for a conclusion. Deductive arguments can be valid or invalid; inductive arguments, strong or weak. A valid argument with true premises is said to be sound. A strong argument with true premises is said to be cogent.

- Evaluating an argument is the most important skill of critical thinking. It involves finding the conclusion and premises, checking to see if the argument is deductive or inductive, determining its validity or strength, and discovering if the premises are true or false. Sometimes you also have to ferret out implicit, or unstated, premises.

- Arguments can come in certain common patterns, or forms. Two valid forms that you will often run into are *modus ponens* (affirming the antecedent) and *modus tollens* (denying the consequent). Two common invalid forms are denying the antecedent and affirming the consequent.

- Analyzing the structure of arguments is easier if you diagram them. Argument diagrams can help you visualize the function of premises and conclusions and the relationships among complex arguments with several subarguments.

• Assessing very long arguments can be challenging because they may contain lots of verbiage but few or no arguments, and many premises can be implicit. Evaluating long arguments, though, requires the same basic steps as assessing short ones: (1) Ensure that you understand the argument, (2) locate the conclusion, (3) find the premises, and (4) diagram it to clarify logical relationships.

Field Problems

1. Find a 150- to 200-word passage purporting to present an argument for a particular view but actually being devoid of arguments. Look in magazine or newspaper letters to the editor or advocacy or political websites. Then rewrite the passage and include an argument for the original view.

2. Visit a website intended to support a particular view on a social or political issue. Using the information on the website, write a 100-word passage containing an argument for a view that the website might endorse.

3. Visit www.townhall.com, www.usatoday.com, or www.csmonitor.com. Find an essay arguing for a particular view, and identify the premises and the conclusion. Decide whether you think the argument a good one. Be prepared to explain why.

Self-Assessment Quiz

Answers appear in "Answers to Self-Assessment Quizzes" (Appendix C).

1. What is a deductive argument? an inductive argument?

2. What is a valid argument? an invalid one? What is a strong inductive argument?

3. What is a sound argument?

Indicate whether the following arguments are deductive or inductive.

4. If you refuse to surrender, then you will be arrested. You refuse to surrender. Prepare yourself: You will be arrested.

5. There's an 80 percent chance that the hurricane will veer northward tomorrow and hit Tampa. So Tampa will probably feel the force of the hurricane tomorrow.

6. Ethel is reckless. She is going to have an accident sooner or later.

7. Whatever Hilary Clinton says is true. She says that the Republicans are weak. So the Republicans are weak.

In each of the following arguments, identify the implicit premise that will make the argument either valid or strong.

8. Jones has never openly criticized any military action against any Middle Eastern nation. He is a warmonger.

9. Maria failed her driving test three times. She's probably not paying attention.

10. If 60 percent of people believe in astrology or tarot cards, the future of the country does not look bright. Grades in college science courses will probably drop dramatically.

For each of the following exercises, provide an example of the argument pattern indicated.

11. *Modus ponens.*

12. *Modus tollens.*

13. Denying the antecedent.

14. Affirming the consequent.

Diagram the following arguments.

15. Cole is up to no good. He's been acting suspiciously for days, and he told Rachel that he was going to steal something valuable.

16. The sitcom *Friends* is becoming really lame. The writing is predictable and plodding. The acting is worse than ever.

17. If dolphins have minds comparable to ours, then these creatures are self-conscious, intelligent, and creative. If they are self-conscious, then they should react appropriately when they see their reflections in a mirror. They do react appropriately. If they're intelligent, they should be able to solve complex problems. They can solve such problems. If they're creative, they should be able to create some form of art. In a rudimentary way, they do create art. They are definitely self-conscious, intelligent, and creative.

18. If the dictum to always tell the truth in all circumstances is a valid moral principle, then it should fit well with our considered moral judgments. But it does not fit well with our considered moral judgments because there are times when lying is actually the right thing to do, as when we lie to save a life. So the dictum to always tell the truth is not a valid moral principle.

19. I don't think that I should vote for any independent candidate in the next election. Independents never win, and I want the person I vote for to win. Also, independents have a tendency to be a little wacky. And we definitely don't need any more wacky politicians in power.

20. Creationism is an inadequate theory about the origins of life. It conflicts with science, and it is incapable of predicting any new facts.

 Integrative Exercises

These exercises pertain to material in Chapters 1–3.

For each of the following passages, indicate whether it contains an argument. If it does, specify the conclusion and premises, any argument indicator words, whether the argument is deductive or inductive, and whether it contains an example of face-saving or group-pressure thinking. Also identify any implicit premises and diagram the argument.

1. If Anne is in town, then she's staying at the Barbary Hotel. She's in town. Therefore, she's staying at the Barbary Hotel.

2. If the death penalty deterred anyone from crime, then there would be a lower crime rate in countries that have the death penalty than in countries that do not. But crime rates are often higher in countries with the death penalty. So the death penalty is really no crime deterrent.

3. "In the wake of the attacks of September 11th, 2001, the governments of Canada and the United States have passed sweeping anti-terrorism bills that effectively lay the groundwork for the criminalization of ideas. One consequence has been . . . the policing of freedom of expression. In Canada, a post–September 11th exhibit of contemporary Arab-Canadian art at the National Museum in Ottawa was abruptly cancelled by the organizers to allow the curators to 'reconsider' the political works on display: the exhibition did go ahead as scheduled, but only after a determined public campaign challenging the museum's actions." [*Alternative Press Review*, Spring 2002]

4. "[Is] there scientific evidence that prayer really works? . . . The problem with . . . any so-called controlled experiment regarding prayer is that *there can be no such thing as a controlled experiment concerning prayer.* You can never divide people into groups that received prayer and those that did not. The main reason is that there is no way to know that someone did not receive prayer. How would anyone know that some distant relative was not praying for a member of the group . . . identified as having received no prayer?" [*Free Inquiry*, Summer 1997]

5. "Going hand in hand with the fundamental dishonesty of America's news media is the second problem: hypocrisy. The news media claims to disdain capitalism and profit, yet most media outlets are part of huge for-profit corporations that engage in fierce, often cutthroat, competition." [Accuracy in Media, www.aim.org, October 28, 2002]

6. "[C]urrent-day Christians use violence to spread their right-to-life message. These Christians, often referred to as the religious right, are well known for violent demonstrations against Planned Parenthood and other abortion clinics. Doctors and other personnel are threatened with death, clinics have been bombed, there have even been cases of doctors being murdered." [Letter to the editor, *Daily Wildcat*, September 17, 2002]

7. Everyone knows how beneficial an operating casino can be to a city of this size. But since establishing a casino here is prohibitively expensive, we need to try to institute gambling on a smaller scale—by placing a few slot machines in government buildings.

8. The financial health of the banking industry will improve dramatically in the next few months. This improvement will immediately lead to more

lenient loan terms for individuals. So it's better to wait a few months to ask a bank for a loan.

9. We evaluated the accuracy of recent news reports on a wide range of news topics. We focused on reports aired or published by three major media outlets. We found that 40 percent of their news reports were highly inaccurate. So, though it's hard to believe, 40 percent of all the news reports that people are exposed to are questionable.

10. A recent poll shows that 76 percent of Americans believe in life after death. In addition, there are thousands of first-person reports of either contacting dead people or seeing their spirits. Life after death is a reality.

11. These are Canada geese. Canada geese mate for life, so these Canada geese are paired up forever.

12. If sex education in the schools can reduce the teen pregnancy rate or help delay the onset of teen sexual activity, I'm all for it. A recent study of several hundred teens showed that sex education in school lowered the incidence of teen pregnancy. We should have sex ed in all public schools.

13. The worst calamity that will befall the world in the next twenty years will be the use of small nuclear weapons by terrorists or rogue states. The death toll from such a state of affairs is likely to be higher than that of any other kind of human devastation. The United Nations just issued a report that comes to the same conclusion. We should act now to prevent the proliferation of nuclear weapons and nuclear-weapons-grade material from falling into the wrong hands.

14. Many surveys show that most people not only believe in "remote viewing" (the ability to observe distant locations without using the physical senses) but also think that science has already proved its existence. This demonstrates that the majority of people are scientifically illiterate. If they understood the least bit about the methods of science and how it reaches conclusions, they would denounce silly ideas like remote viewing—or at least not accept them blindly.

15. Magazines regularly publish articles on "the sexiest man alive" or "the most beautiful woman in the world." All you have to do to see that these claims of superior attractiveness are bunk is to stroll down any main thoroughfare in any nation's capital. There you will see people—male and female—who make the magazines' favorite personifications of beauty or sexiness look like dogs.

16. The biblical story of Noah and the ark is immediately shown to be a fraud or fantasy by one fact: The volume of dung produced by the ark's animals (one pair of everything!) would fill a hundred arks, and shoveling all that stuff overboard would have taken scores of laborers working round the clock for two years.

17. Peanuts are good for you. A million little monkeys can't be wrong.

18. "There is no justice in the world. Amelia Earhart's plane went down, and despite fifty years of looking, no one has ever been able to find her. But

Yasser Arafat's plane goes down, and he's rescued in fifteen minutes." [Jay Leno, *The Tonight Show*]

19. "The following is in response to the letter, 'Let the Middle East fight its own wars.' I can understand the writer's concern about not wanting to start a war with Iraq. However, if Saddam Hussein poses a threat to the whole world—be it with nuclear or germ warfare—shouldn't we Americans take it upon ourselves to help protect the world? Or should we sit back and wait until Saddam is triumphant in developing his nuclear arsenal? Our intervention is considered necessary for all the present turmoil that's been taking place in the Middle East. We are the most intelligent and developed country in the world. We owe it to the lesser-developed counties to be peacekeepers. I ask the writer this: Where would the world be today if the United States had sat back and watched as Adolf Hitler rained terror on Europe?" [Letter to the editor, *Buffalo News*, November 29, 2002]

20. Freedom is a necessary component of the good life. The good life is something that every human being has a right to. Everything that humans have a right to should be acquired by any means necessary. Therefore, any war conducted to secure freedom for any of us is justified.

Critical Thinking and Writing
MODULE 3

FROM THESIS TO OUTLINE

In Module 1, we saw that the second step in writing an argumentative essay (after determining your thesis statement, or conclusion) is creating an outline. Outlines are useful because, among other things, they help avert disaster in the essay-writing phase. Imagine writing two-thirds of your essay, then discovering that the second premise of your argument cannot be supported and is in fact false. You might have to throw out the whole argument and start over.

At the head of your outline, insert your thesis statement, articulating it as clearly and as precisely as possible. At every stage of outlining, you can then refer to the statement for guidance. The premises and conclusion of your argument (or arguments) will constitute the major points of your outline. The following, for example, is the preliminary outline for the essay discussed in Module 2:

THESIS: Allowing coal-burning power plants to emit more sulfur dioxide will most likely increase the incidence of respiratory illnesses.

Seman
Disputants
a magazin
ent ideas a
agreement
graphic" n
"pornogra
Claims
because of
his bride-t
use the bir
smack the
Claims
ous, but th
liberately t
who had b
bake cooki
As a cr
derstand tl
"What doe
obligation
need not a
As a cr
stand exac
mean. Inex
mean, othe
ing is the
others. Go
mentally a
they ask th
an objectiv
put your v
cold. Ofter
unambigu

 Wr

1. Crea
App
port

I. Excessive amounts of sulfur dioxide in the air have been linked to increases in the incidence of asthma and other respiratory illnesses.

II. Many areas of the country already have excessive amounts of sulfur dioxide in the air.

III. Most sulfur dioxide in the air comes from coal-burning power plants.

IV. Therefore, allowing coal-burning power plants to emit more sulfur dioxide will most likely increase the incidence of respiratory illnesses.

After you clearly state the premises, you need to ask yourself whether any of them need to be defended. As we discussed in Module 1, any premise likely to be questioned by your readers will need support. That is, the premise itself will need arguments to back it up, and the supporting arguments should be indicated in your outline. (Some premises, though, may not need support because they are obvious or generally accepted.) As discussed in Chapter 3, you can support a premise (claim) through deductive or inductive arguments with premises made up of examples, analogies, empirical evidence (such as scientific research or trustworthy observations), and authoritative judgments (such as those from reliable experts). Here's how the preceding outline might look with (fictional) supporting arguments clearly shown:

THESIS: Allowing coal-burning power plants to emit more sulfur dioxide will most likely increase the incidence of respiratory illnesses.

I. Excessive amounts of sulfur dioxide in the air have been linked to increases in the incidence of asthma and other respiratory illnesses.

    A. EPA data show an association between high amounts of sulfur dioxide and increased respiratory illnesses.

    B. Cities that monitor air pollution have noted increases in hospital admissions for asthma and other respiratory ills when sulfur dioxide emissions are high.

II. Many areas of the country already have excessive amounts of sulfur dioxide in the air.

    A. Scientists have reported high levels of sulfur dioxide in the air in fifteen major cities.

III. Most sulfur dioxide in the air comes from coal-burning power plants.

    A. Many environmental scientists assert that coal-burning power plants are the source of most sulfur dioxide.

    B. A few owners of coal-burning power plants admit that their plants emit most of the sulfur dioxide in their region.

IV. Therefore, allowing coal-burning power plants to emit more sulfur dioxide will most likely increase the incidence of respiratory illnesses.

I. Excessive amounts of sulfur dioxide in the air have been linked to increases in the incidence of asthma and other respiratory illnesses.

II. Many areas of the country already have excessive amounts of sulfur dioxide in the air.

III. Most sulfur dioxide in the air comes from coal-burning power plants.

IV. Therefore, allowing coal-burning power plants to emit more sulfur dioxide will most likely increase the incidence of respiratory illnesses.

After you clearly state the premises, you need to ask yourself whether any of them need to be defended. As we discussed in Module 1, any premise likely to be questioned by your readers will need support. That is, the premise itself will need arguments to back it up, and the supporting arguments should be indicated in your outline. (Some premises, though, may not need support because they are obvious or generally accepted.) As discussed in Chapter 3, you can support a premise (claim) through deductive or inductive arguments with premises made up of examples, analogies, empirical evidence (such as scientific research or trustworthy observations), and authoritative judgments (such as those from reliable experts). Here's how the preceding outline might look with (fictional) supporting arguments clearly shown:

THESIS: Allowing coal-burning power plants to emit more sulfur dioxide will most likely increase the incidence of respiratory illnesses.

I. Excessive amounts of sulfur dioxide in the air have been linked to increases in the incidence of asthma and other respiratory illnesses.

A. EPA data show an association between high amounts of sulfur dioxide and increased respiratory illnesses.

B. Cities that monitor air pollution have noted increases in hospital admissions for asthma and other respiratory ills when sulfur dioxide emissions are high.

II. Many areas of the country already have excessive amounts of sulfur dioxide in the air.

A. Scientists have reported high levels of sulfur dioxide in the air in fifteen major cities.

III. Most sulfur dioxide in the air comes from coal-burning power plants.

A. Many environmental scientists assert that coal-burning power plants are the source of most sulfur dioxide.

B. A few owners of coal-burning power plants admit that their plants emit most of the sulfur dioxide in their region.

IV. Therefore, allowing coal-burning power plants to emit more sulfur dioxide will most likely increase the incidence of respiratory illnesses.

You should expand your outline until you've indicated how you intend to provide support for each claim that requires it. This level of detail helps ensure that you will not encounter any nasty surprises in the writing phase.

Your essay should somehow address objections or criticisms that your readers are likely to raise, and your outline should indicate how you intend to do this. Answering objections can make your case stronger and lend credibility to you as the writer. Sometimes it's best to address objections where they are likely to arise—in connection with specific premises or arguments. At other times, your essay may be more effective if you deal with objections at the end of it, near the conclusion.

As you work through your outline, don't be afraid to rework your thesis statement or to make changes in arguments. Satisfy yourself that the outline is complete and that it reflects a logical progression of points.

ARGUMENT AND AMBIGUITY

Good writing is clear writing. Writing that lacks clarity is ineffective—not to mention exasperating to readers and sometimes embarrassing to writers. An argument with unclear premises or conclusion is likewise ineffective. The lack of clarity undermines the argument, perhaps even rendering it useless.

Ambiguity is one of the many ways that a piece of writing can be unclear. A term or statement is ambiguous if it has more than one meaning and if the context doesn't reveal which meaning is intended. Consider these claims:

1. Morgan ate the ice cream with relish.
2. Kids make nutritious snacks.
3. A quarter of a million Chinese live on water.
4. John met the girl that he married at a dance.
5. Helen saw the bird with powerful binoculars.
6. Luis hit the boy with a book.
7. The guy was all over the road; I had to swerve a number of times before I hit him.
8. Officers help dog bite victims.
9. Include your children when baking cookies.

All these claims are ambiguous, but they are ambiguous in different ways. Claims 1, 2, and 3 involve *semantic ambiguities.* Semantic ambiguities are due to possible multiple meanings of a word or phase. In claim 1 the phrase "with relish" could mean "accompanied by a condiment" or "with pleasure or delight." In claim 2 the word "make" could mean either "prepare" or "constitute"—a difference between the kids' making food and *being* food. In claim 3 the phrase "live on water" could mean "subsist by ingesting water" or "reside on water"—a distinction between the culinary and the sociological.

Semantic ambiguities often spark unnecessary and tedious debates. Disputants, for example, may disagree dramatically over whether a photo in a magazine is pornographic—but they disagree only because they have different ideas about what the term "pornographic" means. They may actually be in agreement about which photos they find offensive. But to one person, "pornographic" may describe any representation of female nudity. To another person, "pornographic" may refer only to depictions of sexual acts.

Claims 4, 5, and 6 involve *syntactic ambiguities*. Syntactic ambiguities arise because of the sloppy way that words are combined. In claim 4 did John meet his bride-to-be at a dance, or did he marry her at a dance? In claim 5 did Helen use the binoculars, or did the bird use them? In claim 6 did Luis use a book to smack the boy, or did Luis smack a boy who was carrying a book?

Claims 7, 8, and 9 are not plainly either semantically or syntactically ambiguous, but they are unclear (and silly) just the same. In claim 7 was the writer deliberately trying to hit the guy or not? In claim 8 are the officers helping people who had been bitten or using dogs to bite people? In claim 9 are we supposed to bake cookies alongside our children—or bake the children *into the cookies?*

As a critical reader, your job is to be on alert for possible ambiguities, to understand the contexts that can help clear up ambiguities, and to constantly ask, "What does this mean?" If the meaning of a claim is unclear, you are under no obligation to accept it. Likewise, if an argument contains ambiguous claims, you need not accept the argument.

As a critical writer, your job is *not* to suppose that your readers will understand exactly what you mean but to strive to be perfectly clear about what you mean. Inexperienced writers too often assume that because they know what they mean, others will know too. The best corrective for unclear or ambiguous writing is the objective stance—the viewing of your writing from the standpoint of others. Good writers try hard to view their writing as others will, to step back mentally and try to imagine coming to their writing for the first time. In effect, they ask themselves, "Will my audience understand what I mean?" Achieving an objective stance toward your writing is not easy. One thing that helps is to put your writing aside for a day or two after you complete it and then read it cold. Often after this "cooling down" period, passages that you thought were unambiguous turn out to be murky.

Writing Assignments

1. Create an outline for Essay 3 ("The Wrong Ruling on Vouchers") in Appendix A. Specify the thesis statement, each premise, arguments supporting premises, any objections considered, and the conclusion.

2. Study the argument presented in Essay 7 ("Tight Limits on Stem Cells Betray Research Potential") in Appendix A. Identify the conclusion and the premises and objections considered. Then write a two-page critique of the essay's argument.

3. Select an issue from the following list and write a three-page paper defending a claim pertaining to the issue. Follow the procedure discussed in the text for outlining the essay and identifying a thesis and an appropriate argument to defend it. Where necessary, clarify terms.

   * Should same-sex marriages be allowed in all fifty states?
   * In its fight against terrorism, should the federal government be allowed to spy on American citizens by monitoring their email, wiretapping their phones, and checking records from public libraries—all without warrants?
   * Should a city government be allowed to ban art exhibits if they are deemed anti-religious or blasphemous?
   * Does pornography lead to violence against women?

4. Study Essay 13 ("Slouching Toward Chimeras"). Identify the conclusion and premises of the essay's argument, and write a rebuttal to it.

REASONS Part Two

Reasons for Belief
and Doubt

CHAPTER OBJECTIVES

WHEN CLAIMS CONFLICT

- Understand that when a claim conflicts with other claims we have good reason to accept, we have good grounds for doubting it.
- Recognize that if a claim conflicts with our background information, we have good reason to doubt it.
- Appreciate that when we are confronted with a claim that is neither completely dubious nor fully credible, we should proportion our belief to the evidence.
- Realize that it's not reasonable to believe a claim when there is no good reason for doing so.

EXPERTS AND EVIDENCE

- Understand what makes someone an expert and what does not.
- Understand that if a claim conflicts with expert opinion, we have good reason to doubt it.
- Realize that when the experts disagree about a claim, we have good reason to doubt it.
- Be able to recognize fallacious appeals to authority.
- Be able to distinguish true experts from nonexperts by using the four indicators of expertise.

PERSONAL EXPERIENCE

- Understand that it's reasonable to accept the evidence provided by personal experience only if there's no good reason to doubt it.

- Appreciate the importance of the common factors that can give us good reason to doubt the reliability of personal experience—impairment, expectation, and innumeracy.

FOOLING OURSELVES

- Appreciate why we need to resist the human tendency to resist contrary evidence.
- Become sensitive to the possibility of confirmation bias.
- Be alert to the possibility of the availability error.

CLAIMS IN THE NEWS

- Have a basic understanding of how the news media work and what factors influence the claims that they generate.
- Understand the skills involved in evaluating claims in the news.

ADVERTISING AND PERSUASION

- Understand and be able to apply the guiding principle for thinking critically about advertising.
- Be familiar with common ploys of persuasion used in advertising.

---

*Is the argument valid or strong?
How do we know whether we
have good reasons to
accept the premises?
What are good grounds for
accepting a claim that
① is used as a premise or
② stands alone...*

"The whole problem with the world is that fools and fanatics are always so certain of themselves, but wiser people so full of doubts."

—BERTRAND RUSSELL

LET'S REMIND OURSELVES ONCE AGAIN WHY WE'VE COME THIS WAY. If we care whether our beliefs are true or reliable, whether we can safely use them to guide our steps and inform our choices, then we must care about the reasons for accepting those beliefs. The better the reasons for acceptance, the more likely are the beliefs, or statements, to be true. Inadequate reasons, no reasons, or fake reasons (discussed in the next chapter) should lead us not to accept a statement, but to doubt it.

As we saw in earlier chapters, the reasons for accepting a statement are often spelled out in the form of an argument, with the statement being the conclusion. The reasons and conclusion together might compose a deductive argument or an inductive argument. In such cases, the reasons are normally there in plain sight. But in our daily lives statements, or claims, usually confront us alone without any accompanying stated reasons. An unsupported claim may be the premise of an argument (and its truth value may then determine whether the argument is sound or cogent). Or it may simply be a stand-alone assertion of fact. Either way, if we care whether the claim is acceptable, we must try to evaluate the claim as it stands.

Of course, it helps to be knowledgeable about the subject matter of a claim. But understanding and applying some critical thinking principles for assessing unsupported claims can be even more useful. Let's take a close look at these.

Favorite Unsupported Claims

In the Information Age, you don't have to look far for unsupported claims. They jump out at you from all directions. Many of them are a joy to behold because they're so imaginative, unusual, or provocative. They don't offer much of a challenge for critical thinkers, but they sure are fun. The following is a little sampling from cyberspace.

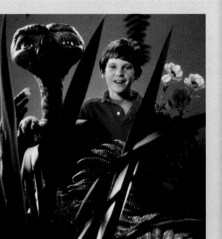

- "Is it strange how, when we are in the middle of summer, it can be raining out, and one day it is very 'hot,' the next day it is 15 degrees cooler, and two days later, it is 'hot' again? Does this seem strange? How about earthquakes in parts of the world, that are so devastating, that if they were to happen here, our whole economy could be ruined. Do you think it is 'odd' that people would suggest that the government can and does control the weather? I know it sounds a little paranoid, but if you do the research to investigate, you will undoubtedly arrive at the same conclusions. Our weather is controlled!"

- "Join the retreat into the Ethiopian mountains—near to the town of Axum—where the Ark of the Covenant is kept. I need some money fairly urgently—so I can visit Axum and start making some preparations. Thanks!"

- "Some of you may be wondering what Aliens and UFO stuff have to do with the Bible. The truth is Aliens and UFOs ARE a BIG part of the Bible, New World Order, and last days deception. Yes they exist, they are the fallen angels who rebelled with Lucifer before and even after the flood, and they are coming back with Lucifer to dominate and control the earth in the last days. To be forewarned, is to be prepared. The Lord has called me forth to inform and warn His people about what is coming."

- "Ever since the first born son of Colonel Charles Lindbergh and Anne Morrow Lindbergh was kidnapped in 1932, the resolution of that 'Crime of the Century' has been the subject of ongoing confusion, argument, and controversy. To this day articles and books are written about it, websites refer to it, and periodicals contain articles bringing into question whether or not the Lindbergh child, Charlie, was murdered or whether the child remained alive after he was kidnapped, as believed to be the case by many people. You may come to agree with me that Charlie was not murdered but was instead raised with another identity. You may also come to believe with me that my belief that I am Charlie is in fact true."

- "Contrary to all reports about a lone drifter named Mark David Chapman who allegedly shot John Lennon in the back December 8, 1980, you'll find ample evidence in the back issues of *Time*, *Newsweek*, and *US News and World Report* magazines to suggest otherwise. Namely, that John Lennon was not only politically assassinated, but that Richard Nixon, Ronald Reagan and, you'd better sit down, horror novelist Stephen King are the three people who can be proven guilty of the crime."

- "The thought screen helmet blocks telepathic communication between aliens and humans. Aliens cannot immobilize people wearing thought screens nor can they control their minds or communicate with them. Results of the thought screen helmet are preliminary. As of June 2000, aliens have not taken any abductees while they were wearing thought screen helmets using Velostat shielding."

- "Dying is as natural as being born. Immortality is a natural physical phenomenon. The study of immortality is an area of science, not faith. Scientific proof has existed for over a century that we all survive the death of our physical bodies, irrespective of our religious beliefs. The Campaign for Philosophical Freedom is working to achieve a philosophical balance in the media, and to increase public awareness of the existence of scientific proof that we all survive death."

- "Conclusions: 1. Life forms exist on the surface of the moon. 2. Lunar-surface life forms can grow into large forms and shapes. Some shapes assume cylindrical, linear and curved profiles. Others are complicated and entangled. 3. Lunar-surface life forms have the capability of attaching to equipment with a potential ability to cause equipment malfunction. 4. Lunar-surface life forms can change size and shape, and can do so quickly. 5. Pressure of the MET wheels on the surface appears to arouse lunar life forms to a state of luminescence. 6. Some 'rocks' which in macro view appear to be like earth-like rocks really are not but, rather, are a build-up of an accumulation of growing life forms. 7. Apollo 14 did land on the moon."

When Claims Conflict

Suppose you come across this claim in a reputable local newspaper:

[Claim 1] The historic Sullivan Building at the corner of Fifth and Main Streets was demolished yesterday to make way for a parking lot.

But say you have very good reasons to believe this claim:

[Claim 2] The historic Sullivan Building at the corner of Fifth and Main Streets was NOT demolished yesterday to make way for a parking lot.

What do you make of such a conflict between claims? Well, as a good critical thinker, you can know at least this: You have good reason to doubt claim 1 and therefore have no good grounds for accepting it. You have good reason to doubt it because it conflicts with another claim you have good reason to believe (claim 2). When two claims conflict, they simply cannot *both* be true; at least one of them has to be false. So this principle comes into play:

If a claim conflicts with other claims we have good reason to accept, we have good grounds for doubting it.

---

① CONFLICTING CLAIMS

①

If a claim conflicts with other claims that we have good reasons to accept, we have good reasons for doubting it...

FURTHER THOUGHT

💡 Fact and Opinion

When we evaluate claims, we often are concerned with making a distinction between facts and opinions. But just what is the difference? We normally use the term *fact* in two senses. First, we may use it to refer to a state of affairs—as in, "Examine the evidence and find out the facts." Second, and more commonly, we use *fact* to refer to *true statements*—as in, "John smashed the dinnerware—that's a fact." Thus, we say that some claims, or statements, are facts (or factual) and some are not. We use the word *opinion*, however, to refer to a *belief*—as in, "It's John's opinion that he did not smash the dinnerware." Some opinions are true, so they are facts. Some opinions are not true, so they are not facts.

Sometimes we may hear somebody say, "That's a matter of opinion." What does this mean? Often it's equivalent to something like, "Opinions differ on this issue" or "There are many different opinions on this." But it also frequently means that the issue is not a matter of objective fact but is entirely subjective, a matter of individual taste. Statements expressing matters of opinion in this latter sense are not the kinds of things that people can disagree on, just as two people cannot sensibly disagree about whether they like chocolate ice cream.

With conflicting claims, you are not justified in believing either one of them until you resolve the conflict. Sometimes this job is easy. If, for example, the competing claims are reports of personal observations, you can often decide between them by making further observations. If your friend says that your dog is sleeping atop your car, and you say that your dog is not sleeping atop your car (because you checked a short time ago), you can see who's right by simply looking at the roof of your car. (Remember, though, that even personal observations can sometimes mislead us, as we'll soon see.)

Many times, however, sorting out conflicting claims requires a deeper inquiry. You may need to do some research to see what evidence exists for each of the claims. In the best-case scenario, you may quickly discover that one of the claims is not credible because it comes from an unreliable source (a subject taken up in the next few pages).

Now suppose that you're confronted with another type of conflict—this time a conflict between a claim and your **background information.** Background information is that huge collection of very well supported beliefs that we all rely on to inform our actions and choices. A great deal of this lore consists of basic facts about everyday things, beliefs based on very good evidence (including our own personal observations and excellent authority), and justified claims that we would regard as "common sense" or "common knowledge." Suppose then that you're asked to accept this unsupported claim:

> Some babies can bench-press a five-hundred-pound weight.

You are not likely to give much credence to this claim for the simple reason that it conflicts with an enormous number of your background beliefs concerning human physiology, gravity, weight lifting, and who knows what else.

Or how about this claim:

> The president of the United States is entirely under the control of the chief justice of the Supreme Court.

This claim is not as outlandish as the previous one, but it too conflicts with our background beliefs, specifically those having to do with the structure and workings of the U.S. government. So we would have good reason to doubt this one also.

The principle exemplified here is:

> *If a claim conflicts with our background information, we have good reason to doubt it.*

Other things being equal, the more background information the claim conflicts with, the more reason we have to doubt it. We would normally—and rightfully—assign a low probability to any claim that conflicts with a great deal of our background information.

You would be entitled, for example, to have some doubt about the claim that Joan is late for work if it conflicts with your background information that Joan has never been late for work in the ten years you've known her. But you are entitled to have very strong doubts about, and to assign very low credibility to, the claim that Luis can turn a stone into gold just by touching it. You could even reasonably dismiss the claim out of hand. Such a claim conflicts with too much of what we know about the physical world.

It's always possible, of course, that a conflicting claim is true and some of our background information is unfounded. So many times it's reasonable for us to examine a conflicting claim more closely. If we find that it has no good reasons in its favor, that it is not credible, we may reject it. If, on the other hand, we discover that there are strong reasons for accepting the new claim, we may need to revise our background information. For example, we may be forced to accept the claim about Luis's golden touch (and to rethink some of our background information) if it is backed by strong supporting evidence. Our background information would be in need of some serious revision if Luis could produce this stone-to-gold transformation repeatedly under scientifically controlled conditions that rule out error, fraud, and trickery.

We need to keep in mind that although our background information is generally trustworthy, it is not infallible. What we assume is a strongly justified belief may be nothing more than prejudice or dogma. We should therefore be willing to re-examine background beliefs that we have doubts about—and to be open to reasonable doubts when they arise.

So it is not reasonable to accept a claim if there is good reason to doubt it. And sometimes, if the claim is dubious enough, we may be justified in dismissing a claim out of hand. But what should we believe about a claim that is not quite dubious enough to summarily discard yet not worthy of complete acceptance? We should measure out our belief according to the strength of reasons. That is,

We should proportion our belief to the evidence.

The more evidence a claim has in its favor, the stronger our belief in it should be. Weak evidence for a claim warrants weak belief; strong evidence warrants strong belief. And the strength of our beliefs should vary across this spectrum as the evidence dictates.

Implicit in all of the foregoing is a principle that deserves to be explicit because it's so often ignored:

It's not reasonable to believe a claim when there is no good reason for doing so.

The famous twentieth-century philosopher Bertrand Russell tried hard to drive this idea home. As he put it, "It is undesirable to believe a proposition when there is no ground whatever for supposing it true."[1] Russell claimed that

---

Handwritten margin notes:

The more background information with which a claim conflicts, the more reason there is to doubt it.

In some cases we might be forced to revise our background information C.S. Peirce on "critical commonsensism..."

What should we do when a claim is not so dubious so as to lead us to reject it? ①

③ We should proportion our belief to the evidence

"A belief which leaves no place for doubt is not a belief; it is a superstition."
—JOSÉ BERGAMÍN

④ It is not reasonable to believe a claim when there is no good reason for doing so. Russell's Principle

"None of my friends could diagnose the symptoms, Doctor. You're my last hope!"

Medical Economics

EXPERT EVIDENCE

①

If a claim conflicts with expert opinion then we have good reason to doubt it

②

When experts disagree about a claim, then we have good reason to doubt it.

if the use of this principle became widespread, social life and political systems would be transformed.

Experts and Evidence

When an unsupported claim doesn't conflict with what we already know, we are often justified in believing it *because it comes from experts.* An **expert** is someone who is more knowledgeable in a particular subject area or field than most others are. Experts provide us with reasons for believing a claim because, in their specialty areas, they are more likely to be right than we are. They are more likely to be right because (1) they have access to more information on the subject than we do and (2) they are better at judging that information than we are. Experts are familiar with the established facts and existing data in their field *and* know how to properly evaluate that information. Essentially, this means that they have a handle on the information and know how to assess the evidence and arguments for particular claims involving that information. They are true authorities on a specified subject. Someone who knows the lore of a field but can't evaluate the reliability of a claim is no expert.

In a complex world where we can never be knowledgeable in every field, we must rely on experts—a perfectly legitimate state of affairs. But good critical thinkers are careful about expert opinion, guiding their use of experts by some commonsense principles. One such principle is this:

If a claim conflicts with expert opinion, we have good reason to doubt it.

This tenet follows from our definition of experts. If they really are more likely to be right than nonexperts about claims in their field, then any claim that conflicts with expert opinion is at least initially dubious.

Here's the companion principle to the first:

When the experts disagree about a claim, we have good reason to doubt it.

If a claim is in dispute among experts, then nonexperts can have no good reason for accepting (or rejecting) it. Throwing up your hands and arbitrarily deciding to believe or disbelieve the claim is not a reasonable response. The claim must remain in doubt until the experts resolve the conflict or you resolve the conflict yourself by becoming informed enough to competently decide on the issues and evidence involved—a course that's possible but usually not feasible for nonexperts.

Sometimes we may have good reason to be suspicious of unsupported claims even when they are purportedly derived from expert opinion. Our doubt is justified when a claim comes from someone deemed to be an expert who in fact is *not* an expert. When we rely on such bogus expert opinion, we commit the fallacy known as the **appeal to authority.**

The fallacious appeal to authority usually happens in one of two ways. First, we may find ourselves disregarding this important rule of thumb: *Just because someone is an expert in one field, he or she is not necessarily an expert in another.* The opinion of experts generally carries more weight than our own—but only in their areas of expertise. Any opinions that they proffer outside their fields are no more authoritative than those of nonexperts. Outside their fields, they are not experts.

We needn't look far for real-life examples of such skewed appeals to authority. Any day of the week we may be urged to accept claims in one field based on

[Handwritten margin notes: Appeal to Authority. Just because someone is an expert in one field, he or she is not necessarily an expert in another... Fallacious appeals to authority]

FURTHER THOUGHT

💡 Are Doctors Experts?

Yes and no. Physicians are certainly experts in the healing arts, in diagnosing and treating disease and injury. They know and understand the relevant facts and they have the wherewithal to make good judgments regarding those facts. But are physicians experts in determining whether a particular treatment is safe and effective? Contrary to what many believe, the answer is, in general, no. Determining the safety and efficacy of treatments is a job for scientists (who may also be physicians). Medical scientists conduct controlled studies to try to ascertain whether Treatment X can safely alleviate Disease A—something that usually cannot be determined by a doctor interacting with her patients in a clinical setting. Medical studies are designed to control all kinds of extraneous variables that can skew the study results, the same extraneous variables that are often present in the doctor's office.

Critical thinkers should keep this distinction in mind because they will often hear people assert that Treatment Y works just because Dr. Wonderful says so.

the opinion of an expert from an unrelated field. An electrical engineer or Nobel Prize–winning chemist may assert that herbs can cure cancer. A radio talk-show host with a degree in physiology may give advice in psychology. A former astronaut may declare that archeological evidence shows that Noah's ark now rests on a mountain in Turkey. A botanist may say that the evidence for the existence of ESP is conclusive. The point is not that these experts can't be right, but that their expertise in a particular field doesn't give us reason to believe their pronouncements in another. There is no such thing as a general expert, only experts in specific subject areas.

Second, we may fall into a fallacious appeal to authority by regarding a nonexpert as an expert. We forget that a nonexpert—even one with prestige, status, or sex appeal—is still a nonexpert. Movie stars, TV actors, renowned athletes, and famous politicians endorse products of all kinds in TV and print advertising. But when they speak outside their areas of expertise (which is almost always the case), they give us no good reason for believing that the products are as advertised. Advertisers, of course, know this, but they hope that we will buy the products anyway because of the appeal or attractiveness of the celebrity endorsers.

Historically the regarding of a nonexpert as an expert has probably been the most prevalent form of the appeal to authority—with disastrous results. Political, religious, tribal, and cultural leaders often have been designated as authorities not because they knew the facts and could correctly judge the evidence but because culture, tradition, or whim dictated that they be regarded as authorities. When these "authorities" spoke, people listened and believed—then went to war, persecuted unbelievers, or undertook countless other ill-conceived projects. If we are to avoid this trap, we must look beyond mere labels and titles and ask, "Does this person provide us with any good reasons or evidence?"

This question, of course, is just another way of asking if someone is a true expert. How can we tell? To be considered an expert, someone must have shown that he or she can assess relevant evidence and arguments and arrive at well-supported conclusions in a particular field. What are the indicators that someone has this essential kind of expertise? There are several that provide clues to someone's ability but do not guarantee the possession of true expertise.

In most fields, the following two indicators are considered minimal prerequisites for being considered an expert:

1. Education and training from reputable institutions or programs in the relevant field (usually evidenced by degrees or certificates)
2. Experience in making reliable judgments in the field (generally the more years of experience the better)

But, unfortunately, people can have the requisite education and experience and still not know what they're talking about in the field in question. Woe be to us, for in the real world there are well-trained, experienced auto mechanics who

History: the dangers of FAA

Who is an expert?

"An expert is a man who has made all the mistakes which can be made in a very narrow field."
—NIELS BOHR

Conditions for expertise

"An expert is someone who knows some of the worst mistakes that can be made in his subject and who manages to avoid them."
—WERNER HEISENBERG

Tom Cruise, Scientology, and Psychiatry

In an infamous interview on the *Today* show, actor Tom Cruise, a well-known follower of the Church of Scientology, declared that psychiatry is a harmful pseudoscience and that psychiatric drugs, especially antidepressants, do not work. The proper approach to depression, he said, is exercise and vitamins. Major mental health organizations swiftly rejected Cruise's claims. The American Psychiatric Association asserted:

> Over the past five years, the nation has more than doubled its investment in the study of the human brain and behavior, leading to a vastly expanded understanding of postpartum depression, bipolar disorder and attention-deficit/hyperactivity disorder. Much of this research has been conducted by the National Institutes of Health and the nation's leading academic institutions.
>
> Safe and effective treatments are available and may include talk therapy, medication or a combination of the two. Rigorous, published, peer-reviewed research clearly demonstrates that treatment works.[2]

So what's a critical thinker to think?

Even without a close examination of the truth of Cruise's claims, we can conclude at least this: (1) Despite his celebrity, his endorsement of the claims does not in itself give us reason to accept them. To think otherwise is to fall for a fallacious appeal to authority. (2) We have reason to doubt his assertions because they conflict with expert opinion. The consensus among the experts (both scientific and medical) is that psychiatry is not a noxious sham and that psychiatric drugs can be effective against depression. We should accept Cruise's view only if there is good reason to do so. Only evidence and argument can establish his case, and few—if any—experts believe this standard has been met.

Do you think that Cruise's affiliation with Scientology is a good reason for rejecting his claims? Why or why not?

Evaluating Web Sources

Can you trust the information you find on the World Wide Web? In most cases, no. But if you understand how to judge the reliability of Web sources, and you're willing to spend some time doing the judging, you can often uncover material that is trustworthy and useful. Finding credible information on the Web takes some effort because, unlike books and magazines, most of the information on the Internet is not screened by editors or fact-checkers or anyone else before it hits cyberspace. *Anyone* can say *anything* on the Web. Thus the watchwords of web research should be *reasonable skepticism*. If you want to know more about evaluating web sources, a good place to start is a college or university library. Many of them have free websites featuring excellent guides to Internet research. Duke University, for example, has such a site (www.lib.duke.edu/libguide/ evaluating_web.htm). Among other things, it offers a checklist of questions to ask about web sources to help you assess their credibility. Some of these questions follow, broken down by category.

AUTHORITY

- Who wrote the page? Look for the author's name near the top or the bottom of the page. If you can't find a name, look for a copyright credit © or link to an organization.
- What are the author's credentials? Look for biographical information or the author's affiliations (university department, organization, corporate title, etc.).
- Could the credentials be made up? Anyone who has visited a chat room knows that people don't always identify themselves accurately.
- Did the author include contact information? Look for an email link, address, or phone number for the author. A responsible author should give you the means to contact him or her.
- Whose website is this? What organization is sponsoring the web page? Look at the domain (.com, .edu, .org, etc.). Look for an "about this site" link. Also look for a tilde (~) in the URL, which usually identifies a personal directory on a website. Be careful of a web page that has a tilde in its URL. Internet service provider sites (AOL, Mindspring, MSN, etc.) and online community sites (GeoCities, Tripod, Angelfire, etc.) feature personal pages. Be careful of web pages from those sites, too.

▼

PURPOSE/INTENDED AUDIENCE

• What is the purpose of the page? Why did the author create it? The purpose could be advertising, advocacy, news, entertainment, opinion, fandom, scholarship, satire, and so on. Some pages have more than one purpose. For example, www.dowjones.com provides free business information but also encourages you to subscribe to the *Wall Street Journal* or other Dow Jones products.

CURRENT?

• Is there a date at the top or bottom of the page? But note: A recent date doesn't necessarily mean the information is current. The content might be years out of date even if the given date is recent. (The last update of the page might have consisted of someone changing an email address or fixing a typo.)

• Is the information up-to-date? This takes a little more time to determine. Compare the information on the web page to information available through other sources. Broken links are one measure of an out-of-date page. In general, information for science, technology, and business ages quickly. Information in the humanities and social sciences ages less quickly. However, old information can still be perfectly valid.

OBJECTIVITY VERSUS BIAS

• Is the author being objective or biased? Biased information is not necessarily "bad," but you must take the bias into account when interpreting or using the information given. Look at the facts the author provides, and the facts the author *doesn't* provide. Are the facts accurately and completely cited? Is the author fair, balanced, and moderate in his or her views, or is the author overly emotional or extreme? Based on the author's authority, try to identify any conflict of interest. Determine if the advertising is clearly separated from the objective information on the page.

SUPPORT

• Does the author support the information he or she uses? Look for links or citations to sources. Some academic web pages include bibliographies.

• Is the support respectable? Does the page cite well-known sources or authorities? Does the page cite a variety of sources? Do other pages on the same topic cite some of the same sources? The web page in question should have a mix of internal links (links to web pages on the same site or by the same author) and external links (links to other sources or experts). If a web page makes it hard for you to check the support, *be suspicious*.[3] ■

do terrible work—and tenured Ph.D.'s whose professional judgment is iffy. Two additional indicators, though, are more revealing:

1. Reputation among peers (as reflected in the opinions of others in the same field, relevant prestigious awards, and positions of authority)
2. Professional accomplishments

These two indicators are more helpful because they are very likely to be correlated with the intellectual qualities expected in true experts. People with excellent reputations among their professional peers and with significant accomplishments to their credit usually are true experts.

As we've seen, we are often justified in believing an unsupported claim because it's based on expert opinion. But if we have reason to doubt the opinion of the experts, then we are not justified in believing the claim based on that opinion. And chief among possible reasons for doubt (aside from conflicting expert opinion) is bias. When experts are biased, they are motivated by something other than the search for the truth—perhaps financial gain, loyalty to a cause, professional ambition, emotional needs, political outlook, sectarian dogma, personal ideology, or some other judgment-distorting factor. Therefore, if we have reason to believe that an expert is biased, we are not justified in accepting the expert's opinion.

But how can we tell when experts are biased? There are no hard-and-fast rules here. In the more obvious cases, we often suspect bias when an expert is being paid by special-interest groups or companies to render an opinion, or when the expert expresses very strong belief in a claim even though there is no evidence to support it, or when the expert stands to gain financially from the actions or policies that he or she supports.

It's true that many experts can render unbiased opinions and do high-quality research even when they have a conflict of interest. Nevertheless in such situations we have reasonable grounds to suspect bias—unless we have good reason to believe that the suspicion is unwarranted. These good reasons might include the fact that the expert's previous opinions in similar circumstances have been reliable or that he or she has a solid reputation for always offering unbiased assessments.

There are, of course, many other possible reasons to doubt the opinion of experts. Any blatant violation of the critical thinking principles discussed in this text, for example, would give us good reason to question an authority's reliability. Among the more common tip-offs of dubious authority are these:

- The expert is guilty of simple factual or formal errors.
- The expert's claims conflict with what you have good reason to believe.
- The expert does not adequately support his or her assertions.
- The expert's writing contains logical contradictions or inconsistent statements.

- The expert does not treat opposing views fairly.
- The expert is strongly biased, emotional, or dismissive.
- The expert relies on information you know is out of date.
- Most other experts in the same field disagree.

The amount of weight you give to any one of these factors—and the subsequent degree of doubt you attach to an expert's opinion—will vary in each case. In general, a single minor error of fact or style does not justify dismissing an expert's entire article that is otherwise excellent. But doubt is cumulative, and as reasons for doubt are added, you may rightfully decide that you are not justified in believing any part of an expert's testimony, regardless of his or her credentials. Depending on your aims, you may decide to check the expert's assertions

Is "Joe the Plumber" a Fallacy?

In the 2008 presidential campaign, Samuel Joseph Wurzelbacher—a 34-year-old plumber and "ordinary guy"—was unexpectedly thrown into the thick of presidential politics. When Barack Obama, the Democratic contender, made a campaign stop in Ohio, Wurzelbacher asked him, "Your new tax plan is going to tax me more, isn't it?" Obama replied that under his plan, taxes would increase for people making over $250,000 per year (a group that did not include Wurzelbacher) and that "when you spread the wealth around, it's good for everybody." John McCain, the Republican candidate, pounced on the conversation, declaring that Wurzelbacher—by then called Joe the Plumber—would be penalized by Obama's tax plan but rewarded by his own. Wurzelbacher endorsed McCain's candidacy, and the McCain campaign began promoting him as a symbol of working-class Americans who would be much better off under a McCain administration.

Wurzelbacher became the star of McCain campaign rallies, a key part of the campaign's strategy, a hero to many Republicans, and the focus of national news coverage. The media were eager to talk to him, and he readily rendered his opinions on taxes, Social Security, and other subjects.

Was this use of Joe the Plumber in a political campaign a fallacious appeal to authority? If he had been presented as an authority on tax policy, that would have been fallacious because he is not an expert; his opinions on the subject carry no more weight than most other people's. (His opinions on plumbing problems, however, may in fact be authoritative.) But mostly the McCain campaign did not take this tack. Instead it seemed to position Joe the Plumber as an *authority on the views of the average guy*. The implicit argument was something like this: The ordinary guy is the real authority on taxes; Joe is the epitome of the ordinary guy; he rejects Obama's tax plan; therefore, we should all reject Obama's tax plan.

The problem with this argument is that (1) Joe may not be average in the relevant sense (his views may or may not represent those of most "average guys") and, (2) even if his views are representative, they may not be right. The view of the average guy may be completely wrong. So the Joe the Plumber gambit is indeed a fallacious appeal to authority, as well as an equally fallacious appeal to popularity. ■

against other sources or to consult an authority with much less evidential or rhetorical baggage.

Finally, keep in mind that there are certain kinds of issues that we probably don't want experts to settle for us. Indeed, in most cases the experts *cannot* settle them for us. These issues usually involve moral, social, or political questions. If

REVIEW NOTES

☑ Conflicting Claims

- If a claim conflicts with other claims we have good reason to accept, we have good grounds for doubting it.
- If a claim conflicts with our background information, we have good reason to doubt it.
- We should proportion our belief to the evidence.
- It's not reasonable to believe a claim when there is no good reason for doing so.
- If a claim conflicts with expert opinion, we have good reason to doubt it.
- When the experts disagree about a claim, we have good reason to doubt it.

we're intellectually conscientious, we want to provide our own final answers to such questions, though we may draw heavily on the analyses and arguments provided by experts. We may study what the experts have to say and the conclusions they draw. But we want ultimately to come to our own conclusions. We prefer this approach in large part because the questions are so important and because the answers we give help define who we are. What's more, the experts typically disagree on these issues. So even if we wanted the experts to settle one of these questions for us, they probably couldn't.

Areas in which experts cannot settle the issue:
① moral
② social
③ political

Personal Experience

We accept a great many claims because they are based on personal experience—our own or someone else's. Personal experience, broadly defined, arises from our senses, our memory, and our judgment involved in those faculties. In countless cases, personal experience is our evidence (or part of the evidence) that something is or is not the case. You believe that Jack caused the traffic accident because you, or someone else, witnessed it. You think that the herbal tea cured your headache because the pain went away after you drank it. You believe that

We accept a great many claims because they are based on personal experience

---

FURTHER THOUGHT

💡 Do Nonexperts Know Best?

Some people have a bias against experts—*all* experts. Their thoughts on the subject might run something like this: "It's the uneducated ones, the simple seekers of knowledge who are the truly wise, for their thinking has not yet been corrupted by ivory-tower learning and highbrow theorizing that's out of touch with the real world. Thus the wisdom of the nonexpert is to be preferred over the expert whenever possible." This attitude is, oddly enough, sometimes embraced by very educated people. There's a strong strain of it, for example, among New Agers and advocates of alternative, or unconventional, medicine.

This nonexpertism is related to the appeal to ignorance discussed in Chapter 5. (The appeal to ignorance says that since there's no evidence refuting a position, it must be true.) The problem is that both tacks, though psychologically compelling, are fallacious. A lack of good reasons—evidence or expert testimony—does not constitute proof of a claim.

The history of science shows that virtually all notable scientific discoveries have been made by true experts—men and women who were fully knowledgeable about their subject matter. There have been many more instances, however, of cocksure nonexperts who proposed theories, cures, and solutions to problems that turned out to be worthless.

Appeal to Ignorance (p. 183 ff)

Nonexpertism

your friend can bend spoons with her mind because you saw her do it at a party. You're sure that the other guy threw the first punch, not you, because that's how you remember the incident. Or you vote to convict the defendant because eyewitness testimony puts him at the scene of the crime with a gun in his hand. But can you trust personal experience to reveal the truth?

The answer is a *qualified* yes. And here's the qualification in the form of an important principle:

> *It's reasonable to accept the evidence provided by personal experience only if there's no good reason to doubt it.*

If we have no good reason to doubt what our personal experience reveals to us, then we're justified in believing it. This means that if our faculties are working properly and our use of them is unimpeded by anything in our environment, we're entitled to accept what our personal experience tells us. If we seem to see a cat on the mat under good viewing conditions—that is, we have no reason to believe that our observations are impaired by, say, poor lighting, cracked glasses, or too many beers—then we're justified in believing that there's a cat on the mat.

The problem is that personal experience, though generally reliable, is not infallible. Under certain circumstances, our senses, memory, and judgment can't be trusted. It's easy enough to identify these circumstances in an abstract way, as you'll see later. The harder job is (1) determining when they actually occur in real-life situations and (2) avoiding them or taking them into account.

The rest of this section is a rundown of some of the more common factors that can give us good reason to doubt the reliability of personal experience.

IMPAIRMENT

This should be obvious: If our perceptual powers are somehow impaired or impeded, we have reason to doubt them. The unambiguous cases are those in which our senses are debilitated because we are ill, injured, tired, stressed out, excited, drugged, drunk, distracted, or disoriented. And just as clear are the situations that interfere with sensory input—when our environment is, say, too dark, too bright, too noisy, or too hazy. If any of these factors are in play, the risk of misperception is high, which gives us reason to doubt the trustworthiness of what we experience.

Memories can be affected by many of the same factors that interfere with accurate perception. They are especially susceptible to distortion if they are formed during times of stress—which helps explain why the memories of people who witness crimes or alleged ghosts are so often unreliable. These situations are understandably stressful.

The impairment of our faculties is complicated by the peculiar way they operate. Contrary to what many believe, they are not like recording devices that make exact mental copies of objects and events in the world. Research suggests

Handwritten margin notes:

Should I trust Personal Experience?

It is reasonable to accept the evidence provided by personal experience only if there is no good reason to doubt it.

Though generally reliable personal experience is not infallible...

① IMPAIRMENT

① Perception

② Memory

"Besides learning to see, there is another art to be learned—not to see what is not."
—MARIA MITCHELL

Tinkering with Your Memory

The memories of eyewitnesses are notoriously unreliable. One reason is that your memory of an event can be altered if you later receive new information regarding the event. Research shows that your memory can be changed in this way, but you won't know it. You will be sincerely convinced that your altered memory is the original memory. Research studies have uncovered this phenomenon again and again. Here's a description of the classic case:

> Once upon a time, a man (whom we'll call Mike) stumbled upon an armed robbery in a hardware store. The robber rummaged around the cluttered store brandishing a silver weapon; finally, he stole all the money. Then, almost as an afterthought, he grabbed a hand calculator and a hammer, placing these in his satchel as he left the store. The police were summoned immediately, but before they arrived, Mike talked to another customer about the robbery. We'll call her Maria. Maria told Mike that she saw the robber grab a calculator and a screwdriver, stuffing them in his satchel as he left the store. The police arrived, and when they questioned Mike, he recounted the robbery at some length: He described in detail the silver weapon, the money, and the calculator. When the police asked him about a tool that they heard had been taken, "Did you see if it was a hammer or a screwdriver?" he said, "Screwdriver."[4]

[handwritten margin note: Our memories are changed by new information...]

that they are more like artists who use bits of sensory data or memory fragments to concoct creative representations of things, not exact replicas. Our perception and memory are *constructive*, which means that what we perceive and remember is to some degree fabricated by our minds. Some of the more blatant examples: You see a man standing in the shadows by the road—then discover when you get closer that the man is a tree stump. You anxiously await a phone call from Aunt Mary, and when the call comes and you hear the person's voice, you're sure it's her—then realize that it's some guy asking for a charitable donation. While in the shower you hear the phone ring—but no one is calling, and the ringing is something your mind is making up.

[handwritten margin note: Our perception and memory are constructive...]

The constructive workings of our minds help us solve problems and deal effectively with our environment. But they can also hinder us by manufacturing too much of our experiences using too little data. Unfortunately, the constructive tendency is most likely to lead us astray precisely when our powers of perception and memory are impaired or impeded. Competent investigators of alleged paranormal phenomena understand this and are rightfully skeptical of paranormal claims based on observations made under dubious conditions like those

[handwritten margin note: Paranormal claims]

Look! Martian Canals

How easy it is for even trained observers to see what isn't there! This famous example, one of many, is explained by psychologist Terence Hines:

> The constructive nature of perception accounts for a famous astronomical illusion—the canals of Mars. These were first reported in 1877 by the Italian astronomer Schiaparelli. They were popularized in the early twentieth century by the American astronomer Percival Lowell. . . . Lowell argued that the canals were constructed by an advanced Martian civilization. It turns out, however, that the canals of Mars don't exist. [Carl Sagan and P. Fox (1975)] have compared the photos taken by *Mariner 9*, which photographed the entire Martian surface, with maps of the canals. When the actual Martian surface is examined, there are no canals

Lowell's drawings of Martian canals.

> and no other physical features that could account for what Schiaparelli and Lowell reported. So, where did the canals come from? Sagan and Fox state that "the vast majority of the canals appear to be largely self-generated by the visual observers of the canal school, and stand as monuments to the imprecision of the human eye-brain-hand system under difficult observing conditions."[5]

mentioned here. Under the right conditions, the mind is very good at showing us UFOs and midnight ghosts that aren't there. Likewise, juries are expected to be suspicious of the testimony of eyewitnesses who swear they plainly saw the dirty deed committed but were frightened, enraged, or a little tipsy at the time.

EXPECTATION

A tricky thing about perception is that we often perceive exactly what we expect to perceive—regardless of whether there's anything there to detect. Ever watch the second hand on an electric clock move—then suddenly realize that the clock is not running at all? Ever been walking through a crowd looking for a friend and hear her call your name—then find out later that she was ten blocks away at the time? Such experiences—the result again of the constructive tendencies of mind—are common examples of how expectation can distort your perceptions.

Scientific research shows that expectation can have a more powerful effect on our experiences than most people think. In numerous studies, subjects who expected to see a flash of light, smell a certain odor, or feel an electric shock did indeed experience these things—even though the appropriate stimuli were never present. The mere suggestion that the stimuli would occur was enough to cause the subjects to perceive, or apparently perceive, things that did not exist.

Our tendency to sometimes perceive things that are not really there is especially pronounced when the stimuli are vague or ambiguous. For example,

[Margin note: Expectations can distort perceptions]

[Margin note: Scientific studies]

" NEWSMAKERS "

Eyewitness Testimony and Injustice

Eyewitness testimony is unreliable. So says a raft of scientific evidence, including this study that made headlines in 2007:

> Brandon L. Garrett, a law professor at the University of Virginia, has, for the first time, systematically examined . . . 200 cases, in which innocent people served an average of 12 years in prison. In each case, of course, the evidence used to convict them was at least flawed and often false —yet juries, trial judges and appellate courts failed to notice.
>
> "A few types of unreliable trial evidence predictably supported wrongful convictions,"

Because of a misidentification, Jerry Miller was convicted of a crime he did not commit and spent twenty-five years in prison. In 2007 he became the 200th prisoner in the United States to be exonerated by DNA evidence.

Professor Garrett concluded in his study, "Judging Innocence," to be published in The Columbia Law Review in January.

> The leading cause of the wrongful convictions was erroneous identification by eyewitnesses, which occurred 79 percent of the time. In a quarter of the cases, such testimony was the only direct evidence against the defendant.[6]

we may perceive completely formless stimuli—clouds, smoke, "white noise," garbled voices, random-patterned wallpaper, blurry photos, lights in the night sky, stains on the ceiling—yet think we observe very distinct images or sounds. In the formlessness we may see ghosts, faces, and words and hear songs, screams, or verbal warnings. We may see or hear exactly what we expect to see or hear. Or the mere suggestion of what we should perceive helps us perceive it. This phenomenon is a kind of illusion known as *pareidolia*. It's the reason some people claim to hear Satanic messages when rock music is played backward, or to observe a giant stone face in fuzzy pictures of the surface of Mars, or to see the perfect likeness of Jesus in the skillet burns on a tortilla.

Scientists are keenly aware of the possible distorting influence of expectancy, so they try to design experiments that minimize it. We too need to minimize it as much as possible. Our strong expectations are a signal that we should double-check our sensory information and be careful about the conclusions we draw from it.

INNUMERACY

When we make an off-the-cuff judgment about the chances of something happening (whether an event in the past or one in the future), we should be extra careful. Why? Because, generally, we humans are terrible at figuring probabilities.

Here's a classic example. Imagine that your classroom has twenty-three students present including yourself. What are the chances that at least two of the students have exactly the same birthday? (Not the same *date of birth*, but the same birthday out of the 365 possible ones.) The answer is neither 1 chance in 365 (1/365), nor 1 in 52 (1/52). It's *1 chance in 2* (1/2, or fifty-fifty)—a completely counterintuitive result.

A common error is the misjudging of coincidences. Many of us often believe that an event is simply too improbable to be a mere coincidence, that something else surely must be going on—such as paranormal or supernatural activity. But we mustn't forget that amazing coincidences occur all the time and, in fact, *must* occur according to elementary laws of statistics. The probability that a particular strange event will occur—say, that an ice cube tossed out of an airplane will hit the roof of a barn—may be extremely low, maybe one in a billion. But that same event given enough opportunities to occur may be highly probable over the long haul. It may be unlikely in any given instance for you to flip a coin and get tails seven times in a row. But this "streak" is virtually certain to happen if you flip the coin enough times.

What are the odds that someone will be thinking of a person she knew, or knew of, from the past twenty-five years then suddenly learn that the person is seriously ill or dead? Believe it or not, such a strange event is likely to occur several times a day. If we make the reasonable assumption that someone would recognize

☑ Personal Experience

- It's reasonable to accept the evidence provided by personal experience only if there's no good reason to doubt it.
- If our perceptual powers are impaired or impeded, we have reason to doubt them.
- Our perception and memory are *constructive*, which means that our minds are capable of manufacturing what we experience.
- We often perceive exactly what we expect to perceive, and this tendency is enhanced when stimuli are vague or ambiguous.
- The gambler's fallacy is the mistake of thinking that previous events can affect the probabilities in the random event at hand.

the names of a few thousand people (both famous and not so famous) from the past twenty-five years and that a person would learn of the illness or death of each of those few thousand people in the twenty-five years, then the chances of our eerie coincidence happening to someone somewhere are pretty good. We could reasonably expect that each day several people would have this experience.[7]

Another error is to think that previous events can affect the probabilities in the random event at hand. This mistake is known as the **gambler's fallacy.** Let's say you toss an unbiased coin six times in a row. On the first toss, the odds are, of course, 1 in 2, or fifty-fifty, that it will land tails. It lands tails. Astoundingly, on the other five tosses the coin also lands tails. That's six tails in a row. So what are the odds that the coin will land tails on the seventh toss? Answer: fifty-fifty. Each toss has exactly the same probability of landing tails (or heads): fifty-fifty. The coin does not remember previous tosses. To think otherwise is to commit the gambler's fallacy. You see it a lot in casinos, sporting events, and—alas—everyday decision making.

The lesson here is not that we should mistrust all judgment about probabilities, but that we shouldn't rely solely on our intuitive sense in evaluating them. Relying entirely on intuition, or "gut feeling," in assessing probabilities is usually not a reason to trust the assessment, but to doubt it.

Fooling Ourselves

As we've seen, it's not reasonable to believe a claim unless we have good reason for doing so. If we care whether our beliefs about the world are reliable, we must base them on the relevant evidence. Beliefs backed by good evidence are more likely to be true, and true beliefs are more likely to help us get what we want out of life.

Gambler's Fallacy

"The first principle
is that you must not
fool yourself—and
you are the easiest
person to fool."
—RICHARD P. FEYNMAN

A scene from *Fairy Tale: A True Story*. Hoaxed twice—once by the original (and charming) English pranksters and once by Hollywood.

Cognitive Errors in assessing Evidence

The kink in this straightforward arrangement is that we too often fail to give evidence its due. We ignore evidence, deny it, manipulate it, and distort it. Somehow there is very little comfort in knowing that everyone occasionally does this dance. What truly is encouraging is that we can learn to be alert to missteps in using and assessing evidence and that we can usually minimize, though not eliminate, the problems. This section looks at three of the most common and most serious mistakes we make when we deal with evidence.

RESISTING CONTRARY EVIDENCE

① RESISTING CONTRARY EVIDENCE

An all too human tendency is to try to resist evidence that flies in the face of our cherished beliefs. We may deny evidence, or ignore it, or reinterpret it so it fits better with our prejudices. Resisting evidence may be psychologically comforting (for a while, anyway), but it thwarts any search for knowledge and stunts our understanding.

As we will see in Chapter 10, the will to resist contrary evidence is especially strong—and tempting—in forays into the paranormal. Remember the study mentioned in Chapter 2 about researchers who showed subjects both evidence for and evidence against the reality of extrasensory perception (ESP)? The subjects who already had doubts about the existence of ESP accurately recalled both kinds of evidence. But the true believers—the subjects who already believed

① Transforming Evidence

Paranormal cases

in ESP—remembered both kinds of evidence as *proving* ESP. They resisted the disconfirming evidence by mentally transforming it into confirming evidence. These results are typical of studies focusing on the paranormal.

Another typical case involves believers in the paranormal who, when confronted with evidence counting against their beliefs, simply refuse to accept it. For example, belief in fairies was given a boost many years ago when two girls presented the world with photographs they had allegedly taken of fairies playing with them in the garden. (The episode was the basis for the 1997 movie *Fairy Tale: A True Story*.) The photos looked fake, with the fairies resembling cutouts from a children's book—which is exactly what they were. But brushing that aside, many (including the renowned writer Sir Arthur Conan Doyle, creator of the fictional Sherlock Holmes) were convinced that the photos showed real fairies. Many years later when the girls were grown, they confessed that the whole thing was a hoax. But some believers—even those who heard the confession first-hand—refused to accept it![8]

But we need not look to the fringes of reality to find instances of the denial of evidence. Scientific research and commonsense experience show that the practice permeates all walks of life. A political activist may refuse to consider evidence that conflicts with his party's principles. A scientist may be so committed to her theory that she refuses to take seriously any data that undermine it. An administrator of a grand program may insist that it is a huge success despite all evidence to the contrary.

Often our resistance to contrary evidence takes a subtle form. If we encounter evidence against our views, we frequently don't reject it outright. We simply apply more critical scrutiny to it than we would to evidence in favor of our views, or we seek out additional confirming information, or we find a way to interpret the data so it doesn't conflict with our expectations.

In one study, proponents and opponents of the death penalty were presented with evidence concerning whether capital punishment deterred crime. Both those opposed to and those in favor of capital punishment were given two types of evidence—(1) some that supported the practice and (2) some that discredited it. Psychologist Thomas Gilovich describes the outcome of the study:

> The results of this experiment were striking. The participants considered the study that provided evidence consistent with their prior beliefs—regardless of what type of study that was—to be a well-conducted piece of research that provided important evidence concerning the effectiveness of capital punishment. In contrast, they uncovered numerous flaws in the research that contradicted their initial beliefs. . . . Rather than ignoring outright the evidence at variance with their expectations, the participants cognitively transformed it into evidence that was considered relatively uninformative and could be assigned little weight.[9]

[Handwritten margin notes: ② Denying Evidence; Fairy Hoax; Everyday examples; Subtle Strategies ① We give more critical scrutiny to evidence that opposes what we believe... ② We reinterpret evidence so it does not conflict with our beliefs...; Death Penalty Study]

There is no cure for our tendency to resist opposing evidence. The only available remedy is our commitment to examine critically our favorite claims—which means trying our best to be even-handed in scrutinizing the evidence we like and the evidence we don't.

LOOKING FOR CONFIRMING EVIDENCE

We often not only resist conflicting evidence, but also seek out and use only confirming evidence—a phenomenon known as *confirmation bias*. When we go out of our way to find only confirming evidence, we can end up accepting a claim that's not true, seeing relationships that aren't there, and finding confirmation that isn't genuine.

In scientific research on confirmation bias, when subjects are asked to assess a claim, they often look for confirming evidence only, even though disconfirming evidence may be just as revealing. For example, in one study, a group of subjects was asked to assess whether practicing before a tennis match was linked to winning the match; another group, whether practicing before a match was linked to losing the match. All the subjects were asked to select the kind of evidence (regarding practice and winning or losing matches) that they thought would be the most helpful in answering the relevant question. Not surprisingly, the subjects deciding whether pre-game practicing was linked to winning focused on how many times players practiced and then won the match. And subjects assessing whether practicing was associated with losing focused on how many times players practiced and then lost the match.[10]

Sometimes we look for confirming evidence even when disconfirming evidence is more telling. For example, take this claim: All swans are white. You can easily find confirming instances; white swans are plentiful and ubiquitous. But even your seeing thousands of white swans will not conclusively confirm that all swans are white because there may be swans in places where you haven't looked. But all you have to do is find one black swan to conclusively show that the claim is false. (People used to believe that the claim was absolutely true—until black swans were discovered in Australia.) In such cases, confirmation bias can lead us way off course.

The moral to this story is that when we evaluate claims, we should look for disconfirming as well as confirming evidence. Doing so requires a conscious effort to consider not only the information that supports what we want to believe but also the information that conflicts with it. We have to seek out disconfirming evidence just as we keep an eye out for confirming evidence—an approach that goes against our grain. We naturally gravitate to people and policies we agree with, to the books that support our views, to the magazines and newspapers that echo our political outlook. Acquiring a broader, smarter, more critical perspective takes effort—and courage.

Handwritten margin notes:

Antidote: be critical of one's favorite beliefs...

(II) LOOKING FOR CONFIRMING EVIDENCE

Confirmation Bias: We tend to look for confirming evidence and ignore evidence that might refute our beliefs

See Weird Things, 69-71

Need to be aware of counterexamples

Antidote: we must train ourselves to look for disconfirming evidence

Epistemic Virtues
① Courage
② Attention
③ Objectivity

PREFERRING AVAILABLE EVIDENCE

Another common mistake in evaluating evidence is the *availability error*. We commit this blunder when we rely on evidence not because it's trustworthy but because it's memorable or striking—that is, psychologically available. In such cases, we put stock in evidence that's psychologically impressive or persuasive, not necessarily logically acceptable. You fall for the availability error if you vote to convict a murder suspect because he looks menacing, not because the evidence points to his guilt; or if you decide that a Honda Civic is an unsafe vehicle because you saw one get smashed in a highway accident; or if, just because you watched a TV news report about a mugging in your city, you believe that the risk of being mugged is extremely high.

Being taken in by the availability error can lead to some serious misjudgments about the risks involved in various situations. Some people (are you one of them?) believe that air travel is more dangerous than many other modes of transportation, so they shun travel by airplane in favor of the automobile. Their conclusion is based on nothing more than a few vivid media reports of tragic plane crashes. But research shows that per mile traveled, flying is far safer than automobile travel. Your chances of dying in a plane crash in 2001 were 1 in 310,560, but the odds of your dying in a car accident were only 1 in 19,075. The fact is, there are plenty of less vivid and less memorable (that is, psychologically unavailable) things that are much more dangerous than air travel: falling down stairs, drowning, choking, and accidental poisoning.[11]

FURTHER THOUGHT

This Is Lunacy!

When there's a full moon, do people get crazy? Do they behave like *lunatics*? Folklore says that they do, and many people believe that there's a lunar effect on the way people act. But numerous studies have shown that there is absolutely no causal connection between the moon and human behavior. So why do so many people believe in lunar power? Part of the reason is the availability error. Strange behavior is more noticeable (and so more available) than normal behavior, so we tend to think that weird behavior is more frequent. And if we look only for confirming instances (and we do), we're likely to believe that the moon is indeed the cause of a lot of peculiar behavior. Of course, many people behave strangely with or without a full moon.

[handwritten margin notes:]

PREFERRING AVAILABLE EVIDENCE
Availability Error: We tend to favor evidence that is memorable and striking...

Examples
1. Air Travel
2. Shark Attacks

Social psychologist John Ruscio provides another example:

Aside from a close miss by what was reported to be a falling airplane part early in *The Truman Show,* I cannot personally recall ever having heard of such an accident, fictitious or real. Students over the years have told me that they recall stories of people having found fallen airplane parts, but not of an actual fatality resulting from such falling parts. Shark attacks, on the other hand, are easily imagined and widely reported. Moreover, in the first movie that comes to my mind, the shark in *Jaws* actually did cause several fatalities. It may come as some surprise, then, to learn that in an average year in the United States thirty times more people are killed by falling airplane parts than by shark attacks.[12]

Environmental Hazards

The availability error is very likely at work in many controversies regarding environmental hazards. Because the alleged hazard and its effects can be easily and vividly imagined and the scientific data on the issue are not so concrete or

---

FURTHER THOUGHT

Research Skills: Judging Sources

To write a good research paper, you need to employ some crucial research skills, the main ones being (1) finding sources of information, (2) evaluating their relevance and quality, and (3) using them effectively to support your arguments. Since this chapter is about assessing the reliability of claims and evidence, it should be very helpful with the second of these. Applying its lessons to this task requires you to do the following:

- **Read critically.** A research paper is not meant to be an information dump, a mere transfer of the words and thoughts of others into your preferred format. It's supposed to be an expression of your own perspective and reasoning, supported and elucidated by trustworthy information gleaned from other sources. The process therefore demands that you read critically, question sources, assess evidence, and be open to changing your mind as the facts warrant.
- **Size up authors and publishers.** Do not thoughtlessly assume that what an author says must be true or that every publisher disseminates trustworthy information. Evaluate the author's credentials, bias, assumptions, motives, and sources. Be suspicious if the author demonstrates poor critical thinking. Gauge publishers mainly by the claims they convey—do the claims conflict with expert opinion, with what you have good reason to believe, with the assertions of other (reputable) publishers, with logic and common sense?

▼

- **Sort out claims.** Ultimately the credibility of a source comes down to the credibility of its claims, including those used as premises and conclusions of arguments. So correctly judging the plausibility of statements is the essential skill in evaluating sources. Remember: It is reasonable (1) to accept claims that fit very well with your background information or that you know are supported independently by authorities or evidence, (2) to accept claims that are adequately supported by the source itself through citations to other credible sources (experts, research, reports, etc.) or through references to supporting facts, (3) to reject claims when there is good reason for believing them false, and (4) to suspend judgment on claims that you are unsure of, for it is unreasonable to accept a claim without good reasons. The only cure for uncertainty about a source's claims is further research and reflection.
- **Compare sources.** Relying exclusively on one source for information is usually a mistake. Consulting a variety of sources helps you put the information in proper perspective, uncover errors and bias, pinpoint consensus and disagreement among experts, and find out where the preponderance of evidence points. Certainly your hunt for sources should be carefully planned and limited, but examining too few of them can lead to views that are one-sided, incomplete, and wrong. ■

memorable, the imagined danger can provoke a public scare even though the fear is completely unwarranted. Brain cancer from the use of cell phones and childhood leukemia from living near power lines—both these putative hazards have provoked fear and public demands for action. But scientific studies have shown these concerns to be groundless. Many environmental hazards are real, of course. But concluding that they exist solely on the basis of scary thoughts is to commit the availability error.

If we're in the habit of basing our judgments on evidence that's merely psychologically available, we will frequently commit the error known as hasty generalization, a mistake discussed in detail in Chapter 8. We're guilty of hasty generalization when we draw a conclusion about a whole group based on an inadequate sample of the group. We fall into this trap when we assert something like this: "Honda Civics are pieces of junk. I owned one for three months, and it gave me nothing but trouble." Our experience with a car is immediate and personal, so for many of us it can be a short step from this psychologically available evidence to a very hasty conclusion. If we give in to the availability error and stick to our guns about lousy Civics in the face of good evidence to the contrary (say, automobile-reliability research done by the Consumer's Union or similar organizations), we should get an F in critical thinking.

Fallacy of Hasty Generalization (199)

Claims in the News

In the Information Age, we are drenched with, well, information. And the news media are a major source of the information that soaks us everyday. Through newspapers, magazines, television, cable, radio, and the Internet, information about what's happening in the world hits us like rain almost every waking hour. The claims, supported and unsupported, just keep coming at us. How can we cope with such an onslaught?

Once again, critical thinking must play a big role. Remember that information is just pieces of data, bundles of claims—not necessarily true, not always useful, and not the same thing as knowledge. Knowledge is true belief supported by good reasons; information doesn't have this vaulted status. And to transform information into knowledge—our most useful commodity—we need critical thinking. Through critical thinking we can make sense of a great deal of the information coming from the news media. As you will see, most of the rest is not relevant and not worth our time.

Let's begin by looking at how the news media work, how and why they generate the claims that they do. Then we'll see how to examine critically these claims embedded in news reports, broadcasts, and multimedia presentations.

INSIDE THE NEWS

The news media include hundreds of newspapers (among the biggest and the best are the *Washington Post,* the *New York Times,* and the *Los Angeles Times*), network news organizations (ABC, NBC, CBS), cable news networks (CNN, MSNBC, and Fox), local and national radio broadcasts, local television news, public television and radio, newsmagazines (notably *Time, Newsweek,* and *U.S. News & World Report*), and numerous news-containing websites. Most news can be found in newspapers, where news stories are generally longer, more comprehensive, and more in-depth than those of any other news source. Newspapers, especially the good ones, devote far more resources to newsgathering and reporting than electronic and Internet media do, usually employing many more reporters and producing many more news stories. A large daily newspaper may contain one hundred thousand words, while a nightly televisions news broadcast may contain less than four thousand. Other kinds of news sources (especially television stations and websites) are far more numerous than newspapers, even though they provide less news and are the primary news sources for millions of people.

But not all news is created equal. Some news stories or reports are good, some are bad; some reliable and informative, some not. Most probably lie somewhere in between. The quality of news reporting depends on many factors, probably most of which are not under the control of the reporters.

*[handwritten margin note:] Information vs. Knowledge
Knowledge is true belief supported by good reasons*

"Everything is being compressed into tiny tablets. You take a little pill of news every day—23 minutes—and that's supposed to be enough."
—WALTER CRONKITE

Foremost among such factors is money. After all, news outlets—whether print, electronic, or web—are businesses with profit margins to maintain, salaries to pay, and stockholders to please. A news organization makes most of its money not from selling its product (news) through subscriptions or direct sales, but from selling opportunities for other companies to advertise to the news outlet's audience. The organization wants a big audience because big audiences can bring in big advertising dollars.

Money

The pressure on the news organizations to turn an acceptable profit is immense and has been growing in the past two decades. The old ideal of journalism as primarily a public service and not a cash cow has seldom been able to withstand the corporate push for profits. The effects of this trend on the nature and quality of the news have been profound. Two veteran newsmen from the *Washington Post* explain some of the changes this way:

News organizations aim to make money

> Most newspapers have shrunk their reporting staffs, along with the space they devote to news, to increase their owners' profits. Most owners and publishers have forced their editors to focus more on the bottom line than on good journalism. Papers have tried to attract readers and advertisers with light features and stories that please advertisers—shopping is a favorite—and by de-emphasizing serious reporting on business, government, the country and the world.
>
> If most newspapers have done poorly, local television stations have been worse. Typically, local stations provide little real news, no matter how many hours they devote to "news" programs. Their reporting staffs are dramatically smaller than even the staffs of shrunken newspapers in the same cities. The television stations have attracted viewers—and the advertising that rewards their owners with extraordinary profits—with the melodrama, violence and entertainment of "action news" formulas, the frivolity of "happy talk" among their anchors and the technological gimmicks of computer graphics and "live" remote broadcasting.
>
> The national television networks have trimmed their reporting staffs and closed foreign reporting bureaus to cut their owners' costs. They have tried to attract viewers by diluting their expensive newscasts with lifestyle, celebrity and entertainment features, and by filling their low-budget high-profit, prime-time "newsmagazines" with sensational sex, crime, and court stories.
>
> All-news cable television channels and radio stations—to which the networks have ceded much of the routine coverage of serious national and foreign news—fill many of their hours as cheaply as

Leonard Downie Jr. and Robert G. Kaiser

Newpapers

Local TV News

Cartoon courtesy of Don Addis.

All news cable TV

Worries re: losing
sources lead reporters
to censor themselves

① Most reporting is
passive reporting...

possible with repetitive, bare-bones news summaries and talk shows that present biased opinions and argument as though they were news.[13]

Deliberately or unconsciously, editors and reporters may skew their reporting so as not to offend their advertisers, their audience, or their stockholders. They may also moderate their reporting to keep their sources of information open. Reporters get a great deal of their news from sources such as government officials, corporate public relations people, and advocacy-group spokespersons. A reporter who irritates these sources by writing stories that they don't like could end up being shunned by the sources. There is always the temptation, then, to craft inoffensive or watered-down stories to please the source. Not all news people give in to the temptation, but many do.

Editors and reporters are the ones who decide what's newsworthy and what isn't. And these decisions can help give us a clearer picture of the world or a more distorted one. The distortion can happen in several ways. First, it can arise when reporters do what we might call passive reporting. Most reporters aren't investigative reporters, going off into the world and digging up the hard facts. Often, the news is simply handed to them by spokespersons and public relations experts hired by governments, corporations, and others who want to get their own version of the facts into the news media. In these situations, reporters may report only what they're told at press conferences or in press releases. The result is canned news that's slanted toward the views of the people who supply it.

A photo's impact on the public psyche can be both strong and controversial. A painful example is this photo and others like it showing the flag-draped coffins of America's war dead returning home from Iraq and Afghanistan. The administration had banned the media from photographing the caskets when they arrived at military bases. Some charged that the administration wanted to keep the photos under wraps for fear they might undermine public support for the war. They think the photos are important reminders of the sacrifices that young men and women have made for their country. Do you think your opinion of the war in Iraq would change if you saw such photos everyday in the news? Would the pictures inform you—or blind you? What do you think about the photo ban?

Second, for a variety of reasons, publishers, editors, producers, and reporters may decide not to cover certain stories or specific aspects of a story. With so much going on in the world, some selectivity is necessary and inevitable. Too often, though, decisions not to cover something can lead the public to conclude that there is nothing happening when in fact something very important is transpiring. During the run-up to the war in Iraq, some massive anti-war protests occurred in the United States and Europe. But, at least at first, the mainstream American news media didn't cover them, leading some observers to accuse the news media of bias in favor of the war. Likewise, some observers complain that the American news media don't cover many international stories that news organizations in other countries cover in depth, such as famines and human rights violations in developing nations. The result, the complaint goes, is that Americans are blithely ignorant of what's really happening in the world. Also, many times the news media forgo covering a story because they deem it too complex or too unexciting for an audience hungry for titillation, scandal, and entertainment. The police chase of a local bandit on Highway 13 may get a full hour of TV coverage, but the federal deficit's effect on middle-income families may get two minutes, if any.

Third, editors, reporters, and producers can dramatically alter our perception of the news by playing certain aspects up or down. Television and radio news broadcasts can make a trivial news item seem momentous just by making it the lead-off story in the broadcast. Or they can make an important story seem inconsequential by devoting only fifteen seconds to it near the end of the broadcast. Newspapers can play the same game by putting a story on the front page with a big headline and compelling photo—or embedding it on page 22 with a tiny headline. Parts of a story can also be arranged for the same effect, with the most telling information mentioned last.

(handwritten margin notes:)
② Selectivity, e.g. lack of international news

③ Emphasis - availability error leads to distortion

FURTHER THOUGHT

💡 Man Shoots Neighbor with Machete

Man shoots neighbor with machete? Yes—so says a headline that actually appeared in a large-circulation newspaper. Probably every newspaper in America has been guilty of running such ambiguously goofy headlines. Here are a few more:

- Iraqi Head Seeks Arms
- Study Finds Sex, Pregnancy Link
- Kicking Baby Considered to Be Healthy
- Typhoon Rips Through Cemetery; Hundreds Dead
- Lack of Brains Hinders Research
- Panda Mating Fails; Veterinarian Takes Over

Pressures on journalists

Every piece of news is filtered through a reporter (as well as an editor or producer), most of whom try hard to get the story right. But they are subject to many pressures—internal and external—to push the story this way or that, to stray far from the laudable ideal of objective reporting based on professional journalistic standards. Reporters can slant the news by using loaded language (discussed in Chapter 5), manipulating the tone of the writing, leaving out (or leaving in) certain details, putting facts in conspicuous (or inconspicuous) positions, inserting arguments and personal opinions, dramatizing parts of the story, and appealing to the reader's prejudices.

Trend for reporters to deliberately make themselves part of the story

Unfortunately, there is a trend these days for reporters to *deliberately* make themselves part of the story—to editorialize as the story's being reported, to try to exhibit attitudes common in the community, to offer subtle value judgments that the audience is likely to approve of. To give an extreme example: On the nightly news, a film clip shows the arrest of picketers in front of a clinic providing abortions, and the reporter on the scene tells the TV audience, "Once again the police are jailing those who try to interfere with women's rights." Or maybe the reporter takes the opposite tack: "Once again the police are jailing protesters exercising their right to protest."

All of this suggests that we should not assume without good reason that a news report is giving us an entirely accurate representation of events. And deciding whether in fact we have good reason is a job for critical thinking.

SORTING OUT THE NEWS

Sometimes you won't be able to tell whether a news report is trustworthy, no matter how carefully you scrutinize it. Your only recourse then is reasonable skepticism. But most times you can at least get a few clues to the report's reliability by taking the following critical approach.

Consider Whether the Report Conflicts with What You Have Good Reason to Believe

A report that conflicts with other reports that you believe are reliable or with facts you already know is not trustworthy. Likewise, a report that conflicts with expert opinion should not be accepted.

Look for Reporter Slanting

Informal Fallacies

Look for slanting in news accounts just as you would look for it in any set of claims. Check for loaded or biased language; arguments or unsupported opinion; emotional appeals; appeals to authority, popularity, and tradition; and biased or subjective tone.

Consider the Source

Ask what the source is of the information presented in the story. Did the reporter uncover the facts herself—or does the information come directly from the government, corporations, or interest groups? How does the reporter know that the information is accurate? Does the information seem to be a simple statement of facts—or a pack of assertions designed to put someone in the best possible light?

Check for Missing Information

Be suspicious if essential facts are not presented in the story or if it seems so heavily edited that the context of remarks is mysterious. Sound bites, for example, are easy to take out of context because they usually have no context.

Look for False Emphasis

The size of headlines, the position of stories, the order in which facts are presented—all these things can give unmerited emphasis to a story or some of its claims. To counteract this tactic, ask if the emphasis is really deserved—or, more broadly, if the story or story part is really as significant as the reporter would have you believe.

Check Alternative News Sources

How can you tell if the news you're getting is incomplete—if there's important news you're not seeing? You can't, unless you check alternative news sources for any missing stories. Reading a variety of newspapers, newsmagazines, journals of opinion, and websites is the best way to ensure that you're getting the big picture. To avoid confirmation bias, and to ensure that you're fully informed, you should read not only those sources that agree with you but also those that don't.

Advertising and Persuasion

Advertising is like air: It is everywhere, so pervasive and so natural that we forget it's there, yet penetrating and changing us every day. Advertising messages hit us rapid-fire and nonstop from television, radio, email, websites, podcasts, movie theaters, magazines, newsletters, newspapers, book covers, junk mail, telephones, fax machines, product labels, billboards, vehicle signs, T-shirts, wall posters, flyers, and who knows what else. Ads permeate all media—print, film, video, television, radio, and cyberspace. Caught in this whirl of words and sounds and images, we can easily overlook the obvious and disconcerting facts behind them: (1) All advertising is designed to influence, persuade, or manipulate us; (2) to an impressive

Avoid confirmation bias by reading alternative news sources....

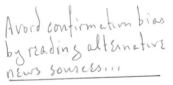

Advertising is designed to influence, persuade or manipulate us...

It is successful

We are oblivious to or deny its effectiveness

degree and in many ways, it *does* successfully influence, persuade, or manipulate us; and (3) we are often oblivious to—or in outright denial about—how effectively advertising influences, persuades, or manipulates us.

The purpose of advertising is to sell products and services, promote causes or candidates, or alter attitudes and opinions. How well advertising does these jobs can be measured in money. Advertising in most media can cost a great deal. A single full-page magazine ad can cost tens of thousands of dollars; a thirty-second TV ad can run into the millions (especially on Super Bowl Sunday). But companies are willing to pay the price because advertising works. The revenues garnered from advertising can outweigh its costs by wide margins; in the case of a magazine ad or a TV spot, the gain could easily be hundreds of thousands or millions of dollars. In addition, advertisers and advertising agencies invest heavily each year in scientific consumer research to determine how to configure ads precisely to elicit the desired response from people. Again, they make these investments because there is a sure payoff: Consumers usually respond just as the research says they will. How do your eyes track across a newspaper ad when you are looking at it? Would you respond better to a TV commercial if the voice-over came from Walter Cronkite or from Jon Bon Jovi? Would the magazine ad be more likely to sell you the cottage cheese if the headline used the word *creamy* instead of *smooth*? Would the ad copy on the junk-mail envelope increase sales if it were red instead of blue? You may not care about any of this, but advertisers do because such seemingly trivial bits of information can help them influence you in ways you barely suspect.

However averse we are (or think we are) to advertising or to its aims, we cannot deny its appeal. We like advertising, at least some of it. We easily can point to ads that annoy us or insult our intelligence, but most of us can also recall ones that are entertaining, funny, inspiring, even informative.

How, then, should good critical thinkers think about advertising? Our guiding principle should be:

> *We generally have good reason to doubt advertising claims and to be wary of advertising's persuasive powers.*

This means that usually the most reasonable response to advertising is a degree of suspicion. If we prefer truth over falsehood, if we would rather not be mistaken or bamboozled, if we want to make informed choices involving our time and money, then a general wariness toward advertising ploys is justified. This principle does not assume that all ad claims are false or that advertising cannot be genuinely informative or useful. It simply says that we should not accept uncritically an ad's message or impact on us.

There are several reasons for this cautious approach. First, recall the purpose of advertising—to *sell or promote something*, whether a product, service, person,

[margin handwritten notes:]
Most reasonable response to advertising is skepticism

① Purpose of advertising: sell or promote something

or idea. To put the point bluntly, though advertising can be both truthful and helpful, its primary function is *not* to provide objective and accurate information to consumers. Advertisers will tell you many good things about their products but are unlikely to mention all the bad. Their main job is *not* to help consumers make fully informed, rational choices about available options. Advertising is advertising—it is not intended to be an impartial search for facts or a program of consumer protection. We are therefore justified in maintaining the same attitude toward advertising that we would toward a complete stranger who wants to sell us a widget: His motives are obviously pecuniary while his commitment to honesty is unknown.

Second, advertising has a reputation for—and a history of—misleading messages. The world is filled with ads that make dubious or false claims, use fallacious arguments (stated or implied), and employ psychological tricks to manipulate consumer responses.

Some of these methods fit neatly in our rundown of fallacies in Chapters 4 and 5. Ads frequently employ fallacious appeals to authority ("As an Olympic gold medal winner, I can tell you that PowerVitamin 2000 really works!"), appeals to emotion ("Enjoy the goodness and warmth of Big-Brand Soup, just like mother used to make"), appeals to popularity ("CNN, America's number-one source for news"), hasty generalizations ("Mothers everywhere will love Softie Diapers—our test mothers sure did!"), and faulty analogies ("As a businessman, I saved General Motors. As president, I can save this country.").

But advertisers also use an array of other persuasive techniques, most of which do not involve making explicit claims or providing good reasons for acting or choosing. The following are some of the more common ones.

[handwritten margin note: ② Advertising has a reputation for and history of misleading messages... Informal fallacies]

"Advertising is the rattling of a stick inside a swill bucket."
—GEORGE ORWELL

IDENTIFICATION

Many ads persuade by simply inviting the consumer to identify with attractive people (real or imagined) or groups. Most ads featuring celebrity endorsements use this ploy. The idea is to get you to identify so strongly with a celebrity that you feel his or her product choices are *your* preferred choices. Without providing a single good reason or argument, endorsement ads say, in effect, that if Christina Aguilera prefers Pepsi, if Halle Berry likes Revlon, if Michael Jordan loves Nike, maybe you should, too.

SLOGANS

Catchy, memorable phrases are the stock-in-trade of advertising. How can we forget "Nike. Just do it" (Nike); "Reach out and touch someone" (AT&T); "Like a rock" (Chevrolet); "Don't

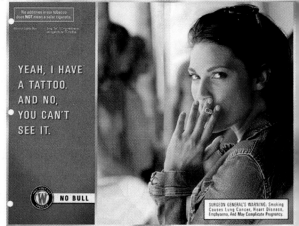

What is the purpose of this ad? Who is the intended audience? The ad mainly uses the ploy of identification: With what kind of person and attitude are you being invited to identify? Do they seem appealing to you? If so, why?

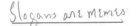
Slogans are memes

leave home without it" (American Express); "Built Ford tough!" (Ford); "Obey your thirst" (Sprite); or "An army of one" (U.S. Army)? Such catchphrases may not say much, but they do get our attention, engender appealing emotions or concepts, and associate them with products or companies—again and again and again. Through repetition that seems to embed themselves in our brains, slogans surreptitiously get us to feel that one product or brand is better than another.

MISLEADING COMPARISONS

In advertising, comparisons can mislead in many ways. Consider these examples:

1. BeSure Tampons are 30% more absorbent.
2. Big sale! The SuperX CD Player for less than the suggested retail price!
3. Simply better-tasting tacos. No question.
4. X Phone lets you call anywhere cheaper. Just 5 cents per minute compared with Y Phone, which charges 10 cents a minute.

The problem with Example 1 is its vagueness, which is of course deliberate. What does "30% more absorbent" mean? Thirty percent more absorbent than they used to be? Thirty percent more absorbent than similar products are? If the latter, what similar products are we talking about? Are BeSure Tampons being compared to the *least* absorbent tampons on the market? The *30%* may seem impressive—until we know to what it actually refers. (Another relevant question is how absorbency was determined. As you might imagine, there are many ways to perform such tests, some of them likely to yield more impressive numbers than others.)

The claim in Example 2 may or may not be touting a true bargain. We would probably view the "Big sale" in a different light if we knew whether the store's *regular* prices are below the suggested retail prices or if *all* stores sell the CD player below the suggested retail.

Example 3 contains the same sort of vagueness we find in Example 1 plus an additional sort of emptiness. The phrase "better-tasting tacos" is a claim about a subjective state of affairs—a claim that *anyone* could make about his or her own gustatory experience. You and a thousand other people might try the tacos and think they taste terrible. So the claim tells you nothing about whether you will like the tacos. The claim would be empty even if it were stretched to "The best-tasting tacos on earth!" In the ad world, such exaggerations are known as *puffery*, which is regarded in advertising law as hype that few people take seriously.

Example 4 is misleading because it tries to compare apples and oranges. The service offered by X Phone is not like that offered by Y Phone. The former gives you bare-bones service for 5 cents a minute; the latter gives you the same plus caller ID, call waiting, and free long distance on weekends. So comparing the two according to the per-minute charge alone is deceptive.

WEASEL WORDS

When advertisers want to *appear* to make a strong claim but avoid blatant lying or deception, they use what are known as *weasel words*. Weasel words water down a claim in subtle ways—just enough to ensure that it is technically true but superficially misleading. Consider:

1. You may have already won a new 2007 Ford pickup truck!
2. Some doctors recommend ginseng for sexual dysfunction.
3. Relieves up to 60 percent of headaches in chronic headache sufferers.

Example 1 is typical junk-mail hype that seems to promise a valuable prize. But the weasel word *may* weakens the claim. Technically, you *may* have actually won since your winning is at least (remotely) possible. But in the typical sweepstakes, the odds of your winning anything are millions to one. Yes, you may have already won—and you are just as likely to get hit by an asteroid tomorrow. Example 2 plays on the weasel word *some*. It is probably true that *some* (meaning at least one) doctors recommend ginseng for sexual dysfunction, but a huge majority of them do not. Using *some*, we could craft an infinite number of technically true but misleading (and ridiculous) claims about what doctors do and don't do. In Example 3 the weasel words are *up to*. Notice that many states of affairs would be consistent with this (vague) statement. It would be true even if just 1 percent of headaches were relieved in almost all headache sufferers.

Other weasels include *as many as, reportedly, possibly, virtually, many, seems,* and *perhaps*. Such words, of course, can have perfectly respectable uses as necessary qualifiers in many contexts. The problems arise when they are used not to qualify but to misguide.

Weasel words

KEY WORDS

appeal to authority

background information

expert

gambler's fallacy

Summary

- Many times we need to be able to evaluate an unsupported claim—a claim that isn't backed by an argument. There are several critical thinking principles that can help us do this. An important one is: *If a claim conflicts with other claims we have good reason to accept, we have good grounds for doubting it.* Sometimes the conflict is between a claim and your background information.

Background information is the large collection of very well-supported beliefs that we rely on to inform our actions and choices. The relevant principle then is: *If a claim conflicts with our background information, we have good reason to doubt the claim.*

- It's not reasonable to accept a claim if there is good reason to doubt it. In the case of claims that we can neither accept nor reject outright: *We should proportion our belief to the evidence.*

- An expert is someone who is more knowledgeable in a particular subject area than most others are. The important principle here is: *If a claim conflicts with expert opinion, we have good reason to doubt it.* We must couple this principle with another one: *When the experts disagree about a claim, we have good reason to doubt it.* When we rely on bogus expert opinion, we commit the fallacy known as the appeal to authority.

- Many claims are based on nothing more than personal experience, ours or someone else's. We can trust our personal experience—to a point. The guiding principle is: *It's reasonable to accept the evidence provided by personal experience only if there's no reason to doubt it.* Some common factors that can raise such doubts are impairment (stress, injury, distraction, emotional upset, and the like), expectation, and our limited abilities in judging probabilities.

- Some of the common mistakes we make in evaluating claims are resisting contrary evidence, looking for confirming evidence, and preferring available evidence. To counteract these tendencies, we need to take deliberate steps to examine critically even our most cherished claims, search for disconfirming evidence as well as confirming, and look beyond evidence that is merely the most striking or memorable.

- Many of the unsupported claims we encounter are in news reports. Reporters, editors, and producers are under many pressures that can lead to biased or misleading reporting. The biggest factor is money—the drive for profits in news organizations, especially those owned by larger corporations or conglomerates. Reporters themselves may introduce inaccuracies, biases, and personal opinions. And the people who produce the news may decide not to cover certain stories (or aspects of stories), which can sometimes provide a skewed or erroneous picture of an issue or event.

- The best defense against being misled by news reports is a reasonable skepticism and a critical approach that involves, among other things, looking for slanting, examining sources, checking for missing facts, and being on the lookout for false emphasis.

- Advertising is another possible source of unsupported or misleading claims. We should realize that we generally have good reason to doubt advertising claims and to be wary of advertising's persuasive powers.

EXERCISES

Exercise 4.1

REVIEW QUESTIONS

1. What is a person's background information?
2. What is the most reasonable attitude toward a claim that conflicts with other claims you have good reason to believe?
3. What degree of probability should we assign to a claim that conflicts with our background information?
* 4. What is the most reasonable attitude toward a claim that is neither worthy of acceptance nor deserving of outright rejection?
5. What is an expert?
6. What should be our attitude toward a claim that conflicts with expert opinion?
7. What should be our attitude toward a claim when experts disagree about it?
8. What is the fallacy of the appeal to authority?
9. According to the text, in most fields, what are the two minimal prerequisites for being considered an expert?
* 10. According to the text, beyond the minimal prerequisites, what are two more telling indicators that someone is an expert?
11. Under what three circumstances should we suspect that an expert may be biased?
12. When is it reasonable to accept the evidence provided by personal experience?
13. What are two factors that can give us good reason to doubt the reliability of personal experience?
14. What is the gambler's fallacy?
15. What are some ways that people resist contrary evidence?
16. What is confirmation bias?
* 17. How can critical thinkers counteract confirmation bias?
18. What is the availability error?
19. What is the connection between availability error and hasty generalization?
20. According to the text, other than reporters and editors themselves, what is the foremost factor influencing the quality of news reporting?
21. According to the text, what are three techniques for critically evaluating the reliability of news reports?
22. What principle should guide our judgments about advertising?

Exercise 4.2

Based on claims you already have good reason to believe, your background information, and your assessment of the credibility of any cited experts, indicate for each of the following claims whether you would accept it, reject it, or proportion your belief to the evidence. Give reasons for your answers. If you decide to proportion your belief to the evidence, indicate generally what degree of plausibility you would assign to the claim.

1. Israeli psychic Uri Geller can bend spoons with his mind.

2. In Russia, some people live to be 150 years old. *(Max 120)*

3. Every year in the United States over three hundred people die of leprosy.

* 4. According to Dr. Feelgood, the spokesperson for Acme Mattresses, the EasyRest 2000 from Acme is the best mattress in the world for back-pain sufferers.

5. Some bars in the suburbs of Chicago have been entertaining their nightly patrons with pygmy hippo tossing. *Not many*

* 6. Every person has innate psychic ability that, when properly cultivated, can enable him or her to read another person's mind.

7. The prime minister of Canada works with the government of the United States to suppress the economic power of French Canadians. *Easily detected/M...*

8. Molly, a thirty-four-year-old bank manager, says that stock prices will plummet dramatically in two months and will trigger another deep year-long recession. *No Expert*

9. A photo exists showing a shark attacking a diver climbing into a helicopter.

* 10. Fifteen women have died after smelling a free perfume sample that they received in the mail.

11. A chain letter describing the struggles of a nine-year-old girl with incurable cancer is circulating on the Internet. The more people who receive the letter, the better the little girl's chances of survival.

12. A report from the National Institutes of Health says that there is no evidence that high doses of the herb ephedra can cure cancer.

13. Giant albino alligators crawl through the underground sewers of New York City.

* 14. Crop circles—large-scale geometric patterns pressed into crop fields—are the work of space aliens.

15. Crop circles are the work of human hoaxers.

16. The prime minister's economic plan to dramatically lower taxes and greatly increase government spending will not cause fiscal deficits.

* 17. Dr. Xavier, a world-famous astrologer, says that the position of the sun, planets, and stars at your birth influences your choice of careers and your marital status.

Handwritten annotations in left margin:
① Reject
② Reject
③ Proportion PFalse
④ Proportion LP
⑤ Reject
⑥ Reject
⑦ Proportion PFalse
⑧ Proportion LF
⑨ Proportion PF
⑩ Proportion MP
⑪ Reject
⑫ Accept
⑬ Reject
⑭ Reject
⑮ Accept
⑯ Proportion LF
⑰ Reject

18. Eleanor Morgan, a Nobel Prize–winning economist, says that modern democratic systems (including developed nations) are not viable.
19. Eating meat rots your colon.
20. The highway speed limit in New York is 65 mph.

(18) Proportion LF
(19) Reject
(20) Accept

Exercise 4.3

For each of the following claims, decide whether you agree or disagree with it. If you agree with it, indicate what evidence would persuade you to reject the statement. If you disagree with it, indicate what evidence would persuade you to accept the statement. In each case, ask yourself if you would really change your mind if presented with the evidence you suggested.

1. Affirmative action should be abolished at all state colleges.
2. Gay marriages should be legally recognized in the United States.
* 3. An alien spacecraft crashed in Roswell, New Mexico, in 1947.
4. Earth is only ten thousand years old.
5. There is life on Mars.
6. Some people can twist their heads around on their necks a complete 360 degrees.
7. On Tuesday, a new computer virus will shut down every network and every PC in the world.
* 8. Meditation and controlled breathing can shrink cancerous tumors.
9. All swans are white.
10. "Corporate welfare"—tax breaks and other special considerations for businesses—should be discontinued.

Exercise 4.4

Examine the following newspaper story and answer the questions that follow.

Work Farce

June 26, 2003—Brazen Department of Education construction employees ripped off the city by clocking in but doing little or no work—instead spending their days at the gym, shopping or moonlighting, a sting operation by Schools Investigator Richard Condon's office found.

Checks of 13 workers—some chosen randomly, others on the basis of complaints—who were monitored beginning last August found eight of them doing little or no work.

The slackers will soon find themselves in handcuffs and unemployment lines, authorities said. . . . Condon charged that time cheating by phantom workers is "common practice."

"Time abuse is a financial drain on the city's public school system. No doubt it plays a role in the overtime that is paid to skilled trade workers," Condon said. . . .

Condon did not release the names of the slackers because they're about to be arrested, he said. Chancellor Joel Klein said they will be fired "immediately."[14]

1. Is the story slanted toward or against a particular group mentioned in the story? How?
2. Are there instances of loaded or biased language or emotional appeals in the story or headline? If so, give examples.
3. What is the main source for this story?

 Field Problems

1. Find a controversial newspaper story posted on the Internet and answer the questions in Exercise 4-4 about it.
2. Write down a claim in which you strongly believe. Select one that pertains to an important social, religious, or political issue. Then indicate what evidence would persuade you to change your mind about the claim.
3. Select a news item or press release from a pro-life website (such as www.covenantnews.com or www.prolifeamerica.com) and a pro-choice one (such as www.choiceusa.org or www.prochoiceamerica.org). Analyze each selection, looking for evidence of bias or slanting—loaded or biased language, unsupported opinion, emotional appeals, omission of relevant but opposing information, and undeserved emphasis on aspects of the story.
4. From a magazine select a full-page ad that uses at least two of the following ploys: (1) misleading comparison, (2) catchy slogan, (3) identification with a celebrity, or (4) weasel words.

Self-Assessment Quiz

Answers appear in "Answers to Self-Assessment Quizzes" (Appendix C).
1. How should a critical thinker regard an unsupported claim that conflicts with a great deal of her background information?
2. State in your own words Bertrand Russell's principle regarding unsupported claims.
3. Name four factors to consider in deciding whether someone should be considered an expert.
4. According to the text, what are some telltale signs that an expert may be biased?

5. Name three types of perceptual impairment that can give us good reason to doubt the reliability of our personal experience.

For each of the following situations and the claim associated with it, indicate whether there may be good reasons to doubt the claim and, if so, specify the reasons.

6. Standing on a street corner in heavy fog, Eve thinks that she sees an old friend walking away from her on the other side of the street. She says to herself, "That's Julio Sanchez."

7. While playing an old rock tune backwards, Elton thinks that he hears a sentence on the tape. It's almost inaudible, but he thinks it says, "Hello, Elton, long time no see."

8. Detective Jones views the videotape of the robbery at the Seven-Eleven, which occurred last night. He sees the robber look into the camera. "I know that guy," he says. "I put him away last year on a similar charge."

For each of the following claims, indicate whether it is: (a) probably true, (b) probably false, (c) almost certainly true, (d) almost certainly false, or (e) none of the above.

9. "Most people are not aware that the cartoonish 'Bigfoot' figure is a distorted product of ancient and modern stories describing a real, but unacknowledged species that is still occasionally observed today in North American forests." [The Bigfoot Field Researchers Organization]

10. "The actual risk of falling ill from a bioterrorist attack is extremely small." [American Council on Science and Health]

11. Nobody in the world is truly altruistic. Everyone is out for himself alone.

12. School violence is caused mainly by hypocrisy on the part of teachers and school administrators.

13. "The world shadow government behind the U.S. government is at it again, destroying U.S. buildings and killing people with staged acts of terrorism [on 9/11/01], the intent of which being—among other things—to start WW III." [Website devoted to 9/11 theories]

14. "What is Pre-Birth Communication? It's something that many people experience, yet very few talk about—the sense that somehow we are in contact with a being who is not yet born! It may be a vivid dream, the touch of an invisible presence, a telepathic message announcing pregnancy, or many other types of encounter. It is a mystery, one that challenges our ideas about ourselves and our children." [Website on "pre-birth communication"]

15. Physicians, drug companies, the food industry, the National Cancer Institute, and the American Cancer Society are all fighting to prevent "natural" cancer cures such as vitamin supplements and herbs from being used by cancer patients.

16. Medieval history is a lie—or, rather, it doesn't exist. Monks made it up based on a corrupt copy of ancient history.

Read the following news story and then answer questions 17–20.

Soldiers Sweep up Saddam's Hit Goons

July 1, 2003—WASHINGTON—U.S. troops captured 319 suspected Ba'ath Party murderers as part of a tough new crackdown on regime diehards yesterday, as Defense Secretary Donald Rumsfeld forcefully denied that the United States is getting into a "quagmire" in Iraq.

Military officials said U.S. forces carried out 27 raids and also seized more than $9 million in cash as well as hundreds of machine guns and grenade launchers over the past two days as part of Operation Sidewinder.

The military offensive is a get-tough display of American power aimed at defeating Saddam Hussein's loyalists and outside terrorists responsible for hit-and-run attacks on U.S. troops and sabotage of Iraq's power and water services. But the Iraqi goon squads continued their guerrilla-style campaign yesterday, ambushing a U.S. Avenger air-defense vehicle in the ultra-tense town of Fallujah, wounding Jeremy Little, an Australian-born sound man for NBC news.

The Pentagon says 65 soldiers have been killed and scores more wounded in a series of ambushes and attacks by Saddam loyalists since the war was declared over May 1.

But at a Pentagon briefing, Rumsfeld tried to counter growing criticism in Congress and in the media over the U.S. policy toward Iraq and angrily denied that the U.S. is getting into another Vietnam War quagmire. . . .

Rumsfeld admitted that fighting in Iraq "will go on for some time," but said "more and more Iraqis" are starting to cooperate with coalition forces in their hunt for Saddam's goon squads.[15]

17. Is the story slanted toward or against a particular group mentioned in the story? How?

18. Are there instances of loaded or biased language or emotional appeals in the story or headline? If so, give examples.

19. What is the main source for this story?

20. Is this story lacking another perspective on the events? Is there more to the story that isn't mentioned? If so, explain.

 Integrative Exercises

These exercises pertain to material in Chapters 1–4.

1. What is a deductive argument? An inductive one?

2. What is a valid argument? A strong one?

3. What is an expert?

4. What is the appeal to authority?

For each of the following arguments, specify the conclusion and premises and indicate whether it is deductive or inductive. If it's inductive, indicate whether it's strong or weak; if deductive, indicate whether it's valid or invalid. If necessary, add implicit premises and conclusions.

5. "Sentencing reforms have produced some perverse results. For example, the primary goal of sentencing guidelines was to reduce the disparity among criminals who committed the same crime. Yet, by equalizing only prison sentences, the guidelines make it impossible for judges to equalize the 'total' penalty, which can include fines and restitution. How these are imposed can vary dramatically among criminals." [Opinion, John Lott, *USA Today*]

6. "We believe that affirmative action has been good for the country because it creates diverse student populations that give everyone a shot at the top—the American promise." [Editorial, *Times Herald-Record*, Middletown, NY]

7. If the United States attacks Syria, it will lose the support of every nation in the world. Fortunately, it will not attack Syria. So it will not lose worldwide support.

8. No one is going to support the prime minister if he backs the United States again in a war. But looks like he is going to back the Americans. Thus, no one will support him.

9. For years, the grass simply would not grow, no matter how much watering or fertilizing she did. But after adding Miracle Sprout, the grass started to grow and spread throughout the property. Miracle Sprout did the trick.

10. "Of course, Banzhaf's argument—that so-called 'fast food' fare, like cigarettes, is addictive and causes illness and death—is ludicrous. Food supports life and only contributes to obesity when it is overused, that is, when we consume more calories (regardless of the source) than are expended in exercise. You will become overweight whether your excess calories come from beer, butter, beans, or burgers." [Editorial, *New York Post*]

11. "The dueling arguments about protecting the flag are familiar. One side says, 'Yes, the flag is a revered symbol, and those who insult it are vulgar fools. But in the end it is freedom that the flag represents, even the freedom to denigrate the nation. To limit free expression would dishonor the meaning of the stars and stripes in a way that flag burners never can.'" [Opinion, *Miami Herald*]

12. "'Yes, replies the other side, freedom is what the flag stands for. But the flag is special. It is sacred, consecrated with the blood of patriots recent and remote. America's detractors can say whatever they please about the nation—only not in this one indefensible way.'" [Opinion, *Miami Herald*]

13. If God be for us, no one can stand against us. If God be against us, we will know only defeat. We continue to see only defeat. God is against us.

14. Vitamin X can lower blood pressure in middle-aged adults. At least four well-controlled scientific studies of nearly three thousand people prove it.

15. Franklin is either evil or crazy. He's definitely not crazy, so he must be evil.

16. If Julio doesn't pay his bills, he will be bankrupt. He will pay his bills. Therefore, he will not be bankrupt.

For each of the following unsupported claims, specify whether it seems worthy of acceptance, rejection, or a degree of belief in between.

17. I saw a ghost last night. I awoke in the middle of the night, looked up, and saw the figure of a woman at the foot of my bed. But I was too drowsy to pay much attention then. I fell back into a deep sleep.

18. My doctor says that drinking ten glasses of water every day can prevent heart disease, diabetes, and high blood pressure.

19. Wearing an evil grin on his face when he was captured, the goon had to be the guy who committed the recent Central Park mugging.

20. The contractor for the giant high-rise says that constructing it makes good economic sense.

Critical Thinking and Writing
MODULE 4

FROM OUTLINE TO FIRST DRAFT

If you have developed a detailed outline, then you have a path to follow as you write. And while you're writing an argumentative essay, having a path is much better than searching for one. Your outline should make the writing much easier.

No outline is a finished work, however. As you write, you may discover that your arguments are not as strong as you thought, or that other arguments would be better, or that changing a point here and there would make an argument more effective. If so, you should amend your outline and then continue writing. The act of writing is often an act of discovery, and good writers are not afraid of revisions or multiple drafts.

Recall from Module 1 that good argumentative essays generally comprise these elements:

Introduction (or opening)
Statement of thesis (the claim to be supported)
Argument supporting the thesis
Assessment of objections
Conclusion

Start your draft with a solid opening that draws your readers into your essay and prepares the way for your arguments. Good openings are interesting, informative, and short. Grab the attention of your readers with a bold statement of your thesis, a provocative quote, a compelling story, or interesting facts. Prepare the way for your arguments by explaining why the question you're addressing is important, why you're concerned about it, or why it involves a pressing problem. Don't assume that your readers will see immediately that the issue you're dealing with is worth their time.

Include a clear statement of your thesis in your opening (in the first paragraph or very close by). In many cases, you will want to tell the reader how you plan to develop your argument or how the rest of the essay will unfold (without going into lengthy detail). In any case, by the time your audience reads through your opening, they should know exactly what you intend to prove and why.

Consider this opening for our imaginary essay on air pollution from Module 3:

> Respiratory experts at the National Institutes of Health say that sulfur dioxide in the air is a poison that we should avoid. Yet the current administration wants to loosen environmental rules to allow coal-burning power plants to emit more sulfur dioxide than they already do. That's a bad idea. The latest evidence shows that letting the plants emit more of this poison will most likely increase the incidence of respiratory illnesses in hundreds of communities.

This opening gets the reader's attention by sounding the alarm about a serious health hazard. It provides enough background information to help us understand the seriousness of the problem. And the thesis statement in the last sentence announces what the essay will try to prove.

The body of your essay should fully develop the arguments for your thesis statement, or conclusion. You should devote at least one paragraph to each premise, though several paragraphs may be necessary. You may opt to deal with objections to your argument as you go along, perhaps as you put forth each premise, or at the end of the essay just before the conclusion. Each paragraph should develop and explain just one idea, which is usually expressed in a topic sentence. Each sentence in each paragraph should relate to the paragraph's main idea. Any sentence that has no clear connection to the main idea should be deleted or revised. Link paragraphs together in a logical sequence using transitional words and phrases or direct references to material in preceding paragraphs.

Here are two paragraphs that might follow the air pollution opening:

Scientists used to wonder whether there is a connection between airborne sulfur dioxide and respiratory illness—but no more. Research has repeatedly shown a strong link between high levels of sulfur dioxide in the air and diseases that affect the lungs. For example, data from studies conducted by the Environmental Protection Agency (EPA) show that when levels of airborne sulfur dioxide in urban areas reach what the EPA calls the "high normal" range, the incidence of respiratory illnesses increases dramatically. According to several EPA surveys of air quality, many major cities (not just Los Angeles) often have high normal levels of sulfur dioxide in the air. In addition, data from health departments in large cities show that when levels of airborne sulfur dioxide are at their highest, hospital admissions for asthma and other respiratory ills also increase.

These findings, however, tell only half the story. Many parts of the country have more than just occasional surges in levels of airborne sulfur dioxide. They must endure unsafe levels *continuously*. New studies from the National Institutes of Health demonstrate that in at least ten major cities, the amount of sulfur dioxide in the air is excessive all the time.

In this passage, a single paragraph is devoted to each premise. Each paragraph develops a single idea, which is stated in a topic sentence. (The topic sentence for the first paragraph: "Research has repeatedly shown a strong link between high levels of sulfur dioxide in the air and diseases that affect the lungs." The second paragraph: "[Many parts of the country] must endure unsafe levels continuously.") Each sentence in each paragraph relates to the topic sentence, and the relationships among the sentences are clear. Likewise the connection between the discussion in the first paragraph and that of the second is apparent. The transitional sentence in the second paragraph ("These findings, however, tell only half the story.") helps bridge the gap between the paragraphs. Both of them help support the thesis statement.

How you end your essay is often as important as how you start it. In short or simple essays, there may be no need for a conclusion. The thesis may be clear and emphatic without a conclusion. In many cases, however, an essay is strengthened by a conclusion, and sometimes a conclusion is absolutely essential. Often without an effective conclusion, an essay may seem to end pointlessly or to be incomplete. The typical conclusion reiterates or reaffirms the thesis statement without being repetitious. Or the conclusion of the essay's argument serves as the conclusion for the whole essay. In long or complex essays, the conclusion often includes a summary of the main points discussed.

Sometimes a conclusion is a call to action, an invitation to the reader to do something about a problem. Sometimes it relates a story that underscores the importance of the essay's argument. Sometimes it highlights a provocative aspect of a claim defended earlier. In all cases it serves to increase the impact of the essay.

The conclusion, however, is not the place to launch into a completely different issue, make entirely unsubstantiated claims, malign those who disagree with you, or pretend that your argument is stronger than it really is. These tacks will not strengthen your essay but weaken it.

DEFINING TERMS

Your essay will do its job only if it is understood, and it will be understood only if the meaning of its terms is clear. As noted in Module 3, sometimes a dispute can hang on the meaning of a single term. Clarify the meaning, and the disagreement dissolves. In an argumentative essay, clarifying terms often comes down to offering precise definitions of words that are crucial to your argument.

There are several different kinds of definitions. A *lexical definition* reports the meaning that a term has among those who use the language. For example, among English-speaking people, the word "rain" is used to refer to (or mean) condensed atmospheric moisture falling in drops, which is the lexical definition. A *stipulative definition* reports a meaning that a term is deliberately assigned, often for the sake of convenience or economy of expression. If you assign a meaning to a familiar term or to a term that you invent, you give a stipulative definition. A *precising definition* reports a meaning designed to decrease ambiguity or vagueness. It qualifies an existing term by giving it a more precise definition. Someone, for example, might offer a precising definition for the word "old" (as it applies to the age of humans) by specifying that "old" refers to anyone over eighty. A *persuasive definition* reports a meaning designed to influence attitudes or beliefs. It is usually not meant to be purely informative but is calculated to appeal to someone's emotions. Someone who opposes abortions for any reason, for example, might persuasively define "abortion" as "the murder of innocent human beings and the rejection of God." Someone who believes that some abortions are morally permissible might define "abortion" as "the termination of a human embryo or fetus."

In general, any definition you offer should decrease vagueness or ambiguity and thereby increase the effectiveness of your writing. Your definitions should also be consistent. If you provide a definition for a term in your essay, then you should stick to that definition throughout. Altering the meaning of a term in mid-essay, or using more than one term to refer to the same thing, can be confusing to the reader—and might even subvert your essay's argument.

Good writers are also very much aware of another kind of meaning—the meaning that comes from a word's *connotations*. Connotations are the feelings, attitudes, or images associated with a word, beyond the literal meaning of the term. Consider these words: "soldier," "warrior," and "grunt." These terms have nearly the same literal meaning, but they differ in the emotions or attitudes they convey. Or what about these terms: "tavern," "saloon," "bar," "watering hole," and "dive." They refer to the same kind of establishment, but the images or emotions conveyed are diverse, ranging from the respectable and pleasant (tavern) to the lowly and odious (dive).

Good writers make use of both the literal meaning of words and their connotations. Connotations, however, can sometimes mislead by obscuring or minimizing the facts. In debates about gun ownership, for example, those who want to restrict gun ownership may characterize their position as "anti-assault weapon." Those opposed to this position may label it as "anti-self-defense." Both these labels are meant to provoke certain attitudes toward the subject matter—attitudes that may not be supported by any evidence or argument. Words used to convey positive or neutral attitudes or emotions in place of more negative ones are known as *euphemisms*. Words used to convey negative attitudes or emotions in place of neutral or positive ones are called *dysphemisms*. Consider the disparate impact on the reader of these pairs of terms, both of which refer to the same thing:

collateral damage	civilian casualties
downsized	fired
revenue enhancements	tax increases
full figured	fat
neutralize	kill
guerrillas	freedom fighters
routed the enemy	made a strategic withdrawal
resolute	pigheaded
emphatic	pushy
sweat	perspire

Keep in mind that euphemisms often perform a useful social purpose by allowing us to discuss sensitive subjects in an unoffensive way. We may spare people's feelings by saying that their loved ones "have passed on" rather than that they "have died," or that their dog "was put to sleep" rather than "killed." Nevertheless, as critical thinkers, we should be on guard against the deceptive use of connotations. As critical writers, we should rely primarily on argument and evidence to make our case.

Writing Assignments

1. Write an alternative opening for Essay 2 ("Marine Parks") in Appendix A. If you want, you may invent quotes or stories.

2. Write an outline for Essay 4 ("The Kalam Cosmological Argument") in Appendix A. Include a thesis statement, each premise, and points supporting each premise.

3. Study Essay 8 ("The Cohabitation Epidemic") in Appendix A. Identify the rhetorical use of any euphemisms or dysphemisms.

4. Select one of the following topics and extract an issue from it that you can write about. Investigate arguments on both sides of the issue, and write a three-page paper defending your chosen thesis.

the morning-after pill	North Korea and nuclear weapons
drug testing	endangered species
vegetarianism	animal rights
the federal deficit	Oscar nominations
same-sex marriages	desecration of the American flag
censorship	date rape
media bias	school prayer
commercial whaling	oil drilling in national wildlife preserves

5. Write a two-page rebuttal to Essay 7 ("Tight Limits on Stem Cells Betray Research Potential") in Appendix A. Use the testimony of experts to help defend your view.

Faulty Reasoning

CHAPTER OBJECTIVES

IRRELEVANT PREMISES

- Learn how to recognize fallacies of irrelevant premises (genetic fallacy, composition, division, appeal to the person, equivocation, appeal to popularity, appeal to tradition, appeal to ignorance, appeal to emotion, red herring, and straw man).
- Understand the concept of burden of proof and when it applies.

UNACCEPTABLE PREMISES

- Learn to recognize fallacies of unacceptable premises (begging the question, false dilemma, slippery slope, hasty generalization, and faulty analogy).

[handwritten margin note: There are many ways an argument can be defective]

A N ARGUMENT IS MEANT TO PROVE A POINT—TO PROVIDE GOOD reasons for accepting a claim. As you know, sometimes an argument succeeds, and sometimes it doesn't. When it doesn't, the problem will be that the premises are false, the reasoning is faulty, or both. In any case, the argument is defective, bad, or bogus—call it what you will. There are countless ways that an argument can be defective. But there are certain types of defective arguments that recur so frequently that they have names (given to them, in many cases, by ancient philosophers or medieval scholars) and are usually gathered into critical thinking texts so students can become aware of them. Such common, flawed arguments are known as **fallacies**, and they are therefore said to be fallacious.

Fallacies are often beguiling; they can *seem* plausible. Time and again they are *psychologically* persuasive, though *logically* impotent. The primary motivation for

[handwritten margin note: Fallacies are psychologically persuasive but logically impotent]

studying fallacies, then, is to be able to detect them so you're not taken in by them.

We can divide fallacies into two broad categories: (1) those that have *irrelevant* premises and (2) those that have *unacceptable* premises.[1] Irrelevant premises have no bearing on the truth of the conclusion. An argument may seem to offer reasons for accepting the conclusion, but the "reasons" have nothing to do with the conclusion. Unacceptable premises are relevant to the conclusion but are nonetheless dubious in some way. An argument may have premises that pertain to the conclusion, but they do not adequately support it. Premises can be unacceptable because they are as dubious as the claim they're intended to support, because the evidence they offer is too weak to adequately support the conclusion, or because they're otherwise so defective that they provide no support at all.

OUT OUT !! YOU DEMONS OF STUPIDITY !!

© 1994 United Feature Syndicate, Inc.

DILBERT: © Scott Adams/Dist. By United Feature Syndicate, Inc.

So in good arguments, premises must be both relevant and acceptable. In fallacious arguments, at least one of these requirements is not met.

In good arguments premises must be:
① relevant
② acceptable

In this chapter we examine numerous fallacies of both types. We won't be able to study all known fallacies—there are just too many. But we will scrutinize the most common ones. By the time you've finished this chapter, you should be able to spot these fallacies a mile away.

Irrelevant Premises

GENETIC FALLACY

The **genetic fallacy** is arguing that a claim is true or false solely because of its origin. For example:

> *You can safely dismiss that alternative energy plan. It's the brainchild of a liberal think tank in Washington.*
>
> *We should reject that proposal for solving the current Social Security mess. It comes straight from the Republican party.*
>
> *Russell's idea about tax hikes for the middle class came to him in a dream, so it must be bunk.*

① Genetic Fallacy

These arguments fail because they reject a claim based solely on where it comes from, not on its merits. In most cases, the source of an idea is irrelevant to its truth. Good ideas can come from questionable sources. Bad ideas can come from impeccable sources. Generally, judging a claim only by its source is a recipe for error.

"One must accept the truth from whatever source it comes."
—MAIMONIDES

Should note cases when the origin is relevant

② Composition

COMPOSITION

The fallacy of **composition** is arguing that what is true of the parts must be true of the whole. The error here is thinking that the characteristics of the parts are somehow transferred to the whole, something that is not always the case. Likewise, the error is committed whenever we assume that what's true of a member of a group is true of the group as a whole. For example,

> *The atoms that make up the human body are invisible. Therefore, the human body is invisible.*
> *Each member of the club is productive and effective. So the club will be productive and effective.*
> *Each note in the song sounds great. Therefore, the whole song will sound great.*
> *Every part of this motorcycle is lightweight; therefore, the whole motorcycle is lightweight.*

Sometimes, of course, the parts do share the same characteristics as the whole. We may safely conclude that since all the parts of the house are made of wood, the house itself is made of wood. We commit the fallacy of composition, though, when we assume that a particular case must be like this.

The fallacy of composition often shows up in statistical arguments. Consider:

Statistical Arguments

> *The average small investor puts $2000 into the stock market every year.*
> *The average large investor puts $100,000 into stocks each year. Therefore, the group of large investors as a whole invests more money in the stock market than the small-investor group does.*

FURTHER THOUGHT

💡 The High Cost of a Fallacy

Did you know that fallacies can sell cars? Take a look at this conversation:

BRUNO: I really like this car. Looks like a babe magnet. Is it very expensive?

SALESPERSON: Oh, the price is very reasonable. You can easily afford it. The payments are only $190 a month.

BRUNO: Wow, I'll take it.

SALESPERSON: (Thinking to himself.) Sucker. He just bought a $30,000 car.

The fallacy of composition strikes again.

Just because the average small investor invests less than the average large investor does not mean that small investors as a group invest less than large investors as a group. After all, there may be many more small investors than large investors.

DIVISION

The flip side of the fallacy of composition is the fallacy of **division**—arguing that what is true of the whole must be true of the parts. The fallacy is also committed when we assume that what is true of a group is true of individuals in the group.

> *This machine is heavy. Therefore, all the parts of this machine are heavy.*
> *Since the committee is a powerful force in Washington politics, each member of the committee is a powerful force in Washington politics.*
> *University students study every conceivable subject. So that university student over there also studies every conceivable subject.*

These arguments are fallacious because they assume that characteristics of the whole must transfer to the parts or that traits of the group must be the same as traits of individuals in the group.

Like the fallacy of composition, the fallacy of division is frequently used in statistical arguments:

> *The average SAT test score of seniors [as a group] is higher than the average SAT score of sophomores. Therefore, this senior's test score must be higher than the score of that sophomore.*

Just because the average score for seniors is higher than the average score for sophomores doesn't mean that any individual senior must have a higher score

---

FURTHER THOUGHT

💡 Bamboozling the Taxpayers

Suppose you hear these words in a speech by a national politician: "My tax cut plan will be a windfall for the American taxpayer. Under my plan, the average tax savings will be $1100 per person. Think of what each of you could do with that much extra income."

Sounds like great news—except that this is an example of the fallacy of division. Just because the tax savings for American taxpayers as a group is an average of $1100 doesn't mean that each individual taxpayer will get $1100. It's possible that only a few taxpayers will get $1100 or more while most won't get any tax break at all.

than any sophomore. The scores of individuals, which make up the average, may vary greatly.

APPEAL TO THE PERSON

The fallacy of **appeal to the person** (or *ad hominem*, meaning "to the man") is rejecting a claim by criticizing the person who makes it rather than the claim itself. For example:

> *Jones has argued for a ban on government-sanctioned prayer in schools and at school-sponsored events. But he's a rabid atheist without morals of any kind. Anything he has to say on the issue is bound to be a perversion of the truth.*
> *We should reject Chen's argument for life on other planets. He dabbles in the paranormal.*
> *You can't believe anything Morris says about welfare reform. He's a bleeding-heart liberal.*

Such arguments are fallacious because they attempt to discredit a claim by appealing to something that's almost always irrelevant to it: a person's character, motives, or personal circumstances. Claims must be judged on their own merits; they are not guilty by association. We are never justified in rejecting a claim because of a person's faults unless we can show how a person's faults translate into faults in the claim—and this is almost never the case. Even when a person's character is relevant to the truth of claims (as when we must consider the merits of testimonial evidence), we are not justified in believing a claim false just because the person's character is dubious. If the person's character is dubious, we are left with no reason to think the claim either true *or* false.

The fallacy of appeal to the person comes in several varieties. One is the personal attack (mentioned earlier), often simply consisting of insults. The gist is familiar enough: Reject X's claims, ideas, or theories because X is a radical, reactionary, extremist, right-winger, left-winger, fool, bonehead, moron, nutbar, or scum of the earth. Whatever psychological impact such terms of abuse may have, logically they carry no weight at all.

Another form of this fallacy emphasizes not a person's character but his or her circumstances. Here someone making a claim is accused of inconsistency—specifically, of maintaining a view that is inconsistent with his or her previous views or social or political commitments.

> *Edgar asserts that evolution is true, but he's an ordained minister in a funda-mentalist church that has taken a firm stand against evolution. So he can't accept this theory; he must reject it.*
> *Madison says she's opposed to abortion, but you can't take her seriously. Her view goes against everything her party stands for.*

Margin notes (handwritten):

④ Appeal to the Person (aka Ad Hominem)

"The broad mass of a nation . . . will more easily fall victim to a big lie than to a small one."
—ADOLF HITLER

ⓐ Personal Attack

ⓑ Character — Circumstances (Inconsistency)

These arguments are fallacious if they're implying that a claim must be true (or false) just because it's inconsistent with some aspect of the claimant's circumstances. The circumstances are irrelevant to the truth of the claim.

When such arguments are put forth as charges of hypocrisy, we get another *ad hominem* fallacy known as **tu quoque** (or "you're another"). The fallacious reasoning goes like this: Ellen claims that X, but Ellen doesn't practice/live by/condone X herself—so X is false. Look:

© Tu Quoque

> A lot of Hollywood liberals tell us that we shouldn't drive SUVs because the cars use too much gas and are bad for the environment. But they drive SUVs themselves. What hypocrites! I think we can safely reject their stupid pronouncements.

But whether someone is hypocritical regarding their claims can have no bearing on the truth of those claims. We may, of course, condemn someone for hypocrisy, but we logically cannot use that hypocrisy as a justification for rejecting their views. Their views must stand or fall on their own merits.

In another variation of circumstantial *ad hominem* reasoning, someone might deduce that a claim is false because the person making it, given his or her circumstances, would be expected to make it. For example:

> Wilson claims that the political system in Cuba is exemplary. But he has to say that. He's a card-carrying communist. So forget what he says.

But whether Wilson is a communist, and whether he would be expected or required to have certain views because of his connection to communism, is irrelevant to the truth of his claim.

Finally, we have the *ad hominem* tactic known as "poisoning the well." In this one, someone argues like this: X has no regard for the truth or has nonrational motives for espousing a claim, so nothing that X says should be believed—including the claim in question. The idea is that just as you can't get safe water out of a poisoned well, you can't get reliable claims out of a discredited claimant. This tack is fallacious because the fact that someone might have dubious reasons for making a claim does not show that the claim is false, nor does it mean that everything that comes out of the "poisoned well" can be automatically dismissed.

④ Poisoning the Well

EQUIVOCATION

⑤ Equivocation

The fallacy of **equivocation** is the use of a word in two different senses in an argument. For example:

> The end of everything is its perfection.
> The end of life is death.
> Therefore, death is the perfection of life.

© Cybercast News Service 2003 Paul Nowak from CNSNews.com

Only man is rational.
No woman is a man.
Therefore, no woman is rational.

Laws can only be created by law-givers.
There are many laws of nature.
Therefore, there must be a Law-Giver,
*   namely, God.*

In the first argument, *end* is used in two different senses. In the first premise it means purpose, but in the second it means termination. Because of this flip-flop in meanings, the conclusion doesn't follow from the premises—but it looks as if it should.

In the second argument, *man* is the equivocal term. In the first premise it means humankind, but in the second, male. So the conclusion doesn't follow, making it appear that a sound argument has banished women's rationality.

In the third argument, *laws* is used in two senses—rules of human behavior in the first premise, regularities of nature (as in "law of gravity") in the second. Consequently, the conclusion trying to establish the existence of God doesn't follow.

The fallacy of equivocation occurs whenever a word has one meaning in one premise and another meaning in another premise or the conclusion. This switch of senses always invalidates the argument.

Equivocation often plays a central part in arguments over abortion because so much depends on the meaning of terms referring to the unborn. Consider:

Everyone agrees that a fetus is a human.
All human beings have a right to life.
Therefore, a fetus has a right to life.

In the first premise, *human* is used in the sense of something having human physical characteristics such as human DNA. In the second premise, the word is used with *beings* in the sense of a person with moral rights. Because of this shift in meaning, the argument fails.

APPEAL TO POPULARITY

The fallacy of the **appeal to popularity** (or to the masses) is arguing that a claim must be true merely because a substantial number of people believe it. The basic pattern of this fallacy is "Everyone (or almost everyone, most people, many people) believes X, so X must be true." For example:

"The exact contrary of what is generally believed is often the truth."
—JEAN DE LA BRUYERE

Most people approve of the government's new security measures, even though innocent people's privacy is sometimes violated. So I guess the measures must be okay.

Of course the war is justified. Everyone believes that it's justified.

The vast majority of Americans believe that there's a supreme being, so how could you doubt it?

These arguments are fallacious because they assume that a proposition is true merely because a great number of people believe it. But as far as the truth of a claim is concerned, what many people believe is irrelevant. Many people used to believe that certain women were witches and should be burned, that slavery was perfectly acceptable, that Earth was the center of the universe, and that bleeding and purging were cures for just about every ill. Large groups of people are no more infallible than an individual is. Their belief in a proposition, by itself, is no indication of truth.

What many other people believe, however, can be an indication of truth if they are experts or have expert knowledge in the issue at hand. If almost all farmers say that the fall harvest will be abundant, ordinarily we should believe them.

Exception: Experts

APPEAL TO TRADITION

⑦ Appeal to Tradition

The **appeal to tradition** is arguing that a claim must be true just because it's part of a tradition. For example:

Acupuncture has been used for a thousand years in China. It must work.

Of course publishing pornography is wrong. In this community there's a tradition of condemning it that goes back fifty years.

Such appeals are fallacious because tradition, like the masses, can be wrong. Remember that an established tradition barred women from voting, stripped African Americans of their civil rights, promoted the vengeful policy of "an eye for an eye," and sanctioned the sacrifice of innocents to the gods.

Be careful, though. Automatically rejecting a claim because it's traditional is not reasonable either. The point is that a tradition should be neither accepted nor rejected without good reason. Knee-jerk acceptance of tradition is as bad as knee-jerk rejection.

Caution: neither should a claim be rejected simply because it is traditional.

APPEAL TO IGNORANCE

⑧ Appeal to Ignorance

The **appeal to ignorance** is arguing that a lack of evidence proves something. In one type of this fallacy, the problem arises by thinking that a claim must be true because it hasn't been shown to be false. For example:

No one has shown that ghosts aren't real, so they must be real.

It's clear that God exists because science hasn't proved that he doesn't exist.

You can't disprove my theory that JFK was killed by LBJ. Therefore, my theory is correct.

The problem here is that a lack of evidence is supposed to prove something—but it can't. A lack of evidence alone can neither prove nor disprove a proposition. A lack of evidence simply reveals our ignorance about something.

In another variation of this fallacy, the breakdown in logic comes when you argue that a claim must be false because it hasn't been proved to be true. Look at these:

> No one has shown that ghosts are real, so they must not exist.
>
> It's clear that God doesn't exist because science hasn't proved that he does.
>
> You can't prove your theory that JFK was killed by LBJ. Therefore, your theory is false.

Again, the moral is: Lack of evidence proves nothing. It does not give us a reason for believing a claim.

"Euphemisms are unpleasant truths wearing diplomatic cologne."
—QUENTIN CRISP

Lack of evidence proves nothing...

" NEWSMAKERS "

Possibly, Maybe, You Never Know

Related to the appeal to ignorance is the argument that because a problem has never been shown not to exist (that is, because the problem is merely possible), we should take steps now to deal with it. Consider this news report:

The head of a prominent cancer research institute has warned his faculty and staff to limit cellphone use because of a possible cancer risk, The Associated Press reports.

Dr. Ronald B. Herberman, the director of the University of Pittsburgh Cancer Institute, notes that while the evidence about a cellphone–cancer link remains unclear, people should take precautions, particularly for children.

"Really at the heart of my concern is that we shouldn't wait for a definitive study to come out, but err on the side of being safe rather than sorry later," Dr. Herberman told The Associated Press.[2]

Research on cell phone use and cancer has been equivocal, with some studies suggesting an association (not a cause-and-effect rela-

Appeals to ignorance involve the notion of **burden of proof.** Burden of proof is the weight of evidence or argument required by one side in a debate or disagreement (in the critical thinking sense). Problems arise when the burden of proof is placed on the wrong side. For example, if Louise declares that "no one has shown that gremlins aren't real, so they must be real," she implicitly puts the burden of proof on those who don't agree with her. She's asserting, in effect, "I say that gremlins are real, and it's up to you to prove I'm wrong." Or to put it another way, "I'm entitled to believe that gremlins are real unless you prove that they're not." But as we saw earlier, this line is just an appeal to ignorance, and the burden of proof for showing that gremlins are real rests with *her*—not with those who don't share her belief. If her claim is unsupported, you need not accept it. If you take the bait and try to prove that gremlins don't exist, you are accepting a burden of proof that should fall on Louise's shoulders, not yours.

Usually, the burden of proof rests on the side that makes a positive claim—an assertion that something exists or is the case, rather than that something does not exist or is not the case. So in general, if a person (the claimant) makes an unsupported positive claim, he or she must provide evidence for it if the claim is to be accepted. If you doubt the claim, you are under no obligation to prove it wrong. You need not—and should not—accept it without good reasons (which the claimant should provide). Of course, you also should not reject the claim without good reasons. If the claimant does provide you with reasons for accepting the claim, you can either accept them or reject them. If you reject them, you are obligated to explain the reasons for your rejection.

APPEAL TO EMOTION

The fallacy of the **appeal to emotion** is the use of emotions as premises in an argument. That is, it consists of trying to persuade someone of a conclusion solely by arousing his or her feelings rather than presenting relevant reasons. When you use this fallacy, you appeal to people's guilt, anger, pity, fear, compassion, resentment, pride—but not to good reasons that could give logical support to your case. Take a look:

> *You should hire me for this network analyst position. I'm the best person for the job. If I don't get a job soon my wife will leave me, and I won't have enough money to pay for my mother's heart operation. Come on, give me a break.*
> *Political ad: If school music programs are cut as part of the new district budget, we will save money—and lose our children to a world without music, a landscape without song. Let the children sing. Vote no on proposition 13.*

As arguments, these passages are fallacious not just because they appeal to strong emotions, but because they appeal to almost *nothing but* strong emotions. They urge us to accept a conclusion but offer no good reasons for doing so. We

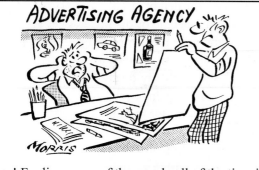

"Phew! Fooling some of the people all of the time is damn hard work."

www.CartoonStock.com

The problem occurs when emotion obscures logic...

may feel compassion for the job hunter and his mother, but those feelings have no bearing on whether he is truly the best person for the job. We may recoil from the idea of children in a stark, tuneless world, but that overblown image and the emotions it evokes in us provide no logical support for the conclusion.

This kind of wielding of emotion in discourse is an example of *rhetoric*, the use of nonargumentative, emotive words and phrases to persuade or influence an audience. Arguments try to persuade through logic and reasons. Rhetoric tries to persuade primarily through the artful use of language. There's nothing inherently wrong with using rhetoric. Its use becomes fallacious, though, when there's an attempt to support a conclusion by rhetoric alone.

But in such cases the fallacy is easily avoided. Good writers often combine arguments with appeals to emotion in the same piece of writing, and no fallacy need enter the picture. A strong argument is presented, and it's reinforced by strong feelings. Consider this piece of persuasive prose:

> I am a mother though my child is dead. He did not die of an incurable disease, of a virus beyond the ken of medical science. He was not taken from me by a foreign enemy while defending his country. No, he was needlessly slaughtered on the highway. A drunk driver ran broadside into his motorcycle. My son was shot fifty feet through the air by the collision and hit the blacktop at forty-five miles per hour.
>
> My son's assassin is not yet out of high school and yet that boy was able to walk into a liquor store and purchase two sixpacks of beer, most of which he drank that evening. This boy does not have the mental capability to graduate from high school in the prescribed time (he was held back in his senior year), and yet the law has given him the right to purchase alcohol and decide for himself what is appropriate behavior with regard to alcoholic consumption. I do not trust most of my adult friends to make such mature judgments. How can anyone trust the eighteen-year-old?
>
> The law must change. Statistics have shown that states which have a minimum drinking age of twenty-one years also have significantly fewer automobile accidents caused by drunken teenagers. I lost my son, but why do any of the rest of us have to suffer as I have? Please, support legislation to increase the drinking age to twenty-one.[4]

There are appeals here to the reader's sympathy and indignation—but also an argument using statistics to support a conclusion about the need for new legislation.

"Discourse on virtue and they pass by in droves; whistle and dance the shimmy, and you've got an audience."

—DIOGENES

RED HERRING

Perhaps the most blatant fallacy of irrelevance is the **red herring**, the deliberate raising of an irrelevant issue during an argument. This fallacy gets its name from the practice of dragging a smelly fish across a trail to throw a hunting dog

---

FURTHER THOUGHT

Emotive Persuasion: Rhetoric at Work

Rhetoric presents us with a large repertoire of techniques for influencing hearts and minds through emotion—while proving nothing through reason. Very often rhetorical devices do nothing more than promote a negative (or positive) attitude toward someone or something, but this ploy can be extraordinarily persuasive. Here are a few popular examples, some of which are also discussed elsewhere in this text.

- **Ridicule**—the use of derision, sarcasm, laughter, or mockery to disparage a person or idea. Ridicule succeeds when it compels you to dismiss people or their claims for no good reason. *Example*: "Trust the *New York Times* to report the news fairly? Right, just like I trust the airlines to be always on time." *Example*: "You think Fox News is fair and balanced? Ha!"

- **Innuendo**—suggesting something denigrating about a person without explicitly stating it. Through innuendo you can indirectly convey the false claim that someone is bad, though you make only true statements. *Example*: "I'm fairly sure that Senator Johnson's youthful indiscretions involving alcohol, marijuana, and crack cocaine probably have no influence on her current public service." *Example*: "I think we can assume that Mr. Abernathy absolutely does not embezzle—anymore." Innuendo was employed in a notorious smear of John McCain in the South Carolina Republican primary in 2000. In a sham telephone survey, voters were asked, "Would you be more or less likely to vote for John McCain if you knew he had fathered an illegitimate black child?"

- **Euphemism and dysphemism**—euphemisms are words used to convey positive or neutral attitudes or emotions in place of more negative ones; dysphemisms are words used to convey negative attitudes or emotions in place of neutral or positive ones. These rhetorical devices work by using the persuasive force of a word's connotations, the feelings and attitudes linked to the word's literal meaning. The devices can mislead, obscure, and confuse. To hide the truth, political, economic, or military leaders might use the euphemism *meaningful downturn in aggregate output* for *recession; revenue enhancement* for *tax increase; downsizing* for *firing;*

▼

armed reconnaissance for *bombing; neutralize* for *kill; alternative interrogation methods* for *torture; collateral damage* for *civilian casualties;* and *soft targets* for *people to kill.*

- **Stereotype**—an unwarranted conclusion—a generalization—about an entire group of people. To stereotype someone is to judge her not as an individual, but as part of a group whose members are thought to be all alike. We think because she is a member of the group, and we assume without good reason that all the members are rude and arrogant, that she must also be rude and arrogant. Stereotypes abound about men and women and probably every known ethnic group. By asserting that someone is part of a stereotyped group, a speaker or writer can induce others to form a baseless, negative opinion of that person. *Example*: "Barack Obama's energy plan can't be worth much. He's an elitist law school professor." ∎

off the scent. The basic pattern is to put forth a claim and then couple it with additional claims that may seem to support it but in fact are mere distractions. For instance:

> *Every woman should have the right to an abortion on demand. There's no question about it. These anti-abortion activists block the entrances to abortion clinics, threaten abortion doctors, and intimidate anyone who wants to terminate a pregnancy.*
>
> *The legislators should vote for the three-strikes-and-you're-out crime control measure. I'm telling you, crime is a terrible thing when it happens to you. It causes death, pain, and fear. And I wouldn't want to wish these things on anyone.*

Notice what's happening here. In the first example, the issue is whether women should have the right to abortion on demand. But the arguer shifts the subject to the behavior of anti-abortion activists, as though their behavior has some bearing on the original issue. Their behavior, of course, has nothing to do with the main issue. The argument is bogus. In the second example, the issue is whether the legislators should vote for a three-strikes crime bill. But the subject gets changed to the terrible costs of crime, which is only remotely related to the main issue. (There's also an appeal to fear.) We can all agree that crime can have awful consequences, but this fact has little to do with the merits and demerits of enacting a three-strikes law.

STRAW MAN

Related to red herring is the fallacy of the **straw man**—the distorting, weakening, or oversimplifying of someone's position so it can be more easily attacked or refuted. A straw-man argument works like this: Reinterpret claim X so that it becomes the weak or absurd claim Y. Attack claim Y. Conclude that X is unfounded. For example:

> David says that he's opposed to the new sodomy laws that make it illegal for consenting adult homosexuals to engage in sex acts in their own homes. Obviously he thinks that gay sex is something special and should be protected so it's allowed to take place just about anywhere. Do you want gays having sex all over town in full view of your children? David does, and he's dead wrong.

" NEWSMAKERS "

The Straw Man Makes Headlines

As noted in Chapter 1, politicians of all parties love to wield the straw-man fallacy. Since the news media rarely make a fuss over someone's employing the trick, a news report that focuses on the fallacy and scolds a politician for using it is, well, newsworthy. The following AP article highlights (fairly or unfairly) the straw man tactics of George W. Bush:

"Some look at the challenges in Iraq and conclude that the war is lost and not worth another dime or another day," U.S. President George W. Bush said recently.

Another time he said, "Some say that if you're Muslim you can't be free."

"There are some really decent people," the president said earlier this year, "who believe that the federal government ought to be the decider of health care . . . for all people."

Of course, hardly anyone in mainstream political debate has made such assertions.

When the president starts a sentence with "some say" or offers up what "some in Washington" believe, as he is doing more often these days, a rhetorical retort almost assuredly follows.

The device usually is code for Democrats or other White House opponents. In describing what they advocate, Mr. Bush often omits

▼

an important nuance or substitutes an extreme stance that bears little resemblance to their actual position.

He typically then says he "strongly disagrees," conveniently knocking down a straw man of his own making.

Mr. Bush routinely is criticized for dressing up events with a too-rosy glow. But experts in political speech say the straw man device, in which the president makes himself appear entirely reasonable by contrast to supposed "critics," is just as problematic.

Because the "some" often go unnamed, Mr. Bush can argue that his statements are true in an era of blogs and talk radio. Even so, "'some' suggests a number much larger than is actually out there," said Kathleen Hall Jamieson, director of the Annenberg Public Policy Center at the University of Pennsylvania.

A specialist in presidential rhetoric, Wayne Fields of Washington University in St. Louis, views it as "a bizarre kind of double talk" that abuses the rules of legitimate discussion.

"It's such a phenomenal hole in the national debate that you can have arguments with nonexistent people," Fields said. "All politicians try to get away with this to a certain extent. What's striking here is how much this administration rests on a foundation of this kind of stuff."

Mr. Bush has caricatured the other side for years, trying to tilt legislative debates in his favor or score election-season points with voters.

Not long after taking office in 2001, Mr. Bush pushed for a new education testing law and began portraying skeptics as opposed to holding schools accountable.

The chief opposition, however, had nothing to do with the merits of measuring performance, but rather the cost and intrusiveness of the proposal.

Campaigning for Republican candidates in the 2002 midterm elections, the president sought to use the congressional debate over a new Homeland Security Department against Democrats.

He told at least two audiences that some senators opposing him were "not interested in the security of the American people." In reality, Democrats balked not at creating the department, which Mr. Bush himself first opposed, but at letting agency workers go without the usual civil service protections.[5]

If you had heard these straw-man arguments, would you have been convinced by some or all of them? How can you tell if a public figure is using this fallacy? How can you avoid being taking in by it?   ∎

Senator Kennedy is opposed to the military spending bill, saying that it's too costly. Why does he always want to slash everything to the bone? He wants a pint-sized military that couldn't fight off a crazed band of terrorists, let alone a rogue nation.

Lawyers for the ACLU have sued to remove the massive Ten Commandments monument from the lobby of the courthouse. As usual, they are as anti-religious as ever. They want to remove every vestige of religion and faith from American life. Don't let them do it. Don't let them win yet another battle in their war to secularize the whole country.

In the first passage, David is opposed to laws prohibiting sexual activity between consenting, homosexual adults in their own homes. His opponent, however, distorts his view, claiming that David is actually in favor of allowing gay sex virtually anywhere, including in public. David, of course, is not asserting this (few people would). This distorted version of David's position is easy to ridicule and reject, allowing his actual view to be summarily dismissed.

REVIEW NOTES

☑ Fallacies with Irrelevant Premises

- **Genetic fallacy:** Arguing that a claim is true or false solely because of its origin
- **Composition:** Arguing that what is true of the parts must be true of the whole
- **Division:** Arguing that what is true of the whole must be true of the parts or that what is true of a group is true of individuals in the group
- **Appeal to the person:** Rejecting a claim by criticizing the person who makes it rather than the claim itself
- **Equivocation:** The use of a word in two different senses in an argument
- **Appeal to popularity:** Arguing that a claim must be true merely because a substantial number of people believe it
- **Appeal to tradition:** Arguing that a claim must be true or good just because it's part of a tradition
- **Appeal to ignorance:** Arguing that a lack of evidence proves something
- **Appeal to emotion:** The use of emotions as premises in an argument
- **Red herring:** The deliberate raising of an irrelevant issue during an argument
- **Straw man:** The distorting, weakening, or oversimplifying of someone's position so it can be more easily attacked or refuted

In the second passage, Senator Kennedy is against the military spending bill on the grounds that it costs too much. His position, though, is twisted into the claim that the military should be pared down so drastically that it would be ineffective even against small groups of terrorists. The senator's views on military spending are thus made to appear extreme or ludicrous. But it is unlikely that Senator Kennedy (or any other senator) wants to see the U.S. military reduced to such a level. He simply wants a less expensive military—not necessarily an ineffective one.

The third passage is typical of the kind of fallacious arguments that crop up in debates over church-state separation. Here, the ACLU wants a monument displaying the Ten Commandments removed from the lobby of a government building, a view that is characterized as anti-religious. But a request that a religious symbol be removed from a government context is not, in itself, necessarily anti-religious. Many have argued, for example, that such requests should be made to protect freedom of religion by preventing the government from giving preferential treatment to one religion over another. Also, wanting to get rid of a religious display on public property is a far cry from wanting to remove "every vestige of religion and faith from American life." Characterizing the ACLU suit as anti-religious, though, is a way to generate strong opposition to it. Note that in church-state debates, the straw-man tack is also used to bolster the other side of the dispute. Those who favor religious displays on government property are sometimes characterized as fanatics who want to turn the government into a theocracy. But, of course, from the fact that people want to allow such a religious display it does not follow that they want anything like a theocracy.

Unacceptable Premises

BEGGING THE QUESTION

The fallacy of **begging the question** (or arguing in a circle) is the attempt to establish the conclusion of an argument by using that conclusion as a premise. To beg the question is to argue that a proposition is true because the very same proposition supports it:

p
Therefore, p.

The classic question-begging argument goes like this:

*God exists. We know that God exists because the Bible says so, and we should
  believe what the Bible says because God wrote it.*

Or, more formally:

The Bible says that God exists.
The Bible is true because God wrote it.
Therefore, God exists.

This argument assumes at the outset the very proposition ("God exists") that it is trying to prove. Any argument that does this is fallacious.

Unfortunately, most question-begging arguments are not as obviously fallacious as "*p* is true because *p* is true." They may be hard to recognize because they are intricate or confusing. Consider this argument:

> *It is in every case immoral to lie to someone, even if the lie could save a life. Even in extreme circumstances a lie is still a lie. All lies are immoral because the very act of prevarication in all circumstances is contrary to ethical principles.*

At first glance, this argument may seem reasonable, but it's not. It reduces to this circular reasoning: "Lying is always immoral because lying is always immoral."

Among the more subtle examples of question-begging is this famous one, a favorite of critical thinking texts:

> *To allow every man unbounded freedom of speech must always be, on the whole, advantageous to the state; for it is highly conducive to the interests of the community that each individual should enjoy a liberty, perfectly unlimited, of expressing his sentiments.*[6]

This argument, as well as the one preceding it, demonstrates the easiest way to subtly beg the question: Just repeat the conclusion as a premise, but use different words.

FALSE DILEMMA

The fallacy of **false dilemma** is asserting that there are only two alternatives to consider when there are actually more than two. For example:

> *Look, either you support the war or you are a traitor to your country. You don't support the war. So you're a traitor.*

This argument contends that there are only two alternatives to choose from: Either you back the war, or you are a traitor. And since you don't back the war,

Whately's Elements of Logic

"Truth, like light, is blinding. Lies, on the other hand, are a beautiful dusk, which enhances the value of each object."
—ALBERT CAMUS

---

② False Dilemma

FURTHER THOUGHT

💡 Are We Begging the Question Yet?

In everyday usage, the phrase "beg the question" often refers to the famous fallacy. But many times it does not. It is sometimes used (some would say misused) to mean something like "prompts the question" or "raises the question," as in, "The rise in the crime rate begs the question of whether we have enough police officers on the job." As a critical thinker, you need to make sure you don't get these two uses confused.

you must be a traitor. But this argument works only if there really are just two alternatives. Actually there are other plausible possibilities here. Maybe you are loyal to your country but don't want to see it get involved in a costly war. Maybe you are a patriot who simply disagrees with your government's rationale for going to war. Because these possibilities are excluded, the argument is fallacious.

Again:

> *Either those lights you saw in the night sky were alien spacecraft (UFOs), or you were hallucinating. You obviously weren't hallucinating. So they had to be UFOs.*

This argument says that there are only two possibilities: The lights were UFOs, or you hallucinated the whole thing. And they must have been UFOs because you weren't hallucinating. But as is the case with the majority of alleged paranormal events, there are many more possible explanations than most people realize. The lights could have been commercial aircraft, military aircraft, meteors, atmospheric conditions, or the planet Venus (which, believe it or not, is often mistaken for a UFO). Since the argument ignores these reasonable possibilities, it's fallacious.

Finally:

> *We must legalize drugs. We either legalize them or pay a heavy toll in lives and the taxpayer's money to continue the war on drugs. And we cannot afford to pay such a high price.*

At first glance, these two alternatives may seem to exhaust the possibilities. But there is at least one other option—to launch a massive effort to prevent drug use and thereby reduce the demand for illegal drugs. The argument does not work because it fails to consider this possibility.

Note that these three arguments are expressed in disjunctive (either-or) form. But they can just as easily be expressed in a conditional (if-then) form, which says the same thing:

> *Look, if you don't support the war, then you are a traitor to your country. You don't support the war. So you're a traitor.*
>
> *If those lights you saw in the night sky were not alien spacecraft (UFOs), then you were hallucinating. You obviously weren't hallucinating. So they had to be UFOs.*
>
> *We must legalize drugs. If we don't legalize them, then we will pay a heavy toll in lives and the taxpayer's money to continue the war on drugs. And we cannot afford to pay such a high price.*

Sometimes we encounter stand-alone disjunctive phrases, rather than full-blown false dilemma arguments. These are false choices often presented as one-liners or headlines in tabloid newspapers, TV news programs, and magazines. For example:

Remember disjunctions can also be expressed as conditionals...

FURTHER THOUGHT

💡 False Dilemmas, Evolution, and Creationism

False dilemmas seem to crop up in all kinds of controversies, including debates in science and philosophy. The following is an example of how the fallacy is thought to arise in the ongoing dispute between creationism and evolution.

> Creationists also assume that any data that counts against evolution counts in favor of creationism. But to argue in this way is to commit the fallacy of *false dilemma*; it presents two alternatives as mutually exclusive when, in fact, they aren't. Gish sets up the dilemma this way: "Either the Universe arose through naturalistic, mechanistic evolutionary processes, or it was created supernaturally." This argument is a false dilemma for a number of reasons. In the first place, there is no need to assume that the universe was created even if evolution is not supported. The universe, as many non-Western peoples believe, may be eternal, that is, without beginning or end. . . . Second, evolution is not the only natural account of creation, and Genesis is not the only supernatural account. Theories of creation are as varied as the cultures that conceived them. Some believe that the universe developed naturally from the void (the Vikings) while others believe that it's the supernatural work of the devil (the Gnostics). Thus, even if the creationists could totally discredit evolution, they would not thereby prove their own position, for there are many other alternatives.[7]

One-liners

Iraq: Quagmire or Failure?
Microsoft: Bad Cop or Evil Giant?
Is the Administration Incompetent or Just Evil?

By limiting the possibilities, these headlines can imply that almost any outlandish state of affairs is actual—without even directly asserting anything.

People are often taken in by false dilemmas because they don't think beyond the alternatives laid before them. Out of fear, the need for simple answers, or a failure of imagination, they don't ask, "Is there another possibility?" To ask this is to think outside the box and reduce the likelihood of falling for simplistic answers.

SLIPPERY SLOPE

③
Slippery Slope

The fallacy of **slippery slope** is arguing, without good reasons, that taking a particular step will inevitably lead to a further, undesirable step (or steps). The idea behind the metaphor, of course, is that if you take the first step on a slippery slope, you will have to take others because, well, the slope is slippery. A familiar slippery-slope pattern is "Doing action A will lead to action B, which will lead to action C, which will result in calamitous action D. Therefore, you should not do action A." It's fallacious when there is no good reason to think that doing action A will actually result in undesirable action D. Take a look at this classic example:

The Domino Theory

> *We absolutely must not lose the war in Vietnam. If South Vietnam falls to the communists, then Thailand will fall to them. If Thailand falls to them, then South Korea will fall to them. And before you know it, all of Southeast Asia will be under communist control.*

This argument was a commonplace during the Cold War. It was known as the domino theory because it asserted that if one country in Southeast Asia succumbed to communism, they all would succumb, just as a whole row of dominoes will fall if the first one is pushed over. It was fallacious because there was no good evidence that the dominoes would inevitably fall as predicted. In fact, after South Vietnam was defeated, they did not fall as predicted.

Here are some more examples:

> *If assault rifles are banned in this country, then handguns will be next. Then sporting rifles will be banned. And ultimately all guns will be banned, and our fundamental freedom to own guns will be canceled out altogether. So if assault rifles are banned, we might as well strike the Second Amendment from the Constitution because it will be worthless.*

> *We must ban pornography in all forms. Otherwise, rape and other sex crimes will be as common as jaywalking.*

REVIEW NOTES

☑ Fallacies with Unacceptable Premises

- **Begging the question:** The attempt to establish the conclusion of an argument by using that conclusion as a premise
- **False dilemma:** Asserting that there are only two alternatives to consider when there are actually more than two
- **Slippery slope:** Arguing, without good reasons, that taking a particular step will inevitably lead to a further, undesirable step (or steps)
- **Hasty generalization:** The drawing of a conclusion about a target group based on an inadequate sample size
- **Faulty analogy:** An argument in which the things being compared are not sufficiently similar in relevant ways

All Americans should be against laws permitting consensual homosexual sex in one's own home. If that kind of thing is allowed, before you know it anything goes—bestiality, prostitution, illegal drug use, and violence.

These arguments follow the basic slippery-slope pattern. They are fallacies not because they assert that one event or state of affairs can inevitably lead to others, but because there is no good reason to believe the assertions. Some arguments may look like slippery-slope fallacies but are not because there is good reason to think that the steps are connected as described. Observe:

If you have Lyme disease, you definitely should get medical treatment. Without treatment, you could develop life-threatening complications. Man, you could die. You should see your doctor now.

This is not a fallacious slippery-slope argument. There are good reasons to believe that the series of events mentioned would actually happen.

HASTY GENERALIZATION

In Chapter 4 we pointed out the connection between the availability error and the fallacy known as **hasty generalization.** In Chapter 8 we will examine hasty generalizations at length. Here we need only recall that we are guilty of hasty generalization when we draw a conclusion about a whole group based on an inadequate sample of the group. This mistake is a genuine fallacy of unacceptable premises because the premises stating the sample size are relevant to the conclusion, but they provide inadequate evidence. For example:

You should buy an iPhone. They're great. I bought one last year, and it has given me nothing but flawless performance.
The only male professor I've had this year was a chauvinist pig. All the male professors at this school must be chauvinist pigs.
Psychology majors are incredibly ignorant about human psychology. Believe me, I know what I'm talking about: My best friend is a psych major. What an ignoramus!
The French are snobby and rude. Remember those two high-and-mighty guys with really bad manners? They're French. I rest my case.
The food at Pappie's Restaurant is awful. I had a sandwich there once, and the bread was stale.

FAULTY ANALOGY

We will also discuss **arguments by analogy** in Chapter 8. Like hasty generalizations, defective arguments by analogy, or **faulty analogies,** are also fallacies

---

Margin notes:

Need to distinguish fallacies from good arguments...

④ Hasty Generalization

"One cool judgment is worth a thousand hasty counsels."
—WOODROW WILSON

Inadequate sample

⑤ Faulty Analogy

Many philosophers think the argument comparing a watch to the universe (the so-called design argument for the existence of God) is a faulty analogy. Why do you suppose they think that?

involving unacceptable premises. An analogy is a comparison of two or more things alike in specific respects. An argument by analogy reasons this way: Because two or more things are similar in several respects, they must be similar in some further respect. For example:

> *In the Vietnam War, the United States had not articulated a clear rationale for fighting there, and the United States lost. Likewise, in the present war the United States has not articulated a clear rationale for fighting. Therefore, the United States will lose this war too.*

> *A watch is a mechanism of exquisite complexity with numerous parts precisely arranged and accurately adjusted to achieve a purpose—a purpose imposed by the watch's designer. Likewise the universe has exquisite complexity with countless parts—from atoms to asteroids—that fit together precisely and accurately to produce certain effects as though arranged by plan. Therefore, the universe must also have a designer.*

In a faulty analogy, the things being compared are not sufficiently similar in relevant ways. Such analogical arguments are said to be weak. For instance, you could argue that:

> *Dogs are warm-blooded, nurse their young, and give birth to puppies.*
> *Humans are warm-blooded and nurse their young. Therefore, humans give birth to puppies too.*

This argument by analogy is about as weak as they come—and a little silly. Dogs and humans are not sufficiently similar in relevant ways (in physiology, for one thing) to justify such a strange conclusion.

[handwritten margin notes:]
Arguments by Analogy are inductive arguments...

A Faulty Analogy results in a weak inductive argument

KEY WORDS

ad hominem	division
appeal to emotion	equivocation
appeal to ignorance	fallacy
appeal to popularity (or to the masses)	false dilemma
	faulty analogy
appeal to the person	genetic fallacy
appeal to tradition	hasty generalization
argument by analogy	red herring
begging the question	slippery slope
burden of proof	straw man
composition	*tu quoque*

Summary

- Certain types of defective arguments that occur frequently are known as fallacies. Fallacies are often psychologically persuasive but logically flawed. We can divide fallacies into two broad categories: (1) those that have *irrelevant* premises and (2) those that have *unacceptable* premises.

- Fallacies with irrelevant premises include the genetic fallacy (arguing that a claim is true or false solely because of its origin), composition (arguing that what is true of the parts must be true of the whole), division (arguing that what is true of the whole must be true of the parts or that what is true of a group is true of individuals in the group), appeal to the person (rejecting a claim by criticizing the person who makes it rather than the claim itself), equivocation (the use of a word in two different senses in an argument), appeal to popularity (arguing that a claim must be true merely because a substantial number of people believe it), appeal to tradition (arguing that a claim must be true or good just because it's part of a tradition), appeal to ignorance (arguing that a lack of evidence proves something), appeal to emotion (the use of emotions as premises in an argument), red herring (the deliberate raising of an irrelevant issue during an argument), and straw man (the distorting, weakening, or oversimplifying of someone's position so it can be more easily attacked or refuted).

- Fallacies with unacceptable premises include begging the question (the attempt to establish the conclusion of an argument by using that conclusion as a premise), false dilemma (incorrectly asserting that only two alternatives exist), slippery slope (arguing, without good reasons, that taking a particular step will inevitably lead to a further, undesirable step or steps), hasty generalization (the drawing of a conclusion about a group based on an inadequate sample of the group), and faulty analogy (an argument in which the things being compared are not sufficiently similar in relevant ways).

 EXERCISES

Exercise 5.1

REVIEW QUESTIONS

1. According to the text, what are the two broad categories of fallacies?
2. What is the genetic fallacy?
3. Can the origin of a claim ever be relevant to deciding its truth or falsity?
* 4. What is the fallacy of composition?
5. What are the two forms of the fallacy of division?
6. Why are appeals to the person fallacious?
7. What type of *ad hominem* argument is put forth as a charge of hypocrisy?
8. What is the fallacy of poisoning the well?
9. What is the fallacy of equivocation?
* 10. Why are appeals to popularity fallacious?
11. What is the appeal to tradition?
12. What are the two forms of the appeal to ignorance?
13. What is the proper response to an appeal to ignorance?
14. What is rhetoric?
* 15. According to the text, is it ever legitimate to use rhetoric and argument together?
16. What is the fallacy of red herring?
17. What is the basic pattern of argument of the straw-man fallacy?
18. What is the fallacy of begging the question?
* 19. Why are people often taken in by false dilemmas?
20. What is the burden of proof?
21. What is the fallacy of slippery slope?

Exercise 5.2

In the following passages, identify any fallacies of irrelevance (genetic fallacy, composition, division, appeal to the person, equivocation, appeal to popularity, appeal to tradition, appeal to ignorance, appeal to emotion, red herring, and straw man). Some passages may contain more than one fallacy, and a few may contain no fallacies at all.

* 1. "Seeing that the eye and hand and foot and every one of our members has some obvious function, must we not believe that in like manner a human being has a function over and above these particular functions?" [Aristotle]

   Composition

2. The federal budget deficits are destroying this country. Just ask any working stiff; he'll tell you.

   Popularity

3. The hippies of the sixties railed against the materialistic, capitalistic system and everyone who prospered in it. But all their bellyaching was crap because they were a bunch of hypocrites, living off their rich mothers and fathers.

   Tu Quoque

4. Gerald says that the legal drinking age should be raised to twenty-two. But what does he know? He drinks like a fish.

   Appeal to the Person

* 5. The *New York Times* reported that one-third of Republican senators have been guilty of Senate ethics violations. But you know that's false—the *Times* is a notorious liberal rag.

   Genetic Fallacy

6. Geraldo says that students who cheat on exams should not automatically be expelled from school. But it's ridiculous to insist that students should never be punished for cheating.

   Straw Man

7. Of course there is a God. Almost every civilization in history has believed in a deity of some kind.

   Appeal to Tradition

8. My sweater is blue. Therefore, the atoms that make up the sweater are blue.

   Division

9. The prime minister is lying about his intelligence briefings since almost everyone surveyed in national polls thinks he's lying.

   Appeal to Popularity

* 10. Kelly says that many women who live in predominantly Muslim countries are discriminated against. But how the heck would she know? She's not a Muslim.

   Appeal to Person

11. A lot of people think that football jocks are stupid and boorish. That's a crock. Anyone who had seen the fantastic game that our team played on Saturday, with three touchdowns before halftime, would not believe such rubbish.

   Red Herring

12. Does acupuncture work? Can it cure disease? Of course. It has been used in China by folk practitioners for at least three thousand years.

   Appeal to Tradition

13. The study found that 80 percent of women who took the drug daily had no recurrence of breast cancer. But that doesn't mean anything. The study was funded in part by the company that makes the drug.

   Genetic Fallacy

* 14. "The only proof capable of being given that an object is visible, is that people actually see it. The only proof that a sound is audible, is that people hear it: and so of the other sources of our experience. In like manner, I apprehend, the sole evidence it is possible to produce that anything is desirable, is that people actually desire it." [John Stuart Mill]

   Equivocation

Appeal to Emotion 15. The new StratoCar is the best automobile on the road. Picture the admiring glances you'll get when you take a cruise in your StratoCar through town. Imagine the power and speed!

Appeal to Ignorance 16. Gremlins exist, that's for sure. No scientist has ever proved that they don't exist.

Appeal to the Person (Tu Quoque) 17. "The most blatant occurrence of recent years is all these knuckleheads running around protesting nuclear power—all these stupid people who do not research at all and who go out and march, pretending they care about the human race, and then go off in their automobiles and kill one another." [Ray Bradbury]

Appeal to Popularity 18. Is the Bible divinely inspired? There can be no doubt that it is, for it has been a best-seller for thousands of years.

Appeal to the Person *19. The former mayor was convicted of drug possession, and he spent time in jail. So you can safely ignore anything he has to say about legalizing drugs.

Appeal to Ignorance 20. I believe that baby-carrying storks are real creatures. No one has ever proved that they don't exist.

Appeal to Emotion (Red Herring) 21. Professor, I deserve a better grade than a D on my paper. Look, my parents just got a divorce. If they see that I got a D, they will just blame each other, and the fighting will start all over again. Give me a break.

Equivocation 22. Only man has morals. No woman is a man. Therefore, no woman has morals.

Composition 23. Every player on the team is the best in the league. So the team itself is the best in the league.

Exercise 5.3

In the following passages, identify any fallacies of unacceptable premises (begging the question, false dilemma, slippery slope, hasty generalization, and faulty analogy). Some passages may contain more than one fallacy, and a few may contain no fallacies at all.

Begging the Question 1. Random drug testing in schools is very effective in reducing drug use because the regular use of the testing makes drug use less likely.

Slippery Slope 2. If today you can make teaching evolution in public schools a crime, then tomorrow you can make it a crime to teach it in private schools. Then you can ban books and other educational materials that mention evolution. And then you can ban the very word from all discourse. And then the anti-science bigots will have won.

 Begging the Question 3. Three thieves are dividing up the $7000 they just stole from the First National Bank. Robber number one gives $2000 to robber number two, $2000 to robber number three, and $3000 to himself. Robber number two says, "How come you get $3000?" Robber number one says, "Because I am the leader." "How come you're the leader?" "Because I have more money."

*4. Either God exists or he does not exist. If he exists, and you believe, you will gain heaven; if he exists and you don't believe, you will lose nothing. If he does not exist, and you believe, you won't lose much. If he does not exist, and you don't believe, you still won't lose much. The best gamble then is to believe. *[handwritten: False Dilemma]*

5. Ivan doesn't talk about his political views. He's got to be either a liberal or a conservative. And he certainly is no liberal. So he must be a conservative. *[handwritten: False Dilemma]*

*6. I used to work with this engineering major. And, man, they are really socially inept. *[handwritten: Hasty General.]*

7. I met these two guys on a plane, and they said they were from Albuquerque. They were total druggies. Almost everyone in that city must be on drugs. *[handwritten: Hasty General.]*

8. Some people are fools, and some people are married to fools. *[handwritten: No Fallacy]*

9. Bill is an investment banker, drives a Cadillac, is overweight, and votes Republican. John is also an investment banker, drives a Cadillac, and is overweight. So John probably votes Republican too. *[handwritten: Faulty Analogy]*

*10. Either we fire this guy or we send a message to other employees that it's okay to be late for work. Clearly, we need to fire him. *[handwritten: False Dilemma]*

Exercise 5.4

For each of the following claims, devise an argument using the fallacy shown in parentheses. Make the argument as persuasive as possible.

1. The federal budget deficit will destroy the economy. (red herring)
2. *Shane* is the best movie Western ever made. (appeal to popularity)
*3. Mrs. Anan does not deserve the Nobel Prize. (appeal to the person)
4. Vampires—the blood-sucking phantoms of folklore—are real. (appeal to ignorance)
5. Internet pornography can destroy this country. (slippery slope)
*6. The Boy Scouts of America should allow gay kids to be members. (begging the question)
7. The United States should attack Iran. (false dilemma)
8. That economics seminar is absolutely the worst course offered at the university. (hasty generalization)
9. Pope John Paul II was a moral giant. (appeal to emotion)
10. The Nigerian court was right to sentence that woman to be stoned to death for adultery. (appeal to popularity)
*11. There are too many guns on the streets because our politicians are controlled by the National Rifle Association and other gun nuts. (red herring)
12. All efforts should be made to ban trade in exotic pets such as tigers. (genetic fallacy)

Field Problems

1. Find a magazine or newspaper letter to the editor that contains at least one fallacy. Identify the fallacy and rewrite the passage to eliminate the fallacy and strengthen the argument. (To effectively rework the argument, you may have to make up some facts.)

2. Select an editorials/letters page from a newspaper (it should contain several opinions on various issues). Scan the entire page, circling and labeling any examples of fallacies. Locate at least three examples.

3. Tune into a TV or radio political talk show—preferably one in which you usually find yourself in strong agreement with the opinions expressed—and identify at least three instances of fallacious reasoning.

Self-Assessment Quiz

Answers appear in "Answers to Self-Assessment Quizzes" (Appendix C). Identify the fallacy or fallacies in the following passages.

1. "[Howard] Dean has leapt beyond criticizing Bush and is now embracing terrorists. He has called Hamas terrorists 'soldiers in a war' and said the U.S. should not take sides between Israel and Palestinian suicide bombers." [Ann Coulter]

2. You think that welfare mothers would actually prefer to have jobs? Prove it, and until you do they are all lazy moochers.

3. Civil rights legislation was furiously opposed by Dixiecrat Strom Thurmond—which proves that it was reasonable and moral.

4. "[George W.] Bush lies about important things like the economy, his tax cuts, his education, our reasons for going to war and drunk driving. But I think he lies only when he feels he has to. He knows that most of the time Fox News, the *Wall Street Journal* and Rush Limbaugh are only too glad to do it for him." [Al Franken]

5. "Jews are part of the Soviet people. They are a fine people, intelligent, very valued in the soviet Union. Therefore, the problem of the Jews in the Soviet Union does not exist." [Mikhail Gorbachev]

6. You can safely ignore Helena's argument for the rights of women because she's a member of the National Organization of Women.

7. You advocate a woman's right to abortion because you do not understand how hideous and monstrous an abortion procedure is, how it tears a living fetus away from the uterine wall, crushes it to bleeding pieces, and sucks it away into oblivion.

8. That is a lousy book. It did not sell well at all.

9. All of us cannot be loved because all of us cannot be the focus of deep affection.

10. "If the parts of the Universe are not accidental, how can the whole Universe be considered as the result of chance? Therefore the existence of the Universe is not due to chance." [Moses Maimonides]

11. This administration is either one of the best or one of the worst. It is certainly not one of the best, so we must count it among those at the bottom of the heap.

12. Atheistic philosophers have been trying for thousands of years to prove that there is no God, and they haven't succeeded yet. This shows that there is indeed a God after all.

13. How can you, with a straight face, argue that animals have rights and expect me to believe you? You eat meat!

14. Judges should not hand down anything but maximum sentences for all convicted criminals. If you start making exceptions, prosecutors will start asking for lighter sentences. Next thing you know, every criminal will be getting off with mere warnings.

15. America—love it or leave it!

16. "I cannot wait until Andy Rooney starts acting his age and retires. What a waste of editorial space. His op-ed column in the Sept. 28 News was so silly." [Letter to the editor, *Buffalo News*]

17. If he truly loved me, he would have written me a letter and said so. He didn't do that, so he obviously hates me.

18. Children were asked to recite the Pledge of Allegiance every day and to include the phrase "under God." That was dead wrong. No child should have to submit to such brainwashing.

19. Ranjit was caught cheating on his final exam. But why should he be punished when a dozen other people cheated last year in the same course?

20. Rush Limbaugh always said that drug users ought to be thrown in jail and shown no mercy. But those words of wisdom come from a guy who has had quite a drug problem himself!

 ## Integrative Exercises

These exercises pertain to material in Chapters 1–5.

For each of the following passages, indicate whether it contains an argument. If it does, specify the conclusion and premises, whether it is deductive or inductive, whether it is a good argument (sound or cogent), and whether it is a fallacy. Some passages may contain no argument.

1. Andrea denies that she is an atheist, so she must be a theist.

2. You say that there are no such things as ghosts, but can you prove that they don't exist?

3. "Didn't Tom Cruise make a stock-car movie in which he destroyed thirty-five cars, burned thousands of gallons of gasoline, and wasted

dozens of tires? If I were given the opportunity, I'd say to Tom Cruise, 'Tom, most people don't own thirty-five cars in their *life*, and you just trashed thirty-five cars for a movie. Now you're telling other people not to pollute the planet? Shut up, sir.'" [Rush Limbaugh]

4. "The large number of female voters for Arnold Schwarzenegger in California announces one thing: the death of feminism. That so many women would ignore his sexual misconduct and vote for him bespeaks the re-emergence of the reckless phallus." [Letter to the editor, *Newsday*]

5. Hillary Clinton supports gun-control legislation. As you know, all fascist regimes of the twentieth century have passed gun-control legislation. We are forced to conclude that Hillary Clinton is a fascist.

6. If Congress bans automatic weapons, America will slide down a slippery slope leading to the banning of all guns, the shredding of the Bill of Rights, and a totalitarian police state.

7. Affirmative action makes for a better society. Everybody knows that, even if they won't admit it.

8. Thinking is like swimming. Just as in swimming it's easy to float on the top but hard to dive deep, it's easy in thinking to float along on the surface of an issue but difficult to use your intellect to delve down into the layers.

9. "If a cell, under appropriate conditions, becomes a person in the space of a few years, there can surely be no difficulty in understanding how, under appropriate conditions, a cell may, in the course of untold millions of years, give origin to the human race." [Herbert Spencer]

10. The chancellor is either a crook or a nut. He is a crook. Thus, he is no nut.

11. Everything must either happen by random accident or by divine intervention. Nothing happens by pure accident, so everything must happen because of divine intervention.

12. Children should never be spanked. Spanking is harmful. I've talked to three mothers about this issue, and they all agree that spanking harms a child's self-esteem and development.

13. The Eagles are the most popular rock group in history because they have sold the most records.

14. My professor says that telling a lie is never morally permissible. But that's ridiculous. The other day I heard him tell a bald-faced one to one of his students.

15. "Not all forms of gender discrimination are unethical. There are a number of exclusively male or female fitness clubs around the country utilized by religious individuals who shun the meat market scene. If a woman wants to spare herself the embarrassment of being ogled in her sports bra while doing thigh-thrusts, it is her right to work out with women only. Similarly, if a man wants to spare himself the temptation of working out with lingerie models, he should be allowed membership to strictly male

fitness clubs. It would be unreasonable to require non-discrimination of these private clubs, or to make them build separate facilities to accommodate everyone." [Letter to the editor, *Arizona Daily Wildcat*]

16. "Highway checkpoints, drug testing, ubiquitous security cameras and now the government's insistence on the use of sophisticated software tools to spy on the American people all point to a single vision. This vision was shared with us years ago, in George Orwell's book *1984*. Big Brother is indeed watching." [Letter to the editor, *Buffalo News*]

17. There are those on campus who would defend a student's right to display a Confederate flag on his or her dorm room door. But there is no such right. Slavery was wrong, is wrong, and always will be wrong.

18. "It is impossible to make people understand their ignorance; for it requires knowledge to perceive it and therefore he that can perceive it hath it not." [Jeremy Taylor]

19. If you give that homeless guy fifty cents today, tomorrow he will want a dollar, then five dollars, then ten, and where will it stop? Before you know it, *you're* homeless.

20. The biblical story of Adam and Eve in the garden of Eden is true. If it weren't true, it would not be in the Bible.

Critical Thinking and Writing
MODULE 5

AN ANNOTATED SAMPLE PAPER

Let's see how the lessons of the four previous modules might be applied in an actual student essay.[8] The following (beginning on page 210) incorporates the main elements of good argumentative papers and, as even the best essays do, exhibits both strengths and weaknesses—many of which are noted in the margins. Read the paper carefully, taking in the annotations as you go, making sure you understand each point before moving on to the next.

Free Speech on Campus

In order to meet the goals and purposes of higher education, free speech must remain intact. Thus, the University of Missouri should not adopt a campus hate speech code. ① The First Amendment protects all speech outside the university setting, and what happens outside of the university setting also should be allowed inside. ② Without an open forum for thought, though it may include hate speech, the university fails in its mission to provide a realistic experience for its students. By abolishing hate speech on university campuses, that open forum for discovery and knowledge is eliminated. As a result, learning and knowledge are stunted. ③ Without the exchange of controversial ideas and opinions, there can be no real change in our society. Experiencing and debating is almost always better than suppressing, because censoring speech can never invoke real change.

The First Amendment protects the right for every person to express opinions about the government and about each other. It actually "protects speech no matter how offensive the content" (Hate Speech on Campus, 1996). Just because something is offensive to one person does not mean it is offensive to another. Justice John M. Harlan wrote in Cohen v. California (1971), "One man's vulgarity is another's lyric" (Free Speech, 1996). In other words, just because something is offensive to one person does not mean that it is offensive by definition.

Speech that is protected outside of the university setting also should be protected inside. Some would argue that hate speech hinders the abilities of minority students to learn, but part of the goal of higher education is to put students out of their comfort zone and to challenge their ways of thinking. In response to a sexual harassment policy being implemented

Seems to be three arguments to discuss but this summary does not make that as clear as it should.

Provides background for first argument.

Thesis statement

Summarizes the arguments to be made.

Needs a more explicit transition to first argument.

Sources cited

Responds to an objection to thesis.

First argument for thesis

at the University of Massachusetts, lawyer Harvey A. Silvergate (1995) wrote a memo to university administrators opposing the proposal.

> One of the primary purposes of a college education and experience is to challenge students, to make them question their comfortable lives and assumptions in short, to discomfort them in one way or another. (Silvergate, 1995)

In the same memo, Silvergate also wrote:

> If I am allowed to say something on the street corner, in a letter to the editor of a newspaper, or on a radio talk show, surely I should be allowed to say it on the campus of the University of Massachusetts.

Not clear how these quotations—which refer to sexual harassment—relate to hate speech.

First argument for thesis

This is equally true for the University of Missouri. What can possibly be gained by excluding an element of real life such as offensive speech from the campus experience? The university would only serve to deceive its students by shielding them from realistic situations while they are in school. This, in turn, only serves to place them into the real world with false expectations.

Alternatively, exploring and debating is almost always better than suppressing. The organization Justice on Campus (1995) contends that:

Introduces quotation

> When we hear speech or see images that offend us, nothing is more human than our urge to suppress or to destroy them. But as deeply human is our need to think and to share our thoughts with others. Censorship is the greatest evil because the censor's goal is to imprison the human spirit.

Second argument for thesis

In addition to providing a realistic picture of nonacademic life, allowing all types of speech on campus encourages an open forum for the discussion of all types of ideas. Discussion of controversial issues and different points of view are the fuel for a useful education. That is why higher education has a responsibility to ensure that all forms of speech are

protected, analyzed, and addressed. "The right of free speech is indivisible. When one of us is denied this right, all of us are denied" (Hate
Speech on Campus, 1996). By denying one point of view, we eliminate
the open forum. A speech code on any university campus only hinders the
ability of students and faculty to fully explore the market of ideas available to them. The University of Missouri is no exception to the idea that
academic freedom is the bedrock of a free society.

*Third argu-
ment for
thesis*

If we do not allow open expression, however hateful it is, then there
can be no change, no growth. Racism, sexism, ageism, etc. are not going
to diminish without being addressed in higher education. As noted by
the ACLU (Hate Speech on Campus, 1995), "Verbal purity is not social
change." Barring certain types of speech would be a seeming quick fix
for issues such as racism, sexism, ageism, and homophobia, which
often comprise hate speech. But racist statements are not the real problem
between the races; racism is. If we bar all racially biased comments on
campus, all we have done is fuel the racism. We have then given hatred
the power to lurk and grow within us instead of communicating and
debating about it in the open.

If hate speech is not allowed to occur openly, the problem of racism
is never addressed. Like racism, hate speech itself is not the problem; hate
is. As members of a society, we must communicate in order to solve problems and grow as individuals. This includes addressing hateful ideas and
opinions. We can make no progress if we do not allow offensive kinds
of speech to exist on campus. By barring them, we run the risk of being
silenced ourselves.

*Conclusion
summarizes main
arguments.*

A hate speech code at the University of Missouri would be detrimental to everyone, from students to faculty. The First Amendment protects all kinds of speech, including the offensive. It does this in order to

*Restatement of
thesis*

ensure that all voices are heard and that all issues can be addressed. To go through college with the idea that offensive speech does not happen is detrimental to students and to the society in which they live. The educational system is based on the idea that communication leads to learning and that learning leads to personal growth. Without the open forum for thought and the freedom to express controversial ideas, a higher education is worthless. Moreover, no one ever solved a controversial gender issue or a racial conflict in silence. There must be communication so that debate can transpire. In order for any change in our society to transpire, offensive speech must be allowed to continue. It can only be addressed and learned from if it is equally protected by the Constitution. Mike Godwin, of the Electronic Frontier Foundation, says, "when it comes to the Bill of Rights, what you don't use, you lose. The First Amendment is a terrible thing to waste" (Comments and quotes, 1995). If anyone has a responsibility to use the freedom granted by the First Amendment, higher education is at the top of the list.

References

American Civil Liberties Union. (1996). Hate speech on campus. [Online]. Available: http://www.aclu.org/library/pbp16.html

American Civil Liberties Union. (1996). Free speech. [Online]. Available: www.aclu.org/issues/freespeech/isfs.html

Justice on Campus. (1996). Comments and quotes on sexual harassment and free speech. [Online]. Available: http://joc.mit.edu/comments.html

Justice on Campus. (1995). Speech codes and disciplinary charges. [Online]. Available: http://joc.mit.edu/roundup.html

Silvergate, H. A. (1995, November 23). Memo from Harvey Silvergate. [Online]. Available: http://joc.mit.edu/amherst/silvergate.112495.txt

Writing Assignments

1. In a one-page essay argue that women are more nurturing and caring than men are. Avoid fallacies. Then write a one-page critique of the first paper, paying special attention to any fallacies you uncover.

2. Write a two-page rebuttal to Essay 8 ("The Cohabitation Epidemic") in Appendix A, pointing out as many fallacies as possible.

3. Write a one-page paper arguing that the speed limit on all U.S. highways should be raised to 70 mph. Include at least three fallacies in the paper. Exchange your paper with a classmate who has done the same assignment. Pinpoint the fallacies in each other's papers.

4. Study Essay 15 ("Time to Think"). Identify the conclusion and premises of the essay's argument, and write a rebuttal to it.

ARGUMENTS

Part Three

Deductive Reasoning: Propositional Logic

 CHAPTER OBJECTIVES

CONNECTIVES AND TRUTH VALUES

- Understand the purpose and uses of propositional logic.
- Understand the meaning, the symbols, and the uses of the four logical connectives—conjunction, disjunction, negation, and conditional.
- Know the definition of *statement* and the distinction between simple and compound statements.
- Know how to translate simple statements into symbolic form.
- Know how to construct a truth table and how to use it to test the validity of arguments.
- Know the situations in which conjunctions, disjunctions, negations, and conditionals are true or false.
- Understand the structure of conditional statements and the various ways in which they can be expressed.

CHECKING FOR VALIDITY

- Know how to determine the validity of very simple arguments using truth tables.
- Be able to use parentheses to express statements in symbolic form.
- Be able to use the short method to evaluate complex arguments.

FOR CENTURIES PHILOSOPHERS, MONKS, SCIENTISTS, LINGUISTS, AND students have been enthralled by logic. Yes, *logic*. For many people—including some great thinkers such as Aristotle, Gottfried Leibniz, and Bertrand Russell—logic has been, ironically, a passion, something deemed worthy of deep study and long devotion. For hundreds of years, logic (along with philosophy) was a required course in universities and was regarded as one of the grand pillars upon which a liberal arts education was based (the others were grammar, rhetoric, arithmetic, music, astronomy, and geometry). Even today scholars continue to be drawn into logic's depths, never seeming to tire of exploration and application.

But why do they bother? Why do they seem to think that logic is anything other than the dry and dusty preoccupation of dry and dusty philosophers? Well, maybe they bother because the study and use of logic, like the study and use of mathematics, is an exercise in exactitude, precision, clarity, and—above all—definite answers. All of which can be very satisfying. Or perhaps they bother because logic is the study of good reasoning or thinking and is therefore concerned with every decision and every judgment we make.

Logic also labors. Out of the study of logic have come discoveries now used in electronic engineering, set theory, linguistics, mathematics, and, of course, philosophy. Investigations in logic have yielded insights that made the invention of digital computers possible.

Of course, what you really want to know is what coursework in logic can do for *you*. Well, in this chapter you get a preliminary answer to that question. Here we take up an exploration of **propositional logic** (or truth-functional logic)—the branch of deductive reasoning that deals with the logical relationships among statements. In propositional logic, we use symbols to represent and clarify these relationships. If you master this material, you should reap at least two rewards right off. The first is a more thorough understanding of the power, precision, and dynamics of deductive reasoning. The second is the ability to evaluate the validity of very complex arguments.

How complex? Take a look at this deductive argument. Can you tell if it's valid?

(1) The United States will be secure and prosperous only if it shares more of its resources with the impoverished or discontented peoples of the world.

"My lawyer says I can sue the school because they're violating my right to be stupid."

© 1996 by Randy Glasbergen.

(2) *The United States will share more of its resources with the impoverished or discontented peoples of the world only if doing so will not significantly reduce Americans' standard of living.*

(3) *If Americans' standard of living is significantly reduced, then either the United States will not be secure and prosperous or it will not share more of its resources with the impoverished or discontented peoples of the world.*

(4) *The United States will not share more of its resources with the impoverished or discontented peoples of the world.*

(5) *Therefore, the United States will not be secure and prosperous.*

If you don't know anything about propositional logic, the only way you can check this argument for validity is to use brute brainpower. You just have to noodle it out, and the noodling will not be easy. But with a grounding in propositional logic, you can figure this one out in straightforward fashion.

Connectives and Truth Values

As we've seen, arguments are composed of statements. In Chapter 3 we used symbols to represent the statements. Each symbol stood not for a logical relationship between statements but for a single statement. Propositional logic takes this symbolization to another level by using symbols to stand not just for statements but also for the *relationships between statements*—relationships that we specified previously with logical connective words, or connectives, such as "if . . . then" and "or." Propositional logic gets this work done by using the symbol language of **symbolic logic**, a branch of logic in its own right.

Because these logical connectives specify the relationships between statements, they shape the *form* of the argument. Recall that the validity of an argument is a matter of the argument's form, which is why we can judge the validity of an argument apart from any consideration of the truth of its premises. So propositional logic helps us assess the validity of an argument without being distracted by nonformal elements such as the language used to express content.

So the symbols used to express an argument are of two types. The first you're already familiar with; they're the letters, or **variables,** you use to represent propositions. For example: If p, then q. (There's no particular distinction in the letters p and q; any letters will do, as long as you use them consistently. That is, once you've chosen p to represent, say, "Alice rode her bike," p must consistently represent this same statement throughout the argument.) The second kind are the symbols for the logical connectives that indicate relationships between statements.

In the digital age when any image can be faked, forged, and Photoshopped, seeing is not always believing, and critical thinking is your only defense against visual sleight of hand. *Top*: In 2004, the presidential campaign of George W. Bush ran a television ad with a photo of a large crowd of soldiers listening to Bush's speech. The campaign doctored the photo by repeating the image of a small group of soldiers to create a composite crowd. *Middle*: During its reign, the Soviet Union tried to remove all public reminders of Leon Trotsky, an early leader of the Russian Revolution who fell out of favor with the Soviets. Trotsky's image was systematically obliterated from photos. *Bottom*: To announce the promotion of Ann Dunwoody to become the first female four-star general in U.S. history, the Army released this picture of her. The photo, however, had been altered from the original to show an American flag in the background and a more youthful looking Dunwoody. Considering the possibilities of image doctoring, what critical thinking principles do you think should guide your viewing of media images?

The following table presents the symbols for, and the meaning of, four logical connectives.

Symbol	Meaning	Example
&	Conjunction (and)	$p \ \& \ q$ Alice rode her bike, and John walked.
v	Disjunction (or)	$p \ v \ q$ Either Alice rode her bike, or John walked.
~	Negation (not)	$\sim p$ Alice did not ride her bike. (or) It is not the case that Alice rode her bike.
→	Conditional (if-then)	$p \rightarrow q$ If Alice rode her bike, then John walked.

These connectives are used in compound statements such as "The air is clean, and the sky is blue" or "If you stay up late, you will sleep in tomorrow." Remember that a **statement** (or claim) is an assertion that something is or is not the case. In other words, it is the kind of thing that can be either true or false. A **simple statement** is one that doesn't contain any other statements as constituents. And a **compound statement** is composed of at least two simple statements.

Every statement has a truth value. That is, a statement is either true or false. Or to be more precise, a true statement has a truth value of *true*, and a false statement has a truth value of *false*. In contrast, questions and exclamations don't have truth values.

Now let's say that we've converted an argument into its symbolic form, and we know all the *possible* truth values of the argument's variables (statements). In other words, we know under what circumstances a statement is true or false due to the influence of the logical connectives. How would this information help us?

It could help us quickly uncover the validity or invalidity of the whole argument. Given the possible truth values of some statements in the argument, and given the statements' relationships with one another as governed by the logical connectives, we could infer the possible truth values of all the other statements. Then we would have to answer just one question: *Is there a combination of truth values in the argument such that the premises could be true and the conclusion false?* If the answer is yes, then the argument is invalid. If there is no such circumstance, the argument is valid.

If you're a little fuzzy on all this, don't worry. It will become clearer to you as you digest the following examples and learn more about the dance between connectives and truth values.

CONJUNCTION

Two simple statements joined by a connective to form a compound statement are known as a **conjunction**. Each of the component statements is called a **conjunct**. For example:

Julio is here, and Juan is here.

Which we symbolize like this:

p & q

The grammatical conjunction *and* is one of several terms that can express logical conjunction. Others include *but, yet, nevertheless, while, also,* and *moreover*. In propositional logic, all these are logically equivalent; they are therefore properly symbolized by the ampersand (&). *Caution:* Make sure the connective really is conjoining two distinct statements and not a set of compound nouns as in "We went to Jack's bar *and* grill" or "Juanita *and* Maria were a team."

To identify the possible truth values of a conjunction, we can create a **truth table,** which is just a graphic way of displaying all the possibilities. Here's the truth table for the conjunction *p & q*:

p	*q*	*p & q*
T	T	T
T	F	F
F	T	F
F	F	F

Above the line in the table, you see a column for each of the component statements and the conjunction itself. The Ts and Fs below the line are abbreviations for true and false. The first two columns of Ts and Fs represent the four possible sets of truth values for the variables. The table shows, in other words, that there are only four combinations of truth values for the pair of variables *p* and *q*: T T, T F, F T, and F F. These are the only combinations possible for a conjunction, which is a two-variable compound.

The last column of Ts and Fs (under *p & q*) shows the truth values for the conjunction given the four possible combinations of truth values of the pair of variables. This means that if you plug into the conjunction every possible pair of truth values, the conjunction will yield only these four truth values: T, F, F, and F.

In ordinary language, this is what each of the rows is saying:

Row 1: When *p* is true and *q* is true, *p & q* is true.
Row 2: When *p* is true and *q* is false, *p & q* is false.

Row 3: When p is false and q is true, p & q is false.
Row 4: When p is false and q is false, p & q is false.

Maybe you've already guessed (by studying the truth table) an important fact about the truth value of a conjunction: *If just one statement in the conjunction is false, the whole conjunction is false; only if both conjuncts are true is the whole conjunction true.* The previous truth table reflects this state of affairs. In the table, we see that p & q is true only when p is true and q is true (in the first row)—and that p & q is false whenever at least one of the component statements is false (in the other three rows). This should make perfect sense to you because in everyday speech, if one-half of a conjunction is false, we would normally regard the *whole* conjunction as false.

It's a good idea to remember the exact sequence of Ts and Fs in the first two columns of the previous truth table. That way you won't have to guess to make sure you include every possible combination of truth values. The first few columns in any truth table are usually entered automatically as guides.

PENGUINS ARE BLACK AND WHITE.
SOME OLD TV SHOWS ARE BLACK AND WHITE.
THEREFORE, SOME PENGUINS ARE OLD TV SHOWS.

—GLASBERGEN

Logic: another thing that penguins aren't very good at.

© 2002 by Randy Glasbergen.

DISJUNCTION

In a conjunction we assert that p and q are both true and that if just one conjunct is false, the whole conjunction is false. But in a **disjunction**, we assert that either p or q is true (though both might be) and that even if one of the statements is false, the whole disjunction is still true. Each statement in a disjunction is called a **disjunct**. For example:

Either Joan is angry, or Ann is serene.

which we symbolize as

$p \lor q$

or

Either Joan or Ann will row the boat.

which we also symbolize as

$p \lor q$

The symbol for disjunction ($\lor$) is called a wedge, which is roughly equivalent to the word *or*. The word *unless* is also sometimes used in place of *or* to form a disjunction, as in "I will go to the movies, unless I stay home." The words either and neither usually signal the beginning of a disjunction.

The truth table for a disjunction looks like this:

p	q	$p \lor q$
T	T	T
T	F	T
F	T	T
F	F	F

The table shows us that $p \lor q$ is true in every possible combination of Ts and Fs—except one, where both p and q are false (in the last row). This situation just reflects the fact that for a disjunction to be true, only one of the disjuncts must be true. The disjunction here, for example, is true if (1) Joan is angry or (2) Ann is serene or (3) Joan is angry and Ann is serene.

An important point to keep in mind is that in English the word "or" has two meanings. It can mean "one or the other, or both," which is called the *inclusive* sense. In this sense, $p \lor q$ means "p or q or both" ("If he's sick or tired, he won't go jogging"). But "or" can also mean "either but not both," which is called the *exclusive* sense. In the exclusive sense, $p \lor q$ means "p or q but not both" ("Either the baby is a boy or a girl"). Standard practice in logic is to assume the inclusive sense when dealing with disjunctions. This approach is reflected in the truth table for a disjunction, and it simplifies the evaluation of disjunctive arguments. It has no effect on our evaluation of disjunctive syllogisms (discussed in Chapter 3); they would be valid forms regardless of whether the disjunction was construed as inclusive or exclusive. Look:

> *Either* p *or* q.
> *Not* p.
> *Therefore,* q.

In the disjunctive syllogism, one of the disjuncts is denied, so the argument is valid in any case. But if one of the disjuncts is affirmed, the argument is invalid when the disjunction is inclusive:

> *Either* p *or* q.
> p.
> *Therefore, not*-q.

Obviously, if the disjunction means "p or q or both," then by affirming p we cannot conclude not-q.

If we know that the disjuncts in a disjunctive premise really are exclusive options ("either a boy or a girl"), then we can safely assume the exclusive meaning of "or" and examine the argument accordingly. Otherwise it's safest to stick to the inclusive sense.

"Logic is not a body of doctrine, but a mirror-image of the world. Logic is transcendental."

—LUDWIG WITTGENSTEIN

Arguments We Have Known and Loved

Virtually every field has its share of well-worn arguments used to establish this theory or that proposition. But the discipline of philosophy—because it is, well, philosophy—is studded from end to end with influential arguments, including some especially famous ones.

If all that exists is matter in motion, then there are no disembodied spirits.
All that exists is matter in motion.
Therefore, there are no disembodied spirits.

Whatever begins to exist has a cause.
The universe began to exist.
Therefore, the universe had a cause, namely God.

There is unnecessary evil in the world.
If there were an all-powerful, all-knowing, all-good being, there would be no unnecessary evil in the world.
Therefore, there is no all-powerful, all-knowing, all-good being.

If it's true that all our actions are determined by an indefinitely long chain of prior events, then people cannot perform free actions.
It's true that all our actions are determined by an indefinitely long chain of prior events.
Therefore, people cannot perform free actions.

We can't be certain that we are not dreaming.
If we can't be certain that we are not dreaming, we cannot be certain that what we sense is real.
If we cannot be certain that what we sense is real, we cannot acquire knowledge through sense experience.
Therefore, we cannot acquire knowledge through sense experience.

NEGATION

A negation is the denial of a statement, which we indicate with the word "not" or a term that means the same thing. For example, the negation of the statement "The price of eggs in China is steep" is

The price of eggs in China is not steep.

or

It is not the case that the price of eggs in China is steep.

or

It is false that the price of eggs in China is steep.

Assuming we use *p* to represent the foregoing statement, here's how we would symbolize its negation:

~*p*

The symbol ~ is called a "tilde," and when we state ~*p* aloud, we say "not-*p*." When it appears in front of a statement, it indicates the reversal of the statement's truth value. A true statement becomes false; a false statement becomes true. One interesting consequence of this reversal is that a *double negation* is the same thing as *no* negation. For example, take the foregoing negation ("The price of eggs in China is not steep"). If you negate this negation ("It is not the case that the price of eggs in China is not steep") you end up with the positive statement, "The price of eggs in China is steep." The truth table for a negation explains why such reversals can happen:

p	~*p*
T	F
F	T

CONDITIONAL

Remember conditional statements? We looked at them when we discussed valid and invalid argument forms (*modus ponens*, denying the antecedent, etc.). The basic form of a conditional is "if . . . then . . ." For example: "If the cat is on the mat, then the rat will stay home." Symbolized, a conditional looks like this: *p* → *q*, where an arrow represents the connective. Recall also that in a conditional, the first part (*p*) is the antecedent, and the second part (*q*) is the consequent.

Notice that a conditional asserts only that if the antecedent is true, then the consequent must be true. It does not assert that the antecedent is actually true or that the consequent is actually true—but only that under specified conditions a certain state of affairs will be actual.

At first, you may find that the truth table for conditionals seems a little odd. But it makes good sense when you think about it:

p	*q*	*p* → *q*
T	T	T
T	F	F
F	T	T
F	F	T

The table shows that a conditional is false in only one situation—when the antecedent is true and the consequent is false. Put more precisely, a conditional statement is false if and only if its antecedent is true and its consequent is false. In all other possible combinations of truth values, a conditional is true—and this is the part that may strike you as odd.

Let's take each of the four combinations in turn and see how they work in this conditional statement: "If George is paid a dollar, then he'll jump out the window." The question we can ask is this: "Under what circumstances is the conditional statement (the whole statement, antecedent and consequent together) true?" Well, it should be clear that if George is indeed paid a dollar, and if he does jump out the window, then the whole conditional would be true. This is the situation in the first row of the truth table.

What about the last row—what if the antecedent is false and the consequent is false? If it is false that George is paid a dollar, and it's false that he jumps out the window, there is no reason to think that the conditional itself is false. George could reasonably assert that the conditional statement isn't false if he isn't paid a dollar and doesn't jump out the window.

George could also reasonably assert that the conditional isn't false even when the antecedent is false and the consequent is true (the situation in the third row). If George isn't paid a dollar, and he still jumps out the window, that doesn't prove that the conditional is false.

This path brings us back to the fact that a conditional statement is false *only* when the antecedent is true and the consequent is false.

Conditional statements can be expressed in ways other than the if-then configuration, the standard form. Here are some conditionals in various patterns with each one paired with the standard-form version:

1. You will fall off that ladder if you're not careful.
   If you're not careful, you will fall off that ladder.
2. Gregory will excel in school, provided that he studies hard.
   If Gregory studies hard, then he will excel in school.
3. Jenna would not have wrecked the car if she had not tried to beat that light.
   If Jenna had not tried to beat that light, she would not have wrecked the car.
4. I'll ride the bus only if I'm late.
   If I ride the bus, then I'm late.
5. Whenever I think, I get a headache.
   If I think, I get a headache.
6. I will walk the dog unless it's raining.
   If it's not raining, I will walk the dog.

Among these patterns, pair 4 and pair 6 are likely to cause you the most trouble. In pair 4, "only if" is the troublesome term. Just remember that "only if" introduces the *consequent* of a conditional. So in "I'll ride the bus only if I'm

> "The art of reasoning becomes of first importance. In this line antiquity has left us the finest models for imitation."
> —THOMAS JEFFERSON

☑ Statements and Connectives

- A simple statement, or claim, is one that does not contain any other statements as constituents. A compound statement is one composed of at least two simple statements.
- Logical connectives

    Conjunction (and): & If just one statement in a conjunction is false, the whole conjunction is false.
    Disjunction (or): v A disjunction is true even if one of the disjuncts is false.
    Negation (not): ~ A negation "reverses" the truth value of any statement.
    Conditional (if-then): → A conditional is false if and only if its antecedent is true and its consequent is false.

- Words used in conditionals

    if—introduces the antecedent; If p, then $q = p \rightarrow q$
    only if—introduces the consequent; p only if $q = p \rightarrow q$
    provided—introduces the antecedent; p provided $q = q \rightarrow p$
    unless—introduces the antecedent; p unless $q = {\sim}q \rightarrow p$
    whenever—introduces antecedent; whenever p, $q = p \rightarrow q$

late," "only if" indicates that the consequent is "I'm late." So the antecedent is "If I ride the bus." You have to move "if" to the front of the antecedent to put the statement in standard form. In pair 6, "unless" is the sticking point. You need to understand that "unless" introduces the antecedent and means "if not." So here "unless it's raining" becomes "if it's not raining" in the antecedent position.

Because of such variations in conditional statements, it's important to translate conditionals into standard form before you try to assess their validity. To do that, you must identify the antecedent and consequent and put them in proper order (antecedent before consequent).

Exercise 6.1

Identify each of the following statements as a conjunction, disjunction, or conditional; identify its component statements; and indicate the symbol used to represent the connective.

* 1. The Democrats raised taxes, and the Republicans cut programs.
  2. Either I walk home, or I drive Ralph's car.
  3. If the Yankees win, they will be in the World Series.
  4. It is not the case that the Yankees won.
* 5. If Taslima can read your mind, then you're in trouble.
  6. The newspaper ad was either misleading, or it was meant as a joke.
* 7. If God is all-powerful, then he can prevent evil in the world.
  8. He supported the revolution, and he was arrested without being charged.

Exercise 6.2

Translate each of the following statements into symbolic form. Use the letters in parentheses to represent each component statement. (Assume that the letters stand for positive statements so that a negated statement is indicated by adding a ~ in front of a letter.)

* 1. Either Herman does his homework, or he goofs off. (p, q)
  2. If Herman does his homework, he will have time to go to the party. (s, t)
  3. It is not the case that Hans had access to the murder weapon. (a)
* 4. People die, but books live forever. (e, f)
  5. Aiming that loaded gun at someone is not a good idea. (c)
  6. Provided Alex returns the money, he will not be prosecuted. (x, y)
  7. Human cloning will become widespread, unless the government interferes. (p, q)
* 8. He will not benefit from instruction, and he will not learn on his own. (g, h)
  9. Buffalo gets a lot of snow in winter, and everybody hates it. (j, k)
  10. His tampering with the judicial system is not appropriate. (b)
  11. You will eventually discover the correct formula if you work systematically. (x, y)
  12. He's either a nut or a brilliant eccentric. (p, q)
  13. If Socrates is a man, he is mortal. (d, e)
* 14. It is not the case that the zoo won't accept any more mammals. (p)
  15. Either disembodied spirits exist, or psychic hoaxes are rampant. (s, t)
  16. Mickey Mouse wanted to get married, but Minnie demurred. (p, q)

Exercise 6.3

Indicate which of the following statements are true and which are false.

  1. Dogs are mammals v Snakes are marsupials
* 2. Alligators are reptiles & Dogs are reptiles

   3. ~ Dogs are reptiles & ~ Alligators are mammals
   4. Dogs can bark → Dogs can talk
   5. Dogs can talk → Dogs are reptiles
 * 6. ~ Dogs are mammals v Snakes are reptiles
   7. ~ Alligators are reptiles → Alligators are mammals
 * 8. Alligators can bark & ~ Dogs are reptiles
   9. ~ ~ Dogs are mammals v Snakes are reptiles
  10. ~ ~ Dogs are mammals → ~ ~ Snakes are reptiles

Exercise 6.4

Indicate which of the following symbolized statements are true and which are false. Assume that the variables a, b, and c are true, and p, q, and r are false.

   1. $a \& p$
 * 2. $b \lor r$
   3. $c \to q$
   4. $\sim b \lor c$
 * 5. $\sim b \to \sim q$
   6. $a \& \sim q$
   7. $b \lor \sim p$
   8. $a \& c$
   9. $b \to \sim c$
 * 10. $p \to \sim r$

Exercise 6.5

Translate each of the symbolic statements in Exercise 6.4 into a statement in English. Assume that the letters stand for positive statements. Answers are provided for 2, 5, and 10.

Exercise 6.6

Translate each of the following statements into symbolic form. Assume that the letters you use stand for positive statements.

   1. If Joshua fought the battle of Jericho, then the walls must have come tumbling down.
 * 2. Either democracy is losing ground in the United States, or it is being enhanced in Third World countries.
   3. Either the ancient Greek temples were built by ancient Greeks, or they were built by Romans who imitated the Greeks.

4. The Egyptian pyramids were not built by ancient alien visitors from space, and they certainly were not built by Egyptians taught by alien visitors from space.

* 5. Science will never triumph over religion unless science can offer a spiritual experience.

6. If World War II was a just war, then the Gulf War was a just war.

7. I will fly to Detroit, but I will not meet you in Dallas.

8. It is not the case that philosophy is dead, and it is not true that science has replaced it.

* 9. Provided I pass my logic course, I will finally be able to fathom political arguments.

10. The federal deficit is out of control, but most Americans are not worried.

Checking for Validity

Now you're ready to put what you've learned about truth tables to use in determining the validity of arguments. The truth-table test of validity is based on an elementary fact about validity that you've already encountered: *It's impossible for a valid argument to have true premises and a false conclusion.* So any procedure that allows us to easily check if the premises are true and the conclusion is false will help us test an argument for validity. Truth tables can do this. Devising truth tables for arguments, then, can reveal the underlying structure—the form—of the arguments, even those that are fairly complex.

SIMPLE ARGUMENTS

Let's start by analyzing a very simple argument involving a conjunction:

Ducks have webbed feet.
Ducks have feathers.
Therefore, ducks have webbed feet and ducks have feathers.

We symbolize the argument like this:

p
q
∴ *p & q*

Here we have each premise and the conclusion represented by variables, giving us a good look at the argument's logical form. The symbol ∴ indicates that a conclusion follows (it's often translated as "therefore"). The argument is, of course, valid—a fact that you can quickly see without the aid of a truth table. But it makes for a simple illustration:

p	q	$p \,\&\, q$
T	T	T
T	F	F
F	T	F
F	F	F

This truth table is a repeat of the one we looked at in the section on conjunctions. The top line of the table shows the argument's two premises and its conclusion with their truth values listed below. Like all truth tables, this one shows every possible combination of truth values for the premises and conclusion.

When dealing with simple arguments, the first two columns of a truth table are guide columns in which the variables, or letters, of the argument are listed, followed by a column for each premise and then a column for the conclusion. In this case, though, the guide columns happen to be identical to the premise columns, so we won't repeat them.

REVIEW NOTES

☑ Common Argument Forms Symbolized

MODUS PONENS (VALID)

$p \to q$
p
$\therefore q$

MODUS TOLLENS (VALID)

$p \to q$
$\sim q$
$\therefore \sim p$

DENYING THE ANTECEDENT
(INVALID)

$p \to q$
$\sim p$
$\therefore \sim q$

AFFIRMING THE CONSEQUENT
(INVALID)

$p \to q$
q
$\therefore p$

HYPOTHETICAL SYLLOGISM
(VALID)

$p \to q$
$q \to r$
$\therefore p \to r$

DISJUNCTIVE SYLLOGISM
(VALID)

$p \lor q$
$\sim p$
$\therefore q$

Now we can ask the big question: "Does the truth table show (in any row) a state of affairs in which the premises of the argument are true and the conclusion false?" If we can find even *one* instance of this arrangement, we will have shown that the argument is invalid. Remember that we are trying to judge the *validity* of an argument, which is a matter of argument *form*. So if we can discover that it's *possible* for a particular argument form to have true premises and a false conclusion, we will know without further investigation that the argument is invalid. Not only that, but we will know that *any* argument of the same pattern is invalid. The truth table can tell us definitively whether an argument is invalid because the table includes every possible combination of truth values. If the truth table doesn't reveal a situation in which the argument has true premises and a false conclusion, then the argument is valid.

As you can see in the previous table, there is no row in which the premises are true (T T) and the conclusion false (F). Therefore, the argument is valid.

Here's a slightly more complex argument:

> *If the icebergs melt, the lowlands will flood.*
> *The icebergs will not melt.*
> *Therefore, the lowlands will not flood.*

You should recognize this argument as an instance of denying the antecedent. Here it is symbolized, with negation and conditional connectives:

$p \rightarrow q$
$\sim p$
$\therefore \sim q$

And here's the argument's truth table:

p	q	$p \rightarrow q$	$\sim p$	$\sim q$
T	T	T	F	F
T	F	F	F	T
F	T	T	T	F
F	F	T	T	T

You can begin checking for validity in a couple of different ways. You can first inspect all rows that have a false conclusion and then see if the premises in that row are true, indicating an invalid argument. Or you can zero in on rows showing all true premises and then check to see if they have false conclusions. In this case, the third row tells the tale: Both premises are true and the conclusion is false. So the argument is invalid, and we need not check any other rows.

> "Logic takes care of itself; all we have to do is to look and see how it does it."
> —LUDWIG WITTGENSTEIN

As we saw earlier, the truth value of a compound statement depends on the truth value of its components. That's why it's a good idea to start out with guide columns in a truth table. The truth value of these variables (letters) determines the truth value of statements that are comprised of the variables. The truth value of these compound units in turn determines the truth value of any larger compound units.

In the truth table just given, the truth value of ~p is the contradictory of p, and the truth value of ~q is the contradictory of q. So whatever the truth value of a statement, the tilde (~) reverses it, from true to false or false to true.

Now let's try this one:

> *Either we fight for freedom or we give in to tyranny.*
> *We won't fight for freedom.*
> *Therefore, we will give in to tyranny.*

FURTHER THOUGHT

From Here to Absurdity

One kind of powerful argument that you frequently encounter is known as *reductio ad absurdum* (reduction to absurdity). The idea behind it is that if the contradictory (negation) of a statement leads to an absurdity or falsehood, then the negation of the statement is false and the statement itself must be true. You must accept the statement because denying it gets you into logical trouble. So if you want to demonstrate that a statement is true (or false), you assume the statement's negation and show that it leads to an absurd or false statement. Here's the form of this type of argument:

$$p$$
$$p \rightarrow q$$
$$\sim q$$
$$\therefore \sim p$$

In plain English, this says: Let's suppose that p is true. If p is true, then q must be true. But there's no way that q can be true. (Or, q being true is absurd.) So it must not be the case that p is true. For example:

> Suppose that water cannot freeze.
> If water cannot freeze, then ice cannot exist.
> But obviously ice does exist.
> Therefore, water can freeze.

Symbolized, it looks like this:

$p \lor q$
$\sim p$
$\therefore q$

And here is its truth table:

p	q	$p \lor q$	$\sim p$	q
T	T	T	F	T
T	F	T	F	F
F	T	T	T	T
F	F	F	T	F

Is this argument valid? To find out, we need to check the table for any row that shows true premises and a false conclusion. The third row is the only one in which both premises are true—but the conclusion is also true. So this argument is valid.

TRICKY ARGUMENTS

Arguments can get more complicated when variables and connectives are intricately combined into larger compounds and when the number of variables increases. In both these situations, truth tables can help you unravel the complexities. Let's examine an argument that has both these wrinkles. We'll go right to the symbolized form:

$p \rightarrow \sim(q \And r)$
p
$\therefore \sim(q \And r)$

Notice in these premises the use of parentheses to join variables. The parentheses enable us to symbolize arguments more precisely and to avoid confusion. In math, there is an obvious difference between $2 \times (3 + 4)$, which equals 14, and $(2 \times 3) + 4$, which equals 10. Likewise, there is a crucial difference between $p \rightarrow \sim(q \And r)$ and $(p \rightarrow \sim q) \And r$. The former symbolization would express a conditional such as "If it rains tomorrow, then Alice and Eric will not go to the movies." But the latter symbolization would represent a very different conditional, such as "If it rains tomorrow, then Alice will not go to the movies, and Eric will go to the movies." Such differences, of course, can affect the truth values of a statement and require a different truth table.

Here's a distinction involving parentheses that's worth committing to memory. Consider these two statements:

~(q & r)
It is not the case that Leo sings the blues and Fats sings the blues.

~q & ~r
Leo does not sing the blues, and Fats does not sing the blues.

The first statement asserts that it is not the case that *both* Leo and Fats sing the blues. That is, it's not true that Leo and Fats are concurrently in the habit of singing the blues. Maybe Leo sings the blues, and Fats doesn't, or vice versa. On the other hand, the second statement says that Leo doesn't sing the blues and neither does Fats. If we hope that at least one of these guys sings the blues, we're out of luck.

Here's another distinction worth knowing. Look at these two statements:

~(q v r)
It is not the case that either Leo sings the blues or Fats sings the blues.

~q v ~r
Either Leo does not sing the blues or Fats does not sing the blues.

The first statement says that neither Leo nor Fats sings the blues. The second statement says that it is not the case that Leo *and* Fats sing the blues.

Correctly symbolizing statements with parentheses is a straightforward business, but it requires close attention to what's being said. Your best clues to where to insert parentheses come from the words *either* and *neither*, conjunction and disjunction words such as *and* and *or*, and the punctuation of the sentences. Notice how the sentence clues in the following statements inform how the statements are symbolized:

If the gods intervene, then neither peace nor war can change the destiny of the nation.

We can symbolize the statements with the following variables:

p—The gods intervene.
q—Peace can change the destiny of the nation.
r—War can change the destiny of the nation.

$p \rightarrow \sim(q \text{ v } r)$

And:

Either Jay Leno is funny or the show is rigged, or the network has made a bad investment.

p—Jay Leno is funny.
q—The show is rigged.
r—The network has made a bad investment.

(*p* v *q*) v *r*

Arguments like these that have three variables instead of two may look formidable, but they're not. The steps you use to check the validity of a three-variable argument are the same ones you apply in two-variable arguments. You devise a truth table, calculate truth values, and check for true premises with a false conclusion. The truth table, of course, has an additional guide column for the third variable, and there are more rows to accommodate the larger number of possible true-false combinations. In a two-variable table there are four rows; in a three-variable table there are eight and thus eight combinations of truth values. Notice how the guide columns are laid out:

p	*q*	*r*
T	T	T
T	T	F
T	F	T
T	F	F
F	T	T
F	T	F
F	F	T
F	F	F

> "Reason in man is rather like God in the world."
> —THOMAS AQUINAS

To remember the truth values in each guide column, think: The first column is four Ts, then four Fs; the second column is alternating pairs of truth values beginning with T T; and the third column is alternating Ts and Fs starting with T.

Now let's test this argument for validity:

If Billy shot the sheriff but he didn't shoot the deputy, then he's guilty of only one crime. But it's not true that he shot the sheriff but didn't shoot the deputy. Therefore, it's not the case that he's guilty of only one crime.

p—Billy shot the sheriff.
q—He shot the deputy.
r—He's guilty of only one crime.

(*p* & ~*q*) → *r*
~(*p* & ~*q*)
∴ ~*r*

And here's the argument's truth table:

	1 p	2 q	3 r	4 p & $\sim q$	5 $(p$ & $\sim q) \to r$	6 $\sim(p$ & $\sim q)$	7 $\sim r$
1	T	T	T	F	T	T	F
2	T	T	F	F	T	T	T
3	T	F	T	T	T	F	F
4	T	F	F	T	F	F	T
5	F	T	T	F	T	T	F
6	F	T	F	F	T	T	T
7	F	F	T	F	T	T	F
8	F	F	F	F	T	T	T

This truth table has seven columns, and you can guess why six of them are there: The first three are the guide columns, and the last three are for the two premises and the conclusion. Column 4 is there because it simplifies the assigning of truth values to columns 5, 6, and 7—it's a component of the two premises. If we wanted, we could add more columns for other components such as $\sim r$, if the additions would make creating the truth table easier.

The truth values for p & $\sim q$ are, of course, determined by the truth values of its conjuncts. If just one conjunct is false, the conjunction is false (as it is in rows 1, 2, and 5 through 8). Only in rows 3 and 4 is the conjunction true. The truth value of the conditional $(p$ & $\sim q) \to r$ is based on the truth values of $(p$ & $\sim q)$ and r, with the conditional being false only when $(p$ & $\sim q)$ is true and r is false (row 4). In all other rows the conditional is true. The truth value of the premise $\sim(p$ & $\sim q)$ is the contradictory of the truth value for $(p$ & $\sim q)$. Likewise, the truth value of $\sim r$ is the contradictory of r.

Is there any row in which the premises are true and the conclusion false? Yes, that's the situation in rows 1, 5, and 7, so the argument is invalid.

STREAMLINED EVALUATION

With truth tables, you can accurately assess the validity of any propositional argument, even some fairly complicated ones. But as the arguments get more complicated (when they have more than two or three variables, for example), you may want a more efficient technique for calculating validity. Here's a good alternative method—one that just happens to be easier to master if you already know the ins and outs of truth tables.

In this approach—what we'll call the *short method*—we don't bother to produce a whole truth table, but we do try to construct some truth-table rows (maybe only one if we're lucky). The basic strategy is based on the same fact we relied on in the truth-table test: It's impossible for a valid argument to have true premises and a false conclusion. So we try to discover if there's a way to make the conclusion false and the premises true by assigning various truth values to the argument's components. That is, we try to prove that the argument is invalid. If we can do this, then we'll have the proof we need.

Let's try the short method on this argument:

~q
p → (q v r)
r
∴ p

First we write out the argument so that the premises and conclusion are in a single row:

$$\text{~q} \qquad p \to (q \text{ v } r) \qquad r \qquad p$$

Now we examine the conclusion. What truth value must we assign to it to ensure that it's false? Obviously the answer is *false*—because there is only one variable in the conclusion, and the conclusion must be false. So we label *p* with an F in the conclusion and everyplace else in the argument. Then our row looks like this:

$$\text{~q} \qquad \underset{\text{F}}{p \to (q \text{ v } r)} \qquad r \qquad \underset{\text{F}}{p}$$

Just one caution: As you work through the short method, you must remember that the truth values you mark under the argument row *apply to the variables (letters) only, not the premises.* To avoid any confusion, if you want you can write the truth values for the premises *above* the argument row. In this way you can indicate either (1) the premise truth values that you're trying for or (2) the premise truth values that result from your truth value assignments.

REVIEW NOTES

☑ The Short Method: Step by Step

1. Write out the symbolized argument in a single row.
2. Assign truth values to the variables in the conclusion to make the conclusion false. (Write the appropriate Ts or Fs below the row.) Assign these truth values to the same variables elsewhere.
3. Consistently assign truth values to variables in the premises. Assign truth values first to premises where specific truth values are "locked in."
4. Try to make assignments that yield a false conclusion and true premises. If you can, the argument is invalid. If not, the argument is valid.

In this argument we can also tell right away that *r must* be true because it's a premise in the argument, and we're trying to see if we can make all the premises true (and the conclusion false). Then we have:

~q	$p \rightarrow (q \lor r)$	r	p
F	T	T	F

Now we look at the first premise because it will be easy to determine its truth value. Since the first premise must be true, and it's a negation, *q* must be false. This fills out the whole argument with truth values:

~q	$p \rightarrow (q \lor r)$	r	p
F	F F T	T	F

We've shown then that the first and third premises are true. And we can now see that the second premise must also be true: The disjunction ($q \lor r$) is true because one of the disjuncts is true (*r*). And the conditional (made up of *p* and the disjunction) is true because a false antecedent (*p*) and a true consequent ($q \lor r$) yields a true conditional.

We have thus shown that this argument can have a false conclusion and true premises—the sign of an invalid argument.

Now let's try the short method on this argument:

$p \rightarrow q$

$q \rightarrow r$

$\sim r$

$\therefore \sim p$

$p \rightarrow q$	$q \rightarrow r$	~r	~p

Again, we start with the conclusion. Since the conclusion is a negation ($\sim p$), we know that there's only one way that the conclusion could be false—if *p* is true. We then must make *p* true everyplace else in the argument:

$p \rightarrow q$	$q \rightarrow r$	~r	~p
T			T

We now turn to the first premise, a simple conditional. The antecedent (*p*) is true, which means that if the conditional is to be true, its consequent (*q*) cannot be false (a true antecedent and a false consequent yields a false conditional). So we're forced to assign these truth values:

$p \rightarrow q$	$q \rightarrow r$	~r	~p
T T	T		T

That leaves just *r* to deal with. Again we are forced to assign a truth value to it. Because the premise is a negation, and it must be true, *r* has to be false. But if *r* is false, the second premise (another simple conditional) must be false (truth values for the premises are shown *above* the argument row):

T	F	T	F
$p \rightarrow q$	$q \rightarrow r$	~r	~p
T T	T F	F	T

So we see that since there is only one way for the conclusion to be false, we are locked into truth values that prevented us from having all true premises. We simply cannot consistently assign truth values to this argument that will give us a false conclusion and true premises. Therefore, this argument is valid.

In using the short method like this, your overall goal is to see if you can prove invalidity in the most efficient way possible. You want to get the job done without a lot of unnecessary steps. The best strategy for doing this is to look for truth value assignments *that cannot be any other way* given the truth value assignments in the conclusion. That is, focus on premises with assignments that are "locked into" the argument by the truth values you've given the conclusion. Make assignments in those premises first, regardless of which premise you start with.

In the foregoing arguments, the conclusions could be made false in only one way, and that made the rest of the work easier. But sometimes a conclusion can be made false in more than one way. In such cases, your strategy should be to try each possibility—each way that the conclusion can be false—until you get what you're after: an argument with true premises and a false conclusion. As soon as you get it, stop. You've proven that the argument form is invalid, and there's no reason to continue making assignments. If you try all the possibilities and still can't prove invalidity, the argument is valid.

Let's take a look at one of these multiple-possibility arguments:

$p \rightarrow q$
$q \vee r$
~q
∴ p & r

$p \rightarrow q$	$q \vee r$	~q	p & r

In this argument the conclusion is a conjunction, which means that it can be made false by any one of these combinations of truth values: F-T, T-F, and F-F. If we make separate rows for each of these possibilities, they look like this:

	$p \rightarrow q$	$q \vee r$	~q	p & r
1	F	T		F T
2	T	F	~q	T F
3	F	F	~q	F F

So can we consistently assign truth values to make the premises true and the conclusion false in any of these rows? We can forget about row 2 because in the first premise, q must be true (to avoid making the conditional false). And if q is true, the third premise would be false. Likewise, we must throw out row 3 because q again must be true (to ensure that the disjunction is true). And if true, we run into the same problem we have in row 2—the third premise must be false. Row 1, though, works. To make the third premise true, we must make q false. And when we assign a truth value of false to q in the rest of the argument, we make the premises true and the conclusion false. Therefore, the argument is invalid.

Exercise 6.7

Construct a truth table for each of the statements in Exercise 6.3. Answers are provided for 2, 6, and 8.

Exercise 6.8

Construct a truth table for each of the following arguments and indicate whether the argument is valid or invalid.

1. $a \& b$
   $\therefore a$

* 2. $p \rightarrow q$
   p
   $\therefore q$

3. $p \lor q$
   p
   $\therefore \sim q$

4. $p \rightarrow q$
   $\sim p$
   $\therefore q$

5. $a \& b$
   $\sim a$
   $\therefore b$

6. $p \rightarrow q$
   $q \rightarrow r$
   $\therefore q$

* 7. $p \rightarrow q$
   $\sim q \& r$
   $\therefore r$

8. $a \lor (b \& c)$
   $\sim(b \& c)$
   $\therefore a$

9. $x \rightarrow y$
   $y \rightarrow z$
   $\therefore x \rightarrow z$

10. $p \rightarrow q$
    $\therefore p \rightarrow (p \ \& \ q)$

11. $a \rightarrow b$
    $b \rightarrow c$
    $\therefore (b \ \& \ c) \ \text{v} \ (a \ \& \ b)$

12. $a \ \text{v} \ (b \rightarrow c)$
    $b \ \& \ {\sim}c$
    $\therefore {\sim}a$

13. $(p \ \text{v} \ q) \rightarrow (p \ \& \ q)$
    $p \ \& \ q$
    $\therefore p \ \text{v} \ q$

* 14. $p \rightarrow q$
    ${\sim}(q \ \text{v} \ r)$
    $\therefore {\sim}p$

15. $d \rightarrow e$
    $e \ \text{v} \ f$
    e
    $\therefore d \ \& \ f$

16. $(p \rightarrow q) \rightarrow (p \rightarrow r)$
    ${\sim}(p \rightarrow q)$
    ${\sim}r$
    $\therefore p$

17. $(d \ \text{v} \ e) \rightarrow f$
    $f \rightarrow (d \ \& \ e)$
    $\therefore (d \ \& \ e) \rightarrow (d \ \text{v} \ e)$

18. ${\sim}(d \ \& \ e)$
    $e \ \text{v} \ f$
    $\therefore {\sim}d \ \& \ e$

19. $d \ \& \ ({\sim}e \rightarrow {\sim}d)$
    $f \rightarrow {\sim}e$
    $\therefore f$

20. $d \ \text{v} \ {\sim}e$
    $f \rightarrow e$
    $\therefore d \rightarrow {\sim}f$

Exercise 6.9

For each of the following arguments, translate it into symbols, construct a truth table, and determine its validity.

1. If there is no rain soon, the crops will die. If the crops die, there will be no food for the coming winter. The crops will not die. Therefore, there will be rain soon.

2. If we give kidnappers the money that they demand, then further kidnappings will be encouraged. If we do not give kidnappers the money that they demand, the kidnappers will kill the hostages. We will not give kidnappers the money that they demand. Therefore, the kidnappers will kill the hostages.

* 3. Jake is the plumber or Jake is the carpenter. Jake is not the carpenter. Therefore, Jake is the plumber.

4. "Men, it is assumed, act in economic matters only in response to pecuniary compensation or to force. Force in the modern society is largely, although by no means completely, obsolete. So only pecuniary compensation remains of importance." [John Kenneth Galbraith, *The New Industrial State*]

5. If the lake freezes, then the lake-effect snow will stop. If the lake-effect snow stops, the streets will be easier to plow. Therefore, the streets will be easier to plow.

6. Either Emilio walks or he takes the train. And either Joann takes the train or she does not take the train. If Emilio walks, then Joann takes the train. Emilio takes the train. So Joann will not take the train.

7. UN peacekeepers will not attack the local militants, provided that the militants behave themselves. The militants will not make trouble if the UN peacekeepers don't attack. Therefore, UN peacekeepers will not attack the local militants, and the militants will not make trouble.

8. "If then, it is agreed that things are either the result of coincidence or for an end, and these cannot be the result of coincidence or spontaneity, it follows that they must be for an end." [Aristotle, *Physics*]

9. Either there is evidence that women of supernatural powers (i.e., witches) exist, or there is no such evidence. If there is no such evidence, then we have no reason to believe in witches. If there is evidence, we do have reason to believe in witches. There is no such evidence. Therefore, we have no reason to believe in witches.

10. Either the herbal remedy alleviated the symptoms, or the placebo effect alleviated the symptoms. If the placebo effect is responsible for easing the symptoms, then the herbal remedy is worthless. The herbal remedy alleviated the symptoms. So the herbal remedy is not worthless.

* 11. Unless both Mary goes and Henry goes, the party will be a disaster. The party will be a disaster. Therefore, both Mary and Henry will not go.

Exercise 6.10

Use the short method to check the validity of the following arguments in Exercise 6.8: 1, 3, 5, 9, 10, 15, 16, and 18. Write the symbolized argument in one row and assign truth values to each variable. Then above the argument row, assign truth values to the premises and conclusion. Answers are provided for 3, 10, and 15.

KEY WORDS

compound statement	statement
conjunct	simple statement
conjunction	symbolic logic
disjunct	truth table
disjunction	variables
propositional logic	

Summary

- In propositional logic we use symbols to stand for the relationships between statements—that is, to indicate the form of an argument. These relationships are made possible by logical connectives such as conjunction (and), disjunction (or), negation (not), and conditional (If . . . then . . .). Connectives are used in compound statements, each of which is composed of at least two simple statements. A statement is a sentence that can be either true or false.

- To indicate the possible truth values of statements and arguments, we can construct truth tables, a graphic way of displaying all the truth value possibilities.

- A conjunction is false if at least one of its statement components (conjuncts) is false. A disjunction is still true even if one of its component statements (disjuncts) is false. A negation is the denial of a statement. The negation of any statement changes the statement's truth value to its contradictory (false to true and true to false). A conditional statement is false in only one situation—when the antecedent is true and the consequent is false.

- The use of truth tables to determine the validity of an argument is based on the fact that it's impossible for a valid argument to have true premises and a false conclusion. A basic truth table consists of two or more guide columns listing all the truth value possibilities, followed by a column for each premise and the conclusion. We can add other columns to help us determine the truth values of components of the argument.

• You can check the validity of arguments not only with truth tables but also with the short method. In this procedure we try to discover if there is a way to make the conclusion false and the premises true by assigning various truth values to the argument's components.

Field Problems

1. Find three deductive arguments on the Internet or in a college newspaper. Symbolize the arguments and determine the validity of each one by making a truth table.

2. Find a deductive argument in one of your textbooks (excluding this one). Symbolize it and create a truth table to test its validity. Then devise a different argument that uses the same argument form as the one you found.

Self-Assessment Quiz

Answers appear in "Answers to Self-Assessment Quizzes" (Appendix C).

1. What are the four logical connectives used in this chapter? How is each one symbolized?

2. Construct the truth table for each logical connective.

3. Under what circumstances is a conjunction false?

4. Under what circumstances is a conditional false?

5. Which of the following symbolized statements are true and which are false? Assume that *a*, *b*, and *c* are true, and *p*, *q*, and *r* are false.

$c \rightarrow q$

$a \mathbin{\&} {\sim}q$

$a \mathbin{\text{v}} {\sim}c$

6. Put the following statement into symbolic form:

You will go far if you study hard.

7. Put the following statement into symbolic form:

Either the Earth is flat or it is hollow.

8. Construct a truth table for each of the following arguments and indicate whether the argument is valid or invalid.

$p \rightarrow q$
$q \rightarrow r$
$\therefore q$

$p \lor (q \ \& \ r)$
$\sim(q \ \& \ r)$
$\therefore p$

9. Translate this argument into symbols, construct its truth table, and indicate whether the argument is valid.

If the temperature rises, then the water will rise. If the water rises, the dam will break. Either the water rises, or it doesn't rise. The water will not rise. Therefore the dam will not break.

10. Translate this argument into symbols, construct its truth table, and indicate whether the argument is valid.

Either Joe goes to the movie, or Julia goes to the movie. If the movie is Gone with the Wind, *then Julia goes to the movie. So if Joe goes to the movie, the movie is not* Gone with the Wind.

Construct arguments in English for each of the following symbolized arguments.

11. $x \rightarrow y$
    $y \rightarrow z$
    $\therefore x \rightarrow z$
12. $a \rightarrow b$
    $\therefore a \rightarrow (a \ \& \ b)$
13. $a \ \& \ b$
    $\sim b$
    $\therefore a$
14. $(p \lor q) \rightarrow (p \ \& \ q)$
    $p \ \& \ q$
    $\therefore p \lor q$
15. $p \rightarrow q$
    $\sim p$
    $\therefore q$

Use the short method to check the validity of the following arguments. Write out the argument in a single row and assign truth values to each variable.

16. $p \rightarrow q$
    $\sim q$
    $\therefore \sim p$

17. $p \& q$
    $q \rightarrow r$
    $\sim q$
    $\therefore r$

18. $p \rightarrow q$
    $q \rightarrow r$
    $\therefore q \rightarrow r$

19. $p \text{ v } (q \& r)$
    $\sim p$
    $\sim q$
    $\therefore r$

20. $a \rightarrow b$
    $b \rightarrow c$
    $\therefore (b \& c) \text{ v } (a \& b)$

 Integrative Exercises

These exercises pertain to material in Chapters 1–6.

1. What is critical thinking?
2. What is an argument?
3. What are the symbols for the four logical connectives, and what do they mean?
4. True or false: A mere assertion or statement of beliefs constitutes an argument.
5. Can a deductive argument guarantee the truth of its conclusion?

For each of the following arguments, specify the conclusion and premises and indicate any argument indicator words. Symbolize the argument and construct a truth table to determine the argument's validity.

6. If there are no clouds tonight, I will be able to see Venus and you will be able to see Saturn. There will be clouds tonight, so you will not be able to see Saturn.

7. If the bill is passed, the public will demand the resignations of all senators involved. The public, though, will never demand the resignations of an elected official. The bill will not be passed.

8. Either the crippled economy or the sex scandals will drive the prime minister from office. If inflation rises, then we will have a crippled economy. Inflation will not rise. Therefore, the sex scandals will drive the prime minister from office.

9. Jones is either crazy or very shrewd. He definitely isn't very shrewd, so he's not crazy either.

10. I will go to market unless the farmer objects, and I will stay home if the cows are sick. The cows aren't sick, therefore I will go to market.

For each of the following arguments, determine whether it is deductive or inductive, valid or invalid, and strong or weak.

11. Either Ellen is shy or she is not. If her cheeks turn red, she's shy. If they don't turn red, she's not shy. Her cheeks are red. Ellen is shy.

12. Assad graduated from Harvard. If he graduated from Harvard, he's probably very competitive. He's probably very competitive.

13. "And certainly if its essence and power are infinite, its goodness must be infinite, since a thing whose essence is finite has finite goodness." [Roger Bacon, *The Opus Majus*]

14. The comet has appeared in the sky every sixty years for the past four centuries. It will appear in the sky again, right on schedule.

15. Use the short method to check the validity of this argument:

$$a \rightarrow b$$
$$\sim b$$
$$\therefore \sim a$$

16. Use the short method to check the validity of this argument:

$$p \rightarrow q$$
$$p$$
$$\therefore \sim q$$

For each of the following arguments, identify the implicit premise that will make the argument valid.

17. The conflict to combat terrorism involves the killing of human beings. Therefore, the conflict cannot be morally justified.

18. The movie *Harry Potter* is a huge box office success. Obviously it is a great film.

19. Tariq prays constantly. He's sure to succeed in all that he does.

20. Senator Moneybags took a bribe. He therefore should be run out of office.

Writing Assignments

1. In a one-page essay, devise a deductive argument in which you argue for (or against) the idea that freedom of speech or the press should be restricted on college campuses.

2. Select an issue from the following list and write a two-page paper defending a claim pertaining to the issue. Use one or more deductive arguments to make your case.

   - Should there be restrictions on who can speak or what can be said at college graduation ceremonies?
   - Should private clubs be permitted to ban members of the opposite sex from membership?
   - Should "In God We Trust" be removed from U.S. currency?
   - Should there be restrictions on what college professors can say in the courses they teach?

3. Outline the argument in Essay 5 ("More Innocents Die When We Don't Have Capital Punishment") in Appendix A, indicating the premises and the conclusion. Determine whether the argument is deductive or inductive.

4. Study Essay 16 ("Torture: Time for Congress to End the Debate") and Essay 17 ("Torture: Severe Interrogations Work"). Decide which essay presents the stronger arguments, and write a paper defending your view.

Deductive Reasoning:
Categorical Logic

 CHAPTER OBJECTIVES

STATEMENTS AND CLASSES

- Understand how categorical logic differs from propositional logic.
- Learn the definitions of *subject term, predicate term, copula, quantifier, quantity,* and *quality.*
- Memorize the four standard-form categorical statements.

TRANSLATIONS AND STANDARD FORM

- Know how to translate ordinary statements into standard categorical form.
- Know how to translate singular statements into standard form.

DIAGRAMMING CATEGORICAL STATEMENTS

- Be able to construct a Venn diagram for any categorical statement.
- Memorize the Venn diagrams for the four standard-form categorical statements.
- Know how to use Venn diagrams to tell if two statements are, or are not, equivalent.

SIZING UP CATEGORICAL SYLLOGISMS

- Understand the structure of categorical syllogisms.
- Know the definition of *major term, minor term, middle term, major premise,* and *minor premise.*
- Know how to check the validity of a categorical argument by drawing Venn diagrams.

A S WE'VE SEEN, IN PROPOSITIONAL LOGIC THE BASIC UNIT OF OUR concern is the statement. Simple statements make up compound statements joined by logical connectives. And the truth value of a compound statement is a function of the truth values of the *component statements*. This important fact is the reason propositional logic is also called truth-functional logic. In *truth-functional logic* we ignore the deeper relationships among the internal parts of a statement.

Categorical logic is different. The basic unit of concern in categorical logic is the *statement component.* We study the relationships not between statements but between the subject and predicate of a statement.

Both types of reasoning are deductive, and in both our ultimate goal is the evaluation of arguments. In propositional logic this task is made easier with truth tables and truth table–like calculations. In categorical logic the primary tools are diagrams and calculation rules.

In categorical reasoning the statements, or claims, of interest are **categorical statements**—those that make simple assertions about categories, or classes, of things. They say how certain classes of things are, or are not, included in other classes of things. For example: "All cows are herbivores," "No gardeners are plumbers," or "Some businesspeople are cheats." Categorical statements like these play their part without the complexities that arise from conjunctive, disjunctive, or conditional statements.

Like propositional logic, categorical logic is inescapable in daily life. Without thinking much about the process, we often use arguments composed of categorical statements. We may reason, for example, that no pocketknives are things permitted on a commercial airplane because no sharp instruments are things allowed on a commercial airplane, and all pocketknives are sharp instruments. In a real-life situation, we wouldn't state the argument so formally (and awkwardly), and we would probably make one of these premises implicit because it's too obvious to mention. Also, this whole process would likely happen in seconds, with the argument zipping through our heads at top speed.

There are several good reasons why categorical logic—first formulated by Aristotle over two thousand years ago—is still around. Chief among these are that (1) we cannot avoid it and (2) we need it. If so, then learning how to use it well can only help us.

"MEMO: It has come to my attention that every time we solve one problem, we create two more. From now on, all problem solving is forbidden."

© 2001 by Randy Glasbergen.

Statements and Classes

The words in categorical statements that name classes, or categories, of things are called *terms*. Each categorical statement has both a **subject term** and a **predicate term.** For example:

> *All cats are carnivores.*

The subject term here is *cats,* and the predicate term is *carnivores.* The statement says that the class of *cats* is included in the class of *carnivores.* We can express the form of the statement like this:

> *All S are P.*

By convention, S stands for the subject term in a categorical statement; P, the predicate term.

This kind of statement—All S are P—is one of four **standard forms of categorical statements.** Here are all four of them together:

1. All S are P. (All cats are carnivores.)
2. No S are P. (No cats are carnivores.)
3. Some S are P. (Some cats are carnivores.)
4. Some S are not P. (Some cats are not carnivores.)

Standard-form statement 2, "No S are P," asserts that no member of the S class is included in the P class (no members of the class of cats are part of the class of carnivores). Statement 3, "Some S are P," asserts that some members of the S class are also members of the P class (some members of the class of cats are also members of the class of carnivores). Statement 4, "Some S are not P," asserts that some members of the S class are not members of the P class (some members of the class of cats are not members of the class of carnivores).

For the sake of simplicity, the terms in these statements about cats are single words, just nouns naming a class. But subject and predicate terms can also consist of noun phrases and pronouns. Noun phrases are used because several words may be needed to specify a class. Sometimes a noun like cats won't do, but a noun phrase like "cats that live outdoors and hunt mice" will.

In standard-form categorical statements, subject and predicate terms can't be *anything but* nouns, pronouns, and noun phrases. Only nouns, pronouns, and noun phrases can properly designate classes. So the statement "All cats are carnivores" is in standard form, but "All cats are carnivorous" is not.

As you might guess, many categorical statements you'll run into don't strictly fit any of these four patterns. But they should—if you want to easily evaluate the validity of arguments containing these statements. So part of the job of assessing such arguments is translating the categorical statements found "in the wild" into

Aristotle (384–322 B.C.E.), the father of formal logic.

the tamer and clearer configurations of the standard forms. The challenge is to do these translations while being faithful to the meaning of the original.

Now, to accurately translate categorical statements, you need to know more about how they're put together. Categorical statements have four parts and several characteristics expressed in these parts. You already know about two of these parts, the subject term and the predicate term. They're joined together by a third part called the **copula,** a linking verb—either "are" or "are not."

The fourth part is the **quantifier,** a word that expresses the **quantity,** or number, of a categorical statement. The acceptable quantifiers are "all," "no," or "some." The quantifiers "all" and "no" in front of a categorical statement tell us that it's *universal*—it applies to every member of a class. The quantifier "some" at the beginning of a categorical statement says that the statement is *particular*—it applies to at least one member of a class.

Categorical statements can vary not only in quantity, but also in the characteristic of **quality,** being either *affirmative* or *negative*. A categorical statement that *affirms* that a class is entirely or partly included in another class is said to be affirmative in quality. A categorical statement that *denies* that a class is entirely or partly included in another class is said to be negative in quality.

With this technical vocabulary we can describe each of the standard forms of statements noted earlier.

1. All S are P. (All cats are carnivores.)

This standard-form statement has a universal quantity and an affirmative quality. It *affirms* that *all* cats are included in the class of carnivores. So we characterize it as a *universal affirmative* statement, or claim.

2. No *S* are *P*. (No cats are carnivores.)

This one *denies* that *all* cats are included in the class of carnivores. Put another way, the whole class of cats is *excluded* from the class of carnivores. It's a *universal negative* statement.

3. Some *S* are *P*. (Some cats are carnivores.)

This one *affirms* that only *some* cats are included in the class of carnivores. It's a *particular affirmative* statement.

4. Some *S* are not *P*. (Some cats are not carnivores.)

This one *denies* that only *some* cats are included in the class of carnivores. It doesn't refer to the whole class of cats, just as statement 3 doesn't refer to the whole class. But it denies, instead of affirms, that the partial class of cats is included in the class of carnivores. It's a *particular negative* statement.

Here are the four standard forms of categorical statements again with their quality and quantity listed:

A: All *S* are *P*. (universal affirmative)
E: No *S* are *P*. (universal negative)
I: Some *S* are *P*. (particular affirmative)
O: Some *S* are not *P*. (particular negative)

Notice that this time the statements are preceded not by numbers but by the letters A, E, I, and O. These letters are the traditional designations for the four logical forms of categorical statements. We can say then, for example, that this or that statement is an A-statement or an O-statement, indicating the pattern of the arguments in an easy shorthand.

Something important to remember, even if it's obvious: All categorical statements should fit into one of these four standard forms, and all statements that do fit into one of these have the *same* form.

Exercise 7.1

For each of the following statements, identify the subject and predicate terms and the name of the form (universal affirmative, universal negative, particular affirmative, or particular negative). Also, state the traditional letter designation for each form (A, E, I, O).

* 1. No scientists are Baptists.
  2. Some plants are trees.
  3. No cats that have lived over fifteen years in a domestic setting are pets free of all health problems.
  4. Some mammals are not whales.
* 5. All theologians who have studied arguments for the existence of God are scholars with serious misgivings about the traditional notion of omnipotence.
  6. No football players are A-students.
  7. All refugees from unstable countries are poor people.
* 8. Some who play the stock market are not millionaires.
  9. No taxpayers from the 2003 tax year are embezzlers.
  10. No U.S. prosecutors who have reviewed the cases of death and injury at the Ace-Westinghouse foundry are friends of corporate America.
  11. All cancer survivors in the clinical study are coffee drinkers.
* 12. Some terrorists are Saudi citizens.
  13. No pro-democracy students in China are outside agitators.
  14. Some congressional Republican leaders are pro-lifers.
  15. Some health care programs proposed in the Senate are not viable options.
* 16. No death-row inmates are death-penalty supporters.
  17. All child-abuse caseworkers are overburdened civil servants.

Translations and Standard Form

This is worth repeating: We translate ordinary statements into standard-form categorical statements so we can handle them more efficiently. We want to handle them efficiently so we can more easily evaluate the validity of arguments composed of categorical statements. Translation is necessary to bring out the underlying structure of statements. It's also important because ordinary language is too imprecise and ambiguous to use in the analysis of statements and arguments. You'll appreciate this fact more as you work with categorical statements.

Translating statements into standard form is a straightforward process consisting of a few simple steps and some rules of thumb. Knowing the steps and

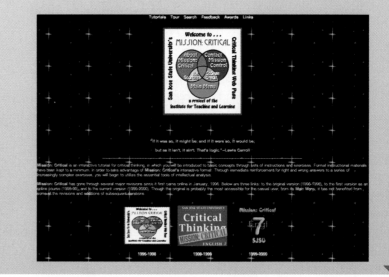

FROM THE WEB

Logic Help!

The Web may be big and crazy, but sanity is always nearby: Many websites offer help in the study of logic. (For a good list of such resources, visit *EpistemeLinks* at http://www.epistemelinks.com/Main/Topics .aspx?TopiCode=Logi.) Here are three that include solid treatment of categorical logic:

• *Mission: Critical* (http://www.sjsu.edu/depts/itl/index.html), an interactive tutorial on the basics of argument, logic, and fallacies, including auto-graded exercises for categorical and propositional logic

- An interactive tutorial on categorical syllogisms and Venn diagrams (http://www.sci.wsu.edu/math/Lessons/Logic/), from Washington State University

- A review of the basics of categorical syllogisms and Venn diagrams at *The Philosophy Pages* (http://www.philosophypages.com/lg/e08a.htm)

the rules is important, but *practice* translating statements is vital if you want to know how to translate fast and accurately. If you don't understand a particular point, you'll have an easier time if you go over it until you do rather than skipping it and looking at it later.

Just as a reminder, here's the pattern of all standard-form categorical statements:

Quantifier . . . Subject Term . . . Copula . . . Predicate Term

You need to know how to handle each of these parts. The copula must always be either "are" or "are not," so you don't have to spend a lot of time trying to determine the correct verb. But pinning down the terms and quantifiers is a little more challenging.

TERMS

In translating statements, your first order of business is usually identifying the terms and ensuring that they designate classes. Once you identify the terms and distinguish the subject term from the predicate term, you'll know in what order the terms must appear in the statement because the subject term must always precede the predicate term. Identifying the terms, though, often involves rewording them so they actually name classes. Consider these translations:

[Original] All dogs are loyal.
[Translation] All dogs are loyal animals.

[Original] Some bachelors waste money.
[Translation] Some bachelors are people who waste money.

[Original] No nations can survive without secure borders.
[Translation] No nations are things that can survive without secure borders.

Sometimes it's easy to locate statement terms but not as easy to tell which is the subject term and which is the predicate term. This can happen when the order of the subject and predicate is reversed:

Beyond the mountains stood the redwood trees.

Here the subject is "the redwood trees." The sentence has a normal variation of subject-predicate order, common in English. If you understand the structure

---

REVIEW NOTES

☑ The Four Standard-Form Categorical Statements

A: All *S* are *P*. (universal affirmative)   "All cats are felines."
E: No *S* are *P*. (universal negative)   "No cats are felines."
I: Some *S* are *P*. (particular affirmative)   "Some cats are felines."
O: Some *S* are not *P*. (particular negative)   "Some cats are not felines."

of such grammatical reversals, then you should be able to identify the true subject and predicate terms.

Difficulty distinguishing subject and predicate terms can also arise when the word "only" is in a statement. For example, which is the subject term and which is the predicate in these A-statements?

1. Only palm readers are wise counselors.
2. Only if something is a dance is it a minuet.
3. Hamburgers are the only entrees.
4. The only crimes prosecuted are murders.

We can figure out statements 1 and 2 by using this formula: *The words "only" and "only if" precede the predicate term in an A-statement.* So the correct translations are:

1. All wise counselors are palm readers.
2. All minuets are dances.

The translations of statements 3 and 4 follow this formula: *The words "the only" precede the subject term in an A-statement.* Therefore the correct translations are:

3. All entrees are hamburgers.
4. All prosecuted crimes are murders.

FURTHER THOUGHT

💡 Standard Form Versus Fuzziness

We take the trouble to translate categorical statements into standard form for several reasons—one of them being that language is fuzzy, fuzzy, fuzzy. The famed logician Bertrand Russell agreed: "Because language is misleading, as well as because it is diffuse and inexact when applied to logic (for which it was never intended) logical symbolism is absolutely necessary to any exact or thorough treatment of our subject" (*Introduction to Mathematical Philosophy*).

We can see a good example of language fuzziness in this type of categorical statement: "All S are not P." Take the statement "All Bigfoot monsters are not apes." Does this mean that (1) no Bigfoot monsters are apes or (2) that some Bigfoot monsters are not apes? Statement 1 is an E-statement; statement 2 is an O-statement. To defeat fuzziness, we have to apply some categorical logic and translate the original sentence into either an E- or O-statement.

"Men are apt to mistake the strength of their feeling for the strength of their argument. The heated mind resents the chill touch and relentless scrutiny of logic."
—WILLIAM E. GLADSTONE

Now, what are the terms in these statements?

5. Harrison Ford is an actor.
6. Toronto is Canada's finest city.
7. Sunday is the first day of the week.
8. *The Matrix* is an amazing movie.
9. Alicia is not a good student.

These are known as **singular statements.** Each one asserts something about a single person or thing, including objects, places, and times. Each subject term is a noun (including proper names), pronoun, or noun phrase referring to an individual, particular item. In a way, the predicate terms specify classes but, alas, the subject terms don't. We can transform such statements, though, into universal statements (A-statements or E-statements). The trick is to think of each subject term as naming a class in which there's just one member. We can, for example, treat the subject term in statement 5 ("Harrison Ford") as designating a class with Harrison Ford as one member of that class, like this:

5. All persons identical with Harrison Ford are actors.

We can translate our other singular statements in similar fashion:

6. All places identical with Toronto are places that are Canada's finest city.
7. All days identical with Sunday are the first days of the week.
8. All things identical with the film *The Matrix* are amazing movies.
9. No persons identical with Alicia are good students.

Now we can see more clearly that statements 5–8 are A-statements and statement 9 is an E-statement.

Granted, translations of ordinary statements into standard-form categorical statements can sometimes sound awkward, as the preceding translations surely do. But when we translate statements, we put them into a form that makes their logical connections transparent—an agreeable state of affairs when we're trying to check the validity of complex arguments.

QUANTIFIERS

Some quantifiers may be in nonstandard form, and some may be unexpressed. Consider these statements:

1. Every soldier is a warrior.
2. Whoever is an artist is a genius.
3. Sharks are good swimmers.
4. Nothing breakable is a warehouse item.
5. Comets are ice balls.

FURTHER THOUGHT

💡 Let Us Count the Ways . . .

Plenty of nonstandard statements are equivalents of categorical statements in standard form.

A-STATEMENT: "ALL S ARE P"

Only celebrities are spoiled brats.
Mathematicians are good acrobats.
Every general is a leader.
Only if something is a plant is it a flower.
Any car is a vehicle.
Something is a breakfast only if it is a meal.
Whatever is a revolver is a weapon.
Every pediatrician is a doctor.
If something is not a vegetable, then it is not a potato.
All dictators are thugs.

E-STATEMENT: "NO S ARE P"

If anything is a weapon, then it is not a flower.
All humans are nonreptiles.
Pontiacs are not doctors.
Nothing that is a mind is a body.
Nothing red is a banana.
None of the vegetables are fruits.
It is false that some vegetables are fruits.

I-STATEMENT: "SOME S ARE P"

There are engineers who are painters.
Most criminals are morons.
Several diplomats are egomaniacs.
At least one survivor is a hero.
A few lotteries are scams.
Many Europeans are Germans.

O-STATEMENT: "SOME S ARE NOT P"

Some philosophers are nonreptiles.
Some nonreptiles are philosophers.
Not all judges are rock stars.
Many conservatives are not Republicans.
Most liberals are not hawks.
There are nonreptile philosophers.
Americans are not always patriots.
A few rock stars are not maniacs.

Each is a universal statement with a nonstandard or unexpressed quantifier. Here are the translations with the proper quantifiers:

1. All soldiers are warriors.
2. All artists are geniuses.
3. All sharks are good swimmers.
4. No breakable things are warehouse items.
5. All comets are ice balls.

Statements 1, 2, and 4 have nonstandard quantifiers; statements 3 and 5 have unexpressed quantifiers. Fortunately, most nonstandard quantifiers are fairly easy to decipher. "Every soldier," for example, obviously means all the soldiers. "Nothing" and "none" mean not any, which refers to all of them, whatever they are. Usually, unexpressed quantifiers are readily understood because of the nature of the terms. The statement "Sharks are good swimmers" clearly refers to all sharks, not just some of them. In some statements, though, the unexpressed quantifier is not obvious—for example, "Berkeley students are liberals." Is it "*All* Berkeley students" or "*Some* Berkeley students"? When in doubt, assume the quantifier that you think would make the statement most likely to be true. In this case, "All Berkeley students . . ." is a sweeping generalization that's unlikely to apply to every single Berkeley student. The claim more likely to be true is "Some Berkeley students . . ."

Now consider these statements:

6. There are government workers who are spies.
7. Most movie stars are snobs.
8. Several politicians are space aliens.

These are all particular categorical statements. Their translations are:

6. Some government workers are spies.
7. Some movie stars are snobs.
8. Some politicians are space aliens.

The quantifier "some" is appropriate in all these statements because, in logic, it means "at least one." We therefore have only two options for expressing quantity in categorical statements: *all* and *less than all*. "Most," "a few," "several," "almost all," and similar terms are all translated as "some." Part of the reason for logic's restrictive definition of "some" is that, in everyday language, "some" is extremely vague. The word could mean "most," "two or three," "ten or more," "many," who knows? Logic, though, needs precision—more precision than is found in ordinary discourse.

Exercise 7.2

Translate each of the following statements into standard categorical form and indicate whether the form is A, E, I, or O.

* 1. All Giants fans are fanatical.
  2. Some government programs are wasteful.
  3. Brave are the soldiers who give their all.
  4. "People who whisper lie." [Swedish proverb]
* 5. Only cell phone companies that keep up with the latest technology are good investments.
  6. Only if something has a back beat is it a rock-and-roll song.
  7. "People with pinched faces often have poisonous hearts." [Chinese proverb]
  8. Nothing that is a snake is a mammal.
* 9. "All intelligent thoughts have already been thought." [Johann Wolfgang von Goethe]
  10. "The only good human is a dead human." [*Planet of the Apes*]
  11. Gregory is a Republican.
  12. Soldiers who broke their legs didn't finish their training.
* 13. Some things are meant to be forgotten.
  14. "There is no excellence without difficulty." [Ovid]
  15. Jonathan is not a very brave pilot.
  16. "All men have sinned." [New Testament]

Exercise 7.3

Follow the instructions given for Exercise 7.2.

* 1. Only poets are guardians of the soul.
  2. Any earthquake is a potential disaster.
  3. "People who wish to salute the free and independent side of their evolutionary character acquire cats." [Anna Quindlen]
* 4. All androids like Commander Data are nonhuman.
* 5. Nothing that satisfies the heart is a material thing.
  6. Some young people are non-Catholics.
  7. Every political party that gets at least 50 percent of the vote in a presidential election is a major player in American politics.
* 8. Most treatments said to be part of "alternative medicine" are unproven.
  9. There are products advertised on the Internet that are unsafe devices.
  10. "People who love only once in their lives are . . . shallow people." [Oscar Wilde]
  11. Some of the members of the Daughters of the American Revolution are from Canada.

* 12. Friday is the only day that gives her any joy.
13. Many socialists are not communists.
14. "All prejudices may be traced to the intestines." [Friedrich Nietzsche]
* 15. The picture hanging on the wall is crooked.
16. Whoever seeks the truth through philosophy is a free person.
17. "He that is born to be hanged shall never be drowned." [French proverb]
18. Only artists are visionaries.
19. Not all writers are poets.
* 20. "A nation without a conscience is a nation without a soul." [Winston Churchill]

Diagramming Categorical Statements

If you want more help in understanding the relationships between subject and predicate terms, you're in luck. You can graphically represent such relationships with the use of **Venn diagrams** (named after British logician and mathematician John Venn). The diagrams consist of overlapping circles, each one representing a class specified by a term in a categorical statement. Here's an example:

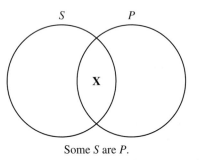

Some *S* are *P*.

This is the diagram for an I-statement: "Some *S* are *P*." The circle on the left represents the class of *S*; the circle on the right, the class of *P*. The area on the left contains only members of the *S* class. The area on the right contains only members of the *P* class. The area where the circles overlap indicates that both *S* members and *P* members are present. The X in the overlapped area, however, gives more specific information: It shows that *at least one S* member is a *P* member. That is, there is at least one *S* that also is a *P*. This diagram, of course, represents *any* statement of the form "Some *S* are *P*"—like, for instance, "Some cars are Fords." The X on the diagram where the circles overlap, then, would indicate that at least one car is a Ford.

Now here's the diagram for an O-statement—"Some *S* are not *P*":

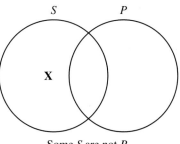

Some *S* are not *P*.

Here the X is in the *S* circle but outside the *P* circle, indicating that at least one *S* is not a *P*. In our car example (in which the *S* circle represents the class of cars and the *P* circle represents the class of Fords), this diagram would indicate that at least one car is not a Ford.

Here's the diagram for an A-statement—"All *S* are *P*":

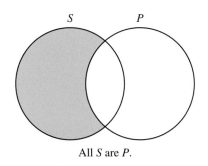

All *S* are *P*.

This diagram asserts that all members of the *S* class are also members of the *P* class. ("All cars are Fords.") Notice that the part of the diagram where the *S* circle does not overlap the *P* circle is shaded, showing that that area is "empty," or without any members. And this means that there are no members of *S* that are not also members of *P*. The remaining part of the *S* circle overlaps with the *P* circle, showing that *S* members are also *P* members.

Finally, the diagram for an E-statement—"No *S* are *P*":

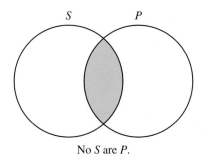

No *S* are *P*.

Here the area where the *S* circle and the *P* circle overlap is shaded (empty), meaning that there is no situation in which *S* overlaps with *P* (in which members of *S* are also members of *P*). So no members of *S* are also members of *P* ("No cars are Fords").

Venn diagrams can come in handy when you want to know whether two categorical statements are equivalent—whether they say the same thing. If the diagrams for the statements are identical, then the statements are equivalent.

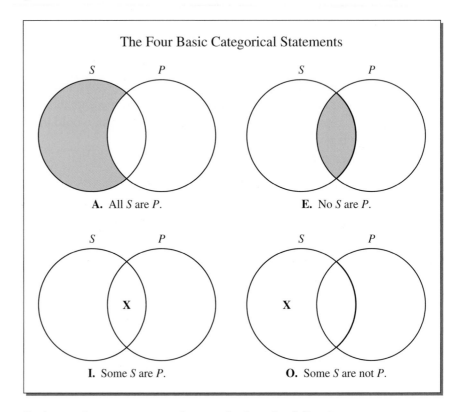

Let's say that you want to know whether the following two statements say the same thing:

No *S* are *P*.
No *P* are *S*.

If you diagram them both, you get your answer:

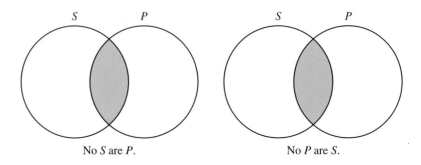

☑ Three Steps to Diagramming a Categorical Statement

1. Draw two overlapping circles, each one representing a term in the statement.
2. Label the circles with the terms.
3. Shade an area of a circle to show that an area is empty; insert an X to show that at least one member of a class is also a member of another class.

You can see that the diagrams are identical—they both show the area of overlap between the two circles as shaded, signifying that there are no members of *S* that are also members of *P*, and vice versa. So the first statement ("No *S* are *P*," an E-statement) says the same thing as the second statement ("No *P* are *S*").

Likewise, if we compare the diagrams for "Some *S* are *P*" (I-statement) and "Some *P* are *S*," we can see that these statements are also equivalent:

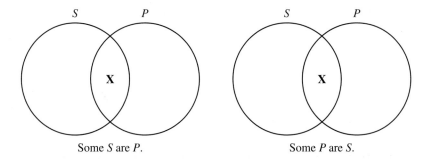

Some *S* are *P*.   Some *P* are *S*.

On the other hand, by comparing diagrams we can see that A-statements and E-statements are *not* equivalent (something you knew already, of course):

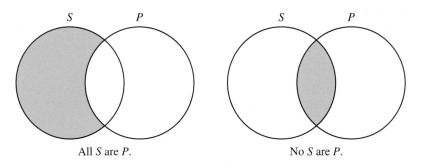

All *S* are *P*.   No *S* are *P*.

Let's examine one final pair of statements:

All *S* are *P*.
No *S* are non-*P*.

The diagrams clearly show that these are equivalent:

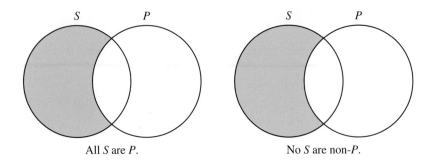

All *S* are *P*.　　　　　　　　No *S* are non-*P*.

Exercise 7.4

Construct Venn diagrams for each of the following statements. Specify both the subject and predicate terms. If necessary, translate the statement into standard form before diagramming (A, E, I, or O).

* 1. No one is exempt from the draft in times of war.
  2. No creed can be inviolable.
  3. No one can join the army when they're sixteen.
  4. Some birds are flightless.
* 5. Nothing is more pitiable than the reasons of an unreasonable man.
  6. Abraham Lincoln is one of the few writers whose words helped turn the world.
  7. Some snakes are not poisonous.
* 8. Some good talkers are good listeners.
  9. It is false that some businessmen are crooks.
  10. Some people with excellent reputations are not persons of excellent character.
  11. Black dogs didn't get fed.
* 12. "Every commander is alone." [Michael Powell]
  13. Rainbows are always misleading.
  14. There are bad apples in every barrel.
  15. "Few friendships could survive the moodiness of love affairs." [Mason Cooley]

Exercise 7.5

Construct Venn diagrams for each statement in the following pairs, then indicate whether the statements are equivalent.

* 1. *P* are *S*; No *S* are *P*.
 2. Some *S* are *P*; Some *P* are *S*.
* 3. All *S* are *P*; All *P* are *S*.
 4. No *S* are *P*; All *P* are non-*S*.
 5. All *S* are *P*; Some *P* are non-*S*.
* 6. All *P* are non-*S*; All *S* are non-*P*.
 7. No non-*S* are *P*; No non-*P* are *S*.
 8. No *S* are *P*; No *P* are *S*.
* 9. Some *S* are not *P*; Some *P* are not *S*.
 10. All *S* are non-*P*; No *P* are *S*.

Sizing Up Categorical Syllogisms

Once you understand the workings of categorical statements, you're ready to explore the dynamics of categorical arguments, or—more precisely—categorical syllogisms. As we saw in Chapter 3, a syllogism is a deductive argument made up of three statements: two premises and a conclusion. A categorical syllogism is one consisting of three categorical statements (A, E, I, or O) interlinked in a specific way. You can see the interlinking structure in this categorical syllogism:

(1) All egomaniacs are warmongers.
(2) All dictators are egomaniacs.
(3) Therefore, all dictators are warmongers.

If we diagram this argument as we did in Chapter 3, we come up with this structure:

$$\frac{1 + 2}{\downarrow}$$
$$3$$

> "Logical consequences are the scarecrows of fools and the beacons of wise men."
> —THOMAS HENRY HUXLEY

But this kind of diagram, though handy in truth-functional logic, isn't much help here because it doesn't reveal the internal components and interlinking structure of the statements. Observe: Each categorical statement has, as usual, two terms. But there are a total of only three terms in a categorical syllogism, each term being mentioned twice but in different statements. So in the preceding argument, *dictators* appears in statements 2 and 3; *egomaniacs,* in 1 and 2; and *warmongers,* in 1 and 3.

In a categorical syllogism, the *major term* of the argument is the predicate term in the conclusion (*warmongers,* in this case). It also appears in one of the premises (premise 1), which is therefore called the *major premise*. The *minor term (dictators)* occurs as the subject term in the conclusion. It also occurs in one of the premises (premise 2), which is therefore called the *minor premise*. And the *middle term (egomaniacs)* appears once in each premise but not in the conclusion. If we map out the argument with the terms labeled in this way, here's what we get:

> *Major Premise: (1) [middle term] [major term].*
> *Minor Premise: (2) [minor term] [middle term].*
> *Conclusion: (3) Therefore, [minor term] [major term].*

(We could have placed the minor premise first and the major premise second because, logically, the order doesn't matter. But by convention we always position the major premise first and the minor premise next.)

We can symbolize this argument form with letters:

(1) All *M* are *P*.
(2) All *S* are *M*.
(3) Therefore, all *S* are *P*.

Here, *M* stands for the middle term; *P* for the major term; and *S* for the minor term.

So a categorical syllogism, then, is one that has:

1. Three categorical statements—two premises and a conclusion.
2. Exactly three terms, with each term appearing twice in the argument.
3. One of the terms (the middle term) appearing in each premise but not the conclusion.
4. Another term (the major term) appearing as the predicate term in the conclusion and also in one of the premises (the major premise).
5. Another term (the minor term) appearing as the subject term in the conclusion and also in one of the premises (the minor premise).

A valid categorical syllogism, like a valid deductive argument of any other sort, is such that if its premises are true, its conclusion *must* be true. (That is, if the premises are true, the conclusion cannot possibly be false.) This fact, of course, you already know. Of more interest now is how we can *check the validity* of categorical syllogisms. Fortunately, there are several ways, the simplest of which is the Venn diagramming method. This technique involves drawing a circle for each term in the argument (giving us three overlapping circles), then diagramming the premises on these circles. If the resulting diagram reflects the assertion in the conclusion, the argument is valid.

Living by the Rules

Drawing Venn diagrams is a good way to both visualize what a syllogism is saying and test it for validity. But you can also check validity without diagrams. One technique is to assess a syllogism's validity by determining if the argument follows certain rules. Some of these rules involve the fine points of syllogistic structure. But others are drawn from simple facts about syllogisms that you probably already know—or have suspected. Here are three such rules:

1. A valid categorical syllogism must possess precisely three terms.
2. A valid categorical syllogism cannot have two negative premises.
3. A valid categorical syllogism with at least one negative premise must have a negative conclusion.

Any standard-form categorical syllogism that breaks even one of these rules is invalid. (On the other hand, a categorical syllogism that does not violate any of these rules is not necessarily valid. It may be defective for other reasons.)

Here are some syllogisms that violate at least one rule:

All snakes are reptiles.
All reptiles are cold-blooded creatures.
Therefore, all lizards are cold-blooded creatures.
(Violates rule 1.)

No criminals are law-enforcement officers.
Some law-enforcement officers are not bank robbers.
Therefore, some bank robbers are not criminals.
(Violates rule 2.)

No Italians are Asians.
Some Eskimos are Italians.
Therefore, some Eskimos are Asians.
(Violates rule 3.)

If you know how to diagram categorical statements, then you can diagram a categorical argument. Remember that since a categorical statement has two terms, we need two circles to diagram it—one circle for each term. And since a categorical syllogism has three terms, we need three circles, overlapping like this:

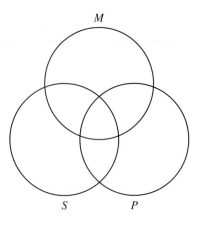

The top circle represents the class designated by the middle term (*M*); the bottom left circle, the minor term (*S*); and the bottom right circle, the major term (*P*). The two lower circles together represent the conclusion since they stand for the relationship between the minor and major terms (*S* and *P*).

Let's diagram our syllogism about dictators and warmongers, diagramming one statement, or premise, at a time. We can start by labeling the diagram like this:

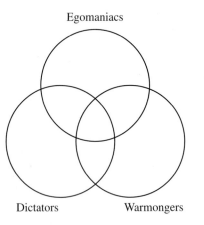

Now, we diagram the first premise ("All egomaniacs are warmongers"). To represent premise 1, we shade the part of the egomaniacs circle that does *not* overlap with the warmongers circle. This signifies that all the existing egomaniacs are also warmongers:

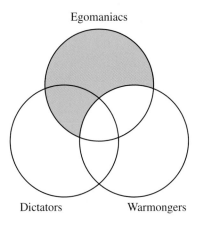

Egomaniacs

Dictators   Warmongers

Then we diagram premise 2 ("All dictators are egomaniacs") by shading the part of the dictators circle that does not overlap with the egomaniacs circle:

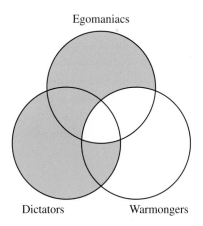

Egomaniacs

Dictators   Warmongers

The resulting combined diagram is supposed to reflect the information in the conclusion ("Therefore, all dictators are warmongers"). We can see that the dictators circle is shaded everywhere—except in the area that overlaps the egomaniac circle. And this is how the syllogism's diagram *should* be shaded to depict the statement "all dictators are warmongers." So the diagram does express what's asserted in the conclusion. The argument is therefore valid. If you diagram the premises of a categorical syllogism and the resulting combined diagram says the same thing as the conclusion, the syllogism is valid. If the diagram does not "contain" the conclusion (if information is missing), the syllogism is invalid.

This syllogism has two universal ("All") premises (both A-statements). Let's diagram one that has a particular ("Some") premise:

All robots are drudges.
Some professors are robots.
Therefore, some professors are drudges.

Here's the diagram properly labeled:

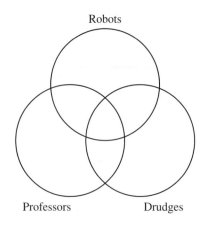

We'll diagram the major premise first ("All robots are drudges")—but not just because it happens to be the first premise. In categorical syllogisms with both a universal and a particular premise, we should always diagram the universal premise first. The reason is that diagramming the particular premise first can lead to confusion. For example, in the argument in question, if we were to diagram the particular premise first ("Some professors are robots"), we would end up with an X in the area where the robots and professors circles overlap. That section, however, is split into two subsections by the drudges circle:

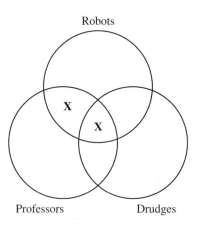

So then the question arises, In which subsection should we place the X? Should we plunk the X into the area overlapping with the drudges circle—or into the part not overlapping with the drudges circle? Our choice *does* affect what the diagram says about the validity of the argument. But if we diagram the universal premise first, then the decision of where to insert the X is made for us

☑ Five Steps to Checking Validity with Venn Diagrams

1. Draw three overlapping circles, each circle representing a term in the syllogism, with the two circles representing the major and minor terms placed on the bottom.
2. Label the circles with the terms.
3. Diagram the first premise. (Diagram universal premises first. When diagramming a particular premise, if it's unclear where to place an X in a circle section, place it on the dividing line between subsections.)
4. Diagram the second premise.
5. Check to see if the diagram represents what's asserted in the conclusion. If it does, the argument is valid; if not, it's invalid.

because there would be only one relevant subsection left (and we can't place an X in a shaded area):

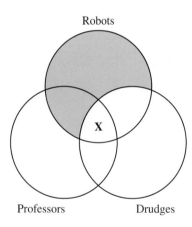

The resulting diagram represents the statement that some professors are drudges, which is what the conclusion asserts. The syllogism, then, is valid.

But sometimes, diagramming the universal premise first still leaves us with a question about where the X should go. Consider this syllogism:

All barbers are singers.
Some Italians are singers.
Therefore, some Italians are barbers.

When we diagram the universal premise first, we see that the section where the Italians and singers circles overlap is divided between a subsection including barbers and a subsection excluding barbers. So the X could go in either subsection, and we have no way of knowing which:

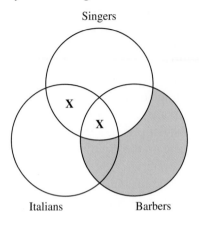

In situations like this, the best approach is to indicate our lack of information by placing the X on the border between the two subsections, like this:

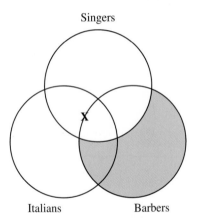

An X placed in this position means that among things that are both Italians and singers, something is either a barber or not a barber. Now, the conclusion says that some Italians are barbers. This conclusion is represented in the diagram only if there's an X *unquestionably* in the area where the barbers and Italians circles overlap. But we don't have an X unquestionably in that region; we have only an X that *may or may not be there*. That is, there's a question of just where the X is. Therefore, the diagram does not assert what the conclusion does, and the argument is invalid.

Exercise 7.6

For each of the following arguments, label the minor term, major term, and middle term. Then translate each syllogism into symbolic form using *S*, *P*, and *M* to represent the terms.

1. No apples are vegetables. Some plants are vegetables. So some plants are not apples.

* 2. All horses are mammals, and no mammals are lizards. Therefore, no lizards are horses.

3. All cars are self-propelled vehicles, and all motorcycles are self-propelled vehicles. Thus, all motorcycles are cars.

4. Some roses are yellow flowers. All roses are plants. Therefore, some plants are yellow flowers.

5. All roads are highways to Rome, but no mere paths are roads. So no mere paths are highways to Rome.

* 6. Some videotapes are not film classics, but all black-and-white movies are film classics. Therefore, some black-and-white movies are not videotapes.

7. All presidents are leaders, but some statesmen are not presidents. So some statesmen are not leaders.

8. All politicians are campaigners. All campaigners are money-grubbers. Therefore all politicians are money-grubbers.

* 9. No elm trees are cacti. Some tall plants are elm trees. So some tall plants are not cacti.

10. All thieves are criminals. All thieves are dangers to society. Therefore, all dangers to society are criminals.

Exercise 7.7

Draw Venn diagrams to test the validity of each of the arguments in Exercise 7.6. Answers are given for 2, 6, and 9.

Exercise 7.8

Translate each of the following arguments into categorical syllogistic form (major premise, minor premise, conclusion), symbolize the argument (using the conventional S, P, M variables), and draw a Venn diagram to test its validity.

* 1. Some architectural structures are nontraditional designs, for all houses are architectural structures, and some houses are nontraditional designs.

2. All bacon burgers are heart attack–inducing foods because all bacon burgers are high-fat foods, and some heart attack–inducing foods are not high-fat foods.

* 3. All worshippers of God are spiritual giants because all worshippers of God are redeemed souls, and all redeemed souls are spiritual giants.

4. Some famous men are not racists since all racists are enemies of justice, and some famous men are not enemies of justice.

5. No persons who are true to the values of this republic are politicians because all politicians are self-promoting egoists. And no self-promoting egoists are persons true to the values of this republic.

6. Some philosophers are musicians. Therefore, some trumpet players are philosophers since all trumpet players are musicians.

7. All opponents of the United States going to war against terrorist states are people opposed to anti-terrorist security arrangements. Some people opposed to anti-terrorist security arrangements are Leftist extremists. Therefore, some opponents of the United States going to war against terrorist states are not Leftist extremists.

* 8. No wimps are social activists because no wimps are people of honest and strong conviction. And all social activists are people of honest and strong conviction.

9. Most people who drive SUVs (sport utility vehicles) are instant-gratification freaks who don't care about the environment or environmental issues. Instant-gratification freaks who don't care about the environment or environmental issues are the true enemies of the planet. Therefore, people who drive SUVs are the true enemies of the planet.

10. Vitamin pills are useless gimmicks promoted as sure-cures for a variety of illnesses. Some useless gimmicks promoted as sure-cures, though, are placebos that can make people feel good. So some vitamin pills are placebos that can make people feel good even if they don't cure anything.

 KEY WORDS

categorical logic	quantity
categorical statement	singular statements
copula	standard-form categorical statement
predicate term	
quality	subject term
quantifier	Venn diagram

Summary

- Every categorical statement has a subject term and a predicate term. There are four standard forms of categorical statements: (1) universal affirmative ("All dogs are mammals"), (2) universal negative ("No dogs are mammals"), (3) particular affirmative ("Some dogs are mammals"), and (4) particular negative (Some dogs are not mammals").

- Categorical statements must be translated into standard form before you can work with them. Translating involves both identifying terms and ensuring that they designate classes as well as determining the quantifiers.
- Drawing Venn diagrams is a good way to visualize categorical statements and to tell whether one statement is equivalent to another.
- A categorical syllogism is an argument consisting of three categorical statements (two premises and a conclusion) that are interlinked in a structured way. The syllogism consists of a major term, minor term, and middle term. The middle term appears once in each premise. The major term appears in one premise and the conclusion, and the minor term appears in the other premise and the conclusion.
- The easiest way to check the validity of a categorical syllogism is to draw a three-circle Venn diagram—three overlapping circles with the relationship between terms graphically indicated. If, after diagramming each premise, the diagram reflects what's asserted in the conclusion, the argument is valid. If not, the argument is invalid.

Field Problems

1. Do a search on the Internet for the term "rant" or "rants." You will get an enormous list of web pages featuring off-the-cuff opinions and tirades on countless topics—everything from religion and politics to celebrity fashion, cheese, bad drivers, Rice Krispies, and many unmentionables. From this mélange, pick out an *invalid* categorical syllogism and write a 100- to 150-word paragraph assessing the soundness of the argument (both its truth and validity) and how it might be rewritten to be made valid.

2. Check recent news reports to find one categorical statement made by either the president of the United States, the U.S. Attorney General, or the Chairman of the Joint Chiefs of Staff. Translate the statement into standard form. (1) Construct a *valid* categorical syllogism using the statement as the conclusion and supplying whatever premises you deem appropriate. Assume that your premises are true. (2) Then construct an *invalid* syllogism using the same statement as the conclusion and supplying premises, also assumed to be true. In both arguments, try to keep the statements as realistic as possible (close to what you may actually read in a news magazine, say).

Self-Assessment Quiz

Answers appear in "Answers to Self-Assessment Quizzes" (Appendix C).

1. What is a quantifier? What are the two quantities that can be expressed in categorical statements?

2. What are the two qualities that can be expressed in categorical statements?

3. What are the four standard-form categorical statements? (Specify them by quality and quantity and by letter designation.)

For each of the following statements, identify the subject and predicate terms, the quality, the quantity, and the name of the form (universal affirmative, universal negative, particular affirmative, or particular negative).

4. Some tax cuts are economic mistakes.

5. No philosophers are five-year-old kids.

6. All patients treated with herbal medicine are Chinese.

7. Some ghost stories are not fabrications devised by true believers.

Translate each of the following statements into standard categorical form and indicate whether the form is A, E, I, or O.

8. Only if something is a watercraft is it a canoe.

9. "Baseball is pastoral." [George Carlin]

10. Sheila is the finest scholar in the department.

11. No one with any sense would drive a car without headlights on a rainy night.

12. "Slow and steady wins the race." [Aesop]

13. A politician is someone who firmly believes that getting elected makes one smart.

14. "A fanatic is someone who can't change his mind and won't change the subject." [Winston Churchill]

Construct Venn diagrams to test the validity of each of the following syllogisms.

15. All *M* are *P*. Some *S* are *M*. Therefore, some *S* are *P*.

16. No *M* are *P*. No *S* are *M*. Therefore, all *S* are *P*.

17. All *P* are *M*. No *S* are *M*. Therefore, no *S* are *P*.

18. Some *P* are not *M*. All *S* are *M*. Therefore, some *S* are not *P*.

19. All *M* are *P*. All *M* are *S*. Therefore, all *S* are *P*.

20. Some *S* are *M*. All *M* are *P*. Therefore, some *S* are *P*.

Integrative Exercises

These exercises pertain to material in Chapters 3–7.

For each of the following arguments, determine whether it is deductive or inductive, valid or invalid, strong or weak. Then diagram it using the lines-and-arrows method discussed in Chapter 3. Also indicate whether the argument contains any appeals to popularity or common practice.

1. "[Sen. John Edwards (D-NC)] brings enough solid assets to the wide-open race [for Democratic presidential nomination] that his credentials are worth examining—even if his shortcomings are also apparent. The first of those assets is geographical. He is currently the only Southerner in the field, and Democrats know their only successful presidential candidates in the past 40 years came from Texas, Georgia, and Arkansas. . . . The second asset is personal. The Democratic field is longer on competence than on charisma. Edwards can light up a room, and he bonds with voters more easily than, say, Sen. John Kerry of Massachusetts." [David S. Broder]

2. "Encouragement of contempt for laws is more dangerous to society than occasional use of marijuana. Severe laws against marijuana do not discourage use of marijuana, but rather breed this contempt not only for drug laws, but for laws in general. Therefore severe laws against marijuana are more dangerous to society than the activity which they are designed to prevent." [A. Blakeslee]

3. Psychic powers (ESP, telepathy, and clairvoyance) are a myth. Hundreds of studies have failed to detect any genuine effects of such phenomena. Numerous case histories and other research over the past one hundred years reveal that most putative "psychics" have turned out to be frauds or incapable of reliably producing the desired results. And no researchers in this field have ever devised a plausible theory that explains how psychic powers work.

4. It is ridiculous for the Supreme Court or any other branch of the government to ban the reciting of school-sponsored (or school-allowed) prayers before football games. In areas of the country where this practice is prevalent, the communities involved are overwhelmingly in favor of such prayers. These recitations are thus the right thing to do—morally and legally.

For each of the following arguments, identify the argument pattern—*modus ponens, modus tollens,* affirming the consequent, denying the antecedent, or none of these.

5. If minds are identical to bodies, then whatever is true of minds is true of bodies, and vice versa. But minds are indivisible (they cannot be divided into parts) and bodies are divisible (we can break down a body into many parts and in many ways). Therefore, minds are not identical to bodies.

6. If Vaughn is boring, then no student can stand to listen to his lectures for more than sixty seconds. Vaughn is not boring, so students can stand to listen to him for more than a minute.

7. If there were structures in nature that were so complex that they could not possibly have evolved through natural selection, then the theory of evolution must be false. There are such structures, however—like the

human eye. Consequently evolution cannot be the right explanation for the existence of the peculiar life forms found on Earth.

Indicate which of the following symbolized statements are true and which are false. Assume that the variables *a, b,* and *c* are true, and *p, q,* and *r* are false.

8. ~*b* v *r*

9. *a* & ~*p*

10. *p* → ~*a*

11. *b* → *r*

For each of the following arguments, specify the conclusion and premises (including any implied premises). Symbolize the argument and construct a truth table to determine the argument's validity.

12. If the nuclear power industry improves its safety record and solves the nuclear waste problem, then it will become the number one source of energy in the world. But it will never be able to change its safety record or solve the waste problem. Consequently the industry will not become the primary source of the world's energy.

13. Either Katharine inherited money from her grandparents or she won the lottery. But she certainly did not inherit money from her grandparents. So she won the lottery.

14. The surgery will be a success if blood loss can be controlled. The surgery is a success and the patient has spoken to the press. So blood loss must have been controlled.

15. If racial justice and equal opportunity are ever to be achieved in the United States, then affirmative action must be instituted in higher education and in civil service employment. If affirmative action is instituted in higher education and in civil service jobs, the income gap between whites and African Americans will disappear. The income gap between whites and African Americans will disappear, so affirmative action will be instituted in higher education and in civil service jobs.

Translate each of the following arguments into categorical syllogistic form (major premise, minor premise, conclusion), symbolize the argument (using the conventional *S, P, M* variables), and draw a Venn diagram to test its validity.

16. Some Muslims are not Sunni Muslims, for some Muslims are Shiite Muslims, and no Shiite Muslims are Sunni Muslims.

17. Some Army soldiers are Rangers, and no Army Rangers are Marine pilots. So some Army soldiers are not Marine pilots.

18. Some sociopaths are not criminals, but all serial killers are criminals. It follows that some sociopaths are not serial killers.

19. Senator Bullhorn will not back any civil rights legislation. He's a former Dixiecrat. And former Dixiecrats never back civil rights legislation.

20. Some Bible believers are fundamentalist Christians, and fundamentalist Christians are always pro-lifers. So some Bible believers are pro-lifers.

Writing Assignments

1. Write a two-page essay arguing either for or against capital punishment. Cast your argument as a categorical syllogism.

2. Write a two-page rebuttal to Essay 5 ("More Innocents Die When We Don't Have Capital Punishment") in Appendix A.

3. Read Essay 4 ("The Kalam Cosmological Argument") in Appendix A, noting the premises and conclusions of any arguments. Write a three-page rebuttal to it.

4. Read Essay 11 ("A Deviance from God's Norm") in Appendix A, identifying the premises and conclusions of any arguments. Write a two-page rebuttal to it.

5. Study Essay 18 ("Freedom of Expression: Protect Student Speech—Even 'Unwise' Bong Banner") and Essay 19 ("Freedom of Expression: Policy Reflects Common Sense") in Appendix A. Decide which essay presents the stronger arguments, and write a paper defending your view.

Inductive Reasoning

CHAPTER OBJECTIVES

ENUMERATIVE INDUCTION

- Know what enumerative induction is and how it's used.
- Learn the definitions of *target population, sample,* and *relevant property.*
- Understand the two ways in which an enumerative induction can fail to be strong.
- Understand the error known as hasty generalization and know how to avoid it.
- Understand the basics of opinion polls and know the definitions of *random sampling, self-selecting sample, margin of error,* and *confidence level.*

ANALOGICAL INDUCTION

- Know how to formulate and evaluate an argument by analogy.
- Know how to use the following criteria to evaluate arguments by analogy: relevant similarities, relevant dissimilarities, the number of instances compared, and diversity among cases.

CAUSAL ARGUMENTS

- Know what causal claims and arguments are.
- Be able to apply Mill's methods to the evaluation of causal arguments.
- Be aware of the ways in which people can make errors in causal reasoning.
- Recognize and know how to avoid the post hoc fallacy.
- Learn the definitions of *necessary* and *sufficient conditions.*
- Be able to distinguish between necessary and sufficient conditions in everyday contexts.

W E NOW PASS FROM AN EXPLORATION OF DEDUCTIVE ARGUMENTS to a close examination of inductive ones—a very small step since both these argument types are common features of our everyday lives. Recall that a deductive argument is intended to provide logically conclusive support for its conclusion, being valid or invalid, sound or unsound. An inductive argument, on the other hand, is intended to supply only probable support for its conclusion, earning the label of "strong" if it succeeds in providing such support and "weak" if it fails. The conclusion of an inductively strong argument is simply more likely to be true than not. If the argument's premises are true, it is said to be cogent. Unlike valid deductive arguments, an inductively strong argument cannot guarantee that the conclusion is true—but it can render the conclusion probably true, even highly likely to be true. Inductive arguments, then, cannot give us certainty, but they can give us high levels of probability—high enough at least to help us acquire knowledge in everything from physics to bird watching.

Deductive logic is the invisible framework on which much of our reasoning hangs and the solid bond that holds together the logical lattices of mathematics, computer science, and other theoretical or abstract disciplines. Inductive reasoning, though, gives us most of what we know about the empirical workings of the world, allowing us in science and in ordinary experience to soar reliably from what we know to what we don't. It allows us to reason "beyond the evidence"—from bits of what is already known to conclusions about what those bits suggest is probably true.

Inductive arguments come in several forms. In this chapter we will examine three of them and focus, as in previous chapters, on how to evaluate their merits in real-life contexts.

Enumerative Induction

As you may have noticed in Chapter 3, sometimes an inductive argument reasons from premises about a group, or class, of things to a conclusion about a single member of the group (that is, from general to particular). For example:

Almost all of the students attending this college are pacifists.
Wei-en attends this college.
Therefore, Wei-en is probably a pacifist.

Eighty-two percent of residents in this neighborhood have been victims of crimes.
Samuel is a resident of this neighborhood.
Therefore, Samuel will probably be a victim of a crime.

Far more inductive arguments, however, reason from premises about individual members of a group to conclusions about the group as a whole (from particular to general). In such cases we begin with observations about some

---

Marginal notes (handwritten):

"The rules of probable inference are the most difficult part of logic, but also the most useful."
—BERTRAND RUSSELL

REVIEW

Reasoning & Areas of Inquiry
(A) Deductive Logic
  (1) Mathematics
  (2) Geometry
  (3) Logic
  (4) Philosophy
(B) Inductive Logic
  (1) Science
  (2) Medicine
  (3) Law
  (4) Philosophy
  (5) Everyday life

Statistical Syllogism
Generalization to a
particular...

Enumerative Induction
Inference from members
of a group (sample) to
to the whole group (target)

"There are lies, damn lies, and statistics. We're looking for someone who can make all three of these work for us."

www.CartoonStock.com

members of the group and end with a generalization about all of them. This argument pattern is called **enumerative induction**, and it's a way of reasoning that we all find both natural and useful.

Most peace activists I know are kind-hearted. So probably all peace activists are kind-hearted.

Every Gizmo computer I've bought in the last two years has had a faulty monitor. Therefore all Gizmo computers probably have faulty monitors.

Forty percent of the pickles that you've pulled out of the barrel are exceptionally good. So 40 percent of all the pickles in the barrel are probably exceptionally good.

More formally, enumerative induction has this form:

X percent of the observed members of group A have property P.
Therefore, X percent of all members of group A probably have property P.

In this formal guise, our pickle argument looks like this:

Forty percent of the observed pickles from the barrel are exceptionally good.
Therefore, 40 percent of all the pickles in the barrel are probably exceptionally good.

Enumerative induction comes with some useful terminology. The group as a whole—the whole collection of individuals in question—is called the **target population** or **target group.** The observed members of the target group are called the **sample members** or **sample.** And the property we're interested in is called the **relevant property** or **property in question.** In the foregoing example, the target group is the pickles in the barrel. The sample is the observed pickles. And the property is the quality of being exceptionally good.

Now, using this terminology we can study arguments by enumeration a little closer. Remember that an inductive argument can not only be strong or weak, but it can also vary in its strength—in the degree of support that the premises give to the conclusion. So argument strength depends on the premises as well as on how much is claimed in the conclusion. Let's look at some examples.

Argument 1
All the corporate executives Jacques has worked for have been crooks.
Therefore, all corporate executives are probably crooks.

The target group is corporate executives, the sample is the corporate executives Jacques has worked for, and the relevant property is being a crook. We

[handwritten marginal notes:]

Terminology
① Target population
② Sample
③ Relevant property

Strength depends on:
① Premises
② How much is claimed in the conclusion

ANALYSIS

don't know how many corporate executives Jacques has worked for, but we must assume from what we know about career paths in corporate America that the number is small, probably no more than a dozen. Neither do we know exactly how many corporate executives there are, but we can safely guess that there are thousands or hundreds of thousands. It should be obvious then that this enumerative inductive falls short on at least one score: The sample is too small. We simply cannot draw reliable conclusions about all corporate executives based on a mere handful of them. The argument is weak.

With such a small sample of the target group, we can't even conclude that *most* corporate executives are crooks. But we can make argument 1 strong by revising the conclusion like this: "*Some* corporate executives are probably crooks." This is a much more limited generalization that requires a more limited supporting premise.

We can fault this argument on another count: The sample is not representative of the target group. With thousands of corporate executives working for thousands of corporations, we must assume that corporate executives—in temperament, morality, demographics, and many other factors—are a diverse lot. It is therefore highly unlikely that Jacques's former bosses are representative of all corporate executives in their crookedness (the relevant property). And if the sample is not representative of the whole, we cannot use it to draw accurate conclusions about the whole. Argument 1 is weak for this additional reason.

Consider this one:

Argument 2

All of the blue herons that we've examined at many different sites in the nature preserve (about two hundred birds) have had birth defects.

Therefore, most of the blue herons in the nature preserve probably have birth defects.

In this argument the target group is the blue herons in the nature preserve, the sample is the two hundred blue herons examined, and the relevant property is having birth defects. We would normally consider this a very strong enumerative induction. Assuming that the premise is true, we would probably be surprised to discover that only a tiny minority of the target group had birth defects. Since the sample was drawn from many parts of the preserve, we would deem it representative of the target group. And due to the general uniformity of characteristics among birds in the wild, we would assume that a sample of two hundred birds would be large enough to strongly support the conclusion. As it stands, argument 2 is strong.

On the other hand, a conclusion asserting that *all* of the target group had birth defects would normally go beyond what the evidence in the premise would support. There could easily be at least some blue herons in the preserve (assuming it to be sufficiently large) that don't have birth defects, even if most do.

① Sample Size

Weak

One could revise the conclusion...

② Representativeness

Weak

"The deductive method is the mode of using knowledge, and the inductive method the mode of acquiring it."
—HENRY MAYHEW

Strong

Question of cogency

So you can see that an enumerative inductive argument can fail to be strong in two major ways: Its sample can be (1) too small or (2) not representative. Of course, it's possible for an enumerative induction to be perfectly strong—but have false premises, in which case the argument isn't cogent. That is, the data (or evidence) stated in the premises could have been misinterpreted, fabricated, or misstated.

SAMPLE SIZE

Let's say that you decide to conduct a survey of college students to determine their attitude toward federal deficits. So you stand around in the student center and query the first five students that pass by. Four out of the five say that deficits don't matter. You conclude: Eighty percent of the student body believe that deficits don't matter. Should you send your findings to the school newspaper—or to CNN?

Hasty Generalization

No way. This survey is a joke—the sample is much too small to yield any reliable information about the attitudes of the students as a whole. This verdict may seem obvious, but just about everyone at one time or another probably makes this kind of mistake, an error known as **hasty generalization.** We're guilty of hasty generalization whenever we draw a conclusion about a target group based on an inadequate sample size. People regularly make this mistake when dealing with all sorts of enumerative inductive evidence—political polls, consumer opinion surveys, scientific studies (especially medical research), quality-control checks, anecdotal reports, and many others.

In our everyday experience, we may casually make, hear, or read hasty generalizations like this:

You should buy a Dell computer. They're great. I bought one last year, and it has given me nothing but flawless performance.

The only male professor I've had this year was a chauvinist pig. All the male professors at this school must be chauvinist pigs.

Psychology majors are incredibly ignorant about human psychology. Believe me, I know what I'm talking about: My best friend is a psych major. What an ignoramus!

The French are snobby and rude. Remember those two high-and-mighty guys with really bad manners? They're French. I rest my case.

The food at Pappie's Restaurant is awful. I had a sandwich there once, and the bread was stale.

In general, the larger the sample, the more likely it is to reliably reflect the nature of the larger group. In many cases our common sense tells us when a sample is or is not large enough to draw reliable conclusions about a particular

FURTHER THOUGHT

💡 Do You Really Need to Know This?

Here's a little reminder—in case you needed one—that many inductive generalizations you come across *are just not worth knowing*, whether they're well founded or not. Consider the following, compliments of DumbFacts.com:

- In the course of a lifetime the average person will grow two meters of nose hair.
- The average American makes six trips to the bathroom every day; that's about two and one-half years of your life down the drain.
- More people use blue toothbrushes than red ones.
- The average adult male shaves off one pound of beard per year.
- Men get hiccups more often than women do.
- In the United States, 55,700 people are injured by jewelry each year.
- According to the World Health Organization, there are approximately 100 million acts of sexual intercourse each day.

target group. A good rule of thumb is this: *The more homogeneous a target group is in traits relevant to the property in question, the smaller the sample can be; the less homogeneous, the larger the sample should be.*

For example, if we want to determine whether cottontail rabbits have teeth, we need to survey only a tiny handful of cottontail rabbits (maybe even just one) because cottontail rabbits are fairly uniform in their physical characteristics. In this sense, if you've seen one cottontail rabbit, you've seen them all. On the other hand, if we want to know the sexual preferences of Hispanics who live in North American suburbs, surveying just a few won't do. Questioning a sample of two or twenty or even two hundred North American suburban Hispanics will not give us a reliable read on the sexual preferences of the target group. In social, psychological, and cultural properties, people are too diverse to judge a large target group by just a few of its members. In biological properties, however, *homo sapiens* is relatively uniform. We need to survey only one normal member of the species to find out if humans have ears.

REPRESENTATIVENESS

In addition to being the proper size, a sample must be a **representative sample**—it must resemble the target group in all the ways that matter. If it does not properly represent the target group, it's a **biased sample.** An enumerative inductive argument is strong only if the sample is representative of the whole.

[Handwritten margin notes:]

The more homogeneous a target group is in traits relevant to the property in question, the smaller the sample can be... The less homogeneous, the larger the sample should be...

Biological properties are fairly homogeneous, psychological and sociological properties are not...

Problem of the biased sample

Many arguments using unrepresentative samples are ludicrous; others are more subtle.

> *College students are glad that Congress is controlled by Republicans. Surveys of the members of Young Republican clubs on dozens of college campuses prove this.*

> *Most nurses in this hospital are burned out, stressed out, and overworked. Just ask the ones who work in the emergency department. They'll tell you they're absolutely miserable.*

> *No one is happy. Almost everyone is complaining about something. Just look at the letters to the editor in any big-city newspaper. Complaints, complaints, complaints.*

To be truly representative, the sample must be like the target group by (1) having all the same relevant characteristics and (2) having them in the same proportions that the target group does. The "relevant characteristics" are features that could influence the property in question. For example, let's say that you want to survey adult residents of Big City to determine whether they favor distributing condoms in high schools. Features of the residents that could influence whether they favor condom distribution include political party affiliation, ethnic background, and being Catholic. So the sample of residents should have all of these features and have them in the same proportions as the target group (residents of Big City). If half the adult residents of Big City are Catholic, for example, then half the sample should consist of residents who are Catholic.

Say that we want to determine how the ten thousand eligible voters in a small town intend to vote in an upcoming presidential election. We survey one thousand of them, which should be more than enough for our purposes. But the voters we poll are almost all over seventy years old and live in nursing homes. Our sample is biased because it does not reflect the makeup of the target group, most of whom are people under forty-five who live in their own homes, work in factories or offices, and have school-age children. Any enumerative argument based on this survey would be weak.

We are often guilty of biased sampling in everyday situations. One way this happens is through a phenomenon called *selective attention* (see Chapters 2 and 4), the tendency to observe and remember things that reinforce our beliefs and to gloss over and dismiss things that undercut those beliefs. We may tell our friends that *The Sopranos* is a lousy TV series because we remember that three episodes were boring—but we conveniently forget the four other episodes that we thought were superb. Or we may be convinced that Dr. Jones is one of the legendary "absent-minded professors." But this generalization seems plausible to us only because we're on the lookout for instances in which the professor's behavior seems to fit the stereotype, and we don't notice instances that contradict the stereotype.

"Public opinion polls are rather like children in a garden, digging things up all the time to see how they're growing."

—J. B. PRIESTLEY

OPINION POLLS

Enumerative inductions reach a high level of sophistication in the form of opinion polls conducted by professional polling organizations. Opinion polls are used to arrive at generalizations about everything from the outcome of presidential elections to public sentiments about cloning babies to the consumer's appetite for tacos. But as complex as they are, opinion polls are still essentially inductive arguments (or the basis of inductive arguments) and must be judged accordingly.

So as inductive arguments, opinion polls should (1) be strong and (2) have true premises. More precisely, any opinion poll worth believing must (1) use a large enough sample that accurately represents the target population in all the relevant population features and (2) generate accurate data (the results must correctly reflect what they purport to be about). A poll can fail to meet this latter requirement through data-processing errors, botched polling interviews, poorly phrased questions, and the like. (See the box "How Survey Questions Go Wrong.")

In national polling, samples need not be enormous to be accurate reflections of the larger target population. Modern sampling procedures used in national

[Handwritten margin notes: Opinion polls are inductive arguments; i.e. Enumerative inductions]

[Handwritten margin notes: An opinion poll must be 1) strong and 2) cogent]

FURTHER THOUGHT

💡 How Survey Questions Go Wrong

Many opinion polls are untrustworthy because of flaws in the way the questions are asked. The sample may be large enough and representative in all the right ways, but the poll is still dubious. Here are a few of the more common problems.

QUESTION PHRASING

Poll results can be dramatically skewed simply by the way the questions are worded. A poll might ask, for example, "Are you in favor of a woman's right to kill her unborn child?" The question is ostensibly about a woman's right to terminate a pregnancy through abortion and is supposed to be a fair measure of attitudes on the question. But the wording of the question practically guarantees that a very large percentage of respondents will answer "no." The controversial and emotionally charged characterization of abortion as the killing of an unborn child would likely persuade many respondents to avoid answering "yes." More neutral wording of the question would probably elicit a very different set of responses.

Another example: A 1995 poll of African Americans discovered that 95 percent of the sample group approved of a local school voucher program.

[Handwritten margin notes: Problems with polls ① Question phrasing ② Question ordering ③ Restricted choices]

▼

To get this huge approval rating, the survey question was worded like this: "Do you think that parents in your area should or should not have the right to choose which local schools their children will attend?" Who would want to give up such a right? No wonder the question elicited an overwhelming number of "shoulds."

Such biased wording is often the result of pollster sloppiness. Many other times it's a deliberate attempt to manipulate the poll results. The crucial test of polling questions is whether they're likely to bias responses in one direction or another. Fair questions aren't skewed this way—or are skewed as little as possible.

QUESTION ORDERING

The order in which questions are asked in a poll can also affect the poll results. Pollsters know that if the economy is in bad shape and they ask people about the economic mess first and then ask them how they like the president, the respondents are likely to give the president lower marks than if the order of the questions was reversed. Likewise, if you're asked specific questions about crimes that have been committed in your home town and then you're asked if you feel safe from crime, you're more likely to say no than if you're asked the questions in reverse order.

RESTRICTED CHOICES

Opinion polls frequently condense broad spectrums of opinions on issues into a few convenient choices. Some of this condensation is necessary to make the polling process manageable. But some of it is both unnecessary and manipulative, seriously distorting the opinions of those polled. Daniel Goleman of the *New York Times* offers this example: "In one survey . . . people were asked if they felt 'the courts deal too harshly or not harshly enough with criminals.' When offered just the two options, 6 percent said 'too harshly' and 78 percent answered 'not harshly enough.' But when a third alternative was added—'don't have enough information about the courts to say'—29 percent took that option, and 60 percent answered 'not harshly enough.'" ■

polls can produce representative samples that are surprisingly small. Polling organizations such as Gallup and Harris regularly conduct polls in which the target group is American adults (more than 187 million), and the representative sample consists of only one thousand to fifteen hundred individuals.

How can a sample of one thousand be representative of almost two hundred million people? By using **random sampling.** To ensure that a sample is truly representative of the target group, the sample must be selected *randomly* from

[margin notes, handwritten:]
Standard samples: 1000-1500 people

Random sampling
In a simple random selection every member of the target group has an equal chance of being selected for this sample...

the target group. In a simple random selection, every member of the target group has an equal chance of being selected for the sample. Imagine that you want to select a representative sample from, say, one thousand people at a football game, and you know very little about the characteristics of this target population. Your best bet for getting a representative sample of this group is to choose the sample members at random. Any nonrandom selection based on preconceived notions about what characteristics are representative will likely result in a biased sample.

Selecting a sample in truly random fashion is easier said than done (humans have a difficult time selecting anything in a genuinely random way). Even a simple process such as your trying to arbitrarily pick names off a list of registered voters is not likely to be truly random. Your choices may be skewed, for example, by unconscious preferences for certain names or by boredom and fatigue. Researchers and pollsters use various techniques to help them get close to true randomization. They may, for instance, assign a number to each member of a population, then use a random-number generator to make the selections.

"I don't have any political opinions - would you like to hear about my symptoms?"

www.CartoonStock.com

FURTHER THOUGHT

💡 Mean, Median, and Mode

If you read enough opinion polls, you will surely encounter one of these terms: mean, median or mode. These concepts are invaluable in expressing statistical facts, but they can be confusing. Mean is simply an average. The mean of these four numbers—6, 7, 4, and 3—is 5 (6 + 7 + 4 + 3 = 20 divided by 4 = 5). The median is the middle point of a series of values, meaning that half the values are above the point and half the values are below the point. The median of these eleven values—3, 5, 7, 13, 14, 17, 21, 23, 24, 27, 30—is 17 (the number in the middle). The mode is the most common value. The mode in this series of values—7, 13, 13, 13, 14, 17, 21, 21, 27, 30, 30—is 13 (the most frequently appearing value).

The notions of mean, median, and mode are often manipulated to mislead people. For example, let's say that the dictator of Little Island Nation (population one thousand) proposes a big tax cut for everyone, declaring

▼

"The so-called science of poll-taking is not a science at all but a mere necromancy. People are unpredictable by nature, and although you can take a nation's pulse, you can't be sure that the nation hasn't just run up a flight of stairs."

—E. B. WHITE

that the mean tax savings will be $5000 (the total tax cut divided by one thousand taxpayers). The Islanders begin to gleefully envision how they will spend their $5000. But then they learn that the mean figure has been skewed higher because of a few millionaires whose tax savings will be $100,000 or more. The tax savings for the vast majority of taxpayers is actually less than $500. The $5000 figure that the dictator tossed out is the true mean—but painfully misleading. To the Islanders, the median tax savings is much more revealing: The median is $400. The mode, the most common figure, is $300. When they get all the facts, the Islanders stage a revolt—the first one in history caused by a better understanding of statistics. ∎

Avoid self-selecting samples...

One approach that definitely does *not* yield a random sample is allowing survey subjects to choose themselves. The result of this process is called a **self-selecting sample**—a type of sample that usually tells you very little about the target population. We would get a self-selecting sample if we publish a questionnaire in a magazine and ask readers to fill it out and mail it in or if during a TV or radio news broadcast, we ask people to cast their vote on a particular issue by clicking options on a website or emailing their responses. In such cases, the sample is likely to be biased in favor of subjects who, for example, just happen to be especially opinionated or passionate; who may have strong views about the topic of the survey and are eager to spout off; or who may simply like to fill out questionnaires. Magazines, newspapers, talk shows, and news programs sometimes acknowledge the use of self-selecting samples by labeling the survey in question as "unscientific." But whether or not that term is used, the media frequently tout the results of such distorted surveys as though the numbers actually proved something.

Even good polls provide only an approximation

So a well-conducted poll using a random sample of one thousand to fifteen hundred people can reliably reflect the opinions of the whole adult population. Even so, if a second well-conducted poll is done in exactly the same way, the results will not be identical to that of the first poll. The reason is that every instance of sampling is only an approximation of the results that you would get if you polled every single individual in a target group. And, by chance, each attempt at sampling will yield slightly different results. If you dipped a bucket into a pond to get a one gallon sample of water, each bucketful would be slightly different in its biological and chemical content—even if the pond's content was very uniform.

Margin of Error: Variations between the values derived from a sample and the true values of the whole target group...

Such differences are referred to as the **margin of error** for a particular sampling or poll. Competently executed opinion polls will state their results along with a margin of error. A presidential poll, for example, might say that Candidate

Dubious Polls

Here's yet another poll with a self-selecting sample. The website for this TV news show noted inconspicuously that "This QuickVote is not scientific and reflects the opinions of only those Internet users who have chosen to participate. The results cannot be assumed to represent the opinions of Internet users in general, nor the public as a whole." The survey is not only based on a self-selecting sample but also contains another results-skewing element. What is it? Why do you think the media insist on conducting such unreliable polls?

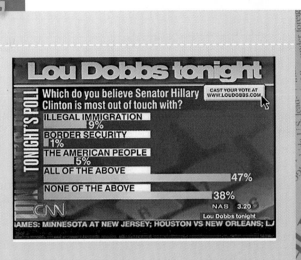

X will receive 62 percent of the popular vote, plus or minus 3 points (a common margin of error for presidential polls). The usual way of expressing this number is 62 percent ±3. This means that the percentage of people in the target population who will likely vote for Candidate X is between 59 and 65 percent.

Connected to the concept of margin of error is the notion of **confidence level.** In statistical theory, the confidence level is the probability that the sample will accurately represent the target group within the margin of error. A confidence level of 95 percent (the usual value) means that there is a 95 percent chance that the results from polling the sample (taking into account the margin of error) will accurately reflect the results that we would get if we polled the entire target population. So if our aforementioned presidential poll has a 95 percent confidence level, we know that there's a 95 percent chance that the sampling results of 62 percent ±3 points will accurately reflect the situation in the whole target group. Of course, this confidence level also means that there's a 5 percent chance that the poll's results will *not* be accurate.

Note that "confidence level" refers only to sampling error, the probability of the sample not accurately reflecting the true values in the target population. It doesn't tell you anything about any other kinds of polling errors such as bias

> "It is the mark of a truly intelligent person to be moved by statistics."
>
> —GEORGE BERNARD SHAW

Polling the Clueless

Sometimes polls end up surveying not the views of people with genuine opinions but what has been called "non-attitudes." This happens when respondents answer polling questions even though they have no real opinion on the subject or no idea what the questions are really about. Presumably, people—being people—would rather give a bogus answer than admit that they are clueless.

In one landmark poll conducted many years ago, respondents were asked, "Some people say that the 1975 Public Affairs Act should be repealed. Do you agree or disagree with this idea?" One-third of those polled offered their opinion on the issue. Trouble was, the Public Affairs Act did not exist. The pollsters made it up.

that can occur because of poorly worded questions or researchers who may consciously or unconsciously influence the kinds of answers received.

Thank you for taking part in this poll, sir. Here's the first question: What the heck makes you so arrogant to think your opinion could have any kind of importance, sir?

www.CartoonStock.com

Sample size, margin of error, and confidence level are all related in interesting ways.

- Up to a point, the larger the sample, the smaller the margin of error because the larger the sample, the more representative it is likely to be. Generally, for national polls, a sample size of six hundred yields a margin of error of ±5 points; a sample of one thousand, ±4 points; and a sample of fifteen hundred, ±3 points. But increasing the sample size substantially to well beyond one thousand does not substantially decrease the margin of error. Boosting the sample from fifteen hundred to ten thousand, for example, pushes the margin of error down to only 1 percent.

- The lower the confidence level, the smaller the sample size can be. If you're willing to have less confidence in your polling results, then a smaller sample will do. If you can accept a confidence level of only 90 percent (a 10 percent chance of getting inaccurate results), then you don't need a sample size of fifteen hundred to poll the adult population.

• The larger the margin of error, the higher the confidence level can be. With a large margin of error (±8, for example), you will naturally have more confidence that your survey results will fall within this wide range. This idea is the statistical equivalent of a point made earlier: You can have more confidence in your enumerative inductive argument if you qualify, or decrease the precision of, the conclusion.

To sum up: An enumerative induction, like any other inductive argument, must be strong and have true premises for us to be justified in accepting the conclusion. A strong enumerative induction must be based on a sample that is both large enough and representative. An opinion poll, as a sophisticated enumerative induction, must use a sufficiently large and representative sample and ensure that the gathered data accurately reflect what's being measured.

REVIEW NOTES

☑ Enumerative Induction

• Target group: The class of individuals about which an inductive generalization is made
• Sample: The observed members of a target group
• Relevant property: The property under study in a target group
• Hasty generalization: The drawing of a conclusion about a target group based on an inadequate sample size
• Biased sample: A sample that is not representative of its target group
• Simple random sampling: The selecting of a sample to ensure that each member of the target group has an equal chance of being chosen
• Margin of error: The variation between the values derived from a sample and the true values of the whole target group
• Confidence level: The probability that the sample will accurately represent the target group within the margin of error

---

Exercise 8.1

For each of the following enumerative inductions, (1) identify the target group, sample, and relevant property; (2) indicate whether the argument is strong or weak; and (3) if it's weak, say whether the problem is a sample that's too small, not representative, or both. Assume that the information provided in the premises of each argument is true.

*1. Two-thirds of the adults in New York City identify themselves as "pro-choice" in the abortion debate. And almost 70 percent of adults in San Francisco do. This makes the situation perfectly clear: A large majority of the people in this country are pro-choice. *Weak NR*

2. Most people are fed up with celebrities who get on their soapbox and air their political opinions. When people on the street have been asked by TV reporters how they feel about this issue, they almost always say that they wish celebrities would keep their opinions to themselves. *Weak NR/S*

3. Doctors used to think that anti-arrhythmic drugs were the cure for irregular heartbeats. They overprescribed these drugs and fifty thousand patients died. Doctors used to believe that the cure for ulcers was a bland diet, but that turned out to be wrong too. Every new treatment we see these days sounds great. But history tells us that they will all turn out to be worthless. *Weak S*

*4. I've asked at least a dozen first-year students at this university whether the United States should go to war with "terrorist" countries, and they all have said no. So most of the students at this university are against such a militant policy. *Weak NR/S*

5. A random, nationwide poll of several thousand gun owners shows that 80 percent of them are opposed to gun-control laws. Thus, most adults oppose gun-control laws. *Weak NR*

6. In every winter for the past twenty years Buffalo has received several feet of snow. Therefore, Buffalo is likely to get several feet of snow in the next fifty winters. *Strong*

7. Most newspaper reports of crimes in Chicago involve alleged perpetrators who belong to racial minorities. Therefore, most crimes in Chicago are committed by racial minorities. *Weak NR*

*8. Eighty-five percent of dentists who suggest that their patients chew gum recommend Brand X gum. Therefore, 85 percent of dentists recommend Brand X gum. *Weak NR*

9. Two hundred samples of water taken from many sites all along the Charles River show unsafe concentrations of toxic chemicals. Obviously the water in the Charles River is unsafe. *Strong*

10. Clearly there is an epidemic of child abductions in this country. In the past year, major network news organizations have reported five cases of children who were abducted by strangers. *Weak NR/S*

11. University fraternities are magnets for all sorts of illegal activity. Last year several frat brothers were arrested at a frat-house party. And this year a fraternity was actually kicked off campus for violating underage drinking laws. *Weak S*

*12. Most Americans are happy with their jobs and derive a great deal of satisfaction from them. A survey of fifteen hundred adults with an annual income of $48,000 to $60,000, employed in various occupations, supports this assertion. When these subjects were asked if they were happy and satisfied with their jobs, 82 percent said yes. *Weak NR*

Handwritten marginal notes:

T: People in country
S: Adults in NY/SF
P: Being pro-choice

T: People in general
S: People questioned by TV reporters
P: being fed up by celebrities who voice opinions

T: medical treatments
S: two cases
P: are worthless

T: students at this university
S: first-year students here
P: being against militant policy

T: American adults
S: several thousand gun owners
P: being opposed to gun control

T: future B winters
S: past 20 B winters
P: B getting several ft. of snow

T: Crimes in Chicago
S: C crimes reported
P: C crimes committed by RM

T: dentists
S: d who recommend chewing gum
P: d who recommend Brand X gum

T: water in Charles River
S: 200 samples from many sites
P: con of toxic chemicals

T: children
S: children reported by news as ab.
P: being abducted

T: university frats
S: at least 2 involved in illegal acts
P: illegal act involving frats

T: Americans
S: those w/incomes 48,000-60,000
P: being happy and satisfied w/job

Exercise 8.2

For each of the enumerative inductions in Exercise 8.1, indicate whether the argument is strong or weak. If it's strong, explain how the sample could be modified to make the argument weak. If it's weak, explain how the sample could be modified to make the argument strong. Keep the modifications as realistic as possible. Answers are supplied for 1, 4, 8, and 12.

Exercise 8.3

For each of the following opinion polls, (1) determine whether the poll results offer strong support for the pollster's conclusion, and, if they don't, (2) specify the source of the problem (sample too small, unrepresentative sample, or nonrandom sampling). Assume that the conducting of each survey is free of technical errors such as mistakes in data processing or improper polling interviews.

* 1. An Internet site featuring national and world news asks visitors to participate in the site's "instant daily poll" of hot topics. The current polling question is: "Should the words 'under God' be stricken from the Pledge of Allegiance if its recitation is required of public school children?" Twelve thousand people visit the site on the day that the poll is taken. Of those, seven thousand answer no to the question. The site concludes that 58 percent of Americans oppose modifying the Pledge.

2. Anita conducts a survey to determine if Americans are willing to support the arts by contributing money directly to local theater groups. One night she and her assistants interview five hundred people who are attending a performance of a musical at the city's biggest theater. To help ensure random selection, they purposely select every other patron they encounter for interviewing. There is only one interview question: "Are you willing to support the arts by giving money to local theater groups?" Ninety-four percent of the interviewees answer yes. Anita later reports that a large majority of Americans are willing to support the arts by giving money to local theater groups.

3. A prominent sociologist wants to determine the sexual attitudes of women aged twenty-five to forty-five. The main question to be explored is whether heterosexual women in this age group feel satisfied with their partners' sexual performance. The sociologist interviews two hundred of her friends who belong to the target group. She also asks two hundred of her female colleagues at her college to complete and return a survey asking the key question. She gets 78 completed surveys back from women in the target group. She finds that 75 percent of all the interviewees say that they are not satisfied with their partners' performance. She concludes that most heterosexual women aged twenty-five to forty-five aren't happy with the sexual performance of their partners.

4. A national polling organization surveys fifteen hundred obstetrician-gynecologists chosen randomly from a national registry of this medical specialty. The survey question is whether obstetrician-gynecologists

provide quality care for pregnant women. Ninety-eight percent of those surveyed say yes. The pollsters conclude that almost all physicians think that obstetrician-gynecologists provide quality care for pregnant women.

5. A national women's magazine publishes a questionnaire on sexual harassment in the workplace. Respondents are asked to complete the questionnaire and mail it in to the magazine. The magazine receives over twenty thousand completed questionnaires in the mail. Sixty-two percent of the respondents say that they've been sexually harassed at work. The magazine reports that most women have been sexually harassed at work.

Exercise 8.4

For each of the following arguments, indicate which conclusions from the accompanying list would be strongly supported by the premise given. Assume that all statements are true.

* 1. Seventy-two percent of the three hundred university students who responded to a questionnaire published in the campus newspaper are opposed to the U.S. president's economic policies.

    a. Some readers of the campus newspaper are opposed to the U.S. president's economic policies.
    b. Seventy-two percent of the students attending this school are opposed to the U.S. president's economic policies.
    c. Some students attending this school are opposed to the U.S. president's economic policies.
    d. Most readers of the campus newspaper are opposed to the U.S. president's economic policies.
    e. Seventy-two percent of the readers of the campus newspaper are opposed to the U.S. president's economic policies.

2. By listening to music, 43 percent of arthritis patients at the Drexell Clinic experience a decrease in pain in their knee and finger joints.

    a. By listening to music, 43 percent of arthritis patients can experience a decrease in pain in their knee and finger joints.
    b. By listening to music, some arthritis patients can experience a decrease in pain in their knee and finger joints.
    c. By listening to music, some arthritis patients at the Drexell Clinic can experience a decrease in pain in their knee and finger joints.
    d. By listening to music, many arthritis patients can experience a decrease in pain in their knee and finger joints.

3. Four out of five of the college's English majors hate anything written by William Faulkner.

    a. Eighty percent of the college's English majors hate anything written by William Faulkner.

   b. Most students at this college hate anything written by William Faulkner.

   c. Most college students hate anything written by William Faulkner.

   d. English majors at this college hate anything written by William Faulkner.

4. Alonzo has been driving his Dodge Spirit for seven years without any problems. His friend has the same kind of car and has been driving it for five years trouble-free.

   a. Dodge Spirits are trouble-free cars.

   b. Most Dodge Spirits are trouble-free cars.

   c. Some Dodge Spirits are trouble-free cars.

   d. Many Dodge Spirits are trouble-free cars.

5. Seventy-seven percent of adults interviewed in three Philadelphia shopping malls (650 people) say they will vote Democratic in the next presidential election.

   a. Most people will vote Democratic in the next presidential election.

   b. Seventy-seven percent of adult residents of Philadelphia will vote Democratic in the next presidential election.

   c. Many people in Philadelphia will vote Democratic in the next presidential election.

   d. A substantial percentage of people who shop at malls in Philadelphia will vote Democratic in the next presidential election.

Exercise 8.5

The following statements suggest modifications to each of the opinion polls in Exercise 8.3. In each case, determine whether the modification (and any associated change in poll results) would make the pollster's conclusion more likely to be true or not more likely to be true.

* 1. Twenty-one thousand people visit the site on the day that the poll is taken (instead of 12,000), and of those, 12,600 answer no to the question (instead of 7000).

2. Anita supplements her research by conducting phone interviews of a random sample of eight hundred adult residents of her city (population one million), asking a slightly modified question: "Are you willing to support the arts by giving money to local theater groups?" She conducts a similar poll in another large city. In both polls, at least 60 percent of respondents say yes.

3. The sociologist interviews three hundred of her friends (instead of two hundred) who belong to the target group, and she asks four hundred (instead of two hundred) of her female colleagues at her college to complete and return a survey asking the key question. Again, 75 percent of respondents say that they are not satisfied with their partners' performance.

4. The national polling organization surveys fifteen hundred physicians of various specialties chosen randomly from a national registry. Ninety-five percent of the respondents say that obstetrician-gynecologists provide quality care for pregnant women.

5. The magazine receives over thirty thousand completed questionnaires in the mail (instead of twenty thousand). Fifty-five percent of the respondents say that they've been sexually harassed at work.

Analogical Induction

An **analogy** is a comparison of two or more things alike in specific respects. In literature, science, and everyday life, analogies are used to explain or describe something. Analogies (often in the form of similes) can be powerful literary devices, both unforgettable and moving:

> . . . *the evening is spread out against the sky*
> *Like a patient etherized upon a table* . . .
>   [T. S. Eliot]

> *As cold waters to a thirsty soul,*
> *so is good news from a far country.*
>   [Proverbs 25:25]

> . . . *Out, out brief candle!*
> *Life's but a walking shadow, a poor player*
> *That struts and frets his hour upon the stage*
> *And then is heard no more. It is a tale*
> *Told by an idiot, full of sound and fury,*
> *Signifying nothing.*
>   [Macbeth, *Act V*]

But an analogy can also be used to *argue inductively for a conclusion*. Such an argument is known as an **analogical induction,** or simply an **argument by analogy.** An analogical induction reasons this way: Because two or more things are similar in several respects, they must be similar in some further respect. For example:

> *Humans can move about, solve mathematical equations, win chess games, and feel pain.*
> *Robots are like humans in that they can move about, solve mathematical equations, and win chess games.*
> *Therefore, it's probable that robots can also feel pain.*

Handwritten margin notes:

Analogy: Comparison of two or more things alike is specific respects...
Analogies have many uses

Analogical Induction
Analogy used to argue inductively for a conclusion...

> "All perception of truth is the detection of an analogy."
> —HENRY DAVID THOREAU

This argument says that because robots are like humans in several ways (ways that are already known or agreed on), they must be like humans in yet another way (a way that the argument is meant to establish).

So analogical induction has this pattern:

Thing A has properties P_1, P_2, P_3 plus the property P_4.
Thing B has properties P_1, P_2, and P_3.
Therefore, thing B probably has property P_4.

Form of Analogical Induction

Argument by analogy, like all inductive reasoning, can establish conclusions only with a degree of probability. The greater the degree of similarity between the two things being compared, the more probable the conclusion is.

Like all inductive arguments conclusion is probable...

Recall that enumerative inductive has this form:

X percent of the observed members of group A have property P.
Therefore, X percent of all members of group A probably have property P.

Thus, the most blatant difference between these two forms of induction is that enumerative induction argues from some members of a group to the group as a whole, but analogical induction reasons from some (one or more) individuals to one further individual. Looked at another way, enumerative induction argues from the properties of a sample to the properties of the whole group; analogical induction reasons from the properties of one or more individuals to the properties of another individual.

Differences between Enumerative Induction & Analogical Induction

Arguments by analogy are probably used (and misused) in every area of human endeavor—but especially in law, science, medicine, ethics, archeology, and forensics. Here are a few examples.

Examples of Analogical Arguments...

Argument 3: Medical Science

Mice are mammals, have a mammalian circulatory system, have typical mammalian biochemical reactions, respond readily to high blood pressure drugs, and experience a reduction in blood cholesterol when given the new Drug Z. Humans are mammals, have a mammalian circulatory system, have typical mammalian biochemical reactions, and respond readily to high blood pressure drugs. Therefore, humans will also experience a reduction in blood cholesterol when given the new Drug Z.

Argument 4: Religion

A watch is a mechanism of exquisite complexity with numerous parts precisely arranged and accurately adjusted to achieve a purpose—a purpose imposed by the watch's designer. Likewise the universe has exquisite complexity with countless parts—from atoms to asteroids—that fit together precisely and accurately to produce certain effects as though arranged by plan. Therefore, the universe must also have a designer.

Argument 5: Law

The case before the court involves a school-sponsored charity drive at which school officials led a public prayer. At issue is whether the school officials were in violation of the Constitutional ban on government support of religion. A similar case—a relevant precedent—involved school-sponsored prayer at a school soccer game, and again at issue was whether the school was in violation of the Constitutional ban on government support of religion. In that case, the high court ruled that the school-sponsored prayer was unconstitutional. Therefore, the high court should also rule in the charity-drive case that the officially led prayer is unconstitutional.

Argument 6: Forensics

Whenever we have observed this pattern in the spatter of blood, we have subsequently learned that the gunshot victim was about four feet from the gun when it was fired and that the victim was facing away from the assailant. In this crime scene, we have exactly the same pattern of blood spatter. Therefore, the victim was about four feet from the gun when it was fired and was facing away from the assailant.

FURTHER THOUGHT

💡 Analogical Induction in Moral Reasoning

In Chapter 11 we'll study in detail the uses of argument and critical thinking in moral reasoning. For now, it's sufficient to know this: When we try to show that a particular action is right or wrong , we often rely on argument by analogy. We argue that since an action is relevantly similar to another action, and the former action is clearly right (or wrong), then we should regard the latter action in the same way. For example, we might propose an argument like this:

Premise 1: Caring more for the members of one's own family than outsiders is morally permissible.

Premise 2: America's policy of giving more aid to its own citizens than those of other countries is relevantly similar to caring more for the members of one's own family than outsiders.

Conclusion: Therefore, America's policy of giving more aid to its own citizens than those of other countries is probably morally permissible.

Here, as in any argument by analogy, the conclusion can be established only with a degree of probability. And we would evaluate its strength the same way we would any other analogical argument.

Arguments by analogy are easy to formulate—perhaps too easy. To use an analogy to support a particular conclusion, all you have to do is find two things with some similarities and then reason that the two things are similar in yet another way. You could easily reach some very loopy conclusions. You could argue this, for instance: Birds have two legs, two eyes, breathe air, and fly; and humans have two legs, two eyes, and breathe air; therefore, humans can also fly. So the question is, how do we sort out the worthy analogical inductions from the unworthy (or really wacky)? How do we judge which ones have conclusions worth accepting and which ones don't?

Fortunately, there are some criteria we can use to judge the strength of arguments by analogy:

1. Relevant similarities
2. Relevant dissimilarities
3. The number of instances compared
4. Diversity among cases

If you find yourself thinking that they make perfect sense, that's probably because you already use these criteria in your own arguments by analogy.

Relevant Similarities

The more relevant similarities there are between the things being compared, the more probable the conclusion. Consider this argument:

> In the Vietnam War, the United States had not articulated a clear rationale for fighting there, and the United States lost. Likewise, in the present war the United States has not articulated a clear rationale for fighting. Therefore, the United States will lose this war too.

There is just one relevant similarity noted here (the lack of rationale). As it stands, this argument is weak; the two wars are only dimly analogous. A single similarity between two wars in different eras is not enough to strongly support the conclusion. But watch what happens if we add more similarities:

> In the Vietnam War, the United States had not articulated a clear rationale for fighting, there was no plan for ending the involvement of U.S. forces (no exit strategy), U.S. military tactics were inconsistent, and the military's view of enemy strength was unrealistic. The United States lost the Vietnam War. Likewise, in the present war, the United States has not articulated a clear rationale for fighting, there is no exit strategy, U.S. tactics are inconsistent, and the military's view of enemy strength is naive. Therefore, the United States will also lose this war.

How do we avoid bad arguments that have loopy conclusions...

CRITERIA FOR ASSESSING ARGUMENTS BY ANALOGY
Criteria for Strength

Weak: just one similarity is noted in this argument

Adding relevant similarities makes argument stronger

Remember to check for cogency

① Similarities must be relevant
② Similarities must be true

Irrelevant similarities

With these additional similarities between the Vietnam War and the current conflict, the argument is considerably stronger. (The premises, of course, may be false, rendering the argument not cogent, even if the inference were strong.) Arguments 3–6 (medical science, religion, law, and forensics) can also be strengthened by citing additional relevant similarities between the things compared.

Notice that this first criterion involves *relevant* similarities. The similarities cited in an analogical induction can't strengthen the argument at all if they have nothing to do with the conclusion. A similarity (or dissimilarity) is relevant to an argument by analogy if it has an effect on whether the conclusion is probably true. The argument on war that was just given mentions five different similarities between the Vietnam War and the present war, and each similarity is relevant because it has some bearing on the probability of the conclusion. But what if we added these similarities?

1. In both wars, some combatants have green eyes.
2. In both wars, some soldiers are taller than others.
3. In both wars, ticket sales to movies in the United States increase.

These factors would make no difference to the probability of the conclusion. They're irrelevant and can neither strengthen nor weaken the argument.

Relevant Dissimilarities

Dissimilarities can weaken the argument

Generally, the more relevant dissimilarities, or disanalogies, there are between the things being compared, the less probable the conclusion. Dissimilarities weaken arguments by analogy. Consider argument 3 (regarding Drug Z). What if we discover that cholesterol-lowering drugs that work in mice almost never work in humans? This one dissimilarity would severely weaken the argument and make the conclusion much less probable.

Hume's Principle
One can criticize an analogical argument by pointing out the dissimilarities...

Example: Watch Argument

Pointing out dissimilarities in an analogical induction is a common way to undermine the argument. Sometimes finding one relevant dissimilarity is enough to show that the argument should be rejected. A familiar response to argument 4 (the watch argument) is to point out a crucial dissimilarity between a watch and the universe: The universe may resemble a watch (or mechanism) in some ways, but it also resembles a living thing, which a watch does not.

The Number of Instances Compared

In the Vietnam War Argument one can introduce more instances, i.e. wars...

The greater the number of instances, or cases, that show the relevant similarities, the stronger the argument. In the war argument, for example, there is only one instance that has all the relevant similarities: the Vietnam War. But what if there were five additional instances—five different wars that have the relevant similarities to the present war? The argument would be strengthened. The Vietnam

War, though it is relevantly similar to the present war, may be an anomaly, a war with a unique set of properties. But citing other cases that are relevantly similar to the present war shows that the relevant set of similarities is no fluke.

Argument 6 (the forensics induction) is an especially strong argument in part because it cites numerous cases. It implies the existence of such instances when it says "Whenever we have observed this pattern . . ."

See Argument 6 (p. 304)

Diversity Among Cases

As we've seen, dissimilarities between the things being compared weaken an argument by analogy. Such dissimilarities suggest that the things being compared are not strongly analogous. And we've noted that several cases (instead of just one) that exhibit the similarities can strengthen the argument. In this criterion, however, we focus on a very different point: The greater the diversity among the cases that exhibit the relevant similarities, the stronger the argument.

The greater the diversity among cases that exhibit the relevant similarities the stronger the argument

Take a look at this argument:

Example

> (1) *In the 1990s a U.S. senator, a Republican from Virginia, was chairman of the commerce committee, had very close ties to Corporation X, had previously worked for Corporation X before coming to office, and was found to have been taking bribes from Corporation X.*
> (2) *In the 1980s another U.S. senator, a Democrat from Texas, was chairman of the commerce committee, had very close ties to Corporation X, had previously worked for Corporation X before coming to office, and was found to have been taking bribes from Corporation X.*
> (3) *In the 1970s another U.S. senator, an Independent from Arkansas with strong religious values, was chairman of the commerce committee, had very close ties to Corporation X, had previously worked for Corporation X before coming to office, and was found to have been taking bribes from Corporation X.*
> (4) *Now the newly elected Senator Jones, a Democrat from New York with strong support from labor unions, is chairman of the commerce committee, has very close ties to Corporation X, and has previously worked for Corporation X before coming to office.*
> (5) *Therefore, Senator Jones will take bribes from Corporation X.*

Here we have several similarities in question, and they exist between the Senator Jones situation (described in premise 4) and three other cases (detailed in premises 1–3). But what makes this argument especially strong is that the cases are diverse despite the handful of similarities—one case involves a Republican senator from Virginia; another, a Democratic senator from Texas; and finally a religious Independent senator from Arkansas. This state of affairs suggests that the similarities are not accidental or contrived but are strongly linked even in a variety of situations.

REVIEW NOTES

☑ Analogical Induction

ANALOGICAL ARGUMENT PATTERN

Thing A has properties P_1, P_2, P_3 plus the property P_4.
Thing B has properties P_1, P_2, and P_3.
Therefore, thing B probably has property P_4.

CRITERIA FOR JUDGING ARGUMENTS BY ANALOGY

1. The number of relevant similarities
2. The number of relevant dissimilarities
3. The number of instances compared
4. The diversity among cases

As you know, an inductive argument cannot guarantee the truth of the conclusion, and analogical inductions are no exception. But by carefully applying the foregoing criteria, we can increase our chances of arriving at well-supported conclusions (or of identifying those conclusions that are not). This is happily the case—even though there is no magic formula for using the criteria in real-life situations.

Exercise 8.6

Evaluate each of the following passages and indicate whether it contains (a) an argument by analogy, (b) a literary analogy, or (c) an enumerative induction. If the passage contains an argument by analogy, indicate the total number of things (instances) being compared, the relevant similarities mentioned or implied, the conclusion, and whether the argument is strong or weak.

Literary

1. Thinking is like a game of chess, in which every piece is related to every other, and every move is part of the realization of a hundred possible strategies.

Literary

* 2. "Duct tape is like the force. It has a light side, a dark side, and it holds the universe together." [Carl Zwanzig]

Enumerative Induction

3. Girls are smarter than boys. Girls in the debate club always argue better than boys. And the mean grade-point average of the girls in the glee club is higher than that of the boys in the club.

Literary

4. "Howard Hughes was able to afford the luxury of madness, like a man who not only thinks he is Napoleon but hires an army to prove it." [Ted Morgan]

5. "Look around the world: contemplate the whole and every part of it: you will find it to be nothing but one great machine, subdivided into an infinite number of lesser machines, which again admit of subdivisions, to a degree beyond what human senses and faculties can trace and explain. All these various machines, and even their most minute parts, are adjusted to each other with an accuracy, which ravishes into admiration all men, who have ever contemplated them. The curious adapting of means to ends, throughout all nature, resembles exactly, though it much exceeds, the production of human contrivance; of human design, thought, wisdom, and intelligence. Since therefore the effects resemble each other, we are led to infer, by all the rules of analogy, that the causes also resemble; and that the Author of Nature is somewhat similar to the mind of men; though possessed of much larger faculties, proportioned to the grandeur of the work, which he has executed. By this argument *a posteriori*, and by this argument alone, do we prove at once the existence of a Deity, and his similarity to human mind and intelligence." [David Hume]

* 6. My brother was always good at arithmetic, so he'll be a whiz at algebra.

7. Tolerating a vicious dictator is like tolerating a bully on the block. If you let the bully push you around, sooner or later he will beat you up and take everything you have. If you let a dictator have his way, he will abuse his people and rob them of life and liberty. If you stand up to the bully just once or—better yet—knock him senseless with a stick, he will never bother you again. Likewise, if you refuse to be coerced by a dictator or if you attack him, his reign will be over. Therefore, the best course of action for people oppressed by a dictator is to resist and attack.

* 8. I like sausage, and I like ham, and I like pork chops. So I will like chitlings.

9. "The brain secretes thought as the stomach secretes gastric juice, the liver bile, and the kidneys urine." [Karl Vogt]

10. George has loved every Chevrolet he has owned in the past five years. So he will probably love the Chevrolet he bought yesterday.

11. How does one know that there exist in the world other minds—that is, others having feelings and other subjective experiences? One can observe that one's own experiences are connected to publicly observable phenomena, that other people exhibit publicly observable phenomena, and therefore other people also must have subjective experiences. For example, one may observe that when one stubs a toe, one feels pain and cries "ouch." Then if other people—who are physically similar to oneself—also stub their toes and cry "ouch," one can conclude that they also experience pain.

* 12. "Character is the foundation stone upon which one must build to win respect. Just as no worthy building can be erected on a weak foundation,

so no lasting reputation worthy of respect can be built on a weak character." [R. C. Samsel]

Exercise 8.7

Evaluate each of the following arguments by analogy, indicating (1) the things (instances) being compared, (2) the relevant similarities mentioned or implied, (3) whether diversity among multiple cases is a significant factor, (4) the conclusion, and (5) whether the argument is strong or weak.

Weak

* 1. Like former president Ronald Reagan, president George W. Bush is a staunch conservative, has strong Christian values, and adheres almost dogmatically to certain conservative principles. President Reagan allowed his fierce fidelity to his principles and values to lead him into a foreign policy disaster, the Iran-Contra debacle. President Bush will likely be involved in a similar foreign policy mess for similar reasons.

Weak

2. The United Nations failed to intervene in Bosnia to prevent massive human rights violations and ethnic cleansing. It also failed to act to stop the murders of close to a million innocent people in Rwanda. The UN will not intervene to stop any widespread slaughter of innocents in Nigeria.

?

3. "If a single cell, under appropriate conditions, becomes a person in the space of a few years, there can surely be no difficulty in understanding how, under appropriate conditions, a cell may, in the course of untold millions of years, give origin to the human race." [Herbert Spencer]

Strong

4. The casinos in Atlantic City have brought a tremendous amount of revenue into both area businesses and local government, without inviting the evils of organized crime and causing the degradation of law and order or quality of life. The same can be said for the Turning Stone casino in Upstate New York, as well as for Casino Niagara in Niagara Falls, Canada. A casino built in Buffalo, New York, will provide all the same benefits without the disadvantages.

Weak

* 5. A well-established moral principle is that one is morally justified in using deadly force in self-defense when one is threatened with death or great pain from an assailant. A disease such as terminal cancer can also threaten one with death or great pain. So suicide—a use of deadly force—must sometimes be morally justified when it is an act of self-defense against an assailant (terminal disease) that threatens death or great pain.

Weak

6. "If we survey the universe, so far as it falls under our knowledge, it bears a great resemblance to an animal or organized body, and seems actuated with a like principle of life and motion. A continual circulation of matter in it produces no disorder: a continual waste in every part is incessantly repaired: The closest sympathy is perceived throughout the whole system. And each part or member, in performing its proper

offices, operates both to its own preservation and to that of the whole. The world, therefore, I infer, is an animal, and the Deity is the soul of the world, activating it and activated by it." [Philo, in Hume's *Dialogues Concerning Natural Religion*]

7. "The mass of men serve the State thus, not as men mainly, but as machines, with their bodies. They are the standing army, and the militia, jailers, constables, *posse comitatus*, &c. In most cases there is no free exercise whatever of the judgment or of the moral sense; but they put themselves on a level with wood and earth and stones, and wooden men can perhaps be manufactured that will serve the purpose as well. Such command no more respect than men of straw, or a lump of dirt." [Henry David Thoreau]

Causal Arguments

Our world is a shifting, multifarious, complicated web of causes and effects—and that's an oversimplification. Incredibly, the normal human response to the apparent causal chaos is to jump in and ask what causes what. What causes breast cancer? What made Malcolm steal the car? What produced that rash on Norah's arm? What brought the universe into existence? When we answer such questions (or try to), we make a **causal claim**—a statement about the causes of things. And when we try to prove or support a causal claim, we make a **causal argument**—an inductive argument whose conclusion contains a causal claim.

> "I would rather discover a single causal connection than win the throne of Persia."
> —DEMOCRITUS

Causal arguments, being inductive, can give us only probable conclusions. If the premises of a strong causal argument are true, then the conclusion is only probably true, with the probability varying from merely likely to highly probable. The probabilistic nature of causal arguments, however, is not a failing or weakness. Causal reasoning is simply different from deductive reasoning, and it is our primary method of acquiring knowledge about the workings of the world. The great human enterprise known as science is concerned mainly with causal processes and causal arguments, and few people would consider this work inferior or unreliable because it was not deductively unshakeable.

"This is a little embarrassing to admit, but everything that happens happens for no real reason."

Enumerative Induction

Causal arguments can come in several inductive forms, some of which you already know about. For example, we sometimes reason about cause and effect using enumerative induction:

> *One time, when I made the aluminum rod come in contact with the rotating*
> *circular-saw blade, sparks flew.*
> *Another time, when I made the aluminum rod come in contact with the rotating*
> *circular-saw blade, sparks flew.*
> *Many other times, when I made the aluminum rod come in contact with the ro-*
> *tating circular-saw blade, sparks flew.*
> *Therefore, making the aluminum rod come in contact with the rotating circular-*
> *saw blade always causes sparks to fly.*

Analogical Induction

Occasionally, we may argue to a causal conclusion using analogical induction:

> *Ten years ago a massive surge in worldwide oil prices caused a recession.*
> *Five years ago a massive surge in worldwide oil prices caused a recession.*
> *Therefore, the current massive surge in worldwide oil prices will cause a recession.*

Most often, though, we use another type of induction in which we reason to a causal conclusion by pinpointing the best explanation for a particular effect. Let's say that after a hailstorm you discover that the roof of your car, which you had left parked outside in the driveway, has a hundred tiny dents in it. You might reason like this: The dents could have been caused by the mischievous kids next door, or by a flock of lunatic woodpeckers, or by the hailstorm. After considering these options (and a few others), you decide that the best explanation (or hypothesis) for the dents is the hailstorm. So you conclude that the hailstorm caused the dents in your car's roof.

Inference to the Best
Explanation...

This is a very powerful and versatile form of inductive reasoning called **inference to the best explanation.** It's the essence of scientific thinking and a mainstay of our everyday problem-solving and knowledge acquisition (whether causal or noncausal). Because of the importance and usefulness of such reasoning, this text devotes three chapters to it in Part 4. So we won't try to cover the same ground here. Instead, we'll concentrate on some other inductive patterns of reasoning that have traditionally been used to assess causal connections.

TESTING FOR CAUSES

J.S. Mill (1806–1873)

MILL'S METHOD's

English philosopher John Stuart Mill (1806-1873) noted several ways of evaluating causal arguments and formulated them into what are now known as "Mill's methods" of inductive inference. Despite their fancy name, however, the methods are basically common sense and are used by just about everyone. They also happen to be the basis of a great deal of scientific testing. Let's look at a few of the more important ones.

Agreement or Difference

A modified version of Mill's *Method of Agreement* says that if two or more occurrences of a phenomenon have only one relevant factor in common, that factor must be the cause.

Imagine that dozens of people stop into Elmo's corner bar after work as they usually do and that ten of them come down with an intestinal illness one hour after leaving the premises. What caused them to become ill? There are a lot of possibilities. Maybe a waiter who had a flu-like illness sneezed into their drinks, or the free tacos had gone bad, or another patron had a viral infection and passed it along via a handshake. But let's say that there is only one relevant factor that's common to all ten people who got sick: They all had a drink from the same bottle of wine. We could then plausibly conclude that something in the wine probably caused the illness.

Public health officials often use the Method of Agreement, especially when they're trying to determine the cause of an unusual illness in a population of several thousand people. They might be puzzled, say, by an unusually large number of cases of rare liver disease in a city. If they discover that all the affected people have the same poison in their bloodstreams—and this is the only common relevant factor—they have reason to believe that the poison is the cause of the liver disease. In such situations, the poison may turn out to have an industrial or agricultural source.

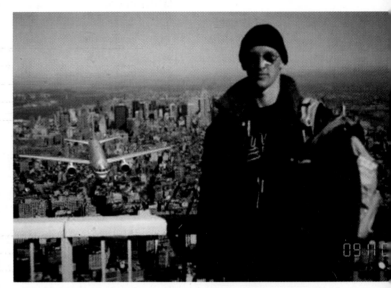

Not long after the September 11, 2001, attacks, this photographic fake started popping up everywhere on the Web, its caption identifying it as a snapshot of a tourist on the observation deck of the World Trade Center, taken just seconds before the first plane struck. The camera, said the caption, was discovered later in the rubble. What reasons could a critical thinker have for concluding that the photo is in fact a sham? (Hint: Some of the more obvious reasons are that the camera would have very likely been destroyed in the disaster, the plane shown is not the kind used in the attack, and the tourist is dressed wrong for the weather [the day was warm]).

Here's a schematic of an argument based on the Method of Agreement:

Instance 1: Factors *a*, *b*, and *c* are followed by *E*.
Instance 2: Factors *a*, *c*, and *d* are followed by *E*.
Instance 3: Factors *b* and *c* are followed by *E*.
Instance 4: Factors *c* and *d* are followed by *E*.
Therefore, factor *c* is probably the cause of *E*.

There's only one factor—factor *c*—that consistently accompanies effect *E*. The other factors are sometimes present and sometimes not. We conclude then that factor *c* brings about *E*.

Mill's (modified) *Method of Difference* says that the relevant factor present when a phenomenon occurs, and absent when the phenomenon does not occur, must be

①
Method of Agreement

If two or more occurrences of a phenomenon have only one relevant factor in common, that factor must be the cause...

the cause. Here we look not for factors that the instances of the phenomenon have in common, but for factors that are points of difference among the instances.

Suppose that the performance of football players on a major league team has been consistently excellent except for six players who've recently been playing the worst games of their careers. The only relevant difference between the high- and low-performing players is that the latter have been taking daily doses of Brand X herbal supplements. If the supplement dosing is really the only relevant difference, we could plausibly conclude that the supplements are causing the lousy performance. (Finding out if the supplements are indeed the only relevant difference, of course, is easier said than done.)

So arguments based on the Method of Difference have this form:

Instance 1: Factors a, b, and c are followed by E.
Instance 2: Factors a and b are not followed by E.
Therefore, factor c is probably the cause of E.

Both Agreement and Difference

If we combine these two reasoning patterns, we get a modified version of what Mill called the *Joint Method of Agreement and Difference*. Using this joint method is, obviously, just a matter of applying both methods simultaneously—a procedure that generally increases the probability that the conclusion is true. This combined method, then, says that the likely cause is the one isolated when you (1) identify the relevant factors common to occurrences of the phenomenon (the Method of Agreement) and (2) discard any of these that are present even when there are no occurrences (the Method of Difference).

Let's apply this combined method to the mystery illness at Elmo's bar. Say that among the ten patrons who become ill, the common factors are that they all drank from the same bottle of wine, and they all had the free tacos. So we reason that the likely cause is either the wine or the tacos. After further investigation, though, we find that other patrons who ate the tacos did not become ill. We conclude that the wine is the culprit.

The schematic for arguments based on the Joint Method of Agreement and Difference is:

Instance 1: Factors a, b, and c are followed by E.
Instance 2: Factors a, b, and d are followed by E.
Instance 3: Factors b and c are not followed by E.
Instance 4: Factors b and d are not followed by E.
Therefore, factor a is probably the cause of E.

Factors a and b are the only relevant factors that are accompanied by E. But we can eliminate b as a possibility because when it's present, E doesn't occur. So b can't be the cause of E; a is most likely the cause.

Handwritten margin notes:

② Method of Difference
The relevant factor present when the phenomenon occurs and absent when the phenomenon does not occur must be the cause...

③ Joint Method of Agreement and Difference
The likely cause is the one isolated when you:
1) identify the relevant factors common to the occurrences of the phenomenon
2) discard any of these that are present even when there are no occurrences

Controlled Trials

You can see the Joint Method of Agreement and Difference at work in modern "controlled trials" used to test the effectiveness of medical treatments. In these experiments, there are two groups of subjects—one known as the experimental group; the other, the control group. The experimental group receives the treatment being tested, usually a new drug. The control group receives a bogus, or inactive, treatment (referred to as a placebo). This setup helps ensure that the two groups are as similar as possible and that they differ in only one respect—the use of the genuine treatment. A controlled trial, then, reveals the relevant factor *common* to the occurrence of the effect, which is the subjects' response to the treatment (Method of Agreement). And it shows the only important difference between the occurrence and nonoccurrence of the effect: the use of the treatment being tested.

Correlation

In many cases, relevant factors aren't merely present or absent during occurrences of the phenomenon—they are closely *correlated* with the occurrences. The cause of an occurrence varies as the occurrence (effect) does. For such situations Mill formulated the *Method of Concomitant Variation*. This method says that when two events are correlated—when one varies in close connection with the other—they are probably causally related.

④

Method of Concomitant Variation

When one event varies in close connection with the other they are probably causally related...

If you observe that the longer you boil eggs, the harder they get (and no other relevant factors complicate this relationship), you can safely conclude that this correlation between boiling and hardening is a causal connection. You have good evidence that the boiling causes the hardening.

In medical science, such correlations are highly prized because direct evidence of cause and effect is so hard to come by. Correlations are often indirect evidence of one thing causing another. In exploring the link between cigarette smoking and lung cancer, for example, researchers discovered first that people who smoke cigarettes are more likely to get lung cancer than those who don't smoke. But later research also showed that the more cigarettes people smoke, the higher their risk of lung cancer. Medical scientists call such a correlation a *dose-response relationship*. The higher the dose of the element in question (smoking), the higher the response (the more cases of lung cancer). This dose-response relationship between cigarette smoking and lung cancer is, when combined with other data, strong evidence that smoking causes lung cancer.

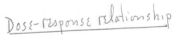

Dose-response relationship

We can represent arguments based on the Method of Concomitant Variation like this:

Instance 1: Factors *a*, *b*, and *c* are correlated with *E*.
Instance 2: Factors *a*, *b*, and increased-*c* are correlated with increased *E*.
Instance 3: Factors *a*, *b*, and decreased-*c* are correlated with decreased *E*.
Therefore, factor *c* is causally connected with *E*.

A very important cautionary note must accompany this discussion of correlation: Correlation, of course, does not always mean that a causal relationship is present. A correlation could just be a coincidence (see later). An increase in home PC sales is correlated with a rise in the incidence of AIDS in Africa, but this doesn't mean that one is in any way causally linked with the other.

FURTHER THOUGHT

 Is It Causal Confusion or ESP?

For over two decades, scientist-writer Susan Blackmore (with degrees in psychology, physiology, and parapsychology) has been investigating the psychology of "psychic," or paranormal, experience. Her central hypothesis has been that people's supposed experience of extrasensory perception, or ESP (telepathy, clairvoyance, and precognition), is the result of errors in causal thinking. Specifically, people tend to mistake coincidence for causal connection. She writes:

Scientist-writer Susan Blackmore

My hypothesis is that psychic experiences are comparable to visual illusions. The experience is real enough, but its origin lies in internal processes, not peculiarities in the observable world. Like visual illusions they arise from cognitive processes that are usually appropriate but under certain circumstances give rise to the wrong answer. In other words, they are a price we pay for using efficient heuristics.

In the case of vision, illusions arise when, for example, depth is seen in two-dimensional figures and constancy mechanisms give the answer that would be correct for real depth. The equivalent in the case of psychic experiences may be the illusion that a cause is operating and an explanation is required when in fact none is. In other words, psychic experiences are illusions of causality. . . .

Experiences of telepathy, clairvoyance, and precognition imply a coincidence that is "too good to be just chance." This is so whether the experience involves dreaming about a person's death and that person dies within a few hours, feeling the urge to pick up one's partner from

[Margin annotations, handwritten:]

Psychic experiences are comparable to visual illusions

Psychic experiences are illusions of causality

the station and in fact he was stranded and needed help, or betting on a horse that later wins a race.

Some people's response to such events is to say, "That was just a chance coincidence"; while others' is to say, "That cannot be chance." In the latter case the person will then look for a causal explanation for the coincidence. If none can be found, a "cause," such as ESP, may be invoked. Alternatively, some kind of noncausal but meaningful connection may be sought, such as Jung's "acausal connecting principle."

There are two possible types of error that may be made here. First, people may treat connected events as chance coincidences, thereby missing real connections between events and failing to look for explanations. Second, they may treat chance events as connected and seek for explanations where none is required. In the real world of inadequate information and complex interactions one would expect errors of both types to occur. It is the latter type that, I suggest, gives rise to experiences of ESP. . . .

One prediction of this approach is that those people who more frequently look for explanations of chance coincidences are more likely to have psychic experiences. Therefore, sheep [believers in ESP] should be those who underestimate the probability of chance coincidences.

It has long been known that probability judgments can be extremely inaccurate. Kahneman and Tversky (1973) have explored some of the heuristics, such as "representativeness" and "availability," that people find coincidences surprising (Fall 1982; Falk and McGregor 1983). Adding specific but superfluous detail can make coincidences seem more surprising, and things that happen to subjects themselves seem more surprising to them than the same things happening to other people. . . .

There is, however, little research relating these misjudgments to belief in the paranormal or to having psychic experiences. Blackmore and Troscianko (1985) found that sheep performed worse than goats [skeptics about ESP] on a variety of probability tasks. For example, in questions testing for responsiveness to sample size, sheep did significantly worse than goats. The well-known birthday question was asked: How many people would you need to have at a party to have a 50:50 chance that two have the same birthday? . . . As predicted, goats got the answer right significantly more often than sheep.

Subjects also played a coin-tossing computer game and were asked to guess how many hits they would be likely to get by chance. The correct answer, 10 hits in 20 trials, seems to be rather obvious. However, the sheep gave a significantly lower mean estimate of only 7.9, while goats gave a more accurate estimate of 9.6.[1]

CAUSAL CONFUSIONS

Mill's methods and other forms of causal reasoning may be common sense, but they're not foolproof. No inductive procedure can guarantee the truth of the conclusion. More to the point, it's easy to commit errors in cause-and-effect reasoning—regardless of the method used—by failing to take into account pertinent aspects of the situation. This section describes some of the more common causal blunders to which we're all prey.

Misidentifying Relevant Factors

A key issue in any type of causal reasoning is whether the factors preceding an effect are truly relevant to that effect. In the Method of Agreement, for example, it's easy to find a preceding factor common to all occurrences of a phenomenon. But that factor may be irrelevant. In the case of Elmo's bar, what if all those who became ill had black hair? So what? We know that hair color is very unlikely to be related to intestinal illness. *Relevant* factors include only those things that could possibly be causally connected to the occurrence of the phenomenon being studied. We could reasonably judge that factors relevant to the intestinal illness would include all the conditions that might help transmit bacteria or viruses.

Your ability to identify relevant factors depends mostly on your background knowledge—what you know about the kinds of conditions that could produce the occurrences in which you're interested. Lack of background knowledge might lead you to dismiss or ignore relevant factors or to assume that irrelevant factors must play a role. The only cure for this inadequacy is deeper study of the causal possibilities in question.

[handwritten margin note: Need to identify relevant factors]

[handwritten margin note: Need background knowledge to identify relevant factors]

Mishandling Multiple Factors

Most of the time, the biggest difficulty in evaluating causal connections is not that there are so few relevant factors to consider—but that there are so many. Too often the Method of Agreement and the Method of Difference are rendered useless because they cannot, by themselves, narrow the possibilities to just one. At the same time, ordinary causal reasoning is frequently flawed because of the failure to consider *all* the relevant antecedent factors. (Later chapters will refer to this problem as the failure to consider alternative explanations.)

Sometimes this kind of oversight happens because we simply don't look hard enough for possible causes. At other times, we miss relevant factors because we don't know enough about the causal processes involved. This again is a function of skimpy background knowledge. Either way, there is no countermeasure better than your own determination to dig out the whole truth.

[handwritten margin note: Sometimes there are too many relevant factors]

"In reality, the most astonishingly incredible coincidence imaginable would be the complete absence of all coincidences."

—JOHN ALLEN PAULOS

Coincidence, Birth Dates, and U.S. Presidents

When we're tempted to say that the conjunction of two events "couldn't be just coincidence," we should think twice. People are often lousy at determining the true likelihood of events. Recall the birth-date problem mentioned in Chapter 4. It's the classic example of misjudged probabilities: In a random selection of twenty-three people, what is the probability that at least two of them will have the same birth date? The answer: 50 percent, or 50-50. People are usually shocked when they hear the answer. Part of the reason is that they typically underestimate how often oddball coincidences occur and fail to see that such strange conjunctions *must* occur from time to time. Here's a succinct explanation of the problem from social psychologist David G. Myers:

> We've all marveled at such coincidences in our own lives. Checking out a photocopy counter from the Hope College library desk, I confused the clerk when giving my six-digit department charge number—which just happened at that moment to be identical to the counter's six-digit number on which the last user had finished. Shortly after my daughter,

Laura Myers, bought two pairs of shoes, we were astounded to discover that the two brand names on the boxes were "Laura" and "Myers."

And then there are those remarkable coincidences that, with added digging, have been embellished into really fun stories, such as the familiar Lincoln–Kennedy coincidences (both with seven letters in their last names, elected 100 years apart, assassinated on a Friday while beside their wives, one in Ford's theater, the other in a Ford Motor

Co. car, and so forth). We also have enjoyed newspaper accounts of astonishing happenings, such as when twins Lorraine and Levinia Christmas, driving to deliver Christmas presents to each other near Flitcham, England, collided.

My favorite is this little known fact: In Psalm 46 of the King James Bible, published in the year that Shakespeare turned 46, the 46th word is "shake" and the 46th word from the end is "spear." (More remarkable than this coincidence is that someone should have noted this!) . . .

"In reality," says mathematician John Allen Paulos, "the most astonishingly incredible coincidence imaginable would be the complete absence of all coincidences." When Evelyn Marie Adams won the New Jersey lottery twice, newspapers reported the odds of her feat as 1 in 17 trillion—the odds that a given person buying a single ticket for two New Jersey lotteries would win both. But statisticians Stephen Samuels and George McCabe report that, given the millions of people who buy U.S. state lottery tickets, it was "practically a sure thing" that someday, somewhere, someone would hit a state jackpot twice. Consider: An event that happens to but one in a billion people in a day happens 2000 times a year. A day when nothing weird happened would actually be the weirdest day of all.[2]   ■

Being Misled by Coincidence

Sometimes ordinary events are paired in unusual or interesting ways: You think of Hawaii, then suddenly a TV ad announces low-cost fares to Maui; you receive some email just as your doorbell sounds and the phone rings; or you stand in the lobby of a hotel thinking of an old friend—then see her walk by. Plenty of interesting pairings can also show up in scientific research. Scientists might find, for example, that men with the highest rates of heart disease may also have a higher daily intake of water. Or women with the lowest risk of breast cancer may own Toyotas. Such pairings are very probably just coincidence, merely interesting correlations of events. A problem arises, though, when we think that there nevertheless must be a causal connection involved.

For several reasons, we may very much want a coincidence to be a cause-and-effect relationship, so we come to believe that the pairing is causal. Just as often we may mistake causes for coincidences because we're impressed or excited about the conjunction of events. The pairing of events may seem "too much of a coincidence" to be coincidence, so we conclude that one event must have caused the other. You may be thinking about how nice it would be for your sister to call you from her home in Alaska—then the phone rings, and it's her! You're tempted to conclude that your wishing caused her to call. But such an event, though intriguing and seemingly improbable, is not really so extraordinary.

Given the ordinary laws of statistics, incredible coincidences are common and must occur. Any event, even one that seems shockingly improbable, is actually very probable over the long haul. Given enough opportunities to occur, events like this surprising phone call are virtually certain to happen to *someone*.

People are especially prone to "it can't be just coincidence" thinking because, for several psychological reasons, they misjudge the probabilities involved. They may think, for example, that a phone call from someone at the moment they're thinking of that person is incredible—but only because they've forgotten about all the times they've thought of that person and the phone *didn't* ring. Such probability misjudgments are a major source of beliefs about the paranormal or supernatural, topics that we address in Chapter 10. (See also the box "Is It Causal Confusion or ESP?" in this chapter.)

Unfortunately, there is no foolproof way to distinguish coincidence from cause and effect. But this rule of thumb can help:

> *Don't assume that a causal connection exists unless you have good reason for doing so.*

Generally, a good reason consists of the passing of one or more standard causal tests (such as the ones we've been discussing)—and being able to rule out any relevant factors that might undermine the verdict of those tests. Usually, when a cause-effect connection is uncertain, only further evaluation or research can clear things up.

Confusing Cause with Temporal Order

A particularly prevalent type of misjudgment about coincidences is the logical fallacy known as ***post hoc, ergo propter hoc*** ("after that, therefore because of that"). We believe that a cause must precede its effect. But just because one event precedes another that doesn't mean that the earlier one *caused* the later. To think so is to be taken in by this fallacy. Outrageous examples of post hoc arguments include: "The rooster crowed, then the sun came up, so the rooster's crowing caused sunrise!" and "Jasmine left her umbrella at home Monday, and this caused it to rain." You can clearly see the error in such cases, but consider these arguments:

Argument 7
After the training for police officers was enhanced, violent crime in the city decreased by 10 percent. So enhanced training caused the decline in violent crime.

Argument 8
An hour after Julio drank the cola, his headache went away. The cola cured his headache.

Argument 9
As soon as Smith took office and implemented policies that reflected his conservative theory of economics, the economy went into a downward slide characterized by

[handwritten margin notes:]
Rule of Thumb
Do not assume that a causal connection exists unless you have good reason for doing so,...

Post Hoc Ergo Propter Hoc

slow growth and high unemployment. Therefore, the Smith policies caused the current economic doldrums.

Argument 10
I wore my black shirt on Tuesday and got an F on a math quiz. I wore the same shirt the next day and flunked my psych exam. That shirt's bad luck.

The conclusion of argument 7 is based on nothing more than the fact that the enhanced training preceded the reduction in violent crime. But crime rates can decrease for many reasons, and the enhanced training may have had nothing to do with the decline in crime. For the argument to be strong, other considerations besides temporal order would have to apply—for example, that other possible causes or antecedent factors had been ruled out; that there was a close correlation between amount of training and decline in crime rates; or that in previous years (or in comparable cities) enhanced training was always followed by decreased violent crime (or no change in training was always followed by steady crime rates).

Argument 8 is also purely post hoc. Such reasoning is extremely common and underlies almost all folk remedies and a great deal of quackery and bogus self-cures. You take a vitamin E capsule, and eight hours later your headache is gone. But was it really the vitamin E that did the trick? Or was it some other overlooked factor such as something you ate, the medication you took (or didn't take), the nap you had, the change in environment (from, say, indoors to outdoors), or the stress reduction you felt when you had pleasant thoughts? Would your headache have gone away on its own anyway? Was it the *placebo effect*—the tendency for people to feel better when treated even when the treatment is fake or inactive? A chief function of controlled medical testing is to evaluate cause-and-effect relationships by systematically ruling out post hoc thinking and irrelevant factors.

Argument 9 is typical post hoc reasoning from the political sphere. Unless there are other good reasons for thinking that the economic policy is causally connected to specific economic events, the argument is weak and the conclusion unreliable.

Argument 10 is 100 percent post hoc and undiluted superstition. There is no difference in kind between this argument and much of the notorious post hoc reasoning of centuries ago: "That girl gave me the evil eye. The next day I broke my leg. That proves she's a witch, and the Elders of Salem should have her put to death!"

Confusing Cause and Effect

Sometimes we may realize that there's a causal relationship between two factors—but we may not know which factor is the cause and which is the effect. We may be confused, in other words, about the answers to questions like these:

Does your coffee drinking cause you to feel stressed out—or do your feelings of being stressed out cause you to drink coffee?

The Deadly *Post Hoc* Fallacy

Despite a growing body of scientific research showing no connection between a measles vaccine and autism in young children, many people have insisted that the vaccine causes the disorder. Some parents of autistic children reasoned that since autism symptoms arose after the children were vaccinated, the vaccine was to blame. As evidence builds against a causal link, the reasoning looks more and more *post hoc*—and dangerous. The latest study confirms previous findings:

Scientists who tried to replicate a study that once tied a measles vaccine with autism said on Wednesday they could not find any link and hope their study will encourage parents to vaccinate their children to combat a rash of measles outbreaks.

Parents' refusals to have their children vaccinated against measles have contributed to the highest numbers of cases seen in the United States and parts of Europe in many years.

Measles kills about 250,000 people a year globally, mostly children in poor nations.

Public health officials have been stressing the safety of the combined measles-mumps-rubella, or MMR, shot and other childhood vaccines in the face of vocal groups who claim the immunizations may cause autism and other problems.

The U.S. Institute of Medicine has issued several definitive reports showing no connection between autism and any vaccinations.[3]

What are the dangers for children of their parents' *post hoc* reasoning? Why do you think some parents would hold to their belief in the vaccine-autism link in the face of contrary scientific evidence? Is the availability error at work here?

Does participation in high-school sports produce desirable virtues such as courage and self-reliance—or do the virtues of courage and self-reliance lead students to participate in high school sports?

Does regular exercise make people healthy—or are healthy people naturally prone to regular exercise?

As you can see, it's not always a simple matter to discern what the nature of a causal link is. Again, we must rely on our rule of thumb: *Don't assume that a causal connection exists unless you have good reason for doing so.* This tenet applies not only to our ordinary experience but to all states of affairs involving cause and effect, including scientific investigations.

Everyday life

In everyday life, sorting cause from effect is often easy because the situations we confront are frequently simple and familiar—as when we're trying to discover what caused the kettle to boil over. Here, we naturally rely on Mill's methods or other types of causal reasoning. But as we've seen, in many other common circumstances, things aren't so simple. We often cannot be sure that we've identified all the relevant factors, or ruled out the influence of coincidence, or correctly distinguished cause and effect. Our rule of thumb, then, should be our guide in all the doubtful cases.

Science

Science faces all the same kinds of challenges in its pursuit of causal explanations. And despite its sophisticated methodology and investigative tools, it must expend a great deal of effort to pin down causal connections. Identifying the cause of a disease, for example, usually requires not one study or experiment, but many. The main reason is that uncovering relevant factors and excluding irrelevant or misleading factors is always tough. This is why we should apply our rule of thumb even to scientific research that purports to identify a causal link. In Chapters 9 and 10, we'll explore procedures for evaluating scientific research and for applying our rule of thumb with more precision.

"Shallow men believe in luck. Strong men believe in cause and effect."
—RALPH WALDO EMERSON

NECESSARY AND SUFFICIENT CONDITIONS

To fully appreciate the dynamics of cause and effect and to be able to skillfully assess causal arguments, you must understand two other important concepts: **necessary conditions** and **sufficient conditions**. Causal processes always occur

---

REVIEW NOTES

☑ Causal Confusions

- Misidentifying relevant factors
- Overlooking relevant factors
- Confusing coincidence with cause
- Confusing cause with temporal order (*post hoc* fallacy)
- Confusing cause and effect

under specific conditions. So we often speak of cause and effect in terms of *the conditions for the occurrence of an event*. Scientists, philosophers, and others go a step further and emphasize a distinction between necessary and sufficient conditions for the occurrence of an event:

> A *necessary* condition for the occurrence of an event is one without which the event cannot occur.
> A *sufficient* condition for the occurrence of an event is one that guarantees that the event occurs.

Suppose you drop a water-filled balloon from atop a building (aiming it at your least favorite professor, of course), and it breaks on the pavement. What are the *necessary* conditions for the breaking of the balloon (the effect)? There are several, including (1) your releasing the balloon, (2) the force of gravity acting on the water, (3) the weakness of the material that the balloon is made of (its breakability), and (4) the hardness of the pavement. If any one of these conditions is not present, the water balloon will not break. To state the obvious: If you don't release the balloon, it won't drop. If gravity is not in force, the balloon won't fall. If the balloon material isn't breakable, it won't, well, break. If the pavement isn't hard enough, even a breakable balloon won't rupture. (For the sake of illustration, this list of necessary conditions is incomplete. Many, if not most, events in nature have large numbers of necessary conditions.)

What are the *sufficient* conditions for the balloon's breaking? Not one of the four conditions by itself is sufficient to cause the balloon to break. None *guarantees* the occurrence of the effect; none suffices to produce the event. But all the necessary conditions combined (these four and others) are sufficient to guarantee the balloon's breaking.

Failing to feed a healthy goldfish for a few weeks is a sure way to kill it. So this deprivation is a sufficient condition for its death, as is removing the water from its fishbowl. But neither taking away the fish's food nor draining its bowl is a necessary condition for a goldfish's death because its death can be caused without resorting to either of these methods. On the other hand, necessary conditions for *sustaining* the fish's life include feeding it, providing it with water to live in, ensuring that the water is properly oxygenated, and so on. Again, in this instance, the whole set of the necessary conditions would constitute a sufficient condition for sustaining the fish's life.

In cases in which a complete set of necessary conditions constitutes a sufficient condition for an event, we say that the conditions are *individually necessary and jointly sufficient* for an event to occur. As the previous examples suggest, however, it's possible to have a set of conditions that are individually necessary but not jointly sufficient. Say some of the conditions necessary for sustaining the goldfish's life are present, but not all of them are. Because some necessary conditions are missing, the sufficient condition for keeping the fish alive would

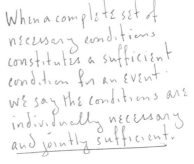

Handwritten margin notes:

Necessary Conditions

Sufficient Condition

① Necessary Conditions

② Sufficient Conditions

When a complete set of necessary conditions constitutes a sufficient condition for an event. we say the conditions are individually necessary and jointly sufficient.

not exist. On the other hand, it's also possible to have a set of conditions that are jointly sufficient but *not* individually necessary. By not feeding a goldfish for weeks we would create a set of conditions sufficient for the death of the fish. But these conditions aren't necessary for the death of a goldfish because we could ensure its death in other ways.

So there are conditions that are necessary but not sufficient for the occurrence of an event, and conditions that are sufficient but not necessary. There are also conditions that are both necessary and sufficient for an event. The Earth's being more massive than the moon is *both* a necessary and sufficient condition for the moon's being less massive than the Earth. A piece of paper's being heated to a sufficiently high temperature in the presence of oxygen is both a necessary and sufficient condition for the combustion of the paper.

In some situations, depending on our interests or practical concerns, we may focus on necessary causal conditions; in other situations, sufficient causal conditions. When we're interested in preventing or eliminating a state of affairs, we often zero in on necessary causal conditions. If you were a scientist trying to discover how to prevent mosquito infestations, you would try to determine the necessary conditions for the occurrence of mosquito infestations. Uncovering and understanding just one necessary condition could give you everything you need to control the problem. If you found out, for example, that a necessary condition for mosquito breeding is standing water, you would need to look no further for an answer. Eliminating the standing water would prevent infestations.

When we're interested in *bringing about* a state of affairs, we're likely to focus on sufficient causal conditions. If you were a doctor devoted to treating clogged arteries in your patients, you would seek out treatments scientifically proven to be sufficient for alleviating the condition. The treatments might include surgery to remove the blockage or a procedure called balloon angioplasty to widen artery passageways.

Your success in appraising causal arguments often depends heavily on your ability to distinguish between statements expressing causes as necessary conditions and statements expressing causes as sufficient conditions. Consider:

> *In the current situation, the president will send in U.S. troops if the United Nations refuses to act.*

This statement says that the condition required for the deployment of U.S. troops is the United Nations' refusing to act. But is this a necessary or sufficient condition? The use of the word "if" by itself signals a sufficient condition. If sufficient condition is what's meant, then the statement says that the UN's refusing to act will automatically trigger the troop deployment. This outcome is assured if the UN refuses.

But if the statement is meant to express the idea that the UN refusal is a necessary condition, then we're talking about a very different situation. If the UN refusal is a necessary condition, then it *will not* unavoidably trigger the troop de-

When interested in preventing or eliminating a state of affairs, look for necessary conditions...

When interested in bringing about a state of affairs look for sufficient conditions

Distinguishing Necessary and Sufficient Conditions

(a) Sufficient condition is introduced by word "if"

ployment because the refusal may not be the *only* necessary condition. The idea of necessary condition is expressed by the phrase "only if" before the stipulated condition. To express necessary condition, the statement should read:

> *In the current situation, the president will send in U.S. troops only if the United Nations refuses to act.*

So depending on the kind of causal condition meant, the statement could describe a war that's sure to happen if the condition obtains—or a war that may not occur even if the condition does obtain.

As you might expect, conditions that are *both* necessary and sufficient are indicated by the phrase "if and only if." For example:

> *The paper will combust if and only if it's heated to a sufficiently high temperature in the presence of oxygen.*

None of this discussion, however, should lead you to think that a causal condition must be *either* necessary or sufficient. It could be neither:

> *Late delivery of the package caused John to miss his deadline.*

> *Ricardo's stubbornness caused the negotiations to break down.*

[margin handwritten notes:]
(b) Necessary condition is introduced by "only if"

(c) Sufficient and necessary conditions are introduced by "if and only if"

(d) Cases where conditions are neither necessary nor sufficient

Exercise 8.8

Analyze each of the following causal arguments. Identify the conclusion and whether the argument appeals to the method of agreement, the method of difference, the joint method of agreement and difference, or correlation. In some cases the conclusion may be implied but not stated. Indicate whether the argument is strong or weak.

1. Forty-five patients were admitted to Mercy Hospital for pneumonia in December. They were all given standard treatment for pneumonia. After five days, thirty of them were well enough to go home. The other fifteen, however, somehow acquired other infections and were not well enough to be released for fourteen days. The only relevant factor common to these fifteen is this: They all stayed in the same ward (different from the ward that the other group stayed in). Something about staying in that ward is the cause of the prolonged illness.

* 2. Research suggests that eating lots of fruits and vegetables may provide some protection against several types of cancer. Studies have revealed that the risk of getting cancer associated with the lowest intakes of fruits and vegetables is twice as high as that associated with the highest intakes. This association holds for several types of cancer, including cancers of the breast, colon, pancreas, and bladder.

[margin handwritten notes:]
(1) Agreement / Strong

(2) Correlation / Strong

③ Joint/Strong

3. "An experimental vaccine prevented women from becoming persistently infected with a [type of human papilloma virus called HPV-16] that is associated with half of all cervical cancers, researchers reported. . . . The study involved 2,392 women from 16 to 23 years in age. Participants were randomly assigned to receive three shots of either an HPV-16 vaccine or a placebo (a dummy substance). The study was double-blinded—that is, neither the investigators nor the study participants knew who got the vaccine and who got the placebo. Participants were followed for an average of 17 months after getting the third shot. . . . [Forty-one] women developed HPV-16 infection—all of these women were in the placebo group. . . . By comparison, no one who got all three vaccine shots developed an HPV-16 infection." [National Cancer Institute]

④ Difference/Strong
The effect is absent
when cause is absent.

4. Getting the endorsement of the teachers' union in this town is absolutely essential to being elected to the school board in this city. No one has ever won a seat on the school board without an endorsement from the teachers' union.

⑤ Difference/Weak

5. For most of the school year the number of disciplinary actions taken weekly because of student misconduct at North High School has remained about the same—roughly ten a week. But for the last month the number of actions per week has gone down considerably—to about six per week. There can be only one reason: Last month the Ten Commandments were posted in the hallway outside the principal's office. This posting was the only significant recent change in the school.

⑥ Joint/Strong

6. In Instance 1, when factors X, Y, and Z were present, E happened. In Instance 2, when factors X, Y, and P were present, E happened. In Instance 3, when factors X and Z were present, E did not happen. In Instance 4, when Z and P were present, E did not happen. And in Instance 5, when X, Z, and P were present, E did not happen. Therefore, Y caused E.

⑦ Correlation/Strong

*7. Educators have frequently noted the connection between education level and salary. The higher a person's education level is, the higher his or her annual salary is likely to be. Education increases people's earning power.

⑧ Joint/Strong

8. "On the 20th May, 1747, I took twelve patients [with] scurvy on board the *Salisbury* at sea. Their cases were as similar as I could have them. They all in general had putrid gums, the spots and lassitude, with weakness of their knees. They lay together in one place, being a proper apartment for the sick in the fore-hold; and had one diet in common to all. . . . Two of these were ordered each a quart of cider a day. Two others took [twenty-five drops of] vitriol three times a day. . . . Two others took two spoonfuls of vinegar three times a day. . . . Two of the worst patients [were given a half pint of sea water daily]. . . . Two others had each two oranges and one lemon given them everyday. . . . The two remaining patients took [small doses of nutmeg, garlic, mustard seed, and a few other ingredients]. The consequence was that the most sudden and visible good effects were perceived from the use of the oranges and lemons; one of

those who had taken them being at the end of six days fit for duty. . . . The other was the best recovered of any in his condition, and being now deemed pretty well was appointed nurse to the rest of the sick. As I shall have occasion elsewhere to take notice of the effects of other medicines in this disease, I shall here only observe that the result of all my experiments was that oranges and lemons were the most effectual remedies for this distemper at sea." [James Lind, *Of the Prevention of the Scurvy*, 1753]

9. On Tuesday fifty-two people ate ham sandwiches at Johnny's Deli, and half of these came down with hepatitis. The board of health discovered that the people who became ill had their ham sandwiches made by Johnny's brother, who had hepatitis at the time. This was the only relevant common element among those who got sick. Seems Johnny's brother was the cause of this outbreak.

9 Difference/Strong
Factor is present when E occurs and absent when E does not occur...

10. Scientists wanted to see whether giving pre-puberty children dietary supplements of calcium could significantly increase the density of the children's bones. (Bone density is a key part of bone strength.) So they selected seventy-one pairs of identical twins and gave one twin of each pair a daily supplement of extra calcium and the other twin a sugar pill (placebo). All the twins had diets that contained adequate amounts of all nutrients. The investigators monitored the twins and their diets for three years. The only relevant difference between the twins was the extra calcium that half of them received. At the end of the three years, the scientists found that the twins who had received the extra calcium had significantly greater bone density. They concluded that the extra calcium caused the increased density.

10 Joint/Strong

11. For years vehicular accidents at the intersection of Fifth and Main Streets have consistently averaged two to four per month. Since a traffic light was installed there, the rate has been one or two accidents every three months. That new traffic light has made quite a difference.

11 Difference/Strong

12. The risk of atherosclerosis (a.k.a. hardening of the arteries) is linked to the amount of cholesterol in the bloodstream (called serum cholesterol). The higher the serum cholesterol levels, the greater the risk of atherosclerosis. There's a causal connection between serum cholesterol levels and risk of atherosclerosis.

12 Correlation/Strong

*13. Investigators tested the performance of four gasoline-powered lawnmowers before and after a tune-up. The machines differed in age, manufacturer, engine type, and controls. The performance of every mower was better after the tune-up, leading the testers to conclude that tune-ups can improve the performance of lawnmowers.

13 Difference/Strong

14. The reason there have been so many terrorist attacks in Western countries in the past ten years is that the rights of Palestinians have been violated by Westerners. Every time large numbers of innocent Palestinians have been jailed, persecuted, or killed in Western countries, there has been a terrorist attack in the West.

14 Agreement/Strong

(15) Difference/Weak

15. Charlie was pretty happy all week, but then he started moping around like he'd lost his dog or something. I think he's upset because he got word that his grades weren't good enough to get into med school.

(16) Agreement/Strong

Having a major war, somewhere in the world causes the price of oil to hit $40 a barrel

* **16.** The price of a barrel of oil on the world market has hit $40 only twelve times in the last thirty years. Sometimes major world economies were in recession, and sometimes they weren't. Sometimes oil production was down; sometimes up. U.S. oil reserves were sometimes sold off; sometimes not. But one thing that was always present when oil hit $40 was that there was a major war going on somewhere in the world.

(17) Difference/Strong

17. Sometimes my television reception is excellent, and sometimes it's terrible. There's only one important factor that seems to make a difference. When the reception is excellent, no other major appliances are running in the house. When it's terrible, at least one major appliance—like the dishwasher—is running. For some reason, running a major appliance interferes with my TV reception.

(18) Joint/Strong

18. In our test, after people washed their hands with Lather-Up Germicidal Soap, no germs whatsoever could be detected on their hands. But under exactly the same conditions, after they washed their hands with Brand X germicidal soap, plenty of germs were found on their hands. Lather-Up is better. *at killing germs*

(19) Agreement/Strong

* **19.** Just five people got As on the midterm exam. The only common factor in their success is that they all studied the night before and reviewed their notes just before walking into class to take the test.

(20) Correlation/Weak

20. The cause of Jackie M's criminal behavior—his involvement in petty theft and assaults—is no mystery. Jackie commits most of his criminal acts when the outdoor temperatures are highest. When outdoor temperatures are lowest, he behaves himself. In fact, the incidence of his criminal behavior rises as the temperature rises. Jackie's problem is that he has a heat-sensitive personality.

Exercise 8.9

For each argument in Exercise 8.8, identify errors in causal reasoning that are most likely to occur in the circumstances indicated. The possibilities include (a) misidentifying or overlooking relevant factors, (b) being misled by coincidence, (c) falling for the *post hoc* fallacy, and (d) confusing cause and effect. Answers are provided for 2, 7, 13, 16, and 19.

Exercise 8.10

For each of the following causal statements, indicate whether the specified cause is (a) a necessary condition, (b) a sufficient condition, (c) a necessary and sufficient condition, or (d) neither a necessary nor a sufficient condition.

(a)

* **1.** Sylvia's being exposed to the influenza virus caused her to get the flu.

(1) 2. Sergio's eagerness to get to the airport caused him to get a speeding ticket.

(a) 3. Giving the roses water and nourishing soil caused them to flourish.

(b) * 4. Chopping off the head of the king put an end to him.

(b) 5. The mighty Casey hit the ball out of the park, winning the game by one run.

(b) 6. The straw broke the camel's back.

(c) 7. The proper combining of sodium and chlorine produced salt, sodium chloride.

(d) 8. Johann got a good grade on the exam because he studied the night before.

(a) * 9. A single spark started the internal combustion engine.

(d) 10. Simone lost weight by exercising regularly.

KEY WORDS

analogy

argument by analogy
  (analogical induction)

biased sample

causal argument

causal claim

confidence level

enumerative induction

hasty generalization

inference to the best
  explanation

margin of error

necessary condition

post hoc, ergo propter hoc

random sample

relevant property

representative sample

sample

self-selecting sample

sufficient condition

target group

Summary

- An inductive argument is intended to provide only probable support for its conclusion, being considered strong if it succeeds in providing such support and weak if it does not.
- Inductive arguments come in several forms, including enumerative, analogical, and causal. In enumerative induction, we argue from premises

about some members of a group to a generalization about the entire group. The entire group is called the target group; the observed members of the group, the sample; and the group characteristics we're interested in, the relevant property.

- An enumerative induction can fail to be strong by having a sample that's too small or not representative. When we draw a conclusion about a target group based on an inadequate sample size, we're said to commit the error of hasty generalization.

- Opinion polls are enumerative inductive arguments, or the basis of enumerative inductive arguments, and must be judged by the same general criteria used to judge any other enumerative induction.

- In analogical induction, or argument by analogy, we reason that since two or more things are similar in several respects, they must be similar in some further respect. We evaluate arguments by analogy according to several criteria: (1) the number of relevant similarities between things being compared, (2) the number of relevant dissimilarities, (3) the number of instances (or cases) of similarities or dissimilarities, and (4) the diversity among the cases.

- A causal argument is an inductive argument whose conclusion contains a causal claim. There are several inductive patterns of reasoning used to assess causal connections. These include the Method of Agreement, the Method of Difference, the Method of Agreement and Difference, and the Method of Concomitant Variation.

- Errors in cause-and-effect reasoning are common. They include misidentifying relevant factors in a causal process, overlooking relevant factors, confusing cause with coincidence, confusing cause with temporal order, and mixing up cause and effect.

- Crucial to an understanding of cause-and-effect relationships are the notions of necessary and sufficient conditions. A necessary condition for the occurrence of an event is one without which the event cannot occur. A sufficient condition for the occurrence of an event is one that guarantees that the event occurs.

Field Problems

1. Design an opinion poll to determine the percentage of people on campus who believe that individuals under age seventeen who commit crimes that carry the death penalty for adults should likewise get the death penalty. Specify all the following parameters: (1) the target group, (2) the makeup and size of the sample, (3) the methods for ensuring a random sample, (4) the methods for ensuring a representative sample, (5) the exact phrasing

of the polling question(s), (6) the method for gathering the responses (telephone survey, "man on the street" poll, email questionnaire, etc.), and (7) the acceptable margin of error. Explain the reasons for your choices.

2. Devise an extended argument by analogy (two hundred to three hundred words) to support the proposition that Earth is not a mere planet of rock and soil but is a living organism, a notion that has come to be known as the gaia theory. You'll need to research this term on the Internet. (The original idea that inspired this view was not that the planet was an organism, but that it *could be usefully viewed* as an organism that is self-regulating.) People who take the idea literally might say, for example, that just as billions of cells in the human body perform the functions that sustain the body, so billions of organisms on Earth perform the functions that sustain the life of Earth. Use several relevant similarities in your argument. Then write a critique of your argument, focusing especially on relevant dissimilarities and the number of relevant similarities.

3. Select a causal argument on a political issue from recent op-ed pages (in newspapers or on websites). Then critique it, explaining why it's strong or weak, specifically noting whether it misidentifies or overlooks relevant factors, confuses cause with coincidence, commits the *post hoc* fallacy, confuses cause and effect, or mishandles or misunderstands necessary and sufficient conditions.

Self-Assessment Quiz

Answers appear in "Answers to Self-Assessment Quizzes" (Appendix C).

1. What is the logical form of enumerative induction, indicated schematically?
2. In enumerative induction, what are the target group, the sample, and the relevant property?
3. What are the two major ways in which an enumerative induction can fail to be strong?
4. What is the logical form of analogical induction, indicated schematically?

For each of the following enumerative inductions, indicate whether the argument is strong or weak. If it's weak, say whether the problem is a sample that's too small, not representative, or both.

5. All the women in my yoga class are against the war. Ninety percent of the members of a national women's group (twelve thousand members) are against the war. And all my women friends are against the war. The fact is, almost all American women oppose this war.

6. Recently there was a racially motivated murder in Texas. Two white men killed a black man. Then another murder of a black man by some racist whites occurred in Louisiana. And in Mississippi an admitted racist

finally was convicted of the murder of a black man that occurred years ago. The South has more racist killers than any other part of the country.

7. Most professors at this college are not grading as strictly as they used to. They now give Bs for work to which they used to assign Cs. The grading standards in American colleges are dropping.

8. The first time Ariana encountered trigonometry, she couldn't understand it. And the first time she read Shakespeare, she didn't get it. She will never understand anything.

9. Americans are quite satisfied with the administration's recent foreign policy decisions. An "instant poll" conducted yesterday on the CNN website got fifteen thousand responses from site visitors—and 95 percent of them said that American foreign policy was on the right track.

10. Judging from what I've seen, anti-war demonstrators are just a bunch of peaceniks left over from the Vietnam War era.

Evaluate each of the following arguments by analogy, indicating (1) the two things being compared, (2) the conclusion, and (3) whether the argument is strong or weak.

11. "Suppose that someone tells me that he has had a tooth extracted without an anaesthetic, and I express my sympathy, and suppose that I am then asked, 'How do you know that it hurt him?' I might reasonably reply, 'Well, I know that it would hurt me. I have been to the dentist and know how painful it is to have a tooth stopped without an anaesthetic, let alone taken out. And he has the same sort of nervous system as I have. I infer, therefore, that in these conditions he felt considerable pain, just as I should myself.'" [Alfred J. Ayer]

12. "As for one who is choosy about what he learns . . . we shall not call him a lover of learning or a philosopher, just as we shall not say that a man who is difficult about his food is hungry or has an appetite for food. We shall not call him a lover of food but a poor eater. . . . But we shall call a philosopher the man who is easily willing to learn every kind of knowledge, gladly turns to learning things, and is insatiable in this respect." [Socrates]

13. "Let us begin with a parable [showing that statements about God have no meaning]. . . . Once upon a time two explorers came upon a clearing in the jungle. In the clearing were growing many flowers and many weeds. One explorer says, 'Some gardener must tend this plot.' The other disagrees, 'There is no gardener.' So they pitch their tents and set a watch. No gardener is ever seen. 'But perhaps he is an invisible gardener.' So they set up a barbed-wire fence. They electrify it. . . . But no shrieks ever suggest that some intruder has received a shock. No movements of the wire ever betray an invisible climber. . . . Yet still the Believer is not convinced. 'But there is a gardener, invisible, intangible, insensible.' . . . At last the Sceptic despairs, 'But what remains of your

original assertion? Just how does what you call an invisible, intangible, eternally elusive gardener differ from an imaginary gardener or even from no gardener at all?'" [Antony Flew]

Analyze each of the following causal arguments. Identify the conclusion and whether the argument is weak or strong. If it's weak, explain why with reference to the material in this chapter.

14. School violence is caused mainly by teens playing violent video games. Incidents of violence in schools have increased as more and more teens are playing violent video games, as the video games themselves have become more graphically and realistically violent, and as the number and variety of video games have expanded dramatically.

15. Smoking and exposure to secondhand smoke among pregnant women pose a significant risk to both infants and the unborn. According to numerous studies, each year the use of tobacco causes thousands of spontaneous births, infant deaths, and deaths from SIDS. Death rates for fetuses are 35 percent higher among pregnant women who smoke than among pregnant women who don't smoke.

16. Why are crime rates so high, the economy so bad, and our children so prone to violence, promiscuity, and vulgarity? These social ills have arisen—as they always have—from the "moral vacuum" created when Americans turn away from religion. Our current slide into chaos started when prayer was banned from public schools and secular humanism swooped in to replace it. And as God has slowly faded from public life, we have got deeper in the hole.

17. The twelve of us went on a hike through the mountains. We all drank bottled water except Lisa, who drank from a stream. Later she got really sick. Some intestinal thing. But the rest of us were fine. We've repeated this adventure many times on other hikes, with all but one of us drinking bottled water and one drinking from a stream. Everything else was the same. Each time, the person who drank from the stream got really ill. Drinking from streams on these hikes causes intestinal illness. Don't do it.

18. Ever since I started drinking herbal tea in the morning, my energy level has improved and I'm a lot calmer during the day. That stuff works.

19. Yesterday my astrological chart—prepared by a top astrologer—said that I would meet an attractive person today, and I did. Last week, it said I'd come into some money, and I did. (Jack paid me that hundred dollars he owed me.) Now I'm a believer. The stars really do rule.

20. Most of the terminal cancer patients in this ward who had positive attitudes about their disease lived longer than expected. Most of the negative-attitude patients didn't live as long as expected. A positive attitude can increase the life expectancy of people with terminal cancer.

⊚ Integrative Exercises

These exercises pertain to material in Chapters 3 and 6–8.

For each of the following arguments, specify the conclusion and premises and indicate whether it is deductive or inductive. If it's deductive, use Venn diagrams or truth tables to determine its validity. If it's inductive, indicate whether it's an enumerative, analogical, or causal induction and whether it's strong or weak. If necessary, add implicit premises and conclusions.

1. It's clear that if the allies accidentally damage any holy sites when they attack enemy forces, the local people will never give the allies any respect or cooperation. The allies, though, will not damage any holy sites. Therefore, the locals will respect the allies and cooperate with them.

2. "By removing the exact-change-only lane at the Black Rock toll barrier, the New York State Thruway Authority has created artificial traffic jams. For 20 years, I have rarely encountered traffic problems at this toll barrier. Now it is a daily occurrence." [Letter to the editor, *Buffalo News*]

3. If people have free will, then they can be held morally responsible for what they do. But—as our judicial system demonstrates—people cannot really be held morally responsible for their actions. Thus, people do not have free will.

4. "If we take in hand any volume; of divinity or school metaphysics, for instance; let us ask, *Does it contain any abstract reasoning concerning quantity or number? No. Does it contain any experimental reasoning concerning matter of fact and existence?* No. Commit it then to the flames; for it can contain nothing but sophistry and illusion." [David Hume]

5. No philosophy majors are persons without a brain. All students without a brain are persons who spend most of their time partying. So no philosophy majors are persons who spend most of their time partying.

6. "The decision to have or not to have a child is mine and mine alone. I am not cattle for the government to order about, demanding that I bring an unwanted child to term. Stripping me of the right to control my own destiny dehumanizes me, period. Anything less than my choice, on my terms, reduces me to property." [Guest opinion, The Onion.com]

7. All politicians are corrupt manipulators, so some corrupt manipulators are effective leaders, since some effective leaders are politicians.

8. If we increase security in the country because of terrorist attacks, then our personal freedoms will be curtailed. If we do not increase security in the country, then terrorist attacks will increase. So either our personal freedoms will be curtailed or terrorist attacks will increase.

9. "A well regulated militia being necessary to the security of a free State, the right of the people to keep and bear arms shall not be infringed." [U.S. Constitution]

10. "World War II would still be going on had we adhered to the rules we now find our troops having to operate under. War is brutal, and innocent folks are going to die in the process. The time has come to realize that we, as a nation, cannot afford another Vietnam. Let's use what means are necessary to win now and deal with the public outcry afterward." [Letter to the editor, *Buffalo News*]

11. [Be careful: This one has an unstated conclusion.] "The U.S. is the only nation-state to have been condemned by the World Court for international terrorism. The U.S. vetoed a UN Security Council resolution calling on governments to observe international law. After deliberately targeting the civilian public health infrastructure, the U.S. military imposes a continuing economic blockade on Iraq which has directly resulted in the deaths of hundreds of thousands of children. The U.S. government is the primary financier and arms supplier for the decades-old Israeli war against the entire Palestinian people." [Editorial, *Alternative Press Review*]

12. Almost all of the owners of restaurants, bars, and clubs in New York City are opposed to the city's total ban on smoking in indoor public places. The vast majority of New Yorkers simply do not like this law.

13. Every student Maria knows who wears glasses also has a high grade-point average. So most students who wear glasses probably have high grade-point averages.

14. "The evils of the world are due to moral defects quite as much as to lack of intelligence. But the human race has not hitherto discovered any method of eradicating moral defects. . . . Intelligence, on the contrary, is easily improved by methods known to every competent educator. Therefore, until some method of teaching virtue has been discovered, progress will have to be sought by improvement of intelligence rather than of morals." [Bertrand Russell]

15. Television is destroying morality in this country. As TV violence, sex, and vulgarity have increased, so have violent crimes, sexual assaults, and violations of obscenity laws.

16. In the past twenty years several Navy planes and a number of ships have disappeared in the Bermuda Triangle. These odd vanishings cannot be mere coincidence. The Bermuda Triangle is the epicenter of mysterious forces unknown to science.

17. "The idea that mainstream corporate media—the broadcast networks and newspaper chains, both those under consolidated ownership and those few that still cling to independence—is consistently liberal is laughable on its face. . . . [The] raft of Bush endorsements from the 'undeniably liberal' papers . . . seems to provide some deniability. Add in the past and current presence of avowed conservatives like Jack Welch at the top of these organizations, look over to the regular political forums of the Sunday talk shows, scan the editorial pages of the supposedly liberal

Washington Post (where conservative pundits overshadow their left colleagues in both numbers and vehemence) and the argument is clearly bogus." [Letter to the editor, Salon.com]

18. Eighty-three percent of the letters to the editor received by this newspaper are adamantly pro-life. And since the *Daily Planet* is the only major newspaper in the city, and it provides the primary forum for discussion of local issues, we must conclude that this town is also overwhelmingly pro-life.

19. The big grandfather clock in the hallway struck midnight—and then the old man died. This doesn't prove that the striking of the clock killed him, but it does show that the two events—the clock's striking and the death of the old man—were somehow causally linked.

20. If the recession continues, people will lose billions of dollars in failed investments. People will indeed lose billions of dollars in failed investments, so the recession will continue.

Writing Assignments

1. In a one-page essay use an enumerative inductive argument to argue that your campus is (or is not) relatively free of crime.

2. Using either enumerative induction or argument by analogy, write a two-page rebuttal to Essay 6 ("Misleading the Patient for Fun and Profit") in Appendix A.

3. In a two-page page essay argue for or against one of these claims:

   • Men are better at science than women are.
   • Everyone does what is in his or her own best interests.
   • Deadbeat dads (fathers who don't or won't pay child support that they are legally obligated to pay) should be put in jail.
   • Sexual harassment is not a problem on this campus.
   • Competition is always a good thing.
   • Pornography should never be banned on a college campus.

4. Study Essay 20 ("Flag Amendment: Congress Nears Choice: Protect Freedom or Stoke Anger?") and Essay 21 ("Flag Amendment: Flag Needs Protection"). Decide which essay presents the stronger arguments, and write a paper defending your view.

EXPLANATIONS Part Four

Inference to the Best Explanation

CHAPTER OBJECTIVES

EXPLANATIONS AND INFERENCE

- Understand what inference to the best explanation is and how it differs from other kinds of induction.
- Know what an explanation (including theoretical explanation) is and how it differs from an argument.
- Appreciate how inference to the best explanation is used in all disciplines and in everyday life.
- Be able to demonstrate how to use inference to the best explanation in many different situations.

THEORIES AND CONSISTENCY

- Know how to check an explanation for internal and external consistency.

THEORIES AND CRITERIA

- Understand the importance of using criteria to judge the adequacy of theories.
- Be able to list and explain the five criteria of adequacy.
- Be able to apply the criteria of adequacy to simple causal theories.
- Know what an ad hoc hypothesis is.

TELLING GOOD THEORIES FROM BAD

- Memorize and explain the four steps in the TEST formula.
- Recognize the importance of considering alternative explanations.
- Be able to use the TEST formula to evaluate theories.

REVIEW

Arguments
— Deductive
— Inductive

Types of Inductive
Arguments...
① Enumerative Induction

② Analogical Induction

REVIEW OF THE BASICS

LET'S TAKE STOCK OF THE INDUCTIVE TERRAIN TRAVELED THUS FAR. In Chapter 8 we closely examined the nature and uses of inductive reasoning. We were reminded that a deductive argument, unlike an inductive one, is intended to provide logically conclusive support for its conclusion. If it succeeds in providing such support, it's said to be valid; if not, invalid. If a valid argument has true premises, it's said to be sound. But an inductive argument is intended to supply only probable support for its conclusion. If it manages to provide such support, it's said to be strong; if not, weak. The conclusion of an inductively strong argument is simply more likely to be true than not. If a strong argument has true premises, it's said to be cogent.

We also saw that inductive arguments come in several forms. One of them is enumerative induction, in which we reason from premises about *some* members of a group to a conclusion, or generalization, about the group *as a whole*. All the swans you have ever seen are white, so *all* swans must be white. Forty percent of the students at your college have a driver's license, so 40 percent of all students everywhere must have a driver's license. (Whether these enumerative inductive arguments are strong or cogent is another matter.)

Another kind of inductive argument is argument by analogy (or analogical induction), in which we reason that since two or more things are similar in several respects, they must be similar in some additional respect. In an analogical induction you might argue that (1) since humans can move about, solve mathematical equations, win chess games, and feel pain, *and* (2) since computers (or robots) are like humans in that they can move about, solve mathematical equations, and win chess games, it's therefore probable that computers can also

---

> ### REVIEW NOTES
>
> ☑ A Look Back at the Basics
>
> - **Statement (claim):** An assertion that something is or is not the case
> - **Premise:** A statement given in support of another statement
> - **Conclusion:** A statement that premises are intended to support
> - **Argument:** A group of statements in which some of them (the premises) are intended to support another of them (the conclusion)
> - **Indicator words:** Words that frequently accompany arguments and signal that a premise or conclusion is present
> - **Deductive argument:** An argument intended to provide conclusive support for its conclusion
> - **Inductive argument:** An argument intended to provide probable support for its conclusion

feel pain. Analogical induction, like all inductive reasoning, can establish conclusions only with a degree of probability.

Finally, we saw that causal arguments—inductive arguments whose conclusions contain causal claims—can be enumerative inductions, analogical inductions, or arguments that rely on Mill's methods and similar kinds of inferences. Reasoning well about causal connections means avoiding numerous common errors, including misidentifying or overlooking relevant factors, confusing coincidence with cause, and committing the post hoc fallacy.

We noted only in passing that there is another kind of inductive reasoning that is so important that a whole section in this text (Part 4) is devoted to it: **inference to the best explanation.** Well, here we are in Part 4, and it's time to delve deep into this kind of inductive reasoning, perhaps the most commonly used form of inference and arguably the most empowering in daily life.

Explanations and Inference

Recall from Chapter 1 that an explanation is a statement (or statements) asserting why or how something is the case. For example: The bucket leaks because there's a hole in it. He was sad because his dog died. She broke the pipe by hitting it with a wrench. These explanations and all others are intended to clarify and elucidate, to increase our understanding. Remember too our discussion of the important distinction between an explanation and an argument. While an explanation tells us *why or how something is the case,* an argument gives us reasons for believing *that something is the case.*

As you've probably already guessed, there are also different kinds of explanations. (See the box "The Lore of Explanations.") For instance, some explanations are what we might call procedural—they try to explain how something is done or how an action is carried out. ("She opened up the engine, then examined the valves, then checked the cylinders.") Some are interpretive—they try to explain the meaning of terms or states of affairs. ("This word means 'dashing' or 'jaunty.'") And some are functional—they try to explain how something functions. ("The heart circulates and oxygenates the blood.")

But the kind of explanation we're concerned with here—and the kind we bump into most often—is what we'll call, for lack of something snappier, a **theoretical explanation.** Such explanations are theories, or hypotheses, that try to explain why something is the way it is, why something is the case, why something happened. In this category we must include all explanations intended to explain the cause of events—the causal explanations that are so important to both science and daily life. Theoretical explanations, of course, are claims. They assert that something is or is not the case.

Now, even though an explanation is not an argument, an explanation can be *part* of an argument. It can be the heart of the kind of inductive argument known

Handwritten margin notes:
③ Causal Arguments

④ Inference to the Best Explanation...

Arguments vs. Explanations

Different kinds of explanations
① Procedural Explanations
② Interpretive Explanations
③ Functional Explanations
④ Theoretical Explanations
Explanations that are theories or hypotheses

An explanation can be part of an argument

Inference to the Best Explanation

①
Schema for Enumerative Induction

②
Schema for Analogical Induction

③
*Schema for Inference to the
Best Explanation...*

Criteria
- Strength
- Cogency

See C.S. Peirce
IBE (Abduction) goes
beyond the evidence;
posits a theory that
introduces something new

as inference to the best explanation. And in this kind of inference, the explanations we use are theoretical explanations.

In inference to the best explanation, *we reason from premises about a state of affairs to an explanation for that state of affairs.* The premises are statements about observations or other evidence to be explained. The explanation is a claim about why the state of affairs is the way it is. The key question that this type of inference tries to answer is, What is the best explanation for the existence or nature of this state of affairs? The best explanation is the one most likely to be true, even though there is no guarantee of its truth as there is in deductive inference.

Recall that enumerative induction has this pattern:

> *X percent of the observed members of group A have property P.*
> *Therefore, X percent of all members of group A probably have property P.*

And that analogical induction has this pattern:

> *Thing A has properties P_1, P_2, P_3 plus the property P_4.*
> *Thing B has properties P_1, P_2, and P_3.*
> *Therefore, thing B probably has property P_4.*

Inference to the best explanation, however, has this pattern:

> *Phenomenon Q.*
> *E provides the best explanation for Q.*
> *Therefore, it is probable that E is true.*

For example:

> *The new quarterback dropped the ball again. The best explanation for that screw-up is that he's nervous. So he's definitely nervous.*

> *The best explanation for Maria's absence today is that she's angry at the boss. Yep, she's mad at the boss.*

> *The defendant's fingerprints were all over the crime scene, the police found the victim's blood on his shirt, and he was in possession of the murder weapon. The only explanation for all this that makes any sense is that the defendant actually committed the crime. He's guilty.*

If the explanations in these arguments really are the best, then the arguments are inductively strong. And if the premises are also true, then the arguments are cogent. If cogent, we are justified in believing that the explanations for the phenomena are in fact correct.

Notice that an inference to the best explanation always goes "beyond the evidence"—it tries to explain facts but does so by positing a theory that is not derived entirely from those facts. It tries to understand the known by putting forth—through inference and imagination—a theoretical pattern that encom-

☑ The Lore of Explanations

An explanation is a statement (or statements) asserting why or how something is the case. In traditional terminology, that which is to be explained in an explanation is called the *explanandum*, and that which does the explaining is called the *explanans*. Take this explanation: "The dog barked because a prowler was nearby." The explanandum is "the dog barked," and the explanans is "a prowler was nearby."

You can categorize explanations in many ways, depending on the kind of explanandum in which you're interested. Here are a few of the more common categories:

- Teleological explanations try to explain the purpose of something, how it functions, or how it fits into a plan. (*Telos* is a Greek word meaning "end" or "purpose.")

  Example: The wall switch is there so you can turn off the lamp from across the room.
  Example: These wildflowers are here as a blessing from God.

- Interpretive explanations concern the meaning of terms or states of affairs. These explanations seek to understand not something's purpose or cause, but rather its sense or semantic meaning.

  Example: When Mary smiled, she was signaling her agreement.
  Example: "Effect" means to accomplish, but "affect" means to influence.

- Procedural explanations try to explain how something is done or how an action is carried out.

  Example: To stop the chemical reaction, Ariana added sulfur.
  Example: He paid his taxes online by downloading the forms, then using his credit card number.

Handwritten margin notes:
Explanendum
Explanans

Types of Explanations
① Teleological

② Interpretative

③ Procedural

passes both the known and unknown. It proposes a plausible pattern that expands our understanding.

The fact that there are *best* explanations, of course, implies that not all explanations for a state of affairs are created equal; some are better than others. Just because you've devised an explanation for something doesn't mean that you're justified in believing that the explanation is the right one. If other explanations are just as good, your explanation is in doubt. If other explanations are better

"WELL WHICH DO YOU THINK IS MORE LIKELY,
YOUR PILLOW IS GROWING HAIR OR YOU'RE
LOSING YOURS?"

www.CartoonStock.com

We often use IBE without even knowing it...

Explanandum: Car won't start

Possible explanans

"A superstition is a
premature explana-
tion that overstays
its time."

—GEORGE ILES

than yours, you are not justified in believing it. But much of the time, after further study or thought, you can reasonably conclude that a particular explanation really is the best explanation. (More on how to evaluate the relative worth of explanations later.) In this way you can come to understand the state of affairs more than you did before.

Inference to the best explanation probably seems very familiar to you. That's because you use it all the time—and need it all the time. Often when we try to understand something in the world, we construct explanations for why this something is the way it is, and we try to determine which of these is the best. Devising explanations helps increase our understanding by fitting our experiences and background knowledge into a coherent pattern. At every turn we are confronted with phenomena that we can only fully understand by explaining them.

Sometimes we're barely aware that we're using inference to the best explanation. If we awaken and see that the streets outside are wet, we may immediately posit this explanation: It's been raining. Without thinking much about it, we may also quickly consider whether a better explanation is that a street-sweeper machine has wet the street. Just as quickly we may dismiss this explanation because we see that the houses and cars are also wet. After reasoning in this fashion, we may decide to carry an umbrella that day.

Let's consider a more elaborate example. Say that you discover that your car won't start in the morning (the phenomenon to be explained). You would like to know why it won't start (the explanation for the failure) because you can't repair the car unless you know what the problem is. You know that there are several possible explanations or theories.

1. The battery is dead.
2. The fuel tank is empty.
3. The starter has malfunctioned.
4. A vandal has sabotaged the car.
5. All or several of the above.

So you try to figure out which theory is the most plausible, that is, most likely to be true. You see right away that there is snow around the car from yesterday's snowstorm—but there are no tracks (not even yours) and no signs of tampering anywhere. So you dismiss theory 4. You remember that you filled up the gas tank yesterday, the fuel gauge says that the tank is full, and you don't see any signs of

Darwin and the Best Explanation

Charles Darwin (1809–1882) offered the theory of evolution by natural selection as the best explanation for a wide variety of natural phenomena. He catalogued an extensive list of facts about nature and showed that his theory explains them well. He argued, however, that the alternative theory of the day—the view that God independently created species—does not explain them. Darwin declared:

Charles Darwin (1809–1882).

> It can hardly be supposed that a false theory would explain, in so satisfactory a manner as does the theory of natural selection, the several large classes of facts above specified. It has recently been objected that this is an unsafe method of arguing; but it is a method used in judging of the common events of life, and has often been used by the greatest natural philosophers.[1]

"For this, indeed, is the true source of our ignorance—the fact that our knowledge can only be finite, while our ignorance must necessarily be infinite."

—KARL POPPER

leakage. So you can safely ignore theory 2. You notice that the lights, heater, and radio work fine, and the battery gauge indicates a fully charged battery. So you discard theory 1. When you try to start the car, you hear a clicking sound like the one you heard when the starter had failed previously. Among the theories you started with, then, theory 3 now seems the most plausible. This means that theory 5 cannot be correct since it entails two or more of the theories.

Which theory is the most plausible?

If you wanted to, you could state your argument like this:

(1) Your car won't start in the morning.

(2) The theory that the starter has malfunctioned is the best explanation for the car's not starting in the morning.

(3) Therefore, it's probable that the malfunctioning starter caused the car not to start in the morning.

Schema

In science, where inference to the best explanation is an essential tool, usually the theories of interest are causal theories, in which events are the things to be explained and the proposed causes of the events are the explanations. Just as we do in everyday life, scientists often consider several competing theories for the same event or phenomenon. Then—through scientific testing and careful thinking—they systematically eliminate inadequate theories and eventually arrive at the one that's rightly regarded as the best of the bunch. Using this form

---

FURTHER THOUGHT

💡 Sherlock Holmes and Inference to the Best Explanation

Sherlock Holmes owed his great success as a detective primarily to inference to the best explanation. He was so good at this kind of inference that people (especially Watson) were frequently astonished at his skill. Holmes, however, was guilty of spreading some confusion about his ability. He called his method deduction, though it was clearly inductive. Holmes in action:

> I knew you came from Afghanistan. From long habit the train of thoughts ran so swiftly through my mind that I arrived at the conclusion without being conscious of intermediate steps. There were such steps, however. The train of reasoning ran, "Here is a gentleman of medical type, but with the air of a military man. Clearly an army doctor, then. He has just come from the tropics, for his face is dark, and that is not the natural tint of his skin, for his wrists are fair. He has undergone hardship and sickness, as his haggard face says clearly. His left arm has been injured. He holds it in a stiff and unnatural manner. Where in the tropics would an English army doctor have seen much hardship and got his arm wounded? Clearly in Afghanistan."[2]

Here Holmes explains how he knew that a man had "gone about in fear of some personal attack within the last twelve-month":

> "You have a very handsome stick," I answered. "By the inscription I observed that you had not had it more than a year. But you have taken some pains to bore the head of it and pour melted lead into the hole so as to make it a formidable weapon. I argued that you would not take such precautions unless you had some danger to fear."[3]

of inference, scientists discover planets, viruses, cures, subatomic particles, black holes—and many things that can't even be directly observed.

And then there are all those other professionals who rely on inference to the best explanation. Physicians use it to pinpoint the cause of multiple symptoms in patients. Police detectives use it to track down law breakers. Judges and juries use it to determine the guilt or innocence of accused persons. And philosophers use it to assess the worth of conceptual theories.

With so many people in so many areas of inquiry using inference to the best explanation, you'd expect the world to be filled with countless theories proposed by innumerable people looking to explain all sorts of things. And so there are. Here's a very brief table of notable or interesting proposed theories and the phenomena they are meant to explain:

Theory	To Explain . . .
Atomic	Behavior of subatomic particles
Germ	Spread of disease
HIV	Cause of AIDS
Oedipus complex	Behavior of men and boys
Placebo effect	Apparent cure of disease
The lone-gunman	Assassination of John F. Kennedy
Violent video games	Violence in children
No official prayer in school	High crime and low morals
El Niño	Bad weather
El Niño	Good weather
Incumbent politicians	A bad economy
Political sex scandals	Immoral behavior of young people

Of course, it's often easy to make up theories to explain things we don't understand. The harder job is sorting out good theories from bad, and that's the topic of the next few pages.

Exercise 9.1

1. What is an explanation?
2. What is inference to the best explanation?
3. Is inference to the best explanation inductive or deductive?
* 4. According to the text, what is a theoretical explanation?
5. What is the basic logical pattern of inference to the best explanation? for enumerative induction? for analogical induction?
6. According to the text, under what circumstances can an inference to the best explanation be deemed strong? cogent?

[Handwritten margin notes:]
Explanations often involve theoretical entities that cannot be observed...

Who uses IBE?
— Scientists
— Physicians
— Police
— Judges/Juries
— Philosophers

7. What is a teleological explanation? interpretive explanation? procedural explanation?

* 8. What is a causal explanation? Are causal explanations used in inference to the best explanation?

9. How does the kind of explanation used in inference to the best explanation differ from a teleological explanation or an interpretive explanation?

10. Have you used inference to the best explanation today? If so, how did you use it? (Supply an example from the events of your day.)

Exercise 9.2

Explanandum is underlined

For each of the following explanations, indicate what state of affairs is being explained and what the explanation is.

1. Most students drop Professor Graham's class because he is so boring.

* 2. We all know that the spotted owl is endangered, and the only explanation for that is the political clout of the logging industry.

3. Why did James say that he saw a ghost in his bedroom? Because he drinks too much and has a vivid imagination.

4. Crimes committed by high school students are increasing because school districts refuse to mandate harsh punishments for criminal acts.

* 5. I'll tell you why the incidence of robbery is up: There aren't enough gun owners in the population.

6. Binge drinking is on the rise at women's colleges. This can best be explained by the permissive attitudes of the deans.

7. Americans are fond of the death penalty, but Europeans are not. Americans just never got over the old Wild West eye-for-an-eye mentality. Europeans never had a Wild West.

* 8. I believe that psychics really can predict the future because many things that psychics have told me have come true.

9. Rock stars make more money than teachers because they are smarter than teachers.

10. Global terrorism is caused by worldwide injustice and deprivation.

Exercise 9.3

For each of the following, determine whether the type of explanation offered is theoretical (the kind used in inference to the best explanation) or nontheoretical (e.g., teleological, interpretive, procedural). Be careful to note any borderline cases (explanations that could be either theoretical or nontheoretical).

1. There is no peace in the Middle East—and there never will be—due to the stubbornness of both sides in the conflict. ① Theoretical
2. "Creation science" is controversial because mainstream scientists hate it. ② Theoretical
*3. Ethics is the critical study of morality. ③ Interpretive
4. John built himself a solar house so he could thumb his nose at the power company. ④ Borderline/Teleological
5. Jack is soaking wet because he stood in the rain. ⑤ Theoretical
6. When Jill raises her hand, that means she's going to ask a question that no one can answer. ⑥ Interpretive
*7. When you experience memory loss, that can only mean one thing: Alzheimer's disease. ⑦ Theoretical
8. I wear this medallion for good luck. ⑧ Borderline/Teleological
9. He got the information through a complicated process of downloading it from the hard drive and putting it on multiple disks. ⑨ Procedural
10. Evil exists in the world because God allows it. ⑩ Borderline/Teleological
11. You are always sick because you don't take care of yourself. ⑪ Theoretical
*12. That painting is without vibrancy or cohesion. Just look at the dull colors and mish-mash of forms. ⑫ Interpretive
13. Jill flunked her courses because she liked to party too much. ⑬ Theoretical
14. Sam has been weight training, so he's pretty buff. ⑭ Theoretical
15. Jane is studying hard so she can get a better job. ⑮ Teleological
16. No one noticed the comet before because of cloud cover. ⑯ Theoretical
17. He broke the lock and pushed open the door—that's how he got in. ⑰ Borderline/Procedural?

Exercise 9.4

In each of the following examples, a state of affairs is described. Devise two theories to explain each one. Include one theory that you consider plausible and one theory that you think is not plausible.

1. Mutilated cows have been found in several pastures in the western United States. In each case organs are missing from the carcasses. There are never any signs of vehicle tracks or footprints. The cause of death is unknown. The method used to remove the organs is also unknown, although the wounds show indications of precision surgical tools.
*2. When Jack came home, he noticed the window in the kitchen was broken, there were muddy footprints on the kitchen floor, and some valuable silverware was missing.
3. Carl has vivid memories of his being in a past life. Sometimes he remembers himself being a stable boy; other times he recalls that he was a Roman soldier. All of these memories come to light only when Carl is under hypnosis.

4. In many Islamic countries women have fewer rights than men do.

5. In the 1980s the number of homeless people in the United States increased dramatically.

* 6. Alice has been taking vitamin C every day for a year, and during that time she has not had a cold or a sore throat.

7. Teenagers are now having sex at earlier ages.

8. Scientists have discovered that there is a direct correlation between fat in people's diets and heart disease. The more fat, the greater the risk of heart disease.

9. The incidence of violent crimes in the United States has decreased in recent years.

Exercise 9.5

Read each of the following passages and answer these questions:

1. What is the phenomenon being explained?

2. What theory is suggested as a possible explanation for the phenomenon?

3. Is the theory plausible? If not, why not?

4. Is there a plausible theory that the writer has overlooked? If so, what is it?

PASSAGE 1

Many people believe that drinking a warm glass of milk at bedtime helps them fall asleep. The reason must be the tryptophan in the milk. Tryptophan is an essential amino acid that is converted into serotonin. Serotonin affects sleep patterns and the perception of pain.

PASSAGE 2

"Shark attacks around the world declined in 2003 for a third straight year, partly because swimmers and surfers grew more accustomed to thinking of the ocean as a wild and dangerous place. . . .

"The University of Florida, which houses the International Shark Attack File, said there were 55 unprovoked attacks worldwide, down from 63 reported in 2002 and lower than the previous year's 68 attacks.

"Four people were killed, compared to three in 2002, four in 2001 and 11 in the year 2000.

"Normally, scientists do not put much stock in year-to-year fluctuations in the number of attacks because they can be affected by such things as the weather and oceanographic conditions that drive bait fish closer to shore.

"But the third consecutive year of decline could indicate a longer term trend, the university said.

"'I think people are beginning to get a little more intelligent about when and where they enter the water,' George Burgess, director of the International Shark Attack File, said in a statement.

"'There seems to be more of an understanding that when we enter the sea, it's a wilderness experience and we're intruders in that environment.'"[4]

PASSAGE 3

"Women who have been coloring their hair for 24 years or more have a higher risk of developing a cancer called non-Hodgkin lymphoma, researchers reported.

"They said their study of 1,300 women could help explain a mysterious rise in the number of cases of the cancer that affects the lymphatic system.

"Writing in the *American Journal of Epidemiology*, they said women who dyed their hair starting before 1980 were one-third more likely to develop non-Hodgkin lymphoma, or NHL, and those who used the darkest dyes for more than 25 years were twice as likely to develop the cancer.

"'Women who used darker permanent hair coloring products for more than 25 years showed the highest increased risk,' Tongzhang Zheng, associate professor of epidemiology and environmental health at Yale School of Medicine, said in a statement.

"Cancer experts note that a person's absolute risk of developing lymphoma is very low, so doubling that risk still means a woman who dyes her hair is very unlikely to develop lymphoma."[5]

PASSAGE 4

Spontaneous human combustion (SHC) is the theory that under certain rare circumstances, a human body mysteriously ignites, burns, and is almost entirely consumed. Investigators have encountered a few cases in which the burnt remains of a human body (usually only a limb or two) are found in an enclosed room, with nearby flammable objects completely unaffected by fire. The other parts of the body, including the torso, are entirely incinerated. There is usually, or always, a source of flame in the room—a lit pipe or candle, for example. And the victim is often elderly, alcoholic, or in some way incapacitated. SHC is the only reasonable explanation for these strange facts.

Theories and Consistency

Very often we may propose a theory as an explanation for a phenomenon, or we may have a theory thrust upon us for consideration. In either case, we will likely be dealing with an argument in the form of inference to the best explanation. The conclusion of the argument will always say, in effect, *this* theory is the

"In making theories, keep a window open so that you can throw one out if necessary."

—BELA SCHICK

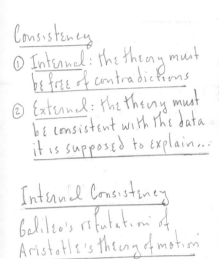

Consistency
① Internal: the theory must be free of contradictions
② External: the theory must be consistent with the data it is supposed to explain...

Internal Consistency
Galileo's refutation of Aristotle's theory of motion

External Consistency

best explanation of the facts. And we will be on the hot seat trying to decide if it really is. How do we do that?

The work is not always easy, but there are special criteria we can use to get the job done. Before we apply these criteria, though, we have to make sure that the theory in question meets the minimum requirement of *consistency*. A theory that does not meet this minimum requirement is worthless, so there is no need to use the special criteria to evaluate the theory. A theory that meets the requirement is eligible for further consideration. Here we are concerned with both *internal* and *external* consistency. A theory that is internally consistent is consistent with itself—it's free of contradictions. A theory that is externally consistent is consistent with the data it's supposed to explain—it fully accounts for the phenomenon to be explained.

If we show that a theory contains a contradiction, we have refuted it. A theory that implies that something both is and is not the case cannot possibly be true. By exposing an internal contradiction, Galileo once refuted Aristotle's famous theory of motion, a venerable hypothesis that had stood tall for centuries. He showed that the theory implied that one falling object falls both faster and slower than another one.

If a theory is externally inconsistent, we have reason to believe that it's false. Suppose you leave your car parked on the street overnight and the next morning discover that (1) the windshield is broken, (2) there's blood on the steering wheel, and (3) there's a brick on the front seat. And let's say that your friend Charlie offers this theory to explain these facts: Someone threw a brick through your windshield. What would you think about this theory?

You would probably think that Charlie had not been paying attention. His theory accounts for the broken windshield and the brick—but not the blood on the steering wheel. You would likely toss his theory out and look for one that was complete. Like this one: A thief broke your windshield with a brick then crawled through the broken window, cutting himself in the process.

REVIEW NOTES

☑ Minimum Requirement: Consistency

• Internal consistency: A theory that is internally consistent is free of contradictions
• External consistency: A theory that is externally consistent is consistent with the data it's supposed to explain

Theories and Criteria

For a moment let's return to our example of the car that won't start. Recall that we examined five possible explanations for the non-start phenomenon:

1. The battery is dead.
2. The fuel tank is empty.
3. The starter has malfunctioned.
4. A vandal has sabotaged the car.
5. All or several of the above.

But what if someone suggested that our analysis of this problem was incomplete because we failed to consider several other possible theories that are at least as plausible as these five? Consider these, for example:

6. Each night, you are sabotaging your own car while you sleepwalk.
7. Your ninety-year-old uncle, who lives a thousand miles away from you, has secretly been going for joyrides in your car, damaging the engine.
8. A poltergeist (a noisy, mischievous ghost) has damaged the car's carburetor.
9. Yesterday, you accidentally drove the car through an alternative space-time dimension, scrambling the electrical system.

What do you think of these theories? More specifically, are the last four theories *really* at least as plausible as the first five? If you think so, *why*? If you think not, *why not*? Remember that a theory's strangeness is no good reason to discount it. It will not do to say that theories 6–9 are too weird to be true. In the history of science plenty of bizarre theories have turned out to be correct. (Quantum theory in physics, for example, is about as weird as you can get.) Earlier we concluded that theory 3 was better (more likely to be true) than 1, 2, 4, and 5. But what criteria did we use to arrive at this judgment? And on the basis of what criteria can we say that theory 3 is any better than theories 6–9? There must be *some* criteria because it is implausible that every theory is equally correct. Surely there is a difference in quality between a theory that explains rainfall by positing some natural meteorological forces and one that alleges that Donald Duck causes weather phenomena.

A simplified answer to the problem of theory choice is this: Just weigh the evidence for each theory, and the theory with the most evidence wins. As we will soon see, the amount or degree of evidence that a theory has is indeed a crucial factor—but it cannot be the sole criterion by which we assess explanations. Throughout the history of science, major theories—from the heliocentric theory of the Solar System to Einstein's General Theory of Relativity—have never been established by empirical evidence alone.

"The Universe is not obliged to conform to what we consider comfortable or plausible."
—CARL SAGAN

[Handwritten margin notes: "Weirdness does not automatically disqualify a theory. In the history of science plenty of bizarre theories have turned out to be correct."]

[Handwritten margin note: "It is important to weigh the evidence but evidence itself cannot be the sole criterion"]

The task of determining the best explanation has another complication. If we accept such extraordinary theories as 6–9 as legitimate possibilities, there must be no end to the number of theories that we could devise to explain the data at hand. In fact, we could come up with an infinite number of possible theories for any phenomenon simply by repeatedly adding one more element. For example, we could propose the one-poltergeist theory (a single entity causing the trouble), a two-poltergeist theory, a three-poltergeist theory, and so on.

Fortunately, despite these complications, there are reasonable criteria and reliable procedures for judging the merits of eligible theories and for arriving at a defensible judgment of which theory is best. Enter: the **criteria of adequacy.** The criteria of adequacy are the essential tools of science and have been used by scientists throughout history to uncover the best explanations for all sorts of events and states of affairs. Science, though, doesn't own these criteria. They are as useful—and as used—among nonscientists as they are among men and women of science.

Applying the criteria of adequacy to a set of theories constitutes the ultimate test of a theory's value, for *the best theory is the eligible theory that meets the criteria*

Criteria of Adequacy

The best theory is the eligible theory that meets the criteria of adequacy better than any of its competitors...

The external world is often invoked as the best explanation for the pattern of our perceptions...

FURTHER THOUGHT

Inference to the Best Explanation and the External World

In Chapters 10 and 11 we will explore in detail how inference to the best explanation can be used to tackle some big issues. Here we just want to mention one of the "big questions" to which philosophers and other thinkers have applied inference to the best explanation.

A problem that has historically occupied thinkers in the history of philosophy is whether we have any good reasons to believe that there is a world outside our own thoughts. That is, is there an *external world* independent of the way we represent it to ourselves? Some people, called skeptics, have denied that we have any such good reasons because we can never get "outside our skins" to objectively compare our subjective experiences with reality. All we know is the nature of our perceptions—which may or may not be linked to the "real world" in any way.

To this puzzle many philosophers have applied inference to the best explanation. They argue that we can indeed know that there is an external reality because that belief is the best explanation of the peculiar pattern of our perceptions. In other words, the best explanation of why we seem to see a tree in front of us is that there *really is a real tree in front of us.*

of adequacy better than any of its competitors. Here, "eligible" means that the theory has already met the minimum requirement for consistency.

All of this implies that the evaluation of a particular theory is not complete until alternative, or competing, theories are considered. As we've seen, there is an indefinite number of theories that could be offered to explain a given set of data. The main challenge is to give a fair assessment of the relevant theories in relation to each other. To fail to somehow address the alternatives is to overlook or deny relevant evidence, to risk biased conclusions, and to court error. Such failure is probably the most common error in the appraisal of theories.

A theory judged by these criteria to be the best explanation for certain facts is worthy of our belief, and we may legitimately claim to know that such a theory is true. But the theory is not then necessarily or certainly true in the way that a sound deductive argument's conclusion is necessarily or certainly true. Inference to the best explanation, like other forms of induction, cannot guarantee the truth of the best explanation. That is, it is not truth-preserving. The best theory we have may actually be false. Nevertheless we would have excellent reasons for supposing our best theory to be a true theory.

The criteria of adequacy are *testability, fruitfulness, scope, simplicity,* and *conservatism.* Let's examine each one in detail.

TESTABILITY

Most of the theories that we encounter every day and all the theories that scientists take seriously are **testable**—*there is some way to determine whether the theories are true or false.* If a theory is untestable—if there is no possible procedure for checking its truth—then it is worthless as an explanatory theory. Suppose someone says that an invisible, undetectable spirit is causing your headaches. What possible test could we perform to tell if the spirit actually exists? None. So the spirit theory is entirely empty. We can assign no weight to such a claim.

Here's another way to look at it. Theories are explanations, and explanations are designed to increase our understanding of the world. But an untestable theory does not—and cannot—explain anything. It is equivalent to saying that an unknown thing with unknown properties acts in an unknown way to cause a phenomenon—which is the same thing as offering no explanation at all.

We often run into untestable theories in daily life, just as scientists sometimes encounter them in their work. Many practitioners of alternative medicine claim that health problems are caused by an imbalance in people's *chi,* an unmeasurable form of mystical energy that is said to flow through everyone. Some people say that their misfortunes are caused by God or the Devil. Others believe that certain events in their lives happen (and are inevitable) because of fate. And parents may hear their young daughter say that she did not break the lamp, but her invisible friend did.

[Handwritten margin notes:]

Evaluation of a particular theory is not complete until alternative or competing theories are considered

IBE cannot guarantee the truth of the best explanation

I. TESTABILITY

There must be some way to determine whether the theories are true or false

Appealing to an unknown X with unknown properties is the same as offering no explanation at all.

Untestable Theories
- chi
- God
- angels
- demons
- gremlins

☑ Criteria of Adequacy

- Testability: Whether there is some way to determine if a theory is true
- Fruitfulness: The number of novel predictions made
- Scope: The amount of diverse phenomena explained
- Simplicity: The number of assumptions made
- Conservatism: How well a theory fits with existing knowledge

Many theories throughout history have been untestable. Some of the more influential untestable theories include the theory of witches (some people called witches are controlled by the Devil), the moral fault theory of disease (immoral behavior causes illness), and the divine placement theory of fossils (God created geological fossils to give the false impression of an ancient Earth).

But what does it mean for a theory to be testable or untestable? A theory is testable *if it predicts something other than what it was introduced to explain.* Suppose your electric clock stops each time you touch it. One theory to explain this event is that there is an electrical short in the clock's wiring. Another theory is that an invisible, undetectable demon causes the clock to stop. The wiring theory predicts that if the wiring is repaired, the clock will no longer shut off when touched. So it is testable—there is something that the theory predicts other than the obvious fact that the clock will stop when you touch it. But the demon theory makes no predictions about anything, *except* the obvious, the very fact that the theory was introduced to explain. It predicts that the clock will stop if you touch it, but we already know this. So our understanding is not increased, and the demon theory is untestable.

Now, if the demon theory says that the demon can be detected with x-rays, then there is something the theory predicts other than the clock's stopping when touched. You can x-ray the clock and examine the film for demon silhouettes. If the theory says that the demon can't be seen but can be heard with sensitive sound equipment, then you have a prediction, something to look for other than clock stoppage.

So other things being equal, testable theories are superior to untestable ones; they may be able to increase our understanding of a phenomenon. But an untestable theory is just an oddity.

FRUITFULNESS

Imagine that we have two testable theories, theory 1 and theory 2, that attempt to explain the same phenomenon. Theory 1 and theory 2 seem comparable in most

[Handwritten margin notes:]
Some untestable theories
- witches
- moral fault theory of disease
- divine placement of fossils

Testability: a theory is testable if it predicts something other than what it was introduced to explain...

Carl Hempel

II. FRUITFULNESS

respects when measured against the criteria of adequacy. Theory 1, however, successfully predicts the existence of a previously unknown entity, say, a star in an uncharted part of the sky. What would you conclude about the relative worth of these two theories?

If you thought carefully about the issue, you would probably conclude that theory 1 is the better theory—and you would be right. Other things being equal, theories that perform this way—that successfully predict previously unknown phenomena—are more credible than those that don't. They are said to be **fruit-ful**, to yield new insights that can open up whole new areas of research and discovery. This fruitfulness suggests that the theories are more likely to be true.

If a friend of yours is walking through a forest where she has never been before, yet she seems to be able to predict exactly what's up ahead, you would probably conclude that she possessed some kind of accurate information about the forest, such as a map. Likewise, if a theory successfully predicts some surprising state of affairs, you are likely to think that the predictions are not just lucky guesses.

[handwritten margin note: All other things being equal, theories that predict previously unknown phenomena are more credible than those that don't predict anything]

FROM THE WEB

The Importance (and Fun) of Crazy Theories

Many theories proposed throughout the history of science have been, well, crazy. That is, they have been unorthodox or heretical, with a shockingly different take on the world. The heliocentric theory of our solar system is a prime example. Some of these crazy theories have turned out to be good theories—they measured up to the criteria of adequacy very well. So a crazy theory is not necessarily a bad theory. Science as a whole has always been open to offbeat explanations, but they had to be judged to have merit. Most crazy theories in science or the fringes of science, though, usually fail the criteria of adequacy miserably. The challenge for scientists and other critical thinkers is to remain open to unorthodox theories but not be afraid to test them through critical reasoning. Besides, offbeat theories are fun. These following theories were gleaned from the Web.

[handwritten margin note: Need to be "open to" but critical of unorthodox theories]

- "It is my belief that Mars was once a beautiful, fertile planet capable of sustaining life, much like our own, until some cataclysmic, global event changed everything. I believe that the survivors went searching for another planet, on which to live, and that they chose the Earth. We are their descendants. They were an advanced civilization who brought their technology with them. Upon reaching Earth, they proceeded to build the same type structures that were familiar to them on Mars. That way, if there were more survivors they'd recognize the structures and know where the others were."

- "Trepanation is the practice of making a hole in the skull. It is sometimes spelled trephination. . . . trepanation was practiced on every continent through every time period and by every race of mankind until the advent of brain surgery in this century. Doctors, today, have been taught that trepanation was done in past centuries for superstitious, magical or religious reasons. They generally look on trepanation as a practice akin to blood letting.

Trepanation: formerly for the release of evil spirits and later for the achievement of enlightenment.

They scoff at it. . . . The risk to benefit ratio would have to have been very favorable for the practice to have been so widely practiced but official investigators haven't been able to see that there is both a rationale and a benefit to this procedure."

- "There is without any doubt whatsoever scientific evidence for the existence of the afterlife. . . . Some of the technical evidence includes: The Electronic Voice Phenomenon (Spirit Voices on Tape), Instrumental Transcommunication (two-way communication with those who crossed over), the SCOLE Experiments, Out of Body Experiences, Near Death Experiences, Empirical Materialisation, Trans and Mental Mediumship; Poltergeists, Xenoglossy and Reincarnation, the Cross-Correspondences, Proxy Sittings."

- Have you ever dreamed of traveling in time? Now you can experience what you have only dreamed of. With the Hyper Dimensional Resonator you can travel into the past or explore the future. The world will be at your beck and call and you will have all the time in the world to explore it. . . . I sell an instrument which can be used for both, out of the body time travel and can also be used to help heal the sick."

All empirical theories are testable (they predict something beyond the thing to be explained). But fruitful theories are testable and then some. They not only predict something, they predict something that no one expected. The element of surprise is hard to ignore.

Decades ago Einstein's theory of relativity gained a great deal of credibility by successfully predicting a phenomenon that was extraordinary and entirely novel. The theory predicts that light traveling close to massive objects (such as stars) will appear to be bent because the space around such objects is curved. The curve in space causes a curve in nearby light rays. At the time, however, the prevailing opinion was that light always travels in straight lines—no bends, no curves, no breaks. In 1919 the physicist Sir Arthur Eddington devised a way to test this prediction. He managed to take two sets of photographs of exactly the same portion of the sky—when the sun was overhead (in daylight) and when it was not (at night). He was able to get a good photo of the sky during daylight because there was a total eclipse of the sun at the time. If light rays really were bent when they passed near massive objects, then stars whose light passes near the sun should appear to be shifted slightly from their true position (as seen at night). Eddington discovered that stars near the sun did appear to have moved and that the amount of their apparent movement was just what the theory predicted. This novel prediction then demonstrated the fruitfulness of Einstein's theory, provided a degree of confirmation for the theory, and opened up new areas of research.

www.CartoonStock.com

EXAMPLE: Einstein's Theory of Relativity predicts light travelling near massive objects would appear bent. Eddington devised a test that successfully confirmed the prediction...

So the moral is that other things being equal, fruitful theories are superior to those that aren't fruitful. Certainly many good theories make no novel predictions but are accepted nonetheless. The reason is usually that they excel in other criteria of adequacy.

SCOPE

III. SCOPE

Suppose theory 1 and theory 2 are two equally plausible theories to explain phenomenon X. Theory 1 can explain X well, and so can theory 2. But theory 1 can explain or predict *only* X, whereas theory 2 can explain or predict X—as well as phenomena Y and Z. Which is the better theory?

We must conclude that theory 2 is better because it explains more diverse phenomena. That is, it has more **scope** than the other theory. The more a theory explains or predicts, the more it extends our understanding. And the more a

The more a theory predicts, the better the theory is

EXAMPLE: Einstein's theory
predicts everything predicted
by Newton's Theory and more

Constructive Perception

theory explains or predicts, the less likely it is to be false because it has more evidence in its favor.

A major strength of Newton's theory of gravity and motion, for example, was that it explained more than any previous theory. Then came Einstein's theory of relativity. It could explain everything that Newton's theory could explain plus many phenomena that Newton's theory could not explain. This increased scope of Einstein's theory helped convince scientists that it was the better theory.

Here's a more down-to-earth example. For decades psychologists have known about a phenomenon called *constructive perception* (discussed in Chapter 4). In

" NEWSMAKERS "

The Best Explanation for Hurricane Katrina?

Some explanations make the news in a big way. In 2008 John Hagee, a prominent evangelical leader and author, publicly endorsed the presidential candidacy of John McCain, immediately thrusting both men into a media-heightened controversy involving some of Hagee's previously stated views. Receiving a large share of the attention was his explanation (later retracted) for the devastation of New Orleans by Hurricane Katrina:

> All hurricanes are acts of God, because God controls the heavens. I believe that New Orleans had a level of sin that was offensive to God, and they were recipients of the judgment of God for that.
>
> The newspaper carried the story in our local area, that was not carried nationally, that there was to be a homosexual parade there on the Monday that the Katrina came. And the promise of that pa-

rade was that it was going to reach a level of sexuality never demonstrated before in any of the other gay pride parades.

So I believe that the judgment of God is a very real thing. I know there are people who demur from that, but I believe that the Bible teaches that when you violate the law of God, that God brings punishment sometimes before the Day of Judgment, and I believe that the Hurricane Katrina was, in fact, the judgment of God against the city of New Orleans.[6]

As an explanation for a physical phenomenon, this theory is as subject to evaluation using the criteria of adequacy as any other theory. What is the leading alternative theory to explain the natural disaster? Which theory, as judged by the criteria, is better? ■

constructive perception what we perceive (see, hear, feel, etc.) is determined in part by what we expect, know, or believe. Studies have shown that when people expect to perceive a certain stimulus (say, a flashing light, a certain color or shape, a shadow), they often *do* perceive it, even if there is no stimulus present. The phenomenon of constructive perception then can be used to explain many instances in which people seem to perceive something when it is not really there or when it is actually very different from the way people think it is.

One kind of case that investigators sometimes explain as an instance of constructive perception is the UFO sighting. Many times people report seeing lights in the night sky that look to them like alien spacecraft, and they explain their perception by saying that the lights were caused by alien spacecraft. So we have two theories to explain the experience: constructive perception and UFOs from space. If these two theories differ only in the degree of scope provided by each

[handwritten margin notes: Constructive Perception Hypothesis (CPH)]

[handwritten margin notes: The strength of CPH vs. theories invoking extraordinary claims, is scope.]

[Handwritten margin note: Jury deliberations often appeal to scope...]

[Handwritten margin note: IV. SIMPLICITY]

[Handwritten margin note: Theories 6-9 lack simplicity]

[Handwritten margin note: Ockham's Razor: Other things being equal the best theory is the one that makes the fewest assumptions...]

[Handwritten margin note: The fewer the number of assumptions, the fewer the ways for a theory to go wrong]

[Handwritten margin note: The fewer assumptions, the less evidence required to support it.]

one, however, we must conclude that the constructive-perception theory is better. (In reality, theories about incredible events usually differ on several criteria.) The constructive-perception theory can explain not only UFO sightings but all kinds of ordinary and extraordinary experiences—hallucinations, feelings of an unknown "presence," misidentification of crime suspects, contradictory reports in car accidents, and more. The UFO theory, however, is (usually) designed to explain just one thing: an experience of seeing strange lights in the sky.

Scope is often a crucial factor in a jury's evaluation of theories put forth by both the prosecution and the defense. The prosecution will have a very powerful case against the defendant if the prosecutor's theory (that the defendant did it) explains all the evidence and many other things while the defense theory (innocence) does not. The defendant would be in big trouble if the prosecutor's theory explains the blood on the defendant's shirt, the eyewitness accounts, the defendant's fingerprints on the wall, and the sudden change in his usual routine—*and* the innocence theory renders these facts downright mysterious.

Other things being equal, then, the best theory is the one with the greatest scope. And if other things aren't equal, a theory with superior scope doesn't necessarily win the day because it may do poorly on the other criteria—or another theory might do better.

SIMPLICITY

Let's return one last time to the scenario about the non-starting car. Recall that the last four theories are:

6. Each night, you are sabotaging your own car while you sleepwalk.
7. Your ninety-year-old uncle, who lives a thousand miles away from you, has secretly been going for joyrides in your car, damaging the engine.
8. A poltergeist (a noisy, mischievous ghost) has damaged the car's carburetor.
9. Yesterday, you accidentally drove the car through an alternative space-time dimension, scrambling the electrical system.

By now you probably suspect that these explanations are somehow unacceptable, and so they are. One important characteristic that they each lack is **simplicity**. Other things being equal, the best theory is the one that is the simplest—that is, the one that makes the fewest assumptions. The theory making the fewest assumptions is less likely to be false because there are fewer ways for it to go wrong. Another way to look at it is that since a simpler theory is based on fewer assumptions, less evidence is required to support it.

Explanations 8 and 9 lack simplicity because they each must assume the existence of an unknown entity (poltergeists and another dimension that scrambles electrical circuits). Such assumptions about the existence of unknown objects, forces, and dimensions are common in occult or paranormal theories. Explanations 6 and

7 assume no new entities, but they do assume complex chains of events. This alone makes them less plausible than the simple explanation of 3, starter malfunction.

The criterion of simplicity has often been a major factor in the acceptance or rejection of important theories. For example, simplicity is an important advantage that the theory of evolution has over creationism, the theory that the world was created at once by a divine being (see Chapter 10). Creationism must assume the existence of a creator and the existence of unknown forces (supernatural forces used by the creator). But evolution does not make either of these assumptions.

Evolution is a simpler theory than creationism

FURTHER THOUGHT

💡 There's No Theory Like a Conspiracy Theory

Conspiracy theories try to explain events by positing the secret participation of numerous conspirators. The assassination of JFK, the terrorist attacks of 9/11, international banking, the Watergate scandal, the inner workings of the U.S. government—all these and more have been the subject of countless conspiracy theories, both elaborate and provocative. Some conspiracy theories, of course, have been found to be true after all. But most of them are implausible. The main problem with them is that they usually fail the criterion of simplicity. They would have us make numerous assumptions that raise more questions than they answer: How do the conspirators manage to keep their activities secret? How do they control all the players? Where is the evidence that all the parts of the conspiracy have come together just so?

Nonetheless, the United States seems to be Conspiracy Central. Here's a short list of things that, we are told, are the center of a massive conspiracy:

The death of Elvis Presley
The assassination of Martin Luther King, Jr.
The Oklahoma City bombing
The death of Princess Diana
The terrorist attacks of September 11, 2001

And here are a few of the alleged cabals that are doing all the dirty deeds:

The U.S. government
The Vatican
The CIA
The Illuminati, a secret society controlling the government
Doctors
The Freemasons

Conspiracy Theories usually fail to meet the criterion of simplicity...

The additional assumptions raise more questions than they answer...

Copernicus vs. Ptolemy

Additional hypotheses must be independently verifiable

Ad Hoc Hypotheses that are not independently verifiable violate the criterion of simplicity

Ad hoc hypotheses always make a theory less simple and therefore less credible...

I. CONSERVATISM

All other things being equal, the best theory is the one that fits best with our established beliefs...

Scientists eventually accepted Copernicus's theory of planetary motion (heliocentric orbits) over Ptolemy's (Earth-centered orbits) because the former was simpler (see Chapter 10). In order to account for apparent irregularities in the movement of certain planets, Ptolemy's theory had to assume that planets have extremely complex orbits (orbits within orbits). Copernicus's theory, however, had no need for so much extra baggage. His theory could account for the observational data without so many orbits-within-orbits.

Sometimes a theory's lack of simplicity is the result of constructing ad hoc hypotheses. An **ad hoc hypothesis** is one that cannot be verified independently of the phenomenon it's supposed to explain. If a theory is in trouble because it is not matching up with the observational data of the phenomenon, you might be able to rescue it by altering it—by positing additional entities or properties that can account for the data. Such tinkering is legitimate (scientists do it all the time) if there is an independent way of confirming the existence of these proposed entities and properties. But if there is no way to verify their existence, the modifications are ad hoc hypotheses. Ad hoc hypotheses always make a theory less simple—and therefore less credible.

CONSERVATISM

What if a trusted friend told you that—believe it or not—some dogs lay eggs just as chickens do? Let's assume that your friend is being perfectly serious and believes what she is saying. Would you accept this claim about egg-laying dogs? Not likely. But why not?

Probably your main reason for rejecting such an extraordinary claim would be that it fails the criterion of **conservatism**, though you probably wouldn't state it that way. (Note: This sense of "conservatism" has nothing to do with political parties.) This criterion says that other things being equal, *the best theory is the one that fits best with our established beliefs.* We would reject the canine-egg theory because, among other things, it conflicts with our well-founded beliefs about mammals, evolution, canine anatomy, and much more. Humans have an enormous amount of experience with dogs (scientific and otherwise), and none of it suggests that dogs can lay eggs. In fact, a great deal of what we know about dogs suggests that they *cannot* lay eggs. To accept the canine-egg theory despite its conflicting with a mountain of solid evidence would be irrational—and destructive of whatever understanding we had of the subject.

Perhaps one day we may be shocked to learn that—contrary to all expectations—dogs do lay eggs. But given that this belief is contrary to a massive amount of credible experience, we must assign a very low probability to it.

We are naturally reluctant to accept explanations that conflict with what we already know, and we should be. Accepting beliefs that fly in the face of our knowledge has several risks:

1. The chances of the new belief being true are not good (because it has no evidence in its favor, while our well-established beliefs have plenty of evidence on their side).

2. The conflict of beliefs undermines our knowledge (because we cannot know something that is in doubt, and the conflict would be cause for doubt).

3. The conflict of beliefs lessens our understanding (because the new beliefs cannot be plausibly integrated into our other beliefs).

So everything considered, the more conservative a theory is, the more plausible it is.[7]

Here's another example. Let's say that someone claims to have built a perpetual motion machine. A perpetual motion machine is supposed to function

[Handwritten margin notes: Risks of accepting claims that conflict with accepted beliefs]

[Handwritten margin notes: See Quine, Web of Belief]

[Handwritten margin notes: Why there cannot be a perpetual motion machine]

Was the Moon Landing a Hoax?

A stunning conspiracy theory says yes. NASA faked the whole thing, you see. Here's NASA's side of the story:

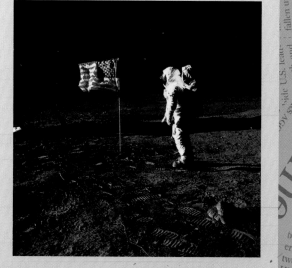

All the buzz about the Moon began on February 15th when Fox television aired a program called *Conspiracy Theory: Did We Land on the Moon?* Guests on the show argued that NASA technology in the 1960s wasn't up to the task of a real Moon landing. Instead, anxious to win the Space Race any way it could, NASA acted out the Apollo program in movie studios. Neil Armstrong's historic first steps on another world, the rollicking Moon Buggy rides, even Al Shepard's arcing golf shot over Fra Mauro—it was all a fake! . . .

According to the show NASA was a blundering movie producer thirty years ago. For example, *Conspiracy Theory* pundits pointed out a seeming discrepancy in Apollo imagery: Pictures of astronauts transmitted from the Moon don't include stars in the dark lunar

[Handwritten margin note: Star Problem]

sky—an obvious production error! What happened? Did NASA film-makers forget to turn on the constellations?

Most photographers already know the answer: It's difficult to capture something very bright and something else very dim on the same piece of film—typical emulsions don't have enough "dynamic range." Astronauts striding across the bright lunar soil in their sunlit spacesuits were literally dazzling. Setting a camera with the proper exposure for a glaring spacesuit would naturally render background stars too faint to see.

Here's another one: Pictures of Apollo astronauts erecting a US flag on the Moon show the flag bending and rippling. How can that be? After all, there's no breeze on the Moon. . . .

Not every waving flag needs a breeze—at least not in space. When astronauts were planting the flagpole they rotated it back and forth to better penetrate the lunar soil (anyone who's set a blunt tent-post will know how this works). So of course the flag waved! Unfurling a piece of rolled-up cloth with stored angular momentum will naturally result in waves and ripples—no breeze required! . . .

The best rebuttal to allegations of a "Moon Hoax," however, is common sense. Evidence that the Apollo program really happened is compelling: A dozen astronauts (laden with cameras) walked on the Moon between 1969 and 1972. Nine of them are still alive and can testify to their experience. They didn't return from the Moon empty-handed, either. Just as Columbus carried a few hundred natives back to Spain as evidence of his trip to the New World, Apollo astronauts brought 841 pounds of Moon rock home to Earth.

"Moon rocks are absolutely unique," says Dr. David McKay, Chief Scientist for Planetary Science and Exploration at NASA's Johnson Space Center (JSC). McKay is a member of the group that oversees the Lunar Sample Laboratory Facility at JSC where most of the Moon rocks are stored. "They differ from Earth rocks in many respects," he added.

"For example," explains Dr. Marc Norman, a lunar geologist at the University of Tasmania, "lunar samples have almost no water trapped in their crystal structure, and common substances such as clay minerals that are ubiquitous on Earth are totally absent in Moon rocks."

"We've found particles of fresh glass in Moon rocks that were produced by explosive volcanic activity and by meteorite impacts over 3 billion years ago," added Norman. "The presence of water on Earth rapidly breaks down such volcanic glass in only a few million years. These rocks must have come from the Moon!"[8]

Margin annotations (handwritten):

Flag Problem

Uniqueness of moon rocks
- No water
- no clay minerals

- Particles of fresh glass

without ever stopping and without requiring any energy input from outside the machine; it is designed to continuously supply its own energy.

Now, this is an intriguing idea—which we shouldn't take too seriously. The problem is that the notion of a perpetual motion machine is not conservative at all. It conflicts with a very well-established belief—namely, one of the scientific laws of thermodynamics. The law of conservation of mass-energy says that mass-energy cannot be created or destroyed. A perpetual motion machine, though, would have to create energy out of nothing. Like any law of nature, however, the law of conservation of mass-energy is supported by a vast amount of empirical evidence. We must conclude, then, that it is extremely unlikely that anyone could escape the law of conservation of mass-energy through the use of any machine. (This fact, however, has not stopped countless optimistic inventers from claiming that they've invented such devices. When the devices are put to the test, they invariably fail to perform as advertised.)

It's possible, of course, that a new theory that conflicts with what we know could turn out to be right and a more conservative theory wrong. But we would need good reasons to show that the new theory was correct before we would be justified in tossing out the old theory and bringing in the new.

Science looks for conservative theories, but it still sometimes embraces theories that are departures (sometimes *radical* departures) from the well-worn, accepted explanations. When this dramatic change happens, it's frequently because other criteria of adequacy outweigh conservatism. We'll explore the creation and evaluation of scientific theories in the next chapter.

Occult or paranormal theories often run afoul of the criterion of conservatism. Take *dowsing,* for instance. Dowsing is the practice of detecting underground water by using a Y-shaped stick (known as a divining rod or dowsing rod), a pendulum, or another device. It's a folk tradition that's hundreds of years old. Dowsers claim to be able to detect the presence of underground water by walking over a given terrain and holding the two branches of the dowsing rod (one in each hand) with its point facing skyward away from the body. (This claim, as it turns out, is unsupported.) When the point of the rod dips toward the ground, that's supposed to indicate that water is beneath

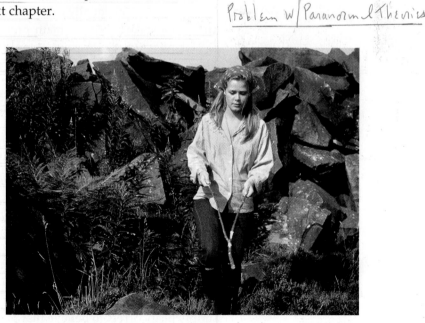
The art of dowsing. What makes the rod dip?

[handwritten margin notes:] A perpetual motion machine would violate law of conservation of mass-energy

Often a new theory that conflicts with established beliefs turns out to be right

Need to weigh the other criteria of adequacy

Problem w/ Paranormal Theories

the dowser. It seems to the dowser (and sometimes to observers) that the rod moves on its own, as though under the influence of some hidden force.

One theory to account for the rod's movements is this: an unknown form of radiation emanating from the underground water pulls on the diving rod, causing it to move. (A well-supported alternative theory is that the movement of the divining rod in the dowser's hands is caused by suggestion and unconscious muscular activity in the dowser.) As it stands, the radiation theory is not testable, fruitful, or simple. But its major failing is its lack of conservatism. The claim about the strange, occult radiation conflicts with what scientists know about energy, radiation, and human sensory systems. It is possible that the dowser's radiation exists, but there is no reason to believe that it does and good reason to doubt it.

We will look at many more examples shortly, but before we go any further, you need to fully understand two crucial points about the nature of theory appraisal.

First, there is no strict formula or protocol for applying the criteria of adequacy. In deductive arguments there are rules of inference that are precise and invariable. But inference to the best explanation is a different animal. There are no precise rules for applying the criteria, no way to quantify how a theory measures up according to each criterion, and no way to rank each criterion according to its importance. Sometimes we may assign more weight to the criterion of scope if the theory in question seems comparable to other theories in terms of all the remaining criteria. Other times we may weight simplicity more when considering theories that seem equally conservative or fruitful. The process of theory evaluation is not like solving a math problem—but more like diagnosing an illness or making a judicial decision. It is rational but not formulaic, and it depends on the dynamics of human judgment. The best we can do is follow some guidelines for evaluating theories generally and for applying the criteria of adequacy. Fortunately, this kind of help is usually all we need. (You'll get this kind of guidance in the following pages.)

Second, despite the lack of formula in theory assessment, the process is far from subjective or arbitrary. There are many distinctions that we successfully make every day that are not quantifiable or formulaic—but they are still objective. We cannot say exactly when day turns into night or when a person with a full head of hair becomes bald or when a puddle in the rain becomes a pond, but our distinctions between night and day or baldness and hirsuteness or puddles and ponds are clearly objective. Of course, there are cases that are not so clear-cut that give rise to reasonable disagreement among reasonable people. But there are also many instances that are manifestly unambiguous. Pretending that these states of affairs are unclear would be irrational. It would simply be incorrect to believe that broad daylight is nighttime or that a puddle is a pond.

[Handwritten margin notes:]

SUMMARY:

① There is no strict formula to apply the criteria

② Despite the lack of a strict formula in theory assessment, the process is far from subjective...

Exercise 9.6

1. When you are trying to decide between two theories, can you just rely on evidence alone to determine which theory is better?

* 2. In theory evaluation, what is the minimum requirement of consistency?

3. According to the text, what is a "best theory"?

4. According to the text, what are the criteria of adequacy?

5. What does it mean for a theory to be testable? fruitful? conservative?

* 6. What does it mean to say that a theory does not have much scope?

7. According to the text, are theories that posit paranormal entities simple? If not, why not?

8. What are the risks involved in accepting a nonconservative theory?

Exercise 9.7

Following are several pairs of theories used to explain various phenomena. For each pair, determine (1) which theory is simpler and (2) which one is more conservative.

1. Phenomenon: A sudden remission of cancer in a patient.
   Theories: Part of the natural cycle of the disease; the result of taking an elixir with "healing properties" unknown to science.

   ① S & C

* 2. Phenomenon: The survival of a group of sailors whose ship sank at sea.
   Theories: Quick action by a group of magic dolphins; quick action by the Coast Guard rescue team.

   ② S & C

3. Phenomenon: The winning of an election by a relatively unknown candidate.
   Theories: A last-minute blitz of TV ads; the candidate's endorsement by a famous convicted murderer.

   ③ Conservative

* 4. Phenomenon: A "precognitive" dream (having one's dream come true).
   Theories: Coincidence; psychic energy emanating from the dreamer.

   ④ S & C

5. Phenomenon: The sudden friendliness of the North Korean government toward the United States.
   Theories: A big change in the leadership of the government; North Korea's realization that democratic capitalism is the way to go.

   ⑤ Conservative

6. Phenomenon: The bizarre and dangerous behavior of your best friend.
   Theories: An allergy attack; the result of taking LSD.

   ⑥ Conservative

* 7. Phenomenon: A hurricane hitting south Florida.
   Theories: El Niño; radiation from outer space.

   ⑦ S & C

8. Phenomenon: A huge drop in the incidence of childhood disease over the last fifty years.
   Theories: Mandatory immunization; lower levels of air pollution.

   ⑧ S & C

"For any scientific theory is born into a life of fierce competition, a jungle red in tooth and claw. Only the successful theories survive—the ones which in fact latched on to the actual regularities in nature."

—BAS VAN FRAASSEN

Telling Good Theories from Bad

Many (perhaps most) explanatory theories that you run into every day are easy to assess. They are clearly the best (or not the best) explanations for the facts at hand. The dog barked because someone approached the house. Your friend blushed because he was embarrassed. The senator resigned because of a scandal. In such cases, you may make inferences to the best explanation (using some or all of the criteria of adequacy) without any deep reflection. But at other times, you may need and want to be more deliberate, to think more carefully about which explanation is really best. In either case, it helps to have a set of guidelines that tells you how your inquiry *should* proceed if you're to make cogent inferences. Here, then, is the **TEST formula,** four steps to finding the best explanation:

Step 1. State the **T**heory and check for consistency.
Step 2. Assess the **E**vidence for the theory.
Step 3. **S**crutinize alternative theories.
Step 4. **T**est the theories with the criteria of adequacy.

(In the next chapter, you will see that this formula is also one way of describing the general approach used in science to evaluate sets of theories.)

Step 1. State the theory and check for consistency. Before you can evaluate an explanatory theory, you must express it in a statement that's as clear and specific as possible. Once you do this, you can check to see if the theory meets the minimum requirement for consistency. If it fails the consistency test, you can have no good grounds for believing that it's correct. And, obviously, if the theory fails step 1, there's no reason to go to step 2.

Step 2. Assess the evidence for the theory. To critically evaluate any theory, you must understand any reasons in its favor—the empirical evidence or logical arguments that may support or undermine it. Essentially, this step involves an honest assessment of the empirical evidence relevant to the truth (or falsity) of the theory. To make this assessment, you must put to use what you already know about the credibility of sources, causal reasoning, and evidence from personal and scientific observations (topics covered in Chapters 4 and 8).

In this step, you may discover that the evidence in favor of a theory is strong, weak, or nonexistent. You may find that there is good evidence that seems to count against the theory. Or you may learn that the phenomenon under investigation did not occur at all. Whatever the case, you must have the courage to face up to reality. You must be ready to admit that your favorite theory has little to recommend it.

Step 3. Scrutinize alternative theories. Inference to the best explanation will not help us very much if we aren't willing to consider alternative explanations. Simply examining the evidence relevant to an eligible theory is not enough.

TEST FORMULA

① Theory's consistency

② Assess Evidence (chapters 4 & 8)

③ Scrutinize alternative theories
Evidence is necessary but not sufficient

Theories can often appear stronger than they really are if we don't bother to compare them with others. To take an outrageous example, consider this theory designed to explain the popularity and seeming omnipresence of an American icon: Mickey Mouse is not an animated character but a living, breathing creature that lives in Hollywood. The evidence for this explanation is the following: (1) Millions of people (mostly children) worldwide believe that Mickey is real; (2) Walt Disney (Mickey's alleged creator) always talked about Mickey as if the mouse was real; (3) millions of ads, books, movies, and TV shows portray Mickey as real; (4) it's possible that through millions of years of Earth history a biological creature with Mickey's physical characteristics could have evolved; and (5) some say that if enough people believe that Mickey is real, then—through psychic wish fulfillment or some other paranormal process—he will become real.

Mickey Mouse Hypothesis (MMH)

Evidence for MMH

Now, you don't believe that Mickey is real (do you?), even in the face of reasons 1–5. But you might admit that the Mickey theory is starting to sound more plausible. And if you never hear any alternative explanations, you might eventually become a true believer. (Anthropologists can plausibly argue that various cultures have come to believe in many very unlikely phenomena and exotic deities in large part because of *a lack of alternative explanations*.)

People come to believe in unlikely phenomena in part because of a lack of alternative explanations

When you do consider an alternative explanation—for example, that Mickey is an imaginary character of brilliant animation marketed relentlessly to the world—the Mickey-is-real theory looks a little silly. And once you consider the evidence for this alternative theory (for example, documentation that Walt Disney created Mickey with pen and ink and that countless marketing campaigns have been launched to promote his creation), the other explanation looks even sillier.

Meme Theory

Step 3 requires us to have an open mind, to think outside the box, to ask if there are other ways to explain the phenomenon in question and to consider the evidence for those theories. Specifically, in this step we must conscientiously look for competing theories, *then apply both step 1 and step 2 to each one of them.* This process may leave us with many or few eligible theories to examine. In any case, it's sure to tell us something important about the strength or weakness of competing theories.

We must consciously look for alternative explanations and apply steps 1 & 2

Many times the criteria of adequacy can help us do a preliminary assessment of a theory's plausibility without our surveying alternative theories. For example, a theory may do so poorly regarding a particular criterion that we can conclude that, whatever the merits of alternative explanations, the theory at hand is not very credible. Such a clear lack of credibility is often apparent when a theory is obviously neither simple nor conservative.

Lack of plausibility might be enough to disqualify an inadequate theory

Skipping step 3 is an extremely common error in the evaluation of explanations of all kinds. It is a supreme example of many types of errors discussed in earlier chapters—overlooking evidence, preferring available evidence, looking only for confirming evidence, and denying the evidence.

Looking for alternative theories goes against our tendency to cling to our favorite theory...

People accept paranormal theories because They cannot think of alternative theories

④ Test theories using Criteria of Adequacy

Step 3 goes against our grain. The human tendency is to grab hold of a favorite theory—and to halt any further critical thinking right there. Our built-in bias is to seize on a theory immediately—because we find it comforting or because we just "know" it's the right one—then ignore or resist all other possibilities. The result is a greatly increased likelihood of error and delusion and a significantly decreased opportunity to achieve true understanding.

Failure to consider alternative theories is the archetypal mistake in inquiries into the paranormal or supernatural (a topic we discuss in Chapter 10). The usual pattern is this: (1) You come across an extraordinary or impressive phenomenon, (2) you can't think of a natural explanation of the facts, and (3) you conclude that the phenomenon must not be natural but paranormal or supernatural. This conclusion, however, would be unwarranted. Just because you can't think of a natural explanation doesn't mean that there isn't one. You may simply be unaware of the correct natural explanation. In the past, scientists have often been confronted with extraordinary phenomena that they couldn't explain—phenomena that were later found to have a natural explanation.

Step 4. Test the theories with the criteria of adequacy. As we've seen, simply toting up the evidence for each of the competing theories and checking to see which one gets the highest score will not do. We need to measure the plausibility of the theories using the criteria of adequacy. The criteria can help us put any applicable evidence in perspective and allow us to make a judgment about theory plausibility even when there's little or no evidence to consider.

By applying the criteria to all the competing theories, we can often accomplish several important feats. We may be able to eliminate some theories immediately, assign more weight to some than others, and distinguish between theories that at first glance seem equally strong.

The best way to learn how to do step 4, as well as steps 1–3, is by example. Watch what happens when we assess the plausibility of theories for the following two phenomena.

REVIEW NOTES

☑ Evaluating Theories: The TEST Formula

Step 1: State the **Theory** and check for consistency.
Step 2: Assess the **Evidence** for the theory.
Step 3: **Scrutinize** alternative theories.
Step 4: **Test** the theories with the criteria of adequacy.

A DOOMED FLIGHT

In 1996, a Boeing 747 jetliner known famously as TWA flight 800 crashed in the Atlantic Ocean off Long Island, New York, killing all 230 people onboard. The incident, like most airline disasters, prompted a search for explanations for the crash and the proliferation of numerous explanatory theories, some of them alleging conspiracy, cover-up, and dark deeds. The FBI, the National Transportation Safety Board (NTSB), and others launched investigations, relying heavily on the criteria of adequacy to sort through competing theories. After many months of inquiry and debate, experts concluded that the probable cause of the crash was mechanical failure.

[handwritten note: Boeing 747 crash in 1996 attributed to mechanical failure...]

Using this incident as inspiration and guide, let's devise another story of a mysterious jetliner crash and examine the main theories to explain it. We will assume that all the facts in the case are known, that all relevant reports are honest (no intent to deceive), and that no other information is forthcoming. In other words, this is a very contrived case. But it suits our purposes here just fine. Here goes.

The (made-up) facts of the case are these: At 7:30 p.m. flight 200, a Boeing 747 departed JFK airport in New York on its way to London and then crashed into the Atlantic about thirty miles off the coast. While in flight, the plane exploded, sending debris over a wide area. The crash happened during a time of heightened awareness of possible terrorist attacks on aircraft.

[handwritten note: CASE STUDY]

Now let's try steps 1–4 on a supposedly popular theory and some of its leading alternatives. Here's the pop theory in question. Theory 1: *A missile fired by a terror-ist brought down the plane.* This one meets the requirement for consistency, so our first concern is to assess the evidence for the theory. Those who favor this theory point to several pieces of evidence. Eyewitnesses said that they had seen a bright streak of light or flame speeding toward the plane. A few people said that they thought they were watching a missile intercept the plane. And a journalist reported on the Internet that the plane had been shot down by a missile fired from a boat.

[handwritten note: Theory 1]

There are, however, some problems with this evidence.

A Boeing 747 in trouble; from the movie *Eraser*.

Problems w/Theory 1

Problems with
the Evidence...

Eyewitness reports of the movements of bright lights in a dark sky are notoriously unreliable, even when the eyewitnesses are experts. Under such viewing conditions, the actual size of a bright object, its distance from the observer, its speed, and even whether it's moving are extremely difficult to accurately determine by sight. Also another phenomenon could have easily been mistaken for a speeding missile: It's known that an explosion rupturing a fuel tank on a 747's wing can ignite long streams of fuel, which from the ground may look like a missile heading toward the plane. In addition, U.S. Coast Guard and Navy ships were in sight of every ship and boat in the area and report no firing of missiles or any other pyrotechnics. Because of the distances involved and other factors, firing a missile from the ground at flight 200 and hitting it was virtually impossible. Finally, an unsupported allegation—whether from a journalist or anyone else—is not good evidence for anything.

Theory 2

Then we have this explanation. Theory 2: *An alien spacecraft shot down the plane*. For the sake of illustration, we will assume that this explanation meets the consistency requirement. The evidence is this: Several people say that they saw a UFO fly near the plane just before the plane exploded. And tapes of radar images show an unknown object flying close to the 747.

These eyewitness accounts suffer from the same weakness as those mentioned in theory 1. Observations under the conditions described are not reliable. Thus many alleged alien craft have turned out to be airplanes, helicopters, blimps, meteors, and even the planet Venus, an extremely bright object in the sky. Radar tapes may show many objects that are "unknown" to untrained observers but are identified precisely by experts. The radar evidence would be more impressive if flight controllers could not account for an object flying close to flight 200.

Theory 3

Theory 3: *A bomb on board the plane exploded, bringing the aircraft down*. This explanation is internally and externally consistent. The main evidence for it is the existence of trace amounts of explosive residue on a few of the recovered aircraft parts. Also, the story of the crash of flight 200 resembles the media account of the crash of another jetliner that's known to have been brought down by an onboard bomb.

This resemblance, though, is only that—it's not evidence that counts in favor of the bomb theory. And the explosive residue is not so telltale after all. Investigators determined that the residues are most likely left over from a security training exercise conducted on the plane a week earlier. Moreover, examination of the wreckage and patterns of damage to it suggests that a bomb was not detonated inside the aircraft.

Theory 4

Theory 4: *A mechanical failure involving the fuel tanks caused the explosion that brought the plane down*. This is an eligible theory. It's backed by evidence showing that an explosion occurred in one of the plane's fuel tanks. Experts know that a short circuit in wiring outside a fuel tank can cause excess voltage in wiring that's inside the tank, igniting the fuel. Investigators found that there was indeed a short circuit in some of the fuel tank wiring. In addition, explosions in several other 747s, some smaller planes, and various machine engines have been linked to faulty wiring in fuel tanks.

Theory 5: *A solar flare disrupted electrical circuits in the plane, releasing a spark that made the fuel tanks explode.* This too is an eligible theory. Solar flares are massive electromagnetic explosions on the surface of the sun. They can sometimes disrupt radio communications, even cause radio blackouts. Theory 5 says that a solar flare so dramatically affected electrical circuits in the plane that a spark was emitted that ignited the fuel. The rationale behind this theory is that flying planes, being closer to the sun, are more susceptible to the powerful effects of solar flares.

The evidence for this theory, however, is nil. There is no good reason to believe that a solar flare could ever cause a spark in an electrical circuit.

Now let's apply the criteria of adequacy to these explanations. We can see right away that all the theories do equally well in terms of testability and fruitfulness. They're all testable, and none has yielded any surprising predictions. Except for theory 4, they also have equal scope because they explain only the phenomenon they were introduced to explain, the crash of flight 200 (and perhaps similar airline crashes). Theory 4, however, has a slight edge because it can explain certain airline crashes as well as explosions in other systems that have wired fuel tanks. So if we are to distinguish between the theories, we must rely on the other criteria.

This is bad news for theories 2 and 5 because they fail the criteria of simplicity and conservatism. The evidence in favor of the alien spacecraft theory is extremely weak. Even worse, it conflicts with a great deal of human experience regarding visitors from outer space. We simply have no good evidence that anyone has ever detected any beings or technology from outer space. Moreover, the probability of Earth being visited by beings from outer space must be considered low (but not zero) in light of what we know about the size of the universe and the physical requirements of space travel. Likewise, the solar flare theory has no evidence to support it, and it too conflicts with what we know. There are no documented cases of solar flares causing sparks in electrical wiring. And neither theory is simple. Theory 2 assumes an unknown entity (aliens), and theory 5 assumes unknown processes (solar flares causing sparks in wiring). These are excellent grounds for eliminating theories 2 and 5 from the running.

That leaves theories 1, 3, and 4, which we must also sort out using the criteria of simplicity and conservatism. They fare equally well in terms of simplicity because none assumes any unknown or mysterious entities or processes. Conservatism, though, is a different story. Neither theory 1 nor 3 accords with the evidence. In each case, existing evidence counts *against* the theory. Theory 4, though, accords well with the evidence. It not only doesn't conflict with what we

[margin notes:]
Theory 5

Criteria of Adequacy

Theory 4 has greater scope than the other four theories

We can appeal to criteria of simplicity & conservatism to disqualify theories 2 & 5

Final Assessment

know, but the evidence also supports the theory in important ways. Theory 4, then, is the best explanation for the crash of flight 200 and the theory most likely to be true. And the explanation we started with, theory 1, is implausible.

AN AMAZING CURE

Homeopathy is an old theory that currently occupies an honored place among advocates of what is often called "alternative medicine"—health practices and hypotheses that are, for the most part, outside the realm of conventional medicine and medical science. Homeopathy is based on the idea that extremely tiny doses of substances that cause disease symptoms in a healthy person can alleviate similar symptoms in a sick person. Samuel Hahnemann (1755–1843), a German physician, was the first to apply this notion systematically. He also added what he called the "law of infinitesimals," the proposition that—contrary to the findings of science—the smaller the dose, the more powerful the medicine. So he treated people with drastically diluted substances—so diluted that, in many homeopathic medicines, not even one molecule of the substance remained. Hahnemann acknowledged this fact but believed that the substances somehow left behind an imperceptible "spirit-like" essence, or memory, that effected cures. This essence was supposed to revitalize the "vital force" in the body.

To be more precise we can state the homeopathic theory like this: *Extremely dilute solutions of substances that produce symptoms in a healthy person can cure those same symptoms in a sick person.* This hypothesis is offered as an explanation of why people taking homeopathic remedies seem to get better. They get better because homeopathy works.

The leading alternative theory is this: *People taking homeopathic remedies feel better because of the placebo effect.* That is, homeopathy does not work as advertised, but people think that it does because of the power of placebos (inactive or fake treatments). The placebo effect is a very well-documented phenomenon in which people given a placebo respond with improvements in the way they feel. Scientists disagree over how much placebos can affect clinical conditions, but there is little doubt that placebos can have at least a modest impact on how people feel, especially their experience of pain.[9] Because placebos can have an effect, they are used in all well-designed clinical trials—that is, studies testing the effectiveness of treatments. (More on clinical testing and placebos in the next chapter.) There are other plausible alternative theories (such as the idea that people feel better because of the natural course of the disease), but we will restrict our analysis to the homeopathy and placebo theories.

Both are eligible theories. They are also both testable, so we must turn to the other criteria to help us judge their worth. The homeopathy theory has yielded no observable, surprising predictions, so it has no advantage in fruitfulness. The placebo theory has yielded several predictions (that a certain percentage

---

Handwritten margin notes:

Homeopathy: theory that tiny doses of a substance that make a healthy person ill can cure a sick person...

Samuel Hahnemann, (1755–1843) appealed to "the law of infinitesimals": the smaller the dose the more powerful the medicine

Theory 1: Homeopathy

Theory 2: Placebo Effect

CRITERIA OF ADEQUACY

"Science is organized common sense where many a beautiful theory was killed by an ugly fact."
—Thomas H. Huxley

of people who suffer from a particular illness and who get a placebo will feel better), but none of these are particularly surprising. The homeopathy theory has no scope because it tries to explain events by positing unknown forces and processes—which doesn't explain anything. The placebo theory, though, does have scope, explaining why people may feel better after trying a homeopathic remedy as well as why people with a variety of illnesses feel better after taking a placebo.

Scope- explains more

But in terms of simplicity, the homeopathy theory is in trouble. Homeopathy postulates both an undetectable essence and an unknown mysterious force. These assumptions alone are serious problems for the theory. The placebo theory, on the other hand, assumes no unknown forces, entities, or processes.

Homeopathy does not do well with criterion of simplicity

Finally, homeopathy runs afoul of the criterion of conservatism. It conflicts with a massive amount of scientific evidence in biochemistry and pharmacology. There is no verified instance of any substance having a stronger effect the more diluted it becomes. There isn't a single documented case of an extremely diluted solution (one in which not one molecule of the original substance remains) affecting any biological system. In addition, all available scientific evidence on the question gives little or no support to homeopathy. (Many studies have been conducted on homeopathic remedies, but several scientific reviews have concluded that the studies are seriously flawed or weak, offering no significant support to the theory.[10])

Homeopathy runs afoul of the criterion of conservatism

We can lay out these assessments as in the following table:

Criteria	Homeopathy	Placebo
Testable	Yes	Yes
Fruitful	No	No
Scope	No	Yes
Simple	No	Yes
Conservative	No	Yes

In the absence of a formula for weighting or ranking criteria, what plausible judgments can we make about the relative strengths of these two theories? It seems that we can ignore the criteria of testability and fruitfulness because both theories seem roughly even on these criteria—or at least no theory has a clear advantage over the other. We have decided, however, that homeopathy has no scope, while the placebo theory does.

Things become more clear when we consider the remaining criteria. There are stark differences between the two theories in simplicity and conservatism. Homeopathy is not simple, and any theory that posits an unknown entity is less plausible than one that does not—unless the other criteria of adequacy can

Homeopathy is not simple & violates criterion of conservatism

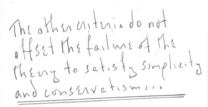
The other criteria do not offset the failure of the theory to satisfy simplicity and conservatism....

somehow offset this disadvantage. But the other criteria are not much help for homeopathy. This judgment—the lack of simplicity and the resulting lower plausibility—seems clear-cut and is based on an unambiguous state of affairs. The homeopathy theory's lack of conservatism is also evident. The plausibility of any theory that flies in the face of such a mountain of established fact is near zero. So homeopathy's score must also be near zero. It is, therefore, a very poor explanation and strikingly inferior to the alternative explanation.

Without a detailed formula, without a weighting system, and without quantifying any criteria, we have arrived at a verdict regarding two competing theories. Deciding among theories is not always so straightforward, of course. But this lack of clear-cut answers is what gives rise to more research and more critical thinking.

Exercise 9.8

Based on what you already know and the criteria of adequacy, determine which theory in each group is most plausible.

1. Phenomenon: A deadly illness striking everyone in a small town.
   Theories: (1) Resurgence of smallpox, (2) poison in the drinking water, (3) a failure to think positively.

2. Phenomenon: A sudden and dramatic drop in the price of most corporate stocks.
   Theories: (1) Rumors of a recession, (2) manipulation of the stock market by one powerful stockholder, (3) particularly nasty weather on the East Coast.

* 3. Phenomenon: Extraordinarily large humanlike footprints in the snow on a mountainside.
   Theories: (1) The legendary man-beast known as the Yeti, (2) falling rocks from the sky, (3) a very big human mountain climber.

4. Phenomenon: The construction of the Egyptian pyramids.
   Theories: (1) The work of clever Egyptian engineers and many slaves, (2) the work of Egyptians with the help of extraterrestrial beings, (3) the work not of the Egyptians but the ancient Romans.

5. Phenomenon: A large increase in the incidence of heart disease among middle-aged women.
   Theories: (1) The result of an increase in violence against women, (2) an increase in the amount of fat consumed by women over age forty-five, (3) an increase in the number of women who marry late in life.

Exercise 9.9

Evaluate the following theories using the TEST formula. As part of your evaluation:

  a. State the claim to be evaluated.
  b. Indicate what phenomenon is being explained.
  c. Specify at least one alternative theory.
  d. Use the criteria of adequacy to assess the two theories and determine which one is more plausible.
  e. Write a paragraph detailing your reasons for your choice. Use your background knowledge to fill in any information about the theories and how well they do regarding each criterion.

1. A religious sect based in Boston predicts that the end of the world will occur on January 1, 2001. The world, of course, did not end then. The leader of the sect explains that the prophesy failed to come true because members of the sect did not have enough faith in it.

2. A small, secret society of corporate CEOs and international bankers runs the economies of the United States and Europe. For its own benefit and for its own reasons the society decides when these nations go into and come out of recession, what levels of production will be achieved by the oil industry, and what each country's gross national product will be. Members of the society are so rich and powerful that they are able to hide the society's activities from public view and operate without the knowledge of governments and ordinary citizens.

3. What is the greatest influence on the course of human history, its social and cultural development? Some say it's powerful ideas like socialism, democracy, human dignity, and scientific method. Some say it's the social movements that embody and promote these ideas. But the greatest influences are wrought by great leaders, who are not necessarily great thinkers. Throughout history, every time a great leader appeared—Moses, Alexander, Caesar, Napoleon, and the like—the world was irrevocably changed regardless of what ideas or social movements were in existence.

4. The primary cause of all wars is fear. When people are afraid of others—because of ignorance or perceived threats—they naturally respond with belligerence and acts of violence. If they have no fear of others, they tend to react rationally and calmly and to seek some sort of fair accommodation.

5. Scientists studied twenty terminal cancer patients, taking note of the overall mental attitudes of the patients. Some of them were characterized as having negative attitudes; they were often angry at their situation and experienced feelings of hopelessness and regret. But other patients were thought to have positive attitudes; they were generally upbeat, optimistic about their treatment, and hopeful. Most of those with positive attitudes lived longer than most of those with negative attitudes. A positive attitude can lengthen cancer patients' lives.

6. Anais said farewell to her favorite uncle as he boarded a plane for Paris. That night she dreamed that he was flying in a jetliner that suddenly ran into a powerful thunderstorm and extreme turbulence. The plane rocked from side to side, then descended rapidly into the night. The

jetliner crashed into a mountain, killing all onboard. When she awoke the next day, she learned that her uncle's plane had encountered violent turbulence on the way to Paris and that several passengers, including her uncle, had been injured during the flight. She had just had one of those rare experiences known as a prophetic dream.

Exercise 9.10

Read the following passages and answer these questions for each one:

1. What is the phenomenon being explained?
2. What theories are given to explain the phenomenon? (Some theories may be unstated.)
3. Which theory seems the most plausible and why? (Use the criteria of adequacy.)
4. Which theory is the least plausible and why?
5. Regarding the most credible theory, what factors would convince you to regard it as even more plausible?
6. Regarding the least credible theory, what factors would convince you to regard it as much more plausible?

PASSAGE 1

"Since Venus rotates so slowly, we might be tempted to conclude that Venus, like Mercury, keeps one face always toward the Sun. If this hypothesis were correct we should expect that the dark side would be exceedingly cold. Pettit and Nicholson have measured the temperature of the dark side of Venus. They find that the temperature is not low, its value being only $-9F$ degrees, much warmer than our stratosphere in broad daylight. It is unlikely that atmospheric currents from the bright side of Venus could perpetually heat the dark side. The planet must rotate fairly often to keep the dark side from cooling excessively."[11]

PASSAGE 2

"Parapsychologists claim man's ability to know when he is being stared at has existed since the time of primitive man and served, in those days, to warn him of impending danger and attack from savage beasts. They also believe this ability still exists in modern men and women today. Skeptics deny this claim and believe it is nothing more than superstition and/or a response to subtle signals from the environment that are not strong enough to let us know exactly what caused them. For example, if we are in a very dark room and we suddenly sense the presence of another person—even though we do not see or hear him—we may know he is there because of the person's shaving lotion, movement of air currents in the room, body heat, etc. In other words if we are warned of another's presence, it is likely due to subtle physical cues in the environment that we normally do not attend to—not to any so-called 'psychic' or paranormal ability!"

"To determine if people can tell when they are being stared at, two demonstrations were completed. In the first, forty individuals were stared at for an average time of 8.6 minutes while they were eating, reading, or watching a computer screen or television. When they finished they were asked if they were aware they were being stared at. Of the forty a total of thirty-five reported they were 'totally unaware that anyone was looking at them.' For the other five there is good reason to believe they also were not aware they were being viewed. In the second demonstration fifty students sat at a table in front of a one-way mirror and were observed by two experimenters, one minute at a time, five times during a twenty-minute observation period. The students' task was to try to guess when they were being stared at and report their degree of certainty. None of the fifty were able to correctly guess when they were being stared at. The mean accuracy score for the group was 1.24; the chance score for guessing was 1.25 out of a total of five guesses."[12]

🔑 KEY WORDS

ad hoc hypothesis	scope
conservatism	simplicity
criteria of adequacy	testability
fruitfulness	TEST formula
inference to the best explanation	theoretical explanation

Summary

- Even though an explanation is not an argument, an explanation can be part of an argument—a powerful inductive argument known as inference to the best explanation. In inference to the best explanation, we reason from premises about a state of affairs to an explanation for that state of affairs.
- To be worthy of consideration, a theory must meet the minimum requirement for consistency.
- We use the criteria of adequacy to judge the plausibility of a theory in relation to competing theories. The best theory is the one that meets the criteria of adequacy better than any of its competitors.
- The criteria of adequacy are testability (whether there is some way to determine if a theory is true), fruitfulness (the number of novel predictions

made), scope (the amount of diverse phenomena explained), simplicity (the number of assumptions made), and conservatism (how well a theory fits with existing knowledge).

• Judging the worth of a theory is a four-step process called the TEST formula: (1) Stating the theory and checking for consistency, (2) assessing the evidence for the theory, (3) scrutinizing alternative theories, and (4) testing the theories with the criteria of adequacy.

Field Problems

1. Many companies have recently marketed products that are supposed to relieve various ills (arthritis, lower back pain, migraine headaches, tennis elbow, etc.) through the use of simple magnets. This "magnetic therapy" is said to work because magnetic fields generated by the magnets act on the body's processes or structures. Look at ads in magazines, on TV, or on the Internet to find a health claim made for one of these products. Then in a 150-word paragraph evaluate the claim in light of the criteria of simplicity and conservatism. Check for any relevant scientific research and information at www.quackwatch.com or www.hcrc.org/sram (*The Scientific Review of Alternative Medicine*).

2. Using the TEST formula, evaluate the theory that people are more likely to behave strangely or violently during a full moon than at other times. Do some research to uncover any evidence pertaining to this theory. Write a 200-word report summarizing your findings.

3. Do Internet research on conspiracy theories concerning the September 11, 2001, attack on the United States. They posit explanations of why or how the attack happened—explanations that are usually shockingly different from the explanations accepted by most Americans. Select one of these alternative theories and compare it to the prevailing standard explanation. Using the TEST formula, decide which theory is more plausible.

Self-Assessment Quiz

Answers appear in "Answers to Self-Assessment Quizzes" (Appendix C).

1. What is the basic pattern of inference to the best explanation? How does this pattern differ from that of enumerative induction? analogical induction?

2. What is the minimum requirement for consistency?

3. What are the criteria of adequacy?

4. According to the text, what does it mean for a theory to be testable or untestable?

5. What is the TEST formula?

6. According to the text, in theory evaluation, when is a theory properly considered the best?

Each of the following theories is offered to explain John's apparently prophetic dream that a distant cousin would die in a plane crash. Indicate which theory (a) lacks simplicity, (b) is not conservative, (c) is untestable, and (d) has the most scope. (Some theories may merit more than one of these designations.)

7. The fact that John's dream happened to be about a plane crash involving his cousin was coincidence. We have many dreams, and some are likely to match real events from time to time.

8. In his dream, John was able to see into the future and "view" the plane crash.

9. The incident was an example of "synchronicity," in which events are paired in unusual but predetermined ways by cosmic forces.

10. John had calculated the odds of the crash even before he dreamed about it, so the dream was not a prophesy, but a memory of his calculation.

Indicate which theory in each of the following groups is most plausible.

11. Phenomenon: The rise in popularity of a newly elected president.
Theories: (1) The so-called honeymoon effect in which a new president enjoys popularity until he or she is involved in serious or controversial decisions, (2) the systematic manipulation of all polling organizations by the president's staff, (3) the influence of a powerful secret society controlling the media.

12. Phenomenon: Your friend has been skipping class, and you haven't seen her in days.
Theories: (1) She's in bed with the flu, (2) she has been kidnapped, (3) she has inherited millions of dollars and has decided to hang out with a better class of friends.

13. Phenomenon: Ships, boats, and planes have been disappearing off the coast of Florida for years.
Theories: (1) Considering the meteorological and atmospheric conditions of the area, it's normal for some craft to be lost from time to time; (2) the craft have been hijacked; (3) the ships, boats, and planes are simply off course.

14. Phenomenon: The rapid spread of an unknown, dangerous, viral disease throughout North America.
Theories: (1) The lack of awareness and defenses against a new mutated virus, (2) bureaucratic bungling at the Centers for Disease Control and Prevention, (3) a massive conspiracy of doctors who want higher fees for treating seriously ill patients.

Evaluate the following theories using the TEST formula. As part of your evaluation, (1) state the claim to be evaluated, (2) indicate what phenomenon is being explained, (3) specify at least one alternative theory, and (4) use the criteria of adequacy to assess the two theories and determine which one is more plausible.

15. People buy high-ticket merchandise because of subliminal advertising—their minds are being influenced by imperceptible stimuli designed by ad execs.

16. Skeptical scientists have never been able to find evidence for cold fusion, try as they may. That's because their skepticism skews their observations.

17. Eleanor won the state lottery twice in nine months. She must have a system that enables her to pick winning numbers.

18. He embezzled that money because his parents were divorced when he was very young.

19. Schoolchildren who do poorly in school are not dumb or handicapped. They perform poorly for one reason only: low or negative expectations of their teachers.

20. The woman has been displaying bizarre behavior for years, but recently she seems worse than ever. She sometimes suddenly begins screaming, saying that there are snakes crawling on the walls. She shakes uncontrollably at the slightest noise. And she has started to bleed from her palms. The priest says that she's possessed by demons, and he's right.

Integrative Exercises

These exercises refer to lessons in Chapters 3 and 6–9.

1. What is a deductive argument?
2. What is a valid argument?
3. What is an inductive argument?
4. What is the logical pattern of *modus ponens*?

For each of the following arguments, specify the conclusion and premises and indicate whether it is deductive or inductive. If it's deductive, use Venn diagrams or truth tables to determine its validity. If it's inductive, indicate whether it's an enumerative, analogical, or causal induction and whether it's strong or weak. If necessary, add implicit premises and conclusions.

5. The problem is that if people realize that they can do their own buying and selling of stocks, they won't use brokers any more. But people don't realize that yet. So people will continue to use brokers.

6. "After days of talking to Shiites in Karbala and Najaf, it is clear to this reporter that there is virtually no undercurrent of anti-Americanism in the heartland of Iraqi Shi'ism. Even some clerics who have just returned from exile in Iran were keen to advertise their goodwill toward the United States." [Amir Taheri, *New York Post*]

7. Every man I know has some kind of hangup about sex. What is it with men? They're all a bunch of sexual neurotics.

8. Either the prime minister sent troops into Iraq to grab the oil there, or he sent them to get rid of Saddam. Obviously, the point was not to take the oil, so the real reason must have been to oust Saddam.

9. "Hence a young man is not a proper hearer of lectures on political science; for he is inexperienced in the actions that occur in life, but its discussions start from these and are about these; and, further, since he tends to follow his passions, his study will be vain and unprofitable, because the end aimed at is not knowledge but action." [Aristotle, *Nichomachean Ethics*]

10. "For every needy illegal immigrant, there is a needy legal immigrant or U.S. citizen who could greatly benefit from educational assistance. Granting in-state tuition to illegal aliens is hardly fair when there are plenty of U.S. citizens and legal immigrants who cannot obtain the same benefits." [Letter to the editor, *Newsday*]

11. No kings are persons without power. All people without power are persons who spend their days being victims. Therefore, no kings are victims.

12. Vulgarity is abroad upon the land, and Hollywood is to blame. As vulgar, sexually explicit, tasteless movies have proliferated, so has the amount of vulgarity increased.

13. He's afraid of her. He avoids her all the time, and he won't look her in the eye.

14. Most teens arrested for committing some act of violence also play a lot of violent video games. These games are causing violent behavior among our youth.

Evaluate each of the following theories and indicate whether it is plausible or implausible.

15. The positions and movements of the stars and planets at the time of your birth can have a powerful effect on your life.

16. Clyde Moran was sent to prison for raping and murdering a woman in her home, and he spent fifteen years behind bars. He was convicted on the testimonial of three witnesses who say that they saw him near the woman's house on the night of the murder. The district attorney now says that recent DNA evidence shows that the man who committed the crime is not Moran. But the word of three good witnesses is good enough for me. Moran killed that woman, and he should stay in prison where he belongs.

17. In Area 51, the famous portion of a military base near Groom Dry Lake in Nevada, the government is concealing real alien visitors or an actual space vehicle used by the visitors to reach Earth.

18. If people are homeless, it's because they chose to be homeless. In America, there are a hundred ways to get out of poverty—if you want to.

19. The large network news organizations have ignored most of the anti-war protests staged since 9/11. Coverage of any anti-war sentiment seems to be against media policy. This can only mean that top network execs have decided together that such coverage is not in their best interests.

20. When the street lights shined on the side of the building, a vague image appeared on the wall, a mixture of shadows and light. Most people say that the image shows the face of Jesus. This image is a holy sign from God.

Writing Assignments

1. In a one-page essay evaluate the theory that all major decisions made by the current U.S. president are politically motivated and have very little to do with the merits of ideas or programs. Use the TEST formula.

2. Think of the last time you caught a cold or the flu. Write a one-page paper evaluating at least two theories that explain how you first came in contact with the virus. Use the TEST formula.

3. Write a two-page paper in which you use the TEST formula to assess two theories concerning so-called reverse speech. One theory is that the reverse-speech phenomenon actually exists (hypothesis 1), as discussed in Essay 9 ("The Demon-Haunted Sentence: A Skeptical Analysis of Reverse Speech") in Appendix A; the other one (hypothesis 2) is the view that people who claim to hear reverse speech messages are part of a conspiracy to make a profit off reverse-speech products and services.

4. Write a paper to rebut the argument in Essay 17 ("Torture: Severe Interrogations Work"). Use at least one argument that is *not* used in Essay 16 ("Torture: Time for Congress to End the Debate").

Judging
Scientific Theories

CHAPTER OBJECTIVES

SCIENCE AND NOT SCIENCE

- Understand why science is not the same thing as technology, ideology, and scientism.

THE SCIENTIFIC METHOD

- Know the five steps of the scientific method.
- Understand the logic of scientific testing.
- Learn why no scientific hypothesis can be conclusively confirmed or conclusively confuted.

TESTING SCIENTIFIC THEORIES

- Using the steps of the scientific method, be able to explain how a scientist would go about testing a simple hypothesis in medical science.
- Understand why scientists use control groups, make studies double-blind, include placebos in testing, and seek replication of their work.

JUDGING SCIENTIFIC THEORIES

- Be able to list the five criteria of adequacy and explain what they mean.
- Understand how to apply the criteria of adequacy to the theories of evolution and creationism and why the text says that evolution is the better theory.

SCIENCE AND WEIRD THEORIES

- Be able to explain why evaluating weird claims might be worthwhile.

MAKING WEIRD MISTAKES

- Understand why it can be so easy to err when trying to evaluate weird theories.
- Be prepared to explain three major errors that people often make when they are trying to assess extraordinary experiences and theories.
- Learn the distinction between logical and physical possibility.

JUDGING WEIRD THEORIES

- Be able to use the TEST formula to evaluate extraordinary theories.
- Understand why eyewitness testimony is often unreliable.

S O THE WORLD IS CHOCKABLOCK WITH CLAIMS IN THE FORM OF explanations—*theoretical explanations*, to be more precise, about why something is the case or why something happens. An overwhelming number of such theories are offered to explain the cause of events: why the window broke, why the moon looks so pale, why Ralph stole the bike, why the stock market tanked. As critical thinkers, we do the best we can in evaluating these theories that come our way, testing them if possible, looking for alternative theories, and applying the criteria of adequacy. As it turns out, science is in the same line of work.

Science seeks to acquire knowledge and understanding of reality, and it does so through the formulation, testing, and evaluation of theories. When this kind of search for answers is both systematic and careful, science is being done. And when we ourselves search for answers by scrutinizing possible theories—and we do so systematically and carefully—we are searching scientifically.

Let's examine the scientific process more closely.

[margin note: When we evaluate theories in everyday life we should be thinking scientifically]

Science and Not Science

First, let's explore what science is *not*.[1]

Science is not technology. Science is a way of searching for truth—a way that uses what's often referred to as *the scientific method.* Technology is not a search for truth; it's the production of products—DVDs, cell phones, wireless computers, robots that sweep the carpet, better mousetraps. Technology applies knowledge acquired through science to practical problems that science generally doesn't care about, such as the creation of electronic gadgets. Technology seeks facts to use in producing stuff. Science tries to understand how the world works not by merely cataloging specific facts but by identifying general principles that both explain and predict phenomena.

This nice distinction gets blurry sometimes when technologists do scientific research in order to build a better product or scientists create gadgets in order to

[margin note: WHAT SCIENCE IS NOT
① Science is not technology
Science is a way of searching for truth --- a way that uses the scientific method
Technology uses scientific research to develop new products]

SEVEN WARNING SIGNS
OF BOGUS SCIENCE...

FURTHER THOUGHT

 Seven Warning Signs of Bogus Science

What would a distinguished scientist tell trial judges who must try to discern whether scientific testimony by an expert is credible? Robert L. Park is that scientist (as well as an author and professor of physics), and he has identified the following clues "that a scientific claim lies well outside the bounds of rational scientific discourse." He cautions, though, that "they are only warning signs—even a claim with several of the signs could be legitimate."

Claims for the existence of Bigfoot rest largely on the shaky underpinning of anecdotal evidence.

1. **The discoverer pitches the claim directly to the media.** The integrity of science rests on the willingness of scientists to expose new ideas and findings to the scrutiny of other scientists. Thus, scientists expect their colleagues to reveal new findings to them initially. An attempt to bypass peer review by taking a new result directly to the media, and thence to the public, suggests that the work is unlikely to stand up to close examination by other scientists.

2. **The discoverer says that a powerful establishment is trying to suppress his or her work.** The idea is that the establishment will presumably stop at nothing to suppress discoveries that might shift the balance of wealth and power in society. Often, the discoverer describes mainstream science as part of a larger conspiracy that includes industry and government. Claims that the oil companies are frustrating the invention of an automobile that runs on water, for instance, are a sure sign that the idea of such a car is baloney.

3. **The scientific effect involved is always at the very limit of detection.** Alas, there is never a clear photograph of a flying saucer, or the Loch Ness monster. All scientific measurements must contend with some level of background noise or statistical fluctuation. But if the signal-to-noise ratio cannot be improved, even in principle, the effect is probably not real and the work is not science.

Thousands of published papers in parapsychology, for example, claim to report verified instances of telepathy, psychokinesis, or precognition.

▼

But those effects show up only in tortured analyses of statistics. The researchers can find no way to boost the signal, which suggests that it isn't really there.

4. **Evidence for a discovery is anecdotal.** If modern science has learned anything in the past century, it is to distrust anecdotal evidence. Because anecdotes have a very strong emotional impact, they serve to keep superstitious beliefs alive in an age of science. The most important discovery of modern medicine is not vaccines or antibiotics; it is the randomized double-blind test, by means of which we know what works and what doesn't. Contrary to the saying, the word "data" is not the plural of "anecdote."

5. **The discoverer says a belief is credible because it has endured for centuries.** There is a persistent myth that hundreds or even thousands of years ago, long before anyone knew that blood circulates throughout the body or that germs cause disease, our ancestors possessed miraculous remedies that modern science cannot understand. Much of what is termed "alternative medicine" is part of that myth.

6. **The discoverer has worked in isolation.** The image of a lone genius who struggles in secrecy in an attic laboratory and ends up making a revolutionary breakthrough is a staple of Hollywood's science-fiction films, but it is hard to find examples in real life. Scientific breakthroughs nowadays are almost always syntheses of the work of many scientists.

7. **The discoverer must propose new laws of nature to explain an observation.** A new law of nature, invoked to explain some extraordinary result, must not conflict with what is already known. If we must change existing laws of nature or propose new laws to account for an observation, it is almost certainly wrong.[2] ∎

② Science is not ideology

"Science is not gadgetry. The desirable adjuncts of modern living, although in many instances made possible by science, certainly do not constitute science."
—WARREN WEAVER

We cannot identify science with a "worldview."

do better scientific research. But, in general, science pursues knowledge; technology makes things.

Science is not ideology. Some people say that science is not a way of finding out how the world works, but a worldview affirming how the world is, just as Catholicism or socialism affirms a view of things. To some, science is not only an ideology, but a most objectionable one—one that posits a universe that is entirely material, mechanistic, and deterministic. On this "scientific view," the world—including us—is nothing more than bits of matter forming a big machine that turns and whirs in predetermined ways. This mechanistic notion is thought to demean humans and human endeavors by reducing us to the role of cogs and sprockets.

But we can't identify science with a specific worldview. At any given time, a particular worldview may predominate in the scientific community, but this fact doesn't mean that the worldview is what science is all about. Predominant world-views among scientists have changed over the centuries, but the general nature of science as a way of searching for truth has not. For example, the mechanistic view of the universe, so common among scientists in the seventeenth century, has now given way to other views. Discoveries in quantum mechanics (the study of sub-atomic particles) have shown that the old mechanistic perspective is incorrect.

Science is not scientism. One definition of *scientism* is the view that science is the only reliable way to acquire knowledge. Put another way, science is the only reliable road to truth. But in light of the reliability of our sense experience under standard, unhindered conditions (see Chapter 4), this claim is dubious. We obviously do know many things without the aid of scientific methodology.

But there is a related point that is not so dubious. Science may not be the only road to truth, but it is an extremely reliable way of acquiring knowledge about the empirical world. (Many philosophers of science would go a step further and say that science is our *most reliable* source of knowledge about the world.) Why is science so reliable? Science embodies to a high degree what is essential to reliable knowing of empirical facts: systematic consideration of alternative solutions or theories, rigorous testing of them, and careful checking and rechecking of the conclusions.

Some would say that science is reliable because it is self-correcting. Science does not grab hold of an explanation and never let go. Instead, it looks at alternative ways to explain a phenomenon, tests these alternatives, and opens up the conclusions to criticism from scientists everywhere. Eventually, the conclusions may turn out to be false, and scientists will have to abandon the answers they thought were solid. But usually, after much testing and thinking, scientists hit upon a theory that does hold up under scrutiny. They are then justified in believing that the theory is true, even though there is some chance that it is flawed.

The Scientific Method

The scientific method cannot be identified with any particular set of experimental or observational procedures because there are many different methods to evaluate the worth of a hypothesis. In some sciences such as physics and biology, hypotheses can be assessed through controlled experimental tests. In other sciences such as astronomy and geology, hypotheses usually must be tested through observations. For example, an astronomical hypothesis may predict the existence of certain gases in a part of the Milky Way, and astronomers can use their telescopes to check whether those gases exist as predicted.

The scientific method, however, does involve several steps, regardless of the specific procedures involved:

1. Identify the problem or pose a question.
2. Devise a hypothesis to explain the event or phenomenon.

> "The essence of science: ask an impertinent question, and you are on the way to a pertinent answer."
> —JACOB BRONOWSKI

[Handwritten margin notes:]
17th century mechanism has been replaced by other views

③ Science is not scientism
Scientism is the mistaken view that science is the only reliable way to knowledge
Science is an extremely reliable way to knowledge

Science is a self-correcting approach to knowledge...

Science is fallibilist

Science is what scientists do.

General Framework

3. Derive a test implication or prediction.
4. Perform the test.
5. Accept or reject the hypothesis.

Scientific inquiry begins with a problem to solve or a question to answer. So in step 1 scientists may ask: What causes X? Why did Y happen? Does hormone therapy cause breast cancer? Does aspirin lower the risk of stroke? How is it possible for whales to navigate over long distances? How did early hominids communicate with one another? Was the Big Bang an uncaused event?

In step 2 scientists formulate a hypothesis that will constitute an answer to their question. In every case there are facts to explain, and the hypothesis is an explanation for them. The hypothesis guides the research, suggesting what kinds of observations or data would be relevant to the problem at hand. Without a hypothesis, scientists couldn't tell which data are important and which are worthless.

Where do hypotheses come from? One notion is that hypotheses are generated through induction—by collecting the data and drawing a generalization from them to get a hypothesis. But this can't be the way that most hypotheses are formulated because they often contain concepts that aren't in the data. (Remember, theories generally reach beyond the known data to posit the existence of things unknown.) The construction of hypotheses is not usually based on any such mechanical procedure. In many ways, they are created just as works of art are created. Scientists dream them up. They, however, are guided in hypothesis creation by certain criteria—namely, the criteria of adequacy we examined in the last chapter. With testability, fruitfulness, scope, simplicity, and conservatism as their guide, they devise hypotheses from the raw material of the imagination.

Remember, though, that scientists must consider not just their favorite hypothesis, but alternative hypotheses as well. The scientific method calls for consideration of competing explanations and for their examination or testing at some point in the process. Sometimes applying the criteria of adequacy can immediately eliminate some theories from the running, and sometimes theories must be tested along with the original hypothesis.

In step 3 scientists derive implications, or consequences, of the hypothesis to test. As we've seen, sometimes we can test a theory directly, as when we simply check the lawnmower's gas tank to confirm the theory that it won't run because it's out of gas. But often theories cannot be tested directly. How would we directly test, for example, the hypothesis that chemical X is causing leukemia in menopausal women? We can't.

So scientists test indirectly by first deriving a test implication from a hypothesis and then putting that implication to the test. Deriving such an observational consequence involves figuring out what a hypothesis implies or predicts.

Handwritten margin notes:

① Pose a question

② Formulate a hypothesis

Since the hypothesis contains concepts that are not in the data (C.S. Peirce), it is misleading to say it is generated through induction. Formulation of a hypothesis requires imagination—not too different from artistic creation...

Need to look for alternative hypotheses

"The whole of science is nothing more than a refinement of everyday thinking."
—ALBERT EINSTEIN

③ Derive test implication

If H is true, what implications would follow? Implication has form of a conditional statement...

Are You Scientifically Literate?

A 2002 survey conducted by the National Science Foundation found that 70 percent of American adults don't understand the scientific process, most believe in things rejected by science, and only about half could correctly answer some basic science questions. Some of the findings:

- Sixty percent agree or strongly agree that some people possess psychic powers.
- Thirty percent believe that some unidentified flying objects (UFOs) are alien spacecraft.
- Only 60 percent reject the scientific validity of astrology, and 43 percent read the astrology charts occasionally in the newspaper.

Here are a few of the science questions that fewer than half of the respondents got right:

- Lasers work by focusing sound waves. (False.)
- Electrons are smaller than atoms. (True)
- The universe began with a huge explosion, the "Big Bang." (True)
- The earliest humans lived at the same time as the dinosaurs. (False)

In addition, only 54 percent knew how long it takes Earth to orbit the sun. (One year)

Scientists ask, "If this hypothesis were true, what consequences would follow? What phenomena or events would have to obtain?"

Recall that we derived test implications in the problem of the car that wouldn't start in Chapter 9. One hypothesis was that the car wouldn't start because a vandal had sabotaged it. We reasoned that if a vandal had indeed sabotaged the car, there would be tracks in the snow around it. But there were no tracks, disconfirming the sabotage hypothesis.

⊗ Refuting a hypothesis

The logic of hypothesis testing, then, works like this. When we derive a test implication, we know that if the hypothesis to be tested (*H*) is true, then there is a specific predicted consequence (*C*). If the consequence turns out to be false (it does not obtain as predicted), then the hypothesis is probably false, and we can reject it. The hypothesis, in other words, is disconfirmed. We can represent this outcome in a conditional, or hypothetical, argument:

> If *H*, then *C*.
> not-*C*.
> Therefore, not-*H*.

This is, remember, an instance of *modus tollens*, a valid argument form. In this case, *H* would be false even if only one of several of its consequences (test implications) turned out to be false.

On the other hand, we would get a very different situation if C turned out to be true:

> If *H*, then *C*.
> *C*.
> Therefore, *H*.

Notice that this is an instance of affirming the consequent, an invalid argument form. So just because C is true, that doesn't necessarily mean that H is true. If a consequence turns out to be true, that doesn't *prove* that the hypothesis is correct. In such a result, the hypothesis is confirmed, and the test provides at least some evidence that the hypothesis is true. But the hypothesis isn't then established. If other consequences for the hypothesis are tested, and all the results are again positive, then there is more evidence that the hypothesis is correct. As more and more consequences are tested, and they are shown to be true, we can have increasing confidence that the hypothesis is in fact true. As this evidence accumulates, the likelihood that the hypothesis is actually false decreases—and the probability that it's true increases.

In step 4 scientists carry out the testing. Usually this experimentation is not as simple as testing one implication and calling it quits. Scientists may test many consequences of several competing hypotheses. As the testing proceeds, some hypotheses are found wanting, and they're dropped. If all goes well, eventually one hypothesis remains, with considerable evidence in its favor. Then step 5 can happen, as the hypothesis or hypotheses are accepted or rejected.

Because scientists want to quickly eliminate unworthy hypotheses and zero in on the best one, they try to devise the most telling tests. This means that they are on the lookout for situations in which competing hypotheses have different test consequences. If hypothesis 1 says that C is true, and hypothesis 2 says that C is false, a test of C can then help eliminate one of the hypotheses from further consideration.

As we've seen, implicit in all this is the fact that no hypothesis can ever be *conclusively* confirmed. It's always possible that we will someday find evidence that undermines or conflicts with the evidence we have now.

Likewise, no hypothesis can ever be *conclusively* confuted. When scientists test hypotheses, they never really test a single hypothesis—they test a hypothesis together with a variety of background assumptions and theories. So a hypothesis can always be saved from refutation by making changes in the background claims. (As we detailed in the previous chapter, sometimes these changes are made by constructing ad hoc hypotheses—by postulating unverifiable entities or properties.) In such situations, no amount of evidence logically compels us to conclusively reject a hypothesis.

But our inability to conclusively confirm or confute a hypothesis does not mean that all hypotheses are equally acceptable. Maintaining a hypothesis in the face of mounting negative evidence is unreasonable, and so is refusing to accept a hypothesis despite accumulating confirming evidence. Through the use of carefully controlled experiments, scientists can often affirm or deny a hypothesis with a high degree of confidence.

[margin handwritten note: (5) Accept or reject hypothesis]

[margin handwritten note: Note Quine-Duhem and the problem of ad hoc hypotheses...]

REVIEW NOTES

☑ Steps in the Scientific Method

1. Identify the problem or pose a question.
2. Devise a hypothesis to explain the event or phenomenon.
3. Derive a test implication or prediction.
4. Perform the test.
5. Accept or reject the hypothesis.

Testing Scientific Theories

Let's see how we might use the five-step procedure to test a fairly simple hypothesis. Suppose you hear reports that some terminal cancer patients have lived longer than expected because they received high doses of vitamin C. And say that the favored hypothesis among many observers is that the best explanation for the patients' surviving longer is that vitamin C is an effective treatment against cancer. So you decide to test this hypothesis: High doses of vitamin C can increase the survival time of people with terminal cancer. (Years ago, this hypothesis was actually proposed and tested in three well-controlled clinical trials.[3]) An obvious alternative hypothesis is that vitamin C actually has no effect on the survival of terminal cancer patients and that any apparent benefits are

[margin handwritten note: Exercise 10.6]

"The grand aim of all science is to cover the greatest number of empirical facts by logical deduction from the smallest number of hypotheses or axioms."
—ALBERT EINSTEIN

due mainly to the placebo effect (the tendency for people to temporarily feel better after they're treated, even if the treatment is a fake). The placebo effect could be leading observers to believe that people taking vitamin C are being cured of cancer and are thus living longer. Or the placebo effect could be making patients feel better, enabling them to take better care of themselves (by eating right or complying with standard medical treatment, for example), increasing survival time.

Now, if your hypothesis is true, what would you expect to happen? That is, what test implication could you derive? If your hypothesis is true, you would expect that terminal cancer patients given high doses of vitamin C would live longer than terminal cancer patients who didn't receive the vitamin (or anything else).

How would you conduct such a test? To begin with, you could prescribe vitamin C to a group of terminal cancer patients (called the experimental group) but not to another group of similar cancer patients (called the control group) and keep track of their survival times. Then you could compare the survival rates of the two groups. But many people who knowingly receive a treatment will report feeling better—even if the treatment is an inactive placebo. So any positive results you see in the treated group might be due not to vitamin C but to the placebo effect.

To get around this problem, you would need to treat both groups, one with vitamin C and the other with a placebo. That way, if most of the people getting the vitamin C live longer than expected and fewer of those in the placebo group do, you can have slightly better reason for believing that vitamin C works as advertised.

But even this study design is not good enough. It's possible for the people conducting the experiment, the experimenters, to unknowingly bias the results. Through subtle behavioral cues, they can unconsciously inform the test subjects which treatments are real and which ones are placebos—and this, of course, would allow the placebo effect to have full reign. Also, if the experimenters know which treatment is the real one, they can unintentionally misinterpret or skew the study results in line with their own expectations.

Double Blind Study

This problem can be solved by making the study *double-blind.* In double-blind experiments, neither the subjects nor the experimenters know who receives the real treatment and who the inactive one. A double-blind protocol for your vitamin study would ensure that none of the subjects would know who's getting vitamin C, and neither would the experimenters.

What if you have a double-blind setup but most of the subjects in the vitamin C group were sicker to begin with than those in the placebo control group? Obviously, this would bias the results, making the vitamin C treatment look less effective—even if it *is* effective. To avoid this skewing, you would need to

Nonintervention (Population) Studies

Not all medical hypotheses are tested by treating (or not treating) groups of patients and analyzing the results (as in the vitamin C example). Many are tested without such direct intervention in people's lives. The former type of study is known as an intervention, or controlled, trial, while the latter is called, not surprisingly, a *nonintervention* study (also an *observational* or *population* study). The basic idea in a nonintervention study is to track the interplay of disease and related factors in a specified population, uncovering associations among these that might lead to better understanding or control of the disease process.

A typical nonintervention study might go like this: For seven years scientists monitor the vitamin E intake (from food and supplements) and the incidence of heart disease of 90,000 women. Evaluation of this data shows that the women with the highest amounts of vitamin E in their diets have a 40 percent lower incidence of heart disease. That is, for reasons unknown, a lower risk of heart disease is associated with a higher intake of vitamin E in women. This study does not show that higher intakes of vitamin E *cause* less heart disease, only that there is a link between them. Perhaps some other factor merely associated with vitamin E is the true protector of hearts, or maybe women who take vitamin E are more likely to do other things (such as exercise) that lower their risk of heart disease.

Generally, nonintervention studies cannot establish cause-and-effect relationships, though they may hint that a causal relationship is present. And sometimes multiple nonintervention studies yielding the same results can make a strong case for a causal connection. Intervention trials, however, *can* establish cause and effect.

Nonintervention studies have led scientists to some of the most important findings in preventive health. It was a series of such studies done over decades, coupled with other kinds of scientific data, that revealed that cigarette smoking caused cancer. And it was such investigations that showed that high blood pressure, high cholesterol, overweight, and smoking are risk factors for heart disease.

Note to critical thinkers: Very often the media misreport the results of nonintervention studies, reading cause and effect into a mere association. For example, if a single nonintervention study finds a link between chewing gum and better eyesight, a headline in the morning paper (or a TV newscaster) may proclaim that "Gum-chewing improves your eyesight!" Maybe, maybe not—but the study would not justify that conclusion.

ensure that each group is as much alike as possible to start—with all subjects being around the same age, same physical condition, same stage of cancer, and so on.

Finally, you would need to run some statistical tests to ensure that your results are not a fluke. Even in the most tightly controlled studies, it's possible that the outcome is the result of random factors that cannot be controlled. Statisticians have standard methods for determining when experiment results are likely, or not likely, to be due to chance.

Suppose you design your study well and you conduct it. The results: The patients receiving the high doses of vitamin C did not live longer than the placebo group. In fact, all the subjects lived about the same length of time. Therefore, your hypothesis is disconfirmed. On the other hand, the alternative hypothesis—that vitamin C has no measurable effect on the survival of terminal cancer patients—is confirmed.

Should you now reject the vitamin C theory? Not yet. Even apparently well-conducted studies can have hidden mistakes in them, or there can be factors that the experimenters fail to take into account. This is why scientists insist on study *replication*—the repeating of an experiment by different groups of scientists. If the study is replicated by other scientists, and the study results hold up, then you can be more confident that the results are solid. In such a case, you could safely reject the vitamin C hypothesis. (This is, in fact, what scientists did in the real-life studies of vitamin C and cancer survival.)

At this point, when evidence has been gathered that can bear on the truth of the hypothesis in question, good scientific judgment is crucial. It's here that consideration of other competing hypotheses and the criteria of adequacy again come into play. At this stage, scientists need to decide whether to reject or accept a hypothesis—or modify it to improve it.

Judging Scientific Theories

As you can see, theory-testing is part of the broader effort to assess the merits of one theory against a field of alternatives. And as you know by now, this broader effort will always involve, explicitly or implicitly, the application of the criteria of adequacy to the theories in question:

Criteria of Adequacy

- Testability: Whether there's some way to determine if a theory is true
- Fruitfulness: The number of novel predictions made
- Scope: The amount of diverse phenomena explained
- Simplicity: The number of assumptions made
- Conservatism: How well a theory fits with existing knowledge

Let's study two important examples to see how scientists manage this task: The first is a classic case from the history of science; the second, a contemporary tale of what many perceive as a battle between science and religion. Notice that the steps itemized by the TEST formula are implicit in the evaluation process.

COPERNICUS VERSUS PTOLEMY

Consider the historic clash between the geocentric (Earth-centered) and the heliocentric (sun-centered) theories of planetary motion. It's difficult to imagine two rival theories that have more profoundly influenced how humanity views itself and its place in the universe.

Copernicus on Ptolemy's System

Copernicus was shocked at how complex and seemingly arbitrary Ptolemy's revered system was. He thought that Ptolemy, through countless revisions and additions, had created not a beautiful model—but a kind of monster. As Copernicus put it,

> It is as though an artist were to gather the hands, feet, head and other members for his images from diverse models, each part excellently drawn, but not related to a single body, and since they in no way match each other, the result would be a monster rather than a man.

Nicolaus Copernicus (1473–1543).

In the beginning was the geocentric view. Aristotle got things going by putting forth the theory that a spherical Earth was at the center of a spherical universe consisting of a series of concentric, transparent spheres. On one celestial sphere we see the sun, the moon, and the known planets. On the outermost sphere we behold the stars. All the heavenly bodies rotate in perfect circles around the stationary Earth. The heavenly bodies are pure, incorruptible, and unchanging; the earth, impure, corruptible, and transient.

Stage One
Aristotle's Geocentric Model

Then came the great astronomer and mathematician Ptolemy, who flourished in Alexandria between 127 and 148 C.E. He discovered inconsistencies in the traditional geocentric system between the predicted and observed motions of the planets. He found, in other words, that Aristotle's theory was not conservative, a crucial failing. So he fine-tuned the old view, adding little circular

Stage Two
Ptolemy's Modified Model

"IT'S BLACK, AND IT LOOKS LIKE A HOLE. I'D SAY IT'S A BLACK HOLE."

© 2002 by Sidney Harris. www.ScienceCartoonsPlus.com

motions (called epicycles) along the planet orbits and many other minor adjustments. He also allowed for an odd asymmetry in which the center of planet orbits was not exactly the center of Earth—all this so the theory would match up to astronomical observations. By the time Ptolemy finished tinkering he had posited eighty circles and epicycles—eighty different planetary motions—to explain the movements of the sun, moon, and five known planets.

The result was a system far more complex than Aristotle's was. But the revised theory worked well enough for the times, and it agreed better than the earlier theory did with observational data. Despite the complications, learned people could use Ptolemy's system to calculate the positions of the planets with enough accuracy to effectively manage calendars and astrological charts. So for fifteen centuries astronomers used Ptolemy's unwieldy, complex theory to predict celestial events and locations. In the West, at least, Earth stood still in the center of everything as the rest of the universe circled around it.

The chief virtue of the Ptolemaic system, then, was conservatism. It fit, mostly, with what astronomers knew about celestial goings-on. It was also testable, as any scientific theory should be. Its biggest failing was simplicity—or the lack thereof. The theory was propped up by numerous assumptions for the purpose of making the theory fit the data.

Enter Nicolaus Copernicus (1473–1543). He was disturbed by the complexity of Ptolemy's system. It was a far cry from the simple theory that Aristotle bequeathed to the West. Copernicus proposed a heliocentric theory in which Earth and the other planets orbit the sun, the true center of the universe. In doing so, he greatly simplified both the picture of the heavens and the calculations required to predict the positions of planets.

Copernicus's theory was simpler than Ptolemy's on many counts, but one of the most impressive was retrograde motion, a phenomenon that had stumped astronomers for centuries. From time to time, certain planets seem to reverse their customary direction of travel across the skies—to move backward! Ptolemy

Strength: Conservatism
Weakness: Lack of Simplicity

Stage Three
Copernicus' Heliocentric Model

"[Natural selection] has no vision, no foresight, no sight at all. If it can be said to play the role of watchmaker in nature, it is the blind watchmaker."

—RICHARD DAWKINS

----

explained this retrograde motion by positing yet more epicycles, asserting that planets orbiting Earth will often orbit around a point on the larger orbital path. Seeing these orbits within orbits from Earth, an observer would naturally see the planets sometimes backing up.

But the Copernican theory could easily explain retrograde motion without all those complicated epicycles. As the outer planets (Mars, Jupiter, Saturn) orbit the sun, so does Earth, one of the inner planets. The outer planets, though, move much slower than Earth does. On its own orbital track, Earth sometimes passes the outer planets as they lumber along on their orbital track, just as a train passes a slower train on a parallel track. When this happens, the planets appear to move backward, just as the slower train seems to reverse course when the faster train overtakes it.

Copernicus's theory, however, was not superior on every count. It explained a great many astronomical observations, but Ptolemy's theory did too, so they were about even in scope. It had no big advantage in fruitfulness over the Ptolemaic system. It made no impressive predictions of unknown phenomena. Much more troubling, it seemed to conflict with some observational data.

One test implication of the Copernican theory is the phenomenon known as *parallax*. Critics of the heliocentric view claimed that if the theory were true, then as Earth moved through its orbit, stars closest to it should seem to shift their position relative to stars farther away. There should, in other words, be parallax. But no one had observed parallax.

Copernicus and his followers responded to this criticism by saying that stars were too far away for parallax to occur. As it turned out, they were right about this, but confirmation didn't come until 1832 when parallax was observed with more powerful telescopes.

Another test implication seemed to conflict with the heliocentric model. Copernicus reasoned that if the planets rotate around the sun, then they should show phases just as the moon shows phases due to the light of the sun falling on it at different times. But in Copernicus's day, no one could see any such planetary phases. Fifty years later, though, Galileo used his new telescope to confirm that Venus had phases.

Ultimately, scientists accepted the Copernican model over Ptolemy's because of its simplicity—despite what seemed at the time like evidence against the theory. As Copernicus said, "I think it is easier to believe this [sun-centered view] than to confuse the issue by assuming a vast number of Spheres, which those who keep the Earth at the center must do."[4]

EVOLUTION VERSUS CREATIONISM

Few scientific theories have been more hotly debated among nonscientists than evolution and its rival, creationism (or creation science). Both theories purport to

Copernicus can explain retrograde motion without invoking Ptolemy's "messy" epicycles

So Copernicus Theory is simpler.

No advantage in either ① fruitfulness or ② scope

TWO PROBLEMS

① Parallax: If the HM were correct, parallax should be observed...

Parallax was not observed until 1832...

② Phases: If the planets orbit the sun, they should show phases

Fifty years later Galileo used his telescope to confirm Venus has phases

"Science is an integral part of culture. It's not this foreign thing, done by an arcane priesthood. It's one of the glories of human intellectual tradition."
—STEPHEN JAY GOULD

"It is a good morning exercise for a research scientist to discard a pet hypothesis every day before breakfast. It keeps him young."
—KONRAD LORENZ

FURTHER THOUGHT

Can You See Evolution?

Critics of the theory of evolution often ask, "If evolution occurs, why can't we see it?" Here's how the National Academy of Sciences responds to this objection (http://books.nap.edu/html/creationism/evidence.html):

> Special creationists argue that "no one has ever seen evolution occur." This misses the point about how science tests hypotheses. We don't see Earth going around the sun or the atoms that make up matter. We "see" their consequences. Scientists infer that atoms exist and Earth revolves because they have tested predictions derived from these concepts by extensive observation and experimentation.
>
> Furthermore, on a minor scale, we "experience" evolution occurring every day. The annual changes in influenza viruses and the emergence of antibiotic-resistant bacteria are both products of evolutionary forces. . . . On a larger scale, the evolution of mosquitoes resistant to insecticides is another example of the tenacity and adaptability of organisms under environmental stress. Similarly, malaria parasites have become resistant to the drugs that were used extensively to combat them for many years. As a consequence, malaria is on the increase, with more than 300 million clinical cases of malaria occurring every year.

explain the origin and existence of biological life on Earth, and each claims to be a better explanation than the other. Can science decide this contest? Yes. Despite the complexity of the issues involved and the mixing of religious themes with the nonreligious, good science can figure out which theory is best. Remember that the best theory is the one that explains the phenomenon and measures up to the criteria of adequacy better than any of its competitors. There is no reason that the scientific approach cannot provide an answer here—even in this thorniest of thorny issues.

Neither the term "evolution" nor the concept began with Charles Darwin (1809–1882), the father of evolutionary theory. The word showed up in English as early as 1647. The ancient Greek philosopher Anaximander (c. 611–547 B.C.E.) was actually the first evolutionary theorist, inferring from some simple observations that humans must have evolved from an animal and that this evolution must have begun in the sea. But in his famous book *The Origin of Species* (1859), Darwin distilled the theory of evolution into its most influential statement.

Scientists have been fine-tuning the theory ever since as new evidence and new insights pour in from many different fields, such as biochemistry and genetics. But the basic idea has not changed: Living organisms adapt to their environments through inherited characteristics, which results in changes in succeeding genera-

First speculations re: Evolution go back to the ancient Greeks, i.e. Anaximander (611–547 BCE)

Charles Darwin (1809–1882)

The Origin of Species (1859)

Hypothesis I: EVOLUTION

tions. Specifically, the offspring of organisms differ physically from their parents in various ways, and these differences can be passed on genetically to their offspring. If an offspring has an inherited trait (such as sharper vision or a larger brain) that increases its chances of surviving long enough to reproduce, the individual is more likely to survive and pass the trait on to the next generation. After several generations, this useful trait, or adaptation, spreads throughout a whole population of individuals, differentiating the population from its ancestors. *Natural selection* is the name that Darwin gave to this process.

Creation science, on the other hand, maintains that (1) the universe and all life was created suddenly, out of nothing, only a few thousand years ago (six thousand to ten thousand is the usual range); (2) natural selection could not have produced living things from a single organism; (3) species change very little over time; (4) man and apes have a separate ancestry; and (5) the earth's geology can be explained by catastrophism, including a worldwide flood.[5]

© 2002 by Sidney Harris. www.ScienceCartoonsPlus.com

The first thing we should ask about these two theories is whether they're testable. The answer is yes. Recall that a theory is testable if it predicts or explains something other than what it was introduced to explain. On this criterion, evolution is surely testable. It explains, among other things, why bacteria develop resistance to antibiotics, why there are so many similarities between humans and other primates, why new infectious diseases emerge, why the chromosomes of closely related species are so similar, why the fossil record shows the peculiar progression of fossils that it does, and why the embryos of related species have such similar structure and appearance.

Creationism is also testable. It too explains something other than what it was introduced to explain. It claims that Earth's geology was changed in a worldwide flood, that the universe is only a few thousand years old, that all species were created at the same time, and that species change very little over time.

Innumerable test implications have been derived from evolutionary theory, and innumerable experiments have been conducted, confirming the theory. For example, if evolution is true, then we would expect to see systematic change in the fossil record from simple creatures at the earlier levels to more complex individuals at the more recent levels. We would expect not to see a reversal of this configuration. And this sequence is exactly what scientists see time and time again.

Hypothesis II: CREATIONISM

CRITERIA OF ADEQUACY

① Testability

Both theories are testable.
Predictions made by creation
science turn out to be false

Creationism, however, has not fared as well. Its claims have not been borne out by evidence. In fact, they have consistently conflicted with well-established scientific findings.

This latter point means that creationism fails the criterion of conservatism—it conflicts with what we already know. For example, the scientific evidence shows that Earth is not six thousand to ten thousand years old—but billions of years old. According to the National Academy of Sciences:

> There are no valid scientific data or calculations to substantiate the belief that Earth was created just a few thousand years ago. [There is a] vast amount of evidence for the great age of the universe, our galaxy, the Solar system, and Earth from astronomy, astrophysics, nuclear physics, geology, geochemistry, and geophysics. Independent scientific methods consistently give an age for Earth and the Solar system of about 5 billion years, and an age for our galaxy and the universe that is two to three times greater.[6]

Creationism also fails the criterion of conservatism on the issue of a geology-transforming universal flood. Again, the National Academy of Sciences:

> Nor is there any evidence that the entire geological record, with its orderly succession of fossils, is the product of a single universal flood that occurred a few thousand years ago, lasted a little longer than a year, and covered the highest mountains to a depth of several meters. On the contrary, intertidal and terrestrial deposits demonstrate that at no recorded time in the past has the entire planet been under water. . . . The belief that Earth's sediments, with their fossils, were deposited in an orderly sequence in a year's time defies all geological observations and physical principles concerning sedimentation rates and possible quantities of suspended solid matter.[7]

Has either theory yielded any novel predictions? Evolution has. It has predicted, for example, that new species should still be evolving today; that the fossil record should show a movement from older, simpler organisms to younger, more complex ones; that proteins and chromosomes of related species should be similar; and that organisms should adapt to changing environments. These and many other novel predictions have been confirmed. Creationism has made some novel claims, as we saw earlier, but none of these have been supported by good evidence. Creationism is not a fruitful theory.

The criterion of simplicity also draws a sharp contrast between the two theories. Simplicity is a measure of the number of assumptions that a theory makes. Both theories make assumptions, but creationism assumes much more. Creationism assumes the existence of a creator and unknown forces. Proponents of creationism readily admit that we do not know how the creator created nor what creative processes were used.

Handwritten margin notes:

② Conservatism
Creation science fails the conservatism criterion

ⓐ Cosmology

ⓑ Geology

③ Fruitfulness
Evolution succeeds where creationism fails

"If we are going to teach creation science as an alternative to evolution, then we should also teach the stork theory as an alternative to biological reproduction."
—JUDITH HAYES

④ Simplicity
Creationism is less simple. It assumes existence of a creator & unknown forces

Gaps in the Fossil Record?

Creationists hold that if evolution were true, then there should be fossil remains of transitional organisms. But, they insist, there are gaps where transitional fossils should be, so evolution didn't happen. But this claim is incorrect. There are transitional fossils:

Gaps in the fossil record are not even a critical test of evolution vs. progressive creation, as evolution also predicts gaps. There are some 2 million described species of living animals, but only 200,000 described fossil species. Thus, it is impossible to provide a minutely detailed history for every living species. This is because, first, the fossil record has not been completely explored. It is pretty hard to overlook a dinosaur bone! Yet, though dinosaurs have been excavated for over 150 years, 40% of the known species were found in the last 20 years or so (*Discover*, March 1987, p. 46). It is likely many more dinosaur species remain to be found. Second, sedimentary rocks were formed locally in lakes, oceans, and river deltas, so many upland species were never fossilized. Third, many deposits that were formed have been lost to erosion. Thus, a complete record is impossible.

In 2006 scientists discovered this 375-million-year-old fossil of a species that spans the gap between fish and land animals.

However, there is a critical test. Evolution predicts that some complete series should be found, while [creationists predict] that

Evolution predicts some complete series should be found whereas creationism predicts none should be found

none should ever be found. In fact, many excellent series exist. The evolution of the horse is known in exquisite detail from *Hyracotherium* (*Eohippus*) to the modern horse (G. G. Simpson, *Horses,* 2nd ed. Oxford, 1961). Scientific creationists have been forced to claim that the series is but allowed variation within a created "kind." If so, then rhinoceroses, tapirs, and horses are all the same "kind," as they can be traced to ancestors nearly identical to *Hyracotherium*! All of these fossils lie in the correct order by both stratigraphic and radioisotope dating.

Another critical test is Darwin's prediction that ". . . our early ancestors lived on the African continent. . . ." (*The Descent of Man*, p. 158). An excellent, detailed series of skulls and some nearly complete skeletons now connect modern man to African australopithecines. Some of the extinct australopithecines had brains about the size and shape of those of chimpanzees.[8]   ∎

⑤ Scope
Evolution explains far more than creationism

Theodosius Dobzhansky: Nothing in biology makes sense except in light of evolution...

Creationism generates more questions than it answers

In this contest of theories, the criterion of scope—the amount of diverse phenomena explained—is probably more telling than any of the others. Biological evolution explains a vast array of phenomena in many fields of science. In fact, a great deal of the content of numerous scientific fields—genetics, physiology, biochemistry, neurobiology, and more—would be deeply perplexing without the theory of evolution. As the eminent geneticist Theodosius Dobzhansky put it, "Nothing in biology makes sense except in the light of evolution."[9]

Virtually all scientists would agree—and go much further:

It helps to explain the emergence of new infectious diseases, the development of antibiotic resistance in bacteria, the agricultural relationships among wild and domestic plants and animals, the composition of Earth's atmosphere, the molecular machinery of the cell, the similarities between human beings and other primates, and countless other features of the biological and physical world.[10]

Creationism, however, can explain none of this. And it provokes, not solves, innumerable mysteries: What caused the worldwide flood? Where did all that water come from? Where did it all go? Why does Earth seem so ancient (when it's said to be so young)? How did the creator create the entire universe suddenly —out of nothing? Why does the fossil record seem to suggest evolution and not creation? So many questions are an indication of diminished scope and decreased understanding.

Note that creationism tries to explain biological facts by appealing to something that's incomprehensible—a creator and his means of creating. The

"My theory of evolution is that Darwin was adopted."
—STEVEN WRIGHT

creationist view is that something incomprehensible using incomprehensible means created the universe. But appealing to the incomprehensible does not increase our understanding. Creationism, then, explains nothing. Creationism has zero scope.

Good scientists must be prepared to admit this much: If creationism meets the criteria of adequacy as well as evolution does, then creationism must be as good a theory as evolution. But creationism fails to measure up to the criteria of adequacy. On every count it shows itself to be inferior. Scientists then are justified in rejecting creationism in favor of evolution. And this is exactly what they do.

Creationism's appeal to an incomprehensible creator results in theory w/zero scope

---

FURTHER THOUGHT

💡 The Clash over "Intelligent Design"

A controversial view known as intelligent design (ID) is the latest conceptual challenge to evolution, maintaining that biological life is much too complex to be fully explained by evolutionary processes. Take a moment to reflect on this synopsis of part of the debate:

Intelligent Design: Born-Again Creationism

> The proponents of intelligent design, a school of thought that some have argued should be taught alongside evolution in the nation's schools, say that the complexity and diversity of life go beyond what evolution can explain.
>
> Biological marvels like the optical precision of an eye, the little spinning motors that propel bacteria and the cascade of proteins that cause blood to clot, they say, point to the hand of a higher being at work in the world.
>
> In one often-cited argument, Michael J. Behe, a professor of biochemistry at Lehigh University and a leading design theorist, compares complex biological phenomena like blood clotting to a mousetrap: Take away any one piece—the spring, the baseboard, the metal piece that snags the mouse—and the mousetrap stops being able to catch mice.
>
> Similarly, Dr. Behe argues, if any one of the more than 20 proteins involved in blood clotting is missing or deficient, as happens in hemophilia, for instance, clots will not form properly.
>
> Such all-or-none systems, Dr. Behe and other design proponents say, could not have arisen through the incremental changes that evolution says allowed life to progress to the big brains and the sophisticated abilities of humans from primitive bacteria.
>
> These complex systems are "always associated with design," Dr. Behe, the author of the 1996 book *Darwin's Black Box*, said in an interview.

▼

Michael Behe on Irreducible Complexity

Behe claims that complex "all or nothing" systems could not evolve by natural selection...

"We find such systems in biology, and since we know of no other way that these things can be produced, Darwinian claims notwithstanding, then we are rational to conclude they were indeed designed."

It is an argument that appeals to many Americans of faith.

But mainstream scientists say that the claims of intelligent design run counter to a century of research supporting the explanatory and predictive power of Darwinian evolution, and that the design approach suffers from fundamental problems that place it outside the realm of science. For one thing, these scientists say, invoking a higher being as an explanation is unscientific.

"One of the rules of science is, no miracles allowed," said Douglas H. Erwin, a paleobiologist at the Smithsonian Institution. "That's a fundamental presumption of what we do."

That does not mean that scientists do not believe in God. Many do. But they see science as an effort to find out how the material world works, with nothing to say about why we are here or how we should live.

And in that quest, they say, there is no need to resort to other-worldly explanations. So much evidence has been provided by evolutionary studies that biologists are able to explain even the most complex natural phenomena and to fill in whatever blanks remain with solid theories.

This is possible, in large part, because evolution leaves tracks like the fossil remains of early animals or the chemical footprints in DNA that have been revealed by genetic research.

For example, while Dr. Behe and other leading design proponents see the blood-clotting system as a product of design, mainstream scientists see it as a result of a coherent sequence of evolutionary events.

Early vertebrates like jawless fish had a simple clotting system, scientists believe, involving a few proteins that made blood stick together, said Russell F. Doolittle, a professor of molecular biology at the University of California, San Diego.

Scientists hypothesize that at some point, a mistake during the copying of DNA resulted in the duplication of a gene, increasing the amount of protein produced by cells.

Most often, such a change would be useless. But in this case the extra protein helped blood clot, and animals with the extra protein were more likely to survive and reproduce. Over time, as higher-order species evolved, other proteins joined the clotting system. For instance, several proteins involved in the clotting of blood appear to have started as digestive enzymes.

By studying the evolutionary tree and the genetics and biochemistry of living organisms, Dr. Doolittle said, scientists have largely been able to determine the order in which different proteins became involved in helping blood clot, eventually producing the sophisticated clotting mechanisms of humans and other higher animals. The sequencing of animal genomes has provided evidence to support this view.

For example, scientists had predicted that more primitive animals such as fish would be missing certain blood-clotting proteins. In fact, the recent sequencing of the fish genome has shown just this.

"The evidence is rock solid," Dr. Doolittle said. . . .

Dr. Behe, however, said he might find it compelling if scientists were to observe evolutionary leaps in the laboratory. He pointed to an experiment by Richard E. Lenski, a professor of microbial ecology at Michigan State University, who has been observing the evolution of E. coli bacteria for more than 15 years. "If anything cool came out of that," Dr. Behe said, "that would be one way to convince me."

Richard Lenski

Dr. Behe said that if he was correct, then the E. coli in Dr. Lenski's lab would evolve in small ways but never change in such a way that the bacteria would develop entirely new abilities.

In fact, such an ability seems to have developed. Dr. Lenski said his experiment was not intended to explore this aspect of evolution, but nonetheless, "We have recently discovered a pretty dramatic exception, one where a new and surprising function has evolved," he said.

Dr. Lenski declined to give any details until the research is published. But, he said, "If anyone is resting his or her faith in God on the outcome that our experiment will not produce some major biological innovation, then I humbly suggest they should rethink the distinction between science and religion."

Dr. Behe said, "I'll wait and see."[11]

Exercise 10.1

REVIEW QUESTIONS

1. How does science differ from technology?
2. What is the scientific method?
3. Can science be identified with a particular worldview?
4. According to the text, what is scientism?
5. According to the text, why is science such a reliable way of knowing?

* 6. What are the five steps of the scientific method?

7. Can hypotheses be generated through induction? Why or why not?

8. What does it mean to derive a test implication from a theory?

* 9. What is the conditional argument reflecting the fact that a theory is disconfirmed?

10. What is the conditional argument reflecting the fact that a theory is confirmed?

11. Can theories be conclusively confirmed? Why or why not?

* 12. Can theories be conclusively disconfirmed? Why or why not?

13. According to the text, is creationism as good a scientific theory as evolution? Why or why not?

Exercise 10.2

For each of the following phenomena, devise a hypothesis to explain it and derive a test implication to test the hypothesis.

1. In a recent study of scientific literacy, women performed better than men in understanding the scientific process and in answering questions about basic scientific facts and concepts.

* 2. Jamal found giant footprints in his backyard and mysterious tufts of brown fur clinging to bushes in the area. Rumors persist that Bigfoot, the giant primate unknown to science, is frequenting the area. Two guys living nearby also claim to be perpetrating a hoax about the existence of the creature.

3. The rates of automobile crashes are higher among teenage boys than any other age group.

4. For months after the tragedy of September 11, there were no major terrorist attacks in the United States.

5. The CIA reviewed the president's state of the union speech before he made it and verified that the intelligence information in the speech was correct. Later it was found that some of the information was erroneous and based on dubious sources.

* 6. Weight trainers swear that the supplement creatine dramatically increases their performance.

7. Many people who take B vitamins for their headaches report a lower incidence of headaches.

8. Recent research confirms a link between diets high in saturated fat and a higher risk of coronary artery disease.

9. When John got home, he found that the lock on his door had been broken and his color TV was missing.

10. The economic gap between the very rich and the very poor widened considerably in 2004.

Exercise 10.3

Using your background knowledge and any other information you may have about the subject, devise a competing theory for each of the following and then apply the criteria of adequacy to both of them—that is, ascertain how well each theory does in relation to its competitor on the criteria of testability, fruitfulness, scope, simplicity, and conservatism.

1. Phenomenon: People report feeling less pain after trying acupuncture.
   Theory: Treatment with acupuncture needles can alleviate pain.

2. Phenomenon: Your mild-mannered friend suddenly going into a violent rage.
   Theory: Schizophrenia.

* 3. Phenomenon: The unexpected melting of massive chunks of the world's glaciers.
   Theory: Local climate changes.

4. Phenomenon: A rare species of fungus grows in only one place in the world—the wing tips of a beetle that inhabits caves in France.
   Theory: Evolution.

5. Phenomenon: As the job market worsens, blacks lose jobs faster than whites.
   Theory: Racial prejudice.

6. Phenomenon: The psychic was able to recount a number of personal details about a recently deceased person he never met.
   Theory: Psychic ability.

* 7. Phenomenon: Almost all of the terrorist attacks in the world in the past five years have been perpetrated by religious fanatics.
   Theory: Religion fosters terrorism.

8. Phenomenon: Twenty patients with severe arthritis pain were prayed for by fifty people, and fourteen out of those twenty reported a significant lessening of pain.
   Theory: Prayer heals.

9. Phenomenon: Over the past year, two terminally ill cancer patients in Broderick Hospital were found to be cancer free.
   Theory: Treatment with a new type of chemotherapy.

10. Phenomenon: Air pollution levels in San Francisco are at their highest levels in years.
   Theory: Increased numbers of SUVs being driven in the San Francisco area.

Exercise 10.4

For each of the following theories, derive a test implication and indicate whether you believe that such a test would likely confirm or disconfirm the theory.

1. Elise has the power to move physical objects with her mind alone.

* 2. Ever since the city installed brighter street lights, the crime rate has been declining steadily.

3. The Ultra-Sonic 2000 pest-control device can rid a house of roaches by emitting a particular sound frequency that humans can't hear.

4. The Dodge Intrepid is a more fuel-efficient car than any other on the road.

5. Practitioners of transcendental meditation (TM) can levitate—actually ascend unaided off the ground without physical means of propulsion.

* 6. Eating foods high in fat contributes more to overweight than eating foods high in carbohydrates.

7. Lemmings often commit mass suicide.

8. The English sparrow will build nests only in trees.

Exercise 10.5

Read the following passages and answer the following questions for each one:

1. What is the phenomenon being explained?

2. What theories are advanced to explain the phenomenon? (Some theories may be unstated.)

3. Which theory seems the most plausible and why? (Use the criteria of adequacy.)

4. Regarding the most credible theory, is there a test implication mentioned? If so, what is it? If not, what would be a good test implication for the theory?

5. What test results would convince you to change your mind about your preferred theory?

PASSAGE 1

"In the past several years, a researcher named David Oates has been advocating his discovery of a most interesting phenomenon. Oates claims that backward messages are hidden unintentionally in all human speech. The messages can be understood by recording normal speech and playing it in reverse. . . . [According to Oates] 'Any thought, any emotion, any motive that any person has can appear backwards in human speech. The implications are mind boggling because reverse speech opens up the Truth.'. . . To our knowledge there is not one empirical investigation of reverse speech in any peer-reviewed journal. If reverse speech did exist it would be, at the very least, a noteworthy scientific discovery. However, there are no data to support the existence of reverse speech or Oates's theories about its implications."[12]

PASSAGE 2

"Michael Behe, a Lehigh University biochemist, claims that a light-sensitive cell, for example, couldn't have arisen through evolution because it is 'irreducibly complex.' Unlike the scientific creationists, however, he doesn't deny that the universe is billions of years old. Nor does he deny that evolution has occurred. He only denies that every biological system arose through natural selection.

"Behe's favorite example of an irreducibly complex mechanism is a mouse trap. A mouse trap consists of five parts: (1) a wooden platform, (2) a metal hammer, (3) a spring, (4) a catch, and (5) a metal bar that holds the hammer down when the trap is set. What makes this mechanism irreducibly complex is that if any one of the parts were removed, it would no longer work. Behe claims that many biological systems, such as cilium, vision, and blood clotting, are also irreducibly complex because each of these systems would cease to function if any of their parts were removed.

"Irreducibly complex biochemical systems pose a problem for evolutionary theory because it seems that they could not have arisen through natural selection. A trait such as vision can improve an organism's ability to survive only if it works. And it works only if all the parts of the visual system are present. So, Behe concludes, vision couldn't have arisen through slight modifications of a previous system. It must have been created all at once by some intelligent designer. . . .

"Most biologists do not believe that Behe's argument is sound, however, because they reject the notion that the parts of an irreducibly complex system could not have evolved independently of that system. As Nobel Prize–winning biologist H. J. Muller noted in 1939, a genetic sequence that is, at first, inessential to a system may later become essential to it. Biologist H. Allen Orr describes the processes as follows: 'Some part (A) initially does some job (and not very well, perhaps). Another part (B) later gets added because it helps A. This new part isn't essential, it merely improves things. But later on A (or something else) may change in such a way that B now becomes indispensable.' For example, air bladders—primitive lungs—made it possible for certain fish to acquire new sources of food. But the air bladders were not necessary to the survival of the fish. As the fish acquired additional features, however, such as legs and arms, lungs became essential. So, contrary to what Behe would have us believe, the parts of an irreducibly complex system need not have come into existence all at once."[13]

Exercise 10.6

Read the following passage about a study conducted on the use of vitamin C to treat cancer. Identify the hypothesis being tested, the consequences (test implication) used to test it, and whether the hypothesis was confirmed or disconfirmed.

PASSAGE 1

"In 1978, the Mayo Clinic embarked on a prospective, controlled, double-blind study designed to test Pauling and Cameron's claims [for the effectiveness of vitamin C]. Each patient in this study had biopsy-proven cancer that was considered incurable and unsuitable for further chemotherapy, surgery, or radiation. The patients were randomized to receive 10 grams of vitamin C per day or a comparably flavored lactose placebo. All patients took a glycerin-coated capsule four times a day.

"The patients were carefully selected so that those vitamin C and placebo groups were equally matched. There were 60 patients in the vitamin C group and 63 in the placebo group. The age distributions were similar. There was a slight predominance of males, but the ratio of males to females was virtually identical. Performance status was measured using the Eastern Cooperative Oncology Group Scale, a clinical scale well recognized by cancer researchers. Most study patients had some disability from their disease, but only a small proportion were bedridden. Most patients had advanced gastrointestinal or lung cancer. Almost all had received chemotherapy, and a smaller proportion had undergone radiation therapy.

"The results were noteworthy. About 25% of patients in both groups showed some improvement in appetite. Forty-two percent of the patients on placebo alone experienced enhancement of their level of activity. About 40% of the patients experienced mild nausea and vomiting, but the two groups had no statistically significant differences in the number of episodes. There were no survival differences between patients receiving vitamin C and those receiving the placebo. The median survival time was approximately seven weeks from the onset of therapy. The longest surviving patient in this trial had received the placebo. Overall, the study showed no benefit from vitamin C."[14]

Science and Weird Theories

What good is science and inference to the best explanation in the realm that seems to lie *beyond* common sense and scientific inquiry—the zone of the extraordinary, the paranormal, and the supernatural? In this land of the wonderfully weird—the interesting and mysterious domain of UFOs, ESP, ghosts, psychic predictions, tarot card readings, and the like—exactly what work can science do?

From reading Chapter 9, you probably have already guessed that science and critical reasoning can be as useful in assessing weird claims as they are in sizing up mundane ones. Inference to the best explanation—whether wielded in science or everyday life—can be successfully applied to extraordinary theories of all kinds. Fortunately for critical thinkers, the TEST formula outlined in Chapter 9 for finding the best theoretical explanation is not afraid of ghosts, monsters, or space aliens. In the next few pages, we will get a good demonstration of these points by examining some extraordinary theories in much greater detail than we have previously.

Science has always been interested in the mysterious, and from time to time it has also ventured into the weird. In the past 150 years, scientists have tested spiritualism, clairvoyance, telepathy, telekinesis (moving physical objects with the mind alone), astrology, dowsing, the Loch Ness monster, faith healing, fire walking, and more. Among these we should also count some bizarre phenomena that scientists never tire of studying —black holes, alternative dimensions of space, and the microworld of subatomic particles (the weirdest of the weird) where the laws of physics are crazy enough to make Alice in Wonderland scream.

"I maintain there is much more wonder in science than in pseudoscience. And in addition, to whatever measure this term has any meaning, science has the additional virtue, and it is not an inconsiderable one, of being true."
—CARL SAGAN

But why should anyone bother to learn how to evaluate weird claims in the first place? Well, for one thing, they are widely believed (see accompanying box) and often difficult to ignore. They are, after all, heavily promoted in countless television programs, movies, books, magazines, and tabloids. And—like claims in politics, medicine, and many other fields—they can dramatically affect people's lives, for better or worse. It's important then for anyone confronted with such popular and influential claims to be able to assess them carefully.

In addition, if you really care whether an extraordinary claim is true or false, there is no substitute for the kind of critical evaluation discussed here. Accepting (or rejecting) a weird claim solely because it's weird will not do. A horselaugh is not an argument, and neither is a sneer. Weird claims often turn out to be false, and, as the history of science shows, they sometimes surprise everyone by being true.

Making Weird Mistakes

So in science and in our own lives, the critical assessment of weird theories is possible—but that doesn't mean the process is without risks. It's easy for a scientist or anyone else to err when thinking about extraordinary claims. Weird claims and experiences have a way of provoking strong emotions, preconceived attitudes, and long-held biases. In the world of the weird, people (including

---

FURTHER THOUGHT

💡 How Many People Believe Weird Things?

In a 2001 National Science Foundation survey:

- Sixty percent of respondents agreed that "some people possess psychic powers or ESP."
- Thirty percent of respondents agreed that "some of the unidentified flying objects that have been reported are really space vehicles from other civilizations."

According to a 2001 Gallup poll:

- Forty-two percent of Americans believe in haunted houses.
- Thirty-eight percent believe in ghosts or spirits of dead people.
- Twenty-eight percent believe that people can communicate with the dead.
- Twenty-eight percent believe in astrology.
- Twenty-six percent believe in witches.

Handwritten margin notes:

Why bother to learn how to evaluate weird claims?

① They are widely believed and difficult to ignore.

② They can dramatically affect people's lives.

③ One should not accept or reject a claim simply on the basis that it is WEIRD.

scientists and other experts) are often prone to the kinds of errors in reasoning we discussed in Chapter 4, including resisting contrary evidence, looking for confirming evidence, and preferring available evidence. Those who contemplate extraordinary things also seem to be especially susceptible to the following errors.

Ⓐ LEAPING TO THE WEIRDEST THEORY

When people have an extraordinary experience, they usually try to make sense of it. They may have a seemingly prophetic dream, see a ghostly shape in the dark, watch their astrologer's prediction come true, think that they've witnessed a miracle, or feel that they have somehow lived another life centuries ago. Then they cast about for an explanation for such experiences. And when they cannot think of a natural explanation, they often conclude that the explanation must be paranormal or supernatural. This line of reasoning is common but fallacious. *Just because you can't think of a natural explanation doesn't mean that there isn't one.* You may just be ignorant of the correct explanation. Throughout history, scientists have often been confronted with astonishing phenomena that they could not explain in natural terms at the time. But they didn't assume that the phenomena must be paranormal or supernatural. They simply kept investigating—and they eventually found natural explanations. Comets, solar eclipses, meteors, mental illness, infectious diseases, and epilepsy were all once thought to be supernatural or paranormal but were later found through scientific investigation to have natural explanations. When confronted then with a phenomenon that you don't understand, the most reasonable response is to search for a natural explanation.

The fallacious leap to a nonnatural explanation is an example of the appeal to ignorance discussed in Chapter 5. People think that since a paranormal or supernatural explanation has not been shown to be false, it must be true. This line, though logically fallacious, can be very persuasive.

The failure to consider alternative explanations is probably the most common error in assessing paranormal claims. As we've seen, this failure can be willful: People can refuse to consider seriously a viable alternative. But honest and intelligent

"TELL THEM ABOUT YOUR PSORIASIS, BETTY. MAYBE THEY CAN CURE IT."

Harley Schwadron.

[Handwritten margin notes:]

Fallacious Leap to Nonnatural Explanations

When one cannot find a natural explanation one is tempted to leap to a weird explanation...

Just because you can't think of a natural explanation doesn't mean there isn't one...

This leap is an example of the Appeal to Ignorance

Need to look for alternatives

people can also simply be unaware of possible natural explanations. Looking for alternative explanations requires imagination and a deliberate attempt to "think outside the box."

B MIXING WHAT SEEMS WITH WHAT IS

Sometimes people leap prematurely to an extraordinary theory by ignoring this elementary principle: *Just because something seems real doesn't mean that it is.* Because of the nature of our perceptual equipment and processes, we humans are bound to have many experiences in which something appears to be real but is not. The corrective for mistaking the unreal for the real is applying another important principle that we discussed in Chapter 4: It's reasonable to accept the evidence provided by personal experience only if there's no good reason to doubt it. We have reason to doubt if our perceptual abilities are impaired (we are under stress, drugged, afraid, excited, etc.), we have strong expectations about a particular experience (we strongly expect to see a UFO or hear spooky noises, for example), and observations are made under poor conditions (the stimuli are vague and ambiguous or the environment is too dark, too noisy, too hazy, etc.). Scientists can falter here just as anyone else can, which is why they try to use research methods that minimize reasons for doubt.

[handwritten margin note: Mixing What Seems With What Is — Perceptual impairment — Pareidolia]

C MISUNDERSTANDING THE POSSIBILITIES

Debates about weird theories often turn on the ideas of possibility and impossibility. Skeptics may dismiss a weird theory by saying, "That's impossible!" Believers may insist that a state of affairs is indeed possible, or they may proclaim, "*Anything* is possible!" Such protestations, however, are often based on misunderstandings.

[handwritten margin note: Misunderstanding the Possibilities]

REVIEW NOTES

☑ **Common Errors in Evaluating Extraordinary Theories**

1. Believing that just because you can't think of a natural explanation, a phenomenon must be paranormal.
2. Thinking that just because something *seems* real, it *is* real. (A better principle: It's reasonable to accept the evidence provided by personal experience only if there's no good reason to doubt it.)
3. Misunderstanding logical possibility and physical possibility. Also, believing that if something is logically possible, it must be actual.

Logical Possibility vs
Physical Possibility

The experts on the subject of possibility (namely, philosophers) often talk about *logical possibility* and *logical impossibility*. Something is logically impossible if it violates a principle of logic (that is, it involves a logical contradiction). Something is logically possible if it does not violate a principle of logic (does not involve a logical contradiction). Anything that is logically impossible can't exist. We know, for example, that there are no married bachelors because these things involve logical contradictions (male humans who are both married and not married). Likewise we know that there are no square circles because they involve logical contradictions (things that are both circles and not circles). We must conclude from all this that, despite what some people sincerely believe, it is not the case that anything is possible. If a weird phenomenon is logically impossible, we needn't investigate it further because it can't exist. Most alleged paranormal phenomena, however, are not logically impossible. ESP, UFOs, reincarnation, dowsing, spontaneous human combustion, out-of-body experiences, and many more generally do not involve any logical contradiction.

Philosophers also refer to *physical possibility* and *physical impossibility*. Something is physically impossible if it violates a law of science. Whatever violates a law of science cannot occur. We know that traveling faster than the speed of light is physically impossible because such an occurrence violates a law of science. Perpetual motion machines are physically impossible because they violate the law of science known as the conservation of mass-energy. Thus, if an extraordinary phenomenon violates a law of science, we know that it cannot be.

Some things that are logically possible, however, are physically impossible. It's logically possible for Vaughn's dog to fly to another galaxy in sixty seconds. This astounding performance does not violate a principle of logic. But it does violate laws of science pertaining to speed-of-light travel and gravitation. It is therefore physically impossible. The upshot of all this is that, contrary to what some people would have us believe, if something is logically possible, that doesn't mean it's physi-

People have been faking UFO photos for decades, insisting the pictures showed the genuine article and attracting a lot of publicity and true believers. This, despite the ease of making fakes. Astronomer Tom Callen created these two with a camera, some UFO models, and Paint Shop Pro. Do these images look as authentic as those you've seen in TV documentaries purporting to have photographic proof of UFOs?

cally possible. That is, if something is logically possible, that doesn't mean it's actual. Many logically possible things may not be real.

Judging Weird Theories

Now let's do a detailed evaluation of two extraordinary theories using the TEST formula from Chapter 9. Recall the procedure's four steps:

Step 1. State the theory and check for consistency.
Step 2. Assess the evidence for the theory.
Step 3. Scrutinize alternative theories.
Step 4. Test the theories with the criteria of adequacy.

Science uses such a procedure to assess all manner of extraordinary explanations, and—by proceeding carefully and systematically—so can you.

TEST Formula

CROP CIRCLES

Crop circles are large-scale geometric designs pressed or stamped into fields of grain. They are often circular but can be almost any shape, ranging from simple patterns to complex pictograms or symbols. They can measure a few feet in diameter or span the length of several football fields. The current wave of popular interest in crop circles began in the 1970s when they started mysteriously appearing overnight in the grain fields of southern England. The crops would be neatly flattened with the stalks pressed together and sometimes impressively interlaced. In the 1980s and 1990s, interest in the phenomenon grew as crop circles proliferated throughout the world, showing up in Europe, Africa, Australia, the United States, and elsewhere. In 2002 Hollywood got into the act by releasing the movie *Signs* starring Mel Gibson. He plays a Pennsylvania farmer who discovers massive crop circles in his fields and is soon drawn into encounters with extraterrestrial beings.

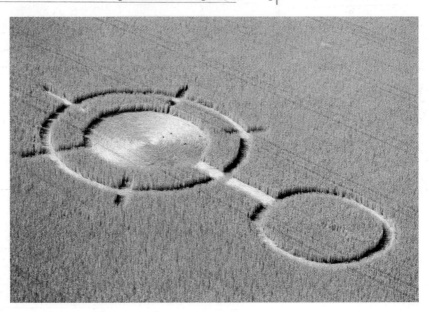

From the beginning, crop circles have been both intriguing and controversial. The controversy has centered mostly on one question: What theory

Stalking the Ghost Hunters

Ghost hunters are haunting North America—on TV shows like the Sci-Fi Channel's *Ghost Hunters* and CNN's *Larry King Live* and through the many ghost-hunter organizations that search creepy houses for restless spirits. But how likely are they to uncover good evidence of ghostly goings-on? Not likely at all, says Benjamin Radford, paranormal investigator and science writer:

> The most famous ghost hunters are two plumbers who moonlight as paranormal investigators, seen in the popular Sci-Fi Channel reality show/soap opera series *Ghost Hunters*. They go to haunted places and find "evidence" of ghosts such as cold spots, photographic anomalies called orbs, and other such spookiness. The two featured investigators, Jason Hawes and Grant Wilson, are proudly blue-collar workers, not egghead Ph.D. scientists, which adds to their strong "regular guy" appeal. While one doesn't need to be a scientist to search for ghosts, the pair (like most ghost hunters) could benefit greatly from a little critical thinking. They claim to be skeptics but are very credulous and seem to have no real understanding of scientific methods or real investigation. (Audiences don't seem to wonder why these "expert" ghost hunters always fail: Even after two seasons and over ten years of research, they still have yet to prove that ghosts exist!). . . .
>
> When it comes to searching for ghosts, you'd think that only the most reliable methods would be used in an attempt to get solid evidence for something as mysterious and elusive as a spirit. Yet, in ghost hunting, often the less scientific the methods and equipment, the more likely a researcher is to find "evidence" for ghosts.
>
> Ghost hunters use a variety of creative—and dubious—methods to detect their quarry's presence, including psychics. Psychics not only claim to locate ghosts but also to communicate with the spirits, who unfortunately don't provide any useful or verifiable information from the afterlife. Virtually all ghost hunter groups claim to be scientific, and most give that appearance because they use high-tech scientific equip-

ment such as Geiger counters, Electromagnetic Field (EMF) detectors, ion detectors, and infrared cameras. Yet the equipment is only as scientific as the person using it; you may own the world's most sophisticated thermometer, but if you are using it as a barometer, your measurements are worthless. Just as using a calculator doesn't make you a mathematician, using a scientific instrument doesn't make you a scientist. . . .

The uncomfortable reality that ghost hunters carefully avoid—the elephant in the tiny, haunted room—is of course that no one has ever shown that any of this equipment actually detects ghosts. The supposed links between ghosts and electromagnetic fields, low temperatures, radiation, odd photographic images, and so on are based on nothing more than guesses, unproven theories, and wild conjecture. If a device could reliably determine the presence or absence of ghosts, then by definition, ghosts would be proven to exist. I own an EMF meter, but since it's useless for ghost investigations—it finds not spirits but red herrings—I use it in my lectures and seminars as an example of pseudoscience. The most important tools in this or any investigation are a questioning mind and a solid understanding of scientific principles.

The ghost hunters' anti-scientific illogic is clear: if one area of a home is colder than another, that may indicate a ghost; if an EMF meter detects a field, that too may be a ghost; if dowsing rods cross, that might be a ghost. Just about any "anomaly," anything that anyone considers odd for any reason, from an undetermined sound to a "bad feeling" to a blurry photo, can be (and has been) considered evidence of ghosts. I was even at one investigation where a ghost supposedly caused a person's mild headache. Because the standard of evidence is so low, it's little wonder that ghost hunters often find "evidence" (but never proof) of ghosts. . . .

[W]hy are ghosts seen wearing clothing? It's one thing to suggest that a person's spirit has a soul that can be seen after death; but do shoes, coats, hats, and belts also have souls? Logically, ghosts should appear naked. The fact that they don't suggests that people's ideas of what ghosts are—and what they look like—are strongly influenced by social and cultural expectations. (For an excellent discussion of this, see Richard Finucane's book *Ghosts: Appearances of the Dead & Cultural Transformation*.)

If ghosts exist, why are we no closer to finding out what they really are, after so much research? The evidence for ghosts is no better today than it was a year ago, a decade ago, or a century ago. Ultimately, ghost hunting is not about the evidence (if it was, the search would have been abandoned long ago). Instead, it's about having fun with friends, telling ghost stories, and the enjoyment of pretending you are searching the edge of the unknown. (It's also about making money selling *Ghost Hunters* T-shirts, books, and videos.) Ghost hunters may be spinning their wheels, but at least they are enjoying the ride.[15]

What thing best explains crop circles

Theory 1: Vortex Theory

best explains the existence of crop circles? Many explanations for the cause of the phenomenon have been offered and debated, with plenty of people making the case for their favorite theory through books, magazine articles, and, of course, the Internet. Let's examine some of these theories and see if we can separate the good from the bad.

Step 1. We begin with a theory that has gotten a great deal of attention from skeptics and believers alike.

Theory 1: Crop circles are created by small whirlwinds of electrified air (a.k.a. wind vortices). The idea here is that crop circles are made by columns of whirling, charged air similar to dust devils or miniature tornadoes. These vortices form above grain fields then plunge to the ground, discharging the electricity and flattening the grain in swirled patterns. But unlike tornadoes, wind vortices leave the stalks of grain undamaged.

> "The most beautiful thing we can experience is the mysterious. It is the source of all true art and science."
> —ALBERT EINSTEIN

FURTHER THOUGHT

💡 The Art of Crop Circles

To many people, crop circles are the work of space aliens, or the result of natural processes, or the mischievous doings of pranksters. But to some, crop circles are an art form. Every year in Britain, serious artists hit the fields and, under cover of darkness, create crop-circle formations that are elegant enough to hang in a museum—if they would fit. John Lundberg, a graphic design artist, is one of these artistic circle makers.

Who—or what—is the artist?

[Lundberg's] group, known as the Circlemakers, considers their practice an art. Lundberg estimates that there are three or four dedicated crop circle art groups operating in the United Kingdom today, and numerous other small groups that make one or two circles a year more or less as a lark.

Circlemakers [www.circlemakers.org] now does quite a bit of commercial work; in early July, the group created a giant crop formation 140 feet (46 meters) in diameter for the History Channel. But they also still do covert work in the dead of night.

Formulating a design and a plan, from original concept to finished product, can take up to a week. "It has to be more than a pretty picture. You have to have construction diagrams providing the measurements, marking the center, and so on," said Lundberg. Creating the art is the work of a night. . . .

"You think about art in terms of authorship and signature," he said. But circle makers never claim credit for specific formations they created. "To do so would drain the mystery of crop circles," he explained. "The art form isn't just about the pattern making. The myths and folklore and energy [that] people give them are part of the art."

Over the last 25 years, the formations have evolved from simple, relatively small circles to huge designs with multiple circles, elaborate pictograms, and shapes that invoke complex non-linear mathematical principles. A formation that appeared in August 2001 at Milk Hill in Wiltshire contained 409 circles, covered about five hectares, and was more than 800 feet (243 meters) across.[16] ∎

Step 2. What is the evidence for this theory? The evidence is indirect. Natural crop-circle vortices are unknown to science, but similar vortices are reported to have been produced artificially in laboratories. A few people claim to have seen the vortices in open fields. An electrified vortex might produce light during discharge, and sure enough eyewitnesses have reported seeing "balls of light" and other light phenomena in or near crop circles. Many crop-circle enthusiasts (known as "cereologists" or "croppies") have photographed what they claim are mysterious lights near crop circles, and the photographs show impressive balls of light and strange glowing arcs. Some croppies also report hearing strange sounds near crop circles (humming noises, for example). Finally, some cereologists have reported that the plants in crop circles differ anatomically from those outside the circles. The joints in stalks, for example, may be bigger in crop-circle plants than in plants growing elsewhere.

This evidence, however, is weak. Producing a vortex in a laboratory does not prove that it exists "in the wild." In fact, there is no good evidence that crop-circle vortices exist in nature. As with most unfamiliar and provocative phenomena, eyewitness accounts of vortices are generally unreliable, especially since people generally don't know what a true crop-circle vortex looks like. Sightings of various light phenomena are not direct evidence for the existence of

[handwritten margin notes:]
Though produced in laboratories, such vortices are not known to occur naturally

Reports of cereologists

Evaluation of the Evidence
No evidence for vortices in nature

"Bloody hell! Crap circles."

www.CartoonStock.com

Crop Circle Vortex Theory
fails to explain the Evidence
not all designs are circles

Theory 2: Extraterrestrials
Does not specify how the
crop circles are made

Rationale similar to
the Design Argument

Evidence: defenders
appeal to complexity
Who else but aliens
produce such designs?

vortices because they can be explained in alternative ways. The lights could come from many other sources, including ball lightning (a documented phenomenon), commercial aircraft, military aircraft, the parachute flares of pranksters, and the flashlights of people making crop circles (there are plenty of people who make crop circles as hoaxes or works of art). The photographs of light phenomena also have alternative explanations. The arcs and balls of light in these photos can be easily produced when the flash reflects off of the camera strap, insects, droplets of water, and the like. Photos of weird lights are also easily faked. Reports of strange sounds, like the reports of weird lights, are not good evidence of vortices at work because the sounds could have several alternative causes (farm machinery, wind, etc.). And even if there are anatomical differences between crop-circle plants and non-circle plants, this would not show that crop circles are made by vortices. At most, it would suggest only that crop-circle plants are different, however the circles are made. (This same point applies to claims about other kinds of differences between crop-circle areas and non-circle locations, including alleged magnetic or soil anomalies. The anomalies, if they exist, do not confirm that crop circles are made in any particular way.)

The biggest problem for the crop-circle vortex theory is that it doesn't explain the evidence. The theory seems adequate to explain circular crop-circle designs (a whirlwind would seem to be just the thing to make a circle on the ground), but not all crop circles are circular. Many are incredibly complex amalgams of squares, triangles, straight lines, and shapes that have no names.

Step 3. Now let's examine a popular alternative theory.

Theory 2: Crop circles are made by extraterrestrial beings (space aliens). This explanation asserts only that crop circles are the work of aliens; it does not specify how the aliens do it. The circles could be created by alien spacecraft, energy beams from space, or "thought energy" from places unknown. This theory has seemed plausible to some people in light of the intricacy and beauty of crop-circle pictograms, with a few croppies insisting that aliens must be communicating in geometrical language. To some, the circles have seemed much too complicated and elegant to be the result of human ingenuity.

The evidence for this alien explanation? The elegant complexity of crop circles has been thought to be pretty good support for the theory. Who else but aliens would create such brilliant masterpieces on such a large scale—masterpieces that are best viewed from the air or space itself? A few people have announced that they found very intricate mathematics in the more elaborate crop-circle

FURTHER THOUGHT

I Confess: I'm a Crop-Circle Prankster

Other than to make great art, why would anyone want to go skulking around in the night to make crop circles in someone's wheat field? Maybe this confession from an unrepentant circle-maker will clear things up:

> I made my first crop circle in 1991. My motive was to prove how easy they were to create, because I was convinced that all crop circles were man-made. It was the only explanation nobody seemed interested in testing. Late one August night, with one accomplice—my brother-in-law from Texas—I stepped into a field of nearly ripe wheat in northern England, anchored a rope into the ground with a spike and began walking in a circle with the rope held near the ground. It did not work very well: the rope rode up over the plants. But with a bit of help from our feet to hold down the rope, we soon had a respectable circle of flattened wheat.
>
> Two days later there was an excited call to the authorities from the local farmer: I had fooled my first victim. I subsequently made two more crop circles using far superior techniques. A light garden roller, designed to be filled with water, proved helpful. Next, I hit on the "plank walking" technique that was used by the original circle makers, Doug Bower and the late Dave Chorley, who started it all in 1978. It's done by pushing down the crop with a plank suspended from two ropes. To render the depression circular is a simple matter of keeping an anchored rope taut. I soon found that I could make a sophisticated pattern with very neat edges in less than an hour.
>
> Getting into the field without leaving traces is a lot easier than is usually claimed. In dry weather, and if you step carefully, you can leave no footprints or tracks at all. There are other, even stealthier ways of getting into the crop. One group of circle makers uses two tall bar stools, jumping from one to another.
>
> But to my astonishment, throughout the early 1990s the media continued to report that it was impossible that all crop circles could be man-made. They cited "cerealogists"—those who study crop circles—and never checked for themselves. There were said to be too many circles to be the work of a few "hoaxers" (but this assumed that each circle took many hours to make), or that circles appeared in well-watched crops (simply not true), or that circle creation was accompanied by unearthly noises (when these sounds were played back, even I recognized the nocturnal song of the grasshopper warbler).[17]

designs. Also, some have reported seeing odd lights in the vicinity of crop circles, and others have claimed that they saw actual alien craft in the night sky not far from the crop-circle fields. A few cereologists have even claimed that they caught sight of UFOs in the process of making crop circles.

This evidence, however, is problematic and has some of the same weaknesses as the wind vortex evidence. The complexity and beauty of crop circles do not lend support to the alien theory because the artistry of the crop formations has an obvious alternative explanation: Humans made them. There are numerous documented cases of humans—either hoaxers or artists—creating stunningly exquisite and elaborate crop circles, some with plenty of mathematics built in. Because the human artist explanation is at least as plausible as the alien artist one, the artistic or intellectual impressiveness of crop circles can give no weight to the alien theory. As mentioned earlier, light phenomena near crop circles also have alternative explanations. Nighttime UFO sightings might seem to be good evidence that aliens are up to something. But they are susceptible to many of the doubt-producing factors that we discussed in Chapter 4: darkness, ambiguous stimuli, lack of cues to the true position and size of moving objects, perceptual construction, stress, strong emotions, expectancy, and more. Eyewitness reports of aliens actually constructing crop circles constitute very weak evidence for theory 2. Such extraordinary reports require reliable corroborating evidence, but no alien activity of any kind has ever been scientifically documented, despite allegations to the contrary.

Many people favor a more down-to-earth theory.

Theory 3: Crop circles are made by humans using ordinary means. This explanation encompasses the creation of crop circles by hoaxers, artists, or any other humans. The relevant evidence suggests that many crop circles have indeed been produced by humans. In 1991 two English artists with a sense of humor, Doug Bower and Dave Chorley, declared that they had been making crop circles for years to fool gullible people who believed in UFOs. They demonstrated their circle-making skills for reporters and television audiences, easily producing very elaborate crop circles in a short time. To create their designs, they used only ropes and planks. They showed that crop circles thought to be way beyond human ability were in fact made by humans using incredibly simple techniques. Their formations fooled many people including at least one prominent cereologist. Many circle-watchers conceded that human hoaxers were making crop circles and that distinguishing "true" circles from fake ones is no cinch. A leading cereologist admitted that 80 percent of crop circles in Britain were made by humans.

It is clear, however, that Bower and Chorley could not have created all the known crop circles. From southern England, crop-circle creation spread all over the globe, appearing in increasing numbers. This spread of the phenomenon, though, seemed to correlate with increased international media coverage of crop circles, suggesting that other humans may have been inspired to copy English

---

Marginal notes:

Reports of space craft

"It is easier to attribute UFO sightings to the known irrationalities of terrestrials than to the unknown efforts of extraterrestrials."
—RICHARD FEYNMAN

Human design as an alternative hypothesis

Problems w/ UFO sightings

Eyewitness reports are weak evidence for reports

Theory 3: Human Designers

Artists and hoaxers

Doug Bower and Dave Chorley admit to making them for years to fool people

Show how they were made using simple techniques

Other humans were inspired to copy English circle-making

circle-making. In addition, many artists have been fascinated by the aesthetics of crop circles and have generated their own masterpieces in grain.

Croppies have argued that humans can't be responsible for some crop circles because there are often no signs of human activity at formation sites (no footprints, paths through the grain, etc.). But as the circle-building of hoaxers suggests, crop circles can be produced by humans without leaving evidence of human activity behind. Hoaxers, for example, can often avoid leaving footprints in a grain field by walking along tramlines, the narrow footpaths created by farm machinery.

Humans can produce crop circles w/o leaving evidence behind...

Also, as suggested earlier, physical anomalies in crop-circle plants or soil do not prove that crop circles are made in any particular way. It's possible that anomalies are produced by the techniques used in human circle-making. Some have suggested, for example, that enlarged joints in grain stalks are the result of the bent stalks baking in the hot sun.

Anomalies in plants pose no problem for Theory Three

Step 4. Now let's see what happens when we apply the criteria of adequacy to these three theories. Theories 1 and 3 seem equal in terms of testability. Both predict something other than what they were introduced to explain. Theory 1, for example, predicts that in the creation of a crop circle, an electrified vortex forms above the formation area—something that should be detectable by the right kind of scientific instruments. Theory 3 is certainly testable because human activity is detectable and measurable. Theory 2 (aliens) may or may not be testable, depending on how alien activity is construed. We will give the theory the benefit of the doubt and say that it too is testable.

CRITERIA OF ADEQUACY

① Testability

Theories 1 and 2 are not fruitful, for they have yielded no surprising predictions. We could argue, though, that theory 3 is fruitful because the creation of specific crop circles at designated times and places has been successfully predicted by hoaxers (the ones who created the circles).

② Fruitfulness

In terms of scope, neither theory 1 nor 2 gets any points. The vortex theory does not explain anything other than the creation of crop circles. Theory 2 could be construed as explaining many things in which aliens are involved (UFO sightings, abductions, UFO crashes, etc.). But positing the existence of mysterious beings that act in mysterious ways for mysterious reasons does not seem to explain much of anything. Theory 3, on the other hand, can be used to explain many strange phenomena because humans, after all, are responsible for many hoaxes and bizarre happenings.

③ Scope
Human Hoax Theory can explain many things

As far as simplicity is concerned, theories 1 and 2 are in deep trouble. Like most paranormal explanations, they both posit the existence of unknown entities (charged, naturally occurring vortices and space aliens). Theory 3 sticks with known entities and processes.

④ Simplicity

On the criterion of conservatism, theories 1 and 2 are again in trouble. There is no good evidence that the hypothesized vortex has ever occurred anywhere. And we have no good reason to believe that either space aliens or

⑤ Conservatism

Eyewitness Testimony and Extraordinary Things

A great deal of the evidence for paranormal phenomena is eyewitness testimony. Unfortunately, research suggests that eyewitness testimony generally can't be trusted—especially when the testimony concerns the paranormal. For example, in some studies people who had participated in séances later gave wildly inaccurate descriptions of what had transpired. Researchers have found that people's beliefs and expectations seem to play a big role in the unreliability of testimony about the paranormal.

Different people clearly have different beliefs and expectations prior to observing a supposed psychic—skeptics might expect to see some kind of trickery; believers may expect a display of genuine psi [parapsychological phenomena]. Some seventy years ago Eric Dingwall in Britain speculated that such expectations may distort eyewitness testimony: The frame of mind in which a person goes to see magic and to a medium cannot be compared. In one case he goes either purely for amusement or possibly with the idea of discovering "how it was done," whilst in the other he usually goes with the thought that it is possible that he will come into direct contact with the other world.

Recent experimental evidence suggests that Dingwall's speculations are correct.

Wiseman and Morris in Britain carried out two studies investigating the effect that belief in the paranormal has on the observation of conjuring tricks. Individuals taking part in the experiment were first asked several questions concerning their belief in the paranormal. On the basis of their answers they were classified as either believers (labeled "sheep") or skeptics (labeled "goats").

In both experiments individuals were first shown a film containing fake psychic demonstrations. In the first demonstration the "psychic" apparently bent a key by concentrating on it; in the second demonstration he supposedly bent a spoon simply by rubbing it.

After they watched the film, witnesses were asked to rate the "paranormal" content of the demonstrations and complete a set of recall questions. Wiseman and Morris wanted to discover if, as Hodgson and Dingwall had suggested, sheep really did tend to misremember those parts of the demonstrations that were central to solving the tricks. For this reason, half of the questions concerned the methods used to fake the phenomena. For example, the psychic faked the key-bending demonstration by secretly switching the straight key for a pre-bent duplicate by passing the straight key from one hand to the other. During

▼

the switch the straight key could not be seen. This was clearly central to the trick's method; and one of the "important" questions asked was whether the straight key had always remained in sight. A second set of "unimportant" questions asked about parts of the demonstration that were not related to the tricks' methods. Overall, the results suggested that sheep rated the demonstrations as more "paranormal" than goats did, and that goats did indeed recall significantly more "important" information than sheep. There was no such difference for the recall of the "unimportant" information.[18]   ■

alien technology have ever visited Earth, let alone created some nice designs in a wheat field.

We can summarize these judgments as in the following table:

Criteria	Vortices	Aliens	Humans
Testable	Yes	Yes	Yes
Fruitful	No	No	Yes
Scope	No	No	Yes
Simple	No	No	Yes
Conservative	No	No	Yes

Summary

We can see immediately that the three theories are equal in testability, but theory 3 wins on all other counts. It is clearly the superior theory. Both the vortex theory and the alien theory fail the test of fruitfulness, scope, simplicity, and conservatism. Of these four criteria, simplicity and conservatism carry the most weight here. In general, the plausibility of a theory is weakened considerably when it posits unknown entities and processes. Likewise, a theory that doesn't fit with what we already know takes a hit in credibility. An unconservative theory, of course, can acquire some credibility if it excels in the other criteria of adequacy. But theories 1 and 2 fall short in all the criteria except testability. We can see then that theories 1 and 2 are not good explanations for crop circles. They are most likely false. Theory 3—human creation of crop circles—is a much better theory.

There are other crop-circle theories that we haven't examined. None of them seem to measure up to the criteria of adequacy as well as theory 3 does. If this is the case, then we can give an even stronger endorsement of theory 3: Crop circles are probably human-made.

Summary

TALKING WITH THE DEAD

Psychic John Edward.

Some people claim that they can communicate with the dead, providing impressive and seemingly accurate information about a person's dead loved ones. They are called psychics (a century ago they were called mediums), and they have gained the respect of many who have come to them in search of messages from the deceased. They are appearing on television programs, publishing books, and offering seminars to thousands. The most famous among these modern-day mediums are psychics James Van Praagh, Sylvia Browne, and John Edward. Their performances assure many people that their loved ones who "have passed over" are fine and that any unsettled issues of guilt and forgiveness can be resolved.

What is the best explanation for these otherworldly performances in which the psychics appear to be in contact with the dead? Several theories have been proposed. One is that the psychics are getting information about the dead and their loved ones ahead of time (before the performances begin). Another is that the psychics are using telepathy to read the minds of the living to discover facts about the dead. But for simplicity's sake let's narrow the list of theories down to the two leading ones.

Step 1. Here's the psychics' theory.

Theory 1: The psychics are communicating information or messages to and from the disembodied spirits of people who have died. In other words, the psychics are doing exactly what they claim to be doing. They are somehow identifying the appropriate deceased spirit, receiving and decoding transmissions from that spirit, conveying the information to the living, and sending messages back to the dead.

Step 2. The main evidence in support of this theory is the psychics' performance. They typically perform before an audience and talk to audience members who have lost loved ones. The psychics appear to know facts about the dead that they could only know if they were actually communicating with the dead. They also seem to inexplicably know things about members of the audience. Often they also provide incorrect information (such as saying that a member of the audience has lost her mother when in fact the mother is very much alive). But their "hits" (times when they produce correct information) occur often enough and seem to be specific enough to impress.

Psychics have rarely been tested scientifically. The few experiments conducted to date have been severely criticized for sloppy methodology. So there is no good scientific evidence to support theory 1. Investigators who have seen the psychics' live performances (not just the edited versions of the TV programs) report that the hit rates (the percentage of hits out of the total number

Ⓐ
Psychics' Theory

". . . we [psychics] are here to heal people and to help people grow . . . skeptics . . . they're just here to destroy people. They're not here to encourage people, to enlighten people. They're here to destroy people."

—JAMES VAN PRAAGH

Why People Believe Psychic Readings

Ray Hyman is professor emeritus of psychology at the University of Oregon and an expert on the scientific investigation of paranormal claims, including psychic readings. Years of research have led him to be skeptical of the validity of psychic readings, but he used to be a true believer. He explains why he went from believer to skeptic:

Now it so happens that I have devoted more than half a century to the study of psychic and cold readings. I have been especially concerned with why such readings can seem so concrete and compelling, even to skeptics. As a way to earn extra income, I began reading palms when I was in my teens. At first, I was skeptical. I thought that people believed in palmistry and other divination procedures because they could easily fit very general statements to their particular situation. To establish credibility with my clients, I read books on palmistry and gave readings according to the accepted interpretations for the lines, shape of the fingers, mounds, and other indicators. I was astonished by the reactions of my clients. My clients consistently praised me for my accuracy even when I told them very specific things about problems with their health and other personal matters. I even would get phone calls from clients telling me that a prediction that I had made for them had come true. Within months of my entry into palm reading, I became a staunch believer in its validity. My conviction was so strong that I convinced my skeptical high school English teacher by giving him readings and arguing with him. I later also convinced the head of the psychology department where I was an undergraduate.

When I was a sophomore, majoring in journalism, a well-known mentalist and trusted friend persuaded me to try an experiment in which I would deliberately read a client's hand opposite to what the signs in her hand indicated. I was shocked to discover that this client insisted that this was the most accurate reading she had ever experienced. As a result, I carried out more experiments with the same outcome. It dawned on me that something important was going on. Whatever it was, it had nothing to do with the lines in the hand. I changed my major from journalism to psychology so that I could learn why not only other people, but also I, could be so badly led astray. My subsequent career has focused on the reasons why cold readings can appear to be so compelling and seemingly specific.

"Death is a part of life, and pretending that the dead are gathering in a television studio in New York to talk twaddle with a former ballroom-dance instructor is an insult to the intelligence and humanity of the living."

—MICHAEL SHERMER

Psychologists have uncovered a number of factors that can make an ambiguous reading seem highly specific, unique, and uncannily accurate. And once the observer or client has been struck with the apparent accuracy of the reading, it becomes virtually impossible to dislodge the belief in the uniqueness and specificity of the reading. Research from many areas demonstrates this finding. The principles go under such names as the fallacy of personal validation, subjective validation, confirmation bias, belief perseverance, the illusion of invulnerability, compliance, demand characteristics, false uniqueness effect, foot-in-the-door phenomenon, illusory correlation, integrative agreements, self-reference effect, the principle of individuation, and many, many others. Much of this is facilitated by the illusion of specificity that surrounds language. All language is inherently ambiguous and depends much more than we realize upon the context and nonlinguistic cues to fix its meaning in a given situation.[19]

HEART

HEAD

LIFE

What is this palm saying? Psychologists think they know.

of statements or questions) are actually much lower than most people realize. They have found hit rates as low as 5 percent with the highest being well under 50 percent. The low hit rate, though, may not be apparent on TV shows because misses are often edited out. Psychics tend to explain their misses with ad hoc hypotheses (explanations that cannot be verified).

Step 3. Here's the main alternative to the psychics' theory.

Theory 2: The psychics are doing "cold reading." Cold reading is a very old skill practiced by fortune-tellers, tarot-card readers, and mentalists (performers who pretend to read minds). When done well, cold reading can astonish and appear to be paranormal. In cold reading, the psychic reader surreptitiously acquires information from people (the subjects) by asking them questions, making statements, observing how people behave, and listening to what they say. Good cold readers always give the impression that the information actually comes from some mysterious source such as the spirits of the departed. Anyone can learn to do cold reading. It doesn't require any exotic skills or special powers. All that's needed is the practiced ability to deftly manipulate a conversation to elicit information from the subject.

Ⓑ
Cold-Reading (312)

Note that theory 2 does not say that the cold reading is necessarily done to deliberately deceive an audience. Cold reading can be done either consciously or unconsciously. It's possible for people to do cold reading while believing that they are getting information via their psychic powers.

To get the relevant information (or appear to have it), a psychic reader can use several cold-reading techniques. These include the following.

1. The reader encourages the subject to fill in the blanks.

   READER: I'm sensing something about the face or head or brow.
   SUBJECT: You're right, my father used to have terrible headaches.

   READER: I'm feeling something about money or finances.
   SUBJECT: Yes, my mother always struggled to pay the bills.

2. The reader makes statements with multiple variables so that a hit is very likely.

"Ahh.. I see your future. Get up, go to work go to bed. Get up, go to work, go to bed. Get..."
www.CartoonStock.com

   READER: I'm feeling that your father was dealing with a lot of frustration, anguish, or anger.
   SUBJECT: Yes, he was always arguing with my brother.

3. The reader makes accurate and obvious inferences from information given by the subject.

   READER: Why was your father in the hospital?
   SUBJECT: He had had a heart attack.
   READER: Yes, he struggled with heart disease for years and had to take heart medication for a long time. You were really worried that he would have another heart attack.

4. The reader asks many questions and treats answers as though they confirmed the reader's insight.

   READER: Who was the person who got a divorce?
   SUBJECT: That was my daughter. She divorced her husband in 1992.
   READER: Because I feel that the divorce was very painful for her, that she was sad and depressed for a while.

5. The reader makes statements that could apply to almost anyone.

> READER: I'm sensing something about a cat or a small animal.
> SUBJECT: Yes, my mother owned a poodle.

With such cold-reading techniques a reader can appear to read minds. Theory 2 is bolstered by the fact that the psychics' amazing performances can be duplicated by anyone skilled in the use of cold reading. In fact, magicians, mentalists, and other nonpsychic entertainers have used cold-reading techniques to give performances that rival those of the top psychics. Regardless of their authenticity, the performances of Van Praagh, Edward, and other psychics seem to be indistinguishable from those based on cold reading. The psychics may indeed be communicating with the dead, but they look like they're using cold-reading techniques.

Step 4. Now we can apply the criteria of adequacy to these two competing explanations. Both theories are testable, and neither has yielded any novel predictions. So we must judge the theories in terms of scope, simplicity, and conservatism. And on each of these criteria, theory 2 is clearly superior. Theory 1 explains only the psychics' performances as described earlier, but theory 2 explains these performances plus other kinds of seemingly psychic readings, including tarot-card reading, fortune-telling, mentalist acts, and old-fashioned spiritualist séances. Theory 1, of course, fails the criterion of simplicity because it assumes unknown entities (disembodied spirits with certain abilities) and unknown processes (communication to and from the dead). Theory 2 makes no such assumptions. Finally, theory 1 is not conservative. It conflicts with everything we know about death, the mind, and communication. Theory 2, though, fits with existing knowledge just fine.

Here are these judgments in table form:

Criteria	Theory 1	Theory 2
Testable	Yes	Yes
Fruitful	No	No
Scope	No	Yes
Simple	No	Yes
Conservative	No	Yes

We must conclude that theory 1 is a seriously defective theory. It is unlikely to be true. Theory 2, however, is strong. It is not only superior to theory 1, but it is also a better explanation than other competing theories we haven't discussed in that it can explain most or all of the psychics' hits. If the cold-reading theory really is better than all these others, then we have good reasons to believe that Van Praagh, Edward, and other psychics perform their amazing feats through simple cold reading.

Exercise 10.7

1. Is it reasonable to accept or reject an extraordinary claim solely because of its weirdness?

2. According to a 2001 Gallup poll, what percentage of Americans believes in haunted houses?

3. Is it reasonable to conclude that a phenomenon is paranormal just because you cannot think of a natural explanation?

* 4. The fallacious leap to a nonnatural explanation is an example of what logical fallacy?

5. According to the text, what is the critical thinking principle that can help you avoid mistaking how something seems for how something is?

* 6. What is logical possibility? logical impossibility?

7. What is physical possibility? physical impossibility?

8. Are dogs that lay eggs logically possible?

9. Is anything possible? If not, why not?

10. What is the four-step method for evaluating a theory?

Exercise 10.8

In each of the following examples, a state of affairs is described. Devise three theories to explain each one. Include two plausible theories that are natural explanations and one competing theory that is paranormal.

1. Jack spent the night in a hotel that had a reputation for being haunted. He slept in the very room (number 666) in which a horrible murder had been committed in the 1930s. He fell asleep thinking about the crime. At 3:00 a.m. he awoke to see the apparition of a man sitting at the foot of his bed.

* 2. Jacques lived in a house built back in the 1940s which was now in disrepair. As he sat reading in the parlor, he heard creaking sounds coming from upstairs.

3. Selena found herself thinking about the camping trip that she went on in Pennsylvania. She was remembering the morning she woke up to find her tent crawling with ladybugs. As she was pondering the ladybugs, she suddenly noticed a ladybug on the windowsill near her chair.

4. Some people report that in the past when they needed help in a risky situation (for example, when they were in a car accident or when they were lost in a crime-ridden neighborhood), they were aided by a stranger who never gave his or her name and who left the scene quickly after rendering assistance. They claim that the stranger must have been their guardian angel.

5. According to a recent survey, 38 percent of Americans believe in ghosts or spirits of the dead.

6. Lil's horoscope said that she would meet someone interesting. Three days after reading it, she did.

* 7. Leroy dreamed that his uncle was killed in Iraq when he stepped on a land mine. When Leroy woke up, he got a call from his mother saying that his uncle had been injured in a car accident in Baghdad.

8. Eleanor has a reputation for acting strangely. Recently when her priest came to visit her in her home, she fell to the floor writhing with convulsions.

9. Nelly made a fresh batch of tortillas. On one of them she noticed that the scorch marks were unusual. She was sure that she could see the face of Jesus in the design made by the scorch marks.

10. Ali was not feeling well. He heard that a crazy woman in his village had put a curse on him because he called her a witch. The next day Ali broke his arm when he slipped and fell against some rocks.

Exercise 10.9

Using your background knowledge and any other information you may have about the subject, devise a competing, naturalistic theory for each paranormal theory that follows, and then apply the criteria of adequacy to both of them—that is, ascertain how well each theory does in relation to its competitor on the criteria of testability, fruitfulness, scope, simplicity, and conservatism.

1. Phenomenon: George and Jan have been married for twenty years. Many times George seems to know exactly what Jan is thinking, as though he could read her mind.
   Theory: George is telepathic.

2. Phenomenon: Yolanda awoke one morning and remembered having a strange dream. She dreamed that space aliens came into her bedroom while she was sleeping and abducted her. The dream seemed extremely vivid. Later in the day, she noticed some scratches on her ankle. She didn't know how they got there.
   Theory: Yolanda was abducted by aliens.

* 3. Phenomenon: In 1917 in Cottingley, England, three girls claimed to have taken photos of fairies who played with them in the garden. The photos showed the girls in the garden with what appeared to be tiny fairies dancing around them. (The 1997 movie *Fairy Tale* was about the girls and their story.)
   Theory: Fairies really do exist, and the girls photographed them.

4. Phenomenon: The Loch Ness monster is alleged to be a large aquatic creature that inhabits one of Scotland's lochs. The creature is unknown to science. People have been reporting sightings of Nessie for hundreds of years. There is no hard evidence proving the existence of the monster.
   Theory: The Loch Ness monster actually exists.

5. Phenomenon: The famous Israeli psychic Uri Geller seems to be able to bend spoons and keys with his mind. He has been performing this feat for

audiences for years. Magicians claim that Geller is a fraud and that they can also bend spoons and keys with simple sleight-of-hand magic tricks.
Theory: Geller's psychic powers enable him to bend metal with his mind.

6. Phenomenon: When there's a full moon people seem to act weird. All you have to do to confirm this is to go downtown and observe people when there's a full moon.
Theory: Through some unknown force, the moon exerts influence on people's behavior.

7. Phenomenon: Some people claim to be psychic detectives, psychics who help law enforcement agencies solve crimes. The psychics sometimes mention the police departments that they have assisted. This psychic detective work is hard to verify, and skeptics claim that either the psychics lie about their successes or they hit upon a solution to a crime by chance.
Theory: The psychic abilities of psychic detectives enable them to solve crimes.

Exercise 10.10

Read the following passages and answer these questions for each one:

1. What is the phenomenon being explained?
2. What theories—stated or implied—are used to explain the phenomenon?
3. Which theory seems the most plausible and why? (Base your judgment on the evidence cited in the passage as well as any other information you might have on the subject, and use the criteria of adequacy.)
4. What kind of evidence would convince you to change your mind about your preferred theory?

PASSAGE 1

"A Ouija board is used in divination and spiritualism. The board usually has the letters of the alphabet inscribed on it, along with words such as 'yes,' 'no,' 'good-bye' and 'maybe.' A planchette (a slidable 3-legged device) or pointer of some sort is manipulated by those using the board. The users ask the board a question and together or one of them singly moves the pointer or the board until a letter is 'selected' by the pointer. The selections 'spell' out an answer to the question asked.

"Some users believe that paranormal or supernatural forces are at work in spelling out Ouija board answers. Skeptics believe that those using the board either consciously or unconsciously select what is read. To prove this, simply try it blindfolded for some time, having an innocent bystander take notes on what letters are selected. Usually, the result will be unintelligible non-sense.

"The movement of the planchette is not due to paranormal forces but to unnoticeable movements by those controlling the pointer, known as the *ideomotor effect*. The same kind of unnoticeable movement is at work in dowsing.

"The Ouija board was first introduced to the American public in 1890 as a parlor game sold in novelty shops."[20]

PASSAGE 2

"Most scientists discount the existence of Bigfoot because the evidence supporting belief in the survival of a prehistoric bipedal apelike creature of such dimensions is scant. The only notable exception is Grover S. Krantz (1931–2002), an anthropologist at Washington State University. For nearly forty years, Krantz argued for the probable existence of Bigfoot, but was unable to convince the majority of scientists. The evidence for Bigfoot's existence consists mainly of testimony from Bigfoot enthusiasts, footprints of questionable origin, and pictures that could easily have been of apes or humans in ape suits. There are no bones, no scat, no artifacts, no dead bodies, no mothers with babies, no adolescents, no fur, no nothing. There is no evidence that any individual or community of such creatures dwells anywhere near any of the 'sightings.' In short, the evidence points more towards hoaxing and delusion than real discovery. Some believers dismiss all such criticism and claim that Bigfoot exists in another dimension and travels by astral projection. Such claims reinforce the skeptic's view that the Bigfoot legend is a function of passionate fans of the paranormal, aided greatly by the mass media's eagerness to cater to such enthusiasm."[21]

PASSAGE 3

"Trickery aside, what about reports of apparent animal ESP? Anecdotal evidence suggests some animals may have precognitive awareness of various types of natural catastrophes, becoming agitated before earthquakes, volcanic eruptions, cyclones, and other events. However, the creatures may actually be responding to subtle sensory factors—like variations in air pressure and tremors in the ground—that are beyond the range of human perception.

"Something of the sort may explain some instances of apparent animal prescience. For example, a Kentucky friend of mine insists that his dogs seem to know when he has decided to go hunting, exhibiting a marked excitement even though they are lodged some distance away from the house. However, it seems possible that they are either responding to some unintended signal (such as recognizing certain noises associated with his getting ready for a hunting trip) or that he is selectively remembering those occasions when the dogs' excitement happens to coincide with his intentions. Another friend says he once had dogs who seemed to know when he was going to take them for a walk, but he decided he must have unconsciously signaled them (such as by glancing in the direction of their hanging leashes)."[22]

PASSAGE 4

"Ever since humans gained the ability to look down at the Earth from airplanes, space shuttles, and satellites, we've discovered a number of unusual markings. We know very little about them. [There are some] mysterious lines that are found on the Nazca Desert of Peru. They stretch for several miles, crossing over cliffs and hills. A Swiss author named Erich von Daniken claims in his book, *Chariots of the Gods*, that these lines were made by aliens who visited the Earth long ago. A German scientist, Maria Reicher, says that von Daniken's idea is ridiculous, and she has her own theory. . . .

"Von Daniken claims that aliens landed in the Nazca Desert back when humans were still evolving from primitive beings. When the alien vehicles touched down, they gouged tracks into the desert plain. According to his theory, the ancient Nazcan natives would have believed that these lines were made by the 'fiery chariots of the sky gods.' They carefully preserved the tracks the 'gods' chariots' had made and even extended them in all directions.

"Maria Reicher believes that the Nazca lines were created by ancient Peruvians to form a kind of calendar. She found that the lines aren't formed by marks in the earth, but by dark, purplish rocks that form borders and rows. The Nazcan people separated these rocks, which litter the desert, from the yellowish sand. Ancient Peruvians depended on the annual spring rains for their very existence. Since they needed time to prepare their fields before rainy season began, they made a point of learning when the seasons changed. Reicher noticed that the lines of rocks point to a place on the horizon where the sun rose and set during the winter and summer solstice—the times when the seasons change. Her theory is that the Nazcans used these lines as a sort of grand astronomical calendar, to help them get ready for the all-important change of seasons."[23]

PASSAGE 5

The renowned prophet Michel Nostradamus (1503–1566) composed a thousand verses that foretold historical events. Here's proof. Verse XXVII reads like this:

> Underneath the cord, Guien struck from the sky,
> Near where is hid a great treasure,
> Which has been many years a gathering,
> Being found, he shall die, the eye put out by a spring.[24]

This is a clear reference to World War II. It means "paratroopers alight near the Nazi's plunder hoard and, captured, they are executed." Some people think that the verses are so vague that anyone can read anything they want into them. But they're not ambiguous at all.

Summary

- Science seeks knowledge and understanding of reality, and it does so through the formulation, testing, and evaluation of theories. Science is a way of searching for truth.
- Science is not a worldview, and we can't identify it with a particular ideology. Science is also not scientism—it is not the only way to acquire knowledge. It is, however, a highly reliable way of acquiring knowledge of empirical facts.

- The scientific method cannot be identified with any particular set of experimental or observational procedures. But it does involve several general steps: (1) identifying the problem, (2) devising a hypothesis, (3) deriving a test implication, (4) performing the test, and (5) accepting or rejecting the hypothesis.
- This kind of theory-testing is part of a broader effort to evaluate a theory against its competitors. This kind of evaluation always involves, implicitly or explicitly, the criteria of adequacy.
- Inference to the best explanation can be used to assess weird theories as well as more commonplace explanations in science and everyday life.
- When people try to evaluate extraordinary theories, they often make certain typical mistakes. They may believe that because they can't think of a natural explanation, a paranormal explanation must be correct. They may mistake what seems for what is, forgetting that we shouldn't accept the evidence provided by personal experience if we have good reason to doubt it. And they may not fully understand the concepts of logical and physical possibility.
- In both science and everyday life, the TEST formula enables us to fairly appraise the worth of all sorts of weird theories, including those about crop circles and communication with the dead, the two cases we examined in this chapter.

Field Problems

1. Find a controversial health or medical theory on the Internet and design a study to test it. Indicate the makeup and characteristics of any group in the study, whether a placebo group is used, whether the study is double-blind, and what study results would confirm and disconfirm the theory.

2. Find a controversial theory in the social sciences on the Internet and design a study to test it. Indicate the makeup and characteristics of any group in the study, whether a placebo group is used, whether the study is double-blind, and what study results would confirm and disconfirm the theory. If the theory is one that you strongly believe, indicate the kind and level of evidence that could convince you to change your mind about it.

3. Do research on the Internet to find information on spontaneous human combustion, the theory that a human body can catch on fire due to an unknown internal chemical or biological process. Apply the TEST formula to evaluate the theory. Consider at least one plausible alternative theory. Look for background information at The Skeptic's Dictionary (http://skepdic.com), the Committee for the Scientific Investigation of Claims of the Paranormal (CSICOP) (www.csicop.org), or *Skeptic Magazine* (www.skeptic.com).

Self-Assessment Quiz

Answers appear in "Answers to Self-Assessment Quizzes" (Appendix C).

1. What is a test implication?
2. Are hypotheses generated purely through induction? Why or why not?
3. When a test implication is disconfirmed, what conditional argument is exemplified?
4. When a test implication is confirmed, what conditional argument is exemplified?
5. Why can't scientific hypotheses be conclusively confirmed?
6. Why can't scientific hypotheses be conclusively disconfirmed?

For each of the following phenomena, devise a hypothesis to explain it and derive a test implication to test the hypothesis.

7. Automobile accidents on Blind Man's Curve have increased lately, especially since the street light was broken and not replaced.
8. Juan was found two hours after the fatal stabbing sitting in Central Park with blood on his shirt.
9. Mysterious lights appeared in the night sky. They looked like alien spacecraft.

For each of the following phenomena, indicate (1) a possible hypothesis to explain it, (2) a possible competing hypothesis, (3) a test implication for each hypothesis, and (4) what testing results would confirm and disconfirm the hypothesis.

10. While camping in the state park, Maria came down with a gastrointestinal illness.
11. The students who were put in a class with two teachers instead of one showed an improvement in their grades.
12. Public health officials report a significant increase in levels of stress in people who live or work in New York City.
13. Since the Vaughn family started using Super Cold-Stopper With Beta-Carotene they have suffered 50 percent fewer colds.

For each of the following hypotheses, specify a test implication and indicate what evidence would convince you to accept the hypothesis.

14. Esther stole the book from the library.
15. Most people—both white and black—are economically better off now than their parents were thirty years ago.
16. The health care system in this country is worse now than it was when Bill Clinton was president.

Each of the theories that follow is offered to explain why an astrological reading by a famous astrologer turned out to be wildly inaccurate. Based on a person's horoscope, he had predicted that the person was a nice man who could work with other people very well. The person turned out to be Josef Mengele, the Nazi mass murderer. Indicate which theory (a) lacks simplicity, (b) is not conservative, (c) is untestable, and (d) has the most scope. (Some theories may merit more than one of these designations.)

17. Theory: Astrology—the notion that the position of the stars and planets at your birth controls your destiny—has no basis in fact.

18. Theory: Astrology works, but the astrologer read the horoscope wrong.

19. Theory: An unknown planetary force interfered with the astrological factors that normally determine a person's destiny.

Evaluate the following theory using the TEST formula. Indicate what phenomenon is being explained. Use your background knowledge to assess the evidence. Specify one alternative theory, use the criteria of adequacy to assess the two theories, and determine which one is more plausible.

20. Joseph has acted strangely for years—always wearing black clothes and sometimes having seizures in public. He's possessed.

Integrative Exercises

These exercises pertain to material in Chapters 3–5 and 8–10.

1. What is an enumerative induction?

2. What is an analogical induction?

3. What is a necessary condition? a sufficient condition?

4. What is the appeal to ignorance?

For each of the following arguments, specify the conclusion and premises. If necessary, add implicit premises and conclusions.

5. "While the time may be right for more privacy in our bedrooms and civil rights protection for gays in the workplace, we don't think most people want our laws rewritten to accommodate same-sex marriage. Instead, they probably agree with Boston Globe columnist Jeff Jacoby, who wrote, 'Sometimes, change destroys. No structure can stand for long when its bearing wall is removed. The bearing wall of marriage—its central and universal characteristic—is its heterosexuality. Knock that down and what is left is ruin.'" [Editorial, *The Tribune-Star*, Terre Haute, IN]

6. "Today in Western New York, more than 46,000 people suffer from Alzheimer's disease or a related dementia. Without a research breakthrough or the development of new treatments in the next few years, 14 million baby boomers nationwide will be victims of the disease, and the cost of their care alone will bankrupt both Medicaid and Medicare. We urge voters to call their senators and representatives to ask them to

commit more funding for Alzheimer's research." [Letter to the editor, *Buffalo News*]

7. "OK, I've been shilly-shallying around here, hesitant to come right out and say what I think, but I'm becoming convinced that our president, the man with his finger on the nuclear trigger, is a bona fide nutcase. I really do. For him to say God told him to strike al-Qaida is just nutso. For him to say God told him to strike at Saddam, ditto. This guy is not dealing with a full deck." [Editorial, SFGate.com]

8. "As to his [Braxton's] reasoning that 'perhaps there is a public-health basis for anti-sodomy laws' since ' . . . scores of thousands of American homosexuals died from engaging in same sexual acts,' there is a bit of a problem. Since heterosexuals also have died from diseases that have directly resulted from sex, then, by Braxton's logic, the Supreme Court would have to ban heterosexual unions as well. With all the conservatives' carping about the intrusiveness of government, one would think that the elimination of laws concerning one's private life would be cause for celebration for a conservative like Braxton." [Letter to the editor, *Newsday*]

For each of the following phenomena, indicate (1) a possible hypothesis to explain it, (2) a possible competing hypothesis, and (3) a test implication for each hypothesis.

9. The accident rate on I-295 has been very high but was reduced considerably after the speed limit was lowered to 60 mph and billboards urged drivers to obey the law.

10. In stressful situations, women appear to adapt better and quicker to the emotional demands of the situation than men do.

11. The percentage of high school seniors engaging in sexual intercourse has risen dramatically in the past six years.

12. The mosquito population in the county has decreased drastically in the past year even though county workers have curtailed the use of insecticides and have stopped urging residents to get rid of standing water on their property, which is a breeding ground for the insects.

Evaluate each of the following theories and indicate whether it is plausible or implausible.

13. Treatment for HIV/AIDS is much more effective than it used to be because of global warming.

14. Six thousand years ago a worldwide flood devastated Earth, killing all but a handful of human beings who survived by building an ark.

15. The universe is so vast, with billions of stars that could have planets that will sustain life, that it is probable that intelligent life exists in other places besides Earth.

16. Transcendental meditation shows us that if enough people meditate together on the prevention of crime, the crime rate in an area will decrease.

Evaluate each of the following theories using the TEST formula. Use your background knowledge to assess the evidence. Specify one alternative theory, use the criteria of adequacy to assess the two theories, and determine which one is more plausible.

17. The United States lost the Vietnam War because the Americans' weapons were inferior to those of the North Vietnamese.

18. The federal deficit is astronomically high because of accounting errors.

19. The conflict between the Israelis and Palestinians is caused by the meddling of the United States and Britain.

20. Everyone who has ever beaten cancer—that is, been cured—has done so because of a wholesome diet.

 Writing Assignments

1. In a one-page essay evaluate the following theories using the TEST formula:
   a. **Phenomenon:** People report feeling less arthritis pain after taking fish oil capsules.
      Theory 1: Fish oil relieves joint pain.
      Theory 2: The placebo effect.
   b. **Phenomenon:** A temporary drop in the crime rate in Des Moines, Iowa, just after a transcendental meditation (TM) group meditated for three days on a lower crime rate.
      Theory 1: TM meditation lowers crime rates.
      Theory 2: Normal fluctuations in Des Moines crime rate.
   c. **Phenomenon:** Fifty patients with severe arthritis pain were prayed for by one hundred people, and twenty-five out of those fifty patients reported a significant lessening of pain.
      Theory 1: Prayer heals.
      Theory 2: Normal pain remission that is characteristic of arthritis.

2. Read Essay 9 ("The Demon-Haunted Sentence: A Skeptical Analysis of Reverse Speech") in Appendix A and write a two-page report in which you craft a succinct statement of the reverse-speech hypothesis, derive a test implication from it, and explain in detail how such a test should be carried out. Include discussion of procedures required to guard against participants cheating during the experiment.

3. Devise two theories to explain the low test scores of most of the students in your calculus course, and then write a two-page paper evaluating the worth of the two theories.

4. Rewrite Essay 10 ("Amityville: The Horror of It All") in Appendix A so that it makes more explicit use of the TEST formula, identifying the phenomenon to be explained and the theories offered to explain it.

5. Write a paper to rebut the argument in Essay 19 ("Freedom of Expression: Policy Reflects Common Sense"). Use at least one argument that is *not* used in Essay 18 ("Freedom of Expression: Protect Student Speech—Even 'Unwise' Bong Banner").

Judging Moral Arguments and Theories

CHAPTER OBJECTIVES

MORAL ARGUMENTS

- Understand the distinction between moral statements, arguments, and theories.
- Learn the difference between moral and nonmoral statements.
- Be familiar with the structure of moral arguments.
- Know the reason why a moral argument requires at least one moral premise.
- Know how to supply the missing moral premise in a moral argument.
- Know how to use the counterexample method to evaluate moral premises.

MORAL PREMISES

- Be able to define moral principle, moral theory, and considered moral judgment.
- Understand how moral premises can be supported or undermined by moral principles, moral theories, and considered moral judgments.
- Know how to use the counterexample method to assess a moral premise.

MORAL THEORIES

- Recognize the differences among moral judgments, principles, and theories.
- Recognize that everyone has a moral theory and that it's important to ensure that your moral theory is coherent.
- Understand the similarities between moral theories and scientific theories.
- Know the three moral criteria of adequacy.
- Know how to apply the moral criteria of adequacy to moral theories.

A COHERENT WORLDVIEW

- Understand what a worldview is and why having a coherent worldview is so important.
- Understand how a worldview can fail to be coherent.
- Know how and why the criterion of internal consistency is applied to worldviews.

W E HAVE COME FAR. WE HAVE SEEN THAT WE CAN PRODUCTIVELY apply critical thinking to everyday claims, arguments, and problems; to explanations in a wide range of subject areas; to scientific theories of all sorts; and to offbeat theories of the paranormal and supernatural kind. Now we can go even further. We can now venture into a vast and complex sphere that is often thought to be off limits to critical reasoning: *morality*. Morality concerns beliefs about right and wrong, good and bad, and just and unjust. It's an aspect of life that we deal with every day because we have little choice. In countless situations we must decide what we ought to do or not do, what is moral or immoral, and what is good or bad. To do these things, we are forced to accept or reject moral statements, make and criticize moral arguments, and wrestle with moral theories.

In this process of contending with moral issues, we inevitably formulate our own moral theory—our own beliefs about what morality is or is not, what actions are right or wrong, and what things are good or bad. To an astonishing degree, our moral theory charts the course of our lives. If the course matters, then we must try to fashion the best moral theory we can.

If we are to be intellectually mature, we also must try to integrate the results of these moral analyses and deliberations into a comprehensive picture of reality, what is known as a worldview. A **worldview** is a philosophy of life, a set of beliefs and theories that helps us make sense of a wide range of issues in life. It defines for us what exists, what should be, and what we can know. We all have a worldview, and our notions about morality are an important part of it. A good critical thinker tries to ensure that his or her worldview contains no internal contradictions and that it offers reliable guidance in dealing with the world.

So in this chapter, we set out to apply critical thinking to some big ideas and broad questions. We explore procedures for evaluating moral discourse—specifically, moral judgments, principles, arguments, and theories—and look at ways that we can incorporate our understanding into a coherent worldview.

Moral Arguments

A moral argument, like any other kind of argument, has premises and a conclusion. The premises (and sometimes the conclusion) may be implied, not stated,

"A system of morality which is based on relative emotional values is a mere illusion, a thoroughly vulgar conception which has nothing sound in it and nothing true."

—SOCRATES

Emotivism: the theory
that moral claims are not
statements, i.e. have no
truth value, but are simply
expressions of emotion

Criticisms
① If emotivism were true,
then there would be no
moral disagreements
② If emotivism were true,
then nothing would be
right or wrong...

FURTHER THOUGHT

Is Moral Reasoning Possible?

Some people claim that reasoning about morality is not possible because moral statements are not statements at all. This view is a moral theory known as *emotivism*. Emotivism says that moral statements are just not the kinds of things that can be true or false. They are more like exclamations such as "Hooray!" or "Bah!" They are expressions of emotion, not statements of fact. So according to emotivism, the sentence "Capital punishment is wrong" means something like "Capital punishment—boo!"

But this theory has been severely criticized by moral philosophers. They contend, for example, that in several ways the theory conflicts with our experience of the moral life. Our everyday moral experience seems to suggest that we sometimes have moral disagreements with others. The notion that we do have disagreements seems to most people like a simple matter of common sense. But according to emotivism, moral disagreements are impossible. Since moral utterances are not statements, they cannot contradict one another. If you say "ice cream—yes!" and someone else says "ice cream—yuk!" the two of you are not disagreeing; you're just venting. But our moral experience seems to show that in moral disagreements we are doing much more than expressing emotion. In addition, emotivism says that nothing is good or bad, right or wrong, because these terms don't refer to anything. But our moral experience appears to suggest that some things really are good or bad, right or wrong. Many moral philosophers believe that these considerations show that emotivism must be mistaken.

Critics who take this line of argument against emotivism admit that our commonsense moral experience may be misleading. It's possible that emotivism is correct after all. Commonsense views of the world have been wrong in the past. But, these critics assert, we are justified in believing what common sense tells us unless we have good reason to doubt it.

Conclusion of a moral
argument is a moral
statement...

① Moral Statements:
assert that an action
is right or wrong or
that something is
either good or bad...
a) forbidden
b) permissable
c) obligatory

and they may be simple or complex—just as in other arguments. Moral arguments, however, differ from nonmoral ones in that their conclusions are moral statements. In general, a **moral statement** is a statement asserting that an action is right or wrong (moral or immoral) or that something (such as a person or motive) is good or bad. Here are some moral statements:

• Serena should keep her promise to you.
• It is wrong to treat James so harshly.
• Abortion is immoral.
• We ought to protect Liu from the angry mob.
• My father is a good man.

Moral statements are plainly different from nonmoral, or descriptive, statements. Nonmoral statements do not assert that something is right or wrong, good or bad—they simply describe a state of affairs without giving it a value one way or the other. Compare these nonmoral statements with the moral statements just given:

- Serena did not keep her promise to you.
- James was treated harshly.
- Some people think abortion is immoral.
- Liu was protected from the angry mob.
- My father tried to be a good man.

The standard moral argument is a mixture of moral and nonmoral statements. At least one premise is a moral statement that asserts a general moral principle or moral standard. At least one premise makes a nonmoral claim. And the conclusion is a moral statement, or judgment, about a particular case (usually a particular kind of action). For example:

Argument 1

(1) It is wrong to inflict unnecessary pain on a child.
(2) Spanking inflicts unnecessary pain on a child.
(3) Therefore, spanking is wrong.

In this simple argument, premise 1 is a moral statement, affirming a general moral principle. Premise 2 is a nonmoral statement describing the nature of a specific kind of action. And the conclusion is the moral statement that the argument is intended to establish. It is about a specific kind of action.

A standard moral argument has this form for good reason. In a moral argument, we simply cannot establish the conclusion (a moral statement) without a moral premise. A moral argument with only nonmoral premises does not work.

FURTHER THOUGHT

Moral and Nonmoral Statements

Is this a moral statement: "I am opposed to abortion"? How about this one: "I feel very strongly that abortion is wrong"? Actually in many contexts, statements like these are not meant to be moral statements at all; they are not meant to assert that an action is right or wrong or that a person is good or bad. They are used instead to report on someone's state of mind. Saying that you feel a certain way toward an action is not the same thing as stating that the action is wrong. But be careful. Sometimes statements like these really are meant as moral statements. Context will usually tell you which kind of statement is intended.

Handwritten margin notes:

② Non-Moral Statements: are descriptive statements

In a moral argument at least one premise contains a moral claim and at least one premise contains a non-moral claim...

Is/Ought
Hume claims that you cannot derive a moral statement (ought) from a non-moral statement (is)

The premises of a moral argument must contain a moral statement...

We need to distinguish:
① asserting moral statements
② reporting one's beliefs

[Margin note: A non-argument with only non-moral premises is an invalid argument]

To put it another way, we cannot infer what *should be* or *ought to be* (in the conclusion) from statements about *what is*. Suppose the previous argument reads like this (and there are no missing premises):

> *Spanking inflicts unnecessary pain on a child.*
> *Therefore, spanking is wrong.*

The premise doesn't say anything about right or wrong; it just makes a descriptive claim. The conclusion, though, does assert something about right or wrong. So the conclusion is not supported by the premise; it does not follow from the descriptive statement.

Here's another example:

[Margin note: EXAMPLE ① Moral arguments require a moral premises...]

> *Torturing prisoners of war is a case of intentional mistreatment.*
> *Prisoners of war should not be tortured.*

This argument fails because the moral premise is missing. We need a moral premise to connect the nonmoral premise to the conclusion, like this:

Argument 2
No prisoner of war should ever be intentionally mistreated.
Torturing prisoners of war is a case of intentional mistreatment.
Prisoners of war should not be tortured.

FURTHER THOUGHT

Can't We All Just Get Along?

Despite the prevalence of moral disagreements on countless issues, there is a surprising amount of agreement on basic moral principles. Often, the bone of contention in moral arguments is not the moral premises (which may be widely accepted), but the nonmoral ones. In debates about "pulling the plug" on severely comatose patients, for example, all parties may agree that murder is wrong but disagree about the nature of comatose patients. Some may insist that comatose patients are entities that can be murdered (because they are fully human, true persons, etc.); others, that comatose patients are not the kind of entities that can be murdered (because they are not persons, for example). So there may not be as much moral disagreement in the world as you might think. Here's a list of moral principles that both parties in moral debates often accept:

[Margin note: IMPORTANT! In many cases moral disagreements are not about the moral premises but about the non-moral statements...]

- **Personal benefit:** Acknowledge the extent to which an action produces beneficial consequences for the individual in question.
- **Principle of benevolence:** Help those in need.

- **Principle of harm:** Do not harm others.
- **Principle of honesty:** Do not deceive others.
- **Principle of lawfulness:** Do not violate the law.
- **Principle of autonomy:** Acknowledge a person's freedom over his/her actions or physical body.
- **Principle of justice:** Acknowledge a person's right to due process, fair compensation for harm done, and fair distribution of benefits.
- **Rights:** Acknowledge a person's rights to life, information, privacy, free expression, and safety.[1]   ■

In the standard moral argument, we also need a nonmoral premise. Remember that the conclusion is a moral statement (judgment) about a particular kind of action. The moral premise, however, is a statement expressing a general moral principle about a much broader class of actions. In order to infer the narrower conclusion from a much broader premise, we need a nonmoral statement to bridge the gap. For example, from the general moral principle that "no prisoner of war should ever be intentionally mistreated," we cannot conclude that "prisoners of war should not be tortured" unless there is a nonmoral premise stating that torturing prisoners of war is a type of intentional mistreatment. Likewise from the general moral principle that "murder is wrong," we cannot conclude that "abortion is wrong" unless there's a factual premise telling us that abortion is murder.

Now, very often when you encounter moral arguments, they are abbreviated and missing the moral premise (the general moral principle), like the arguments discussed earlier:

> *Spanking inflicts unnecessary pain on a child.*
> *Therefore, spanking is wrong.*

> *Torturing prisoners of war is a case of intentional mistreatment.*
> *Prisoners of war should not be tortured.*

Usually, the moral premise is missing because it's implicit. In such cases, to make sense of the argument, you must supply the implicit premise. Sometimes you may automatically add the implicit premise in your head without bothering to properly fill out the argument. But if you want to carefully evaluate moral arguments, it's best to spell out any missing premises. Implicit moral premises are often dubious and need to be studied closely. General moral principles that are taken for granted may turn out to be unfounded or incomplete. Also, laying everything out on the table like this is essential if you want to improve the argument—an important exercise if you care that your positions on moral issues are well supported.

The simplest approach to identifying implicit premises is to treat moral arguments as deductive. (Notice that arguments 1 and 2 are valid deductive

"Do everything ethically ... within reason, of course."

www.CartoonStock.com

arguments.) Your task, then, is to supply plausible premises that will make the argument valid. (We used this same procedure in Chapter 3 for finding implicit premises.) Consider this argument:

Cloning humans is unnatural.
Therefore, cloning humans is morally wrong.

As it stands, this argument is not valid, and we can see right away that the missing premise is a general moral principle. A plausible premise to make this argument valid, then, is "Anything unnatural is morally wrong," a general moral principle. The revised version is:

EXAMPLE I

Argument 3
Anything unnatural is morally wrong.
Cloning humans is unnatural.
Therefore, cloning humans is morally wrong.

Here's another incomplete argument:

Meg lied to her sister for no good reason.
Therefore, Meg should not have lied to her sister.

EXAMPLE II

To make this argument valid and to supply a general moral principle, we can add this premise:

Argument 4
One should not lie without good reason.
Meg lied to her sister for no good reason.
Therefore, Meg should not have lied to her sister.

"So, if we can support our [moral] judgments with good reasons, and provide explanations of why these reasons matter, and show that the case on the other side is weak, what more in the way of 'proof' could anyone possibly want?"
—JAMES RACHELS

Another advantage to treating moral arguments as deductive (and to supplying explicit premises that will make the arguments valid) is ease of analysis. Generally, moral arguments are easier to appraise and modify when they are deductive. And if they are deductively valid, you know that any flaws in the arguments will likely be the result of false premises. For example, if you have a deductively valid argument, and the conclusion is false, you know that at least one of the premises is false.

Often the problematic premise is the missing premise...

Moral Premises

In good arguments the inferences are valid or strong and the premises—whether nonmoral or moral—are true. This latter stipulation means that to make good arguments, you must ensure that the premises are backed by good reasons and are not simply assumed without warrant. To evaluate arguments, you must check the premises for these same qualities. As noted in previous chapters, accurately assessing the truth of nonmoral premises depends mostly on your knowledge of the subject matter, including the results of relevant scientific research, the analyses of reliable experts, and the content of your background information. Gauging the truth of moral premises (moral principles) mostly involves examining the support they get from three sources: (1) other moral principles, (2) moral theories, and (3) considered moral judgments.

The appeal to another moral principle (usually a more general or higher-level principle) is probably the most common way to support a moral premise. Often the more general principle is extremely credible or accepted by all parties so that further support for it is unnecessary. Sometimes it is controversial so that it too is in need of support. Suppose the moral premise in question is, "A dying patient in intolerable and untreatable pain should be allowed to commit suicide with a physician's help." Some would say that this claim is derived from, or is based on, the higher (and more widely accepted) principle of autonomy—the notion that a person has an inherent right of self-determination, a right to make autonomous choices about his or her own life and death. Others would support the premise by appealing to the principle of beneficence, or mercy: If we are in a position to relieve the severe suffering of another without excessive cost to ourselves, we have a duty to do so. They would interpret this principle as sanctioning the physician's role in helping a competent, hopelessly ill patient to die. To try to show that the premise is false, someone might appeal to a sanctity-of-life principle, asserting that human life is sacred and should be preserved at all costs. When such higher principles are brought in, the truth of the original premise often becomes clear—or not. They cannot be the court of final appeal in ethics, for they too can be tested by reasoned argument showing why they should or should not be believed.

Reasons for accepting or rejecting a moral premise can also come from a moral theory, a general explanation of what makes an action right or what makes a person or motive good (see the next section). For example, traditional utilitarianism is a moral theory asserting that

"BUT ISN'T IT MORE IMPORTANT to LEARN How to BE A DECENT HUMAN BEING?"

www.CartoonStock.com

[Handwritten margin notes:]

Truth of Moral Premises
(A) Other moral principles
(B) Moral theories
(C) Considered moral judgments

(A)
Appeal to Other Moral Principles

A dying patient in intolerable and untreatable pain should be allowed to commit suicide w/ a physician's help
① Principle of autonomy
② Principle of beneficence

To show principle is false one might appeal to the sanctity of life principle.

Ⓑ
Appeal to Moral Theories
① Utilitarianism
② Kantian Moral Theory

Ⓒ
Considered Moral Judgments

Appeal to moral common sense

We can assess a moral principle the same way we would assess any other universal generalization: look for a counterexample

Premise 2 is questionable because it would rule out the use of antibiotics

right actions are those that produce the greatest happiness for all concerned. To support the assisted suicide premise, you could appeal to the theory, arguing that the least amount of unhappiness (pain and suffering) for all concerned (patient, physician, and family) would result if the physician helped the patient die. To counter your argument, someone would need to show that your happiness calculations were incorrect (for example, that assisted suicide actually causes more unhappiness in the long run), or that utilitarianism itself is an inadequate theory, or that other theories or considerations are more important or relevant than utilitarian factors.

A moral premise can also be supported or undermined by our *considered moral judgments*. These are moral judgments that we consider credible after we carefully and dispassionately reflect on them. Pertaining to either specific cases or general statements, they constitute what philosophers have called our moral common sense. They are not infallible guides to morality, but unless we have good reasons for doubting their soundness, we are entitled to trust them. Some of our considered judgments may seem undeniable, even self-evident—for example: "Inflicting unnecessary, undeserved suffering on someone is wrong"; "Torturing children for the fun of it is immoral"; "Treating people harshly merely because of the color of their skin is unjust."

Moral principles, theories, and judgments relate to one another in interesting ways (a topic we explore in the following pages). For now, it's enough to note that we can evaluate moral premises by seeing if they conflict with principles, theories, or judgments that we have good reason to trust. Specifically, we can assess a moral premise the same way we might assess any other kind of universal generalization—by trying to think of counterexamples to it. Consider this deductively valid argument, a modified version of argument 3:

Argument 5

(1) *The medical cloning of humans is unnatural because it is something that would not occur without human intervention.*

(2) *All actions that are unnatural and that are not done for religious reasons should not be done.*

(3) *The medical cloning of humans is never done for religious reasons.*

(4) *Therefore, cloning humans should not be done.*

Premise 2 is the general moral principle here. Is it true? At the very least it is questionable. We know that it's questionable because we can think of counterexamples to it. That is, we can think of instances in which the principle seems not to hold. For example, what about the use of antibiotics to treat infections? The use of antibiotics is unnatural as defined in the argument (they are a good example of human intervention in the natural course of illness), and few would claim that antibiotics are employed for religious reasons. (The term "for religious reasons" is vague, but we will assume for the sake of this example that it means something like "as an integral part of established religious practice.") But despite its unnaturalness, the use of antibiotics seems to be morally acceptable to almost everyone. At any rate, it is difficult to imagine what a plausible argument against antibiotics would be like. So premise 2 appears to be false. We could probably refute premise 2 by using many other counterexamples, such as wearing clothes, drinking bottled water, and riding a bicycle.

NB: Non-moral premises cannot also be false...

Moral Theories

Very often when we assess moral arguments and in other ways think critically about morality, we are trying to come to a moral judgment about a particular issue or kind of action. We deliberate because we want to understand what's right or wrong, good or bad. Our moral judgments may appear as premises or conclusions in our arguments or as sturdy pillars of our moral common sense. They may be justified by appeals to general moral principles, which in turn may gain credibility from the most reliable of our moral judgments. But what of moral theories? In the previous section we saw how a moral theory can strengthen or weaken a moral premise. Yet that's only part of the story.

As we have seen, theories of morality are attempts to explain what makes an action right or what makes a person or motive good. They try to specify what all right actions and all good things have in common. As such, they can give support, guidance, or validation to our moral decision making, shaping our moral principles, judgments, and arguments. Traditional utilitarianism (mentioned earlier) is a well-known example of a moral theory. Another is the divine command theory, the view that what makes an action right is that God commands it or wills it. Ethical egoism asserts that right actions are those that promote one's own best interests.

Interestingly enough, we all have a moral theory. Whether we articulate it or not, we all have some kind of view of what makes actions right or persons good. Even the notion that there is no such thing as right or wrong is a moral theory. Even the idea that all moral theories are worthless or that all moral judgments are subjective, objective, relative, or meaningless is a moral theory. The critical question, then, is not whether you have a moral theory but whether the theory you have is a good one.

We all have a moral theory

Moral theorizing is a fact of the moral life. We do moral theorizing when we ponder what rightness or goodness means, or try to furnish basic justification for a moral standard, or resolve a conflict between principles, or gauge the credibility of moral intuitions, or explain why an action is right or wrong. To theorize is to step back from the specifics of a case and try to see the larger pattern that can help us make sense of it all.

Moral theorizing is a fact of the moral life...

Despite the importance of moral theories, they are not the ultimate authority or sole referee in moral reasoning. A theory gives us very general norms, but morality is about more than just generalities—it's also about the particulars of individual moral judgments. How do the general and the particular fit together?

How do the general and the particular fit together?

"In my view moral theorizing is something that real people do in everyday life. It is not just the domain of professors, expounding in their lecture halls. Moral theorizing can be found on the highways and byways, practiced by everyone from bartenders to politicians."

—DALE JAMIESON

Here is one way. Suppose you must decide whether an action is morally permissible. From a plausible moral theory, you draw general guidance in the form of moral principles that apply to the case. If the principles appear to sanction conflicting decisions, you turn again to the theory for understanding in how to resolve the inconsistency. At the same time you consult your considered moral judgments. If your theory and your considered judgments lead you to the same conclusion, you have good reason to believe that the conclusion is correct. If your theory and considered judgments diverge, you must decide which is more credible. If the implications of your theory seem more plausible, you may decide to revise your considered judgments to cohere better with the theory. If your judgments seem more plausible, you may decide to alter your theory accordingly. If your credible judgments conflict drastically with your theory, you may be justified in giving up the theory altogether.

EVALUATING MORAL THEORIES

As you may have gathered, several moral theories vie for our allegiance, each one with a distinctive take on morality and with different implications for

---

FURTHER THOUGHT

Critiquing Moral Theories

Most moral philosophers don't buy the idea that one moral theory is as good as any other. They spend a good deal of time evaluating moral theories to gauge their worth, and some theories don't fare very well under this scrutiny. Here, for example, are some typical criticisms of three controversial moral theories.

SUBJECTIVE RELATIVISM

This view states that what makes an action right for someone is that it is approved by that person. Moral judgments are relative to what each person believes. If you say that stealing is wrong, then it's wrong (for you). If someone else says that stealing is right, then it's right (for her). Moral philosophers, though, think that the theory has several problematic implications. For example, the theory implies that each person is morally infallible. If you truly approve of an action, then it's right, and you cannot be wrong. Subjective relativism also makes moral disagreement nearly impossible. You disagree with others when you think they are mistaken. But according to subjective relativism, no one could be mistaken. These and other implications, critics say, render the theory implausible.

CULTURAL RELATIVISM

This view claims that what makes an action right is that it's approved by one's culture. If your culture deems something to be right, it's right. Moral truth is relative to cultures. As you might expect, this view is criticized for many of the same problems that plague subjective relativism. It implies that cultures are infallible. This means that if most people living in Nazi Germany during World War II had approved of the extermination of the Jews, then the Holocaust was morally right. It seems, though, that societies are no more infallible than individuals are. What's more, cultural relativism implies that it would be impossible to disagree with one's culture and be right. Social reformers such as Martin Luther King, Jr., or Gandhi could not claim that an action approved by society is wrong, for if society approves of it, the action is right. For these and other reasons, most moral philosophers view cultural relativism as a questionable moral theory.

ETHICAL EGOISM

In this view, what makes an action right is that it promotes one's own best interests. It doesn't imply that you should do anything you want because, in the long run, that may not be in your own best interest. Ethical egoism could even condone altruism on the grounds that being nice to other people is in your best interest. Critics, however, say that the theory is implausible because it sanctions all sorts of abominable acts. For example, if it's in your best interest to kill your boss, and if you could do it without suffering any negative consequences (such as getting caught), then ethical egoism says that your moral duty is to kill him. ∎

moral issues. Moral philosophers remind us that theories also differ in quality: All moral theories are not created equal. Some theories are better than others. This fact immediately prompts two questions: Which moral theory is best, and how can we judge that it is the best? Recall that we asked this type of question in Chapters 9 and 10 when we discussed inference to the best explanation and several types of theories (everyday, scientific, and weird). The answer in this chapter is the same as the answer in those chapters: To identify the best theory, we must compare competing theories and use the criteria of adequacy to appraise their worth. The criteria of adequacy that we use in judging moral theories are a little different from those we use to assess other types of theories, though the two sets of criteria have much in common. In significant ways, too, moral theories are much like scientific theories, and the process of theory evaluation is similar in both cases.

How are moral theories like scientific theories? Recall that scientific theories try to explain the causes of events, everything from tumor growth to exploding

[handwritten margin note: We judge moral theories by appealing to criteria of adequacy]

Moral Theories attempt to explain what makes an action right or what makes a person good...

Plausible moral theory must be consistent with the data: our considered moral judgments

Criterion 1: Consistency with considered moral judgments

Reflective Equilibrium

Criterion 2: Consistency with our experience of the moral life
1) making moral judgments
2) having moral disagreements
3) sometimes acting immorally

stars. A plausible scientific theory is one that's consistent with all the relevant data. A theory explaining the cause of a fatal illness, for example, must take into account facts about patient symptoms, medical test results, medical histories, environmental factors, and more. Moral theories, on the other hand, try to explain what makes an action right or what makes a person good. A plausible moral theory must also be consistent with the relevant data. The data that moral theories try to explain are our considered moral judgments, the moral judgments we accept after we reason about them carefully. Any plausible moral theory must be consistent with those considered moral judgments. As we have seen, they are fallible and revisable, but we are entitled to believe them unless we have good reason to doubt them. If a moral theory is seriously inconsistent with them—if, for example, it approves of obviously immoral acts (such as inflicting pain on innocent children for no good reason or treating equals unequally)—it is dubious, perhaps even fatally flawed, and deserving of radical revision or rejection. So the first criterion of adequacy for moral theories is: *consistency with considered moral judgments.*

In science (and many other fields of inquiry) there is an interesting relationship between theory and data. The data have an impact on the theory because the theory explains the data. A good theory, on the other hand, can lead scientists to reject certain data. Scientists want the data and theory to match up as closely as possible. They want the match to be so close that significant changes in either the data or theory aren't necessary. Moral theories work this way too. As suggested earlier, our moral data (our considered moral judgments) influence our moral theory. And our moral theory can lead us to accept or reject certain data. Ideally, we want the fit between data and theory to be as close as possible. In other words, we want to achieve what moral philosophers refer to as a "reflective equilibrium" between facts and theory. We want the fit to be so close that significant adjustments in either data or theory are not necessary.

In addition to being consistent with the data, a plausible scientific theory must also be conservative. It must be consistent with background information—that is, with well-founded beliefs such as reliable scientific findings and well-established theories. Plausible moral theories must also be consistent with the relevant background information—that is, with our experience of the moral life. Whatever else our moral experience involves, it certainly includes (1) making moral judgments (we do this constantly), (2) having moral disagreements (we occasionally do this), and (3) sometimes acting immorally (we recognize that we are not morally perfect). If a moral theory suggests that we do not have these experiences, we must view the theory with suspicion. Another criterion of adequacy for moral theories, then, is *consistency with our experience of the moral life.*

Now, it's possible that our experience of the moral life is an illusion, only seeming to involve making moral judgments, having moral disagreements, and getting into moral disagreements. But unless we have good reason to believe that our moral experience is an illusion, we are justified in accepting it at face value.

A scientific theory gains in credibility if it helps to solve problems (has fruitfulness and scope). A plausible moral theory must also help to solve problems. That is, it must help us make moral decisions, especially those that involve moral dilemmas, instances where moral principles or moral judgments are in conflict. After all, the reason we want a moral theory is that it helps guide our actions and reconcile clashing moral beliefs. A moral theory that offers no help with such moral problems is said to be *unworkable*. Unworkable moral theories are inferior. So a final criterion of adequacy for moral theories is *workability in real-life situations*.

Criterion 3: Workability in real-life situations...

REVIEW NOTES

☑ Moral Criteria of Adequacy

1. Consistency with our considered moral judgments
2. Consistency with our experience of the moral life
3. Workability in real-life situations

TWO IMPORTANT THEORIES

Now let's see how we can use these criteria to take the measure of two fundamentally different theories: traditional utilitarianism and Kantian ethics.

Traditional utilitarianism was founded by Jeremy Bentham (1748–1832) and later refined by John Stuart Mill (1806–1873). Bentham's idea was that right actions are those that achieve the greatest happiness for the greatest number. He declared that by this simple standard all actions could be judged. Many people embraced the theory, for it seemed so much more rational than moral theories of the time, which often rested on dubious assumptions. In the nineteenth century, traditional utilitarianism inspired reformers who worked to abolish slavery, eliminate child labor, and increase recognition of women's rights.

① UTILITARIANISM
Jeremy Bentham (1748–1832)
J.S. Mill (1806–1873)

To be more precise, traditional utilitarianism says that what makes an action right is that it maximizes overall happiness, everyone considered. Acting morally in any given situation, then, involves calculating how much happiness can be produced by several possible actions, identifying the persons who will be affected by those actions, and opting for the one action that produces the greatest amount of happiness in the world. Notice that what matters in utilitarianism is the *consequences* of an action—not whether the action breaks a rule or violates some abstract principle. If happiness is maximized by a particular action, then the action is morally right, regardless of any other considerations. By the lights of utilitarianism, the end justifies the means.

Right action: one that maximizes overall happiness, everyone considered...
① How much happiness is produced by possible actions?
② Who will be affected by those actions?
③ Choose action that will result in greatest happiness.

CRITERIA OF ADEQUACY

① *It meets Criterion 2*

② *Critics point out it seems*
   to fail Criterion 3

How does traditional utilitarianism fare when judged by the moral criteria of adequacy? For starters, the theory does seem to be consistent with key aspects of our experience of the moral life. The theory assumes that we can and do make moral judgments, have moral disagreements, and act immorally.

Some critics, however, have questioned whether traditional utilitarianism is a workable theory because calculating amounts of happiness seems to be extremely difficult or impossible. For example, each action we perform has consequences in-

" NEWSMAKERS "

Relativism and Honor Killings

In recent years, stories like this one have been appearing in the news with shocking frequency:

> Fawaz later recalled that his wife, Zahra, was sleeping soundly on her side and curled slightly against the pillow when he rose at dawn and readied himself for work at his construction job on the outskirts of Damascus. It was a rainy Sunday morning in January and very cold; as he left, Fawaz turned back one last time to tuck the blanket more snugly around his 16-year-old wife. Zahra slept on without stirring, and her husband locked the door of their tiny apartment carefully behind him.

Zahra's grave in Damascus.

Zahra was most likely still sleeping when her older brother, Fayyez, entered the apartment a short time later, using a stolen key and carrying a dagger. His sister lay on the carpeted floor, on the thin, foam mattress she shared with her husband, so Fayyez must have had to kneel next to Zahra as he raised the dagger and stabbed her five times in the head and back: brutal, tearing thrusts that shattered the base of her skull and nearly severed her spinal column. Leaving the door open, Fayyez walked downstairs and out to the local police station. There, he reportedly turned himself in, telling

▼

the officers on duty that he had killed his sister in order to remove the dishonor she had brought on the family by losing her virginity out of wedlock nearly 10 months earlier.

"Fayyez told the police, 'It is my right to correct this error,'" Maha Ali, a Syrian lawyer who knew Zahra and now works pro bono for her husband, told me not long ago. "He said, 'It's true that my sister is married now, but we never washed away the shame.'"[2]

Fayyez had committed an honor killing, a murder for the sake of a family's honor, usually involving the slaying of a sister, wife, or daughter thought to have disgraced the family by immoral behavior. Nowadays women are killed for having an extramarital affair, having premarital sex, being flirtatious, being raped or sexually abused, or otherwise violating some cultural taboo. The United Nations Population Fund estimates that each year about 5000 honor killings are committed in countries all over the globe. They have occurred in the United States, Europe, Africa, and the Middle East, mostly in Muslim communities where they are generally approved of or at least tolerated to some degree.

Fawaz, Zahra's widower.

Honor killings have presented a disquieting challenge to Western cultural relativists, who are committed to saying that the murders are morally permissible if they are approved by the culture involved. But this view often conflicts with that of the relativists' own culture, which may endorse universal human rights (including women's rights) and strongly condemn such murders.

Do you believe that honor killings are wrong—even in those cultures that approve of them? On what grounds? If you are a relativist, are you a consistent one, conceding that honor killings are right if one's culture sanctions them? If you think they are objectively wrong, do you also judge other heinous acts wrong even though they are culturally sanctioned? ■

How do we quantify happiness?
How do we compare short and long-term consequences?

Criterion 1: It seems to conflict with our considered moral judgments...
What if maximizing happiness required the violation of an individual's rights?

Duties: Can one break a promise in order to maximize happiness???

Yet utilitarianism captures an important insight: the notion that consequences matter

Possible to modify the theory

definitely into the future. If this is the case, then at what point should we make our calculation of the happiness produced? Should we figure into our calculations the happiness that will accrue by next Tuesday? next year? next decade? Some actions may produce very little happiness in the short run but a great deal of happiness over the long haul. Some actions work the other way round—big short-term benefits, no long-term payback. Traditional utilitarianism offers no help in resolving this problem, and so critics have accused the theory of being unworkable.

Many moral philosophers think that the theory faces a much bigger problem than unworkability: It seems to conflict with many of our considered moral judgments. For instance, the theory seems inconsistent with our considered moral judgments involving rights. We tend to think that certain things should not be done to people even if doing them would produce the greatest amount of happiness in the world. We would not think it right to falsely accuse and punish an innocent person just because doing so would make a whole town of people happy. We would not think it right to torture one person just because the action would make a dozen other people extremely happy. Our considered moral judgments say that such actions are wrong, but traditional utilitarianism says they may be right.

Suppose two possible actions will produce exactly the same amount of overall happiness. But one of the actions involves the violation of someone's rights or causes a serious injustice. According to utilitarianism, the two actions are equally right. But to many, this evaluation of the situation seems to conflict with our considered moral judgments.

The same kind of conflict arises in regard to moral duties. Most of us believe that we have certain duties to other people that often seem more weighty than considerations of happiness. For example, we believe that in general we have a duty to keep our promises to people. But traditional utilitarianism does not recognize any such duties. It says that our only goal should be to maximize happiness—regardless of whether we have to break a promise to do it.

So for these reasons (and a few others), many critics have accused the theory of being acutely inconsistent with relevant moral data. They believe that any theory that runs afoul of the criterion of consistency in this way cannot be correct.

But take note: Even the fiercest critics of utilitarianism have admitted that the theory does seem to capture something essential to moral theories—the notion that the consequences of actions are indeed relevant to moral judgments. Probably very few people would want to say that in moral decision making the consequences of their actions never matter.

For the record, the sketch of traditional utilitarianism given here has been oversimplified so we can focus on the process of theory assessment. Over the years, utilitarians have modified the theory to make it more plausible. Critics, however, still claim that the theory is flawed . . . but that's another story.

In radical contrast to utilitarianism and other theories basing rightness on the consequences of actions, the moral theory of Immanuel Kant (1724–1804) says that rightness does not depend at all on the production of happiness or on the satisfaction of human desires. For Kant, rightness is not defined by an action's results, but by its form—that is, by the nature of the action itself. Harming the innocent is wrong not because it causes unhappiness, but because of the kind of action it is. Morality is about conforming your actions to universal moral rules derived from reason and doing so for duty's sake alone. Your actions are right only if they are consistent with such rules, and you deserve praise for right actions only if you act solely from a sense of duty.

In Kantian ethics, the moral rules (or duties) are expressed as categorical imperatives—that is, as commands that apply without exception (categorically, or absolutely) and without regard to a person's preferences or goals. Kant says that we can infer all our duties from one moral principle, the ultimate categorical imperative. He formulates it in several ways but supposes that they are all equivalent. His first formulation says, "Act only on that maxim through which you can at the same time will that it should become a universal law."³ On Kant's view, our actions imply general moral rules, or maxims. To tell a lie for personal gain is essentially to act according to a maxim that says something like, "It's morally permissible to lie to someone to promote your own interests." To determine if an action is permissible, we need to ask ourselves if we could consistently will that the maxim of our action become a universal moral law that applies to everyone. We must ask, "Could all humankind, with logical consistency, act on the maxim, and would we be willing to have them do that?" If the answer is yes on both counts, the action is morally permissible; if not, it is prohibited.

Here is Kant's illustration of properly applying this formulation. Suppose that to borrow money from a friend (money that you know you will never pay back), you falsely promise to repay the loan. Is this behavior permissible? To find out, you must ask if you could consistently will that the maxim of your action become a universal law. The maxim of your action is, "Whenever you need money that you know you cannot pay back, make a lying promise to obtain the loan." What would happen if everyone acted according to this maxim? Everyone would make lying promises to get a loan, but everyone would also know that the promises were empty—and the practice of loaning money based on a promise would cease to exist. The result is a contradiction: The universal making of lying promises would end the practice of promising. Thus you cannot consistently will that the maxim of your action become a universal law, so making a lying promise to borrow money is prohibited.

This bare sketch of only one formulation of the categorical imperative does not do justice to Kant's theory, but it's enough for an illustration of how we might apply the moral criteria of adequacy.

[Handwritten margin notes:]

Ⅱ

DEONTOLOGICAL ETHICS

Immanuel Kant (1724-1804)

An action's rightness does not depend on results, the production of happiness or the satisfaction of desires.

Morality is about conforming actions to universal moral rules

Centrality of duty...

Categorical Imperative

Act only on that maxim through which you can at the same time will that it should become a universal law...

Example: The attempt to universalize false promising renders all promises empty; i.e. it undermines promising

Attempt to universalize false promising would end the practice of promising...

CRITERIA OF ADEQUACY

① Kant's theory passes
Criterion 2...

② Problems w/ Criterion 1

Kant's theory is absolute
and does not allow
for exceptions...

One fact that seems obvious is that the theory easily passes the second criterion: It is generally consistent with our experience of the moral life. According to Kantian ethics, we do form moral judgments, have moral disagreements, and err in our moral beliefs. Any flaws in the theory are more likely to arise from the first criterion; sure enough, critics insist that the theory is not consistent with our considered moral judgments. One argument for this conclusion starts from Kant's claim that the moral rules are absolute—that is, they must be obeyed without exception (or as he says, we have "perfect" duties). He asserts, for example, that we have an absolute duty not to lie or to kill the innocent, regardless of the consequences of observing the rule. Suppose a crazed killer wants to murder an innocent man who takes refuge in your house. The killer knocks at your door and asks you if the man is hiding inside. If you tell the truth, the innocent man will be murdered; if you lie, he will be saved. What would Kant have you do in a case like this? His answer is unequivocal: You must tell the truth though it leads to the murder of an innocent person. How does this absolutism fit with our moral common sense? Not very well, critics say. Our considered moral judgments seem to suggest that, in general, saving an innocent life has far more moral value than blindly adhering to an absolute rule. Moral common sense seems to affirm that doing our duty for duty's sake—though generally a worthy aim—is sometimes less important than avoiding tragic consequences. Kant would have us do our duty though the heavens fall, but that view appears inconsistent with moral judgments that we have good reasons to trust.

Given enough space, we could review the responses that Kant's defenders have offered to this criticism (and to others). And we could dwell on the formulation of the categorical imperative that some consider Kant's greatest insight—the principle of respect for persons. But this brief treatment will have to do.

Between utilitarianism and Kantian ethics, which theory is better and why? An adequate answer to that question would be anything but brief. Comparing the virtues and vices of these two theories, and then deciding which one is preferable, would require a great deal of careful analysis and critical thinking. But however the task proceeds, it is sure to involve applying to both theories some telling criteria of adequacy (either the three criteria discussed here, or variations on them, and perhaps others). Such an investigation would show that neither theory is perfect (no theory is) and would likely yield an edifying conclusion such as (1) one theory is more plausible than the other, or (2) both theories are seriously defective, or (3) the best elements of both can be blended into a new theory, or (4) one of the theories is an especially good candidate for modification to eliminate shortcomings.

Applying the criteria is not like solving a mathematical equation or following a set of instructions to build a gasoline engine. There is no rigid rubric for using or weighting the criteria to sort good theories from bad. But like

Some possibilities for
assessing the theories

the scientific criteria of adequacy, these standards do give us guidance in making reasonable judgments about the objective strengths and weaknesses of theories.

A Coherent Worldview

Making a coherent and powerful worldview for yourself is the work of a lifetime, requiring reflection, critical thinking, and (often) personal anguish. So there is no way that this chapter—or *any* chapter, book, or person—can provide you with ready-made content for your worldview. But we can trace out some characteristics that any good worldview should possess.

A worldview is a massive intellectual construct with many elements. We can get a handle on it, though, by thinking of it as primarily a composite of theories —theories about morality, God, science, mind, personhood, society, knowledge, and much more. We all have our own beliefs about these things, and our most general beliefs often congeal into theories. Since worldviews are framed out of theories, good worldviews will, as a minimum requirement, consist of good theories. So much of the job of devising a good worldview consists of ensuring that our theories are the best theoretical explanations available. We do that, of course, by putting our theories to the test as we have in previous chapters.

But there's more to crafting a plausible worldview than that. Recall our discussion of theories and inference to the best explanation in Chapter 9. We saw that a theory helps increase our understanding by fitting our beliefs into a coherent pattern. When some of our most fundamental beliefs conflict with one another, the relevant theory is in trouble and our understanding is decreased. After all, if two of our beliefs are inconsistent with one another, we know that at least one of them must be false. To achieve true understanding, we must somehow resolve the inconsistency. Likewise, if the theories that make up our worldview are inconsistent with one another, there is obviously something wrong with our worldview. At least one of our theories must be flawed, and some of our beliefs must be wrong. Our understanding of the world is decreased, and our prospects for success (however we define it) are dimmed. A crucial criterion, then, for judging a worldview is *internal consistency*—the requirement that the theories composing our worldview do not conflict.

> "The Answer to the Great Question of . . . Life, the Universe and Everything . . . [is] Forty-Two."
> —DOUGLAS ADAMS

> "Reason and free inquiry are the only effectual agents against error."
> —THOMAS JEFFERSON

© 2002 by Sidney Harris. www.ScienceCartoonsPlus.com

How can our best theories conflict? Here are some ways:

- *Our moral theory can conflict with our view of human freedom.* Most people believe that persons can be held morally responsible for their actions—as long as they act freely. That is, persons can be praised or blamed only for those actions over which they have control. But many people also think that humans *cannot* act freely, that they do not have free will. They believe in causal determinism, the view that every event in the universe has a cause (is determined). This means that everything that happens (including human actions) has a preceding cause, so that the chain of causes stretches back into the indefinite past—out of our control. Many would see this situation as an unacceptable conflict between their moral theory and their view of the way the world is.

- *Our theory about the existence of God can conflict with our scientific theory about the nature of the universe.* Some people argue that God must exist because everything has a cause, including the universe, and the only thing that could have caused the universe is God. Modern physics, however, shows that some things in the universe (namely, certain subatomic particles) often occur uncaused, so it's not true that everything has a cause. Thus, in this instance science seems to be at odds with a certain brand of theology.

- *Our theory about the mind can be in conflict with theories of personal survival after death.* Some believe that people can live on in some ethereal form (as souls or disembodied minds, for example) after death. This notion accords well with the idea that the mind (our true essence) is the kind of thing that can exist independently of the body. But this kind of survival after death would not be possible if the mind is identical to the body, as some people believe.

The work of building plausible worldviews will always involve eliminating inconsistencies. If you really want to understand the world and your place in it, you must wrestle with these inconsistencies. Reconciling conflicting beliefs (by eliminating them or modifying them) is a necessary condition for creating theories and a worldview that can successfully guide your thinking, your choices, and your deeds.

With this discussion, we now come full circle to a theme that bubbles up in the first few pages of this book and flows through each chapter to this final paragraph: Every statement, every theory, and every worldview is fair game for critical thinking. No claim can be considered immune to critical inquiry, revision, and rejection. We will probably never be able to evaluate the truth of all our beliefs, but we violate the spirit of critical reasoning and do ourselves a disfavor if we cordon them off and post a sign that says "Off Limits!" If truth is what we seek, if knowledge is our goal, we should be willing to turn the light of critical thinking on any dark corner anywhere. This point is especially relevant to the development of worldviews, which too often are thought to be the unalterable givens of clan and culture, ideologies carved in the pillars of the mind forever. Our worldviews are far too important not to subject them to intelligent, reasoned reflection.

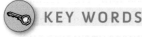

KEY WORDS

moral statement   worldview

Summary

- A moral argument is an argument in which the conclusion is a moral statement. A moral statement is a statement asserting that an action is right or wrong (moral or immoral) or that a person or motive is good or bad.

- In a moral argument, we cannot establish the conclusion without a moral premise. A standard moral argument has at least one premise that asserts a general moral principle, at least one premise that is a nonmoral claim, and a conclusion that is a moral statement.

- Often a moral premise in a moral argument is implicit. The best approach to identifying the implicit premises is to treat moral arguments as deductive. Your job, then, is to supply plausible premises that will make the argument valid.

- Gauging the truth of moral premises (moral principles) mostly involves examining the support they get from three sources: (1) other moral principles, (2) moral theories, and (3) considered moral judgments.

- We can assess the truth of a moral premise the same way we might assess any other kind of universal generalization—by trying to think of counterexamples to it.

- Theories of morality are attempts to explain what makes an action right or what makes a person good. We test moral theories the same way we test any other theory—by applying criteria of adequacy to a theory and its competitors. The criteria of adequacy for moral theories are (1) consistency with considered moral judgments, (2) consistency with our experience of the moral life, and (3) workability in real-life situations.

- Worldviews are composites of theories, including theories of morality. A good worldview must consist of good theories. But it also must have internal consistency—the theories composing our worldview must not conflict.

- Our worldviews are far too important not to subject them to intelligent, reasoned reflection.

EXERCISES

Exercise 11.1

REVIEW QUESTIONS

1. What is a moral theory?
2. According to the text, what is a worldview?
3. What is a moral statement?
4. What is the basic structure of a standard moral argument?
* 5. Why can't we infer a moral statement from nonmoral statements alone?
6. Why is it important to spell out implicit premises in a moral argument?
7. What technique can we use to determine whether a general moral principle is true?
8. What is a moral judgment?
* 9. According to the text, what precisely does a moral theory try to explain?
10. According to the text, what are the criteria of adequacy for appraising moral theories?
11. According to the text, how are moral theories like scientific theories?
12. Who founded the moral theory known as traditional utilitarianism?
* 13. According to the text, what is a crucial criterion for judging a worldview?

Exercise 11.2

Specify whether the following statements are moral or nonmoral.

NM * 1. Joan worries whether she's doing the right thing.
NM 2. When the government restricts freedom of the press, it harms every citizen.
M 3. The government should not restrict freedom of the press.
NM 4. Paul was sure that he saw Gregory steal the book from the library.
M 5. Because of the terrible results of the bombing, it's clear that the entire war effort was immoral.
M * 6. The Church should never have allowed pedophile priests to stay in the priesthood.
M 7. The officer was justified in using deadly force because his life was threatened.
NM 8. The officer used deadly force because his life was threatened.
M * 9. Lying is wrong unless the lie involves trivial matters.
M 10. The officials should never have allowed the abuse to continue.

Exercise 11.3

In each of the following passages, add a moral premise to turn it into a valid moral argument.

1. Noah promised to drive Thelma to Los Angeles, so he should stop belly-aching and do it.

    People should keep promises

2. The refugees were shot at and lied to, and the authorities did nothing to stop any of this. The authorities should have intervened.

    Authorities have a moral obligation

3. There was never any imminent threat from the Iraqi government, so the United States should not have invaded Iraq.

    US is justified in invading only when country poses i. threat

* 4. The Indian government posed an imminent threat to Pakistan and the world, so the Pakistanis were justified in attacking Indian troops.

    when a country poses an i threat

5. Burton used a gun in the commission of a crime; therefore he should get a long prison term.

    Anyone who uses a gun to commit a crime deserves...

6. Ellen knew that a murder was going to take place. It was her duty to try to stop it.

    Anyone who knows that a murder will take place...

7. Ahmed should never have allowed his daughter to receive in vitro fertil-ization. Such a procedure is unnatural.

    Any procedure that is unnatural should not be used...

8. The doctors performed the experiment on twenty patients without their consent. Obviously, that was wrong.

    Doctors should never experiment on people without their consent

* 9. What you did was immoral. You hacked into a database containing personal information on thousands of people and invaded their privacy.

    Hacking into a DB is immoral

10. Ling spent all day weeding Mrs. Black's garden for no pay. The least Mrs. Black should do is let Ling borrow some gardening tools.

    If someone does another person a favor, that person is obligated)...

Exercise 11.4

Use counterexamples to test each of the following general moral principles.

1. Anything that is unnatural is immoral.
2. It is always and everywhere wrong to tell a lie.
* 3. In all circumstances the killing of a human being is wrong.
4. In all situations in which our actions can contribute to the welfare, safety, or happiness of others, we should treat all persons equally.
5. Any action that serves one's own best interests is morally permissible.
6. Any action that is approved of by one's society is moral.
* 7. Assisted suicide is never morally justified.
8. Whatever action a person approves of is morally right.
9. Making a promise to someone incurs a moral obligation to keep the promise in all circumstances.

10. Any action done for religious reasons is morally acceptable because religious reasons carry more weight than secular ones.

Exercise 11.5

Identify the moral argument in each of the following passages. Specify the premises and the conclusion, adding implicit premises where needed.

1. The movie *Lorenzo's Oil* is about a family's struggle to find a cure for their young son's fatal genetic disease, an illness that usually kills boys before they reach their eleventh birthday. The script is based on the true story of a family's attempt to save Lorenzo, their son, from this fatal genetic disease through the use of a medicinal oil. The movie is a tear-jerker, but it ends on a hopeful note that suggests that the oil will eventually cure Lorenzo and that the oil is an effective treatment for the genetic disease. The problem is, there is no cure for the disease and no good scientific evidence showing that the oil works. But the movie touts the oil anyway—and gives false hope to every family whose son suffers from this terrible illness. Worse, the movie overplays the worth of the oil, seriously misleading people about the medical facts. The movie, therefore, is immoral. It violates the ageless moral dictum to, above all else, "do no harm." *Lorenzo's Oil* may be just a movie, but it has done harm nonetheless.

2. "I, like many of my fellow Muslims, was appalled by the latest bombings in Saudi Arabia ('Among the Saudis, Attack Has Soured Qaeda Supporters,' front page, Nov. 11). Yet I was disturbed to get the sense that Saudis were angered by this latest act of barbarity because the targets were mainly Arab and Muslim.

   "You quote one person as saying of the bombing in Riyadh in May, 'At that time it was seen as justifiable because there was an invasion of a foreign country, there was frustration.' Another says, 'Jihad is not against your own people.'

   "Regardless of whether the victims are Muslim or not, the vicious murder of innocent human beings is reprehensible and repugnant, an affront to everything Islam stands for. Any sympathy for Al Qaeda among the minority of Saudis should have evaporated after the May bombings in Riyadh, and it should have surprised no one in Saudi Arabia that Al Qaeda would attack a housing complex full of Arabs and Muslims.

   "That is what Al Qaeda is: a band of bloodthirsty murderers." [Letter to the editor, *New York Times*]

3. John and Nancy Jones had a two-year-old son who suffered from a serious but very curable bowel obstruction. For religious reasons, the Joneses decided to treat their son with prayer instead of modern medicine. They refused medical treatment even though they were told by several doctors that the child would die unless medically treated. As it turned out, the boy did

die. The Joneses were arrested and charged with involuntary manslaughter. Were the Joneses wrong to refuse treatment for their son? The answer is yes. Regardless of what faith or religious dogma would have the Joneses do, they allowed their child to die. According to just about any moral outlook, the care of a child by the parents is a fundamental obligation. Above all other concerns, parents have a duty to ensure the health and safety of their children and to use whatever means are most likely to secure those benefits. The Joneses ignored this basic moral principle. They were wrong—and deserve whatever punishment the state deems appropriate.

Exercise 11.6

Read the following description of a moral theory and answer the questions that follow.

> **The Ethics of Love Theory**
> According to the Ethics of Love Theory, what makes an action right is that it is based on love toward others. Love is the only universal moral good. In any situation where a moral choice must be made, this theory says that we must ask ourselves: "Which action would demonstrate the greatest degree of love for others, everyone considered?" So in this theory, actions that demonstrate love (such as respecting others, telling the truth, treating people equally, caring for them, protecting them from harm) would always be preferred over actions that do not demonstrate love (discriminating against persons, lying to them, harming them, stealing from them, ignoring them if they ask for help). Also, actions that demonstrate great love (such as risking your life to save theirs) would be preferred over those that exhibit only small degrees of love (such as being courteous).

1. Is this theory consistent with our considered moral judgments? Is it consistent with our judgments regarding the punishment of criminals? acts of war? providing for one's family as opposed to providing for all persons equally? If the theory conflicts with our considered moral judgments, provide an example demonstrating the conflict.

2. Is this theory consistent with our experience of the moral life? According to this theory, are moral judgments possible? Can we have moral disagreements? Can we ever act immorally?

3. Is this theory workable? Does it help you make moral decisions in these situations?

    a. Your beloved mother has a terminal illness which causes her unimaginable pain, and she begs you to kill her.

    b. You promise to buy your beloved spouse a car, but a half dozen homeless people beg you to give them the money that you had set aside for the car.

c. You are a doctor who must decide which of one hundred patients should receive a life-saving organ transplant. You can choose only one, though you love all of them. Some are elderly; some, in great pain; some, very young; and some, Nobel laureates.

4. What is your final assessment of the ethics of love theory? Is it a good theory? Is it a better theory than traditional utilitarianism?

Field Problems

1. Check the Internet to find out about rule-utilitarianism, a moral theory meant to be an improvement over traditional utilitarianism. (A place to start is The Internet Encyclopedia of Philosophy, www.utm.edu/research/iep. See the entry "Moral Philosophy.") Write a three-hundred-word assessment of the theory, using the moral criteria of adequacy.

2. From a newspaper opinion/editorial page (including letters to the editor) select a passage containing a moral argument. Write a brief assessment of the argument, identifying the premises and conclusion, adding implicit premises (to make the argument valid), and stating whether the revised argument is sound or unsound.

3. Go to the opinion/editorial section of www.usatoday.com and select a short article on an important moral issue. Analyze the article's argument, identifying premises and the conclusion, and determine whether the argument is a good one.

Self-Assessment Quiz

Answers appear in "Answers to Self-Assessment Quizzes" (Appendix C).

1. What is a moral statement?
2. What are the elements of a standard moral argument?
3. According to the text, what are the moral criteria of adequacy?
4. According to the text, how can you test whether a general moral principle is true?
5. Is it possible to derive a moral statement from a nonmoral statement?

In each of the following passages, add a moral premise to turn it into a valid moral argument.

6. Of course we should have offered protection to the Kurds. They were in grave danger and they asked for our help.
7. The supplement manufacturers knew that the herb ephedra was dangerous, so they should have removed it from the market.

8. The Democrats insulted the president. They should have never been allowed to do that.

9. The Smiths were consenting adults who were having sex in the privacy of their own home. These actions by the Smiths are morally permissible.

10. Randi killed his neighbor, and the killing was not in self-defense. He should not have committed such an act.

Use counterexamples to test each of the following general moral principles.

11. Lying is wrong under all circumstances.

12. People who commit crimes should not be punished—they should be retrained to act legally.

13. All humans, whatever their circumstances, have full moral rights.

14. All creatures that are alive and sensitive to stimulation are equally valuable and should be accorded equal respect.

15. The morally right action is the one that produces the most happiness, everyone considered.

16. Right actions are those that are in one's own self-interest.

Defend the following actions from a utilitarian standpoint.

17. Medical experimentation on a patient without her consent.

18. Taking food, shelter, and other resources from rich people and distributing them equally among poor people.

Evaluate each of the following arguments.

19. Any form of expression or speech that offends people of faith should not be tolerated. *Penthouse* magazine definitely offends people of faith. Ban it!

20. Anyone who disagrees with the basic moral dictums of the prevailing culture should be censored. Dr. Tilden's graduation speech clearly was inconsistent with the prevailing moral opinions on campus. She should be reprimanded.

 Integrative Exercises

These exercises pertain to material in Chapters 3, 5, and 8–11.

For each of the following arguments, specify the conclusion and premises and indicate where possible whether it is cogent or sound. Also, determine whether any fallacies are used and, if so, name them.

1. Ninety percent of famous scientists do not believe in God, so 90 percent of all scientists probably do not believe in God.

2. If Vaughn buys that flat-screen TV, he will spend all of his time watching television. And if he spends all of his time watching television, he will get fat. Well, Vaughn did buy that flat-screen TV. Therefore, he will get fat.

3. Anyone who runs away from an automobile accident should be arrested. Janet ran away from an automobile accident. She should be arrested.

4. I found five jellybeans in the yard this morning, and I found thirty more in the kitchen this afternoon. So I've found thirty-five jellybeans today.

5. Ann is taller than Jacob, and Jacob is taller than Jane. Therefore, Ann is taller than Jane.

6. "I write in response to the Nov. 4 *News* article, 'Plans for group home, storage facility opposed.' As the sister and guardian of a profoundly retarded woman who lives in a group home, I can assure the gentlemen quoted that their fears are very much unfounded. The home in which my sister resides is large, lovely, brand new, well staffed and well maintained. It does nothing but enhance the community, bring neighbors together and create a wonderfully diverse neighborhood." [Letter to the editor, *Buffalo News*]

7. "Scrawling 'Rape all Asian bitches and dump them' on classroom walls is not a hate crime, and graffiti should be protected by the First Amendment, according to assistant professor of communication Laura Leets. This is outrageous. I hope Ms. Leets is simply arguing from a narrow legalistic interpretation and is merely insensitive to the tremendous hurt such graffiti can inflict, not to mention the additional damage caused when a professor on campus defends it. Words can be just as destructive as physical violence. Drawing a technical distinction between the two is at best insensitive, at worst evil." [Letter to the editor, *Stanford Magazine*]

8. We have interviewed one hundred NBA players, and seventy of them admit to extramarital affairs. So most NBA players are adulterers.

9. You think you're going to drive cross-country in that 1978 Chevy disaster-on-wheels? Forget it. It's old, has 150,000 miles on it, and has worn belts and bad cylinders.

10. Take it easy. Joyce will arrive soon to give you a lift into town, just as she promised. She has never broken a promise, and her car is in excellent shape.

11. Yolanda took the money from petty cash even though she had plenty of money in her pocket. People shouldn't steal unless they are destitute. She shouldn't have taken that money.

12. There is one principle we can never avoid: We should never do anything to disrespect human life. The artificial use of human cells—as scientists are now doing in stem cell research—shows a complete disregard for human life. Stem cell research is immoral.

13. Hank is a Harvard grad. Therefore, he's probably intelligent and well educated.

14. This new BMW will give you a sense of style, assurance, and class. See your BMW dealer today.

15. The depiction of Hollywood stars in movies puffing away on cigarettes is teaching our kids to smoke. Recent research reveals a cause-and-effect relationship between exposing children to movie smoking and their subsequent decision to take up the habit.

For each of the following phenomena, (1) devise two theories to explain it, and (2) apply the criteria of adequacy to them to determine which theory is best.

16. The number of delayed and canceled flights in the airline industry has tripled in the last year.

17. After taking a new food supplement known as Max10, hundreds of people have reported having more energy, feeling more alert, and having an enhanced sense of well-being.

18. Ever since the average classroom size at Wellington High dropped from forty-two to twenty-five, grades have improved dramatically and discipline problems are at an all-time low.

19. Over the past ten years there has been a surprising rise in the incidence of leukemia in children who live in the Saxton area.

20. Multiracial neighborhoods seem much friendlier than neighborhoods that are segregated or are dominated by one ethnic or cultural group.

 Writing Assignments

1. Complete Exercise 11.6 and then write a two-page essay assessing the worth of the ethics of love theory. Use the moral criteria of adequacy.

2. Write a one-paragraph summary of the moral argument put forth in Essay 6 ("Misleading the Patient for Fun and Profit") in Appendix A. Be sure to identify clearly the argument's premises and conclusion.

3. Write a two-page assessment of the moral theory known as ethical egoism (discussed in the box "Critiquing Moral Theories"). Use the moral criteria of adequacy.

4. Read Essay 11 ("A Deviance from God's Norm") in Appendix A, outline its argument, and write a two-page essay in rebuttal. As part of your critique, identify any fallacies used by the author.

5. Read Essay 14 ("The Right to Ridicule") in Appendix A and outline its argument. Decide whether you agree with the author and write a two-page essay giving reasons for your view.

APPENDIX A

Essays for Evaluation

ESSAY I

Death Penalty Discriminates Against Black Crime Victims

USA TODAY
APRIL 29, 2003

Death penalty opponents have long complained that minorities are more likely to be executed than whites convicted of the same crime. Now a new study points up another troubling racial difference between who lives and who dies: the color of the victim.

While blacks and whites are murdered in roughly equal numbers in the USA, the killers of white people are six times as likely to be put to death, according to a statistical analysis released last week by the anti–death penalty human rights organization Amnesty International USA. It found that of 845 people executed since the U.S. resumed capital punishment in 1977, 80% were put to death for killing whites, while only 13% were executed for killing blacks.

The findings point to one chilling conclusion: The criminal justice system places a higher value on the lives of whites than on the lives of blacks and other minorities. That means minorities who are victims of violent crimes are also victimized by a legal system that fails to provide them the "equal protection of the laws" they are guaranteed under the 14th Amendment to the Constitution.

The report adds to the troubling evidence of racial discrimination against minority victims that has surfaced in other, state-level studies over the past year:

- In Illinois, juries have been three times as likely to sentence a person to death if the victim is white rather than black. Then-Gov. George Ryan cited those findings in January, when he commuted 167 death sentences to life imprisonment.
- In Maryland, the death penalty is four times as likely to be imposed when the victim is white rather than black. But a moratorium on executions imposed by the outgoing governor has been revoked by his successor.

Other studies in New Jersey, North Carolina, Pennsylvania, Texas and Virginia have shown similar results, as did a review a decade ago by the U.S. General Accounting Office, the investigative arm of Congress.

Other research suggests race-based differences in administering justice are not unique to the death penalty. A major study published by Stanford University in 1995 found that prosecutors tended to stereotype nonwhite crime victims as less-convincing witnesses, and cases involving nonwhite victims were more likely to be dismissed or result in plea-bargains to lesser penalties.

The Supreme Court banned the death penalty in 1972 after finding it was imposed arbitrarily. Five years later executions resumed based on the court's 1976 ruling that new laws would guide judges and juries to mete out death sentences evenhandedly.

The record since then shows the court was right the first time. When a victim's skin color is key in deciding who is put to death, the system not only violates constitutional protections but also is corrupt.

A better alternative to the death penalty is life imprisonment without parole. It protects society from those who commit heinous crimes without perpetuating a deadly system of unequal justice based on race.

Writing Assignments for this essay: Chap. 1, #1; Chap. 1, #2

ESSAY 2

Marine Parks

BILL DALY

The issue of whether we should allow marine parks to stay open has been widely debated in our community recently. It is an important issue because it concerns fundamental moral and economic questions about the way we use our native wildlife. A variety of different arguments have been put forward about this issue. This essay will consider arguments for having marine parks and point to some of the problems with these views. It will then put forward reasons for the introduction of laws which prohibit these unnecessary and cruel institutions.

It has been argued that dolphin parks provide the only opportunity for much of the public to see marine mammals (Smith, 1992). Most Australians, so this argument goes, live in cities and never get to see these animals. It is claimed that marine parks allow the average Australian to appreciate our marine wildlife. However, as Smith states, dolphins, whales and seals can be viewed in the wild at a number of places on the Australian coast. In fact, there are more places where they can be seen in the wild than places where they can be seen in captivity. Moreover, most Australians would have to travel less to get to these locations than they would to get to the marine parks on the Gold Coast. In addition, places where there are wild marine mammals do not charge an exorbitant entry fee—they are free.

Dr. Alison Lane, the director of the Cairns Marine Science Institute, contends that we need marine parks for scientific research (*The Age*, 19.2.93). She argues that much of our knowledge of marine mammals comes from studies which were undertaken at marine parks. The knowledge which is obtained at marine parks, so this argument goes, can be useful for planning for the conservation of marine mammal species. However, as Jones (1991) explains, park research is only useful for understanding captive animals and is not useful for learning about animals in the wild. Dolphin and whale biology changes in marine park conditions. Their diets are different, they have significantly lower life spans and they are more prone to disease. In addition, marine mammals in dolphin parks are trained and this means that their patterns of social behaviour are changed. Therefore research undertaken at marine parks is generally not reliable.

It is the contention of the Marine Park Owners Association that marine parks attract a lot of foreign tourists (*The Sun-Herald*, 12.4.93). This position goes on to assert that these tourists spend a lot of money, increasing our foreign exchange earnings and assisting our national balance of payments. However, foreign tourists would still come to Australia if the parks were closed down. Indeed, surveys of overseas tourists show that they come here for a variety of other reasons and not to visit places like Seaworld (*The Age, Good Weekend*, 16.8.93). Tourists come here to see our native wildlife in its natural environment and not to see it in cages and cement pools. They can see animals in those conditions in their own countries. Furthermore, we should be promoting our beautiful natural environment to tourists and not the ugly concrete marine park venues.

Dolphin parks are unnecessary and cruel. The dolphins and whales in these parks are kept in very small, cramped ponds, whereas in the wild they are used to roaming long distances across the seas. Furthermore, the concrete walls of the pools interfere with the animals' sonar systems of communication. In addition, keeping them in pools is a terrible restriction of the freedom of fellow creatures who may have very high levels of intelligence and a sophisticated language ability. Moreover, there are many documented cases of marine mammals helping humans who are in danger at sea or helping fisherman with their work.

In conclusion, these parks should be closed, or at the very least, no new animals should be captured for marine parks in the future. Our society is no longer prepared to tolerate unnecessary cruelty to animals for science and entertainment. If we continue with our past crimes against these creatures we will be remembered as cruel and inhuman by the generations of the future.

Bibliography

The Age, 19.2.93.

The Age, Good Weekend, 16.8.93.

Jones, G. (1991). "The Myths About Animal Research in Marine Parks." In *Scientific Australian*, Vol. 12, No. 3.

Smith, H. (1992). "Marine Parks: Good for Business, Good for Australia." In *Leisure Business Review*, Vol. 24, No. 4.

The Sun-Herald, 12.4.93.

Writing Assignments for this essay: Chap. 1, #3; Chap. 4, #1

ESSAY 3

The Wrong Ruling on Vouchers

NEW YORK TIMES
JUNE 28, 2002

The country has been waiting for several years now to see how the Supreme Court would rule on school vouchers. Yesterday, in a 5-to-4 decision, the court issued a sweeping ruling upholding Cleveland's school voucher program. It was a bad decision on constitutional grounds, and a bad one for American education.

In theory, Cleveland's voucher program allows children to use state stipends to go to any school they want. In practice, the choice it offers them is between a failing public school system and the city's parochial schools. This is not a choice that the Constitution intended public tax money to underwrite.

The problem with the Cleveland program begins with the size of the stipends, which are capped at $2,250. That is far less than most private schools cost. But it is just right for parochial schools where, for a variety of reasons, tuition is far lower. Not surprisingly, fully 96.6 percent of students end up taking their vouchers to religiously affiliated schools.

Once students enroll in those schools, they are subjected to just the sort of religious training the First Amendment forbids the state to underwrite. In many cases, students are required to attend Mass or other religious services. Tax dollars go to buy Bibles, prayer books, crucifixes and other religious iconography. It is hard to think of a starker assault on the doctrine of separation of church and state than taking taxpayer dollars and using them to inculcate specific religious beliefs in young people.

The majority argues that the Cleveland program does not, as a technical matter, violate the First Amendment because it is parents, not the government, who are choosing where the money goes. But given the reality of education in Cleveland, parents do not have the wealth of options that would make their selection of religious schools meaningful. And in any case, the money ultimately comes from taxpayers, and therefore should not be directed—by whatever route—to finance religious training.

This ruling does as much damage to education as it does to the First Amendment. A common argument for vouchers is that they improve public schools by forcing them to compete for students. What is holding the public schools back, however, is not lack of competitive drive but the resources to succeed. Voucher programs like Cleveland's siphon off public dollars, leaving struggling urban systems with less money for skilled teachers, textbooks and computers. They also skim off some of the best-performing students, and the most informed and involved parents, from public schools that badly need their expertise and energy.

Yesterday's decision also undermines one of the public school system's most important functions: teaching democracy and pluralism. In public schools, Americans of many backgrounds learn together. In the religious schools that Cleveland taxpayers are being forced to sponsor, Catholics are free to teach that their way is best, and Jews, Muslims and those of other faiths can teach their coreligionists that they have truth on their side. As Justice John Paul Stevens wrote in dissent, "Whenever we remove a brick from the wall that was designed to separate religion and government, we increase the risk of religious strife and weaken the foundation of our democracy." This court has removed many bricks.

Writing Assignments for this essay: Chap. 2, #1; Chap. 3, #1

ESSAY 4
The Kalam Cosmological Argument
THEODORE SCHICK

Although it may be possible for the universe to be infinitely old, many believe that the universe was created less than fifteen billion years ago in a cataclysmic explosion known as the "big bang." The existence of such a creation event explains a number of phenomena including the expansion of the universe, the existence of the cosmic background radiation, and the relative proportions of various sorts of matter. As the theory has been refined, more specific predictions have been derived from it. A number of these predictions have recently been confirmed. Although this is a major scientific achievement, many believe that it has theological implications as well. Specifically, they believe that it provides scientific evidence for the existence of God. Astronomer George Smoot suggested as much when he exclaimed at a press conference reporting the findings of the Cosmic Background Explorer (COBE) satellite, "If you're religious it's like looking at the face of God." Why? Because something must have caused the big bang, and who else but God could have done such a thing? Astronomer Hugh Ross, in his book *The Creator and the Cosmos,* puts the argument this way: "If the universe arose out of a big bang, it must have had a beginning. If it had a beginning, it must have a beginner."* And that beginner, Ross believes, is God.

The Kalam cosmological argument follows along these lines. It goes like this:

1. Whatever begins to exist has a cause.
2. The universe began to exist.
3. Therefore, the universe had a cause, namely God.

This argument gets its name from the Arabic word *Kalam* which means "to argue or discuss." It originated with Islamic theologians who sought to challenge the Greek view of the eternity of matter.

The Kalam cosmological argument doesn't require that everything have a cause, only those things that begin to exist. Since God is eternal, he doesn't require a cause. The universe, however, is not eternal. So it does require a cause.

As with the traditional cosmological argument, however, the Kalam cosmological argument gives us no reason for believing that the first cause is God. The universe that came from the big bang is finite, and it doesn't take a being of

---

* Hugh Ross, *The Creator and the Cosmos* (Colorado Springs: Navpress, 1995) 14.

infinite power to create a finite universe. The same goes for the properties of intelligence and goodness. So even if the Kalam cosmological argument did prove the existence of a first cause, it doesn't prove the existence of God.

There's reason to believe it doesn't even prove the existence of a first cause, however, for modern physics explicitly repudiates premise 1 and provides good reason for rejecting premise 2.

Remarkably enough, modern physics rejects the claim that whatever begins to exist has a cause. On the contrary, it maintains that things like subatomic particles can come into existence without a cause. As physicist Edward Tryon tells us:

> . . . quantum electrodynamics reveals that an electron, positron, and photon occasionally emerge spontaneously in a perfect vacuum. When this happens, the three particles exist for a brief time, and then annihilate each other, leaving no trace behind. . . . The spontaneous, temporary emergence of particles from a vacuum is called a vacuum fluctuation, and is utterly commonplace in quantum field theory.*

Vacuum fluctuations are random events, and random events have no cause. So anything produced by a vacuum fluctuation is uncaused.

What's even more remarkable is that according to modern physics, the universe itself could be the result of a vacuum fluctuation! Tryon explains:

> If it is true that our Universe has a zero net value for all conserved quantities, then it may simply be a fluctuation of a vacuum, the vacuum of some larger space in which our universe is imbedded. In answer to the question of why it happened, I offer the modest proposal that our Universe is simply one of those things which happen from time to time.†

According to Tryon, universes happen; they come into existence spontaneously without being caused to exist.

Wouldn't a universe produced by a vacuum fluctuation violate the Law of Conservation of Mass-Energy? Not if the total amount of mass-energy of the universe is zero. How is that possible? Physicist Paul Davies explains:

> There is a . . . remarkable possibility, which is the creation of matter from a state of zero energy. This possibility arises because energy can be both positive and negative. The energy of motion or the energy of mass is always positive, but the energy of attraction, such as that due to certain types of gravitational or electromagnetic fields is negative. Circumstances can arise in which the positive energy that goes to make up the mass of newly created particles of matter is exactly offset by the negative energy of gravity or electromagnetism. . . . Some have suggested that there is a deep cosmic principle at work which requires the universe to have exactly zero energy. If that is so, the cosmos can follow the path of least resistance, coming into existence without requiring any input of matter or energy at all.‡

---

*Edward Tryon, "Is the Universe a Vacuum Fluctuation?" *Nature* 246 (1973) 396–397.
† Tryon 397.
‡ Paul Davies, *God and the New Physics* (New York: Simon and Schuster, 1983) 31–32.

If our universe has zero total energy, as measurements seem to indicate, it could be the result of a vacuum fluctuation. But if it was the result of a vacuum fluctuation, it was not caused to exist by anyone or anything.

The second premise of the Kalam cosmological argument says that the universe began to exist. Evidence for the big bang is usually presented as evidence for this claim. But the fact that the big bang occurred doesn't prove that the universe began to exist, for the big bang may itself have been the result of a prior big crunch!

It has long been known that if the amount of matter in the universe is great enough, then the universe will someday stop expanding and start contracting. Eventually, all the matter in the universe will be drawn back to a single point in what has come to be known as "the big crunch." Because matter supposedly cannot be crushed out of existence, the contraction cannot go on indefinitely. At some point the compressed matter may bounce back in another big bang. If so, the big bang would have been caused by a prior big crunch rather than by some supernatural being.

The view that the universe oscillates between periods of expansion and contraction in an endless—and beginningless—cycle of creation and destruction is a very Eastern one. Hindus, for example, believe that everything in the universe—as well as the universe itself—undergoes a continuous process of death and rebirth. For them, time is circular; the beginning and end are one and the same. Thus the notion of a first cause makes no sense. Only for those who have a linear view of time is the question of the origin of the universe a problem.

Recent estimates indicate that there is not enough mass in the universe to stop its expansion. So the big bang may not have been the result of a prior big crunch. But even if the universe as a whole never contracts, we know that certain parts of it do. When a star has used up its fuel, the force of gravity causes it to contract. If the star is massive enough, this contraction results in a black hole. The matter in a black hole is compressed toward a point of infinite density known as a "singularity." Before it reaches the singularity, however, some physicists, most notably Lee Smolin, believe that the matter in the black hole may start expanding again and give rise to another universe. In a sense, then, according to Smolin, our universe may reproduce itself by budding off. He writes:

> A collapsing star forms a black hole, within which it is compressed to a very dense state. The universe began in a similarly very dense state from which it expands. Is it possible that these are one and the same dense state? That is, is it possible that what is beyond the horizon of a black hole is the beginning of another universe?
>
> This could happen if the collapsing star exploded once it reached a very dense state, but after the black hole horizon had formed around it. . . .
>
> What we are doing is applying this bounce hypothesis, not to the universe as a whole, but to every black hole in it. If this is true, then we live not in a single universe, which is eternally passing through the same recurring cycle of collapse and rebirth. We live instead in a continually growing community

of "universes," each of which is born from an explosion following the collapse of a star to a black hole.*

Smolin's vision of a self-reproducing universe is an appealing one. It suggests that the universe is more like a living thing than an artifact and thus that its coming into being doesn't require an external agent.

Smolin's theory is simpler than the God hypothesis because it does not postulate the existence of any supernatural entities. It is also more conservative because it doesn't contradict any laws of science. In addition, it is potentially more fruitful because it is possible to draw testable predictions from it. Other things being equal, the simpler, the more conservative, and the more fruitful a theory, the better. So even if the big bang occurred fifteen billion years ago, we don't have to assume that it was caused by God.

Writing Assignments for this essay: Chap. 4, #2; Chap. 7, #3

ESSAY 5

More Innocents Die When We Don't Have Capital Punishment

DENNIS PRAGER

A couple of weeks ago, three New Hampshire prisoners, one a convicted murderer, escaped from prison. What if the murderer had murdered again? On whose hands would the victim's blood have been?

One of the most common, and surely the most persuasive, arguments against capital punishment is that the state may execute an innocent person. One reason for its effectiveness is that proponents of capital punishment often do not know how to respond to it.

That's a shame. For while the argument is emotionally compelling, it is morally and intellectually shallow.

First of all, there is almost no major social good that does not lead to the death of innocent individuals. Over a million innocent people have been killed and maimed in car accidents. Would this argue for the banning of automobiles? To those whose criterion for acceptable social policy is that not one innocent die, it should.

If it were proven that a strictly enforced 40-mile-per-hour speed limit on our nation's highways would save innocent lives, should we reduce highway limits to 40 miles per hour? Should all roller coasters be shut down because some innocents get killed riding on them?

Anyone whose criterion for abolishing capital punishment is saving innocent lives should be for a 40-mile-per-hour speed limit and for abolishing roller coasters.

But death-penalty abolitionists aren't. And that is why they cannot logically build their case against capital punishment on the argument that an innocent may die. They accept a large number of social policies that kill innocents.

---

* Lee Smolin, *The Life of the Cosmos* (New York: Oxford University Press, 1997) 87–88.

Therefore, if abolitionists were intellectually honest, they would have to argue that capital punishment achieves no social good or that it is immoral to kill any murderers, not that it must be abandoned because an innocent may die.

But they do not make those arguments because they know that most Americans do not share their view that killing a murderer is immoral and that all murderers deserve to live. So they make the emotional but intellectually dishonest argument that, sure, some murderers ought be put to death, but we just can't do that because an innocent person may one day die.

The abolitionist argument that an innocent might be killed is false for a second reason. Far more innocent people have already died because we did not execute their murderers. The abolitionist has convinced himself, and a sincere but gullible public, that only a policy of capital punishment threatens innocent lives, while abolition of capital punishment threatens no innocent lives. That is entirely untrue.

Murderers who are not executed have murdered innocent people—usually fellow prisoners. And the very real possibility of escape from prison means that murderers threaten far more innocent lives than capital punishment does.

So here is the bottom line: If the escaped New Hampshire murderer had murdered someone, would opponents of capital punishment have acknowledged that the blood of that victim was on their hands? I doubt it. They believe that only advocates of capital punishment can have blood on their hands, when and if the state executes an innocent person. But they, the abolitionists, somehow have no blood on their hands when a convicted murderer murders an innocent.

As a proponent of capital punishment, I fully acknowledge my moral responsibility for any innocent person executed by the state. It is time that the abolitionists confronted their responsibility for every innocent already murdered and yet to be murdered by murderers who should have been executed. Or at least let them drop this false argument and state the truth: They believe murderers should never be killed.

Writing Assignments for this essay: Chap. 6, #3; Chap. 7, #2

ESSAY 6
Misleading the Patient for Fun and Profit
LEWIS VAUGHN

Romance is in the air. The media, the public, the gurus, and the hucksters have gazed upon acupuncture, homeopathy, chelation therapy, herbal concoctions, magnetic therapy, and any other treatments called "alternative medicine" . . . and have *fallen in love.* So, as in any romance, current talk about a beloved "alternative" therapy is usually marked by uncritical acceptance, blind commitment, feverish thinking, and occasional cooing.

In this atmosphere, there are two politically incorrect questions that you must never utter: (1) *Is this true?* (Are there good grounds for believing this claim?) and

(2) *Is this right?* (Is it morally permissible to use or promote this treatment?) We are told that to ask question 1 (and the relevant accompanying questions about evidence and reasons for believing) is to reveal an annoying and pernicious bias in favor of Western science and rational ways of knowing. It is to show a callous disregard for the kind of validation that can come from people's subjective experiences. It is—worst of all—to give offense to those who have strong beliefs about the effectiveness of a treatment.

Fortunately, scientists—being the pigheaded realists that they are—have persisted in asking question 1 and have thus discovered, among other things, that acupuncture is no better than placebo, homeopathy doesn't work, and chelation therapy can kill you.

Question 2, however, is almost never asked. One version of it is particularly rare: Is it ethical to recommend or promote an unproven treatment—one that has little or no scientific evidence supporting its efficacy?

The issue is important because companies, advertisers, special interest groups, magazines, newspapers, television talk shows, health practitioners, and others often do promote remedies and health practices that are unproven. This practice—for better or worse—can have enormous consequences for all of us.

Most medical scientists and health officials oppose the practice, sometimes warning that there isn't yet enough evidence to recommend a certain treatment to the public. Promoters of unproven treatments strongly disagree and sometimes ridicule officials for being "overly cautious" or "too conservative." Their most plausible arguments usually involve an appeal to the relative costs and benefits of a treatment. "What's the harm?" they may ask. "If the treatment itself is harmless, why shouldn't suffering people be given a chance to try it? There may be no strong evidence that it works, but if it does, the benefits to many people would be substantial. The costs to people—in terms of potential physical harm—are low. So on balance, it's best to urge people to try it; the possible benefits outweigh the possible costs." Promoters may believe that this argument is especially strong if the treatment has some preliminary evidence in its favor or if the monetary outlay for the treatment is low.

But is this really a good argument? Many on both sides in the debate would probably agree that weighing costs and benefits is a valid way to judge the issue. (This approach is based on the fundamental ethical insight that we ought to do what's likely to benefit people and avoid doing what's likely to harm them.) So the question reduces to whether promoting unproven treatments is likely to result in a net benefit to people. Does the promoter's argument show that his promoting leads to such benefit?

Actually, his argument fails. It fails because it's too simplistic, neglecting to take into account important factors in the cost-benefit equation.

One such factor is *probability*. Few people would judge a treatment solely on the magnitude of its proposed benefit or harm. Most would want to take into account the probability that the proposed effects would happen. Someone may claim that rubbing a stone on your belly will cure cancer. The alleged benefit is enormous—but the likelihood of receiving this benefit is almost nil. If someone wanted to sell you such a "cancer-curing" stone for ten dollars, would you buy it? Probably not. The proposed benefit is great but not likely to happen. The cost, though, is a sure thing: if you want the stone, you'll have to pay the price. So on balance, the likely cost, though small, outweighs the unlikely benefits, though great.

But what's the probability that any unproven remedy will be effective? The evidence relating to the remedy can't tell us; by definition, it's too weak to help us figure probabilities. We can, however, make a reasonable assumption. Scientists know that the chances of new hypotheses being correct are very low simply because it's far easier to be wrong than to be right. For the same reason, the likelihood of new health claims turning out to be true is also low. Historically, most health hypotheses, when adequately tested, have been found to be false. In drug testing, for example, scientists may begin with thousands of substances proposed as medicines, some with preliminary evidence in their favor. In the end, after assessing them all, only a meager handful are proven effective in humans. Some promoters misjudge the cost-benefit of recommending a treatment because they either overestimate the probability of its effectiveness or don't consider the factor at all. They seem to assume that the odds of any proposed remedy being effective are close to 50-50, especially if there's some preliminary evidence in its favor. This assumption is false.

When we plug realistic probabilities into our moral equation, the wisdom of promoting unproven treatments becomes suspect. Even if an unproven treatment has considerable possible benefits, is harmless, and costs little, it may be no bargain. In general, given the realistic probabilities, the most likely prospect is that the treatment will be ineffective. So, in fact, the odds are excellent that people who buy the treatment will waste their time and money. The likely cost outweighs the unlikely benefits. Promoting the treatment is not likely to result in a net benefit for people, but net harm. The possible benefit of a ten-dollar "cancer-fighting" rock may be great, but the low probability of its working makes buying it a bad deal. Promoting it would be unethical.

Clearly, the higher the cost of an unproven treatment, the less likely that promoting it will result in a net benefit. But there's more to the cost of an unproven treatment than many promoters realize. The monetary cost can vary tremendously and may not be low at all. (Many unconventional treatments cost hundreds or even thousands of dollars.) Other costs include the direct physical harm that a treatment can cause (nearly all treatments—drugs, surgery, herbs, vitamins, and others—cause some side effects). There's also an indirect cost: A few people (maybe many people) may take the promoter seriously and stop, postpone, or refuse a proven therapy to try the unproven one—a gamble that sometimes has tragic consequences. Then there's the very real emotional pain that false hope can often bring. In these ways, even a harmless therapy can cause harm. All these costs must be factored into the cost-benefit equation. Usually, they just make the promoter's argument weaker.

But, some will say, what about the placebo effect, the well-documented phenomenon of people tending to feel better after being given a bogus or inactive treatment? If someone who tries an unproven treatment experiences the placebo effect and therefore feels better, doesn't this mean that there is benefit to trying an unproven treatment after all? Doesn't the placebo effect thus change our moral equation?

The placebo effect (which happens in 30% or more of cases) would change the equation if it were unequivocally beneficial. But it is not. First, the placebo effect does not happen in every case. In fact, it is probable that in most cases it does not happen. Even when it does, it is often of short duration. So there is no guarantee that anyone will benefit from a placebo in any particular case. Second, placebos can cause adverse side effects (when they do, they're called nocebos). So they're not uniformly helpful. Third, placebo effects can encourage people to continue to use an ineffective treatment when more effective treatments are available. Placebo effects, after all, are not cures, but temporary feel-good phenomena. Fourth, placebo effects often inspire people to promote a remedy to friends and relatives—even though the remedy may be ineffective or harmful. This simply multiplies the problems that accrue to use of placebos. So in the promotion of unproven treatments, the placebo effect is usually not a point in the promoter's favor. Our moral equation still stands—generally *against* the promotion of merit- less remedies.

Now, it's possible that a person could apply the cost-benefit approach in her own life and rightly conclude that she *should* try an unproven remedy. She could calculate that any possible benefit, though very unlikely, is well worth the cost because no other treatment is possible or because she considers the cost inconsequential. Promoters, however, aren't privy to such personal information about those who try unproven remedies. Promoters can only weigh the prob- able impact of their actions on other people. If they do so honestly, they'll have to conclude that, generally, promoting unproven treatments does more harm than good.

Writing Assignments for this essay: Chap. 2, #2; Chap. 8, #2; Chap. 11, #2

ESSAY 7

Tight Limits on Stem Cells Betray Research Potential
USA TODAY
AUGUST 8, 2002

A year ago, President Bush received widespread applause for a savvy compro- mise on stem-cell research that appeared to offer something for everyone.

Medical researchers and the desperate patients who depend on them were promised enough of the uniquely malleable cells to test their potential to cure devastating diseases. Abortion opponents and others worried about the expand- ing ethical frontiers of medical science won assurances that the government would do nothing to encourage the deliberate creation of human embryos that would then be destroyed in stem-cell research.

The key to the compromise: Bush's claim that "more than 60" lines of stem cells are currently available for federally funded research, enough to meet scientists' needs. Restricting federal support to pre-existing sources of stem cells, the president said, would allow the nation to "explore the promise and potential of stem-cell research without crossing a fundamental moral line."

But a year later, the facts are getting in the way of the administration's assurances to researchers. Of the original 64 stem-cell lines counted by officials at the National Institutes of Health (NIH) last August, only five are now fully available to researchers, according to institutions that own rights to the self-replicating colonies of cells. Twelve others are available with some limitations, according to NIH. More than a dozen of the stem-cell lines remain largely untested; many of the others may never be available because of reasons ranging from legal disputes over ownership to medical problems with the colonies.

Yet instead of acknowledging the slow progress and looking for ways to fulfill the promised research opportunities, the Bush administration denies there's a problem. That response allows stem-cell research to whiz ahead overseas, while government-backed research in the USA moves at a glacial pace.

Among the problems:

- The NIH has funded only four new research efforts involving stem cells, none of which is fully underway. More such proposals in the pipeline are even further from start-up.
- The NIH has approved two dozen researchers' requests for federal funding to expand existing research projects to include embryonic stem cells, but only half have received government funds.
- The few lines of stem cells available to researchers lack sufficient genetic diversity to provide researchers with a full understanding of how they work.
- All of the cell lines on Bush's approved list were mixed with mouse cells, a process that taints their use as potential treatments.
- More than a dozen of the lines are largely untested and may never develop adequately for use in the lab.
- Researchers who have access to administration-approved stem-cell lines must spend precious time proving that their federal and private funds don't intermingle. Though the administration eased those rules this spring, scientists still complain that needless hurdles remain.

The administration claims that the slow progress is only natural in a new area of science. But during the past year, it says, it has made great strides in building a foundation to support stem-cell research.

In fact, the administration has created a network of legal agreements with the private owners of stem-cell lines that eventually should make it easier for researchers to gain access to the precious cells. It also has trained researchers to properly handle them.

Even so, such valuable legwork will go to waste if limits on government-backed research enable private labs and foreign researchers to race ahead of U.S. scientists who are restricted in their access to potentially lifesaving breakthroughs. Little wonder that Harvard researcher Douglas Melton reports problems attracting promising young scientists to the field.

The troubles trace back to the same cause: Bush's strict limits on the stem-cell lines that qualify for federal funding.

Proposals to expand the stem-cell lines ignite passionate ethical concerns. The most common is the specter that human embryos will be created and then destroyed solely for research.

The concern is valid. But the controversy is avoidable.

Today, there are thousands of unwanted human embryos left from attempts at in-vitro fertilization. Destined for destruction anyway, the embryos could re-invigorate the nation's stem-cell research program if Bush would extend federal funding to include stem cells from these sources.

Yet Bush's spokesmen say he is comfortable with his decision and doesn't plan to loosen the rules. To the contrary, a Bush-appointed bioethics panel is pushing for stronger limits on the cells' use, a step that would further slow research. To their credit, neither the administration nor Congress has shown much interest in pursuing those plans.

Where they need to focus their interest is on a new plan that would produce the significant medical progress Bush promised a year ago. The record increasingly shows that the old rules must go.

Writing Assignments for this essay: Chap. 3, #2; Chap. 4, #5

ESSAY 8

The Cohabitation Epidemic

NEIL CLARK WARREN

A few summers ago, tennis stars Andre Agassi and Steffi Graf announced that their first child would be born. "This is a very exciting time for us," Agassi said. "We are so happy to be blessed with this gift." No one seemed to notice—or care—that the couple wasn't married. Only a generation ago, this revelation would have raised eyebrows.

Yes, things have changed dramatically over the past few decades. According to the U.S. Census Bureau, 1 million people were in "unmarried-partner households" in 1970. The number rose to 3.2 million in 1990. And in 2000, the figure soared to 11 million. Now, half of all Americans ages 35 to 39 have lived with someone outside of marriage, according to researcher Larry Bumpass. Make no mistake: We are witnessing a major societal shift before our very eyes.

When an epidemic reaches this level of societal acceptance, many well-meaning people begin to ask, "Should we accept cohabitation as another social trend akin to fast food, cell phones and casual Fridays?" You may be wondering whether all this hubbub about living together is much ado about nothing. As a psychologist who has worked with singles and married couples for 35 years, I think our alarm over this issue is much ado about a lot.

Who Cohabits and Why

Typically, people who cohabit fall into two categories. First, there are those who have little or no intention of getting married. They simply want to enjoy the benefits of living together—the availability of sex, combined financial resources, shared household responsibilities and so on. This arrangement allows for a "quick exit" if things turn sour. The second group are those who see living together as a trial marriage—a half-step toward the altar. These people say, "We'll live together first and see how it goes." They consider it prudent to take a test drive before signing on the dotted line.

Though I don't want to oversimplify a complex issue, I believe there are three primary reasons why these couples forgo or delay marriage:

1. Marriage has lost a lot of its luster in our society. The truth is, many people have never seen a successful, thriving marriage, mainly because great marriages are becoming scarce. Several years ago, I conducted a survey in which I asked 500 individuals to tell me about the marriage they most admired. To my dismay, nearly half said they couldn't recommend even one healthy, exemplary marriage! With such a dearth of model marriages, it's understandable why so many young people hesitate to take the plunge.

2. Beyond the lack of model marriages, millions of people have suffered significant pain from broken marriages. One researcher estimates that 70 percent of all Americans have been impacted by divorce—either their parents' or their own. When a broken marriage devastates someone's life, she or he may figure that getting married is just too risky.

3. The majority of singles have lost confidence in their ability to correctly judge a highly compatible and thus long-lasting match. Yet their needs for companionship, sexual satisfaction and economic sufficiency motivate them to search for a person with whom they can have at least a temporary partnership.

So Why Bother with Marriage?

We can certainly argue against cohabiting from a biblical standpoint, because numerous Scriptures admonish us to avoid sexual immorality and to keep marriage sacred (Hebrews 13:4, 1 Corinthians 6:18, 1 Thessalonians 4:3). But let's be realistic: Many couples who live together don't care about biblical principles, and even faith-oriented people often ignore what the Bible says. This is why psychological and other social science research becomes so critical. The findings of this research overwhelmingly support marriage over cohabitation. Consider:

Marriage vows serve as glue that holds people together. Numerous empirical studies destroy the myth that living together is good preparation for marriage, thus reducing the risk of divorce. In fact, one study involving 3,300 cases found that people who cohabited prior to marriage had a 46 percent higher marital failure rate than noncohabiters.

Think about it. The fundamental agreement upon which live-in relationships are based is conditional commitment. This attitude says, "I'll stick with you as long as things go well. But if we run into problems, all bets are off." Relationships that begin with a quasi-commitment carry the same mind-set into marriage. When things become trying, as inevitably they will from time to time, the spouses say goodbye.

As David Popenoe and Barbara Dafoe Whitehead wrote in their extensive review of recent literature, "Virtually all research on the subject has determined that the chances of divorce ending a marriage preceded by cohabitation are significantly greater than for a marriage not preceded by cohabitation."

Marriage provides the most stability for children. Few live-in couples intend to have children, but it often happens. More than a quarter of unmarried mothers are cohabiting at the time of their children's birth. Further, two-thirds of children who end up in stepfamilies have parents who are cohabiting rather than married.

This means that each year thousands of children are born or moved into families where Mom and Dad's commitment to each other is tenuous or, at least, informal. These children, during their most vulnerable developmental stages, are deprived of the security that comes from knowing their parents have pledged themselves to each other for a lifetime. To make matters worse, 75 percent of all children born to cohabiting parents will experience their parents' separation before they reach age 16. Only about one-third of children born to married parents face a similar fate.

Marriage offers promised permanence. Most wedding vows still include the promise to "love, honor and cherish in sickness and in health, in plenty or in want, till death do us part." One reason this is so important: The best relationships require partners who are genuine and authentic—who can be their real selves. The promised permanence of marriage allows just that: "I'll stick with you even when I come to know the real you, with all your imperfections and shortcomings." But how can two individuals be authentic and genuine if they think their partner may bolt at the first sign of trouble? With the conditional commitment of live-in relationships, partners are left wondering, If I'm not who my partner wants me to be—if he sees my faults—will he pack his bags and leave?

Marriage creates healthier individuals. Scores of studies have shown that married people are better off emotionally, physically, financially and vocationally than unmarried partners. For example, annual rates of depression among cohabiting couples are more than three times what they are among married couples. And women in cohabiting relationships are significantly more likely than married women to suffer physical and sexual abuse.

Marriage partners are more likely to be faithful. Four times as much infidelity is reported among cohabiting men than among married men. Moreover, one married woman in a hundred reports having had an affair in the past year, compared to 8 percent of cohabiting women.

Amid the alarming statistics about cohabitation, we can confidently tell singles that a "trial marriage" is unnecessary. In addition to the research showing the detriments of living together, several studies have discovered—with 80 percent to 94 percent accuracy—the variables that predict which marriages will thrive and which will not. This means unmarried couples can know in advance if they have a better-than-average chance of succeeding in marriage. With this available information, hopefully the cohabitation trend will begin to cycle downward.

Writing Assignments for this essay: Chap. 4, #3; Chap. 5, #2

ESSAY 9

The Demon-Haunted Sentence: A Skeptical Analysis of Reverse Speech

TOM BYRNE AND MATTHEW NORMAND

In the past several years, a researcher named David Oates has been advocating his discovery of a most interesting phenomenon. Oates claims that backward messages are hidden unintentionally in all human speech. The messages can be understood by recording normal speech and playing it in reverse. This phenomena, reverse speech, has been discussed by Oates in a number of books, magazines, newspapers, and radio programs, and even on television with Larry King and Geraldo Rivera. His company, Reverse Speech Enterprises, is dedicated to profiting from his discovery. The basics of Oates's theory are outlined in his book *Reverse Speech: Hidden Messages in Human Communication*. He also outlines his theories on Reverse Speech Enterprise's large and detailed Web page (http://www.reversespeech.com). The following quotes taken from that page define the main characteristics and implications of reverse speech; similar statements can be found in his publications.

> Human speech has two distinctive yet complementary functions and modes. The Overt mode is spoken forwards and is primarily under conscious control. The Covert mode is spoken backward and is not under conscious control. The backward mode of speech occurs simultaneously with the forward mode and is a reversal of the forward speech sounds.

> These two modes of speech, forward and backward, are dependent upon each other and form an integral part of human communication. . . .

> Covert speech develops before overt speech. Children speak backwards before they do forwards. . . .

> Reverse speech is the voice of truth and it is complementary with forward speech. The two modes occur simultaneously yet are formed in different areas of the mind. Simply, forward speech is from the left brain and Reverse Speech is from the right brain. . . . If a lie is spoken forwards, the truth may be spoken backwards. Any thought that is on a person's mind has the potential to appear in Reverse Speech. . . . It can reveal hidden memory and experiences. . . . Employers can use it for employee selection, lawyers for deposition analysis, reporters for politicians' speeches. Its applications are endless. . . . Put simply, the discovery of reverse speech means that the human mind is no longer private. Any thought, any emotion, any motive that any person has can appear backwards in human speech. The implications are mind boggling because reverse speech opens up the Truth.

It is the great potential for harm evident in the last and most disturbing item that prompted this article. We argue that there is no scientific evidence for the phenomena of reverse speech; and that the use of reverse speech as lie detection in courts of law or any other forum, as advocated by Oates, is entirely invalid and unjust.

The burden of proof for any phenomenon lies upon the shoulders of those claiming its existence. To our knowledge there is not one empirical investigation of reverse speech in any peer-reviewed journal. If reverse speech did exist it would be, at the very least, a noteworthy scientific discovery. However, there are no data to support the existence of reverse speech or Oates's theories about its implications. Although descriptions of "research papers" are available on the Reverse Speech Web site, there is no good indication that Oates has conducted any scholarly or empirical investigation. We found only two outside analyses of reverse speech. The first, Newbrook and Curtain, is a Web-published document discussed below, and the other is a brief review of Oates's aforementioned book that appeared in *Library Journal*. The reviewer, Susan Brombacher, concluded that Oates's theories are difficult to prove and that he seems more interested in making a profit than educating others. We concur with both points. The Reverse Speech Web page contains a plethora of merchandise and services available to consumers at considerable prices. These include reverse-play tape recorders ($225), T-shirts ($18), signed copies of Oates's book ($29.95), and various training workshops ($850–$1,500). Furthermore, we believe that the reason the phenomenon of reverse speech is difficult to prove is it does not exist.

The very existence of reverse speech is ecologically invalid. "Backwards" language does not convey meaning to a listener—in other words it does not make any sense. This has been put to empirical test. Subjects who hear recordings of words played backwards are unable to report what words they heard. The ability to communicate through language is an incredibly complex marvel of evolution. If reverse speech existed, it would not be comprehensible and would have no practical value. Therefore, there would be no selection mechanism by which it would evolve. It would truly be a "miracle." And, as for all miracles, we do not have a shred of supporting evidence.

We are not claiming that reverse speech is a simple hoax. In fact it is quite possible that Oates and his followers are convinced of its existence. As far back as the 1930s, controlled scientific studies were conducted demonstrating the tendency for people to "hear" things that were not there. One of the methods employed to study such phenomena was the verbal summator, as described by the American psychologist B. F. Skinner. The verbal summator consisted of a phonograph (or tape) of random vowel sounds that were grouped together in such a way as to not produce any systematic phonetic groupings. These random phonetic sounds were arranged into patterns that approximated common stress patterns in everyday conversation.

After such strings of nonsense syllables were arranged, they were played for subjects at barely audible volume levels. After repeatedly listening to these sounds, subjects reported "hearing" the phonograph or the tape "say" things. These sentences, or sentence fragments, did not actually exist and, as such, were considered to be utterances that were already strong in the subject's repertoire.

Put another way, they were "projecting" their own thoughts onto the sounds they were hearing.

Oates frequently plays examples of reversed-speech phrases in which the listener can hear what appears to be meaningful speech. It is not difficult to hear something that sounds like English phrases when they have been pointed out. However, as in messages heard from the verbal summator, the phonemes may sound similar to a meaningful phrase but are really sound salad. A listener expecting to hear a certain phrase will likely do so. In their critique of Oates's theories, Newman and Curtain conducted a simple experiment in which subjects under various conditions tried to detect examples of reverse speech from Oates's audiotapes. As expected, they found that subjects who were told what to listen for were much more successful in hearing the phrases than those not expecting what they would hear. This is analogous to seeing a certain image in a cloud formation only after another person has pointed it out. Fortunately, most of us recognize that a cloud that looks like Elvis is not really Elvis. Backward phonemes, however, may convincingly sound like a real sentence and are not as readily dismissed as coincidence.

Oates's claims have dangerous implications. He states not only that reverse speech is real but also that it always "tells" the truth. He calls it the "ultimate lie detector test." Although some types of nonverbal communication (e.g., facial expressions) may be of limited use for lie detection, the search for a surefire mechanism that uncovers whatever truths lie in the unconscious is best left to science fiction writers and kept out of courts of law; no such mechanism exists. Adding to the insidious nature of these claims, Oates states that one has to be specially trained to hear reverse speech; those who pay him a hefty sum and go through his training can then serve as expert witnesses and command hefty sums themselves. As expert witnesses they could analyze testimony played backwards and inform a court what a witness is truly saying. The judge and jury, not having the training, will be unable to verify this information. The potential damage could be enormous since the "truth" may be invented from the subjective interpretation of nonsense syllables. Furthermore Oates advocates the use of reverse speech not simply as a lie detector, but as a useful tool for psychotherapists. Although Oates states that he and his colleagues "are not therapists," he describes the goal of one of his training programs as to "Prepare the student to establish their own therapeutic practice" (available at http://www.reversespeech.cpm/courses.shtml). It seems that no matter what Oates and his colleagues call themselves, they are engaging in practices that most people would deem clinical in nature. Advocating therapy based on such questionable theories is unethical.

Hopefully the questionable validity of reverse speech will be recognized before history repeats itself. Not so long ago, belief in facilitated communication, another invented form of communication, led to witch-hunt investigations based on information that had absolutely no basis in reality. In facilitated communication, a nonspeaking individual receives assistance from a "facilitator" who guides his or her hands across a keyboard so that a message can be typed. Curiously, many nonspeaking individuals who seemed to benefit from facilitated communication did not have motor deficits. Therefore, it was unclear why motor assistance would help them communicate. Controlled studies repeatedly demonstrated that the facilitator in fact manifested the messages communicated by the nonverbal individuals either intentionally or unintentionally. As stated by Gorman, "When the assisting facilitator could not see or hear the questions presented, autistic individuals could not communicate correct answers, and what was typed was actually what the facilitator saw."

Far from being innocuous, facilitated communication led to false accusations of sexual abuse and resulting court trials that severely disrupted the lives of innocent people. It is easy to see how reverse speech has the same maleficent potential as facilitated communication. The person trained to hear reverse messages could intentionally or unintentionally report that speech contains hidden incriminating evidence. Many people are not prepared to refute such contrived evidence.

The danger of facilitated communication was recognized, and it is no longer considered to be scientifically valid by most professionals working in the disability field. In 1994, the American Psychological Association adopted a resolution stating that facilitated communication is a controversial and unproved communicative procedure with no scientifically demonstrated support for its efficacy. We advocate a similar stance on reverse speech. Without validation of its existence, the potential for harm greatly exceeds any benefits. Until that time, we should not allow the use of reverse speech in any situation in which important decisions must be made.

Writing Assignments for this essay: Chap. 9, #3; Chap. 10, #2

ESSAY 10

Amityville: The Horror of It All

JOE NICKELL

The bestselling book *The Amityville Horror: A True Story* was followed by a movie of the same title and a sequel, *Amityville II: The Possession*. Although the original event proved to be a hoax, that fact does not seem well known to the general public. . . . Now a new book sheds new light on the sordid affair and reviews the multiple-murder case that preceded it. Written by Ric Osuna, it is titled *The Night the DeFeos Died: Reinvestigating the Amityville Murders*.

The saga began on November 13, 1974, with the murders of Ronald DeFeo Sr., his wife Louise, and their two sons and two daughters. The six were shot while they slept in their home in Amityville, New York, a community on Long Island. Subsequently the sole remaining family member—Ronald Jr., nicknamed "Butch"—confessed to the slaughter and was sentenced to twenty-five years to life. Just two weeks after his sentencing late the following year, George and Kathy Lutz and their three children moved into the tragic home where— allegedly—a new round of horrors began.

The six-bedroom Dutch Colonial house was to be the Lutzes' residence for only twenty-eight days. They claimed they were driven out by sinister forces that ripped open a heavy door, leaving it hanging from one hinge; threw open windows, bending their locks; caused green slime to ooze from a ceiling; peered into the house at night with red eyes and left cloven-hooved tracks in the snow outside; infested a room in mid-winter with hundreds of houseflies; and produced myriad other supposedly paranormal phenomena, including inflicting a priest with inexplicable, painful blisters on his hands.

Local New York television's Channel 5 "investigated" the alleged haunting by bringing in alleged psychics together with "demonologist" Ed Warren and his wife Lorraine, a professed "clairvoyant." The group held a series of séances in the house. One psychic claimed to be ill and to "feel personally threatened" by shadowy forces. Lorraine Warren pronounced that there was a negative entity "right from the bowels of the earth." A further séance was unproductive but psychics agreed a "demonic spirit" possessed the house and recommended exorcism (Nickell 1995).

In September 1977 *The Amityville Horror: A True Story* appeared. Written by Jay Anson, a professional writer commissioned by Prentice-Hall to tell the Lutzes' story, it became a runaway best seller. Anson asserted: "There is simply too much independent corroboration of their narrative to support the speculation that they either imagined or fabricated these events," although he conceded that the strange occurrences had ceased after the Lutzes moved out.

Indeed, a man who later lived there for eight months said he had experienced nothing more horrible than a stream of gawkers who tramped onto the property. Similarly the couple who purchased the house after it was given up by the Lutzes, James and Barbara Cromarty, poured ice water on the hellish tale. They confirmed the suspicions of various investigators that it was a bogus admixture of phenomena: part traditional haunting, part poltergeist disturbance, and part demonic possession, including elements that seemed to have been lifted from the movie *The Exorcist*.

Researchers Rick Moran and Peter Jordan (1978) discovered that the police had not been called to the house and that there had been no snowfall when the Lutzes claimed to have discovered cloven hoofprints in the snow. Other claims were similarly disproved (Kaplan and Kaplan 1995).

I talked with Barbara Cromarty on three occasions, including when I visited Amityville as a consultant to the *In Search Of* television series. She told me not only that her family had experienced no supernatural occurrences in the house, but that she had evidence the whole affair was a hoax. Subsequently I recommended to a producer of the then-forthcoming TV series *That's Incredible*, who had called for my advice about filming inside the house, that they have Mrs. Cromarty point out various discrepancies for close-up viewing. For example, recalling the extensive damage to doors and windows detailed by the Lutzes, she noted that the old hardware—hinges, locks, doorknob, etc.—were still in place. Upon close inspection, one could see that there were no disturbances in the paint and varnish (Nickell 1995).

In time, Ronald DeFeo's attorney, William Weber, told how the Lutzes had come to him after leaving the house, and he had told them their "experiences" could be useful to him in preparing a book. "We created this horror story over many bottles of wine that George Lutz was drinking," Weber told the Associated Press. "We were creating something the public wanted to hear about." Weber later filed a two-million-dollar lawsuit against the couple, charging them with reneging on their book deal. The Cromartys also sued the Lutzes, Anson, and the publishers, maintaining that the fraudulent haunting claims had resulted in sightseers destroying any privacy they might have had. During the trials the Lutzes admitted that virtually everything in *The Amityville Horror* was pure fiction (Nickell 1995; Kaplan and Kaplan 1995).

Now Ric Osuna's *The Night the DeFeos Died* adds to the evidence. Ronald DeFeo's wife Geraldine allegedly confirms much of Weber's account. To her, it was clear that the hoax had been planned for some time. Weber had intended to use the haunting claims to help obtain a new trial for his client (Osuna 2002, 282–286).

As to George Lutz—now divorced from his wife and criticized by his former stepsons—Osuna states that "George informed me that setting the record straight was not as important as making money off fictional sequels." Osuna details numerous contradictions in the story that Lutz continues to offer versions of (286–289).

For his part, Osuna has his own story to tell. He buys Ronald "Butch" DeFeo's current story about the murders, assuring his readers that it "is true and has never been made public" (18, 22). DeFeo now alleges that his sister Dawn urged him to kill the entire family and that she and two of Butch's friends had participated in the crimes.

In fact, Butch maintains that Dawn began the carnage by shooting their domineering father with the .35-caliber Marlin rifle. Butch then shot his mother, whom he felt would have turned him in for the crime, but claims he never intended to kill his siblings. He left the house to look for one of his friends who had left the scene and, when he returned to find that Dawn had murdered her sister and other two brothers, he was enraged. He fought with her for the gun and sent her flying into a bedpost where she was knocked out. He then shot her.

Osuna tries to make this admittedly "incredible" tale believable by explaining away contradictory evidence. He accepts DeFeo's claim that he altered the crime scene and asserts that the authorities engaged in abuses and distortions of evidence to support their theory of the crimes. Even so, Osuna concedes that "Butch had offered several different, if ludicrous, versions of what had occurred" (33), and that he might again change his story. But he asserts that "Too much independent corroboration exists to believe it was just another one of his lies" (370).

I remain unconvinced. Butch DeFeo has forfeited his right to be believed, and his current tale is full of implausibilities and contradictions. Osuna appears to me to simply have become yet another of his victims.

References

Anson, Jay. 1977. *The Amityville Horror: A True Story*. New York: Bantam Books.

Kaplan, Stephen, and Roxanne Salch Kaplan. 1995. *The Amityville Horror Conspiracy*. Lacyville, Pa.: Belfrey Books.

Moran, Rick, and Peter Jordan. 1978. The Amityville Horror Hoax, *Fate,* May, 44–46.

Nickell, Joe. 1995. *Entities: Angels, Spirits, Demons, and Other Alien Beings*. Amherst, N.Y.: Prometheus Books, 122–129. (Background for the present article has been abridged from this source.)

Osuna, Ric. 2002. *The Night the DeFeos Died: Reinvestigating the Amityville Murders*. N.p.: Xlibris Corporation.

Writing Assignment for this essay: Chap. 10, #4

ESSAY II
A Deviance from God's Norm

RICHARD LAND

Recently, Senator Rick Santorum was attacked by the liberal media, politicians, and pro-homosexual groups for comments he made about a case being argued currently before the US Supreme Court.

The plaintiff in this case, who was arrested by Houston sheriff's deputies and fined for engaging in homosexual behavior outlawed in Texas, is attempting to have Texas' anti-sodomy law ruled unconstitutional. When asked by an Associated Press reporter to state his opinion about homosexual behavior, Mr. Santorum referred to the Supreme Court case and commented that activities like sodomy, "undermine the basic tenets of our society and the family."

In return for stating his honest opinion Mr. Santorum has been subjected to an endless, venomous diatribe. Liberals and pro-homosexual groups have decided that Mr. Santorum is bigoted and intolerant and no longer worthy material for Senate leadership. The treatment Mr. Santorum has endured for stating his opinion—which by the way, is the opinion of the vast majority of Americans—serves as a vivid reminder of the tactics of his attackers.

Because the homosexual-rights groups have been unable to persuade the majority of Americans that homosexuality is good for us, they have resorted to attacking anyone who speaks the majority opinion. In so doing the gay thought police have revealed themselves for what they really are—bullies who threaten and intimidate those who dare to speak out against them.

We must ask who the real bigots are here. In America, speaking one's mind is a Constitutionally-protected right. The real bigots are those who label anyone who disagrees with them as bigoted and intolerant and attack them for sharing their beliefs. Mr. Santorum has not called for anyone's resignation or dismissal. His detractors have. Once again, the homosexual-rights groups have revealed that they are the real bigots.

Our society has the responsibility and the right to discourage the practice of homosexuality. The Judeo-Christian teaching on this is clear. Homosexuality is a deviance from God's norm. It is neither normal nor healthy behavior. Lest anyone think that this theological position is merely sectarian, it is important to note that even the renowned theologian Wolfhart Pannenberg concluded that when the church has "ceased to treat homosexual activity as a departure from the biblical norm" it "would no longer stand on biblical ground but against the unequivocal witness of Scripture" and "would thereby have ceased to be one, holy, catholic, and apostolic."

Furthermore, any attempt to equate homosexuality with race or ethnicity should offend all of us. There is no evidence that homosexuality is an inborn trait, in spite of numerous efforts to prove the contrary. Homosexuality has many contributing causes, but it is obviously not to be equated with race or ethnicity. A person's ethnicity is what one is, whereas homosexual behavior is what one does.

As Christians, we will continue to support politicians who speak out against homosexuality and to oppose those who support special rights for homosexuals and who seek to support societal approval of homosexual behavior. I applaud Mr. Santorum for courageously sharing his beliefs. We hope other politicians will be emboldened by his stand to hold firm to their convictions about the immorality of homosexual behavior and resist the bullying and intimidation tactics of radical homosexual-rights groups.

Writing Assignments for this essay: Chap. 7, #4; Chap. 11, #4

ESSAY 12

Marriage Still Evolving, as Ever

BUFFALO NEWS
APRIL 2, 2006

The refrain echoes from pulpit to parishioner, from megaphone to protester, from blogger to reader: Marriage is a bond between a man and a woman, and *only* that.

In most cases, perhaps 90 percent, it is. But as New York prepares for a Court of Appeals decision this summer that could legalize or pave the way for gay marriage, people might want to try getting their heads around the idea that marriage is and has been many things. But it never was engraved in romantic, heterosexual—even monogamous—marble. Marriage is an evolving, dynamic, living arrangement.

Marriage only recently, say in the last 150 years, focused on two people in love. Before that, it was more often than not—at all income levels—a forced or coerced arrangement about status, property or power. You could be a prince or a pauper, but your father was often trying to enhance his kingdom, or diet, by hooking you up with someone who could help him do that.

There was a time when women entering marriage lost all their rights to their husbands, something most women today would find laughable. Even more extreme, women at one time, as part of marriage, became a man's property. There were laws in this country that said marriage protected men against accusations of spousal rape. If you were a woman, your husband could rape you with impunity. Marriage, by law or custom, was restricted along racial or religious lines. "Intermarriage" was viewed as hurting or weakening a race, religion or group.

Finally, marriage used to be unviolable, something impossible to split. Today divorce is routine, with half ending before death do us part. That may or may not be good for society, children and spouses, but it shows how marriage is still evolving.

So when supporters talk about gays and lesbians marrying—and thereby gaining an estimated 1,500 rights that accrue to married people but are routinely denied to gays—it's more evolution. You may not agree; you may believe that *only* men and women should marry. But as more states approve, it might help to understand marriage's history and its dynamic place in our lives by examining its fluid reality.

Writing Assignment for this essay: Chap. 2, #4

ESSAY I3
Slouching Toward Chimeras
JEREMY RIFKIN

What happens when you cross a human and a mouse? Sounds like the beginning of a bad joke but, in fact, it's a serious high tech experiment recently carried out by a research team headed by a distinguished molecular biologist, Irving Weissman, at Stanford University's Institute of Cancer/Stem Cell Biology and Medicine. Scientists injected human brain cells into mouse fetuses, creating a strain of mice that were approximately 1 percent human. Dr. Weissman is actively considering a follow-up experiment that would produce mice whose brains are 100 percent human.

What if the mice escaped the laboratory and began to proliferate in the outside environment? What might be the ecological consequences of mice who think like human beings, let loose in nature? Dr. Weissman says he would keep a tight rein on the mice and if they showed any signs of humanness he would kill them. Hardly reassuring.

In a world where the bizarre has become all too commonplace, few things any longer shock the human psyche. But, experiments like the one that produced a partially humanized mouse at Stanford University stretch the limits of human tinkering with nature to the realm of the pathological.

The new research field at the cutting edge of the biotech revolution is called chimeric experimentation. Researchers around the world are combining human and animal cells and creating chimeric creatures that are part human and part animal, reminiscent of the ancient Greek chimeric myths of human-animal hybrids.

The first such chimeric experiment occurred many years ago when scientists in Edinburgh, Scotland fused together a sheep and goat embryo—two completely unrelated animal species that are incapable of mating and producing a hybrid offspring in nature. The resulting creature, called a Geep, was born with the head of a goat and the body of a sheep.

Now, scientists have their sights trained on breaking the final taboo in the natural world—crossing humans and animals to create new human-animal hybrids of every kind and description. Already, aside from the humanized mouse, scientists have created pigs with human blood running through their veins and sheep with livers and hearts that are mostly human.

The experiments are designed to advance medical research. Indeed, a growing number of genetic engineers argue that human-animal hybrids will usher in a golden era of medicine. Researchers say that the more humanized they can make research animals, the better able they will be to model the progression of human diseases, test new drugs, and harvest tissues and organs for transplantation into human bodies. What they fail to mention is that there are other equally promising and less invasive alternatives to these kinds of bizarre experiments including sophisticated computer modeling to study diseases and test the effectiveness and toxicity of drugs as well as in vitro tissue culture, nanotechnology, and artificial prostheses to substitute for human tissue and organs. When it comes to chimeric experimentation, then, the question is, at what price?

Some researchers are speculating about human-chimpanzee chimeras— creating a humanzee. A humanzee would be the ideal laboratory research animal because chimpanzees are so closely related to human beings. Chimps share 98 percent of the human genome and a fully mature chimp has the equivalent mental abilities and consciousness of a four-year-old human child. Fusing a human and chimpanzee embryo—a feat researchers say is quite feasible—could produce a creature so human that questions regarding its moral and legal status would throw 4,000 years of human ethics into utter chaos.

Would such a creature enjoy human rights and protections under the law? For example, it's possible that such a creature could cross the species barrier and mate with a human. Would society allow inter-species conjugation? Would a humanzee have to pass some kind of "humanness" test to win its freedom? Would it be forced into doing menial labor or be used to perform dangerous activities?

The horrific possibilities are mind-boggling. For example, what if human stem cells—the primordial cells that turn into the body's 200 or so cell types—were to be injected into an animal embryo and spread throughout the animal's body into every organ? Some human cells could migrate to the testes and ovaries where they could grow into human sperm and eggs. If two of the chimeric mice were to mate, they could potentially conceive a human embryo. If the human embryo were to be removed and implanted in a human womb, the resulting human baby's biological parents would have been chimeric mice.

Please understand that none of this is science fiction. The American National Academy of Sciences, the country's most august scientific body, issued guidelines for chimeric research on April 25, anticipating a flurry of new experiments in the burgeoning field of human-animal chimeric experimentation. What would be the ramifications of creating hundreds, even thousands, of new life forms that are part human and part other creature? Creatures that could mate, reproduce, and repopulate the Earth?

Bio-ethicists are already clearing the moral path for human-animal chimeric experiments, arguing that once society gets past the revulsion factor, the prospect of new, partially human creatures has much to offer the human race. And, of course, this is exactly the kind of reasoning that has been put forth time and again to justify what is fast becoming a macabre journey into a monstrous Brave New World in which all of nature can be ruthlessly manipulated and reengineered to suit the momentary needs and even whims and caprices of just one species, the Homo sapiens. But now, with human-animal chimeric experiments, we risk even undermining our own species' biological integrity in the name of human progress.

With chimeric technology, scientists now have the power to rewrite the evolutionary saga—to sprinkle parts of the Homo sapiens species into the rest of the animal kingdom as well as fuse parts of other species into our own genome and even to create new human subspecies and superspecies. Are we on the cusp of a biological renaissance, as some believe, or sowing the seeds of our own destruction? Perhaps it is time to ask what we mean by progress.

Writing Assignment for this essay: Chap. 3, #4

ESSAY 14
The Right to Ridicule
RONALD DWORKIN

The British and most of the American press have been right, on balance, not to republish the Danish cartoons that millions of furious Muslims protested against in violent and terrible destruction around the world. Reprinting would very likely have meant—and could still mean—more people killed and more property destroyed. It would have caused many British and American Muslims great pain because they would have been told by other Muslims that the publication was intended to show contempt for their religion, and though that perception would in most cases have been inaccurate and unjustified, the pain would nevertheless have been genuine. True, readers and viewers who have been following the story might well have wanted to judge the cartoons' impact, humor, and offensiveness for themselves, and the press might therefore have felt some responsibility to provide that opportunity. But the public does not have a right to read or see whatever it wants no matter what the cost, and the cartoons are in any case widely available on the Internet.

Sometimes the press's self-censorship means the loss of significant information, argument, literature, or art, but not in this case. Not publishing may seem to give a victory to the fanatics and authorities who instigated the violent protests against them and therefore incite them to similar tactics in the future. But there is strong evidence that the wave of rioting and destruction—suddenly, four months after the cartoons were first published—was orchestrated by Muslim leaders in Denmark and in the Middle East for larger political reasons. If that analysis is correct, then keeping the issue boiling by fresh republications would actually serve the interests of those responsible and reward their strategies of encouraging violence.

There is a real danger, however, that the decision of the British and American press not to publish, though wise, will be wrongly taken as an endorsement of the widely held opinion that freedom of speech has limits, that it must be balanced against the virtues of "multiculturalism," and that the Blair government was right after all to propose that it be made a crime to publish anything "abusive or insulting" to a religious group.

Freedom of speech is not just a special and distinctive emblem of Western culture that might be generously abridged or qualified as a measure of respect for other cultures that reject it, the way a crescent or menorah might be added to a Christian religious display. Free speech is a condition of legitimate government. Laws and policies are not legitimate unless they have been adopted through a democratic process, and a process is not democratic if government has prevented anyone from expressing his convictions about what those laws and policies should be.

Ridicule is a distinct kind of expression; its substance cannot be repackaged in a less offensive rhetorical form without expressing something very different from what was intended. That is why cartoons and other forms of ridicule have for centuries, even when illegal, been among the most important weapons of both noble and wicked political movements.

So in a democracy no one, however powerful or impotent, can have a right not to be insulted or offended. That principle is of particular importance in a nation that strives for racial and ethnic fairness. If weak or unpopular minorities wish to be protected from economic or legal discrimination by law—if they wish laws enacted that prohibit discrimination against them in employment, for instance—then they must be willing to tolerate whatever insults or ridicule people who oppose such legislation wish to offer to their fellow voters, because only a community that permits such insult as part of public debate may legitimately adopt such laws. If we expect bigots to accept the verdict of the majority once the majority has spoken, then we must permit them to express their bigotry in the process whose verdict we ask them to accept. Whatever multiculturalism means—whatever it means to call for increased "respect" for all citizens and groups—these virtues would be self-defeating if they were thought to justify official censorship.

Muslims who are outraged by the Danish cartoons note that in several European countries it is a crime publicly to deny, as the president of Iran has denied, that the Holocaust ever took place. They say that Western concern for free speech is therefore only self-serving hypocrisy, and they have a point. But of course the remedy is not to make the compromise of democratic legitimacy even greater than it already is but to work toward a new understanding of the European Convention on Human Rights that would strike down the Holocaust-denial law and similar laws across Europe for what they are: violations of the freedom of speech that that convention demands.

It is often said that religion is special, because people's religious convictions are so central to their personalities that they should not be asked to tolerate ridicule of their beliefs, and because they might feel a religious duty to strike back at what they take to be sacrilege. Britain has apparently embraced that view because it retains the crime of blasphemy, though only for insults to Christianity. But we cannot make an exception for religious insult if we want to use law to protect the free exercise of religion in other ways. If we want to forbid the police from profiling people who look or dress like Muslims for special searches, for example, we cannot also forbid people from opposing that policy by claiming, in cartoons or otherwise, that Islam is committed to terrorism, however misguided we think that opinion is. Certainly we should criticize the judgment and taste of such people. But religion must observe the principles of democracy, not the other way around. No religion can be permitted to legislate for everyone about what can or cannot be drawn any more than it can legislate about what may or may not be eaten. No one's religious convictions can be thought to trump the freedom that makes democracy possible.

Writing Assignment for this essay: Chap. 11, #5

ESSAY 15
Time to Think

MARK FRANEK

As high school juniors file into classrooms for their SAT's on Saturday, there will probably be some chatter about how more than 4,000 of last fall's tests were scored too low. What they probably won't be aware of is how many of their fellow students may end up with higher scores because they are allowed more time to take the test. Last year, more than 40,000 of the two million SAT takers were granted special accommodations, mainly because of learning disabilities. This represents a doubling in the past decade and a half.

In a perfect world, accommodations on the SAT would level the playing field for all test-takers with learning disabilities. Is that the case? The College Board, the overseer of the SAT, declines to give figures on the family incomes of students who get extra time.

It would be a good guess, however, that such accommodations are not being awarded fairly across race and socioeconomic lines—it generally takes a lot of time, energy and, in some cases, money to get on the accommodations list in the first place. A student must have his learning disability documented by a psychologist, and then use the accommodations recommended by the psychologist on tests at his own high school.

The trend in requesting extensions troubles many schools and teachers. While they made no mention of requests for accommodations, more than 200 high school administrators in January submitted a petition to the College Board that criticized the length of the test and asked the board to give students the option of taking each of the test's three sections (writing, math and critical reading) on different days.

But this recommendation would succeed only in making an already unfair situation worse by increasing the overall cost of the test for students. The SAT is not too long—it's too short. The fairest solution would be to make it untimed for everyone.

Extra-time accommodations fall into two categories: time and a half (so the regular 3 hour 45 minute test swells to just over five and a half hours) and double time. But when scores are reported to colleges, there is no indication whether students had the usual amount of time, or more.

This lack of transparency is untenable. If we continue to look to the SAT as a major gatekeeper to the nation's colleges and universities, we need to understand what got us to this point and also have an honest discussion about the potential solutions.

Back in 1999, a California man named Mark Breimhorst sued over the long-standing practice of flagging SAT scores as "obtained under special conditions" when test takers were given extra time. Mr. Breimhorst, who needed accommodations on tests because he has no hands, argued that this practice violated the rights of students with disabilities by potentially identifying them as disabled to admissions officers (the human gatekeepers) and thus forcing disabled test takers to forgo accommodations.

It was an effective argument, and the College Board, after some foot-dragging, agreed to drop the notation in 2002. What has been happening ever since is a little hard to quantify, but it is happening in just about every high school. More students are documenting their learning disabilities and using accommodations in their classes, the prerequisite set by the College Board for using accommodations on the SAT. For the record, I am not against accommodations for students at their own schools. In my 15 years of teaching, when students have asked me for an extension on an assignment for any reasonable reason, I have given them one.

But what my colleagues and I are noticing is that accommodations for the SAT in other areas—using tests with large type, for example—are not increasing nearly as quickly as extended time (the College Board said it couldn't say if this was the case). It is clear to all of us on the inside that what is driving this phenomenon is the pressure cooker known as the SAT.

The solution is simple: keep the test to one day but end the time limits. The College Board can surely reduce the number of overall questions on the test (there are now a whopping 170, mostly multiple choice, plus one essay) and design them so that they go from embarrassingly easy to impossible except for the top percentile of students to answer even without a deadline.

That goal should be to give everyone a chance to tackle every question and eliminate time as a factor—thereby accommodating the learning style of all children, including those with disabilities. The College Board needs to take its test back to the drawing board. The answers to these design challenges and issues of fairness may not be as easy as multiple choice, but they can be found.

Writing Assignment for this essay: Chap. 5, #4

ESSAY 16

Torture: Time for Congress to End the Debate

USA TODAY
NOVEMBER 13, 2007

Does "waterboarding"—an interrogation technique that simulates drowning—constitute torture?

Yes, says Malcolm Wrightson Nance, a former Navy survival instructor who was waterboarded as part of a training exercise. "It is an overwhelming experience that induces horror and triggers frantic survival instincts," Nance told a congressional panel.

Not sure, says Michael Mukasey, who was confirmed as attorney general last week after the question boiled over at his confirmation hearings.

Now that Mukasey has been sworn in, the issue shouldn't be allowed to fester. Congress, which is considering several measures to prohibit waterboarding, should move promptly to eliminate any lingering doubt about where America stands.

The debate, of course, is about more than just one technique. At base is the smoldering question of whether the United States can devise a system to extract valuable information from suspected terrorists without abandoning its basic values.

Since 9/11, the Bush White House has planted itself on one side of that debate, pushing no-holds-barred, "enhanced" interrogation methods, including waterboarding, against prime terror suspects.

Congress has been on the other side, sort of. It has deplored torture but never explicitly outlawed waterboarding. Many lawmakers wanted to have it both ways: To be on record against torture, but to avoid blame if there's a terror attack that conceivably might have been averted.

In 2005, Congress passed a law banning "cruel, inhuman or degrading treatment" of detainees. It was sponsored by Sen. John McCain, R-Ariz., a Vietnam prisoner of war who was tortured. But that measure, and a 2006 law that was supposed to set interrogation limits, left the boundaries murky. The 2006 law allowed the White House to preserve its CIA interrogation program and the ability to define what methods are used. The Bush Justice Department did the rest: Two secret memos in 2005, revealed last month by the *New York Times*, fudged whatever rules Congress had set.

Those who would preserve methods such as waterboarding say they are sometimes necessary to get information from terrorism suspects. The White House claims its practices have yielded useful information. But details are classified, so it's impossible to judge.

On a practical level, torture is rarely effective. Suspects will say just about anything to escape pain. The British, French and Israelis have tried torture at various points and found that over time, the means compromised the ends. All abandoned it.

Further, torture encourages similar abuse of captured Americans.

Defenders of torture counter by raising the "ticking bomb" scenario. If Osama bin Laden were captured, they ask, wouldn't you favor doing anything to disrupt attacks he had planned? Well, yes. But that is an extraordinarily rare circumstance that the public might accept as an aberration. Barring torture in other circumstances is the only way to prevent it from becoming routine.

What the country needs most is a clear, consistent policy against waterboarding and its ilk. The new attorney general could provide that in a legal opinion. Even better, Congress could lay it down as the law of the land.

Writing Assignment for this essay: Chap. 6, #4

ESSAY 17

Torture: Severe Interrogations Work

TRENT FRANKS

America's distinguishing hallmark, its bedrock foundation, is that we hold to the self-evident truth that all men are created by God, which imparts to each of them equal, inestimable and eternal value.

The first and foremost purpose of our government is to defend the lives and constitutional rights of all Americans.

Tragically, at times in our history, we have crossed paths with those who do not value innocent life or freedom. We now face a merciless jihadist ideology that threatens the peace and security of the entire human family. The tactic of this insidious enemy is to secretly plot and carry out horrifying acts of violence upon our innocent civilians. Our greatest challenge in defeating them is knowing what their next evil act might be.

This has placed America in the crushingly painful position of having to resort to severe interrogations with certain terrorists during those times when no other alternative exists and hundreds or thousands of innocent lives may be at stake.

In the case of Khalid Sheikh Mohammed, the suspected 9/11 mastermind, severe interrogation was successfully used to glean critical intelligence that saved countless innocent lives. Mohammed stayed quiet for months, often answering questions with Koranic chants. According to an article in the Aug. 13 issue of *The New Yorker*, interrogators eventually waterboarded him—for just 90 seconds. Mohammed "didn't resist," said one CIA veteran. "He cracked real quick."

Mohammed's revelations helped authorities arrest at least six major terrorists, including some who may have been plotting attacks that could have taken the lives of thousands of innocent Americans, according to the *National Review Online*.

My definition of severe interrogation has never included—nor would I ever condone—torture. Torture of prisoners in American custody is a felony, and if a prisoner dies in that process, the perpetrator is subject to the death penalty. This is as it should be.

However, we should not tie the hands of those who are given charge to defend us all when, in rare circumstances, they are forced to choose between waterboarding a known terrorist or allowing him to proceed to inflict massive, torturous and hideous brutality upon thousands of innocent U.S. civilians.

Writing Assignments for this essay: Chap. 6, #4; Chap. 9, #4

ESSAY 18

Freedom of Expression: Protect Student Speech—Even "Unwise" Bong Banner

USA TODAY
MARCH 21, 2007

The 18-year-old high school student in Juneau, Alaska, who unfurled a "BONG HiTS 4 JESUS" banner on a sidewalk across from his school when the Olympic torch passed by in 2002 says he was merely trying to provoke his school's strict principal and get himself on TV.

If that was the goal, he certainly succeeded. The principal did get angry. Concluding that "bong hits" clearly meant pot smoking, she crumpled up the banner, suspended the student for 10 days and touched off a free-speech dispute that's pending before the U.S. Supreme Court. The case sounds like something out of *Ferris Bueller's Day Off*, the 1986 film featuring a wise-cracking senior who bedevils the dean of students. But the court's decision, likely to come by the end of June, is expected to be an important marker of the limits of student expression—one that should be settled in the student's favor.

As any principal knows, kids often say and do things adults find dumb and offensive; when that happens at school, it's reasonable to restrict disruptive speech that interferes with education. But the bong-banner incident neither took place on school property nor disrupted classroom activity.

Teachers and principals have to make tough calls like these every day, and their authority extends off campus to school-connected events such as field trips or football games. Yet the courts have appropriately set a high bar for limiting student speech: Their standard is a landmark 1969 Supreme Court ruling that allowed students to wear black arm bands to protest the Vietnam War, because students didn't give up their free speech rights "at the schoolhouse gate" unless their actions significantly disrupted or interfered with school activities.

In the Juneau case, the school board, joined by the Bush administration, is asking the court to lower that bar by redefining "disruption" to mean not just interfering with the educational environment, but also interfering with the school's "educational mission." They make a superficially appealing case. The principal found the bong banner obnoxious and embarrassing, particularly in light of the school's anti-drug policy, and she saw no reason not to discipline students for flouting that policy, even off school grounds.

But where to draw the line? How can the court best balance the principal's need to control her school against students' right to express their opinions, particularly political or religious opinions? Several religious groups filed briefs on the student's behalf.

When the case was argued Monday before the Supreme Court, the justices bantered about what other banners would or wouldn't be permissible: "Vote Republican"? "Smoke Pot, It's Fun"? "Rape is Fun"? "Extortion is Profitable"?

They reached no obvious conclusions, and there was no claim that "BONG HiTS 4 JESUS" was articulate, reasoned or much more than the nonsensical statement the student intended when he took a slogan he saw on a snowboard and turned it into a banner meant to anger an authority figure.

But the line around protected speech is appropriately wide, even when it's subversive or sophomoric. The student's attorney was on target when he told the justices that this sort of expression is "the kind of speech we must tolerate, no matter how unwise it is."

If students don't shed their free-speech rights at the schoolhouse gate, they surely don't on the public sidewalk across the street from the school.

Writing Assignment for this essay: Chap. 7, #5

ESSAY 19

Freedom of Expression: Policy Reflects Common Sense

KENNETH W. STARR

One year ago, the U.S. Court of Appeals for the 9th Circuit issued a decision that confounded school boards and administrators nationwide. A conscientious public high school principal enforced a longstanding student conduct policy against a student entrusted to her care. For that entirely appropriate action, the 9th Circuit subjected her to the prospect of punitive damages.

Principal Deborah Morse was in charge of a school event celebrating the Olympic Torch Relay as it arrived in Alaska for the first time ever. The event occurred during school hours. The assembled student body (accompanied by teachers and administrators) lined both sides of the street in front of the school. Cheerleaders were in uniform. The pep band played. And four students acted as torchbearers. At the very moment that the torch (and television cameras) arrived in front of the school, then-senior high school student Joseph Frederick unfurled his now-famous banner festooned with the slang marijuana reference, "BONG HiTS 4 JESUS."

Principal Morse reasonably determined on the spot that Frederick's obtrusive sign violated school policy prohibiting students from advocating the use of substances that are illegal to minors. This policy expressly applied to on- and off-campus activities. School rules such as this are commonplace throughout the country.

For decades, local school officials, acting *in loco parentis*, have relied on these policies to convey that illegal substances are wrong and harmful. In view of the staggering drug problem in America—half of high school students use drugs illegally by graduation, often on school property—policies that keep pro-drug messages out of the school environment reflect common sense.

Frederick certainly may have a First Amendment right to display his banner on his own time, out of school. But in stealing the focus of a school event for his own drug-promoting publicity stunt, he ran afoul of a reasonable regulation. It would be unwise for the Supreme Court to follow the 9th Circuit in rendering such rules unenforceable. The Court should not compound further the problem by allowing a lifelong educator like Deborah Morse to be saddled with the specter of a draconian civil damages lawsuit.

Writing Assignments for this essay: Chap. 7, #5; Chap. 10, #5

ESSAY 20

Flag Amendment: Congress Nears Choice: Protect Freedom or Stoke Anger?

USA TODAY
JUNE 20, 2006

In early June an allegedly drunken man in West Haven, Conn., yelled racial epithets and tore up an American flag while arguing with police and passersby. Earlier in the spring, instances of vandalism involving flags were reported in New Hampshire and New York.

Those three episodes of 2006—as compiled by the Citizens Flag Alliance, a group pushing for a constitutional amendment to protect the flag—constitute the raging menace of flag desecration.

In fact, they show what a non-issue flag desecration is.

Instances are rare and easily addressed by local laws. They hardly require the extraordinary act of amending the Constitution. . . .

But in a Congress unwilling to address important matters—its own ruinous spending and flagrant corruption to name just two—symbolism is the politically convenient substitute for substance. The Senate will soon take up an amendment to stop flag burning, and the vote is expected to be razor close. The House of Representatives has passed it, meaning that it could soon be sent to state legislatures, where it would be ratified if three-quarters approve.

While it's tempting to dismiss this as trivial election-year posturing, the precedent is troubling. It would for the first time alter the cornerstone of American freedom, the Constitution's First Amendment.

That is not a small matter. The First Amendment is the reason Americans are free to say what they think. It is also the reason people here can worship as they wish, associate with whomever they please, and get news and information from a free and independent press. It gives citizens a right to have grievances redressed. To limit those rights especially for so trivial a reason is to say they are no longer sacrosanct.

They should be. They are what makes America unique.

If Congress banned something as pathetic as flag desecration to score political points, surely it would consider limiting other unpopular speech.

The amendment's wording virtually guarantees that outcome. Would it, for instance, cover depictions of flags as well as actual cloth banners? Would sitting on a flag patch sewn onto the back of a pair of jeans count?

And what about the issue of flying a flag upside down? This has already become the preferred form of protest for people pushing for everything from an immediate withdrawal from Iraq to better psychiatric care for veterans. These protesters often say that they respect the values the flag represents, but that they believe those values are being subverted by people in power. Does this country really want to criminalize such a nuanced form of political dissent?

These issues would be left to legislation drafted by future Congresses and interpreted by courts. All of that, in turn, would weaken individual rights that are at the Constitution's heart.

And for what gain? Proponents of an amendment say the flag is such an important symbol of American democracy that it deserves a special status. But the Connecticut flag burner was charged with seven offenses ranging from public consumption of alcohol to criminal mischief. Surely, that is sufficient.

In fact, what makes the flag so special is this: It stands for a nation that deems individual liberties so important, it tolerates unpopular minority opinion.

The main threat to the flag comes not from the occasional burning of Old Glory. It comes from those who would sacrifice the principles the flag represents.

Writing Assignment for this essay: Chap. 8, #4

ESSAY 2I

Flag Amendment: Flag Needs Protection

DIANNE FEINSTEIN

On the morning of February 24, 1945, when I was a 12-year-old girl, I picked up a copy of the *San Francisco Chronicle*. On its cover, there was a full-page picture of the now iconic Joe Rosenthal photograph of American marines raising the United States flag at Iwo Jima.

For me and for the nation, the photograph was a jolt of electricity boosting our morale during the terrible island-to-island Pacific battles of World War II. The sight of those troops hoisting Old Glory forever cemented my view of our flag.

Today, our flag remains a vibrant symbol of our democracy, our shared values, our commitment to justice, and our eternal memory of those who have sacrificed to defend these principles. It is because of all that our flag embodies that I have co-sponsored the Flag Protection Amendment. . . .

Throughout our nation's history, the flag has been protected by law. In 1989, 48 of our 50 states had statutes restricting flag desecration. In 1974, Supreme Court Justice Byron White wrote that: "(T)here would seem to be little question about the power of Congress to forbid the mutilation of the Lincoln Memorial or to prevent overlaying it with words or other objects. The flag is itself a monument, subject to similar protection."

I agree with Justice White; the American flag is our monument in cloth.

But its protection ended in 1989, when the U.S. Supreme Court struck down a Texas law prohibiting flag desecration. Congress responded by passing the Flag Protection Act of 1989, but the Supreme Court struck down that law as well. The only way to restore protection to the flag is to amend the Constitution. Otherwise, any legislation passed by Congress would be struck down.

The Flag Protection Amendment would not prohibit flag burning. Rather, the Amendment would simply return to Congress the ability to protect the flag as it has been protected throughout most of this nation's history.

Some opponents of the Flag Protection Amendment argue that we must choose between trampling on the flag and trampling on the First Amendment. I strongly disagree.

There is no idea or thought expressed by the burning of the American flag that cannot be expressed equally well in another manner. This Amendment would leave both the flag and free speech safe.

Writing Assignment for this essay: Chap. 8, #4

Chapter 1

Exercise 1.1

1. Critical thinking is the systematic evaluation or formulation of beliefs, or statements, by rational standards.
4. Critical thinking operates according to rational standards in that beliefs are judged by how well they are supported by reasons.
6. The critical in critical thinking refers to the exercising of careful judgment and judicious evaluation.
8. A statement is an assertion that something is or is not the case.
11. An argument is a group of statements in which some of them (the premises) are intended to support another of them (the conclusion).
14. In an argument, a conclusion is a statement that premises are intended to support.
17. No.
19. Indicator words are words that frequently accompany arguments and signal that a premise or conclusion is present.
23. Look for the conclusion first.

Exercise 1.2

1. No statement.
4. No statement.
7. Statement.
10. No statement.

Exercise 1.3

1. Argument.
   Conclusion: He should avoid her.

4. No argument.
7. No argument.
11. Argument.
    Conclusion: Don't outlaw guns.
15. Argument.
    Conclusion: Noisy car alarms should be banned.

Exercise 1.4

1. Argument.
   Conclusion: Faster-than-light travel is not possible.
   Premise: Faster-than-light travel would violate a law of nature.
4. Argument.
   Conclusion: The flu epidemic on the East Coast is real.
   Premise: Government health officials say so.
   Premise: I personally have read at least a dozen news stories that characterize the situation as a "flu epidemic."
7. No argument.
10. No argument.

Exercise 1.5

3. Premise: Freedom of choice in all things is a basic moral right.
   Premise: Abortion is no different than scraping off a few cells from one's skin, and a woman certainly has the right to do that.
6. Premise: Vaughn has admitted that he knows nothing about animals.
   Premise: The Society for the Prevention of Cruelty to Animals has declared Vaughn a dummy when it comes to animals.
9. Premise: The Internet has led to the capture of more terrorists than anything else.
   Premise: The U.S. Attorney General has asserted that the Internet is the best friend that anti-terrorist teams have.
12. Premise: All the top TV critics agree that *The Sopranos* is the greatest series in TV history.
    Premise: I have compared *The Sopranos* to all other TV series and found that the show outshines them all.

Exercise 1.6

2. Conclusion: School vouchers have decreased the quality of education in four states.
4. Conclusion: As a married person, you are happier than people who aren't married.
8. Conclusion: The government does not do anything about pornography on the Internet even though kids have access to all kinds of porn.

Exercise 1.7

1. Argument.
   Conclusion: The Religious Right is not pro-family.
   Premise: Concerned parents realize that children are curious about how their body works and need accurate, age appropriate information about the human reproductive system.
   Premise: Thanks to Religious Right pressure, many public schools have replaced sex education with fear-based "abstinence only" programs that insult young people's intelligence and give them virtually no useful information.

3. Argument.
   Conclusion: There is no archeological evidence for the [biblical] Flood.
   Premise: If a universal Flood occurred between five and six thousand years ago, killing all humans except the eight on board the Ark, it would be abundantly clear in the archeological record.
   Premise: The destruction of all but eight of the world's people left no mark on the archeology of human cultural evolution.

Chapter 2

Exercise 2.1

1. For critical thinking to be realized, the process must be systematic, it must be a true evaluation or formulation of claims, and it must be based on rational standards.

5. We take things too far when we accept claims for no reason.

7. You are most likely to let your self-interest get in the way of clear thinking when you have a significant personal stake in the conclusions you reach.

11. Group pressure can affect your attempts to think critically by allowing your need to be part of a group or your identification with a group undermine critical thinking.

14. A worldview is a set of fundamental ideas that help us make sense of a wide range of issues in life.

17. Critical thinking is concerned with objective truth claims.

21. Reasonable doubt, not certainty, is central to the acquisition of knowledge.

Exercise 2.2

1. Self-interest.
4. Group pressure (in this case, the we-are-better-than-them type).
7. Group pressure.
10. Self-interest.

Exercise 2.3

1. a. The charges are false.
    c. Important evidence that would exonerate Father Miller was not mentioned in the newspaper account.
3. a. A study from Harvard shows that women are less violent and less emotional than men.
6. No good reasons listed.

Exercise 2.4

1. Better-than-others group pressure; Possible negative consequence: Failure to consider other points of view; discrimination against people who disagree with Ortega.
3. It's not entirely clear what the group's motivations are. This passage could easily be an example of better-than-others group pressure.
7. Appeal to popularity. Possible negative consequence: Overlooking other factors that might be a lot more important than popularity.

Exercise 2.5

1. Face-saving; Possible negative consequences: Poor academic performance due to overconfidence; embarrassment of failure after being so cocky; alienation of friends.
2. Self-interest; Possible negative consequences: Wasting the taxpayer's money; being thrown out of office for misconduct.

Chapter 3

Exercise 3.1

4. Deductive.
8. Sound.
12. No.

Exercise 3.2

2. Step 1: Conclusion: She has a superior intellect.
    Premises: Ethel graduated from Yale. If she graduated from Yale, she probably has a superior intellect.
    Step 2: Not deductively valid.
    Step 3: Inductively strong.
    Step 4: Does not apply.
6. Step 1: Conclusion: Thus, every musician has a college degree.
    Premises: Every musician has had special training, and everyone with special training has a college degree.
    Step 2: Deductively valid.
    Step 3: Does not apply.
    Step 4: Does not apply.

9. Step 1: Conclusion: So some actors who sing also play a musical instrument.
        Premises: Some actors sing, and some play a musical instrument.
  Step 2: Not deductively valid.
  Step 3: Not inductively strong.
  Step 4: Intended to be deductive.

15. Step 1: Conclusion: So it's impossible for androids to have minds.
        Premises: If minds are identical to brains—that is, if one's mind is nothing but a brain—androids could never have minds because they wouldn't have brains. Clearly, a mind is nothing but a brain.
  Step 2: Deductively valid.
  Step 3: Does not apply.
  Step 4: Does not apply.

Exercise 3.3

3. Valid.
8. Valid.
14. Invalid.
18. Valid.
23. Invalid.

Exercise 3.4

I.
1. Senator Greed was caught misusing campaign funds.
5. She's not incompetent.
9. The engine started right away.

II.
3. Sixty percent of the teenagers in several scientific surveys love rap music.
6. Assad's fingerprints are on the vase.
9. The murder rates in almost all large cities in the South are very high.

Exercise 3.5

1. Valid; *modus tollens.*
6. Valid; *modus tollens.*
9. Valid; *modus ponens.*

Exercise 3.6

2. If Lino is telling the truth, he will admit to all charges.
  Lino is telling the truth.
  So he will admit to all charges.
  If Lino is telling the truth, he will admit to all charges.
  He will not admit to all charges.
  So he is not telling the truth.

5. If religious conflict in Nigeria continues, thousands more will die.
The religious conflict in Nigeria will continue.
Therefore, thousands more will die.
If religious conflict in Nigeria continues, thousands more will die.
Thousands more will not die.
Therefore, religious conflict in Nigeria will not continue.

9. If solar power can supply six megawatts of power in San Francisco
(which is certainly not the sunniest place in the world), then solar power
can transform the energy systems in places like Texas and Arizona.
Solar power can supply six megawatts of power in San Francisco.
So solar power can transform the energy systems in places like Texas and
Arizona.
If solar power can supply six megawatts of power in San Francisco
(which is certainly not the sunniest place in the world), then solar power
can transform the energy systems in places like Texas and Arizona.
But solar power cannot transform the energy systems in places like Texas
and Arizona.
So solar power cannot supply six megawatts of power in San Francisco.

Exercise 3.7

4. If the Queen of England were a man, she would be mortal.
She is mortal.
Therefore, the Queen of England is a man.

If *a*, then *b*.
b.
Therefore, *a*.

5. If Bill Clinton was the president of the U.S. in 1970, then he would be an
American.
Bill Clinton was not president of the U.S. in 1970.
Therefore, he is not an American.

If *a*, then *b*.
Not *a*.
Therefore, not *b*.

7. If Vaughn is a dog, he is a mammal.
He is a mammal.
Therefore, he is a dog.

If *a*, then *b*.
b.
Therefore, *a*.

8. If ducks are sea turtles, then they are at home in the water.
Ducks are not sea turtles.

Therefore, ducks are not at home in the water.

If *a*, then *b*.
Not *a*.
Therefore, not *b*.

11. If Chicago is the capital of Illinois, then Chicago is in Illinois.
Chicago is in Illinois.
Therefore, Chicago is the capital of Illinois.

If *a*, then *b*.
b.
Therefore, *a*.

Exercise 3.8

1. (1) The stores are closed. (2) We have no money. (3) And we have no way of traveling to any place of business. (4) Therefore, we are just not going to be able to go shopping right now.

4. (1) If the pipes are busted, there will be no running water. (2) The pipes are busted. (3) And if all the water is rusty, we won't be able to use it anyway, (4) and all the water is rusty. (5) So we have no useable water at this point.

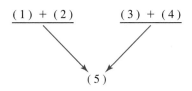

Exercise 3.9

6. (1) If Marla buys the house in the suburbs, she will be happier and healthier. (2) She is buying the house in the suburbs. (3) So she will be happier and healthier.

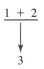

10. (1) The existence of planets outside our solar system is a myth. (2) There is no reliable empirical evidence at all showing that planets exist outside our solar system.

$$2 \downarrow 1$$

17. (1) There are at least two main views regarding the morality of war. (2) Pacifism is the view that no war is ever justified because it involves the taking of human life. (3) Just-war theory is the view that some wars are justified for various reasons—mostly because they help prevent great evils (such as massacres, "ethnic cleansing," or world domination by a madman like Hitler) or because they are a means of self defense. (4) I think that our own moral sense tells us that sometimes (in the case of World War II, for example) violence is occasionally morally justified. (5) It would be hard for anyone to deny that a war to prevent something like the Holocaust is morally right. [Implied conclusion] (6) Just-war theory is correct.

$$4 \downarrow 6$$

20. (1) The picnic will probably be spoiled because (2) there is a 90 percent probability of rain.

$$2 \downarrow 1$$

Exercise 3.10

1. Conclusion: The idea that God is required to be the enforcer of the moral law is not plausible.

   Premises: (4) In the first place, as an empirical hypothesis about the psychology of human beings, it is questionable. (5) There is no unambiguous evidence that theists are more moral than nontheists. (6) Not only have psychological studies failed to find a significant correlation between frequency of religious worship and moral conduct, but convicted criminals are much more likely to be theists than atheists. (7) Second, the threat of divine punishment cannot impose a moral obligation. (8) Might does not make right.

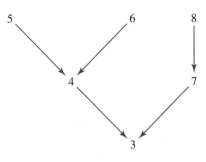

Chapter 4

Exercise 4.1

4. We should proportion our belief to the evidence.
10. Two additional indicators are reputation among peers and professional accomplishments.
17. By making a conscious effort to consider not only information that supports what we believe, but also the information that conflicts with it.

Exercise 4.2

4. Proportion belief to the evidence; the claim is not dubious enough to dismiss out of hand, and not worthy of complete acceptance. Low plausibility.
6. Reject it; it conflicts with a great deal of background information.
10. Proportion belief to the evidence; the claim is not dubious enough to dismiss out of hand, and not worthy of complete acceptance. Moderate plausibility.
14. Reject it; it conflicts with a great deal of background information.
17. Reject it; it conflicts with a great deal of background information.

Exercise 4.3

3. Do not agree. Persuasive evidence would include the body of an alien or the alien craft itself, both scientifically documented as being of extraterrestrial origin.
8. Do not agree. Persuasive evidence would include several double-blind, controlled trials demonstrating that meditation and controlled breathing shrink tumors.

Chapter 5

Exercise 5.1

4. The fallacy of composition is arguing that what is true of the parts must be true of the whole.
10. They are fallacious because they assume that a proposition is true merely because a great number of people believe it, but as far as the truth of a claim is concerned, what many people believe is irrelevant.
15. Yes.
19. People are often taken in by false dilemmas because they don't think beyond the alternatives laid before them.

Exercise 5.2

1. Composition.
5. Genetic fallacy.
10. Appeal to the person.
14. Equivocation.
19. Appeal to the person.

Exercise 5.3

4. False dilemma.
6. Hasty generalization.
10. False dilemma.

Exercise 5.4

3. Jones says that Mrs. Anan deserves the Nobel prize. But he's a friend of hers. Clearly then Mrs. Anan does not deserve the Nobel prize.
6. In light of ethical considerations, the Boy Scouts of America should allow gay kids to be members. The reason is that banning gay kids from the organization would be in conflict with basic moral principles.
11. There are too many guns on the streets because our politicians are controlled by the National Rifle Association and other gun nuts. We don't want the NRA telling us what to do.

Chapter 6

Exercise 6.1

1. Conjunction; Components: The Democrats raised taxes, The Republicans cut programs; &
5. Conditional; Components: Taslima can read your mind, You're in trouble; →

7. Conditional; Components: God is all-powerful, He can prevent evil in the world; →

Exercise 6.2

1. $p \vee q$
4. $e \,\&\, f$
8. $\sim g \,\&\, \sim h$
14. $\sim\sim p$

Exercise 6.3

2. False.
6. True.
8. False.

Exercise 6.4

2. True.
5. True.
10. True.

Exercise 6.5

2. Either John is home or Mary is home.
5. If the sun is not shining, then we will not go outside.
10. If the day goes well, then we will not regret our efforts.

Exercise 6.6

2. $p \vee q$
5. $\sim a \rightarrow \sim b$
9. $p \rightarrow q$

Exercise 6.7

2. Alligators are reptiles and dogs are reptiles.

a	d	$a \,\&\, d$
T	T	T
T	F	F
F	T	F
F	F	F

6. Either dogs are not mammals, or snakes are reptiles. [Hint: To avoid confusion, you can *add* columns after the guide columns, such as the one for ~*d* in this truth table. This extra column reminds you that the truth values for ~*d* are the flip side of those for *d*.]

d	*s*	~*d*	~*d* v *s*
T	T	F	T
T	F	F	F
F	T	T	T
F	F	T	T

8. Alligators can bark, and dogs are not reptiles.

a	*d*	~*d*	*a* & ~*d*
T	T	F	F
T	F	T	T
F	T	F	F
F	F	T	F

Exercise 6.8

2. Valid.

$p \rightarrow q$
p
$\therefore q$

p	*q*	*p* → *q*	*p*	*q*
T	T	T	T	T
T	F	F	T	F
F	T	T	F	T
F	F	T	F	F

7. Valid.

$p \rightarrow q$
$\sim q \& r$
$\therefore r$

	p	q	r	~q	p → q	~q & r	r
1	T	T	T	F	T	F	T
2	T	T	F	F	T	F	F
3	T	F	T	T	F	T	T
4	T	F	F	T	F	F	F
5	F	T	T	F	T	F	T
6	F	T	F	F	T	F	F
7	F	T	T	T	T	T	T
8	F	F	F	T	T	F	F

14. Valid.

$p \rightarrow q$
$\sim(q \lor r)$
$\therefore \sim p$

	p	q	r	~p	p → q	~(q v r)	~p
1	T	T	T	F	T	F	F
2	T	T	F	F	T	F	F
3	T	F	T	F	F	F	F
4	T	F	F	F	F	T	F
5	F	T	T	T	T	F	T
6	F	T	F	T	T	F	T
7	F	F	T	T	T	F	T
8	F	F	F	T	T	T	T

Exercise 6.9

3. Jake is the plumber or Jake is the carpenter. Jake is not the carpenter. Therefore, Jake is the plumber.

$p \lor c$
$\sim c$
$\therefore p$

p	c	p v c	~c	p
T	T	T	F	T
T	F	T	T	T
F	T	T	F	F
F	F	F	T	F

Valid.

11. Unless both Mary goes and Henry goes, the party will be a disaster. The party will be a disaster. Therefore, both Mary and Henry will not go.

$\sim(m \& h) \to p$
p
$\therefore \sim(m \& h)$

	m	h	p	$\sim(m \& h)$	$\sim(m \& h) \to p$	p	$\sim(m \& h)$
1	T	T	T	F	T	T	F
2	T	T	F	F	T	F	F
3	T	F	T	T	T	T	T
4	T	F	F	T	F	F	T
5	F	T	T	T	T	T	T
6	F	T	F	T	F	F	T
7	F	F	T	T	T	T	T
8	F	F	F	T	F	F	T

Invalid.

Exercise 6.10

3. $p \lor q$
   p
   $\therefore \sim q$

$$\begin{array}{ccc} \text{T} & \text{T} & \text{F} \\ p \ \lor \ q & p & \sim q \\ \text{T} \quad \text{T} & \text{T} & \text{T} \end{array}$$

Invalid.

10. $p \to q$
    $\therefore p \to (p \& q)$

$$\begin{array}{cc} \text{F} & \text{F} \\ p \ \to \ q & p \ \to \ (p \ \& \ q) \\ \text{T} \quad \text{F} & \text{T} \quad \text{T} \quad \text{F} \end{array}$$

Valid.

15. $(d \lor e) \to (d \& e)$
    $\sim(d \lor e)$
    $\therefore \sim(d \& e)$

$$\begin{array}{ccc} \text{T} & \text{F} & \text{F} \\ (d \ \lor \ e) \to (d \ \& \ e) & \sim(d \ \lor \ e) & \sim(d \ \& \ e) \\ \text{T} \quad \text{T} \quad \text{T} \quad \text{T} & \text{T} \quad \text{T} & \text{T} \quad \text{T} \end{array}$$

Valid.

Chapter 7

Exercise 7.1

1. S = scientists, P = Baptists; universal negative; E.
5. S = theologians who have studied arguments for the existence of God, P = scholars with serious misgivings about the traditional notion of omnipotence; universal affirmative; E.
8. S = people who play the stock market, P = millionaires; particular negative; O.
12. S = terrorists, P = Saudi citizens; particular affirmative; I.
16. S = death row inmates, P = death penalty supporters; universal negative; E.

Exercise 7.2

1. All Giants fans are fanatics [or, are people who are fanatical]. A.
5. All good investments are cell phone companies that keep up with the latest technology. A.
9. All intelligent thoughts are thoughts that have already happened. A.
13. Some things are memories meant to be forgotten. I.

Exercise 7.3

1. All guardians of the soul are poets. A.
4. All androids like Commander Data are nonhumans. A.
5. No things that satisfy the heart are material things. E.
8. Some treatments said to be part of "alternative medicine" are treatments that are unproven. I.
12. All days that give her any joy are Fridays. A.
15. All pictures identical with the one hanging on the wall are things that are crooked. A.
20. All nations without a conscience are nations without souls. A.

Exercise 7.4

1. No persons are persons exempt from the draft in times of war.
   S = persons; P = persons exempt from the draft in times of war.

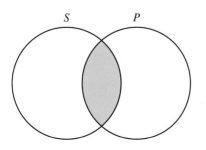

5. No things are things more pitiable than the reasons of an unreasonable man.
   S = things; P = things more pitiable than the reasons of an unreasonable man.

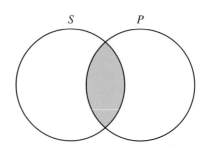

8. Some good talkers are good listeners.
   S = good talkers; P = good listeners.

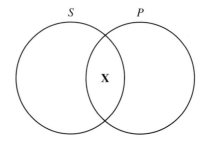

12. All commanders are persons who are alone.
    S = commanders; P = persons who are alone.

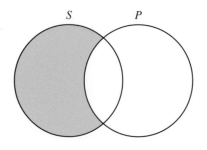

Exercise 7.5

1. No *P* are *S*; No *S* are *P*.

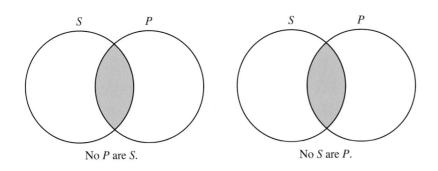

No *P* are *S*. No *S* are *P*.

Equivalent.

3. All *S* are *P*; All *P* are *S*.

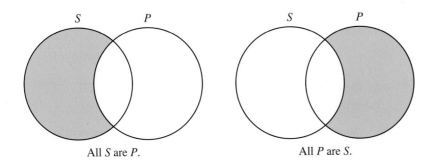

All *S* are *P*. All *P* are *S*.

Not equivalent.

6. All *P* are non-*S*; All *S* are non-*P*.

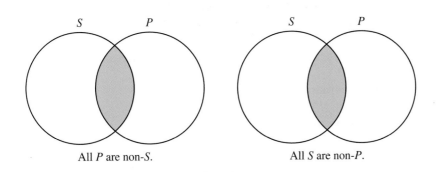

All *P* are non-*S*. All *S* are non-*P*.

Equivalent.

9. Some *S* are not *P*; Some *P* are not *S*.

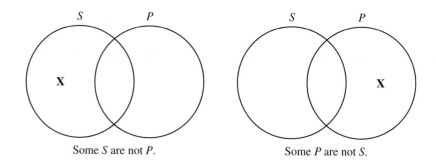

Some *S* are not *P*.   Some *P* are not *S*.

Not equivalent.

Exercise 7.6

2. All horses are mammals, and no mammals are lizards. Therefore, no lizards are horses.
   Minor = lizards (*S*)
   Major = horses (*P*)
   Middle = mammals (*M*)

   > All *P* are *M*.
   > No *M* are *S*.
   > Therefore, no *S* are *P*.

6. Some videotapes are not film classics, but all black-and-white movies are film classics. Therefore, some black-and-white movies are not video-tapes.
   Minor = black-and-white movies (*S*)
   Major = videotapes (*P*)
   Middle = film classics (*M*)

   > Some *P* are not *M*.
   > All *S* are *M*.
   > Therefore, some *S* are not *P*.

9. No elm trees are cacti. Some tall plants are elm trees. So some tall plants are not cacti.
   Minor = tall plants (*S*)
   Major = cacti (*P*)
   Middle = elm trees (*M*)

   > No *M* are *P*.
   > Some *S* are *M*.
   > Therefore, some *S* are not *P*.

Exercise 7.7

2. All *P* are *M*.
   No *M* are *S*.
   Therefore, no *S* are *P*.

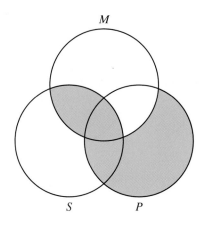

   Valid.

6. Some *P* are not *M*.
   All *S* are *M*.
   Therefore, some *S* are not *P*.

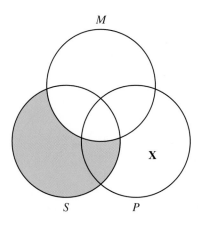

   Invalid.

9. No *M* are *P*.
Some *S* are *M*.
Therefore, some *S* are not *P*.

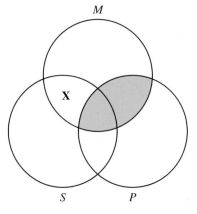

Valid.

Exercise 7.8

1. Some architectural structures are nontraditional designs, for all houses are architectural structures, and some houses are nontraditional designs.

   Some houses are nontraditional designs.
   All houses are architectural structures.
   Therefore, some architectural structures are nontraditional designs.

   Some *M* are *P*.
   All *M* are *S*.
   Therefore, some *S* are *P*.

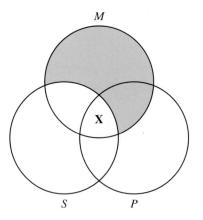

Valid.

3. All worshippers of God are spiritual giants because all worshippers of God are redeemed souls, and all redeemed souls are spiritual giants.

All redeemed souls are spiritual giants.
All worshippers of God are redeemed souls.
Therefore, all worshippers of God are spiritual giants.

All *M* are *P*.
All *S* are *M*.
Therefore, all *S* are *P*.

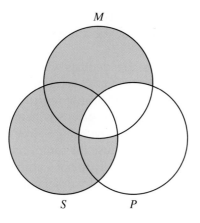

Valid.

8. No wimps are social activists because no wimps are people of honest and strong conviction. And all social activists are people of honest and strong conviction.

All social activists are people of honest and strong conviction.
No wimps are people of honest and strong conviction.
Therefore, no wimps are social activists.

All *P* are *M*.
No *S* are *M*.
Therefore, no *S* are *P*.

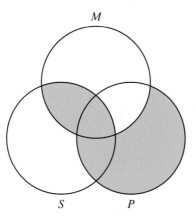

Valid.

Chapter 8

Exercise 8.1

1. Target group: people in the country; sample: adults in New York and San Francisco; relevant property: being "pro-choice" in the abortion debate. The argument is weak because the sample is not representative.

4. Target group: students at this university; sample: first-year students at this university; relevant property: being against such a militant policy. The argument is weak because the sample is both too small and not representative.

8. Target group: dentists; sample: dentists who suggest that their patients chew gum; relevant property: recommending Brand X gum. The argument is weak because the sample is not representative.

12. Target group: Americans; sample: adults with an annual income of $48,000–$60,000; relevant property: being happy and satisfied with one's job. The argument is weak because the sample is not representative. (Middle-income workers are likely to have attitudes toward job satisfaction that are different from those of workers in other income brackets, especially lower ones.)

Exercise 8.2

1. Weak. To ensure a strong argument, randomly draw the sample from the entire U.S. population, not just from a couple of bicoastal cities.

4. Weak. To ensure a strong argument, randomly draw a sample of several hundred students from the whole university population, not just the first-year students.

8. Weak. To ensure a strong argument, randomly draw the sample from the set of all dentists, not just the dentists who recommend gum.

12. Weak. To ensure a strong argument, randomly draw the sample from the set of all American workers, including respondents representative of all income groups.

Exercise 8.3

1. Does not offer strong support for the conclusion. The problem is nonrandom—and therefore nonrepresentative—sampling.

Exercise 8.4

1. a, c.

Exercise 8.5

1. Not more likely to be true.

Exercise 8.6

2. Literary analogy.
6. Argument by analogy. Two things being compared; relevant similarity: working with numbers; conclusion: "he'll be a whiz at algebra"; weak argument.
8. Argument by analogy; four things being compared; relevant similarity: being pork; conclusion: "I will like chitlings"; weak argument.
12. Argument by analogy; two things being compared; relevant similarity: being foundations; conclusions: "no lasting reputation worthy of respect can be built on a weak character"; strong argument.

Exercise 8.7

1. Instances being compared: the personality traits of Ronald Reagan and George W. Bush; relevant similarities: staunch conservatism, strong Christian values, almost dogmatic adherence to conservative principles; diversity among cases not a significant factor; conclusion: "President Bush will likely be involved in a similar foreign policy mess for similar reasons"; weak argument (because of several unmentioned dissimilarities).
5. Instances being compared: Having terminal cancer and being threatened by an assailant; relevant similarities: being threatened with death or great pain; diversity among cases not a significant factor; conclusion: "suicide must sometimes be morally justified when it is an act of self-defense against a terminal disease that threatens death or great pain." This is a strong argument—*if* all the relevant similarities and dissimilarities have indeed been taken into account. A critic could argue, though, that killing oneself in self-defense is just not relevantly similar to killing another human in self-defense. The critic, then, would have to specify what the significant difference is.

Exercise 8.8

2. Conclusion: "Research suggests that eating lots of fruits and vegetables may provide some protection against several types of cancer." Correlation. The argument is strong. The conclusion is a limited claim ("*may* provide some protection . . . "), which the stated correlation could easily support.
7. Conclusion: "Education increases people's earning power." Correlation. The argument is strong.
13. Conclusion: "Tune-ups can improve the performance of lawnmowers." Method of difference. The argument is strong.
16. Conclusion: [Implied] "Having a major war somewhere in the world causes the price of oil to hit $40 a barrel." Method of Agreement. The argument is strong if all relevant factors have been taken into account, which may not be the case.

19. Conclusion: [Implied] "Only five students got As on the midterm exam because they studied the night before the exam and reviewed their notes just before walking into class to take the test." Method of Agreement. The argument is strong.

Exercise 8.9

2. a, d.
7. a.
13. a.
16. a, b, d.
19. a, b.

Exercise 8.10

1. a.
4. b.
9. a.

Chapter 9

Exercise 9.1

4. A theoretical explanation is an explanation that serves as a theory, or hypothesis, used to explain why something is the way it is, why something is the case, or why something happened.
8. A causal explanation is a kind of theoretical explanation. Like all theoretical explanations, causal explanations are used in inference to the best explanation.

Exercise 9.2

2. The state of affairs being explained is the endangered status of the spotted owl. The explanation is the powerful influence of the logging industry.
5. The state of affairs being explained is the incidence of robberies. The explanation is that there aren't enough gun owners.
8. The state of affairs being explained is the many times that psychics have seemed to predict the future. The explanation is that psychics really can predict the future.

Exercise 9.3

3. Interpretive.
7. Theoretical.
12. Interpretive.

Exercise 9.4

2. Theory 1: Jack's house was burglarized.
   Theory 2: Jack's dog went on a rampage.
6. Theory 1: Alice was not exposed to any germs.
   Theory 2: Vitamin C supercharged Alice's immune system.

Exercise 9.6

2. The minimum requirement of consistency is the criterion that any theory worth considering must have both internal and external consistency—that is, be free of contradictions and be consistent with the data the theory is supposed to explain.
6. A theory that does not have much scope is one that explains very little—perhaps only the phenomenon it was introduced to explain and not much else.

Exercise 9.7

2. The second theory is both simpler and more conservative.
4. The first theory is both simpler and more conservative.
7. The first theory is both simpler and more conservative.

Exercise 9.8

3. Theory 3.

Chapter 10

Exercise 10.1

6. (1) Identify the problem or pose a question, (2) devise a hypothesis to explain the event or phenomenon, (3) derive a test implication or prediction, (4) perform the test, (5) accept or reject the hypothesis.
9. If H, then C. Not-C. Therefore, not-H.
12. No. Hypotheses are tested together with other hypotheses. A hypothesis can always be saved from refutation by making changes in one of the accompanying hypotheses.

Exercise 10.2

2. Hypothesis: Two guys are perpetrating a Bigfoot hoax. Test implication: If the two guys are perpetrating a hoax, then monitoring their behavior day and night should yield evidence of hoaxing activity.
6. Hypothesis: Creatine dramatically increases the performance of weight trainers. Test implication: If creatine increases performance, then giving creatine to weight trainers in a controlled way (in a double-blind controlled trial) should increase various measures of performance in the

trainers compared to weight trainers who get a placebo (inactive substance).

Exercise 10.3

3. Theory: Local climate changes.
Competing theory: Heat from volcanic activity around the planet is melting the glaciers.
Both theories are about equal in terms of testability, fruitfulness, and scope. The volcanic theory, however, is neither simple nor conservative. It's not simple because it assumes an unknown process. It's not conservative because it is not consistent with what is known about the effects of heat from volcanoes.

7. Theory: Religion fosters terrorism.
Competing theory: Terrorists commit terrorist acts because they are insane.
Both theories are about equal in terms of testability, fruitfulness, scope, and simplicity. The insanity theory, though, is not conservative. It conflicts with what we know about those who commit terrorist acts. In general, terrorists may be fanatical, but they do not seem to be clinically insane.

Exercise 10.4

2. Test implication: If brighter street lights decrease the crime rate, then reducing the brightness of the lights (while keeping constant all other factors, such as police patrols) should increase the crime rate. The test would likely confirm the theory.

6. Test implication: If eating foods high in fat contributes more to overweight than eating foods high in carbohydrates, then over time people should gain more body weight when they are eating X number of grams of fat per day than when they are eating the same number of grams of carbohydrates per day.

Exercise 10.7

4. The appeal to ignorance.
6. Something is logically impossible if it violates a principle of logic; something is logically possible if it does not violate a principle of logic.

Exercise 10.8

2. Theory 1: The aging of the building materials in the house caused creaking.
Theory 2: The wind blowing against the house caused the creaking.
Theory 3: A ghost caused the creaking.

7. Theory 1: A coincidental matching between the dream and real events made the dream seem prophetic.
Theory 2: Leroy had the same dream every night because he was concerned about his uncle, so there was a good chance that the dream would match something in reality.
Theory 3: The dream was a genuine prophetic dream.

Exercise 10.9

3. Alternative theory: As a prank, the girls cut drawings of fairies out of a book, posed them in the garden, and took photos of themselves with the cutouts. Then they claimed that the photos showed actual fairies. Both theories seem to be about equal in testability and fruitfulness. The prank theory has more scope because faked photos can explain many other phenomena, including many different kinds of paranormal hoaxes. The fairy theory is neither simple nor conservative. Fairies are unknown to science, and claims about their existence conflict with many things that we know.

Chapter 11

Exercise 11.1

5. We cannot infer what should be or ought to be from what is.
9. Moral theories try to explain what makes an action right or what makes a person good.
13. Internal consistency—the requirement that the theories composing our worldview do not conflict.

Exercise 11.2

1. Nonmoral.
6. Moral.
9. Moral.

Exercise 11.3

4. The Indian government posed an imminent threat to Pakistan and the world. When a foreign government poses an imminent threat to Pakistan and the world, Pakistanis are justified in attacking that government. So the Pakistanis were justified in attacking Indian troops.
9. Hacking into a database containing personal information on thousands of people and invading their privacy is immoral. You hacked into a database containing personal information on thousands of people and invaded their privacy. Therefore, what you did was immoral.

Exercise 11.4

3. Killing another human being in self-defense is morally permissible. So it is not the case that in all circumstances the killing of a human being is wrong.

7. If helping someone to commit suicide would somehow save the lives of millions of people, the act would seem to be morally permissible. So it is not the case that assisted suicide is never morally justified.

APPENDIX C

Answers to Self-Assessment Quizzes

Chapter 1

1. A group of statements in which some of them (the premises) are intended to support another of them (the conclusion).
2. Premise indicators: *because, due to the fact that, inasmuch as.* Conclusion indicators: *therefore, it follows that, it must be that.*
3. b. Read the story and write a complete review of it.
4. c. Campus speakers should be allowed to speak freely without being shouted down.
5. No argument.
6. Argument. Conclusion: War can solve problems.
7. Argument: President Bush is not slashing domestic spending.
8. Conclusion.
9. Premise.
10. Conclusion
11. Premise.
12. Conclusion
13. Premise: DNA evidence is unreliable. Premise: Unreliable evidence should not be used in cases of capital murder.
14. Premise: No computer has yet been able to converse with a human being well enough to be indistinguishable from humans. Premise: Such a feat requires consciousness, and machines cannot even in principle produce consciousness.
15. Premise: All of Nostradamus's predictions have come true. Premise: The prediction about September 11 was unambiguous and specific.
16. 10.
17. 6, 7, 9.
18. 1, 2, 3, 5.
19. 8.
20. 4, 11.

Chapter 2

1. Systematic process, involving genuine evaluation or formulation of beliefs, gauged according to rational standards.
2. A surge of strong emotions.
3. We may ignore facts that contradict our beliefs and search out facts that support them.
4. The we-are-better pressure.
5. A philosophy of life, a set of fundamental ideas that helps us make sense of a wide range of important issues in life.
6. Reasonable doubt.
7. Failure to look for opposing evidence increases the chance of error.
8. Face-saving.
9. Face-saving.
10. Self-interested thinking.
11. Group pressure.
12. Group pressure.
13. Group pressure.
14. Self-serving.
15. Group pressure.
16. Face-saving.
17. Group pressure.
18. Subjectivist fallacy.
19. Subjectivist fallacy.
20. Social relativism.

Chapter 3

1. Deductive argument: intended to provide logically conclusive support for its conclusion. Inductive argument: intended to provide probable, not conclusive, support for its conclusion.
2. Valid argument: a deductive argument that succeeds in providing conclusive support for its conclusion. Invalid argument: a deductive argument that fails to provide conclusive support for its conclusion. Strong inductive argument: an inductive argument that succeeds in providing probable, but not conclusive, logical support for its conclusion.
3. Sound argument: a deductively valid argument that has true premises.
4. Deductive.
5. Inductive.
6. Inductive.
7. Deductive.
8. Anyone who doesn't openly criticize any military action against any Middle Eastern nation is a warmonger.

9. The most likely reason for Maria's failing her driving test three times is that she's not paying attention.

10. People who believe in astrology or tarot cards do not do well in college science courses.

11. If the job is worth doing, then it's worth doing well. The job is worth doing. Therefore, it's worth doing well.

12. If Austin is happy, then Barb is happy. Barb is not happy. Therefore, Austin is not happy.

13. If Einstein invented the steam engine, then he's a great scientist. Einstein did not invent the steam engine. Therefore, he is not a great scientist.

14. If Buffalo is the capital of New York, then Buffalo is in New York. Buffalo is in New York. Therefore, Buffalo is the capital of New York.

15. Cole is up to no good. He's been acting suspiciously for days, and he told Rachel that he was going to steal something valuable.

16. The sitcom *Friends* is becoming really lame. The writing is predictable and plodding. The acting is worse than ever.

17. If dolphins have minds comparable to ours, then these creatures are self-conscious, intelligent, and creative. If they are self-conscious, then they should react appropriately when they see their reflections in a mirror. They do react appropriately. If they're intelligent, they should be able to solve complex problems. They can solve such problems. If they're creative, they should be able to create some form of art. In a rudimentary way, they do create art. They are definitely self-conscious, intelligent, and creative.

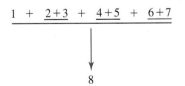

18. If the dictum to always tell the truth in all circumstances is a valid moral principle, then it should fit well with our considered moral judgments. But it does not fit well with our considered moral judgments because there are times when lying is actually the right thing to do, as when

we lie to save a life. So the dictum to always tell the truth is not a valid moral principle.

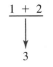

19. I don't think that I should vote for any independent candidate in the next election. Independents never win, and I want the person I vote for to win. Also, independents have a tendency to be a little wacky. And we definitely don't need any more wacky politicians in power.

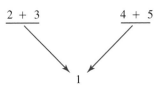

20. Creationism is an inadequate theory about the origins of life. It conflicts with science, and it is incapable of predicting any new facts.

Chapter 4

1. If a claim conflicts with her background information, she has good reason to doubt it.
2. It is not desirable to believe a statement when there is no good reason for doing so.
3. (1) Education and training from reputable institutions or programs in the relevant field; (2) experience in making reliable judgments in the field; (3) reputation among peers (as reflected in the opinions of others in the same field, relevant prestigious awards, and positions of authority); and (4) professional accomplishments.
4. The expert is guilty of blatant violations of the critical thinking principles or of simple factual or formal errors; the expert's claims conflict with what you have good reason to believe; the expert does not adequately support his or her assertions; the expert's writing contains logical contradictions or inconsistent statements; the expert does not treat opposing views fairly; the expert is strongly biased, emotional, or dismissive; the expert relies on information you know is out of date.
5. Impairment due to environmental factors, fatigue, and stress.

6. Reasons for doubt due to low visibility.
7. Reasons for doubt due to vague stimuli.
8. There may or may not be reasons for doubt; the main factor is the reliability of memory.
9. Almost certainly false.
10. Probably true.
11. Almost certainly false.
12. Almost certainly false.
13. Almost certainly false.
14. Almost certainly false.
15. Almost certainly false.
16. Probably false.
17. Yes. Slanted in favor of U.S. policy in Iraq.
18. Yes. Loaded or biased language includes "Ba'ath Party murderers," "Iraqi goon squads," and "regime diehards."
19. The Pentagon.
20. The story lacks the perspective of nonadministration sources and less biased reporters. Some aspects not mentioned: details about specific criticisms of U.S. policy, casualties among Iraqis, evidence for Rumsfeld's claims.

Chapter 5

1. Straw man.
2. Appeal to ignorance.
3. Appeal to the person.
4. Appeal to the person.
5. Red herring.
6. Appeal to the person.
7. Appeal to emotion.
8. Appeal to popularity.
9. Begging the question.
10. Composition.
11. False dilemma.
12. Appeal to ignorance.
13. Appeal to the person.
14. Slippery slope.
15. False dilemma.
16. Hasty generalization.
17. False dilemma.
18. Straw man.
19. Red herring.
20. Appeal to the person.

Chapter 6

1. Conjunction, &; disjunction, v; negation, ~; conditional, →.
2.

Conjunction:

p	q	p & q
T	T	T
T	F	F
F	T	F
F	F	F

Disjunction:

p	q	p v q
T	T	T
T	F	T
F	T	T
F	F	F

Negation:

p	$\sim p$
T	F
F	T

Conditional:

p	q	$p \rightarrow q$
T	T	T
T	F	F
F	T	T
F	F	T

3. When just one statement in the conjunction is false.
4. When the antecedent is true and the consequent is false.
5. $c \rightarrow q$ false
   a & $\sim q$ false
   a v $\sim c$ true

6. $p \rightarrow q$

7. $p \vee q$

8.

Invalid:

$p \rightarrow q$

$q \rightarrow r$

$\therefore q$

p	q	r	$p \rightarrow q$	$q \rightarrow r$	q
T	T	T	T	T	T
T	T	F	T	F	T
T	F	T	F	T	F
T	F	F	F	T	F
F	T	T	T	T	T
F	T	F	T	F	T
F	F	T	T	T	F
F	F	F	T	T	F

Valid:

$p \vee (q \,\&\, r)$

$\sim (q \,\&\, r)$

$\therefore p$

p	q	r	$(q \,\&\, r)$	$p \vee (q \,\&\, r)$	$\sim (q \,\&\, r)$	p
T	T	T	T	T	F	T
T	T	F	F	T	T	T
T	F	T	F	T	T	T
T	F	F	F	T	T	T
F	T	T	T	T	F	F
F	T	F	F	F	T	F
F	F	T	F	F	T	F
F	F	F	F	F	T	F

9. If the temperature rises, then the water will rise. If the water rises, the dam will break. Either the water rises, or it doesn't rise. The water will not rise. Therefore the dam will not break.

Invalid

$p \rightarrow q$

$q \rightarrow r$

$q \vee \sim q$

$\sim q$

$\therefore \sim r$

p	q	r	$p \to q$	$q \to r$	$q \lor \sim q$	$\sim q$	$\sim r$
T	T	T	T	T	T	F	F
T	T	F	T	F	T	F	T
T	F	T	F	T	T	T	F
T	F	F	F	T	T	T	T
F	T	T	T	T	T	F	F
F	T	F	T	F	T	F	T
F	F	T	T	T	T	T	F
F	F	F	T	T	T	T	T

10. Either Joe goes to the movie, or Julia goes to the movie. If the movie is *Gone with the Wind*, then Julia goes to the movie. So if Joe goes to the movie, the movie is not *Gone with the Wind*.

Invalid

$p \lor q$

$r \to q$

$\therefore p \to \sim r$

p	q	r	$p \lor q$	$r \to q$	$p \to \sim r$
T	T	T	T	T	F
T	T	F	T	T	T
T	F	T	T	F	F
T	F	F	T	T	T
F	T	T	T	T	T
F	T	F	T	T	T
F	F	T	F	F	T
F	F	F	F	T	T

11. $x \to y$

   $y \to z$

   $\therefore x \to z$

If it rains, the roof will leak. If the roof leaks, the carpet will be ruined. Therefore, if it rains, the carpet will be ruined.

12. $a \to b$

   $\therefore a \to (a \,\&\, b)$

If I am late, she will be late. Therefore, if I am late, then both of us will be late.

13. $a \,\&\, b$

   $\sim b$

   $\therefore a$

John is in the boat, and Maria is in the boat. Maria is not in the boat. Therefore, I am in the boat.

14. $(p \lor q) \to (p \& q)$
    $p \& q$
    $\therefore p \lor q$

If either the profits fall or the sales go down, then both the profits will fall and the sales will go down. Both the profits will fall and the sales will go down. Therefore, either the profits will fall or the sales go down.

15. $p \to q$
    $\sim p$
    $\therefore q$

If the sky clears, the game proceeds. The sky does not clear. Therefore, the game proceeds.

16. $p \to q$
    $\sim q$
    $\therefore \sim p$

$p \to q$		$\sim q$	$\sim p$
T	F	F	T

Invalid

17. $p \& q$
    $q \to r$
    $\sim q$
    $\therefore r$

$p \& q$		$q \to r$		$\sim q$	r
T	T	T	F	T	F

Valid

18. $p \to q$
    $q \to r$
    $\therefore q \to r$

$p \to q$		$q \to r$		$q \to r$	
	T	T	F	T	F

Valid

19. $p \lor (q \& r)$
    $\sim p$
    $\sim q$
    $\therefore r$

$p \lor (q \& r)$			$\sim p$	$\sim q$	r
T	F	F	T	F	F

Valid

20. $a \rightarrow b$
    $b \rightarrow c$
    $\therefore (b \& c) \lor (a \& b)$

$a \rightarrow b$	$b \rightarrow c$	$(b \& c) \lor (a \& b)$
F F	F	F F F

Invalid

Chapter 7

1. A word that expresses the quantity, or number, of a categorical statement. Universal and particular.
2. Affirmative and negative.
3. A: All S are P. (universal affirmative)
   E: No S are P. (universal negative)
   I: Some S are P. (particular affirmative)
   O: Some S are not P. (particular negative)
4. Some tax cuts are economic mistakes.
   Subject term: tax cuts; predicate term: economic mistakes; quality: affirmative; quantity: particular; name: particular affirmative.
5. No philosophers are five-year-old kids.
   Subject term: philosopher; predicate term: five-year-old kids; quality: negative; quantity: universal; name: universal negative.
6. All patients treated with herbal medicine are Chinese.
   Subject term: patients treated with herbal medicine; predicate term: Chinese people; quality: affirmative; quantity: universal; name: universal affirmative.
7. Some ghost stories are not fabrications devised by true believers.
   Subject term: ghost stories; predicate term: fabrications devised by true believers; quality: negative; quantity: particular; name: particular negative.
8. Only if something is a watercraft is it a canoe.
   All canoes are watercraft. A
9. "Baseball is pastoral." [George Carlin]
   All things identical with baseball are things that are pastoral. A
10. Sheila is the finest scholar in the department.
    All persons identical with Sheila are the finest scholars in the department. A
11. No one with any sense would drive a car without headlights on a rainy night.
    No persons with sense are persons who would drive a car without headlights on a rainy night. E

12. "Slow and steady wins the race." [Aesop]
    All races won are races run slowly and steadily. A
13. A politician is someone who firmly believes that getting elected makes one smart.
    All politicians are persons who firmly believe that getting elected makes them smart. A
14. "A fanatic is someone who can't change his mind and won't change the subject." [Winston Churchill]
    All fanatics are persons who can't change their mind and won't change the subject. A
15. All *M* are *P*. Some *S* are *M*. Therefore, some *S* are *P*.
    Valid.

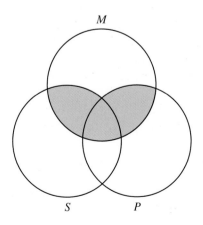

16. No *M* are *P*. No *S* are *M*. Therefore, all *S* are *P*.
    Invalid.

17. All *P* are *M*. No *S* are *M*. Therefore, no *S* are *P*.
Valid.

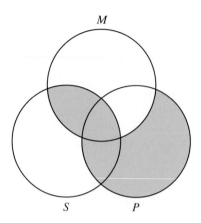

18. Some *P* are not *M*. All *S* are *M*. Therefore, some *S* are not *P*
Invalid.

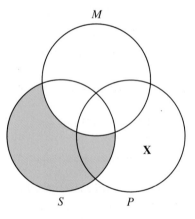

19. All *M* are *P*. All *M* are *S*. Therefore, all *S* are *P*.
Invalid.

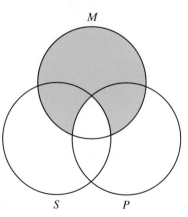

20. Some *S* are *M*. All *M* are *P*. Therefore, some *S* are *P*.
    Valid.

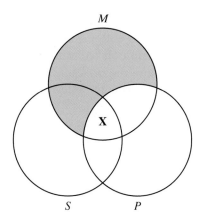

Chapter 8

1. X percent of the observed members of group A have property P.
   Therefore, X percent of all members of group A probably have
   property P.
2. Target group: The class of individuals about which an inductive generalization is made.
   Sample: The observed members of a target group.
   Relevant property: The property under study in a target group.
3. Its sample can be (1) too small or (2) not representative.
4. Thing A has properties P1, P2, P3 plus the property P4.
   Thing B has properties P1, P2, and P3.
   Therefore, thing B probably has property P4.
5. All the women in my yoga class are against the war. Ninety percent of
   the members of a national women's group (twelve thousand members)
   are against the war. And all my women friends are against the war. The
   fact is, almost all American women oppose this war.
   Weak. Not representative.
6. Recently there was a racially motivated murder in Texas. Two white men
   killed a black man. Then another murder of a black man by some racist whites occurred in Louisiana. And in Mississippi an admitted racist
   finally was convicted of the murder of a black man that occurred years
   ago. The South has more racist killers than any other part of the country.
   Weak. Small sample; not representative.
7. Most professors at this college are not grading as strictly as they used to.
   They now give Bs for work to which they used to assign Cs. The grading
   standards in American colleges are dropping.
   Weak. Not representative; probably small sample.

8. The first time Ariana encountered trigonometry, she couldn't understand it. And the first time she read Shakespeare, she didn't get it. She will never understand anything.
   Weak. Small sample; not representative.

9. Americans are quite satisfied with the administration's recent foreign policy decisions. An "instant poll" conducted yesterday on the CNN website got fifteen thousand responses from site visitors—and 95 percent of them said that American foreign policy was on the right track.
   Weak. Not representative.

10. Judging from what I've seen, anti-war demonstrators are just a bunch of peaceniks left over from the Vietnam War era.
    Weak (if "what I've seen" means personally witnessed). Small sample; not representative.

11. "Suppose that someone tells me that he has had a tooth extracted without an anaesthetic, and I express my sympathy, and suppose that I am then asked, 'How do you know that it hurt him?' I might reasonably reply, 'Well, I know that it would hurt me. I have been to the dentist and know how painful it is to have a tooth stopped without an anaesthetic, let alone taken out. And he has the same sort of nervous system as I have. I infer, therefore, that in these conditions he felt considerable pain, just as I should myself.'" [Alfred J. Ayer]
    Two things compared: experiences of tooth extraction; conclusion: that the other person was in considerable pain; strong.

12. "As for one who is choosy about what he learns . . . we shall not call him a lover of learning or a philosopher, just as we shall not say that a man who is difficult about his food is hungry or has an appetite for food. We shall not call him a lover of food but a poor eater. . . . But we shall call a philosopher the man who is easily willing to learn every kind of knowledge, gladly turns to learning things, and is insatiable in this respect." [Socrates]
    Two things compared: philosopher and eater; conclusion: that a philosopher is someone easily willing to learn every kind of knowledge; strong.

13. "Let us begin with a parable [showing that statements about God have no meaning]. . . . Once upon a time two explorers came upon a clearing in the jungle. In the clearing were growing many flowers and many weeds. One explorer says, 'Some gardener must tend this plot.' The other disagrees, 'There is no gardener.' So they pitch their tents and set a watch. No gardener is ever seen. 'But perhaps he is an invisible gardener.' So they set up a barbed-wire fence. They electrify it. . . . But no shrieks ever suggest that some intruder has received a shock. No movements of the wire ever betray an invisible climber. . . . Yet still the Believer is not convinced. 'But there is a gardener, invisible, intangible, insensible.'. . . At last the Sceptic despairs, 'But what remains of your original assertion? Just how does what you call an invisible, intangible,

eternally elusive gardener differ from an imaginary gardener or even from no gardener at all?'" [Antony Flew]
Two things compared: belief in an elusive gardener and belief in God. conclusion: that talk of an undetectable being such as God is meaningless. Weak.

14. School violence is caused mainly by teens playing violent video games. Incidents of violence in schools have increased as more and more teens are playing violent video games, as the video games themselves have become more graphically and realistically violent, and as the number and variety of video games have expanded dramatically.
Conclusion: School violence is caused mainly by teens playing violent video games. Weak. Overlooking relevant factors, failing to rule out coincidence.

15. Smoking and exposure to secondhand smoke among pregnant women pose a significant risk to both infants and the unborn. According to numerous studies, each year the use of tobacco causes thousands of spontaneous births, infant deaths, and deaths from SIDS. Death rates for fetuses are 35 percent higher among pregnant women who smoke than among pregnant women who don't smoke.
Conclusion: Smoking and exposure to secondhand smoke among pregnant women pose a significant risk to both infants and the unborn. Strong.

16. Why are crime rates so high, the economy so bad, and our children so prone to violence, promiscuity, and vulgarity? These social ills have arisen—as they always have—from the "moral vacuum" created when Americans turn away from religion. Our current slide into chaos started when prayer was banned from public schools and secular humanism swooped in to replace it. And as God has slowly faded from public life, we have got deeper in the hole.
Conclusion: Serious social ills occur because Americans turn away from religion. Weak. Overlooking relevant factors, failing to rule out coincidence.

17. The twelve of us went on a hike through the mountains. We all drank bottled water except Lisa, who drank from a stream. Later she got really sick. Some intestinal thing. But the rest of us were fine. We've repeated this adventure many times on other hikes, with all but one of us drinking bottled water and one drinking from a stream. Everything else was the same. Each time, the person who drank from the stream got really ill. Drinking from streams on these hikes causes intestinal illness. Don't do it.
Conclusion: Drinking from streams on these hikes causes intestinal illness. Strong.

18. Ever since I started drinking herbal tea in the morning, my energy level has improved and I'm a lot calmer during the day. That stuff works.
Conclusion: Herbal tea boosts energy and calms the nerves. Weak. Overlooking relevant factors, failing to rule out coincidence, possibly confusing cause and effect.

19. Yesterday my astrological chart—prepared by a top astrologer—said that I would meet an attractive person today, and I did. Last week, it said I'd come into some money, and I did. (Jack paid me that hundred dollars he owed me.) Now I'm a believer. The stars really do rule.
Conclusion: The stars rule. Weak. Failing to rule out coincidence.

20. Most of the terminal cancer patients in this ward who had positive attitudes about their disease lived longer than expected. Most of the negative-attitude patients didn't live as long as expected. A positive attitude can increase the life expectancy of people with terminal cancer.
Conclusion: A positive attitude can increase the life expectancy of people with terminal cancer. Weak. Failing to rule out other relevant factors, failing to rule out coincidence, possibly confusing cause and effect.

Chapter 9

1. Inference to the best explanation:

Phenomenon Q.
E provides the best explanation for Q.
Therefore, it is probable that E is true.

Enumerative induction:

X percent of the observed members of group A have property P.
Therefore, X percent of all members of group A probably have property P.

Analogical induction:

Thing A has properties P1, P2, P3 plus the property P4.
Thing B has properties P1, P2, and P3.
Therefore, thing B probably has property P4.

2. A standard of internal and external consistency that a theory must meet to be eligible for further consideration.

3. Testability: Whether there is some way to determine if a theory is true.
Fruitfulness: The number of novel predictions made.
Scope: The amount of diverse phenomena explained.
Simplicity: The number of assumptions made.
Conservatism: How well a theory fits with existing knowledge.

4. With testable theories there is a way to determine whether they are true or false; untestable theories cannot be checked.

5. Four steps to finding the best explanation:

Step 1. State the Theory and check for consistency.
Step 2. Assess the Evidence for the theory.
Step 3. Scrutinize alternative theories.
Step 4. Test the theories with the criteria of adequacy.

6. The best theory is the eligible theory that meets the criteria of adequacy better than any of its competitors.

7. d

8. a, b

9. a, b

10. a

11. Phenomenon: The rise in popularity of a newly elected president. (1) The so-called honeymoon effect in which a new president enjoys popularity until he or she is involved in serious or controversial decisions.

12. Phenomenon: Your friend has been skipping class, and you haven't seen her in days. (1) She's in bed with the flu.

13. Phenomenon: Ships, boats, and planes have been disappearing off the coast of Florida for years. (1) Considering the meteorological and atmospheric conditions of the area, it's normal for some craft to be lost from time to time.

14. Phenomenon: The rapid spread of an unknown, dangerous, viral disease throughout North America. (1) The lack of awareness and defenses against a new mutated virus.

15. (1) People buy high-ticket merchandise because of subliminal advertising—their minds are being influenced by imperceptible stimuli designed by ad execs. (2) The purchase of high-ticket merchandise. (3) Normal advertising and sales ploys influence people to purchase high-ticket merchandise. (4) The alternative theory is more plausible

16. (1) In cold fusion research, skepticism skews scientists' observations. (2) The lack of evidence for cold fusion. (3) Cold fusion does not exist. (4) The alternative theory is more plausible.

17. (1) Eleanor must have a system that enables her to pick winning numbers. (2) Eleanor's winning the state lottery twice in nine months. (3) Coincidence. (4) The coincidence theory is more plausible.

18. (1) The embezzlement was caused by the divorce of his parents when he was very young. (2) The embezzlement. (3) He embezzled because he needed the money to pay debts. (4) The alternative theory is more plausible.

19. (1) Schoolchildren do poorly in school because of the low or negative expectations of their teachers. (2) Poor performance of school children. (3) Students do poorly because teachers want them to fail. (4) The expectations theory is more plausible.

20. (1) The woman is possessed. (2) The woman's bizarre behavior, including stigmata (bleeding from the palms). (3) The woman suffers from some form of psychosis, which can manifest itself in many strange symptoms, including bleeding from the skin. (4) The alternative theory is more plausible.

Chapter 10

1. An observational consequence implied or predicted by a hypothesis.
2. No. Hypotheses often contain concepts that aren't in the data.
3. If H, then C.
   not-C.
   Therefore, not-H.
4. If H, then C.
   C.
   Therefore, H.
5. It's always possible that we will someday find evidence that undermines or conflicts with the evidence we have now.
6. A hypothesis can always be saved from refutation by making changes in the background claims.
7. Hypothesis: Lack of sufficient lighting on Blind Man's Curve is contributing to an increase in automobile accidents. Test implication: If the hypothesis is true, ensuring sufficient lighting on Blind Man's Curve should cause a decrease in accidents.
8. Hypothesis: Juan did the fatal stabbing. Test implication: If the hypothesis is true, at least some of the blood on his shirt is likely to belong to the victim, which a DNA test can confirm.
9. Hypothesis: The lights were coming from a meteor fireball breaking up in the atmosphere, and the claim of alien spacecraft was the result of misinterpretation caused by viewer expectation and poor viewing conditions. Test implication: If the hypothesis is true, scientists should be able to confirm that a meteor fireball did enter the atmosphere at the time the mysterious lights were said to appear.
10. (1) Maria drank contaminated water from the creek. (2) Maria ate poisonous berries. (3) The water from the creek contained toxins that can cause gastrointestinal illness, and Maria drank some; Maria ate berries that were poisonous and known to cause gastrointestinal illness. (4) Evidence that Maria drank the water and that it contained the suspected toxins would confirm the hypothesis; failure to detect the toxins would disconfirm the hypothesis.
11. (1) Students pay more attention with two teachers in the class. (2) Students get more individual attention from the teachers. (3) Students concentrate more on their studies when two teachers are in the class; when there are two teachers, they spend more time with each student. (4) Evidence that students were paying more attention would confirm the hypothesis; evidence that students did not pay more attention would disconfirm the hypothesis.
12. (1) Higher levels of air pollution cause more stress. (2) An increase in crime causes more stress. (3) Air pollution levels have increased,

and they contribute to stress; crime has increased, and the amount of crime correlates with stress. (4) Evidence of pollution causing stress and of a significant increase in pollution would confirm the hypothesis; evidence showing no change in air pollution levels would disconfirm it.

13. (1) Super Cold-Stopper With Beta-Carotene prevents colds. (2) The Vaughns have been exposed less often to people with colds. (3) Taking Super Cold-Stopper With Beta-Carotene decreases the incidence of colds; the Vaughns have come in contact with fewer people with colds. (4) Evidence that the product does in fact decrease the incidence of colds would confirm the hypothesis; a failure to demonstrate this effect in well-controlled studies would disconfirm the hypothesis.

14. Esther stole the book from the library.
Test implication: Esther should be seen on security cameras stealing the book. Evidence: Video from the security camera clearly showing Esther stealing the book.

15. Most people—both white and black—are economically better off now than their parents were thirty years ago.
Test implication: Economic data from the past thirty years should show significant increases in several indicators of economic well-being. Evidence: Data from several trustworthy sources showing the relevant changes in the indicators.

16. The health care system in this country is worse now than it was when Bill Clinton was president.
Test implication: There should be significant declines in several standard measures of the quality of a health care system, including the number of people who have access to health care, the effectiveness of medical treatments, and infant mortality rates. Evidence: Reliable data from nonpartisan sources that show the relevant declines.

17. d

18. a, b

19. a, b, c

20. Theory: Joseph is possessed. Phenomenon: Joseph's strange behavior. Alternative theory: Joseph is an epileptic. The evidence for the possession theory is almost nonexistent. Strange behavior, common among humans, is not evidence for possession, and science has demonstrated that seizures are an indication not of possession but of epilepsy and other neurological disorders. The epilepsy theory is testable; the possession theory is not. The possession theory is a failure in fruitfulness, scope, simplicity, and conservatism; the epilepsy theory does well by these criteria. The latter is the better theory.

Chapter 11

1. A moral statement is a statement asserting that an action is right or wrong (moral or immoral) or that something (such as a person or motive) is good or bad.

2. At least one premise is a moral statement that asserts a general moral principle or moral standard. At least one premise makes a nonmoral claim. And the conclusion is a moral statement, or judgment, about a particular case (usually a particular kind of action).

3. Consistency with our considered moral judgments; consistency with our experience of the moral life; workability in real-life situations.

4. By trying to think of counterexamples to it.

5. No.

6. Of course we should have offered protection to the Kurds. They were in grave danger and they asked for our help. *And it is our duty to offer protection to people if they are in grave danger and they request our help.*

7. The supplement manufacturers knew that the herb ephedra was dangerous. *If a company is aware that its product is dangerous, it is obligated to remove it from the market.* So they should have removed it from the market.

8. The Democrats insulted the president. *Insults to the president should never be allowed.* They should have never been allowed to do that.

9. The Smiths were consenting adults who were having sex in the privacy of their own home. *Sex between consenting adults in the privacy of their own home is morally permissible.* These actions by the Smiths are morally permissible.

10. Randi killed his neighbor, and the killing was not in self-defense. *Killing someone except in self-defense is morally wrong.* He should not have committed such an act.

11. Lying is wrong under all circumstances. *Counterexample: Lying to save the lives of a thousand people.*

12. People who commit crimes should not be punished—they should be retrained to act legally. *Counterexample: Adolf Hitler committed massive crimes against humanity. Wasn't he deserving of punishment?*

13. All humans, whatever their circumstances, have full moral rights. *Counterexample: Do insane individuals have full moral rights? murderers? people in comas?*

14. All creatures that are alive and sensitive to stimulation are equally valuable and should be accorded equal respect. *Counterexample: Is it just as wrong to kill a goldfish as it is a horse? Should we give turtles the same respect we give to children?*

15. The morally right action is the one that produces the most happiness, everyone considered. *Counterexample: Is it morally right to arbitrarily imprison and torture an innocent person if doing so will produce the most happiness for the most people?*

16. Right actions are those that are in one's own self-interest. *Counterexample: Murdering a friend could conceivably be in your own best interest—would it therefore be morally permissible?*

17. Medical experimentation on a patient without her consent. *Defense: If the experimentation could save hundreds of lives and would have no major negative consequences for the experimenters or for society, it would be justified.*

18. Taking food, shelter, and other resources from rich people and distributing them equally among poor people. *Defense: A more equal distribution of resources would result in greater happiness for a greater number.*

19. Any form of expression or speech that offends people of faith should not be tolerated. *Penthouse* magazine definitely offends people of faith. Ban it! *Evaluation: The first premise is dubious, for it would have us violate the autonomy of persons—by, for example, dramatically curtailing freedom of speech.*

20. Anyone who disagrees with the basic moral dictums of the prevailing culture should be censored. Dr. Tilden's graduation speech clearly was inconsistent with the prevailing moral opinions on campus. She should be reprimanded. *Evaluation: The first premise runs counter to several plausible moral principles, including respect for autonomy, freedom of speech and conscience, and tolerance.*

NOTES

Chapter 1

1. Robert Plummer, "Will Fake Business Blogs Crash and Burn?" *BBC News*, 22 May 2008, <http://news.bbc.co.uk/2/hi/business/7287413.stm> September 5, 2008.

Chapter 2

1. Francis Bacon, "Idols of the Mind," in *Novum Organum, The Works*, 3 vols., ed. and trans. Basil Montague (Philadelphia: Parry & MacMillan, 1854).

2. *Ibid.*

3. Bertrand Russell, *Let the People Think* (London: William Clowes, 1941), 2.

4. W. K. Clifford, "The Ethics of Belief," in *The Rationality of Belief in God*, ed. George I. Mavrodes (Englewood Cliffs, NJ: Prentice-Hall, 1970), 159–60.

5. Shirley MacLaine, *It's All in the Playing* (New York: Bantam Books, 1987), 171–72.

6. For a thorough review of various forms of relativism, see Theodore Schick and Lewis Vaughn, *How to Think About Weird Things*, 3d ed. (Mountain View, CA: Mayfield Publishing, 1999), 68–92.

Chapter 3

1. This step-by-step procedure is inspired, in part, by Greg Bassham et al., *Critical Thinking: A Student's Introduction* (San Francisco: McGraw-Hill, 2002), 56–62.

2. Elias E. Savellos, *Reasoning and the Law: The Elements* (Belmont, CA: Wadsworth, 2001), 59–60.

3. This procedure is inspired, in part, by Brooke Noel Moore and Richard Parker, *Critical Thinking*, 6th ed. (Mountain View, CA: Mayfield Publishing, 2001), 274–75.

Chapter 4

1. Bertrand Russell, *Let the People Think* (London: William Clowes, 1941), 1.

2. American Psychiatric Association, news release, "APA Responds to Tom Cruise's Today Show Interview," June 27, 2005.

3. Duke University Libraries, "Guide to Library Research," <www.lib.duke.edu/libguide/evaluating_web.htm> (February 6, 2004).

4. Elizabeth Loftus and Hunter G. Hoffman, "Misinformation and Memory, The Creation of New Memories," *Journal of Experimental Psychology: General* 118(1) (March 1989):100–104.

5. Terence Hines, *Pseudoscience and the Paranormal* (Buffalo, NY: Prometheus Books, 1988), 170.

6. Adam Liptak, "Study of Wrongful Convictions Raises Questions Beyond DNA," *New York Times*, 23 July 2007.

7. This example inspired by L. W. Alvarez, letter to the editors, *Science* (June 18, 1965):1541.

8. Hines, *Pseudoscience and the Paranormal*, 4–5.

9. Thomas Gilovich, *How We Know What Isn't So* (New York: The Free Press, 1991), 54.

10. J. Cocker, "Biased Questions in Judgment of Covariation Studies," *Personality and Social Psychology Bulletin* 8 (June 1982):214–20.

11. National Safety Council, "What Are the Odds of Dying?" <www.nsc.org> (June 12, 2004).

12. John Ruscio, "Risky Business," *Skeptical Inquirer* (March 2000).

13. Leonard Downie Jr. and Robert G. Kaiser, *The News About the News* (New York: Vintage Books, 2003), 9–10.

14. "Work Farce," *New York Post*, June 26, 2003.

15. "Soldiers Sweep Up Saddam's Hit Goons," *New York Post*, July 1, 2003.

Chapter 5

1. The inspiration for this unconventional categorization comes primarily from Ludwig F. Schlecht, "Classifying Fallacies Logically," *Teaching Philosophy* 14(1) (1991):53–64 and Greg Bassham et al., *Critical Thinking: A Student's Introduction* (San Francisco: McGraw-Hill, 2002).

2. Tara Parker-Pope, "Prominent Cancer Doctor Warns About Cellphones," *New York Times*, 24 July 2008, <http://well.blogs.nytimes.com/2008/07/24/prominent-cancer-doctor-warns-about-cellphones/?scp=2&sq=herberman%20st=cse>, September 11, 2008.

3. Robert T. Carroll, "The Paralyzing Precautionary Principle," *The Skeptic's Dictionary*, 26 July 2008, <http://www.skepdic.com/skeptimedia/skeptimedia20.html>, September 11, 2008.

4. W. Ross Winterowd and Geoffrey R. Winterowd, *The Critical Reader, Thinker, and Writer* (Mountain View, CA: Mayfield Publishing, 1992), 447–48.

5. Associated Press, "The President and the Straw Man," *CBS News*, 18 March 2006, <http://www.cbsnews.com/stories/2006/03/18/politics/main1419363.shtml>, September 11, 2008.

6. Reported in Richard Whately, *Elements of Logic* (London: Longmans, Green, and Co., 1826).

7. Theodore Schick and Lewis Vaughn, *How to Think About Weird Things*, 3d ed. (Mountain View, CA: Mayfield Publishing, 1999), 192.

8. Student paper reproduced by permission of Mitchell S. McKinney, University of Missouri, <http://www.missouri.edu/~commpjb/comm104/Sample_Papers/Free_Speech/free_speech.html>.

Chapter 8

1. Susan Blackmore, "Psychic Experiences: Psychic Illusions," *Skeptical Inquirer* 16:367–76.

2. David G. Myers, "The Power of Coincidence," *Skeptic Magazine* 9(4) (September 2002).

3. Julie Steenhuysen, Reuters, "U.S. Study Clears Measles Vaccine of Autism Link," September 4, 2008.

Chapter 9

1. Charles Darwin, *The Origin of Species* (New York: Collier, 1962), 476.

2. Arthur Conan Doyle, *A Study in Scarlet* (New York: P. F. Collier and Son, 1906), 29–30.

3. Arthur Conan Doyle, "The 'Gloria Scott,'" *Memoirs of Sherlock Holmes* (London: George Newnes, 1894).

4. "Shark Attacks Are Down for Third Year in a Row," <CNN.com> (January 29, 2004).

5. "Study Examines Cancer Risk from Hair Dye," <CNN.com> (January 28, 2004).

6. John Hagee, interview on *National Public Radio*, 18 September 2006, <http://www.npr.org/templates/story/story.php?storyId=6097362>, September 15, 2008.

7. W. V. Quine and J. S. Ullman, *The Web of Belief* (New York: Random House, 1970), 43–44.

8. NASA, "The Great Moon Hoax," Science@NASA website, <http://science.nasa.gov>.

9. For the latest research and discussion on the placebo effect, see A. Hrobjartsson and P. C. Gotzsche, *New England Journal of Medicine* 344 (2001):1594–1602; J. C. Bailar, "The Powerful Placebo and the Wizard of Oz," *New England Journal of Medicine,* 344 2001:1630–32, and Keith Bauer, "Clinical Use of Placebo," <www.ama-assn.org> (July 2001), journal discussion.

10. See C. Hill and F. Doyan, "Review of Randomized Trials of Homeopathy," *Review of Epidemiology* 38 (1990):139–42; Report, Homoeopathic Medicine Group, Commission of the European Communities, December 1996; J. Wise, "Health Authority Stops Buying Homeopthy," *British Medical Journal* 314 (1997):1574; K. Linde et al., "Are the Clinical Effects of Homeopathy Placebo Effects?" Lancet 350(9081) (Sept. 20, 1997):824.

11. Fred L. Whipple, *Earth, Moon and Planets* (Boston: Harvard University Press, 1968).

12. Robert A. Baker, "Can We Tell When Someone Is Staring at Us?" *Skeptical Inquirer,* March/April 2000.

Chapter 10

1. I owe the inspiration and general outline for this section to Theodore Schick, Jr., in Theodore Schick, Jr., and Lewis Vaughn, *How to Think About Weird Things,* 4th ed., 2005.

2. Excerpted from Robert L. Park, "The Seven Warning Signs of Bogus Science," *Chronicle of Higher Education,* 31 January 2003, <http://chronicle.com/free/v49/i21/21b02001.htm>, September 15, 2008.

3. See Stephen Barrett et al., *Consumer Health,* 6th ed. (New York: WCB/McGraw-Hill, 1993), 239–40.

4. Thomas S. Kuhn, *The Copernican Revolution: Planetary Astronomy in the Development of Western Thought* (Cambridge, MA: Harvard University Press, 1957), 179.

5. Section 4a of Act 590 of the Acts of Arkansas of 1981, "Balanced Treatment for Creation-Science and Evolution-Science Act."

6. National Academy of Sciences, *Science and Creationism* (Washington, DC: National Academy Press, 1998).

7. *Ibid.*

8. George S. Bakken, "Creation or Evolution?" National Center for Science Education website, <www.ncseweb.org>.

9. Theodosius Dobzhansky, quoted in National Academy of Sciences, *Science and Creationism*, 'lihttp://books.nap.edu'mt.

10. National Academy of Sciences, "Preface," in *Science and Creationism.*

11. Kenneth Chang, "In Explaining Life's Complexity, Darwinists and Doubters Clash," *New York Times,* August 22, 2005.

12. Tom Byrne and Matthew Normand, "The Demon-Haunted Sentence," *Skeptical Inquirer,* March/April 2000.

13. Theodore Schick and Lewis Vaughn, *How to Think About Weird Things,* 3d ed. (San Francisco: McGraw-Hill, 2002), 190–91.

14. Stephen Barrett, "High Doses of Vitamin C Are Not Effective as a Cancer Treatment," <Quackwatch.com> (July 6, 2003).

15. Benjamin Radford, "Reality Check: Ghost Hunters and 'Ghost Detectors,'" *Skeptical Inquirer,* 2006, <http://www.csicop.org/specialarticles/shady-science.html>, September 16, 2008.

16. Hillary Mayell, "Crop Circles: Artworks or Alien Signs?" *National Geographic News,* August 2, 2002.

17. Matt Ridley, "Crop Circle Confession," *Scientific American,* August 2002.

18. Richard Wiseman, Matthew Smith, and Jeff Wiseman, "Eyewitness Testimony and the Paranormal," *Skeptical Inquirer,* November/December 1995.

19. Ray Hyman, "How Not to Test Mediums," *Skeptical Inquirer,* January/February 2003.

20. Robert T. Carroll, "Ouija Board," The Skeptic's Dictionary, <http://skepdic.com> (October 27, 2003).

21. Robert T. Carroll, "Bigfoot," The Skeptic's Dictionary, <http://skepdic.com> (October 27, 2003).

22. Joe Nickell, "Psychic Pets and Pet Psychics," *Skeptical Inquirer,* November/December 2002.

23. NOVA Online, "Hot Science, Alien Evidence?" <www.pbs.org/wgbh/alienactivity> (October 27, 2003).

24. Henry Roberts, *The Complete Prophesies of Nostradamus* (Great Neck, NY: Nostradamus, 1969), 18, as cited in Andrew Neher, *The Psychology of Transcendence* (Englewood Cliffs, NJ: Prentice Hall, 1980), 188.

Chapter 11

1. "Ethics," Internet Encyclopedia of Philosophy, <www.utm.edu/research/iep>.

2. Katherine Zoepf, "A Dishonorable Affair," *New York Times,* 23 September 2007, <http://www.nytimes.com/2007/09/23/magazine/23wwln-syria-t.html?scp=15& pagewanted=print>, September 16, 2008.

3. Immanuel Kant, *Groundwork of the Metaphysic of Morals,* trans. H. J. Paton (New York: Harper & Row, 1964), 88.

GLOSSARY

ad hoc hypothesis: A hypothesis, or theory, that cannot be verified independently of the phenomenon it's supposed to explain. Ad hoc hypotheses always make a theory less simple—and therefore less credible.

ad hominem **(appeal to the person):** The fallacy of rejecting a claim by criticizing the person who makes it rather than the claim itself. *Ad hominem* means "to the man."

affirming the antecedent: *See modus ponens.*

affirming the consequent: An invalid argument form:

> If *p*, then *q*.
> *q*.
> Therefore, *p*.

analogical induction: *See* argument by analogy.

analogy: A comparison of two or more things alike in specific respects.

antecedent: The first part of a conditional statement (If *p*, then *q*.), the component that begins with the word *if*. See **conditional statement.**

appeal to authority: The fallacy of relying on the opinion of someone deemed to be an expert who in fact is *not* an expert.

appeal to common practice: The fallacy of accepting or rejecting a claim based solely on what groups of people generally do or how they behave (when the action or behavior is irrelevant to the truth of the claim).

appeal to emotion: The fallacy of using emotions in place of relevant reasons as premises in an argument.

appeal to ignorance: The fallacy of arguing that a lack of evidence proves something. In one type of this fallacy, the problem arises by thinking that a claim must be true because it hasn't been shown to be false. In another type, the breakdown in logic comes when you argue that a claim must be false because it hasn't been proved to be true.

appeal to popularity (or to the masses): The fallacy of arguing that a claim must be true merely because a substantial number of people believe it.

appeal to the person: *See ad hominem.*

appeal to tradition: The fallacy of arguing that a claim must be true just because it's part of a tradition.

argument: A group of statements in which some of them (the premises) are intended to support another of them (the conclusion).

argument by analogy (analogical induction): An argument making use of analogy, reasoning that because two or more things are similar in several respects, they must be similar in some further respect.

background information: The large collection of very well supported beliefs that we all rely on to inform our actions and choices. It consists of basic facts about everyday things, beliefs based on very good evidence (including our own personal observations and excellent authority), and justified claims that we would regard as "common sense" or "common knowledge."

begging the question: The fallacy of attempting to establish the conclusion of an argument by using that conclusion as a premise. Also called arguing in a circle.

biased sample: A sample that does not properly represent the target group. *See* **representative sample.**

burden of proof: The weight of evidence or argument required by one side in a debate or disagreement.

categorical logic: A form of logic whose focus is categorical statements, which make assertions about categories, or classes, of things.

categorical statement: A statement, or claim, that makes a simple assertion about categories, or classes, of things.

causal argument: An inductive argument whose conclusion contains a causal claim.

causal claim: A statement about the causes of things.

claim: A statement; an assertion that something is or is not the case.

cogent argument: A strong inductive argument with all true premises.

composition: The fallacy of arguing that what is true of the parts must be true of the whole. The error is thinking that the characteristics of the parts are somehow transferred to the whole, something that is not always the case.

compound statement: A statement composed of at least two constituent, or simple, statements.

conclusion: In an argument, the statement that the premises are intended to support.

conditional statement: An "if-then" statement; it consists of the antecedent (the part introduced by the word *if*) and the consequent (the part introduced by the word *then*).

confidence level: In statistical theory, the probability that the sample will accurately represent the target group within the margin of error.

conjunct: One of two simple statements joined by a connective to form a compound statement.

conjunction: Two simple statements joined by a connective to form a compound statement.

consequent: The part of a conditional statement (If *p*, then *q*.) introduced by the word *then*.

conservatism: A criterion of adequacy for judging the worth of theories. A conservative theory is one that fits with our established beliefs.

copula: One of four components of a standard-form categorical statement; a linking verb—either "are" or "are not"—that joins the subject term and the predicate term.

criteria of adequacy: The standards used to judge the worth of explanatory theories. They include *testability, fruitfulness, scope, simplicity,* and *conservatism.*

critical thinking: The systematic evaluation or formulation of beliefs, or statements, by rational standards.

deductive argument: An argument intended to provide logically conclusive support for its conclusion.

denying the antecedent: An invalid argument form:

If *p,* then *q.*
Not *p.*
Therefore, not *q.*

denying the consequent: *See **modus tollens.***

dependent premise: A premise that depends on at least one other premise to provide joint support to a conclusion. If a dependent premise is removed, the support that its linked dependent premises supply to the conclusion is undermined or completely canceled out.

disjunct: A simple statement that is a component of a disjunction.

disjunction: A compound statement of the form "Either *p* or *q.*" A disjunction is true even if only one disjunct is true, and false only if both disjuncts are false.

disjunctive syllogism: A valid argument form:

Either *p* or *q.*
Not *p.*
Therefore, *q.*

In the syllogism's second premise, either disjunct can be denied.

division: The fallacy of arguing that what is true of the whole must be true of the parts. The error is thinking that characteristics of the whole must transfer to the parts or that traits of the group must be the same as traits of individuals in the group.

enumerative induction: An inductive argument pattern in which we reason from premises about individual members of a group to conclusions about the group as a whole.

equivocation: The fallacy of using a word in two different senses in an argument.

expert: Someone who is more knowledgeable in a particular subject area or field than most others are.

explanation: A statement or statements intended to tell why or how something is the case.

fallacy: An argument form that is both common and defective; a recurring mistake in reasoning.

false dilemma: The fallacy of asserting that there are only two alternatives to consider when there are actually more than two.

faulty analogy: A defective argument by analogy.

fruitfulness: A criterion of adequacy for judging the worth of theories. A fruitful theory is one that makes novel predictions.

gambler's fallacy: The error of thinking that previous events can affect the probabilities in the random event at hand.

genetic fallacy: The fallacy of arguing that a claim is true or false solely because of its origin.

hasty generalization: The fallacy of drawing a conclusion about a target group based on an inadequate sample size.

hypothetical syllogism: A valid argument made up of three hypothetical, or conditional, statements:

> If p then q.
> If q, then r.
> Therefore, if p, then r.

independent premise: A premise that does not depend on other premises to provide support to a conclusion. If an independent premise is removed, the support that other premises supply to the conclusion is not affected.

indicator words: Words that frequently accompany arguments and signal that a premise or conclusion is present.

inductive argument: An argument in which the premises are intended to provide probable, not conclusive, support for its conclusion.

inference: The process of reasoning from a premise or premises to a conclusion based on those premises.

inference to the best explanation: A form of inductive reasoning in which we reason from premises about a state of affairs to an explanation for that state of affairs:

> *Phenomenon Q.*
> *E provides the best explanation for Q.*
> *Therefore, it is probable that E is true.*

invalid argument: A deductive argument that fails to provide conclusive support for its conclusion.

logic: The study of good reasoning, or inference, and the rules that govern it.

margin of error: The variation between the values derived from a sample and the true values of the whole target group.

modus ponens **(affirming the antecedent):** A valid argument form:

> If p, then q.
> p.
> Therefore, q.

modus tollens **(denying the consequent):** A valid argument form:

> If p, then q.
> Not q.
> Therefore, not p.

moral statement: A statement asserting that an action is right or wrong (moral or immoral) or that something (such as a person or motive) is good or bad.

necessary condition: A condition for the occurrence of an event without which the event cannot occur.

peer pressure: Group pressure to accept or reject a claim based solely on what one's peers think or do.

philosophical skepticism: The view that we know much less than we think we do or nothing at all.

philosophical skeptics: Those who embrace philosophical skepticism.

***post hoc, ergo propter hoc* ("after that, therefore because of that"):** The fallacy of reasoning that just because B followed A, A must have caused B.

predicate term: The second class, or group, named in a standard-form categorical statement.

premise: In an argument, a statement, or reason, given in support of the conclusion.

property in question: *See* **relevant property.**

propositional logic: The branch of deductive reasoning that deals with the logical relationships among statements.

quality: A characteristic of a categorical statement, based on whether the statement affirms or denies that a class is entirely or partly included in another class. A categorical statement that affirms is said to be affirmative in quality; one that denies is said to be negative in quality.

quantifier: In categorical statements, a word used to indicate the number of things with specified characteristics. The acceptable quantifiers are "all," "no," or "some." The quantifiers "all" and "no" in front of a categorical statement tell us that it's *universal*—it applies to every member of a class. The quantifier "some" at the beginning of a categorical statement says that the statement is *particular*—it applies to some but not all members of a class.

quantity: In categorical statements, the attribute of number, specified by the words "all," "no," or "some."

random sample: A sample that is selected randomly from a target group in such a way as to ensure that the sample is representative. In a simple random selection, every member of the target group has an equal chance of being selected for the sample.

red herring: The fallacy of deliberately raising an irrelevant issue during an argument. The basic pattern is to put forth a claim and then couple it with additional claims that may seem to support it but in fact are mere distractions.

relevant property (property in question): In enumerative induction, a property, or characteristic, that is of interest in the target group.

representative sample: In enumerative induction, a sample that resembles the target group in all relevant ways. *See* **biased sample**.

sample (sample member): In enumerative induction, the observed members of the target group.

scope: A criterion of adequacy for judging the worth of theories. A theory with scope is one that explains or predicts phenomena other than that which it was introduced to explain.

simple statement: A statement that doesn't contain any other statements as constituents. *See* **compound statement.**

simplicity: A criterion of adequacy for judging the worth of theories. A simple theory is one that makes minimal assumptions.

singular statements: In categorical logic, statements that assert something about a single person or thing, including objects, places, and times.

slippery slope: The fallacy of arguing, without good reasons, that taking a particular step will inevitably lead to further, undesirable steps.

social relativism: The view that truth is relative to societies.

sound argument: A deductively valid argument that has true premises.

standard-form categorical statement: In categorical logic, a categorical statement that takes one of these four forms:

1. All S are P. (All cats are carnivores.)
2. No S are P. (No cats are carnivores.)
3. Some S are P. (Some cats are carnivores.)
4. Some S are not P. (Some cats are not carnivores.)

statement (claim): An assertion that something is or is not the case.

stereotyping: Drawing conclusions about people without sufficient reasons.

straw man: The fallacy of distorting, weakening, or oversimplifying someone's position so it can be more easily attacked or refuted.

strong argument: An inductive argument that succeeds in providing probable—but not conclusive—support for its conclusion.

subjective relativism: The idea that truth depends on what someone believes.

subjectivist fallacy: Accepting the notion of subjective relativism or using it to try to support a claim.

subject term: The first class, or group, named in a standard-form categorical statement.

sufficient condition: A condition for the occurrence of an event that guarantees that the event occurs.

syllogism: A deductive argument made up of three statements—two premises and a conclusion. *See modus ponens and modus tollens.*

symbolic logic: Modern deductive logic that uses symbolic language to do its work.

target group (target population): In enumerative induction, the whole collection of individuals under study.

testability: A criterion of adequacy for judging the worth of theories. A testable theory is one in which there is some way to determine whether the theory is true or false—that is, it predicts something other than what it was introduced to explain.

TEST formula: A four-step procedure for evaluating the worth of a theory:

Step 1. State the Theory and check for consistency.
Step 2. Assess the Evidence for the theory.
Step 3. Scrutinize alternative theories.
Step 4. Test the theories with the criteria of adequacy.

theoretical explanation: A theory, or hypothesis, that tries to explain why something is the way it is, why something is the case, or why something happened.

truth-preserving: A characteristic of a valid deductive argument in which the logical structure guarantees the truth of the conclusion if the premises are true.

truth table: A table that specifies the truth values for claim variables and combinations of claim variables in symbolized statements or arguments.

tu quoque **("you're another"):** A type of *ad hominem* fallacy that argues that a claim must be true (or false) just because the claimant is hypocritical.

valid argument: A deductive argument that succeeds in providing conclusive support for its conclusion.

variables: In modern logic, the symbols, or letters, used to express a statement.

Venn diagrams: Diagrams consisting of overlapping circles that graphically represent the relationships between subject and predicate terms in categorical statements.

weak argument: An inductive argument that fails to provide strong support for its conclusion.

worldview: A philosophy of life; a set of fundamental ideas that helps us make sense of a wide range of important issues in life. A worldview defines for us what exists, what should be, and what we can know.

Photos

Front matter and part opening photos © Alex Staroseltsev/shutterstock.com.
Chapter opening photos © GlowImages/gettyimages.com.

p. 5   Danny Wilcox Frazier/Redux Pictures
p. 15   mistydawnphoto/Shutterstock
p. 16   (top) Frontpage/Shutterstock
p. 16   (bottom) White house photo by Eric Draper
p. 18   Getty Images
p. 19   New Line
p. 37   National Portrait Gallery, London
p. 39   NASA, H. Ford (JHU), G. Illingworth (UCSC/LO), M.Clampin (STScI), G. Hartig (STScI), the ACS Science Team, and ESA
p. 46   Will Counts Collection: Indiana University Archives
p. 47   © Marc Asnin/CORBIS SABA
p. 48   From The New York Times, November 26, 2008 © 2008 The New York Times All rights reserved. Used by permission and protected by the Copyright Laws of the United States. The printing, copying, redistribution, or retransmission of the Material without express written permission is prohibited.
p. 51   PCL/Alamy
p. 69   The Art Archive
p. 70   ©The New Yorker Collection 1980 James Stevenson from cartoonbank.com. All Rights Reserved.
p. 71   Associated Press
p. 83   Courtesy of the Library of Congress, LC-USZ6-1852
p. 89   Courtesy of Friends of Hillary
p. 125   (top) © Steve Schapiro/CORBIS OUTLINE
p. 125   (bottom) © Bettmann/CORBIS
p. 131   PhotoDisc
p. 133   China Photos/Getty Images
p. 137   J.D. Pooley/Getty Images
p. 142   Lowell Observatory Archives
p. 143   Used with kind permission of Lisa Ross and The Innocence Project
p. 146   Icon
p. 149   PolyGram

Essays

INDEX